MW00609849

Contemporary Africana Theory, Thought and Action

CONTEMPORARY AFRICANA THEORY, THOUGHT AND ACTION
A Guide to Africana Studies

Edited by

Clenora Hudson-Weems

Africa World Press, Inc.

P.O. Box 1892   P.O. Box 48

Trenton, NJ 08607   Asmara, ERITREA

Africa World Press, Inc.

P.O. Box 1892
Trenton, NJ 08607

P.O. Box 48
Asmara, ERITREA

Copyright © 2007 Clenora Hudson-Weems
First Printing 2007

All rights reserved. No part of this publication may be reproduced, stored in a retrieval system or transmitted in any form or by any means electronic, mechanical, photocopying, recording or otherwise without the prior written permission of the publisher.

Book and cover design: Saverance Publishing Services

Library of Congress Cataloging-in-Publication Data

Contemporary Africana theory, thought, and action : a guide to Africana studies / edited by Clenora Hudson-Weems.
    p. cm.
Includes bibliographical references and index.
ISBN 1-59221-309-X (cloth) -- ISBN 1-59221-310-3 (pbk.)
    1. African Americans--Study and teaching. 2. African Americans--Historiography. 3. African Americans--Intellectual life. 4. Blacks--Study and teaching. 5. Blacks--Historiography. 6. Blacks--Intellectual life. 7. Africa--Study and teaching. 8. African diaspora. 9. Pan-Africanism. I. Hudson-Weems, Clenora.
E184.7.C66 2007
305.896'073--dc22
                        2007013643

TO MY COLLEAGUES WHO HAVE BEEN PATIENT IN AWAITING THE RELEASE OF THIS VERY SIGNIFICANT PUBLICATION. WE OFFER THIS BODY OF INFORMATION AS A COLLECTIVE EFFORT IN PRESENTING NEW POSSIBILITIES FOR A BETTER WORLD GLOBALLY. IT IS OUR SINCEREST HOPE THAT OUR EFFORTS TO BRIDGE THE GAP BETWEEN PARADIGMS AND PRACTICE WILL OFFER PLAUSIBLE SOLUTIONS TO OUR DILEMMA AS AN AFRICANA PEOPLE BOTH INSIDE AND OUTSIDE THE ACADEMY.

IN MEMORY OF THREE CONTRIBUTORS WHO HAVE PASSED ON:

DR. RICHARD K. BARKSDALE

DR. JACOB CARRUTHERS

DR. MARIA K. MOOTRY

FURTHER WORKS BY THE EDITOR

The Emmett Till Continuum: Physical and Intellectual Lynchings. AuthorHouse (2007)

The Definitive Emmett Till: Passion and Battle of a Woman for Truth and Intellectual Justice, AuthorHouse (2006)

Emmett Till: The Sacrificial Lamb of the Civil Rights Movement, AuthorHouse (2006); Bedford Publishers (1994, 2000)

Africana Womanist Literary Theory, Africa World Press (2004)

Africana Womanism: Reclaiming Ourselves, Bedford Publishers (1993)

Toni Morrison, Co-authored with Wilfred D. Samuels, Prentice-Hall (1990)

TABLE OF CONTENTS

Foreword   xi
Robert E. Weems, Jr.

Introduction   1
Clenora Hudson-Weems

PART I: THEORIES

1. Africana Thought-Action: An Authenticating Paradigm for
   Africana Studies   17
   Clenora Hudson-Weems

2. Afrocentricity and Transformation: Understanding a Movement   29
   Molefi Kete Asante

3. Kush and Kemet: The Pillars of African-Centered Thought   43
   Jacob Carruthers

4. Black Male/Female Relationships: The Lens Model   59
   Delores P. Aldridge

5. Africana Womanism and the Critical Need for Africana
   Theory and Thought   75
   Clenora Hudson-Weems

PART II: BLACK STUDIES: BEGINNINGS AND EVOLUTION

6. William Leo Hansberry and African Studies Beginnings in the
   United States   89
   Kwame Alford

7. Africology: Considerations Concerning a Discipline   105
   Winston A. Van Horne

8. Africology: From Social Movement to Academic Discipline   129
   William E. Nelson, Jr.

9. Foundations of a "Jazz" Theory of Africana Studies   145
   James B. Stewart

PART III: THE BLACK AESTHETIC

10. The Garvey Aesthetic   163
Tony Martin

11. Legacy Revisited: Visual Art and the Black Liberation Struggle   177
H. Ike Okafor-Newsum

12. Critical Theory and Problems of Canonicity in African
American Literature   193
Richard K. Barksdale

PART IV: HEGEMONIC DISCOURSES

13. Global Africa and Comparative Leadership: Walter Rodney,
Julius K. Nyerere and Martin Luther King, Jr.   203
Ali A. Mazrui

14. Emmett Till: The Modern Civil Rights Movement   219
Clenora Hudson-Weems

15. Ebonics: Re-Claiming and Re-Defining Our Language   241
Robert L. Williams

16. Politico-Psychological Control and Oppression of Blacks
through the Media   251
Talmadge Anderson

17. From Africa to Afrocentric Innovations Some Call Jazz   261
Karlton Edward Hester

PART V: TOWARD AFRICANA WOMANISM

18. *Nommo*/Self-Naming, Self-Defining, and the History of
Africana Womanism   289
Clenora Hudson-Weems

19. Africana Womanism: The Coming of Age   309
Daphne Ntiri-Quenum

20. Africana Womanism, An African Legacy: It Ain't Easy
Being a Queen   319
Barbara A. Wheeler

21. Frances Watkins Harper: Eminent Pre-Africana Womanist   333
Anne Steiner

22. Common Bonds from Africa to the U. S.: Africana Womanist Literary Analysis   343
Betty Taylor Thompson

23. Gloria Naylor's *Mama Day*: An Africana Womanist Reading   359
Adele S. Newson-Horst

Table of Contents

PART VI: CONSTRAINTS AND SOLUTIONS

24. Tragic Ambivalence: African American Confusion Regarding Economic Self-Interest   375
Robert E. Weems, Jr.

25. Education for Liberation: Public Black Colleges Under Siege Desegregation versus Affirmative Action   391
Alvin O. Chambliss, Jr.

26. Confronting Racialized Bioethics: The New Contract on Black America   419
Maria K. Mootry

27. Reparation Phase III: Re-Instituting the Primary Collective Vision/Will of African Americans   433
Obedike Kamau

28. Nguzo Saba (The Seven Principles)   445
Maulana Karenga

Epilogue: The Paradox is in the Paradigm: The "Bell Curve," Another Entity in the Legacy of American Oppression   459
Irene Thompson

Afterword: 463
Mark Christian

About the Contributors   467

Index   473

FOREWORD

Robert E. Weems, Jr.

As African Americans find themselves into the new millennium, I am reminded of the title of one of the progressive hip-hop group Public Enemy's most popular songs; "Don't Believe the Hype." During the past century, African Americans indeed experienced significant gains in such important areas as education, politics, and overall civil rights. Yet, because the benefits associated with the partial desegregation of America were not distributed equally among blacks, there remain large pockets of poverty, despair, and anger within the national African American community. Moreover, ongoing assaults against Affirmative Action programs, if successful, will no doubt increase poverty, despair, and anger in Black America.

In this context, this book appears at a crucial juncture in African American history. The chapters in this expansive work, clearly written from an African-centered (or Africana) perspective, represent a guide for thoughtful African Americans seeking to successfully navigate the troubled waters that lie before us.

For those who might question the pessimistic tone of this analysis, a couple of points are worth noting. During the 1990s, the United States witnessed an unprecedented era of prosperity. Low unemployment, inflation, and interest rates, coupled with a rising stock market (corporate profits), created an economic situation so strong that significant benefits even "trickled down" to African Americans. Yet, recent events related to the U. S. economy reveal the validity of the maxim "what goes up, must come down."

Since it appears we are in the midst of a major economic downturn during the first decade of the new millennium, history suggests that African Americans will be hit especially hard. For instance, at the advent of the Great Depression, African American workers were the first to be laid off. Considering that black workers had only recently made occupational advances during the World War I labor shortage, this represented a blatant verification of the historic truism relating to post-slavery African American workers, "last hired – first fired." Likewise, since Clarence Thomas and his colleagues on the Supreme Court soon ruled that in the 1990s employers do not have to comply with Affirmative Action principles, it appears clear that African American workers (on all occupational levels) will be unduly affected by a worsening economy.

Although this work features contributions from scholars in a variety of disciplines, the underlying theme is that today's African Americans must recapture and perpetuate the spirit of cooperation that enabled us to overcome the tribulations of our collective past. In the truest sense of the term *Sankofa*, contemporary African Americans must rediscover and re-employ the survival tools used by our ancestors to successfully deal with the tribulations in our present and future.

INTRODUCTION

Clenora Hudson-Weems

Until the lions have their histories, tales of hunting will always glorify the hunter.

– African Proverb

This comprehensive collection covering myriad fields is the first of its kind. The array of seminal chapters are by national and international stellar scholars and theorists, with a couple of budding ones. Compiled for the purpose of addressing from an African-centered perspective the critical issues confronting Black survival and growth – physically, politically, economically, intellectually, socially, and spiritually – this book puts forth workable solutions to our global plight, guiding us as to where we need to go in both thought and action in order that we and our future generations can have a healthier, unified, strong Black community. Since long-existing Eurocentric theory is not a construct upon which to build our lives as Africana people, there is a critical need to enhance existing models and to examine and go beyond them. Projected to be the blueprint for a more positive and authentic Africana existence, both physically and mentally, this comprehensive collection represents the fruition of a growing collective Africana paradigm for this new millennium. The seed for this seminal work, my 1997 presentation at Temple University and its subsequent publication entitled "Africana Womanism and the Critical Need for Africana Theory and Thought," for T*he Western Journal of Black Studies* summer 1997, has clearly set into motion this critical ball of ideological warfare for the growth and survival of Black life and Black minds.

Divided into six distinct parts, with the foreword by Robert E. Weems, Jr., an introduction, an epilogue by Irene Thompson, and an afterword by Mark Christian, this multi-faceted volume could render an invaluable service, both inside and outside of the Academy, particularly as we find ourselves today in the midst of vast pandemonium – moral debates, ideological confusion, disillusion, and devastation regarding the global destiny of Africana people. Thus, the ideologies espoused in each section, if adhered to, could positively lead us out both theoretically and practically into this new millennium. The organization and the various categories grew out of the ideological framework. The book is structured in a way that reflects the process toward a wholistic understanding and appreciation of Africana life and history. The knowledge acquired could culminate in an authentic, constructive, wholistic existence. In short, the intellectual, theoretical framework, which is a step-by-step categorical setup, explicates the order in which each issue is confronted, beginning with the first section, in which Africana theories are defined and articulated, and leading up to the last section, in which solutions and resolutions are explicated and reflected.

Part I, which is entitled Theories, establishes a methodological framework for authentic Africana thought and action, which is the very basis for rational existence. The volume opens with Hudson-Weems' "Africana Thought-Action: An Authenticating Paradigm for Africana Studies." After presenting an overview of major Africana paradigms, from Black Aestheticism, to Afrocentricity, to Africana Womanism, and more, the article then calls for the ultimate paradigm shift from thought to thought-action as a means of bringing these two poles together.

Chapter 2 moves from the overview and ultimate goal of thought-action to the focus on the long-standing concept of African-centeredness, as espoused by such pioneers in this discourse, as African-centered historians like Cheikh Anta Diop, John Henik Clarke, Yosef Ben-Jochannan, Chancellor Williams, and Charshee McIntyre. The concept became more popularized with the development of Afrocentricity, the terminology advanced by Molefi Kete Asante, who gave it substance and direction. In the opening chapter, "Afrocentricity and Tranformation: Understanding a Movement," Asante examines how Afrocentricity emerged as a leading paradigm in the analysis of African phenomena. Exploring the concept within the framework of self-determination, he suggests that Afrocentricity is concerned with the subject-place of African people within any given context, with the following governing and organizing elements: (1) an intense interest in psychological location as determined by symbols, motifs, rituals, and signs, (2) a commitment to finding the subject-place of Africans in any social, political, economic, or religious phenomenon, (3) a defense of African cultural elements as historically valid in the context of art, music, and literature, (4) a celebration of "centeredness" and agency and a commitment to lexical refinement that eliminates pejoratives about Africans or other people, and (5) a powerful imperative from historical sources to revise the collective text of African people. He then addresses contemporary issues Afrocentrically, such as the Modern Civil Rights Movement and Black Studies Programs and their leaders, insisting that Afrocentric intellectuals remain true to the legacy of the tradition passed down from Kush and Kemet, which anticipates the next chapter by Jake Carruthers.

Reflecting further on the origins of African centeredness, then, is Jacob Carruthers in the third chapter, "Kush and Kemet: The Pillars of African-centered Thought," in which he documents and proposes Kush (ancient Ethiopia) and Kemet (ancient Egypt) as the foundation pillars of African centered thought for over two centuries. This longtime political scientist and Egyptologist holds that such North American and Caribbean pioneering thinkers as Richard Allen, Prince Hall, David Walker and Martin Delany set forth the tradition followed since the late eighteenth century. Revised after World War II by such scholars as J. C. deGraft – Johnson, Cheikh Anta Diop, George G.M. James, and Chancellor Williams, the tradition was reinforced by the Black Studies movement in the sixties. Carruthers further asserts that the incorporation of Nile Valley civilization as the classical foundation of African scholarship was the focus for this two-hundred-year-old intellectual history. Hence, he concludes that the 1994 call for Nile Valley based African-centeredness echoes Richard Allen's 1794 evocation of the Princes of Egypt and the hands of Ethiopia in 1794. Contending that the intellectual framework for the present phase of the project was largely developed by Diop over his forty year productive career, Carruthers insists that the agenda inherited by African scholars must be to continue exploring the arguments set forth by both Diop and his predecessors, culminating in an African-centered World History, which Diop referred to as the African Human Sciences.

In the fourth chapter, "Black Male and Female Relationships: The Lens Model," Delores P. Aldridge contextualizes the critical stance of Black male and female relationships upon which the very foundation of Black life and all other systems rest. This chapter addresses the question of gender-specific issues from an Africana womanist perspective) as advanced by Clenora Hudson-Weems), and their relationship to and impact upon the family, which puts forth the theoretical lens model and role of the Black family, and Black male and female relationships. Positing the Black male-female relationship as a dyad existing within the social context of American society, the author asserts that the male-female bond is an essential one that serves to cement the basic unit of the family and provides an indicator of the quality of social life of members of the group. The pressures and stresses of Black life in America, she observes, affect the quality and prospects of existing relationships as well as the possibilities of future relationships. While Black male-female relationships must always be analyzed within the context of society with all of the structural variables that shape and mold the individual, and thus the relationships, Aldridge's African-centered Lens model set forth here is one which demonstrates the interplay of American institutional values and interpersonal factors that determine Black male-female relationships. This context sets the stage for defining a framework for analyses of Black men, Black women, and their relationships. The chapter concludes with recommendations for building strong Black male-female relationships and reducing the stresses on fragile or nonexistent ones.

This section closes with Chapter Five by Clenora Hudson-Weems, who reclaimed, renamed and redefined Africana women activists by creating a paradigm – Africana Womanism – relative to their true and complex collective role in society. In this chapter, "Africana Womanism and the Critical Need for Africana Theory and Thought," the author reaffirms the call made by Carruthers and Asante and moves on to a theoretical framework much like Aldridge, to ensure that the experiences of women of African descent in particular are presented and interpreted in an African-centered framework. The first part of the chapter focuses on the urgency of worldwide Africana scholars, and theorists in particular, to create their own paradigms and theoretical constructs so that works by Black writers may be analyzed and interpreted more accurately so as to maintain their original meaning, along with their value, particularly as it relates to positive instructions for our current and future lives. She insists that an authentic paradigm utilizing African-centered theories must be applied in the analysis of all Africana texts for the further creation of accuracy in our lives as well as in our works. The last section of the selection emphasizes the unique aspect of the Black experience with particular attention given to the Africana woman. Thus, the chapter reinforces both the general theoretical (Africana) and the focused theoretical (Africana womanism), anticipating a global rubric whose criticality will be discussed in more detail in the following sections.

Part II, entitled Black Studies: Beginnings and Evolution presents the much needed historical backdrop concerning the origins and nature of U. S. Africana Studies. Chapter Six, "William Leo Hansberry and African Studies Beginnings in the U. S.," was written by Kwame Alford in which he discusses Hansberry's initiation, establishment, and development of African Studies as an academic discipline, growing out of his interdisciplinary research experience at Harvard University and his first appointment as professor and director of the Department of Negro History at Straight

University. With this important chapter, we witness how Hansberry's unique and unrivaled credentials enabled him to launch an unprecedented self-promotional campaign as an Africanist. Alford, who holds the Hansberry papers, also discloses how this expert on Africa implemented an outreach program that sought moral and financial support from mainstream and Black organizations, culminating in a more public career for himself, thereby enabling him to effect a promotional campaign for a mass movement to establish African/Black Studies programs at historically Black colleges and universities.

The conceptualizer of "Africology," Winston Van Horne in Chapter Seven, "Africology: Considerations concerning a Discipline," scrutinizes a three-sided question in relation to Africology as an academic discipline: Is Africology really an academic discipline, given the interests and purposes in culture, political economy, and society that it serves? What measures of intellectual stringency ought to ground inquiry and discourse in the discipline? Is its scholarship an open or closed domain of inquiry and discourse? The essay concludes by observing that there is no incongruity between measures of intellectual stringency and openness in inquiry and discourse, on the one hand, and an array of social, cultural, economic, and political interests and purposes of Africology on the other.

In Chapter Eight William E. Nelson, Jr., offers academia his master undertaking, "Africology: From Social Movement to Academic Discipline," in which he carries the discipline of Africology to its next level, analyzing the emergence and implementation of Black Studies as an academic discipline within higher educational institutions in the United States. He looks at its evolution within the context of social movements and the institutionalization of Eurocentric disciplines in higher education. In contrast to traditional social science disciplines based on white elite domination of the political order, Black Studies, (Africology) represents a grassroots movement that functioned as an alternative and corrective to mainstream values and practices. Nelson holds that as a discipline, Africology called into question the methods and epistemological assumptions of traditional social science, and provided a prism through which people of African descent can correctly interpret the world around them. He argues that the search for knowledge through Africology must be reinforced by a commitment to social action. As an organic force, Africology must reach beyond the classroom to address the profound social, economic, political, and cultural needs of the entire Black community and must seek to change the value systems of students and faculty members. Africology must also seek to establish a "professional" discipline, while avoiding the elitist predilections of traditional disciplines. The author concludes that it must remain attached to its revolutionary roots, seeking to produce system-level change, simultaneously providing concrete benefits to African people in the precincts, neighborhoods, and cities where they live.

Part II closes with Chapter Nine by James B. Stewart, which is entitled "Foundations of a 'Jazz' Theory for Africana Studies." Stewart moves broadly to interject the artistic aesthetic and a creative explanation, using jazz as a metaphor to describe the field and function of Africana Studies. The metaphor encompasses characteristics of jazz music, performances and techniques of the musicians, demographics and socialization of the performers, audience involvement, consumption patterns, and musicological analysis. In this analysis, a musical composition performed by a jazz ensemble is treated as the analog of an interdisciplinary investigation by a team of African Studies specialists, with individual instruments used as the counterparts to individual academic disciplines. Moreover, the jazz model synthesizes the more useful features of scientific and humanistic models while overcoming some of their most debilitating weaknesses. The author contends that jazz relaxes requirements associated with knowledge generation and verification to assign a crucial role to improvisation in generating new insights, which imposes structure on artistic and humanistic endeavors by focusing attention on collective, rather than individual outputs. He proposes that structured dialogues between Africana Studies scholars and jazz composers and performers offer further exploration of both the theoretical and operational implications of the model.

A logical follow-up to understanding one's historical context is to move to the position of effecting change. Part III, entitled The Black Aesthetic, focuses on the function of Black art, which is to bring about a moral, political, and social transformation for the liberation of Black people, and the need for a Black Aesthetic in order to contain what, why, and how we think and do. This section begins with Chapter Ten by Tony Martin, entitled "The Garvey Aesthetic," in which the author establishes Garvey as the precursor, particularly in terms of style and content, of the Black Aesthetic and the Black Arts Movements of the sixties. Here the author advocates that the true function of Black art is to advance Black people via positive, conscious literature. In this selection, Martin focuses on Garvey, the political and literary figure, within the context of other such luminaries of the period as W. E. B. DuBois, Claude McKay, Paul Robeson, Langston Hughes, and Zora Neale Hurston.

Next is Chapter Eleven, a thought-provoking selection by H. Ike Okafor-Newsum, "Legacy Revisited: Visual Art and the Liberation Struggle," in which he renders an interesting discussion of the role of visual art in the Black experience in the United States. It presents the way in which art facilitates Black identity formation and political struggle. This astute writer/artist emphasizes the importance of Africa and Africentric sensibility in the production and social function of African American art.

Part III closes with the pivotal Chapter Twelve by the late Richard K. Barksdale, "Critical Theory and Problems of Canonicity in African American Literature," which is an insightful essay that appeared in his 1992 swan song book, *Praisesong of Survival*. Here Barksdale calls for Black scholars' utilization of our own critics who express an interest in the importance of the historical, political, and social context of our literature. He attacks the tendency of high-profile scholars at major universities today to embrace this new critical wave of a fascination with European theorists in their criticism. He comments on the politics of employment, publications, and academic credibility, depending upon the references and sources used in mainstream critical assessments of literature. He outlines recommendations for expanding and broadening the African American literary canon by first "ignoring deconstruction, post-structural textual exegesis, and continental hermeneutics," contending that "American literature cannot effectively survive critical approaches that stress authorial depersonalization and the essential unimportance of racial history, racial community, and racial traditions." He advocates "the politics of survival," with a return to the original mission of the African American literary tradition, which focuses on political content aiming at liberation rather than on impressive form aiming at nothing more.

Part IV, entitled Hegemonic Discourses, presents dialogues on the critical understanding of how cultures are constituted, how they function and change over time, as well as discussions on fixed cultural components and their adaptations to new cultural constructs. Chapter Thirteen opens this section with a very timely and appropriate inaugural lecture for the Walter Rodney Professor at the University of Guyana, delivered in Georgetown, Guyana, in 1998 by Ali A. Mazrui. This lecture, entitled "Global Africa and Comparative Leadership: Walter Rodney, Julius K, Nyerere and Martin Luther King, Jr.," takes a comparative look at leadership across three parts of the Black world (Africa, Black America and the Caribbean), and espouses a concept that recognizes these links while humanizing them by analyzing three leaders from three parts of Global Africa. The essay discusses the ethnic distinctions between dual societies (like Guyana and Rwanda) and plural societies (like Tanzania and the United States), and the implications for stability and political participation. According to Mazrui, Rodney tried to fuse Pan-Africanism with class analysis; Nyerere tried to fuse African Traditions with modern socialism (*ujamaa*); King tried to fuse Gandhism with Christianity. The marriage of

Marxism with Leninism in the 20th century was a disaster. Rodney did not live long enough to discover that the only way of saving Marxism was to de-Leninize it. But Martin Luther King's concept of Gandhism appears not to need to be de-Christianized so far. Hence, Gandhi's soul force and King's dream are joint pilgrims.

Chapter Fourteen, "Emmett Till: The Modern Civil Rights Movement," is a reprint of Clenora Hudson-Weems's third chapter of *Emmett Till: The Sacrificial Lamb of the Civil Rights Movement* (1994), which grew out of her 1988 Ford Doctoral Dissertation at the University of Iowa. She was the first to establish the 1955 brutal lynching of Emmett Louis "Bobo" Till, a fourteen-year-old Black Chicago youth, as the true catalyst of the modern Civil Rights Movements of the fifties and the sixties. His naive act, whistling at a twenty-one-year old white woman, Carolyn Bryant, in Money, Mississippi, proved to be the ultimate American taboo for which he paid the ultimate price. Because this incident, the true ugliness of American racism, has been historically swept under the rug, the author has unearthed it as a lost chapter in the historical account of the Modern Civil Rights Movement, thereby resurrecting Till's martyrdom to the prominence it deserves.

Chapter Fifteen, "Ebonic: Re-Claiming and Re-Defining Our Language," follows, which is written by Robert L. Williams. Here, the author – who coined the term *Ebonics* by combining the words *ebony* (Black) and *phonics* (speech sounds) – explicates the process that he undergoes in redefining Black language from an Africana perspective. The paper demolishes the stereotypical negative connotation of Black speech as an inferior language. In so doing, it not only rescues our image as a people, but more important, it rescues the integrity, dignity, and destiny of our children, our future generations, whose ultimate survival is dependant upon a quality education too long denied them. *Ebonics* is defined as the linguistic continuation of Africa in Black America, thereby representing a reclamation of African American Africanity in the process of granting our children their future and their sense of positive identity.

The sixteenth chapter, written by Talmadge Anderson, is entitled "Politico-Psychological Control and Oppression of Blacks through the Media." Discussing how the media manipulates our minds and dictates our reality, the author contends that control and oppression can be effected upon an individual or a people through forced (involuntary) or induced (voluntary) socialization. Formal subordination may result involuntarily from the enactment of social codes and laws, law enforcement, imprisonment, or slavery. Similarly a person or group may be induced voluntarily to submit to control or to accept a social stigma or condition from the socialization effects of education (mis-education) and the media. While the white-dominated film and print media industries attempted to stereo-type, define, and psychologically control Blacks during the early part of the twentieth century, the electronic media, television has emerged as the prime socialization and control agent since the 1960s. The author discusses how positive definitions and liberated roles are assigned to whites and, conversely, negative, subordinate, and oppressive images are attributed to Blacks in the media. Media promotion and perpetuation of definitions and imagery of White omniscience and supremacy, then, may induce some Blacks voluntarily and subconsciously to submit to social and political control, economic dependency, and oppression. Anderson concludes that only if the negative definitions and imagery of the media are rejected and not internalized will psychological liberation and politico-economic empowerment be realized for African Americans.

The section closes with Chapter Seventeen, in which the author offers a discussion on one of the most important entities in the celebration, con-solation and healing of Black life – music. Explicating this powerful phe-nomenon is Karlton Edward Hester in "From Africa to Afrocentric Inno-vations Some Call Jazz," a reminder that much of the music that drives the music industry and contemporary world culture has Afrocentric origins. He focuses on the need for reclaiming jazz, one of the most sought-after forms of music, an African/African American musical genre, which too frequently gets identified as a master type within the broader context of American music. The author contends that controversy surrounding the ownership of "jazz" and other African American music involves an inter-section of residual "slave mentality" (insisting that African Americans contribute little to world society) combined with a perpetual exploitation of artistic innovations that result from African American creativity. Exam-ining the evolution of African American music within the context of the socio-cultural history, Hester concludes that the most salient aspects of the evolution of innovative "Black" music suggest the success of "jazz" and other African American music has led to many Eurocentric capitalists and institutions claiming ownership and control. Racism and sexism provoke illogical responses and behavior throughout society. Be that as it may, the innovators of jazz remain Scott Joplin, Louis Armstrong, Mary Lou Williams, Billie Holiday, Duke Ellington, Count Basie, Ella Fitzgerald, Charlie Parker, Dizzy Gillespie, Miles Davis, John Coltrane, Donald Byrd, Cecil Taylor, Ornette Coleman, and other African American masters.

Since the woman is revered as the culture bearer, it is appropriate that we look more closely at her role in the making of a civilized space for her people. Hence, Part V, Toward Africana Womanism, reflects vision-ary endeavors, looking at the world in an aesthetic, political and spiritual respect, and seeks a wholistic interpretation of the cultural forces at work. Part V presents an array of perspectives concerning the Africana woman, her role and presence in her own family, or community, and in the collective struggle for liberation. This section opens with Chapter Eighteen, a seminal chapter by Clenora Hudson-Weems, who conceptualized the paradigm. "*Nommo*/Self- Naming, Self-Defining, and the History of Africana Womanism" makes clear the need for Africana women to properly name *(nommo)* themselves and define their reality for the ultimate survival of their families/communities. She explicates the evolution of Africana Womanism – how it came to be and where it stands in the academy today – by tracing the activities of the theory from its inception in 1985 to the present. She documents the evolution of Africana Womanism from terminology, to definition, to application, and finally to practice, as demonstrated by the launching of the Africana Womanism Society in Pittsburgh, September 2004.

In Chapter Nineteen, entitled "Africana Womanism: The Coming of Age," Daphne Ntiri-Quenum (who wrote the introduction to Hudson-Weems' *Africana Womanism: Reclaiming Ourselves)* provides a review and update of the impact of Africana Womanism since its launching in the mid 1980s at national conventions, and culminating in the 1989 publication "Cultural and Agenda Conflicts in Academia: Critical Issues for Africana Women's Studies" (*WJBS*), thereby announcing in print the terminology and concept of Africana Womanism, and finally the 1993 release of the first edition of the book itself. Ntiri-Quenum examines the conflicts between traditional feminism and what Hudson-Weems terms Africana Womanism in terms of their impact upon Black women and their loyalties to family, community, and social change. She asserts that race and class are the super ordinate issues for the Africana womanist who grapples with family and community survival and growth – while feminism, and by extension Black feminism, appear more compatible with the interest of Western ideals of female centrality. Ntiri-Quenum focuses on the activities surrounding the Africana womanist movement and particularly on the literature on this paradigm for the authentic Black woman. The wide adoption of the text at institutions of higher learning around the United States and abroad attest to its validity, credibility and relevance to studies of women and Africana studies. Ntiri-Quenum concludes that central to the ultimate goal of Black family survival is the need for appropriate labels and the need to promote cultural identity and collective consciousness among Africana women, which form the core of Hudson-Weems' arguments.

"Africana Womanism – An Africana Legacy: It Ain't Easy Being A Queen," Chapter Twenty was written by Barbara Wheeler. In this well-informed paper, Wheeler presents a litany of exciting legendary African queens dating back to antiquity. In recapitulating their heroic activities, she shows how these women have served as positive models for Black women since the beginning of humankind. Their historical race-based activities as Black women have effectively informed the very creation of the authentic paradigm of Africana Womanism, a methodology and theoretical construct for all women of African descent. With this perspective, enhanced by these unforgettable, powerful models, scholars are better able to change the way we as a collective family look at Black women historically, currently, and in the future.

Chapter Twenty-One, Anne Steiner's "Frances Watkins Harper: Eminent Pre-Africana Womanist," traces the political/literary activities of the subject during slavery. In this chapter, the careful scholar illustrates that in Harper's focusing on the goal of racial progress in her life and in her literary works, she evolves as an eminent pre-Africana womanist, which validates the notion that Africana women, dating back even before the advent of feminism, have been engaging in a race-based, rather than a gender-based movement as a number one priority. The paper analyzes specific aspects of Harper's life and works to illustrate their convergence with the Africana womanist paradigm, which is a prioritized race, class, and gender agenda, which in and of itself negates the common notion that addressing gender issues is an exclusive for feminism.

Chapter Twenty-Two, "From Africa to the United States: An Africana Womanist Literary Analysis," in which Betty Taylor Thompson meticulously explores the commonalities of Africana women, globally regarding their concerns, backgrounds, images, visions, and methodology, thereby culturally binding their creative productions. Through an exploration of texts – Flora Nwapa's *Efuru*, Mariama Ba's *So Long a Letter*, Tsitsi Dangarembga's *Nervous Conditions,* Toni Morrison's *Song of Solomon,* and Gloria Naylor's *Women of Brewster's Place* and *Bailey's Cafe* – the author finds an Africana womanist perspective demonstrated in the way in which the concerns of the women in these works are addressed. For example, Thompson points out the tendency of Africana women to surround themselves with sisterly and family support as they attempt to negotiate their way through the triple-faced problem of race, class, and gender prejudice. She concludes that the answer to the problems besetting Africana women is rooted in their mutual bonding and support

Part V closes this section with a highly scholarly and thought-provoking fresh interpretation of Gloria Naylor's most authentic Africana novel, *Mama Day. Mama Day*: An Africana Womanist Reading," Chapter Twenty-Three, written by Adele S. Newson-Horst, renders a successful application of Africana Womanist theory to a Black woman's text. This critical chapter situates the novel within the framework of Africana Womanism, which advances the cooperation of the Black male and female as well as community in the liberation of its characters. The paper posits literary Africana Womanism and African Heritage as key enablers of an "authentic" existence, in terms of Black consciousness, as revealed in the novelist's seminal work.

The last section, Part VI, Constraints and Solutions, presents ideas and strategies for correcting the plight of Africana people the world over. Under the title "Uhuru: Liberation Strategies for the New Millennium," this section opens with a chapter reflecting the importance of economics empowerment for the true freedom and independence of Blacks in the United States, and it closes with an expansion of this same urgent issue to a global level. In the opening selection, Chapter Twenty-Four, "A Tragic Ambivalence: African American Confusion Regarding Economic Self-Interest," Robert E. Weems, Jr., picks up where he left off in his book *Desegregating the Dollar*. He discusses one of the greatest dilemmas facing the African American community entering the new century, which is confusion regarding economic self-interest. At one end of the ideological spectrum, he contends, some believe that African Americans' only hope for substantive progress is through the aggressive development of more individually owned Black business enterprises, while others contend that African Americans' best hope lies in the destruction of the capitalist system and the establishment of an egalitarian socialist state. Weems observes that, while African Americans have been caught in an intellectual stalemate concerning the "correct" formula for black economic empowerment, other groups, with more clearly defined goals, have made considerable economic inroads in our community. He asserts that despite the difficulty of the situation, viable strategies do exist that *can* economically revitalize the African American community, such as African Americans' drawing inspiration and instruction from both a Western (white) and a traditional African method of economic cooperation. Consumer cooperatives, along with the rotating credit concept (which the Yoruba call *esusu*), appear to offer African Americans real opportunities to substantively pursue our economic self-interest. The author cautions, however, that for these concepts to work, we, as contemporary African Americans, must re-acquaint ourselves with the high level of "cooperation" that enabled our forebears to survive centuries of slavery and U. S. apartheid.

In Chapter Twenty-Five, Alvin O. Chambliss, Jr., in his in-depth analysis of the plight of historical Black public colleges in America, champions their cause in "Liberation via Equal Education: Public Black

Colleges under Siege – Desegregation versus Affirmative Action." Taking on the U.S. Justice Department, NAACP-DF, and the One DuPont Circle educational establishment in America in support of public Black colleges, Chambliss offers here the first definitive higher education desegregation piece by a civil rights lawyer. In this chapter, he makes a case for the need to keep these institutions in existence in the midst of all the controversy surrounding the desegregation of Black schools. Too frequently, the desegregation of Black Schools becomes a case of their merging with white institutions of higher learning, thereby losing their identity as Black institutions, which must abandon their original mission for mentoring and educating Black youths. This discussion on desegregation extends to alternatives to Affirmative Action as well, in which Chambliss offers new directions and proposes a new Civil Rights agenda centered around public Black colleges in the nineteen southern border states, since the original Civil Rights agenda was not set by us for us.

An awesome and highly controversial subject today, bioethics, is the critical issue debated in Chapter Twenty-Six by the late Maria K. Mootry in her thought-provoking work entitled "Confronting Racialized Bioethics: The New Contract on Black America." Mootry, considered the original racialized bioethicist, discusses how the powers- that-be impose the destinies of our physical being in areas such as genetic engineering and body-parts donations, a crucial subject she developed more fully in the forthcoming book, *Brain Games: Race, Bioethics and the Seduction of the American Mind* (AuthorHouse). This chapter gives an analysis of why the American Dream has failed the African American on a number of levels – continuing acts of racial violence, middle-class white America's withdrawal from liberal policies, and new kinds of intellectual racism. Offering possible solutions to these problems, Mootry proposes a concept of racial principalism.

The issue of the long-sought-after controversial reparation for Black people is the subject of Chapter Twenty-Seven entitled "Reparation – Phase III: Re-Instituting the Primary Collective Vision/Will of African Americans" by Obedike Kamau. This chapter argues that the history of Africans in America can be divided into three broad phases, and that in each of the first two, there was a clear-cut collective Black vision. The collective vision for the first phase, which ran from 1619 to 1865, was the abolition of chattel slavery or "freedom." The collective vision for the second phase, which ran from 1866 to 1968, was the elimination of legal discrimination or "equality." The chapter goes on to suggest that in this, the third phase, the collective vision should be national self-determination; reparations paid by the U.S. government to the descendants of enslaved

Africans should be the primary bridge to reach this goal. The chapter also compares the political and social situations that have existed in each of the phases and discusses why determining a collective vision is more difficult contemporarily than it was in the past. The chapter ends with an in-depth discussion of how the issue of Black Reparations can be dealt with by Africana Studies practitioners. It closes with a creative hip hop piece written by the author, which addresses reparations historically for African American people entitled "I Want My Money!"

Chapter Twenty-Eight, the final chapter in Part Six, is entitled "Nguzo Saba: The Seven Principles from *Kawaida*," in which Maulana Karenga articulates the very defining aspect of our existence as an African people. The author closes the dialogue with a celebration of our value system and commitment, which is derived from our historical collective consciousness and dauntless strength. The Seven Principles explicated – Umoja (Unity), Kugichagulia (Self-Determination), Ujimaa (Collective Work Responsibility), Ujaama (Cooperative Economics) Nia (Purpose), Kuumba (Creativity), Imani (Faith) – then becomes the foundation for the Kwanza celebration, which is an annual seven day event leading up to the new year. The key notion for this educational celebration is that it be not limited to a week, but rather should form the foundation of our actions for the entire year.

An Epilogue follows, entitled "The Paradox is in the Paradigm: The 'Bell Curve,' Another Entity in the Legacy of American Oppression" by Irene Thompson, in which she offers poignant commentary on the ploys and contradictions "inherent" in the racist American system wherein the racist theory of "inherent" race inferiority postulated in the idea of "the Bell Curve."

Finally, this comprehensive volume ends with an Afterword, written by Mark Christian, which expounds upon the implications and overall value of this work for budding Africana scholars and future Africana scholarship. The author here focuses on the usefulness of African-centered tools of analysis with global political importance. He concludes that with our own blueprint as laid out by our own Africana scholars and their paradigms as presented in this expansive work, scholars can continue to write without the influence and dictates of the master's tools, resulting ultimately in dismantling the domination of critical and theoretical presence in academia for Black scholarship.

PART I

*T*HEORIES

African American literature cannot effectively survive critical approaches that stress authorial depersonalization and the
essential unimportance of racist history, racial community, and
racist traditions. (Barksdale, "Critical Theory" 37)

In *Loose Canons*, [Henry Louis] Gates wages his battle against
the African-centered discourse through the time-tested strategy
of nonrecognition… (Carruthers, *Intellectual Warfare* 204)

1

AFRICANA THOUGHT-ACTION: AN AUTHENTI-
CATING PARADIGM FOR AFRICANA STUDIES

Clenora Hudson-Weems

> As we approach the last hour leading up to the next millennium,
> I can not stress enough the critical need today for Africana
> scholars throughout the world to create our own paradigms
> and theoretical frameworks for assessing our works. We need
> our own Africana theorists, not scholars who duplicate or use
> theories created by others in analyzing Africana texts (Hudson-
> Weems, "Critical Need," 79)

From Black Aestheticism to Afrocentricity to Africana Womanism is far more than a mere paradigm shift. It represents the reigning authentic (culturally connected or conscious) paradigms for Africana Studies, spanning the last forty years. Since the searing sixties, the field of Africana Studies has been engaging in an on-going struggle for its rightful place in the Academy. The 1960s marked the beginning of the Black cultural revolution, during which time, Blacks for the first time, demanded to be included in the curriculum at national predominately white colleges and universities. While there was an interest in African Studies at predominantly Black colleges and universities, like Howard University in Washington, D.C. and Straight College (Now Dillard University since 1931) in New Orleans, LA, spearheaded by William Leo Hansberry beginning in 1920, as documented by Kwame Alford in "William Leo Hansberry and Black Studies Beginnings," no such demands, until now, were placed on white institutions. (Alford in *Contemporary Africana Theory*, 2006). Institutions in the forefront of accepting Africana Studies as a legitimate area of study include San Francisco State University, the home of the nation's first Black Studies Program, under the directorship of Nathan Hare; Cornell University, under the directorship of James Turner, which has to this day one of the most pronounced Centers for Africana Studies and Research; Brandeis University, under the directorship of Ronald W. Walters; and Harvard University, under the directorship of Ewart Guinere, to name a few. This was, indeed, a fervent period for Black intellectual and political activities. As stated in an edited volume by Arvarh E. Strickland and Robert E. Weems, Jr., *The African American Experience: An Historiographical and Bibliographical 'Guide*, "Descriptively called the era of Black Nationalism, Black Aesthetics, and the Black Arts Movement, it was an era of definition and affirmation, a period when Blacks created their own paradigms and their own criteria for their own distinct art." (Hudson-Weems, "Literary Tradition, 131). This was particularly illuminating in the positions taken by key figures during that time, like Malcolm X, Addison Gayle and Amiri Baraka, among many other scholars and activists. Continuing to establish authentic paradigms, as dictated by the demands of conscious Africana people, is highly critical today if we truly hope to move forward in the direction of positive survival and existence.

In engaging in authentic theorizing in Africana Studies, "the primary area of focus for the curricula are social/behavioral, historical and cultural studies" (Aldridge and Young, 7). And one of the most defining areas listed here for assessing the trends and movements of every day occurrences is literature, since literature itself is charged with the responsibility, though not always met, of reflecting life. For the sixties, we have at the forefront of the Black Arts Movement, its prime mover, Amira Baraka, who, like his predecessor of the turn of the century, W.E.B. DuBois, commanded that art and politics are inseparable. In a powerful charge in opposition to the reigning theory of *l'art pour l'art* (art for art's sake), DuBois proclaimed,

> Thus, all Art is propaganda and ever must be, despite the wailing of the purists. I stand in utter shamelessness and say that whatever art I have for writing has been used always for propaganda for gaining the right of black folk to love and enjoy. I do not care a damn for any art that is not used for propaganda. But I do care when propaganda is confined to one side while the other is stripped and silent (DuBois quoted in *Call and Response*, 854).

Amiri Baraka and Larry Neal, in their anthology, *Black Fire*, took up that charge and insisted on the three-fold dynamics of the Black Arts Movement, the sister to the Black Power Movement led by Stokely Carmichael. According to Neal, "the artist and the political activist are one" (Hill, *Call and Response*, 1366). The three-fold function of the Black Arts Movement was to entertain, as all art must do; to educate, as has been the rule of art in general; and finally to arouse to political action, which was and continues to be our ultimate mission as visionaries for our people. If this mission is achieved, then we have realized true Black Art. Complimenting these guidelines as articulated by DuBois, Neal, Baraka and others, is the theory of Black Aestheticism, which was refined by Addison Gayle in his edited volume, *The Black Aesthetic*. According to Patricia Liggins Hill, general editor of *Call and Response: The Riverside Anthology of the African American Literary Tradition*, "the Black Aesthetic [is] a black criterion for judging the validity and/or beauty of a work of art... " (Hill, 1365).

During the seventies, we witnessed a paradigmatic shift from the collective call for activism to an interlude of individualism, as "the civil rights protest movement began losing strength as attention shifted from gaining equal rights for African Americans as a whole to the quest for individual rights (Hudson-Weems, "Literary Tradition, 133). An inauthentic paradigmatic shift, this persuasion highlighted the victories of the individual, who had embraced the Eurocentric ways of being, rather that the African centered quests and triumphs of Africana people collectively. Fortunately, however, the eighties ushered in a refocus on the collective with the ascendance of Afrocentricty and its continuing growth and development, marked by the works of Molefe Kete Asante, who coined, advanced, and popularized the term as an authentic Africana paradigm. Clearly the Afrocentrics felt the pressures of the Eurocentrics in their efforts to discredit the Black Arts/Black Power Movements and the Black Aesthetics, which was gaining strength and momentum against their racist tactics of exclusion. According to Hill,

> Largely as a result of the failure of many white-socioeconomic and political institutions to meet the needs of American blacks, the Afrocentricity Movement, which seeks to put African values and ideals at the center of African American life and education, came to life in the 1980s. The members of this movement, including scholars John Henrik Clarke and Molefi Kete Asante, want to replace the Eurocentric worldview, which they feel rules the schools, with an Afrocentic one. In its call for pride in the African heritage and "blackness," Afrocentiricity is a resurgence of the Black Power and Black Arts Movements of the 1960s (*Call and Response*, 1351).

In the nineties, the late Dr. Jacob H. Carruthers, founding director of the Association for the Study of Classical African Civilization (ASCAC) and founding member and director of the Kemetic (Egyptian) Institute in Chicago, accurately articulated in his seminal swansong text, *Intellectual Warfare*, the distinction between the authentic Africana scholars and theorists and the mainstream Black scholars who adopt Eurocentric tool for their analysis of Black life. According the Asa G. Hilliard III, Fuller E. Callaway Professor of Education at Georgia State University, in a book jacket endorsement, the author presents "essays that expose the tap-roots of 'the mess that we are in" (Hilliard quoted in *Intellectual Warfare*). Today, we are witnessing the continuing struggle in the re-establishment and validation of the field of Africana Studies and research into the new millennium. This current stage for Africana Studies is marked by a growing battle among theorists whose subjects revolve around some aspect of Africana life, history, culture or otherwise, explicating in some way workable solutions to our existence as a people and the survival of our future generations.

As we consider this critical field of study, it becomes clear that there needs to be a marriage between the ideals from the Academy, with authentic Africana scholars spear-heading and controlling its direction, and the activism from the communities, with the masses voicing and demanding their urgent needs and concerns. In this troubled world of the critical battles for ownership of our minds and possessions, we must realize that this is not a new war, but rather an on-going one, one over which we must at some time ultimately take total control. *Contemporary Africana Theory and Thought: A Guide to Africana Studies* (2006), an engaging volume consisting of a myriad of authentic Africana theorists, puts forth their contributions in addressing and resolving our dilemma. The following is a small sampling of the scholars and their paradigmatic persuasions (excluding Asante, Carruthers, and Aldridge, all discussed in this piece) found in this seminal collection:

1. William E. Nelson, Jr., Professor of Political Science and Research Professor of African American and African Studies at Ohio State University, examines in "Africology: From Social Movement to Academic Discipline" the evolution of Africology (a term coined by Winston van Horne, former Chair of the Department of Africology at the University of Wisconsin-Milwaukee) within the context of social movements and the institutionalization of Eurocentric disciplines in the Academy.

2. James B. Stewart, Professor of Labor Studies and Industrial Relations, African American Studies, and founding Director of Black Studies at Penn State University, explicates in "Foundations of a 'Jazz' Theory for Africana Studies." the artistic aesthetic and a creative connection between jazz as a metaphor and the function of Africana Studies.

3. Tony Martin, foremost international Garveyite scholar and Professor of History at Wellesley College, expounds on the role of Black art in advancing moral, and social nuances for Black liberation as explicated in "The Garvey Aesthetic" from his *Literary Garveyism*.

4. Richard K. Barksdale, long-standing Black Aesthetic critic who edited the first Black Aesthetic anthology, *Black Writers of America: A Comprehensive Anthology*, took the position in "Critical Theory and the Problems of Canonicity in African American Literature" that "we ignore deconstruction, poststructual exegesis, and continental hermeneutics. African American literature cannot effectively survive critical approaches that stress a-historical depersonalization and the essential unimportance of racial history, racial community, and racial traditions" (Barksdale, *Praisesong*, 36).

5. Ali A. Mazrui, the Albertt Schweitzer Professor in Humanities, Chair of Global Studies and Director of the Institute of Global Cultural Studies at SUNY-Binghamton, conducts a comparative study of Black leadership in Africa, America and the Caribbean. He contends that Julius Nyerere's attempt to bring about a union between African Traditions with modern socialism, and Walter Rodney's attempts at fusing Pan-Africanism with class analysis were unsuccessful. However, he asserts that Martin Luther King Jr.'s efforts in bringing together Gandhism and Christianity proved successful.

6. Talmadge Anderson, founding editor of *The Western Journal of Black Studies* And Professor Emeritus in Comparative American Cultures and Marketing at Washington State University, shows how the media controls our minds via forced (involuntary) or induced (voluntary) socialization in "Politico-Psychological Control and Oppression of Blacks through the Media."

7. Economic historian at the University of Missouri-Columbia, Robert E. Weems, Jr., in "A Tragic Ambivalence: African American Confusion Regarding Economic Self-Interest,"discusses Africana people's greatest dilemma today – confusion surrounding economic self-interest. He surmises that there is hope through the economic revitalization of the African American community, inspired and directed by a Western (white) and a traditional African method of economic cooperation.

8. Atty. Alvin O. Chambliss, Jr., "the last Civil Rights Attorney," who was the lead council in the *Ayers versus Fordice* Supreme Court Decision, discusses the plight of historical Black colleges and universities and calls for the survival of these institutions and their original mission for mentoring and educating Black youths.

9. Maulana Karenga, Professor and Chair of the Department of Black Studies at California State University-Long Beach, explicates in "Kawaida" the Seven Principles – Umoja (Unity), Kugichagulia (Self-Determination), Ujimaa (Collective Work Responsibility), Ujaama

(Cooperative Economics) Nia (Purpose), Kuumba (Creativity), Imani (Faith) – the foundation for the Kwanza celebration, which he started as an annual seven day event leading up to the new year.

Clearly these authentic Africana ideals are in concert with collective activism and offer possible solutions to global issues confronting Africana people.

Authentic paradigms command authentic agendas, and an excellent starting point for this consideration is Africana Womanism, a theory put forth by Hudson-Weems, "the first African American woman intellectual to formulate a position on Africana womanism," in the eighties (*Call and Response*, 1811). According to Zulu Sofola, distinguished as Nigeria's first female playwright, in the Foreword to the first three editions of *Africana Womanism: Reclaiming Ourselves*,

> Africana Womanism not simply a scholarly work, one of those in the mainstream, but our own. It is a new trail, blazed with incontrovertible revelations on the African heritage and gender question. Hudson-Weems bravely takes the bull by the horns, confronts the Eurocentric avalanche of words on questions of gender, and puts forward the Afrocentric point of view (xvii).

It spans from correct terminology, to clear definition, to appropriate application, and finally to actual practice, constant in ensuring that the experiences of Africana women are articulated in an African-centered framework: "The primary goal of Africana women, then, is to create their own criteria for assessing their realities, both in thought and in action" (Hudson-Weems, *Africana Womanism*, 50). Self-naming (*nommo*) and self-definition are at the helm of this process. Africana womanism, then, stands as an exemplar for such a strategy for our liberation via a collective struggle with Africana men, women and children. Hence,

> Africana womanism is just that mission realized. It could enable us to galvanize our thoughts and ideas for the survival of our psyches and bodies. It could enable us to leave a lasting legacy for future generations of Africana people, so that they will not be left with a void leading down the long and tiring journey of starting from scratch for solutions to our seemingly bleak destiny.

> *Africana Womanist Literary Theory* is more than an ideal; it is a reality. For already countless activists and scholars alike have come to the forefront in seizing the opportunities this paradigm has to offer its children—the global Africana community. It has withstood the test of debate and contempt and has preserved through many attempts to silence and even destroy

its momentum. Through it all, it has prevailed and has victori-
ously rendered an authentic workable agenda for all women of
African descent, which brings with it its male counterparts and
its children (*AWLT*, 132).

Africana womanism, coming out of the rich legacy of African womanhood,
then, is an authentic paradigm, with its own unique agenda, true to the
prioritization of race, class, and gender. From its very historical and cultural
context, it is family-centered, not female-centered, and it is first and foremost concerned with race empowerment rather than female empowerment,
which, in reality, is a part of, not separate from, the wholism of Africana
life. For this reason, the study of Africana women must be an integral part
of Africana Studies. In *Africana Womanism*, this issue is explored:

> Many have debated the question of whether Africana Women's
> Studies should fall under the Women's Studies or Black or
> Africana Studies programs or departments. Given that ethnic
> identification precedes gender identity in the name Africana
> Women's Studies, it seems plausible that the race factor is
> more crucial. Therefore, the consensus of many that Africana
> Women's Studies should fall under the umbrella of Black or
> Africana Studies seems more valid. (Hudson-Weems, *Africana
> Womanism*, 77).

Further, theorist Delores Aldridge, the Grace T. Hamilton Professor of
Sociology and Black Studies at Emory University, asserts in "Towards
Integrating Africana Women into Africana Studies:" "And so it is from
this perspective of Africana womanism that this discourse is developed"
(Aldridge, *Out of the Revolution* 193). To be sure, Africana womanism
had its beginnings, it has had its impact, and its clarity in its direction will
prove to be advantageous in getting us to where we want to go. Thus,

> In 1985, I took up the lonesome challenge of [Iva] Carruthers's
> observation [... And so we sit idly by and let whites turn Harriet
> Tubman and Rosa Parks into supporters for White feminism as
> opposed to race defenders. (1980: 18)] in an attempt to reclaim
> the rich legacy of Black women's family-centered political
> activism dating back to Africa, culminating in the refinement of
> a paradigm relative to that place for Africana women.... I cannot
> stress enough the importance of Africana men and women
> working together towards the fruition of total liberation—the
> emancipation of our minds as well as our bodies (Hudson-
> Weems, "Entering the New Millennium" 8).

That said, we can now shift to a focus on the flip side of the coin, the Africana man. His plight is interconnected with that of the Africana woman,

who, like her male counterpart, must combat the issue of racism first. A supreme paradigm of this level of struggle is the case of Emmett Till, double victim of racism as a male and as a child. This fourteen-year-old Black Chicago youth was brutally lynched on August 28, 1955 in Money, Mississippi for whistling at a twenty-one-year old white woman, Carolyn Bryant. His horrific death and the subsequent response to that incident became the catalyst of the Civil Rights Movement of the fifties and the sixties. Theoretically speaking, the most critical issue in this scenario was the need for properly assessing this horrific incident within an historical matrix. Ignoring and underplaying it, rather than examining and accurately interpreting it as the true catalyst of the Civil Rights Movement. have proven to be disadvantageous for Africana people. For example, Africana people would no doubt be more advanced in our liberation struggle today had we understood and acted upon that level of struggle we were at during the fifties, that is understanding that vicious racism should not be tolerated. There was no need to sanitize the impetus for the movement, making it more palatable for the dominant culture. There was and yet remains, instead, the need to question and even topsy-turvy mainstream methods of analysis and interpretation as dictated by the dominant culture. Hence, we should not avoid the ugly, symbolized in the bloated face of Emmett Till, as it resonates our predicament. Rather we should, today and yesterday, confront it head on so that we can effect positive change immediately for not only our survival today, but for that of our future generations as well.

Because we have failed, both in thought and in action, to properly address our reality as an oppressed people, we find that our oppression continues yet today. That is the unpleasant price we pay. And therefore, we are witnessing a Till Continuum on all fronts. In considering the following rhetorical questions surrounding our on-going dilemma as an oppressed Africana people in the wake of the Katrina Disaster and the Plight of Black farmers and Our Land Legacy today, we should gain some invaluable insights into the nature of our oppression and how we can end this unfortunate generational predicament once and for all:

1. Why was the traditional interpretation of Rosa Parks' December 1, 1955 refusal to relinquish her bus seat three months after Emmett Till's August 28, 1955 brutal lynching promoted as the inception of the Civil Rights Movement of the fifties and the sixties? Believe it or not, Till's murder was a *cause celebre* during that time!

2. Why does every generation of Black people have to start all over again, financially speaking, at ZERO? The plight of Black farmers

and land owners, who are losing 9,000 acres per week, demonstrates why so many of our children inherit poverty!

3. Why is Affirmative Action fair for Black people? Equal access to the system means that we want what is fair, not always what is equal!

4. Why does the dominant culture feel comfortable when Blacks are grossly under-represented in the media (television, magazines, etc.)? No one expects Black representation!

5. Why is the dominant culture comfortable with a minimum, if not zero, number of Black employees, etc.? Even Blacks like to be the only one!

6. Why is the truth about the origins of civilization concealed? No real demands are made for the nose and the lips of the Sphinx, which was ordered to be blown off by Napoleon to conceal the identity of the people who created it, to be returned from the British museum!

7. Why were there so many victims of the Katrina hurricane? The Louisiana Black population!

8. Why did the Katrina hurricane become the Katrina disaster? The mysteries and controversy surrounding the levees!

9. Why were the Katrina victims called refugees? Black citizenship is still being questioned?

10. Why were the Katrina victims denied help – food, water and dignity? In the case of Blacks, charity does not start at home!

11. Why is New Orleans reminiscent of Hilton Head? See the similarities in a very few years!

12. Why were the acts of Black Katrina victims seeking survival called looting? Black is Black!

13. Why were the acts of white Katrina victims seeking survival called survival tactics? White is white!

14. Why were the Katrina victims not handled expediently in the same manner that the victims of 911 were handled? Look closely at the victims!

15. Why is the notion of Reparations shunned when it is demanded for Blacks? The Japanese and the Jews got theirs; why not Blacks?

16. Why are there no attempts to restore the dignity, integrity and land of Native Americans? Let bygones be bygones!

17. Why are Blacks and Native Americans being forced off or lynched for their land? Three words—coal, oil or gold!

18. Why are the public schools in the Black communities so under budgeted and the teachers are so inexperienced and insensitive? Separate and Unequal!

19. Why are Black and Native American kids forced into high school drop-outs status? The Prison Industrial Complex awaits their arrival!

20. Why is there still racial profiling? No matter what car you drive, you still be Black!

21. Why do so many Blacks who succeed seek out the company and acceptance of whites? Comfort seeks approval.

22. Why do many successful Blacks chose to forget their origins? No need to harp on race!

23. Why do Blacks trust white expertise, advice, etc. over their own? There are crooks among us all!

24. Why are the constitutional rights of Blacks and Native Americans not protected? For example, dig up the burial grounds of Native Americans and it's called archeological conservation!

25. Why are there culture vultures? Britney Spears and Justin Timberlake are grooving to so-called Pop music, while it is really Black Rhythm and Blues!

26. Why do Blacks accept things only after whites do? White is right!

27. Why do Blacks seek white approval? Whites are the standard setters!

28. Why does it take so long for Blacks to speak out against racial injustices? Let's not play the race card again!

29. Why do so many academics sell out? Intimidation, job insecurity and identity problems!

30. Why? Why? Oh Why?

If you know the answers to the above rhetorical questions and are willing to articulate them, as well as act upon them, then solutions to your problems and those of your children and their children as well, all true products of generational victimization, have been resolved.

In conclusion, Africana Thought-Action, which forges a marriage between the Black community and its academic constituents, is an authentic workable paradigm for Africana Studies and its people. If put into practice, we can at last hope to witness the fruition of authentic Africana ideas and existence for Africana people both inside and outside of the Academy. We can, then, be proud to say that we as true Africana scholars are no longer simply theorizing and dialoguing about our plight and possible solutions to it. We are now taking charge and joining our people in an active move toward ensuring that our long-existing status as an oppressed people cease NOW!

REFERENCES

Aldridge, Delores P. "Toward Integrating Africana Women into Africana Studies" in *Out of the Revolution: The Development of Africana Studies.* Delores P. Aldridge and Carlene Young, Eds. New York: Lexington Books, 2000, 191-204.

Aldridge, Delores P. and Carlene Young. Introduction to *Out of the Revolution: The Development of Africana Studies.* New York: Lexington Books, 2000, 3-12.

Carruthers, Iva. E. "Africanity and the Black Woman" in *Black Books Bulletin,* 6(1980): 14-20:71.

Carruthers, Jacob H. *Intellectual Warfare.* Chicago: Third World Press, 1999.

DuBois, W.E.B. "Criteria of Negro Art" in *Call and Response: The Riverside Anthology of the African American Literary Tradition.* Hill, Patricia Liggins, General Editor. Boston and New York: Houghton Mifflin Company, 1998, 850-855.

Hill, Patricia Liggins, General Editor. *Call and Response: The Riverside Anthology of the African American Literary Tradition.* Boston and New York: Houghton Mifflin Company, 1998.

Hudson-Weems, Clenora. "The African American Literary Tradition" in *The African American Experience.* Arvarh E. Strickland and Robert E. Weems, Editors. Connecticut: Greenwood Press, 2001, 116-143.

_____. "Africana Womanism and the Critical Need for Africana Theory and Thought" in *The Western Journal of Black Studies,* Vol 21, No. 2, 1987: 70-84.

_____. "Africana Womanism: Entering the New Millennium" in *State of the Race, Creating Our 21st Century: Where Do We Go from Here?* Boston: Diaspora Press, 2004, 7-26.

_____. *Africana Womanism: Reclaiming Ourselves.* Troy, MI: Bedford Publishers, 1993.

_____. *Africana Womanist Literary Theory.* Trenton, NJ: Africa World Press, 2004.

Sofola, Zulu, "Foreword to *Africana Womanism: Reclaiming Ourselves.*" Troy, MI: Bedford Publishers, 1993.

2

AFROCENTRICITY AND TRANSFORMATION: UNDERSTANDING A MOVEMENT

Molefi Kete Asante

A frocentricity is an intellectual perspective deriving its name from the centrality of African people and phenomena in the interpretation of data. Maulana Karenga, a major figure in the Afrocentric Movement, says "it is a quality of thought that is rooted in the cultural image and human interest of African people." The Afrocentric school was founded in the late 20th century with the launching of the book *Afrocentricity,* where theory and practice were merged as necessary elements in a rise to consciousness. Among the early influences were Kariamu Welsh, Abu Abarry, C. T. Keto, Linda James Myers, J. A. Sofola, and others. Afrocentricty examined some of the same issues that confronted a group calling themselves the Black Psychologists who argued along lines established by Bobby Wright, Amos Wilson, Na'im Akbar, Kobi Kambon, Wade Nobles, Patricia Newton, and several other psychologists. African American scholars trained in political science, history, and sociology such as Leonard Jeffries, Tony Martin, Vivian Gordon, Kwame Nantambu, Barbara Wheeler, James Turner, and Charshee McIntyre, greatly influenced by the works of Yosef Ben-Jochannon and John Henrik Clarke, had already begun the process of seeking a non-European way to conceptualize the African experience prior to the development of Afrocentric theory.

On the other hand, Afrocentricity found its inspirational source in the philosophy of Kawaida, a concept founded by Maulana Karenga in the sixties, that establishes a set of values – Nguzo Saba, the Seven Principles – guiding an African-centered way of engaging and viewing the world. Kawaida's long-standing concern that the cultural crisis is a defining characteristic of twentieth century African reality in the diaspora, as the nationality crisis is the principal issue on the African continent. Afrocentricity sought to address these crises by repositioning the African person and reality from the margins of European thought, attitude, and doctrines to a centered, positively located place within the realm of science and culture.

Afrocentricity finds its grounding in the intellectual and activist precursors who first suggested culture as a critical corrective to a displaced agency among Africans. Recognizing that Africans in the diaspora had been deliberately de-culturalized and made to accept the conqueror's codes of conduct and modes of behavior, the Afrocentrist discovered that the interpretative and theoretical grounds had also been moved. Thus synthesizing the best of Alexander Crummell, Martin Delaney, Edward Wilmot Blyden, Marcus Garvey, Paul Robeson, Anna Julia Cooper, Ida B. Wells-Barnett, Larry Neal, Carter G. Woodson, Willie Abraham, Frantz Fanon, Malcolm X, Cheikh Anta Diop, and the later W. E. B. DuBois, Afrocentricity projects an innovation in criticism and interpretation. It is in some senses a paradigm, a framework, and a dynamic. It is not a worldview, however, and should not be confused with Africanity, which is essentially the way African people – any African people – live according to customs, traditions, and mores of their society. One can be born in Africa, follow African styles, and modes of living, and practice African religion and still not be Afrocentric; to be Afrocentric one has to have a self-conscious awareness of the need for centering. Thus, those individuals who live in Africa and recognize the de-centering of their minds because of European colonization may self-consciously choose to be demonstratively in tune with their own agency. If so, this becomes a revolutionary act of will that cannot be achieved merely by wearing African clothes or having an African name.

SCHOOL OF THOUGHT

Among contemporaries the works of Maulana Karenga, Abu Abarry, Chinweizu, Ngugi wa Thiong'o, J. A. Sofola, Ama Mazama, Aboubacry Moussa Lam, Terry Kershaw, Walter Rodney, Leachim Semaj, Danjuma Modupe, Kwame Nantambu, Errol Henderson, Runoko Rashidi, Charles Finch, Nah Dove, Marimba Ani, Aisha Blackshire-Belay, Theophile Obenga, and Oba T'shaka have been inspiring in defining the nature of the principal Afrocentric school of thought. The principal motive behind their intellectual works seems to be the use of knowledge for the cultural, social, political, and economic transformation of African people by suggesting the necessity for a re-centering of African minds in a way that brings about a liberating consciousness. Indeed, Afrocentricty contends that there could be no social or economic struggle that would make sense if African people remained enamored with the philosophical and intellectual positions of white hegemonic nationalism as it relates to Africa and African people. At base therefore the work of the Afrocentric school of thought is a political one, in the sense that all social knowledge has a political purpose. No one constructs or writes about re-positioning and re-centering merely for the sake of self-indulgence; none could afford to do so because the African dispossession appears so great and the displacing myths so pervasive that simply to watch the procession of African peripheralization is to acquiesce in African de-centering.

The Afrocentrist contends that passion can never be a substitute for argument as argument should not be a substitution for passion. Afrocentric intellectuals may disagree over the finer points of interpretation and over some facts, but the overall project of relocation and reorientation of African action and data has been the rational constant in all Afrocentric work. Interest in African people is not sufficient for one's work to be called "Afrocentric." Indeed Afrocentricity is not merely the discussion of African and African American issues, history, politics, or consciousness; any one may discuss these issues and yet not be an Afrocentrist. Furthermore, it is not a perspective based on skin color or biology and should not be confused with melanist theorists, who existed before the Afrocentrists, and whose emphasis tends to be on biological determinism. Danjuma Modupe of Hunter College has posited agency, centeredness, psychic integrity, and cultural fidelity as the minimum four theoretical constructs that are necessary for a work to be called Afrocentric. Thus, what is clear is that neither a discussion of the Nile Valley civilizations (an argument against white racial hierarchy) nor of how to develop economic productivity in African American communities is sufficient for a discourse to be considered Afrocentric. Operations that involve the Afrocentric framework, identified by the four theoretical constructs, represent an Afrocentric methodology. As in every other case the presentation of theory and methodological considerations implies avenues for criticism. Those criticizing Afrocentricity are more effective when the criticism derives from the definitions established by the proponents of Afrocentricity themselves; otherwise it is possible for criticism to devolve into low-level intellectual sniping at points considered irrelevant by most Afrocentrists. For example, the debate over extraneous issues such as "was Aristotle black?" or "was Cleopatra black?" has nothing at all to do with Afrocentricity. What is more revelant for the Afrocentrist is the question, "what is the *location* of the person asking such questions or the location of the person needing to answer them?"

THE EMERGENCE

Although a number of writers and community activists growing out of the Black Power Movement of the sixties had increasingly seen the need for a response to marginality, Afrocentricity did not emerge as a critical theory and a literary practice until the appearance of two small books by the Amutefi Publishing Company in Buffalo, New York. The press published Kariamu Welsh's *Textured Women, Cowrie Shells, Cowbells,and Beetiesticks* in 1978 and Molefi Kete Asante's book *Afrocentricity* in 1980. These were the first self- conscious markings along the intellectual path of Afrocentricity, that is, where the authors, using their own activism and community organizing, consciously set out to explain a theory and a practice of liberation by re-investing African agency as the fundamental core of African sanity. Welsh's book was a literary practice growing out of her choreographic method/technique known as *umfundalai,* projected in her dances at the Center for Positive Thought, which she directed. On the other hand, the book Afrocentricity was the first time that the theory of Afrocentricity had been launched as an intellectual idea. It was written from observations and textual analyses of what intellectual activists such as Welsh, Maulana Karenga, and Haki Madhubuti were doing with social transformation in community organizations. Rather than use political organization for the sake of organization, they had articulated a cultural base to the organizing principle. This had a more telling effect on and a more compelling attraction to African people. Based in the lived experiences of African people in the Caribbean, Africa, and elsewhere in the diaspora, the Afrocentric idea had to be concerned with nothing less than the relocation of subject-place in the African world after hundreds of years of living on the imposed and ungrounded terms of Europe.

Unlike the Negritude Movement to which the Afrocentric Movement is often compared, Afrocentricity has not been limited to asking artistic questions. Indeed the cultural question as constructed by the Afrocentrists is not merely literature, art, music, and dance, but the entire process whereby Africans are socialized to live in the modern world. Thus, economics is a cultural question as much as religion and science in the construction of the Afrocentrists. This is why Afrocentrists tend to pose three sets of questions. How do we see ourselves and how have others seen us? What can we do to regain our own accountability and to move beyond the intellectual and cultural plantation that constrains our economic, political, and scientific development? What allied theories and methods may be used to rescue those African ideas and ideals that are marginalized by Europe and thus in the African's mind as well? These have become the crucial questions that have aggravated our social and political worlds and agitated the brains of the Afrocentrists.

FIVE DISTINGUISHING CHARACTERISTICS

As a cultural configuration, the Afrocentric idea is distinguished by five characteristics. Essentially, these have remained the principal features of the Afrocentric theory since its inception in the late 1970s:

(1) an intense interest in psychological location as determined by symbols, motifs, rituals, and signs;

(2) a commitment to finding the subject-place of Africans in any social, political, economic, architectural, literary, or religious phenomenon with implications for questions of sex, gender, and class;

(3) a defense of African cultural elements as historically valid in the context of art, music, education, science, and literature;

(4) a celebration of centeredness and agency and a commitment to lexical refinement that eliminates pejoratives about Africans or other people;

(5) a powerful imperative from historical sources to revise the collective text of African people.

While numerous writers have augmented and added to the central tendency of the Afrocentric theory, it has remained concerned with resolving the cultural crisis as a way of achieving economic, political, and social liberation. A group of thinkers including Ama Mazama, Abu Abarry, Aisha Blackshire-Belay, Kariamu Welsh Asante, Clenora Hudson-Weems, Miriam Maat Ka Re Mo'hges, Katherine Bankole, Cynthia Lehman, Ayi Kwei Armah, Terry Kershaw, Clovis Semmes, Danjuma Modupe, Nilgun Anadolu Okur, C. T. Keto, Molefi Asante, and their students have located the terms of Afrocentricity in the vital areas of linguistic, historical, sociological, and dramatic interpretations of phenomena. This tendency has been called the Temple Circle of Afrocentricity. For example, Abarry has examined orature and libation oratory in African cultural history in connective ways, thus avoiding the disconnected discourses usually found about Africa. Others such as Mekada Graham and Jerome Schiele have concentrated on the social transformative aspects of centrality, believing that it is possible to change the conditions of the socially marginalized by teaching them to see their own centrality and thus empower themselves to confront their existential and material situations. Afrocentrists believe that there is a serious difference between commentary on the activities of Europeans, past and present, and the revolutionary thrust of gaining empowerment through the re-orientation of African interests. There is no rush to discover in Europe the answers for the problems that Europe created for the African condition, psychologically, morally, and economically. Afrocentrists do not shun answers that may emerge in the study of Europe but what Europeans have thought and how Europeans have conceived their reality can often lead to further imprisonment of the African mind. Thus, Afrocentrists call for the liberation of the mind from any notion that Europe is teacher and Africa is pupil; one must contest every space and locate in that space the freedom for Africa to express its own truths. This is not a biologically determined position. It is a culturally and theoretically determined one. That is why there are now Afrocentrists who are European and Asian, and one can find Africans who are not Afrocentric. The new work on Du Bois by the Chinese Afrocentrist Ji Yuan and the work of Cynthia Lehman on the Egyptian texts are examples of non-Africans exploring the various dimensions of centeredness in their analyses of African phenomena. It is consciousness, not biology that decides how one is to apprehend the intellectual data because the key to the Afrocentric idea is orientation to data, not data themselves. Where do you stand when you seek to locate – that is, interrogate – a text, phenomenon, or person?

OBJECTIVITY-SUBJECTIVITY

Perhaps because of the rise of the Afrocentric idea at a time when Eurocentric scholars seemed to have lost their way in a dense forest of deconstructionist and postmodernist concepts challenging the prevailing orthodoxies of the Eurocentric paradigm, we have found a deluge of challenges to the Afrocentric idea as a reaction to postmodernity. But it should be clear that the Afrocentrists, too, have recognized the inherent problems in structuralism, patriarchy, capitalism, and Marxism with their emphasis on received interpretations of phenomena as different as the welfare state and e.e. cummings' poetry. Yet the issues of objectivity and subject-object duality, central pieces of the Eurocentric project in interpretation, have been shown to represent hierarchies rooted in the European construction of the political world.

Afrocentrists claim that the aim of the objectivity argument is always to protect the status quo, because the status quo is never called upon to prove its objectivity, only the challengers to the status quo are asked to explain their objectivity. And in a society where white supremacy has been a major component of the social, cultural, and political culture, the African will always be in the position of challenging the white racial privileged status quo, unless, of course, he or she is co-opted into defending the economic, literary, critical, political, social, or cultural status quo. In each case the person will be defending the reality created by Eurocentrists.

It is the subversion of that configuration that is necessary to establish a playing field based on equality. To claim that those who take the speaker or subject position vis-B-vis others counted as audiences and objects on the same footing is to engage in intellectual subterfuge without precedence. On the other hand, it is possible – as the Afrocentrists claim – to create community when one speaks of subject-subject, speaker-speaker, audience-audience relationships. This allows pluralism without hierarchy.

As applied to race and, racism this formulation is clear in its emphasis on subject-subject relationships. Of course, this subject-subject relationship is almost impossible in a racist system or in the benign acceptance of a racist construction of human relationships as may be found in the American society and is frequently represented in the literature of several scholars who have African ancestry but who are clearly uncomfortable with the fact. White supremacy cannot be accommodated in a normal society and therefore when a writer or scholar or politician refuses to recognize or ignores the African's agency he or she allows for the default position, white supremacy, to operate without challenge and thus participates in a destructive mode for human personality. If African people are not given subject place, then we remain objects without agency, intellectual beggars without a place to stand. There is nothing essentially different from this enslavement than the previous historical enslavement except our inability to recognize the bondage. Thus, you have a white-subject and black-object relationship expressed in sociology, anthropology, philosophy, political science, literature, and history rather than a subject-subject reality. It is this marginality that is rejected in the writings of Afrocentrists.

DIOPIAN INFLUENCE

The late Cheikh Anta Diop did more than anyone else to reintroduce the African as a subject in the context of African history and culture. It was Diop's singular ambition as a scholar to reorder the history of Africa and to reposition the African in the center of his or her own story. This was a major advance during the time that so many African writers and scholars were rushing after Europe to prove Europe's own point of view on the rest of the world. Diop was confident that the history of Africa could not be written without throwing off the falsifications of Europe. Doing this was not only politically and professionally dangerous but it was considered to be impossible given the hundreds of years of accumulated information in the libraries of the West.

To begin with, Diop had to challenge the leading scholars of Europe, meet them in their intellectual home arena, defeat their arguments with science, and establish Africa's own road to its history. That he achieved his purpose has meant that the scholars who have declared themselves Afrocentrists have done so with the example of Diop marching before in splendor. His key contention was that the ancient Egyptians laid the basis of African and European civilization and that the ancient Egyptians were not Arabs or Europeans, but as Diop would say "Black Africans" to emphasize that there should be no mistake. These "Black Africans" of the Nile Valley gave the world astronomy, geometry, law, architecture, art, mathematics, medicine, and philosophy. The ancient African Egyptian term *seba* first found in an inscription on the tomb of Antef I from 2052 B.C.E. had as its core meaning in the *Medu Neter,* the "reasoning style of the people."

What Diop taught his students and readers was that Europe pronounced itself the categorical superior culture and therefore its reasoning often served the bureaucratic functions of "locking" Africans into a conceptual cocoon that at first glance seems harmless enough. Nevertheless, the prevailing positions, often anti-African, were supported by this bureaucratic logic. How can an African liberate himself or herself from these racist structures? Afrocentrists take the position that this is possible, essential, but can only happen if we search for answers in the time-space categories that are anti-hegemonic. These are categories that place Africa at the center of analysis of African issues and African people as agents in our own contexts. Otherwise, how can we ever raise practical questions of improving our situation in the world? The Jews of the Old Testament asked, How can you sing a new song in a strange land? The Afrocentrists ask, How can the African create a liberative philosophy from the icons of mental enslavement?

AFROCENTRICITY AS A CORRECTIVE AND CRITIQUE

There are certainly political implications here because the issue of African politics throughout the world becomes one of securing a place from which to stand, unimpeded by the interventions of a decaying Europe that has lost its own moral way in its reach to enslave and dispossess other people. This is not to say that all Europe is bad and all Africa is good. To even think or pose the issue in that manner is to miss the point. For Africans and Native Americans, Europe has been dangerous. It is five hundred years of danger, and I am not now talking of physical or economic danger, though that history is severe enough, but of psychological and cultural danger, the danger that kills the soul of a people. I surmise that a people's soul is dead when it can no longer breathe its own air, or speak its own language, and when the air of another culture seems to smell sweeter. Following Frantz Fanon, the Afrocentrists argue that it is the *assimiladoes,* the educated elite, whose identities and affiliations are often killed first. Fortunately their death does not mean the people are doomed; it only means they can no longer be trusted to speak what the people know because they are dead to the culture, to the human project.

Therefore, Afrocentricity stands as both a corrective and a critique. Whenever African people, who collectively suffer the experience of dislocation, are relocated in a centered place (that is, with agency and accountability), then we have a corrective. By re-centering the African person as an agent, we deny the hegemony of European domination in thought and behavior and then Afrocentricity becomes a critique. On one hand, we seek to correct the sense of place of the African, and on the other hand, we make a critique of the process and extent of the dislocation caused by the European cultural, economic, and political domination of Africa and African peoples. It is possible to make an exploration of this critical dimension by observing the way European writers have defined Africa and Africans in history, political science, anthropology, and sociology. To condone the definition of Africans as marginal, "fringe" people in the historical processes of the world, including the African world, is to abandon all hope of reversing the degradation of the oppressed.

Thus, the aims of Afrocentricity as regards the cultural idea are not hegemonic. Afrocentrists have expressed no interest in one race or culture dominating another; they express an ardent belief in the possibility of diverse populations living on the same earth without giving up their fundamental traditions except where those traditions invade other people's space. This is precisely why the Afrocentric idea is essential to human harmony. The Afrocentric idea represents a possibility of intellectual maturity, a way of viewing reality that opens new and more exciting doors to human understanding. I do not object to viewing it as a form of historical consciousness, but more than that, it is an attitude, a location, an orientation. To be centered is to stand some place and to come from some place; the Afrocentrist seeks for the African person the contentment of subject, active, agent place.

PRINCIPAL CONCEPTS

Afrocentricity represents a reaction against several tendencies. It spurns the limited analysis of Africans in the Americas as Europeans as well as the notion that Africans in the Americas are not Africans. Rather, it concentrates on what Afrocentrist Danjuma Modupe of Hunter College calls the Condition-Effects-Alleviation Complex and the global formation. Modupe contends that the communal cognitive will is activated by cultural fidelity to that will, but cultural fidelity to that will is also fidelity to Afrocentricity itself. He is one of the leading proponents of the view that Afrocentric consciousness is necessary for psychological liberation and cultural reclamation. This view is shared by numerous Afrocentrists.

There are four areas of inquiry in Afrocentricity: cosmological, axiological, epistemological, and aesthetics. A person seeking to locate a person, event, or phenomenon will have to utilize one of these forms for inquiry. Accordingly, the Afrocentrist places all phenomena within one of these categories. The term cosmological refers to the myths, legends, literatures, and oratures that interact at a mythological or primordial level with how African people respond to the cosmos. How are racial or cultural classifications developed? How do we distinguish between Yoruba and African Brazilian? How do gender, class, and culture interact at the intersection of science? The epistemological issues are those that deal with language, myth, dance, or music, for example, as they confront the question of knowledge and proof of truth. What is the rational structure of Ebonics as an African language, and how does it present itself in the African American's behavior and culture? *Axiology* refers to the good and the beautiful as well as to the combination that gives us right conduct within the context of African culture. This is a value issue. Since Afrocentricity is a trans-generational and transcontinental idea, as Van Horne of the University of Wisconsin-Milwaukee suggests, it utilizes aspects of the philosophies of numerous African cultures to arrive at its ideal. "Beauty is as beauty does" is considered an African American adage, but similar proverbs, statements, and sayings are found throughout the African world where beauty and goodness are often equated. *Aesthetics* as an area of inquiry is closely related to the issue of value. Afrocentrists have isolated, as in the work of Kariamu Welsh-Asante, seven senses of the Afrocentric approach to aesthetics: polyrhythm, dimensionality and texture, polycentrism, repetition, curvilinearity, epic memory, wholism. Welsh-Asante contends that these elements are the leading aspects of any inquiry into African plastic art, sculpture, dance, music, and drama. A number of Afrocentric scholars have delved into a discussion of ontology, the study of beingness, as another issue of inquiry. This should not be confused with the idea of personalism in the original Afrocentric construction of philosophical approaches to Afrocentric cultural theory (critical methodology) and Afrocentric methodology (interpretative methodology). In my earlier writings on Afrocentricity, I contended that the European and Asian worlds might be considered materialistic and spiritualistic whereas the dominant emphasis in the African world was personalism. This was not to limit any cultural sphere but to suggest the most prominent ways that large cultural communities respond to their environments.

Maulana Karenga has identified seven areas of culture. These cultural elements are frequently used by Afrocentrists as well as practitioners of Kawaida when conceptualizing areas of intellectual organization. They are history, mythology, motif, ethos, political organization, social organization, and economic organization. Used most often in the critical analysis of culture, these organizing principles are applied to fundamental subject fields of social, communication, historical, cultural, economic, political, and psychological fields of study whenever a student wants to determine the relationship between culture and a given discipline.

THE DISCIPLINE OF AFRICOLOGY

Finally the Afrocentrists have determined that a new discipline, africology, emerges from the various treatments of data from the Afrocentric perspective. Africology is defined as the Afrocentric study of African phenomena. It has three major divisions: cultural/aesthetics, social/behavioral, and policy/action. Under cultural/aesthetic the scholar can consider at a minimum three key elements to culture and aesthetics: epistemic, scientific, and artistic dimensions. In terms of epistemic dimensions the Afrocentrist examines ethics, politics, psychology, and other modes of behavior. The scientific dimensions includes history, linguistics, economics, and other methods of investigation. The artistic dimension involves icons, art, motifs, symbols, and other types of presentation.

REFERENCES

Achebe, Chinua. *Things Fall Apart*. London: Heineman, 1957.

Asante, Molefi Kete. *Afrocentricity*. Trenton: Africa World Press, 1988.

_____. *The Afrocentric Idea*. Philadelphia: Temple University Press, 1987.

_____. Kemet, *Afrocentricity and Knowledge*. Trenton: Africa World Press, 1990.

_____. *Malcolm X and other Afrocentric Essays*. Trenton: Africa World Press, 1993.

Asante, M. K., and Abu Abarry. *African Intellectual Heritage*. Philadelphia: Temple University Press, 1996.

Asante, M. K., and Kariamu Asante (Eds.) *African Culture: The Rhythms of Unity*. Trenton: Africa World Press, 1990.

Asante, M. K., and Mark Mattson. *African American Atlas*. New York: Macmillan, 1998.

Baker, Houston. *The Journey Back: Issues in Black Literature and Criticism*. Chicago: University of Chicago Press, 1980.

Blackshire-Belay, Carol Aisha, ed. *Language and Literature in the African American Imagination*. Westport, Conn..: Greenwood Press, 1992.

Cerol, Marie -Josee. *Introduction to Guadaloupean Creole*

Chinweizu. *Decolonising the African Mind*. London: Pero, 1987.

Diop, Cheikh Anta. *The African Origin of Civilization*. New York: Lawrence Hill, 1976.

_____. *Civilization or Barbarism: An Authentic Anthropology*. Translated from the French by Yaa-Lengi Meema Ngemi, edited by Harold J. Salemson and Marjolin de Jager. New York: Lawrence Hill, 1991.

_____. Drake, St. Clair. *Black Folk Here and There: An Essay in History and Anthropology*. Vol. 1. Los Angeles: Center for Afro-American Studies, 1987.

Forbes, Jack D. *Africans and Native Americans*. Urbana: University of Illinois Press, 1993.

Gates, Henry Louis, Jr. *The Signifying Monkey*. New York: Oxford University Press, 1988.

Harris, Joseph. E.,ed. *Global Dimensions of African Diaspora*. Washington: Howard University, 1982.

Holloway, Joseph E. and Winifred K. Vass, *The African Heritage of American English*. Bloomington: Indiana University Press, 1993.

Jean, Clinton M. *Behind Eurocentric Veils: The Search for African Realities*. Amherst: University of Massachusetts Press, 1991.

Kambon, Kobi. *The African Personality in America: An African Centered Framework*. Tallahassee, Fla.: Nubia Nation Publications, 1992.

Karenga, Maulana. *Introduction to Black Studies*. 2nd edition. Los Angeles: University of Sankore Press, 1993.

_____. *Kawaida Theory*. Los Angeles: University of Sankore Press, 1995.

Keto, C. Tsehloane. *The Africa-Centered Perspective of History*. Blackwood, N. J.: K. A. Publications, 1989.

Marable, Manning. *African and Caribbean Politics: From Kwame Nkrumah to Maurice Bishop*. London: Verso, 1987.

Martin, Tony. *Race First: The Ideological and Organizational Struggles of Marcus Garvey and the Universal Negro Improvement Association*. 1st edition, Dover, MA: The Majority Press, 1986.

Morrison, Toni. *Beloved*. New York: Random House, 1990.

Myers, Linda James. *Understanding the Afrocentric Worldview*. Dubuque, Iowa: Kendall-Hunt, 1988.

Nascimento, Abdias do. *Racial Democracy in Brazil: Myth or Reality*. Ibadan: Sketch Publishing, 1977. Nascimento, Elisa Larkin. *Pan-Africanism and South America: Emergence of a Black Rebellion*. Buffalo: Afrodiaspora, 1980.

Ngugi wa Thiong'o. *Decolonising the Mind*. London: Heinemann, 1987.

_____. *Moving the Centre: The Struggle for Cultural Freedoms*. London: Curry/ Heineman, 1993.

Okur, Nilgun. *Contemporary African American Drama: From Black Arts to Afroentricity*. New York: Garland Press, 1997.

Richards, Dona Marimba. *Yurugu: An Africa-Centered Critique of European Domination*. Trenton: Africa World Press, 1993.

Rodney, Walter. *How Europe Underdeveloped Africa*. Washington, D.C.: Howard University Press, 1986.

Thompson, Vincent B. *Africa and Unity: The Evolution of Pan Africanism*. London: Longman, 1969.

Walters, Ronald. *Pan-Africanism in the African Diaspora: An Analysis of Modern Afrocentric Political Movements*. Detroit: Wayne State University Press, 1993.

Welsh-Asante, Kariamu. *African Dance*. Lawrenceville, N. J.: Africa World Press, 1996.

Welsh-Asante, Kariamu, ed. *The African Aesthetic: Keeper of the Traditions*. Westport, Conn.: Greenwood Press, 1993.

West, Cornel. *Race Matters*. Boston: Beacon Press, 1992.

Williams, Chancellor. *The Destruction of Black Civilization*. Chicago: Third World Press, 1988.

Wilson, William Julius. *The Declining Significance of Race*. Chicago: University of Chicago Press, 1985.

Woodson, Carter G. *The Mis-Education of the Negro*. Trenton: Africa World Press, 1990.

Wright, Richard. *Native Son*. New York: Harper and Row, 1966.

Ziegler, Dhyana, ed. *Molefi Kete Asante and Afrocentricity: In Praise and Criticism*. Nashville: Winston-Derek, 1994.

3

KUSH AND KEMET: THE PILLARS OF AFRICAN-CENTERED THOUGHT

Jacob Carruthers

INTRODUCTION

> The dreadful insurrections they have made are enough to con-
> vince a reasonable man – princes shall come forth from Egypt
> and Ethiopia shall stretch out her hand unto God. (Jones and
> Allen, 37-38)

The Nile Valley civilizations of Kush (ancient Ethiopia) and Kemet (ancient Egypt) have been the foundation pillars of African-centered thought for over two centuries. In his autobiography published in 1789, Olaudah Equiano used Ethiopia as a synonym for Africa. Five years later, in 1794, Reverend Absalom Jones and Reverend Richard Allen implicitly adopted the Haitian Revolution and evoked Egypt and Ethiopia as metaphors for the enslaved and oppressed African peoples, especially in the United States of America (Jones and Allen, 37-38). Prince Hall in 1797 also linked the Haitian Revolution, then in progress, to the biblical Ethiopia stretching forth her hand (Hall, 49). David Walker, in his *Appeal,* prophesied that the "God of the Ethiopians" would redeem the African peoples from oppression (Walker, 20). Walker went on to connect modern Africa (enslaved and "free") to the civilization of Kemet. And so it went throughout the nineteenth-century liberation struggle. Even Frederick Douglass employed the metaphors of Black Nile Valley civilizations in his rhetorical defense of African humanity.

After the Civil War and the formal dismantling of the chattel slave system, while the neo-white supremacy system called segregation was being put into place, Martin Delany extensively explored the Ancient Nile Valley civilization and ended his treatise by citing from the Bible, "Princes shall come out of Egypt: Ethiopia shall soon stretch forth her hands unto God."[1] At the beginning of the twentieth-century Casely Hayford appropriated the metaphor when he wrote the novel *Ethiopia Unbound.*

Hayford's work was probably a major inspiration for Marcus Garvey who claimed the heritage of Kush and Kemet as African foundations.[2] In 1922 Leo Hansberry launched his courses on ancient African civilization with emphasis on Kush and Kemet (1974).

The year 1954 is significant not only because of milestone political events in the Pan African world; on the continent the Gold Coast (now Ghana) was granted internal self rule under the government of Kwame Nkrumah who had led an effective decolonization struggle for several years; in the United States the NAACP won its first great victory against the legal segregation system. Equally significant were three scholarly works; J. C. deGraft-Johnson, a Ghanian professor published *African Glory*, George G. M. James, of Caribbean origin, a professor at the historically black Arkansas A M and N College, published *Stolen Legacy* and Cheikh Anta Diop, the Senegalese scholar, published *Nations Negres et Culture*.[1] All three works were anchored in the intergenerational African intellectual tradition of the Anteriority of Black Nile Valley Civilizations *vis-a-vis* Africa and the world.

The Black Studies movement of the 1960s was in essence a call for African-centered education. This became clear when a group of scholars and students launched the African Heritage Studies Association in 1968. One of their objectives was the "Reconstruction of African history and cultural studies along Afrocentric lines."[3] This development was inescapably bound to the traditional foundations of the African Heritage of Kush and Kemet; the founding elder and first president of AHSA was John Henrik Clarke.

The works and lectures of Dr. Clarke,[4] Dr. Chancellor Williams (*The Destruction of Black Civilization*), Dr. Yosef ben Jochannan (*Black Man on the Nile and His Family*), and Professor John G. Jackson (*Introduction to African Civilization*), extended the tradition through the 1970s and 1980s. This tendency was augmented when the Association of African Historians began the publication of the *Afrocentric World Review* in the winter of 1973. Perhaps the most comprehensive attempt at articulation of this tendency is found in the works of Molefi Asante beginning in the early 1980s. In the winter of 1980, my essay "Reflections on History of the Afrocentric World View" was published in *Black Books Bulletin*. All of these streams flow from and back into the deep well of the ancient Nile Valley.

The organization of the Association for the Study of Classical African Civilizations (ASCAC) clearly reflected the emerging self-conscious African-centered phase of Pan African nationalism. The Association was organized at the First and Second Ancient Egyptian Studies conferences. Dr. Maulana Karenga, who hosted the first ASCAC conference, insisted on inclusion of the idea of "Classical" African civilizations to emphasize the importance of the ancient Nile Valley heritage. The Kemetic (or ancient Egyptian) Institute of Chicago and the Institute of Pan African Studies of Los Angeles were the organizational bases out of which ASCAC emerged. African-centered education with an emphasis on Kemetic civilization was put forth as one of the major faces of the association. There should be little disagreement that so far the battle for African-centered education has been the greatest intellectual engagement in the last decade of the twentieth century. Thus, the call for Nile Valley based African-centeredness in 1994 is a vibrant echo of the evocation of the Princes of Egypt and the hands of Ethiopia two centuries ago in the 1794 by our intellectual ancestors Richard Allen and Absalom Jones.

CHEIKH ANTA DIOP: THE CHAMPION OF A BLACK KEMET

In 1954 when he published his first major work *Nations Negres et Culture*, Cheikh Anta Diop had already developed the general scheme for his scientific project for the reclamation of Kemet as a fundamental pillar of the African world heritage. Twenty years later, when he introduced the English translation of his thesis, he wrote: "The history of Black Africa will remain suspended in air and cannot be written correctly until African historians dare to connect it with the history of Egypt... it will be impossible to build African humanities, a body of African human sciences, so long as that relationship does not appear legitimate" (Diop, *African Origin,* xiv).

The scientific nature of Diop's project is significant because by 1981 when he published his last major work, *Civilization ou Barbarie*, he was aware of the two-centuries-long tradition of the Kushitic-Kemetic-continental African/African diasporian connections. In that last work reflecting on his life-long project, he wrote that "for us the new, important fact is less to have stated that the Egyptians were Blacks...than to have contributed to making this idea a conscious historical fact for Africans and the world, and especially making it an operational scientific concept: this is where our predecessors did not succeed" (*Civilization or Barbarism,* 2). Indeed, 125 years before *Nations Negres et Culture*, one of his African predecessors, David Walker, had not only claimed (or rather assumed) Black Egypt as a basic fact, he had demanded that Africans begin to throw off the veil of ignorance by first taking "a retrospective view of the arts and sciences – the wise legislators – the Pyramids, and other magnificent buildings – the turning of the channel of the river Nile by the sons of Africa... among whom learning originated, and was carried thence into Greece" (Walker, 19). Walker also anticipated the Two Cradle Theory, another Diopean formulation.[5] In the *Appeal,* Walker asserted: "The whites have always

45

been an unjust, jealous unmerciful avaricious and blood-thirsty set of beings, always seeking after power and authority – we see them all over the confederacy of Greece... cutting each other's throats – trying to subject each other to wretchedness and misery – to effect, which, they used all kinds of deceitful, unfair and unmerciful means" (Walker, 16-17). Thus, in 1829 Walker embraced the anteriority of a Black Egypt in world civilization and distinguished between the worldviews of whites and blacks. In his instruction, Walker revised a tendency that had emerged in the thought of his mentor Reverend Richard Allen a generation earlier. During the nineteenth century this framework guided the thoughts of Hosea Easton and Martin Delany and several others.[6] It is in this context that we will review Diop's contribution.

Diop's project contained not only a plan for his own scholarship but even more significantly a challenge to all African scholars. In a 1976 interview he restated his proposition: "Ancient Egyptian culture enjoys a position vis-B-vis present day African cultures analogous to the role which Greco-Latin culture plays in regard to contemporary Western culture. Could you imagine a western scholar researching in western history without referring to Greco-Latin culture? Could his work be considered as scientific. The same applies to African scholars in respect to ancient Egypt" ("BBB Interviews," 31). The "body of African human sciences" that Diop spent his life developing and promoting would not merely stand as an immobile monument to a glorious African past, but as he put it, "the vital function of a body of African human sciences is to develop a sense of collective belonging through a reinforcement of culture" ("BBB Interviews" 31-32). In other words, the "Black Egypt" project is directed toward the creation of what Diop defined as a new African who "will have felt another man born within him, moved by an historical conscience, true creator, a Promethean bearer of a new civilization and perfectly aware of what the whole world owes to his ancestral genius in *all* domains of science, culture and religion" (*Civilization*, 6).

Thus, the higher objective of a scientifically defined Black Egypt was for Diop not merely to inform Africans and others but to transform African peoples, psychologically, historically and culturally. This process of retaking the Nile Valley through scientific methodology would nullify the European intellectual atrocities that were designed to deform and mutilate the African culture.

The cultivation of a classical base for African civilization is legitimate in its own right; that is, it represents the truth of the matter. Furthermore, all civilizations have classical antecedents; for example, China and the age of Confucius; Judaism and the era of Abraham and his progeny; Islam and the time of the Prophet; Christianity and the days of Jesus and his disciples; Europe and the Greek antiquity. In the case of Africa, however, the project is more vital because of the European intellectual onslaught to remove Africans from history largely through the denial of the Africanity of Kemet.

Diop's twentieth-century project was directed toward the same war that Allen and Walker had fought in the eighteenth and nineteenth centuries. The war was the result of the intellectual blitzkrieg committed by the great European thinkers who invented the doctrine of white supremacy in the middle of the eighteenth century in order to justify three hundred years of exploitation of Africa and the unfortunate and indefinite continuation of exploitations in Africa. In fact, the final atrocities were perpetrated by G.W.F. Hegel in *The Philosophy of History* in the same decade that David Walker wrote his *Appeal*. The *Appeal* was an instructional manual to teach African people how to fight their intellectual war. In his instruction, Walker explained the nature of the war by focusing on Thomas Jefferson's *Notes on Virginia*. "Mr. Jefferson declared to the world that we are inferior to the whites both in the endowment of our bodies and our minds" (Walker, 10). Jefferson had spent several months in France where the doctrine of white supremacy was hammered out in the discourses of Voltaire and Montesquieu.[7] This invention was spread to Britain through David Hume (*Essays*) who studied in France as a protégé of Montesquieu. A little later the doctrine was echoed and circulated in Germany by the German philosopher Immanuel Kant, who was an admirer of the ideas of Hume. One could easily conclude that the doctrine was the product of an international European philosophical conspiracy. Thirty-eight years before Jefferson brought the doctrine across the Atlantic in 1788, Benjamin Franklin had anticipated the new orthodoxy when he opposed the increase of the "sons of Africa" in the British colonies on economic, cultural and aesthetic grounds.[8]

Diop's battle, however, was focused primarily on a narrower target. He began with the deconstruction of the pioneer, modern Egyptologists (*African Origin*) who according to him were "guilty of a deliberate falsification of the history of humanity" (*Civilization or Barbarism*, 1). The connection between these Egyptologists who had produced "the ludicrous and vicious falsifications and the authors of the philosophical doctrine of white supremacy" should be clarified although Diop did not detail the linkages (*Civilization or Rarbarism*). As Diop asserted before this campaign started for "all the writers who preceded (them) and all the contemporaries of the ancient Egyptians, the Black identity of the Egyptian was an evident fact" (*Civilization and Barbarism*, 1). The critical fact is that this falsification

47

by the modern Egyptologists occurred about the time that Hegel added the final touches to the project Montesquieu had begun almost one hundred years earlier. For Hegel, the logical solution to the question raised about "Negro" inferiority was the removal of Africans "proper" from history (Hegel). In order to do this correctly, Africa had to be removed from ancient Egypt and Egypt had to be removed from "Africa proper." From the thought of this new European orthodoxy, the civilization of Egypt – which was so highly regarded by the ancient Jews and Greeks (who were considered the pillars of the modern western civilization) – could not have been authored by an inferior race. Therefore, history had to be falsified. The solution was historicide, that is, the destruction of a people's history. Diop called the crime "mental murder" (*Civilization and Barbarism*, 2). This problem occupied Diop throughout his career. In his first major publication he examined the history of the campaign throughout the nineteenth century. Twenty years later, in 1974, he confronted an international group of Egyptologists at a symposium on the peopling of ancient Egypt.[9] At that time Professor Diop revised his earlier critique by adding paleontological and other scientific data supporting his claim that the ancient Nile Valley dwellers were indeed black. His disciple Théophile Obenga supported Dr. Diop's arguments through an impressive linguistic study, "The Genetic Linguistic Relationship between Egyptian and Modern Negro." Diop's revised argument was later presented in an essay (Origin of the Ancient Egyptian) that was published in volume 2 of the *General History of Africa*. The discourse was further extended in *Civilization or Barbarism* where Diop devoted the first four chapters to the discussion. Although Diop asserted that the "battle is practically won," he pointed out that "there will always be some rearguard actions (including) some Africans who are strutting around... giving us some pinpricks and some lessons in 'scientific objectivity'" (*Civilization and Barbarism*, 2).

Diop's thesis concerning the study of Kemetic civilization is indeed the beginning point for African-centered scholarship. There are two dimensions to Diop's mandate in this regard. First the project is necessary in order to restore African history or, rather, Africans to history. As he put it:

The return to Egypt in all domains is the necessary condition for reconciling African civilizations with history, in order to be able to construct a body of modern human sciences, in order to renovate African culture. Far from being a reveling in the past, a look toward the Egypt of antiquity is the best way to conceive and build our cultural future. In re-conceived and renewed African culture, Egypt will play the same role that Greco-Latin antiquity plays in Western culture. (*Civilization and Barbarism*, 3)

The second dimension is the role of Kemetic civilization in world history. Again Diop argued:

> Insofar as Egypt is the distant mother of Western cultures and sciences, as will emerge from the reading of this book, most of the ideas that we call foreign are oftentimes nothing but mixed up, reversed, modified, elaborated images of the creations of our African ancestors, such as Judaism, Christianity, Islam, dialectics, the theory of being, the exact sciences, arithmetic, geometry, mechanical engineering, astronomy, medicine, literature (novel, poetry, drama), architecture, the arts, etc. (Diop, *Civilization and Barbarism,* 14).

In other words, our champion Diop, has provided a framework for African-centered scholars to develop the "African human sciences" in their full dimensions.

THE AFRICAN-CENTERED INTELLECTUAL AGENDA

Let us now restate some of the significant arguments for a classical foundation for African history. The discourse emphasizes five major premises: (1) Ancient Nile Valley civilizations (Kush and Kemet) were authored and maintained by African peoples, that is, Black people; (2) Kemet was colonized and founded by Kushites; (3) Kemetic civilization was the transmitter of some of the major ideas of civilization to the various cultures of tri-continental antiquity, especially the so-called pillars of Western civilization the Greeks and Hebrews; (4) ironically in view of 3), the ancient cultures of Eurasians are in significant ways diametrically opposed to the cultures of ancient Africans as per Diop's idea of the Two Cradles of Civilization; and (5) African peoples are united culturally, linguistically, and historically from antiquity to the present, from ancient Memphis to modern Soweto and throughout the diaspora. Let us now summarize each of these arguments.

Black Egypt

The people of the Nile Valley, the Kushites and the Kemites, were Africans or black people in the same sense that the terms are used to identify peoples of presumed African descent today. In fact the term Negro, which means "black" in Spanish, was the term of choice used by the Europeans thinkers who invented white supremacy.

Indeed, we are called black because we are of African descent. In terms of the continental populations, these "full-blooded" Africans are collectively referred to as "black Africa." In the diaspora we have been referred to and have defined ourselves variously as Africans, Blacks, Negroes, colored, Afro-Americans and more recently, African Americans (with and without a hyphen). David Walker got to the point when he asserted "Egyptians were Africans... such as we are – some of them yellow and others dark" (Walker, 8). Since the complexions of these various African peoples in time and space range from light browns to dark browns, and hair texture varies from loose curly to tight curly, and facial features are diverse, no typical portrait depicts the multitude that enjoys the distinction of blackness as a racial designation. Thus the Kemites were as black as the diverse peoples of Black Africa are today.

The only non-black people who have lived in Africa for a great length of time and are not generally known as invaders are the Berbers of North Africa. In antiquity these people were depicted as quite distinct from the people of the Nile Valley. In Kemetic iconography they appear as fair-skinned people who contrast sharply with the deep browns and blacks of Kushitic and Kemetic people. Although these people have been treated variously by archaeology, most African-centered scholars have attributed their presence to early migrations from Europe and Asia. The descendants of those ancient "Libyans" resemble many of the modern inhabitants of Egypt because of the invasions and migrations across Northern Africa of Phoenicians, Greeks, Persians, Romans, Arabs, and Turks.

The African-centered position further argues that the populations of Kemet and Kush were African or black in the same sense that the populations of Hellas or Roma were white. All scholars know that some cross-continental biological infusions took place in all of the loci of antiquity. But however swarthy some Greeks may have been, Hellas is considered to be a European or white civilization. In like manner, the ancient Jews and Mesopotamians are considered Asian, white, yellow, and/or brown. Thus, Hegel's demand that ancient Egypt does not belong to Africa must be refuted.

It is true that the Kemites and Kushites were not black supremacists, that is, they did not invent a racial theory to explain their cultural or political superiority over non-Africans. They were, nonetheless, aware of their complexion or color and left an irrefutable record of this in their iconography. Neither are the champions of African-centered thought black supremacists. We, like Diop and our fore-parents, would not even be engaged in this project had not the modern European philosophers waged their campaigns of historicide and cultural genocide. No one would have doubted the Africanity of the Kemites and Kushites had not the Montesquieus told lies about "Negro inferiority"; had not the Hegels dishonestly asserted that Egypt was no part of Africa and that Africans had no history. Had not these lies been told, African scholars would face a significantly different task.

The Kushitic Origin of Pharaonic Civilization

The Kushites – who were called Ethiopians by the ancient Greeks – have been considered the founders of Kemetic civilization from antiquity down to the present. The Greek term Ethiopia also had a more general meaning, for example, it inferred to all of the peoples considered today as "Black Africans," and even all peoples with black skins such as the Dravidians of India. The African-centered perspective holds that the civilization of Kemet had its origin in inner Africa, specifically and more immediately in people from Kush, and more generally from black Africa. The research of Bruce Williams (*Excavations*: 1986) as well as the younger and more liberal Egyptologists[10] so overwhelmingly supports this assertion that we no longer have to detail our arguments in this regard.

Suffice it to say that when Piankhy and Shabaka marched down the Nile from Napata in Kush to the Mediterranean Sea, they were not only considered liberators by the multitude, they were also viewed as restorers of the ancient way. Furthermore, those Kushites, who ushered in what John Henrik Clarke calls "Kemet's Last Walk in the Sun," conceived their mission as recreating what their ancestors had created at the beginning of history. Let us recall that Pharaonic civilization lasted for another one thousand years in Kush after it fell in Kemet when the Eurasians began their invasions. Ironically, Pharaonic civilization had its dawn and dusk in Kush.

THE ANTERIORITY OF AFRICAN CIVILIZATION

Again, David Walker got the idea underway when he asserted that "learning originated among the sons of Africa" (19). The testimony of the Greek writers and ancient Jewish scribes concerning their intellectual debts to Kemet is so extensive that this point is also beyond debate. Diop well summarized the significance of the argument: "Instead of presenting itself to history as an insolvent debtor, the Black world is the very initiator of the 'Western' civilization flaunted before our eyes today. Pythagorean mathematics, the theory of the four elements of Thales of Miletus, Epicurean materialism, Platonic idealism, Judaism, Islam, and modern science are rooted in Egyptian cosmogony and science" (*African Origin,* xiv).

THE TWO-CRADLE THEORY

In accepting the truth of the anteriority of African civilization, we should not claim every moment of Greek or Jewish thought. After all, Mesopotamian civilization had a profound impact on their cultures. Mesopotamian culture in both its Sumerian and its Babylonian-Assyrian phases, articulated the major cultural theme shared throughout Eurasian antiquity, such as, fundamental alienation (Carruthers, "Outside Academia").

Indeed, were one to generalize about the characteristics which Professor Diop attributes to the Northern Cradle (Eurasia), the term alienation or estrangement is absolutely appropriate. In contrast, the African worldview is based on unicity or Umoja as Maulana Karenga has asserted. This trait of alienation runs throughout the history of European thought from Plato through Marx to Foucault.[11] After taking an inventory of European basic ideas, we should not want to claim them all.

THE GENETIC RELATIONSHIP BETWEEN KEMET AND INNER AFRICA

Diop's definitive exploration of the cultural, linguistic, and historical unity of Africa in time and space is a major aspect of his life work. Two of his major works – *Cultural Unity of Black Africa* and *Pre-colonial Black Africa* – are devoted to his thesis in this regard. But the concept of African unity is dominant in all of his major works. The continuity with which Diop so patiently and scientifically explored his ideas on cultural unity was anticipated by Martin Delany, who, following David Walker, explored all facets of the African perspective. In 1879, Delany, summarizing the issue, put it this way: "the enquiry naturally presents itself: How do the Africans of the present day compare in morals and social polity with those of ancient times: We answer that those south of the 'Sahara,' uncontaminated by influence of the coast...are equal in... moral integrity to the ancient Africans. Those people have all the finer elements of the highest civilization" (Delany, 90). We must bear in mind that Delany not only extensively researched ancient Kemetic and Kushitic civilizations in the context of world history, he also traveled to West Africa and studied African culture and languages first-hand. Delany, together with Walker and Diop, provided a role model for our scholarly project.

Although our intellectual ancestors and elders from Prince Hall through John Henrik Clarke have overthrown many barriers and won many major battles, the war is still in progress and we must not diminish our efforts. Our intellectual enemies are continually attempting to discredit our champions and theories by distortions and character assignation. Even more menacing, they try to divide us by various enticements.

These opponents have great power over the educational, research and communications industries; like the Pied Piper they are luring some of our brighter children with the symbols of the Good Life, academic rank and tenure, top salary, lucrative royalties and above all, "honorable" mention. Those of us at the center of the movement have been given carrot-and-stick treatment. We have received offers of grants if only we abandon Egypt and embrace Kush. Some of us, such as Len Jeffries and Tony Martin, have been accused of anti-Semitism. In other words, "*A luta continua.*"

In the face of the continuing warfare we must commit ourselves to following our strategy to ultimate victory. In regard to the five premises of the classical African foundation we must under no circumstances inflict wounds on ourselves. This means we must continue to refine the statements in keeping with what Diop called the scientific method. In other words, we should concentrate on concrete facts for evidence supporting our assertions rather than cultivate the occult, unattached to the world we experience. This does not deny the spiritual basis of all existence. It merely emphasizes the necessity of developing an episteme derived from serious study rather than charismatic from inspiration. The problem with charismatic leadership is that usually we have only the word of the prophet that it was really God whispering the instructions. Some critics point out that surely God would have instructed those who were expected to follow as well as the leaders.

A great deal of work remains to be done. An African world history must be developed. David Walker outlined the project in 1829, Hosea Easton restated that historical sketch in 1837, Martin Delany extensively revised the tradition in 1879. Cheikh Anta Diop provided a sociological framework for such a history, especially in *Precolonial Black Africa* and *Civilization or Barbarism*. Finally, Chancellor Williams put forth a bold philosophy for an African history of the world. Our task is to build on these works and produce an account of world history that will permit us to wean us from European scholarly tales.

We must also concentrate on what Diop called the African Human Sciences. We need to develop scholarly disciplines that are appropriate to our quest for intellectual freedom. Certain ancient European disciplines such as political science are so at odds with the wisdom of Nile Valley civilization that they should probably be abandoned. Others, such as egyptology, were conceived in white supremacy and must be rejected outright. All of the European disciplines should be carefully examined and critiqued. More important we must develop strategies to study Divine Speech, Good Speech, Governance, Medicine, and Instruction, all major disciplines in the living African tradition.

A final reprisal is proclaimed in the subtitle of Diop's last major work. The French subtitle of *Civilization ou Barbarie* is *Anthropoligie sans complaisance*. Leonard Jeffries has translated this subtitle as *Anthropology without compromise*. We cannot afford to snatch defeat from the jaws of victory through compromise with the enemy. Let us not confuse victory with a superficial arrangement that looks like victory but in reality is defeat, like the replacement of colonization with neo-colonialism. Indeed, compromise has done our project more damage than hand-to-hand combat. We are appreciative that the European archaeologists have offered us Kush and a few pharaohs, but we must not forget that we must take the entire Nile Valley together with the rest of Africa. While we accept rank and tenure in their universities let us not relent in our project to establish the African University in the image of the *Peru-ankhs* (the houses of life) of Kemet.

THE AFRICAN-CENTERED REBIRTH

Like the ancient father Khety in his instruction, Diop has called us to the greatest office in the land (Simpson, 1973). The office to which we are appointed affords us an opportunity to advance the African liberation campaign. First let us look at the connection between the modern progenitors of the African-centered worldview and the worldview itself.

The correspondence between Dr. Diop's instruction (*Toward the African Renaissance*) and an ancient Kemetic tradition of *Wheme Mesu* is remarkable (Carruthers, "Whm"). The term *Wheme Mesu* means Repetition of the Birth and was used by the 12th dynasty Pharaoh *Amen M Hat* as the theme for the era of history he introduced. *Wheme Mesu* was a metaphor for the perennial evocation of the model of *Sep Tepy*, the First Occasion or the birth of the National Civilization. This theme embodied the idea that the divine order must be constantly renewed; the principles of the beginning must be reaffirmed; the source must be revisited; the civilization must be restored; that which was in disarray must be repaired. The coronation of the pharaoh was based on a celebration of this theme. Each ascending monarch restored *Maat* (Truth, Order) to her seat while at the same time he or she dispelled *isft* (disorder). In fact all great celebrations embraced this principle of the ever-recurring creation; the Kemetic cosmic drama was incorporated into every aspect of life.

The African-centered focus is also embodied in the thought of the authors of the return to foundations among Africans in the modern Western diaspora. Africans who found themselves mired in the oppression of the chattel slave system reinforced by the intellectual tyranny of doctrinal white supremacy and cultural genocide began to retrieve the ancient cultural foundations. They erected an outline of history that has informed African thought for the past two centuries. In so doing they inadvertently embraced the spirit of rebirth endemic to the African way. Thus, those pioneers answered Diop's evocation 150 years before he was born.

The fact that Diop, James, and deGraft-Johnson were pursuing this time – honored path – unknown to each other and more or less unacquainted with the long history of their implicit project – is affirmation of the legitimacy of the return to the deep well of Kemetic civilization. Tracing this historic theme through five thousand years of the history of African peoples in the context of world history is a priority for African scholars. In order for us to fulfill the optimistic prophesy of our project we must rescue the stream of continuity from the obscurity to which our adversaries have relegated it. In other words, in order to obtain the African future, we must fully restore our living tradition.

Endnotes

1. Martin Delany, *The Origin of Races and Color,* (Baltimore: Black Classics Press), 1991, 95, citing Psalms 68:31.
2. Marcus Garvey, *Philosophy and Opinions of Marcus Garvey,* 1: 56, 2: 18.
3. African Heritage Studies Association 23rd Annual Conference Program, 1994.
4. See John Henrik Clarke, *Africans at the Crossroads: Notes for an African World Revolution.* His major themes are explored in this text.
5. See Vulindlela Wobogo. "Diop's Two Cradle Theory and the Origin of White Racism," *Black Books Bulletin* 4: 4 (winter 1976): 20-29, 72.
6. See Jacob Carruthers, "Reflections on the History of the Afrocentric World-view," 4.
7. See Voltaire, *Candide, Part One,* Ben Ray Redman.
8. See Benjamin Franklin, "Observations concerning the Increase of Mankind," 225.
9. See *The Peopling of Ancient Egypt and the Deciphering of Meroitic Script: The General History of African Studies and Documents.*
10. Ibid.
11. Marimba Ani, *Yurugu:* (1994) is an excellent analysis of European thought from antiquity to the present.

References

African Heritage Studies Association 23rd Annual Conference Program. Chicago, 1994.

Afrocentric World Review, vol. I, No. 1 Winter 1973.

Ani, Marimba. *Yurugu.* Trenton: Africa World Press, 1994.

Ben Jochannan. Yosef. *Black Man on the Nile and His Family.* New York: Alke-bulan Books, 1970.

The Bible.

Carruthers, Jacob. "Outside Academia." *Journal of Black Studies* 22. 4 (June 1992): 459-476.

_____. "Reflections on the History of the Afrocentric Worldview." *Black Books Bulletin* 7. 1 (1980): 4-7, 13, 25.

_____. "Whm Msw: ASCAC and the Spirit of African History." *Kemetic Voice* 2. 5 (April 1994): 1, 8-9, 17.

Clarke, John Henrik. *Africans at the Crossroads: Notes for an African World Revolution.* Trenton: Africa World Press, 1991.

deGraft-Johnson, J. C. *African Glory: The Story of Vanished Negro Civilizations.* New York: Walker, 1954.

Delany, Martin R. *The Origin of Races and Color.* Baltimore: Black Classics Press, 1991.

Diop, Cheikh Anta. *African Origin of Civilization: Myth or Reality,* Westport, Lawrence Hill & Co., 1974.

_____. "BBB Interviews: Cheikh Anta Diop." *Black Books Bulletin* 4. 4 (winter 1976): 30

_____. *Civilization or Barbarism: An Authentic Anthropology.* New York: Lawrence Hill, 1991.

_____. *Nations Negres et Culture.* 2 vols. Paris Presence Africaine, 1979.

_____. "Origin of the Ancient Egyptians." *General History of Africa* vol. 2, *Ancient Civilizations of Africa,* ed. G. Mohtar. London: Heinemann, 1981.

_____. *Towards the African Renaissance: Essays in African Culture and Development, 1946-1960.* Translated by Egbuna P. Madum. London: Karnak House, 1996.

Easton, Hosea. "A Treatise on the Intellectual Character and Civil and Political Condition of the Colored People of the United States," ed. Dorothy Porter. In *Negro Protest Pamphlets,* New York: Arno Press, 1969.

Equiano, Olaudah. *Equiano's Travels: His Autobiography. The Interesting Narrative of the Life of Olaudah Equiano or Gustavus Vassa, the African,* Abridged and edited by Paul Edwards. London: Heinemann, 1969.

Franklin, Benjamin. "Observations Concerning the Increase of Mankind." *Papers of Benjamin Franklin* 4 July 1750-June 1753, 4: 225-34.

Garvey, Marcus Mosiah. *Philosophy and Opinions of Marcus Garvey.* Edited by Amy Jacques-Garvey. 2 vols. 1923, 1925. Dover, Mass.: The Majority Press, 1969.

General History of Africa Vol. II Ancient Civilizations of Africa. Edited by G. Moktar. London: Heinemann, 1981.

Hall, Prince. "A Charge Delivered to the African Lodge June 24, 1797 at Menotony," Edited by Thomas Frazier

Hansberry, Leo. *Pillars in Ethiopian History.* Edited by Joseph E. Harris. Washington, D.C.: Howard University Press, 1974.

Hegel, Georg W. F. *A Philosophy of History.* New York: Dover, 1956.

Hume, David. *Essays Moral, Political and Literary.* New York: Liberty Classics, 1912.

Jackson, John G. *Introduction to African Civilizations.* Secaucus, N. Jersey: Citadel Press, 1974.

James, George G. M. *Stolen Legacy.* San Francisco: Julian Richardson, 1976.

Jefferson, Thomas. *Notes on the State of Virginia.* Edited by William Peden. Chapel Hill: University of North Carolina Press, 1955.

Jones, Absalom, and Richard Allen. "A Narrative of the Proceedings of the Black People during the Late Awful Calamity in Philadelphia." In *A Documentary History of the Negro People in the United States*, Herbert Aptheker. ed. New York: Citadel Press, 1951.

Kant, Imanuel. "Observations on the Feeling of the Beautiful and Sublime," translated by John T. Goldthwart. Berkeley and Los Angeles: University of California Press, 1991.

Montesquieu, Baron de. *The Spirit of the Laws.* New York: Hofner, 1965.

Obenga, Théophile. "The Genetic Linguistic Relationship between Egyptian (Ancient Egyptian and Coptic) and Modern Negro-African Languages." In *The Peopling of Ancient Egypt.*

The Peopling of Ancient Egypt and the Deciphering of Meroitic Script: The General History of Africa, Studies and Documents I, Ghent; UNESCO, 1978.

Simpson, W. K., ed. "Satire of the Trades." In *The Literature of Ancient Egypt.* New Haven: Yale University Press, 1973.

Voltaire. *Candide, Part One,* Ben Ray Redman. In *The Portable Voltaire*, ed. New York: Viking Press, 1949.

Walker, David. *David Walker's Appeal, In Four Articles Together With A Preamble, to the Coloured Citizens of the World, but in Particular, and Very Expressly to Those of the United States of America.* Baltimore: Black Classics Press, 1993.

Williams, Bruce. *Excavations between Abu Simbel and the Sudan Frontier.* Chicago: University of Chicago Press, 1986.

Williams, Chancellor. *Destruction of Black Civilization: Great Issue of a Race from 4500 BC to 2000 AD.* Chicago: Third World Press, 1974.

4

BLACK MALE-FEMALE RELATIONSHIPS: THE LENS MODEL

Delores P. Aldridge

I. INTRODUCTION

The dynamic interplay between Black males and females within relationships is a subject that warrants serious research and analysis. It is
also a topic that provokes lively discussion, for the subject is like religion
or politics – every one has an opinion and is convinced that his or her
perspective is the correct one. Added to this is the fact that male-female
relationships, while interpersonal, exist within the social context of American society. The question of how each gender impacts and influences the
overall characteristics of the other presents a formidable expository challenge. A series of questions indicating meaningful areas of investigation
may then be posed:

(1) Are male-female relationships important?
(2) Is it significant to isolate as well as focus upon the dynamic interplay
of Africana male-female relationships?
(3) What is a useful model or framework for explaining male-female relationships?
(4) What are some recommendations for maintaining sound relationships
and for healing weak or damaged ones?
(5) What relevance, if any, does the understanding of African American
male-female relationships have to do with the understanding of other
relationships in the American society?

CORNERSTONE OF SOCIETY

Male-female relationships are indispensable to the maintenance and
development of human society. The male-female bond is an essential one
and serves to cement the basic unit of the family. These bonds are indicators of the quality of social life and preserve the cohesiveness of the group.
Moreover, male-female relationships provide a vista for discovering

stages of personal development, identity, and the revelation of who people really are. More significant, particularly for the Africana family, they are a measure of a people's capacity for struggle and social construction. As a fundamental unit of the nation, relationship and weaknesses determine the nation's capacity to define, defend, and develop its interests.

AN OVERVIEW

Black male-female relationships are critical to society and its institutions whether the analysis begins from a perspective of nuclear families or of single-parent households. Sensitive research and appropriate methodologies recognize the presence or absence of males in households as indicators of larger social conditions that define the environment in which relationships are forged. Viewed within the social context, relationships are relatively stable or unstable, sturdy or fragile. Physical characteristics of family units provide empirical evidence of the types of adjustments Blacks make in response to pressures and conditions created by a social environment they do not control, and the impact of which they are relatively powerless to change.

Within the context of a malevolent social order, it may be necessary and quite rational for Black mothers rather than fathers to socialize Black male children. This is consistent with their future roles as a marginal "subspecies" within the society that requires atypical behaviors and conditioning. Psychological proclivities resulting from such structural adjustments within the family alter the texture and functioning of Black male-female relations, especially as compared to mainstream ideals. Environmental circumstances and objective social possibilities based on demographic facts and power relations in society create a different psychological frame of reference for Black male-female relations. To lose sight of this basic postulate jeopardizes the legitimacy of scholarship in this field.

A typical shortcoming of views that approach the Black female-headed family as a deficit model can be found in the notion that it is a deviant version of the nuclear standard and, therefore, doomed to internal dysfunctions. This view, entirely external to the subject of study, embodies the general systems approach (Berrien, 1968), which does not appreciate the requirement for improvisation arising from the growing scarcity of socially viable black males. Moreover, this view abstracts away from coercive forces that give rise to innovative family structure. Because innovation is not recognized as a response to external conditions, it is incorrectly characterized as a deformity inherent in black family life.

Two notable circumstances result from the flawed methodology described above. First, there is a lack of sensible and sensitive research on the structure, dynamics, and outcomes of role socialization in the black female-headed family. Second, the evolutionary strengths of these innovations have yet to be captured in the official vocabulary of research literature.

The union of Black men and women remains the pivotal event in guaranteeing reproduction of the race. In explicating the importance of male compatibility for the Africana woman, Hudson-Weems asserts: "positive male companionship is of great interest to the Africana woman-ist in general, for she realizes that male and female relationships are not only comforting but the key to perpetuating the human race. Without each other, the human race becomes extinct" (*Africana Womanism* 67).

In understanding and appreciating the consequences of how the woman is treated within personal relationships (and by extension within society in general), Toure's observations are equally significant. "The treatment of women is a barometer of the fairness and compassion of social institu-tions, a mirror that reflects the economic and social conditions, the levels of political, cultural and moral development of a given country" (Toure, 72). In other words, the treatment of women in relationships is the true measure of social and moral decency. One indicator of the image of black women protected by the mass media, including the latest entertainment format, musical video – has the advantages of being familiar, easily acces-sible, and abundant enough to justify critical analysis.

The standard of beauty communicated by mass media (television, magazines, newspapers, and so on), and only partly contradicted by publi-cations such as *Essence* magazine, has much to do with setting the criteria of beauty for many black women and black men, which too frequently affects Black male-female relationships. Considering the strict limitations on acceptable standards of beauty and behavior imposed by the majority society on black politics, culture, and morality, the mere survival of Black male-female relationships is in itself remarkable.

THE SIGNIFICANCE

Aldridge (1989, 1991) found that prior to the late 1970s focus on the dyad was relatively infrequent. Focus was monadic on males or females rather than on the relationships between the two. Over the last several decades, however, there has been a growing body of scholarly and lit-erary writings on black male-female relationships. A brief bibliography would include writings from sociology (Aldridge, 1984, 1989; 1991; Staples, 1978; Rodgers-Rose, 1980; Jackson, 1971; Scott, 1976; Hare and Hare, 1985); from psychology (Tucker, 1979; Noble, 1978; White, 1984; Young, 1986, 1989); political science (Karenga, 1982; Wilcox, 1979); social welfare (Gary, 1981); psychiatric literature (Welsing, 1974; Poussaint, 1979; Grier and Cobbs, 1968); and works of fiction (Wallace, 1979; Jordan, 1977). Perspectives range from Afrocentric (Asante, 1980, 1981; Karenga, 1982) to a popular treatise (Wallace, 1979).

Despite disciplinary, ideological, and stylistic differences, a concern with Black male-female relationships is central to all these works. A central and recurring theme is survival, and the amazement at the ability of black relationships to survive in the face of enormous odds. An awareness of historical problems, exacerbated by recent social conditions lends a sense of urgency to the analyses set forth. The difficulty of forming relationships due to the scarcity of viable males (Jackson, 1971) and the mutually degrading games that increasingly define the mating ritual (Staples, 1978) emerge as two persistent problems jeopardizing black male-female relationships. The pressures and stresses of black life in America affect the quality and prospects of existing relationships as well as the possibilities for future relationships.

A review of the literature mentioned above leads to the dramatic conclusion that black male-female relationships are probably no more problem-ridden than other male-female relationships. However, the complexities of life and one's socio- economic status contribute to the stability or lack of stability in black male-female relationships and the ability to engage in effective problem solving. Thus, black male-female relationships must always be analyzed within the context of U.S. society. Karenga's (1982) observations of black male-female relationships are most instructive as he, too, points out that these relationships are probably no more problem-ridden than other male-female relationships and that life, itself, is characterized by problems and problem-solving. He cautions that any criticism of black male-female relationships must always be an analysis of the U.S. society with all of the variables that shape and mold individuals and their relationships.

This context sets the stage for defining a framework appropriate for serious analyses of black men, black women, and their relationships. Accordingly, the following postulates are set forth for developing a dynamic framework:

(1) Black males and females in a racist society have an experience that is different from that of whites. Accordingly, our relations have to be viewed within a context where we as a people have existed in a system that has denied and deformed our history and humanity primarily based on the specious concept of race and hierarchies of races.

(2) Sexual and gender oppression is as much an issue for African American men as it is for African American women. Racism and sexism are

interactive and inseparable for them, for both are oppressed in similar and yet different ways. Thus, a different analysis of sexism and black men is needed than that for, by, and of white men.

(3) Demographics is a primary determinant of developing relationships between African American males and females. There is a significant shortage of available/desirable men for black women.

(4) Capitalism and racism have generated situational inequities and sustained oppression which define the lives of people of African descent in America.

(5) Judaeo-Christianism, rooted in the social and cultural experiences of Jews, whites, and men provides images and models that encourage identification with white men as leaders/heroes thus being superior to black men and to women of all hues.

To understand the past, present, or future development and behavior of black males and females in America, these postulates draw attention to personal factors involved in the dyad while also scrutinizing American society itself.

AN AFRICAN-CENTERED LENS MODEL

The interplay of institutional values and interpersonal factors form a dynamic African-centered lens conceptual framework or model for explaining black male-female relationships. What the lens model does is to bring together various individual and societal factors to provide a wholistic model focusing upon the nature and substance of gender relations between Black men and women. Aldridge began developing this model with her work dating back to 1984 and is now refining the model and naming it the Lens Model.

INSTITUTIONAL VALUE SYSTEMS

American society is defined by and derived from core or dominant values-values that have impacted its different sub-cultural groups in different ways. The African-centered dynamic lens model presented in this discourse focuses on these values as being counter-productive for black male-female relationships. Capitalism, racism, sexism, and the Judaeo-Christian ethic comprise the four-pronged institutional or structural value component of the model. Capitalism may be defined as a socio-economic system in which private ownership is the primary means of satisfying human needs. Another characteristic of capitalism is a strong and continuous pursuit of profit. The emphasis upon private ownership tends to shape the view of human relationships, such as, the conceptual conversion of human beings into things to be owned or an attitude in which people may subconsciously be viewed as objects for purchase and resale.

Racism may be defined as a system of denial and deformation of a people's history and humanity based primarily on the specious concept of race and hierarchies of races. Racism in America was born from European feelings of racial superiority and bred within the moral contradiction between Christian concepts and economic beliefs. Slavery represented an attempt to dehumanize of both the proponents and those who were enslaved. On the other hand, slavery represented the extension of private ownership and profit theories into the realm of human relationships. In the contemporary world, neo-colonialism links capitalism and racism, resulting in nations that dominate and nations that are owned by the dominators. In this context it is important to understand that capitalism and racism extend their influence from the intra-personal system to the world system of human organization.

Sexism is the social system and resultant practice of using gender or sex as an a-ascriptive and primary determinant in the establishment, maintenance, and explanation (that is, justification,) of relationships and exchanges. As a system, sexism is composed of assumptions and acts, theories, and practices that imply and impose unequal, oppressive and exploitative relationships based upon gender. When capitalism and racism are reviewed for their effects upon human relationships, it may be seen that sexism converts the dominated into a subordinate feminine stereotype, one waiting to be used.

The Judaeo-Christian tradition is a religious system that has its roots in Judaism and Christianity and draws heavily upon the cultural and social experiences of Jews, whites, and males. The tradition encourages identification with males as leaders and heroes, but more important, it emphasizes the leader-hero tradition as being one with white males and their socio-economic experiences. Thus, any man who does not comply with such an ideal falls short within the value construct of American society. A racist, sexist, capitalist, and Judaeo-Christian macro-system forms the basic structural value system component of the African-centered dynamic model. Following this component, the next step is to set forth the interpersonal dimensions of the dynamic lens model.

INTERPERSONAL FACTORS

Within the context of a racist, sexist, capitalist and Judeo-Christian society, four major factors shape communication and interaction between black males and black females: the scarcity of black men, differential socialization of males and females, sexism and women's liberation, and the modes of interacting. These variables, then, comprise the interpersonal component of the African centered conceptual model.

SCARCITY OF AVAILABLE OR DESIRABLE BLACK MALES

Jackson (1971) draws attention to the shortage of black males by constructing a paradigm based on the following factors: black males have a higher rate of infant mortality; a shorter life expectancy, a high rate of accidents and homicide; they form a disproportionate segment of the prison population and are a significant segment of the drug-addicted population. Staples (1978) reports that there is only one viable, acceptable black male for every five black females, excluding married, imprisoned and, homosexual Black males. Data from the 1977 census indicates that there were 732, 000 more Black females than black males in the 22-24-year-old age range during 1977. More recent census data shows no closure of this gap has occurred (U.S. Bureau of Census, 1990). The shortage is complicated by the fact that so many black males lack the necessary skills to secure and maintain jobs that provide enough income to contribute to the well being of spouses and families (Wilson, 1996). In 1960, there were seventy employed civilian black men for every hundred black women. In 1990, there were forty employed civilian black men for every hundred Black women. Between the 1960s and 1990s, the percentage of Black female-headed households rose as black male unemployment increased and more Black males dropped out of the labor force and out of family life. According to Wilson, "For the first time in the 20th century most adult men in many inner city ghetto neighborhoods are not working in a typical week."(xiii). In a capitalistic society, the measure of an individual's worth is significantly linked to status in the economy. Where males are unable to maintain relevant status in a capitalist, sexist society, there are complications for interactions in the male-female dyad.

Such a profile captures the grim environment confronting Black male-female relationships. Against this backdrop many eligible black men are aware of the imbalance and play a power game with Black women, demanding relationships based on terms that are advantageous to the male. If Black women fail to buy into the power game, interracial courtship is an option that is becoming increasingly available to those who are so inclined. It comes as no surprise, therefore, that the Black woman sees interracial heterosexual relations as a personal rejection of her own desirability.

The Impact of Differential Socialization

Jourard (1971) explored the deadening aspects of the male role, advancing the notion that the socially defined male role requires men to appear tough, objective, striving, achieving, unsentimental, and emotionally unexpressive. If behind this social persona a man cries, he will be viewed as unmanly by others. The contradiction between the ways in which black men are expected to present themselves in small and large group situations and their real emotions is a key to understanding the nature of being a black male in America. The learned tendency of males to mask their true feelings makes it difficult for black men to achieve insight into and empathy with black women.

To the extent that women require expressions of intimate and personal emotions in exchange for their availability as social and sexual partners, the non-expressive or limited expressiveness in males may create difficult situations, as observed by Braithewaite (1981). To properly execute his role as an object of female interest, the black man must be successful at something (for which society ill prepares him), expressing gentleness, emotions, tenderness, and verbal affection toward women, while simultaneously projecting an image of strong, unexpressive coolness.

According to Braithewaite, the high degree of verbal facility among Black men makes it easy for them to create an initial impression of genuine feelings, and thus, to easily establish relationships with women. As the relationship continues and the woman becomes more familiar with the male's ways, however, it becomes increasingly difficult for the black male to camouflage his absence of genuine feelings for his partner. The male must constantly "fake it" and express sentiments he really does not feel. This may explain sudden physical attacks upon one's partner, which are generally followed by loving apologies. Given that the male continuously runs the risk of "blowing his cover" (with the outcome a terminated relationship), it becomes plain that the key issue is not one of one of entering into relationships with women, but rather sustaining relationships with them.

According to Tucker (1979), success with women is important to many men because they are engaged in covert competition with other men. The goal is to avoid peer ridicule and to be perceived as "hip." Given this process, women become targets and the communication structure whereby they become targets assumes the status of an end in itself rather than a means to an end. The process is in many ways dysfunctional to black men. They fear that the expression of emotion leaves them vulnerable, which leads them to reject those emotions, and to suppress an important aspect of human fulfillment.

The pattern of initial contact and verbal gaming as described above are behaviors typical of individuals who internalize basic premises of capitalism and sexism. The woman becomes an object; one gains in profit as one "scores" on an increasing number of women. Real emotions are suppressed or exorcized. The body becomes the object of buying and selling. The inner person is reduced to the status of a toy, available for the man's amusement and pleasure.

Tucker suggests that women can help men by emphasizing different standards for measuring manhood. Instead of rewarding "cool," they may reward responsiveness, support, caring, and honesty. Further, they can encourage black men to confront and struggle with their emotions instead of concealing them. Black women can share with black men a confidence that a man is found to be more attractive when he shares his feelings with women. Men are not always receptive to this kind of effort, but they tend to respect women who succeed, more than those women who are meek, and compliant, and who lack the strength to make demands. Over the last several decades, women have become less compliant in expressing themselves due in part to the rise of the women's liberation movement of the 1960s.

THE IMPACT OF SEXISM AND WOMEN'S LIBERATION

With the advent of the women's liberation movement (though, admittedly, largely subscribed to by white women more than Black women), the subject of sexism has taken on importance among Black people. Sexism has become a focus of discussion among Black males, though the dialogue is inhibited by the perception that it represents yet another assault upon the beleaguered Black male. Staples (1979) argues that female equality involves not only personal relationships but also political and economic relationships. Changing sex-role socialization may be the most effective way to reduce conflicts and inequalities between black men and black women in relationships.

Black women fight an ever-present war against sexism and racism in the context of a Judaeo-Christian capitalistic society. While the Black church has been considered a strong counterforce to EuroAmerican domination, the church itself has not always exercised strong influence in building positive Black male-female relations. The Black church has often institutionalized worship of the white male, defining sexist roles for men and enthroning duty above love. In doing so, it has often treated females in a manner that was not uplifting and positive, exhibiting many tendencies of sexism in its treatment of its women (Grant, 1982). This position of the Black church in the context of a Judaeo-Christian ethic complicates further the nature of sexism operating in black male-female relationships.

The recognition of sexism and the fight for its eradication receives mixed reactions. Staples (1979) is among those who characterize feminism as a divisive force within the oppressed Black American community. Lorde

(1979) supports feminism, arguing that Black women bear the onus of sexism and must assert themselves in an effort to eliminate this oppression. She goes on to suggest that black women must decide the extent and effect of sexism in their community. If this behavior constitutes a pathology, they must define its dimensions. According to Lorde, "Creative relationships of which Staples speaks are to the benefit of black males, considering the sex ratio of males and females." Salaam (1979) contends that the struggle against sexism is not a threat to black masculinity. Forces that assault the humanity and dignity of black women also diminish black men.

A chorus of voices have risen to criticize feminism (LaRue, 1970; Duberman, 1975; Gordon, 1987; Hudson-Weems, 1989, 1993). The arguments may be summarized as follows:

(1) Black people as a race need to be liberated from racism.
(2) Feminism creates negative competition between the black male and the black female for economic security.
(3) White women hoard the benefits of the struggle from black women.
(4) Feminism facilitates increased tension in the already strained interpersonal atmosphere in which black men and black women interact.

The views expressed above suggest that women's liberation impedes the black liberation movement and, therefore, intensifies the problems between Black males and females. The chief problem with women's liberation, as this movement currently operates, is its conservative posture and its endorsement of the social and economic status quo. Women's liberation operates comfortably within the capitalist economic arrangement and the basic goals of the white male power structure. It simply wants a greater representation of females within that structure. Questions regarding the appropriateness and humaneness of power relations based on race and class are not on the agenda.

Black liberation requires that both males and females openly and courageously seek mutual liberation. To achieve this goal, its adherents must operate outside of and as change agents for the traditions serving capitalist and sexist norms. Within the context of Black male-female relations, liberation has a far more complex task than that assumed by women's liberation. To achieve a lovingly free movement within and between black males and females, the parties must create conditions that are at once nonexploitative and non-sexist, drawing from the best cultural traditions of black people as a whole.

INTERACTION: SEEKING NEW MODALITIES

Good relationships between black males and black females grow out of a conscious struggle for change. A good relationship is a stable association defined by its positive sharing and by mutual investment in the emotional and psychological well-being of both partners. African American women have the responsibility to select partners who affirm their strengths, capabilities, and potentials. The complementary nature of the support provided by each member of the relationship sustains a resilience and a positive assertion of love, respect, and trust that is enabling rather than diminishing (Young, "Psychodynamics," 220). Fanon expresses it this way: "The person I love will strengthen me by endorsing my assumption of my manhood [womanhood], while the need to earn the admiration or the love of other will erect a value-making superstructure on my whole vision of the world"(41).

The belief by many who are either seeking partners or caught in dehumanizing relationships, that the quality of life available to one is dependent on the acceptance of unacceptable conditions imposed by another is a contradiction of fundamental values inherent in the African-American experience (Young, "Psychodynamics," 221). Young goes on to explain that it is a denial of one's own sense of self and responsibility to self to refuse to allow any person to abrogate integral self-esteem (Young, "Psychodynamics" 221). White captures the essence of the matter in the following description:

> The ideal male-female relationship within extended family networks and in the Black community at large would be one characterized by the Afro-American values of interdependence, cooperation, and mutual respect, without a fixed classification of household, economic, and social responsibilities based on sex. Male-female relationships that are built on a bond of sharing, nurturance, tenderness, and appreciation have the strong psychological foundation necessary to cope with the social and economic stresses that usually confront Black couples living in a country dominated by Euro-Americans (73).

RECOMMENDATIONS AND CONCLUSIONS

Building strong black male-female relationships and reducing the stresses on fragile or nonexistent ones depend, in large measure, upon the successful implementation of meaningful and realizable recommendations that emerge from careful study and analysis. Such analysis is embraced in the dynamic African-centered lens model, grounded in institutional and interpersonal components, set forth in this chapter. Recommendations and possibilities emanating from the model are provided below.

RECOMMENDATIONS

Strengthening black male-female relationships requires a long-term, sustained effort aimed at all the political, economic, cultural, and social forces impacting black men and women in the American society. As Martin Luther King, Jr. put it: "We are caught in an inescapable network of mutuality tied in a single garment of destiny. Whatever affects one directly affects all indirectly." Recommendations are that:

(1) Social scientists develop and explore researchable questions examining the nature and context of Black male-female relations.

(2) Demographers focus attention on the scarcity of black males as a national phenomenon with its potential grave consequences for the race, and its deleterious effect on Black women.

(3) Black men and women address unsatisfactory interpersonal relationships by participating in personal growth and human relations group sessions.

(4) Universities develop and include a course on male and female relationships as part of their general education curriculum.

(5) Black civil rights organizations and professional, civic, fraternal, and philanthropic groups place on their program agendas, the issue of strategies for strengthening relationships between black men and black women.

(6) The Black media use its power to work diligently at countering, instead of at promoting, the negative images of black men and black women and their relationships.

(7) The Black church examines its own role in promoting male-female conflict.

The Black church must also move to concentrate efforts over the next decade on developing in the following areas:

(1) ministries aimed at building strong and healthy families through initiatives to improve the quality of relationships between black men and black women.

(2) programs aimed at preparing men and women for marriage, including helping men and women deal with their relationships with their own families of origin.

(3) rites of passage programs aimed at preparing young men and young women for manhood and womanhood, and motherhood and father-

hood. For material on rites of passage, refer to Kunjufu (1984); Hare and Hare (1985); Warfield-Coppick , Moore, et. al.(1987); and Lewis (1988), to name a few.

CONCLUSION

The dynamic African-centered lens model is a comprehensive, multifaceted one that provides an approach to understanding the complexity of the relations between black males and females. These relationships cannot be fully explained solely with an interpersonal model. Nor can they be understood from an institutional or structural model alone, as earlier advocated by Aldridge, 1984. Rather, a model is required that embraces both interpersonal and social structural components (Aldridge, 1991). This chapter, then, provides a model specifically for analyzing black male-female relationships. It does so fully recognizing, however, that for maximum positive development, there must be a change in the fabric of American social relations since that is the social backdrop against which black male-female relationships are acted out. Transforming the values inherent in black male-female relationships are, in the final analysis, part of the larger need to transform American society and the human values associated with its legacy of inequality.

References

Aldridge, Delores P. *Black Male-Female Relationships: A Source Book*. Dubuque, Iowa: Kendall/Hunt, 1989.

_____. *Focusing: Black Male-Female Relationships*. Chicago, Ill.: Third World Press, 1991.

_____. "Toward an Understanding of Black Male-Female Relationships," *The Western Journal of Black Studies*. vol. 8, no. 4, 1984: 184-191.

Asante, Molefi. *Afrocentricity: The Theory of Social Change*. Buffalo, N.Y.: Amulefi, 1980.

_____. "Black Male and Female Relationships: An Afrocentric Context." In *Black Men*, L. E. Gary, ed. Beverly Hills, CA: Sage, 1981.

Berrien, F. Kenneth. *General and Social Systems*. New Brunswick, N.J.: Rutgers University Press, 1968.

Braithewaite, Ronald L. "Interpersonal Relations between Black Males and Black Females." Gary, ed. *Black Men*. Beverly Hills, CA: Sage, 1981.

Duberman, Lucile. *Gender and Sex in Society*. New York: Praeger, 1975.

Fanon, Franz. *Black Skin – White Masks*. New York: Grove, 1967.

Gary, Lawrence E., ed. *Black Men*. Beverly Hills, Calif.: Sage Publications, 1981.

Gordon, Vivian V. *Black Women, Feminism, and Black Liberation: Which Way?* Chicago: Third World Press, 1987.

Grant, Jacquelyn. "Black Women and the Church." In G. T. Hull, P. B. Scott and B. Smith, *All the Women Are White, All the Blacks Are Men, but Some of Us Are Brave*, ed. Old Westbury, N.Y.: Feminist Press, 1982, 141-52.

Grier, W., and P. Cobbs. *Black Rage*. New York: Basic Books, 1968.

Hare, Julia. "Black Male-Female Relationships." *Sepia* (November 1979).

Hare, Nathan, and Julia Hare. *Bringing the Black Boy to Manhood: The Passage.* San Francisco: The Black Think Tank, 1985.

Hudson-Weems, Clenora. *Africana Womanism: Reclaiming Ourselves*. Troy, Mich.: Bedford, 1993.

_____. "Cultural and Agenda Conflicts in Academia: Critical Issues in Africana Women's Studies." *The Western Journal of Black Studies*. vol. 13 no. 4, 1989: 185-89.

Jackson, Jacquelyn. "But Where Are the Black Men?" *Black Scholar* 4, 1971: 34-41.

Jordan, June. *Things That I Do in the Dark*. New York: Random House, 1077.

Jourard, Sidney. *Transparent Self.* New York: Jan Nostrand, 1971.

Karenga, Maulana. *Introduction to Black Studies*. Inglewood, Calif.: Kawaida, 1982.

Kunjufu, J. *Developing Positive Self-Images and Discipline in Black Children.* Chicago: African American Images, 1984.

Ladner, Joyce. *Tomorrow's Tomorrow: The Black Woman*. New York: Doubleday, 1972.

LaRue, Linda. "Black Liberation and Women's Lib." *Transaction* vol. 8 no. 1, 1970: 59-63.

Lerner, Gerda. *Black Women in White America*. New York: Vintage Books, 1973.

Lewis, Mary C. *Herstory: Black Female Rites of Passage*. Chicago: African American Images, 1988.

Liebow, Elliot. *Talley's Corner*. Boston: Little, 1967.

Lorde, Audrey. "Feminism and Black Liberation." *The Black Scholar*. Vol. 10, no. 8,9, 1979: 17-20.

Noble, Jeanne. *Beautiful Also Are the Souls of My Black Sisters: A History of Black Women in America*. Englewood Cliffs, N.J.: Prentice-Hall, 1978.

Poussaint, Alvin. "White Manipulation and Black." *The Black Scholar*. vol. 10 no. 8,9, 1979: 52-55.

Rodgers-Rose, LaFrancis. "Dialectics of Black Male-Female Relationship." In *The Black Woman*, ed.. L. Rodgers-Rose. Beverly Hills, Calif.: Sage, 1980: 251-63.

Salaam, Kalamu. "Revolutionary Struggle/Revolutionary Love." *The Black Scholar*. Vol. 10 no. 8,9. 1979: 20-24.

Scott, Joseph. "Polygamy: A Futuristic Family Arrangement for African-Americans." *Black Books Bulletin,* 1976: 13-19.

Staples, Robert. *The Black Woman in America.* Chicago: Nelson-Hall, 1973.

_____. "Masculinity and Race: The Dual Dilemma of Black Men." *Journal of Social Issues.* Vol.34 no. 1, 1978: 169-183.

_____. "A Rejoiner: Black Feminism and the Cult of Masculinity: The Danger Within." *The Black Scholar.* Vol. 10 no. 8,9. 1979.

Toure, Sekou. *Toward Full Reafricanization.* Paris: Presence Africaine, 1959.

Tucker, Robert. *Why Do Black Men Hide Their Feelings?* New York: Dial Press, 1979.

U.S. Bureau of the Census. *Statistical Abstract of the United States, 1990.* Washington, D.C.: Government Printing Office, 1990.

Wallace, Michelle. *Black Macho and the Myth of the Superwoman.* New York: Dial Press, 1979.

Warfield-Coppock, Nsenga, M. Moore,. et al. *Transformations: Rites of Passage Manual for African American Girls.* New York: Star Press, 1987.

Welsing, Frances. "The Cress Theory of Color Confrontation and Racism." *The Black Scholar.* Vol. 5, 1974: 32-40.

White, Joseph L. *The Psychology of Blacks: An Afro-American Perspective.* Englewood Cliffs, N.J.: Prentice-Hall, 1984.

Wilcox, Preston. "Is There Life for Black Leaders after ERA?" *Black Male/Female Relationships.* Vol. 2 no. 1, 1979: 53-55.

Wilson, William J. *When Work Disappears: The World of the New Urban Poor.* New York: Knopf, 1996.

Young, Carlene."Afro-American Family: Contemporary Issues and Implications for Social Policy." In *On Being Black: An In-Group Analysis,* ed. David Pilgrim. Wyndham Hall Press, 1986.

_____. "Psychodynamics of Coping and Surviving of the African American Female in a Changing World," *Journal of Black Studies.* Vol. 20 no 2, 1989: 208-223.

5

AFRICANA WOMANISM AND THE CRITICAL NEED
FOR AFRICANA THEORY AND THOUGHT

THIS CHAPTER IS A REPRINT WITH PERMISSION FROM THE *WESTERN JOURNAL OF BLACK STUDIES* (VOLUME 21, NUMBER 2—SUMMER 1997, 79-84)

Clenora Hudson-Weems

As we enter this new millennium, I cannot stress enough the critical need today for Africana scholars throughout the world to create our own paradigms and theoretical frameworks for assessing our works. We need our own Africana theorists, not scholars who duplicate or use theories created by others in analyzing Africana texts. Indeed, developing paradigms and critical theories, which is our true mission, makes possible for better monitoring interpretations of our works in an effort to keep them both authentic and accurate in order to maintain their originality in meaning and value. The problem, however, is that contrary to white or European theorists, who justifiably approach their literature from the perspective of the centrality of their culture, Eurocentrism, most Africana scholars use theories that are alien and have not been passed through our cultural matrix or lens. While we may have the primary texts, such as the huge body of material by Zora Neale Hurston, we do not on the whole extract from them our own African-centered theories to analyze and explicate the many layers of interpretations that lie within. Instead, we take the Procrustean approach, via superimposing alien or outside theories and methodologies as a primary means of analyzing and interpreting our texts from a so-called legitimate, universally theoretical perspective. Be it known that this ruling perspective in reality is none other than just another perspective. Interestingly, the dominant culture sees absolutely no need to apply our theories in the analysis of their texts.

For the moment, then, let us demystify the European theorists, who situate their analyses within the construct of the centrality of Europe. Ferdinand de Saussure, a French linguist, "considered linguistics to be concerned with a social institution. He identified language as a system of signs [and] he proposed a distinct set of sciences within semiology, now generally known as semiotics" (Makaryk, 467). This system of signs/

words has a signifier (word itself) and the signified (the "meaning" of the word). He stresses that language does not convey reality and thus, calling a thing a desk does not necessarily make it so. He contends that there are two oppositions, which are language (*langue*), "an abstract system maintained by a social group," and speech (*parole*), "the manifestations of that system" (Makaryk, 467). While all of this information is good, and just a given for that matter, focusing exclusively on the external parameters of form rather than content, which is the message, the critical component for us, makes it clear that form here is, in fact, more important than the content, which inauthenticates our focus, since we are at a critical juncture in life regarding our destiny as an oppressed people.

Clifford Geertz, another European theorist, a cultural anthropologist who "construes culture as a text, something to be read and interpreted," (Makaryk, 331) is more involved with the milieu or cultural textual analysis. While his theory is at least ostensibly somewhat compatible with our text because of the emphasis on culture, we must be cautioned that it can only be so if it is endemic, that is, from an insider's perspective, which is not generally the case. For sure, we are familiar with the established reputation of traditional anthropologists and the traditional non-endemic work that they have created, usually studying so-called "primitive" cultures from the perspective of the outsider. This is essentially the problem with studies by such renowned anthropologists like Franz Boas and Margaret Mead, for example. Although Hurston was considered a protégée of Boas, she provided only a taxonomy within which she might place and categorize the oral literature in which she was totally immersed, a prism through which mainstream culture might better understand oral literature. To be sure, Hurston was an anthropologist long before she met Boas. She, of course, took anthropology to a higher level, almost to a divine place as an endemic anthropologist. Needless to say, then, nothing new will come from this kind of structural analysis for us.

Jacque Lacan, a French linguist, psychoanalysis and philosopher, stresses how mind and memory come together in associational links, that is the stream of consciousness technique. This novel form, which explores the mental activity of the characters, was first introduced by French writer Du Jardin in his novel *We're to the Woods No More*. It was later used by Virginia Woolf in her novels *To the Lighthouse*, *Mrs. Dallaway*, and *The Waves*, and also by James Joyce in his enormously lengthy 900 plus page novel, *Ulysses*, exploring a single day of the mental as well as the physical activities of his characters. It was used even later by William Faulkner with all of the material exploring the mental activity of the idiot, Benji, in his novel *The Sound and the Fury*. Here again demonstrated is the emphasis on style and form rather than on content, which, while it is important in and of itself, is not the primary thing for us as Africana people.

Jacques Derrida, a French theorist from Algeria, who is a deconstruc-tionist critic with poststructural textual analysis, puts together theories concerning binary oppositions that are infinitely interchangeable, minus the third realm, which is the real or the effect on others. His response to the significance of the colors black and white in South Africa on the issue of apartheid was that there is no difference and that they are one and the same since they are infinitely interchanging. As others, we, too, should be a bit skeptical here. In fact, his response marked the beginning of his decline as a literary critic. To be sure, the inapplicability of this theory for us should be clear, since Black is always Black and white is certainly always white with all its limitations and privileges respectively.

Another European theorist, Milhail Bakhtin, a Russian formalist, who offers a corrective to the linguist, comes closest, but not close enough, to a theory that could possibly work for Africana texts, with his emphasis on language as imbedded in the social context, the social context being the key component for us. He stresses the element of dialogue, "a model of creativity which assumed that the interaction of at least two embodied voices or personalities was the *sine qua non* for genuine consciousness" (Makaryk, 243). Bakhtin proposes a dialogic process of communication, a kind of "call and response" if you will, which we know comes from African tradition, with the many voices, "polyglossia," which is the poly-morphous stage of the voice, the spirit of the carnival, the "carvinalesque," and the world of topsy-turveydom, all of which are familiar within the African construct with emphasis on orality. In other words, there is no particular need to cite this theorist, since the primary components used have always been an integral part of Africana life, thought and philosophy. Hence, there is no need for Africana texts to be analyzed and explicated via the use of outside theory. To be sure, all of these theorists place Europe and whiteness at the center of their analysis, which we as Africana people should find somewhat problematic for an Africana perspective.

Clearly what we have here is what Dr. Richard K. Barksdale calls, in his collection of lectures and essays *Praisesong of Survival*, and specifi-cally in the selection entitled "Critical Theory and Problems of Canonicity in African American Literature," a fascination with "French-based theo-ries of textual criticism" (Barksdale, 36) on the part of American theorists, emphasizing the propensity toward "ignoring history and personal experi-ence" while emphasizing "an ivory towerish sense of intellectual mysti-fication" (Barksdale 36).... I neither desire nor need to imbue my analy-ses with these or other white critics like Lentricchia who, for example, "argues against the social isolation engendered by textual deconstruction and encourages the use of theories advanced by Gramsci and Foucault for promoting individual empowerment" (Barksdale, 37). We obviously have our own critics who express an interest in the importance of the historical, political, and social context of our literature. For example, while Alaine Locke calls for "l'art pour l'art," insisting that "the Black artist should take a purely aesthetic approach to written material," (Hill, 788), W. E. B. DuBois, whom Patricia Liggins Hill, general editor of *Call and Response* and herself a Black Aesthetician, calls a progenitor of the Black Arts Movement and the Black Aesthetics of the searing sixties, asserts in a 1926 *Crisis* article that "we do not believe in art simply for art's sake" (Hill, 789). Further in "Criteria of Negro Art" in *The Crisis*, DuBois contends that "all Art is propaganda and ever must be, despite the wailing of the purists. I stand in utter shamelessness and say that whatever art I have for writing, has been used always for propaganda, for gaining the right of black folk to love and enjoy... The ultimate judge has got to be you" (Hill, 790). Later, in his "Dramatis Personae" in 1930, DuBois asserts that "All art is propaganda and without propaganda there is no true art" (Hill, 790). Moreover, according to Barksdale, "Richard Wright's assessment that all literature is a protest against something and that without a protesting and politicized literature, needed changes will never be recognized, discussed, or successfully implemented" (Barksdale, 34). Barksdale then says of himself and his co-editor of the anthology *Black Writers of America: A Comprehensive Anthology*, "we were more on fire with political energy than inspired by literary insight.... Kinnamon and I forged a black literary canon full of political content.... For me a literary act is a political act" (Barksdale, 34). Be that as it may, Barksdale sees too clearly the broader picture, which he outlines in his last lecture in Baltimore, November 1989 at the Langston Hughes Society conference, which he founded. Shortly after his keynote address, he received a scathing letter from one of our well-known Black deconstructionist critics, condemning him as an "out dated race man" regarding his perspective on the matter of theory. Unfortunately, however, that letter of attack went unanswered, for in less than a month, Barksdale, who verbally expressed to his wife that he was very disappointed that a young Black scholar whom he had encouraged would disregard the true legacy of Africana literature, suffered the first of many strokes which ultimately caused his death. Moreover, even if he did disagree with Barksdale's accurate assessment regarding Africana theory and thought, the fact that he would do so in such a way as to insult a senior mentor was both unacceptable and unexpected, since from an Africana reality, respect and reverence of one's elders reign supreme. Be that as it may, according to Barksdale,

> A major problem in African American literary canon formation, however, is the burgeoning influence of the very fanciful critical theories... spreading throughout our major graduate schools.... Teachers who have developed skills in these new areas of critical interpretation quickly attract advisees... They not only have become the major dissertation directors, but they have a very strong voice in search and hiring decisions.... . Indeed, one wonders whether PMLA has not become completely enamored of the dense and jargon-ridden style and format practiced by the critical theorist....
>
> So critical theorists have built power bases of influence in many departments of literature, not only in the literary bastions of the East and the West coasts, but throughout the departments of the Big Eight and Big Ten universities. Where the universities have publishing presses, critical theorists also usually exercise some influence on publishing decisions, either as press readers or members of press boards. (Barksdale, 35-36)

What we are talking about here is the awesome politics of employment and publications, as well as one's credibility, visibility, and viability in academe. We have Dr. Barksdale's wife, Dr. Mildred Barksdale, to thank for preserving both her husband's last speech and the condescending letter of response, the former being published during his declining three years plus in his invaluable collection, *Praisesong of Survival*.

Barksdale's astute insights into the true nature and impact of this new critical wave led him to an authentic position, and thus, what follows is his outlined recommendations for expanding and broadening our African American literary canon. He proposes that

> we ignore deconstruction, poststructual textual exegesis, and continental hermeneutics. African American literature cannot effectively survive critical approaches that stress authorial depersonalization and the essential unimportance of racial history, racial community, and racial traditions.... I believe not in avoiding history but in elucidating history. Admittedly, I am that old-fashioned kind of historical critic who still stresses the three M's – the man, the moment, the milieu—in approaching a literary work; and when we get to the text, I stress more M's – matter, manner, mode, meaning.... So, I recommend that as we build our literary canon for the tomorrows that lie ahead in the next century, we remain ever mindful of the need to utilize the politics of survival. This is something to be found in the text of

our history that ahistorical theorists like a Derrida, a Gramsci,
or a Lacan would not begin to understand (Barksdale, 37-8).

What Barksdale is advocating, then, is that we return to the original
mission of the African American literary tradition, which was signaled in
the form of the slave narrative, beginning with Olaudah Equiano's *The
Interesting Narrative of the Life of Olaudah Equiano or Gustavus Vassa,
the African, Written by Himself.* The slave narrative was, indeed, political
as it set out to inform the public of the sad psychological and physical conditions of enslaved Africana people with hopes of galvanizing empathetic
supporters for abolishing this evil system of total brute subjugation. And
is not the political exactly the essence and the objective of Harriet Beecher
Stowe's *Uncle Tom's Cabin*? This tradition was to continue for centuries,
addressing the conditions of the oppressed on whatever the level of racial
oppression of that particular time. Indeed, this is to continue until racial
oppression is no more. Clearly, we have not reached that point as of yet,
and thus, the need for continued emphasis lives on, with a clear focus on
content rather than form.

Like Barksdale and others before him, as a Black Aesthetics critic
and theorist, I take for my analysis of Africana texts an African-centered
theory, grounded in Africana thought and action, and hence, what I am
proposing, like Afrocentric scholar Molefe Asante and

> other great Afrocentric scholars before him (Cheikh Anta Diop,
> John Henry Clark, Juself Ben-Jochannan, and Chancellor Wil-
> liams to name a few), is an Afrocentric perspective on Africana
> issues – putting Africa at the center of the lives and concepts
> of Africanans. In this same way, Africana Womanism com-
> mands an African-centered perspective of Africana women's
> lives – their historical, current, and future interaction with their
> community, which includes their male counterparts" (Hudson-
> Weems. 47).

Like the dominant culture in preserving the integrity of its culture and
art, we need these kinds of theories, African-centered, for our own survival
and the survival of our culture and history. At every instance, we should
ask the questions, and which of the theories we embrace are maps for
analyzing all texts, which work for our unique experiences in this racially
hostile world. In other words, the cultural context, which is all embrac-
ing, such as language, history, dress, behavior, values and principles, is of
utmost importance. We do not have the luxury of spending excessive time
on external nuances, like form, at the risk of sacrificing internal nuances,
such as content and meaning. Thus, our own critical theories for analyzing
our own critical experiences are needed so that we can begin to create

institutions of ideas, Black thought, for housing and disseminating our life experiences, historically, currently and futuralistically.

Institutions like the University of Wisconsin-Milwaukee (where Winston van Horne, the conceptualizer of the discipline of Africology, the study of Africa and its people everywhere, teaches) as well as Temple University (where Molefe Asante is the founding director of the first department to offer a Ph.. D. in African American Studies), could perhaps offer such an opportunity for creating true institutions of Africana ideas. A Ph.D. in African American/Africana Studies utilizing white theory is counterproductive, to say the least. If mainstream theories and methodologies should take center stage at such African-centered institutions or programs, then why establish an African-centered Ph.D. program at all? With this in mind, the following are only some of the valid theories and approaches that a Department of Afrocology/Africana/Black/Pan-African/African American Studies could find strengthening for its unique programs:

Black Aesthetics Continuum – Patricia Liggins Hill-University of San Franciso, Department of English

Kawida – Maulana Karenga-Chair of Black Studies at California StateUniversity-Long Beach

Literary Garveyism-Tony Martin-Wellesley College

Africology – Winston van Horne-Chair of the Department of Africology, University of Wisconsin-Milwaukee

Afrocentricity – Molefi Asante-Temple University

Politics of Survival – Richard K. Barksdale-Professor Emeritus, University of Illinois-Urbana

Africana Womanism – Clenora Hudson-Weems-University of Missouri-Columbia, Department of English

Nkrumaist Literary Theory – Doreatha Drummond Mbalia-University of Wisconsin-Milwaukee, Department of Africology

Groundation in Africana Literary Texts-Wilfred Samuels-Chair of Ethnic Studies,University of Utah

Economic Self Interest-Robert E. Weems, Jr.-University of Missouri-Columbia, Department of History

Anthropology, Memory, and Cultural Resistance-

Ayana-Director of Black World Studies, Loyola University Chicago

Liberation via Equal Education-Alvin O. Chambliss, Jr.-Thurgood Marshall School of Law, Texas Southern University

Racialized Bioethics-Maria Mootry-Director of African American Studies, University of Illinois at Springfield
New Black Liberalism-Lewis Randolph-Ohio University, Department of Political Sciences
Jazz Reclamation in Africana Studies-James B. Stewart-Vice Provost, Pennsylvania State University

Rather than make a futile attempt to discuss and develop all of these theories (all of which will be presented by the above theorists in a forthcoming book entitled *Contemporary Africana Theory and Thought: Into the Next Millennium*, of which I am editor), my mission here is to focus exclusively on the theory of Africana Womanism, which I named, defined and refined. Notice that I do not say I created the idea of Africana Womanism, for it has always been in existence. Going back to pre-American slavery and even to Africa, Africana women have been both African and family-centered, key components of Africana womanism, concerned with the welfare of the entire family as their top priority. I simply named it and refined a paradigm relative to the role of the Africana woman within the constructs of the modern women's movement so that we do not get confused or displaced concerning our true roles in the lives of our families and communities. We are and have always been copartners with our male counterparts in the liberation struggle for our entire people – men, women, and children. And this reality remains a top priority for all true Africana people.

With this in mind, then, what is A fricana Womanism?

> Neither an outgrowth nor an addendum to feminism, Africana Womanism is not Black feminism, African feminism, or Walker's womanism that some Africana women have come to embrace. Africana Womanism is an ideology created and designed for all women of African descent. It is grounded in African culture, and therefore, it necessarily focuses on the unique experiences, struggles, needs, and desires of Africana women.... The primary goal of Africana women, then, is to create their own criteria for assessing their realities, both in thought and in action. (Hudson-Weems, 24, 50)

Indeed, Africana Womanism by its very definition is African-centered, as it places Africa at the center of this analysis as it relates to Africana women. Even in the naming, Africa is at the center, for in African cosmology, *nommo* is the proper naming of a thing which calls it into existence. Thus, the terminology Africana womanism (not Black feminism, womanism, or any other term) more appropriately fits the Africana woman, who is both self-namer and self-definer. It is true that if you do not name and define yourself, someone else surely will. And it is equally true that if you buy a terminology, you likewise buy its agenda. And the agenda for the Africana woman is, indeed, distinguishable from all other female-based theories primarily because of its insistence upon the prioritizing of race, class, and gender (respectively). To be sure, this family-centered, race-empowerment agenda is in direct contravention to any other brands of feminism, which are female-centered and concerned above all else with female empowerment. In spite of the fact that Black feminists, for example, call for simultaneity in combating race, class, and gender oppression, most of their energy goes into combating female subjugation as a priority. Even white feminist, Bettina Aptheker, objectively sees the picture. She appropriately contends that

> When we place women at the center of our thinking, we are going about the business of creating an historical and cultural matrix from which women may claim autonomy and independence over their own lives. For women of color, such autonomy cannot be achieved in conditions of racial oppression and cultural genocide.... In short, "feminist," in the modern sense, means the empowerment of women. For women of color, such an equality, such an empowerment, cannot take place until the communities in which they live can successfully establish their own racial and cultural integrity (Aptheker, 13).

Even if one finds it hard to conceive of prioritizing race, then class, and then gender, one need only to look as Sojourner Truth's oration "And Arn't I a Woman" in which she unpremeditatedly engaged in a self-actualization speech wherein she had to deal with first things first. Before she could begin to address the issue of the absurdity of female subjugation, which was her initial intention when she went to the all-white convention of women in Akron, Ohio in 1951, she had to deal with her ostracism based on her color, race, followed by class:

> "Well, chillun, whar dar is so much racket, dar must be something out o'kilter. I t'ink dat 'twixt de niggers of de Souf an' de women at de Norf' all a-talkin' bout rights, de white men will be in a fix pretty soon... Dat man ober dar say dat women needs to be helped into carriages, and lifted ober ditches, and to have de best place everywhere. Nobody eber helped me into carriages, or ober mud puddles, or give me any best place. And ain't I a woman?... I have borne thirteen chillun, and seen 'em mos' all sold off to slavery, and when I cried out with my mother's grief, none but Jesus heard me! And ain't I a woman?... Den dat little man in black dar, he say women can't have as much rights as men 'cause Christ wan't a woman. Where did your Christ

come from? Where did your Christ come from? From God and
a woman! Man had nothin' to do wid Him" (Truth, 104).

Clearly the gender issue was the last to be addressed here, only after she
dealt with the issue of race and class.

Further emphasizing the race factor was Maria W. Stewart who, two
decades before Truth's famous oration, expanded the same work of Black
cultural nationalism in 1831 by emphasizing the leadership role that Black
women must play in the Black liberation struggle, thereby picking up
where David Walker left off (before his untimely and mysterious death),
with his emphasis on Black male leadership in the liberation struggle. This
pre-Africana womanist advised, "Black women to unite to express and
further develop their full potential as women and as culture bearers. Speaking before the African-American Female Intelligence Society, she charges
black women with the survival and enrichment of the black community"
(Hill, 397). Moreover, abolitionist Frances Harper, too, emphasized race
as a priority for Africana people: "when the two forces [abolitionists and
feminists] became split over the issue of which group, black men or white
women, should be franchised... [she contended] that obtaining the ballot
for part of the race was far better than none [and] passionately pleaded
for the greater urgency of black men's attainment of the vote" (Hill, 346-
47). Likewise, with Harriet Tubman, the underground railroad conductor
who went South nineteen times during the 1850s to help free Black men,
women, and children, and Ida B. Wells, the anti-lynching crusader who
began her investigations in 1892 because two male friends were lynched in
Memphis, Tennessee, because they became competitors to a white grocery
store owner, Black liberation was the number one priority. Indeed, all of
these pre-Africana womanist activists found themselves engaging in race
issues as a top priority.

A critical issue regarding the independent name Africana womanism,
which has none of the baggage with which feminism is being confronted,
is the venomous beginnings of feminism. In 1870, the Fifteenth Amendment to the Constitution was ratified, giving Black men the right to vote.
Wherea Black women were jubilant in this victory for the Africana family,
realizing that a vote in the Black community was a vote in our community,
white women, on the other hand, some of whom had benevolently fought to
abolish slavery, believing that their benevolent activity would benefit them
as well in acquiring full-fledged citizenship with the right to vote, were
angry and thus, their liberal posture radically shifted to a racist one: "For
example, staunch conservative suffragist leader Carrie Chapman Catt and
other women of her persuasion insisted upon strong Anglo Saxon values

and White supremacy. They were interested in banding with White men to secure the vote for pure Whites, excluding not only Africanans but White immigrants as well" (Hudson-Weems. 21). Not only did they desire this chain of action, but they strategized as well, contending in *The Free and the Unfree* that "there is but one way to avert the danger. Cut off the votes of the slums and give it to women.... as a counterbalance to the foreign vote, and as a means of legally preserving White supremacy in the South" (Carol and Nobel, 296). With these clear racist overtones and the emphasis on female empowerment, it is evident that Africana women cannot claim the feminist agenda as theirs own when our entire race is suffering and dying as we speak. Observe South African activist Ruth Mompati, who talks about going into a large auditorium and witnessing the decomposed bodies of all the innocent Black children who were victims of apartheid. She contends that

> the South African woman, faced with the above situation, finds
> the order of her priorities in her struggle for human dignity and
> her rights as a woman dictated by the general political struggle
> of her people as a whole. The national liberation of the black
> South African is a prerequisite to her own liberation and eman-
> cipation as a woman and a worker (Mompati, 112-13).

To be sure, creating an authentic theory for Africana people and for Africana women in particular, reflecting our true level of struggle, is crucial, lest we continue to lose ourselves, and particularly our women (in this case) to someone else's struggle. Note the June 1995 U.S. Supreme Court deci-sion on Affirmative Action Set-Asides. Those that were racially defined were ruled unconstitutional; those based on gender equality were ruled fine and legal. Indeed, what will be the fate of the Black woman who is defined by race first, as all people are? Needless to say, when the feminist has real-ized all her demands, when she is at the top, the Black woman will still be Black, poor, and on the bottom. She will then find herself trying to reenter her community to rejoin her people in the struggle for race parity, only after much precious time and effort have been wasted. Her posture, then would be what it has been from the beginning, that of Africana Womanism, an African-centered paradigm, a theory created for an African-centered perspective. It is clear that we need to operate from the start with Africa at the center of all analyses concerning Africana life and thought, thereby eliminating futile efforts in appropriating outside constructs. To be sure, an authentic paradigm must be mandatory for Africana theorists so that our lives and texts could be accurately construed and interpreted.

"SANKOFA" – Go back and fetch the lessons of our past!

References

Aptheker, Bettina. "Strong Is What We Make Each Other: Unlearning Racism within Women's Studies." *Women's Studies Quarterly*, 9:4 (Winter), 1981, 13-16.

Barksdale, Richard K. "Critical Theory and Problems of Canonicity in African American Literature" in *Praisesong of Survival*. Urbana and Chicago, Illinois: University of Illinois Press, 1992, 32-38.

Carroll, Peter N. and David W. Nobel. *The Free and the Unfree: A New History of the United States*. New York: Penguin Books, 1977.

Hill, Patricia Liggins, general editor. *Call and Response: The Riverside Anthology of the African American Literary Tradition*. Boston: Houghton Mifflin, 1997.

Hudson-Weems, Clenora. *Africana Womanism: Reclaiming Ourselves*. Troy, Mich: Bedford, 1993.

Makaryk, Irena R., general ed. *Encyclopedia of Contemporary Literary Theory*. Toronto: University of Toronto Press, 1993.

Mompati, Ruth. "Women and Life under Apartheid" in *One Is Not a Woman, One Becomes: The African Woman in a Transitional Society*. Daphne Williams Ntiri, ed. Troy, Mich: Bedford, 1982, 108-113.

Truth, Sojourner. "And Arn't I a Woman." In *Narrative of Sojourner Truth*. New York: Arno and the *New York Times*, 1968.

PART II
Black Studies: Beginnings and Evolution

It was during the summer of 1969 that the Institute of the Black World organized a two-month project for faculty and students to organize a curriculum prototype that would define the conceptual parameter and explain the scholarly method and purpose for what was generally being referred to as Black Studies. (Turner, *The Next Decade* v)

6

WILLIAM LEO HANSBERRY AND AFRICAN STUDIES BEGINNINGS IN THE UNITED STATES

Kwame Alford

William Leo Hansberry's early years (1894-1916) and his search for Africa occurred during what historian Rayford W. Logan described as the nadir of post-slavery race relations. The initial stages in his development as an academician and intellectual resulted from the foundation he received from his family, from the tradition of resistance and Black nationalism in the African American community in Mississippi, and from the succession of committed administrators and educators at Alcorn State University. In addition, his early development in Mississippi coincided with "Negrophobia" among whites, the period of constitutional disfranchisement of African Americans and the rise of Jim Crow. Nevertheless, Hansberry emerged, committed to study African peoples in Africa and the diaspora. While attending high school and college at Old Atlanta University, Hansberry discovered and read W.E.B. Du Bois's book *The Negro* (1915), which gave him new insight and unleashed a relentless fervor toward African Studies.

Subsequently young Leo migrated from Atlanta, Georgia, to Cambridge, Massachusetts, to Harvard University and its library (1916-1920), on a mission to read all of the books suggested on Du Bois's reading list. His Harvard tenure marked a fundamental turning point in his life. While he read the books on Du Bois's list he matured as a student and gained academic momentum. His program of study, supported by the classes in which he matriculated, served as the basis for his interdisciplinary approach to the study of ancient African history. His advisor, the distinguished Harvard anthropologist Earnest A. Hooton, provided encouragement and direction and further inspired Hansberry to expand his research into a more systematic approach. During the 1920-1921 academic school year he secured a teaching position at Straight University in New Orleans, Louisiana (now Dillard University). The period between 1920 and 1922 represented the evolutionary and developmental stages of the discipline of African Studies. While his Harvard laboratory served as the origins of the discipline, his first academic appointment served as the first opportunity for development and implementation. Hansberry completed the bachelor of science degree requirements in June 1920 and arrived at Straight University in the fall, where he established African Studies as an interdisciplinary discipline. His courses included anthropology and African archaeology. Concurrently, he initiated a promotional campaign that projected him into the public eye as an expert on Africa.

Hansberry's course repertoire consisted of several essential components, introduced in promotional circulars and leaflets. He issued a statement that resembled course descriptions, asserting that his courses entailed the study of the fundamentals of Negro History of ancient and modern times, the study of the physical and mental differences of races, and an analysis of the important theories of the environmental and biological causes of these differences (Hansberry, *Announcing;* Hansberry, *Circular*; Coleman, 12). Further, Hansberry's April 1921 circular stated that his courses examined and investigated "the influence of Negro and Negroid peoples, on the Paleolithic and Neolithic cultures of Southern Europe, their role in the pre-Chaldean cultures and dynastic civilization of Egypt; a survey of Negro and Negroid civilizations of ancient Ethiopia (Nubia) the purely Negro (according to MacIver) and partly Negro civilizations of ancient Rhodesia and finally the Negro civilizations of Yorubaland (Nigeria) and of the ancient medieval Sudan" (Hansberry, *Circular*; Coleman 12). These courses provided the foundation for a systematic lecture tour that he initiated and conducted during the spring of 1921. This represented the early developmental stages of a paradigm. Hansberry sent promotional announcement materials explaining his intentions, but more specifically his vision for African Studies. His leaflets read, "Announcing an Effort to Promote the Study and Facilitate the Teaching of the Fundamentals of NEGRO LIFE AND HISTORY" (Hansberry, *Announcing*; Harris 5,6; Coleman, 12). Hansberry sent these announcements mostly to African American organizations all over the United States during the 1920-1921 academic school year. Subsequently, he embarked on a travel schedule to many colleges, universities, churches, and Colored Young Mens Christian Association (YMCA) centers for African Americans. He visited fifty-three schools and spoke to more than twenty-one thousand students and teachers. The most revealing aspect of this tour was in Hansberry's open recruitment of students and teachers interested in developing African Studies courses. He meticulously qualified their levels of interest with a flyer questionnaire that accompanied the African Studies promotional materials. The flyer requested that each prospective school, college, or university include an African Studies program in their curriculum. Consequently, Hansberry perceived himself as a "renaissance man – a race man."

Clearly, his ideas of promoting the study of Negro Life and History coincided with Carter Godwin Woodson's (1875-1950) own undertaking. In 1915 and 1916, Woodson founded the Association for the Study of Negro Life and History (ASNLH) and the *Journal of Negro History*. Woodson dedicated his life to the advancement of African Americans through the promotion of Black History. Propagandizing the Black past through the association and the *Journal of Negro History* functioned as Woodson's special form of social activism. He employed a method that simply promoted and exhibited the facts of Black History through the channels of scientific research and education. Woodson's Black History movement, while similar to Hansberry's ideas for an African Studies movement, broadened its base to include the majority of African Americans and heightened the Black community's racial pride and cultural consciousness.

During the early stages of the Black History movement, Hansberry and Woodson developed a professional association and mutual respect for one another. Woodson solicited and employed Hansberry as agent of the association. According to historian Joseph E. Harris, Hansberry spoke throughout the South on behalf of Woodson and the ASNLH. This early lecture apprenticeship and his appreciation of Woodson as a scholar bolstered Hansberry's confidence and vision. Sharing Woodson's vision and using Du Bois and Woodson as guideposts, Hansberry surged ahead with his own strategy for an African Studies movement, including professional faculty and staff development as a major component of his campaign. He gave importance to this component because of the negative opinions of Africa and Africans held by African Americans and the great majority of Americans of all backgrounds – caused by the absence of "accessible material on the subject" and of a curriculum of correction and inclusion (Hansberry *Announcing*). His analysis of the situation remained constant and served as a foundation for his lifelong efforts.

Hansberry, the young teacher and student of Africa, publicized his analysis of how the negative opinions of Africa affected peoples of African descent, while providing strategies and solutions to this problem. This analysis evolved into the developmental stages of the discipline. Consequently, he planned to employ "a scientific approach to solving the very unfavorable tradition around the Negro race." Hansberry's scientific approach appealed to both the general and the academic communities alike. As their awareness increased, he conveyed to them that the "evidence is now [currently] available which establishes that the Negro people have a glorious and honorable past. And are in no sense an inferior type of man" (Hansberry, *Announcing*) In his leaflet he made these assertions and presented the problem in four stages. First, his message examined African American organizations and historically Black colleges and universities, and their lack of commitment to African/Black Studies programs. Hansberry's definition of the problem included a critique of the lack of scientific research and scholarship in the educational system in the United States. He criticized administrations and administrators, faculty and staff of colleges and universities, and specifically historically black colleges and universities for their inaction and non-support for a discipline-based study of Africa and peoples of African descent. It is interesting that Woodson agreed with Hansberry's analysis based on his own experience of teaching at black colleges.

Second, Hansberry acknowledged the tradition of self-trained historians. He chided that their earlier efforts at vindicating the Black past received no appreciation or praise. These acknowledgments reflected Hansberry's own knowledge and appreciation for the efforts of the forerunners of the promotion of Black history. In the nineteenth century, and prior to the work of Du Bois and Woodson, African Americans such as Martin Robinson Delany, David Walker, Alexander Crummell, Frederick Douglass, and George Washington Williams published works on the Black experience in Africa and America. As a student of history, Hansberry clearly affirmed the tradition of these self-trained historians. Moreover, he received inspiration from Crummell's American Negro Academy (1897), Woodson's ASNLH, and Du Bois's political activism. Third, Hansberry asserted that people of African descent derived their lack of self-assurance, self-confidence, and self-respect from a deficiency in knowledge of their heritage. Fourth and more pointedly, Hansberry contended that the previously outlined conditions stemmed from the inaccessibility of and difficulty in acquiring adequate and accurate information, and in securing trained teachers in African/Black Studies. After defining the problem in systematic detail, he provided a hypothesis, which led to a proposal and ultimately a solution. He surmised that a serious program of awareness collective of recent findings on Africa and its cultures, at "schools and colleges," solved the problems of access, self-respect, and self-confidence for "the race."

He planned a lecture tour to schools and colleges in regular session during April and May, and visits to the summer schools during June and July (1921). This lecture tour comprised and unveiled Hansberry's efforts to convey the significance of ancient African civilizations to teachers and students, while encouraging them to commit to formal study. He placed the responsibility of the elevation of blacks economically, culturally, and educationally squarely on the shoulders of the college-trained leadership, Du Bois's "Talented Tenth" and based on this principle, Hansberry's main objective remained the recruitment and cultivation of efficient teachers in the discipline of African/Black Studies.

Hansberry's strategy forecasted the establishment of a bureau or foundation that promoted African/Black History/Studies through investigations and expeditions of an independent character. This bureau or foundation, he calculated, needed active stimulus from public lectures, published magazines, while simultaneously supplying schools with text and reference books, manuals, maps, and illustrated materials. Hansberry's vision combined the essentials of Du Bois's "Talented Tenth" principle, Marcus Mosiah Garvey's black nationalism, Booker T. Washington's idea of self-reliance and the importance of character, and Woodson's idea of the restoration of the historical memory of people of African descent (race pride), all into one undertaking.

Hansberry's discourse, at this early stage of his life, provides a glimpse of his character and vision. It seemed that he embraced Du Bois's theory of the Talented Tenth and his ideal of pan-Africanism, and Garvey's ideals of race pride and literary black nationalism. For example, in his public announcements Hansberry asserted that "Africa holds the secrets of man's physical and cultural beginnings; it is therefore the superlative enigma of history. The black man enjoys distinct natural advantages which warrant him in taking the lead in the solution of this great problem" (Hansberry, *Announcing* 1921).

This polemical style of discourse served as a benchmark for his future leanings toward African Nationalism, and the idea of self-determination for all African people in general, under the umbrella of pan-Africanism. Most important, his plan for the implementation of African Studies/Black history programs at historically black colleges and universities constituted, according to Hansberry, the characteristics of a "movement." As a reminder to the Talented Tenth, he surmised that this movement "[roots itself] in the hearts of the people, [and] will continue to go forward of its own inherent power." Further, he reminded them that their leadership in this movement required a fervent commitment to the welfare of the black majority. Finally, he implored future leaders to embrace their training seriously (Hansberry, *Announcing* 1921).

In his April 1921 circular, Hansberry acknowledged that his concentration grounded itself in "the general and particular phases relating to Ancient and Modern Africa." Hansberry conveyed that his main interest centered on the "significant part the black people of the earth played in the creating of the original and fundamental elements of higher human culture and the very notable, though little known, role they had played in its distribution and maintenance throughout the world" (Hansberry, *Circular* 1921). Moreover, he identified himself as "a member of this particular racial group [African]" and as a student of Dr. Earnest A. Hooton, anthropologist of the Peabody Museum of Harvard University. Besides his racial identity, Hansberry assigned qualification, merit, and legitimacy to his interests with his association with Hooton. In this regard, he enthusiastically conveyed that,

> I made a fairly careful survey of the more important reports and accounts of the Archaeological discoveries and anthropological studies covering the finds of the past hundred years in Egypt, Asia and Southern Europe, and of the last twenty-five years in Nubia, the Sudan, Nigeria, and Rhodesia. The discovery and study of Pre-historic man in Southern Europe, the finds of Petrie, Naville and others in the Nile valley; the work of deMorgan and Dieulafoy in Persia; the studies of [Randall-] MacIver of the old ruins of Rhodesia; the revelations of the old Arabic, Songhay and Haussa manuscripts found in Central Africa; and finally the startling discoveries of Frovenuis in Nigeria; may be cited as some of the important cases in point. (Hansberry, *Circular* 1921)

While he buttressed his program with the enthusiasm of his students at Straight University, Hansberry reassured himself of the timeliness of his actions with the details in his circular. The circular further explained the illustrated lecture series in detail, that originally appeared in the leaflet announcement. The first lecture encompassed the physical and mental differences of various races of people. The second lecture consisted of a survey of "Negro and Negroid peoples," influence on and contribution to the origin, development, distribution, and maintenance of the higher forms of human cultures in prehistoric and historic periods of the world. Last of all, he proposed three concluding lectures that promoted appropriate linkages between them. The third, fourth, and fifth lectures covered the the forces and causes that led to the extinction or destruction of ancient African civilizations; the historical and contemporary relationships between modern Africa and Europe; and the history of Africans in the Western world, with special emphasis on the African presence in the two Americas and the Caribbean Islands or West Indies. Here, Hansberry demonstrated his belief that African diaspora studies should be included within African Studies.

Hansberry subsequently received encouraging replies, mostly from the directors of summer schools at historically black colleges and universities. Some of these schools included Hampton Normal and Agricultural Institute in Hampton, Virginia (later Hampton Institute and now Hampton University); State College at Orangeburg, South Carolina (later South Carolina State College and now South Carolina State University); Florida Agricultural and Mechanical College for Negroes in Tallahassee, Florida (now Florida Agricultural and Mechanical University); and Tuskegee Normal and Industrial Institute (later Tuskegee Institute and now Tuskegee University). Most of them initiated special arrangements in anticipation of the lecture series outlined in Hansberry's outreach program. Although some schools reacted with generally positive responses, he knew that this undertaking needed a large funding base. His approach to the lecture tour involved a mass financial solicitation effort directed at organizations engaged in the uplift of people of African descent. He remained steadfast on this approach because he refused to charge admission for the lectures. Hansberry maintained that an admission charge sent a message that "such arrangements... might deter many teachers from attending. [and] give the project the appearance of a money-making effort" (Hansberry, *Circular* 1921). Therefore, he absorbed the majority of the expense.

During this period Hansberry cultivated two important relationships. First, he sent a copy of the circular to James Weldon Johnson, executive secretary of the National Association for the Advancement of Colored People (NAACP). The founding of the NAACP in 1910 served as one of the many responses to the declining status of African Americans in early twentieth-century America. In the first years of its existence, the founders committed the new organization to an increase in industrial opportunities, to greater police protection for blacks and to the crusade against lynching and the lawlessness harassing African Americans. In 1916 Johnson joined the NAACP and its seventy branches and nine thousand members as field secretary. Four years later, his efforts increased the NAACP's membership tenfold (to ninety thousand). In 1920 Johnson assumed the position of executive secretary. In the 1920s he guided the NAACP to a reputable position among organizations involved in the uplift of African Americans in general, and in civil rights in particular.

Second, a tentative offer from the Universal Negro Improvement Association (UNIA) reached Hansberry during his 1921 lecture tour. Marcus Mosiah Garvey (1887-1940) founded the UNIA in 1911 in Jamaica, British West Indies. Garvey dedicated the organization to the premise that blacks must achieve equality by becoming independent of white society and form their own governments and nations. Influenced by Booker T.

Washington's plan of self-reliance, Garvey arrived in the United States in 1916 and organized his first branch of the UNIA in Harlem, New York. His movement benefitted from preexisting back-to-Africa and Pan-Africanist sentiments among African Americans. During the peak of his popularity in the early 1920s, Garvey stressed emigration, separation, respect for blackness, and economic self-help. Some sources contend that either an official of the UNIA or Garvey himself contacted Hansberry directly. Garvey's unique aggressiveness in securing "lieutenants" to ward off the competition with Du Bois and the NAACP provides credence to this assumption. Hansberry declined the offer due to "the somewhat skeptical attitude... of the public (African Americans in particular) towards this organization [the UNIA]." He further rationalized that the NAACP possessed a "more thoroughly grounded public confidence and therefore [was] better suited to support this movement" (Hansberry, *Circular* 1921). Consequently, Hansberry solicited additional support and guidance from his mentor, Du Bois. He sent Du Bois a copy of the same circular and letter that Johnson received. Finally, he asked Du Bois to exert any influence necessary with Johnson and the NAACP, and to act as a reliable reference. Du Bois supported Hansberry's strategy for African Studies as an academic discipline and a mass movement and remained one of his main allies throughout his career. In this capacity Du Bois provided Hansberry consistent advice and counsel. As their interests converged, they mentored and counseled each other.

Spring 1921 brought several other options for Hansberry's continued seasoning as a budding Africanist. At the encouragement of Hooton he applied for and received a Winthrop Fellowship in Harvard's School of Anthropology. Aware of his teaching responsibilities and lecture tour, he prepared for the fellowship tenure at Harvard for the 1921-1922 academic school year. He also published "The Material Culture of Ancient Nigeria," in the *Journal of Negro History* of July 1921. This article represented a major departure from previous African American historians' views and research of the ancient past. Historian James G. Spady contended that this article remains the first publication to survey an ancient African civilization outside the Nile Valley region, treated thoroughly by an African American. Spady further stated that "the level of transdisciplinary knowledge exhibited in this work is unparalleled" (Spady, "Diop," 300). With clarity and preciseness Hansberry combined historical, anthropological, archaeological, and cultural approaches in one model. During his fellowship tenure at Harvard, Hansberry planned to implement this model to complete the research outlined in his circular. Ironically, his options increased and placed him at a temporary crossroad.

Hansberry's notoriety grew immensely during the 1921-1922 academic school year. Several universities and organizations – including Garvey and the UNIA, Old Atlanta University, and Howard University – courted him simultaneously. He returned to Harvard in September 1921, resumed his studies, and continued reading the books suggested on the list in Du Bois's *The Negro*. At this point he compiled the notes that provided the baseline for his African Studies textbook. The compilation of his research notes collected while at Harvard constituted the core of his textbook outline. This textbook outline represented Hansberry's initial stimulus at developing and implementing his solution to the lack of an African/Black Studies curriculum in public education in the United States. Dubbed the "Little Nile" Hansberry also organized the Nile Club during his stints at Harvard to foster intellectual discussion on African history. Unfortunately, Harvard's School of Anthropology underfunded his research fellowship, which forced him into an early withdrawal at the end of the fall term. He also declined a second offer from Garvey and the UNIA, and also from President Myron Adams of Old Atlanta University.

Even though Hansberry declined a position within Garvey's UNIA, he continued direct contact with Garvey through one of the editors of the *Negro World* (the official organ of the UNIA) William H. Ferris. He sent Ferris an editorial that appeared in the 11 February, 1922, edition of the *Negro World*. According to Spady, Hansberry, while still a faculty member at Straight University, advanced "the first known internationally published account of his investigations in far-reaching dimensions." In this account Hansberry boldly declared that the widely accepted depiction of the "lazy and shiftless African savage" existed in a climate of ignorance. He conveyed that his course in Anthropology at Harvard and his subsequent analysis of the Harvard Expedition into Ethiopia, revealed that "the African...[possessed] great physical energy and mental ability, and remarkable kinds of arts and crafts...[The African also lived] under well-ordered social and political institutions of his own making...which are of great age" (Spady, "Diop," 300). Hansberry's declaration displayed a consistency between his early radicalism and his polemical discourse. He also joined a distinguished roster of historians who wrote for the *Negro World,* including Woodson, Ferris, John Edward Bruce, Hubert Henry Harrison, Joel Augustus Rogers, and Arthur A. Schomburg. For Marcus Garvey, the *Negro World's* readership, and the UNIA membership, Hansberry's declaration also provided a link between the public intellectual, the lay person, and the trained scholar – The Talented Tenth.

Despite the negative opinions concerning Garvey in some spheres of the African American leadership, Hansberry continued his association with him. Nevertheless, Hansberry's appeal also increased. Specifically, President Adams of Old Atlanta University and an official at Howard University kept in close contact with Hansberry during his resumed lecture series. President Adams offered him the chairmanship of the combined departments of history and sociology, a post previously held by Du Bois, with the rank of associate professor and a salary of $175.00 per month, for ten months ($1750.00), plus room, board, and laundry. Howard University eventually offered Hansberry a salary of $500 for the 1922-1923 academic school year, $1250.00 less than Old Atlanta University's offer. By the summer of 1922, Adams attempted desperately, but unsuccessfully, to reach Hansberry in Cambridge, Massachusetts. He finally contacted him in Petersburg, Virginia. Although Hansberry declined the offer, Adams respected Hansberry and asked his advice concerning two other candidates, J. P. Murchison of Biddle Memorial Institute (now Johnson C. Smith University) and William Miles Brewer, a 1919 graduate of Harvard University. Further, Adams asked Hansberry to consider teaching at Old Atlanta University sometime in the near future.

Unfortunately for President Adams and Old Atlanta University, Hansberry never really considered going back to Atlanta for career purposes. Clearly, he focused ever intently on expanding his academic credentials and research base in order to better equip himself for further growth and the development of the discipline of African Studies. However, by the 1921-1922 academic school year, Hansberry's contact base expanded and thrust him out onto an irreversible path more focused on research, academic growth, intellectual development, and teaching. Consequently, during his lecture tour in 1921, Howard University's administration aggressively recruited him and by 1922, Hansberry received a contract and accepted a position as a "special part-time lecturer." He arrived at Howard University in 1922 during the Harlem Renaissance period. Hansberry's contemporaries included Howard professors Alain Locke, Sterling Brown, Rayford Logan, Charles Wesley, Ralph Bunche, along with others such as W.E.B. Du Bois, Claude Mckay, Langston Hughes, and Carter Godwin Woodson.

From 1922 to 1959, Hansberry taught African History and Studies at Howard, while also continuing his post-graduate work. During this period he conducted museum and first-hand field research in Europe and Africa and held community and university symposia. According to historian Joseph E. Harris of Howard University, "the number and identity of everyone who benefitted from Professor Hansberry's counsel and assistance will never be known." (21). He sent or lent an abundance of reference materials to colleagues, friends, and others including W.E.B. Du Bois, Nnamdi Azikiwe of Nigeria, Kwame Nkrumah of Ghana, Haile Selassie of Ethiopia, Carter

Godwin Woodson, Charles Wesley, Joel Augustus Rogers, Charles Siefert, and others. Hansberry founded the African Bibliographic Center and the African American Institute, and he served as chairman of the Governing Council of Africa House in Washington, D.C. These last two entities gave birth to the publication *the Africa Report*, which is still in existence today. As the field of modern-day African/Black History and Studies grew in the 1950s and 1960s, Hansberry expanded his course offerings and intensified his research.

In a wider context, Hansberry follows in the tradition of the scholarly interest in Africa among African Americans that dates back to the late nineteenth and early twentieth centuries. Defined as the 'vindicationist' tradition or 'vindicationism' by St. Clair Drake (in *Black Folk Here and There* 1987, 1990), Hansberry's work capped the earlier attempts at vindicating the black past by such organizations as Alexander Crummell's American Negro Academy (1897) and Carter G. Woodson's Association for the Study of Negro Life and History (1915).

Moreover, Hansberry sought to legitimize his approach to the study of Africa and earn a doctorate at Oxford University, simultaneously. During his attempt to attain professional recognition on the eve of World War II through the 1940s and early 1950s, the intellectual and academic communities and philanthropic organizations that supported area and ethnic studies (Negro Studies) effectively excluded Hansberry and his early development of the discipline of African Studies. Pointedly, the decline of African Studies at historically black colleges and universities from the 1920s through the 1940s witnessed an embracement of the subject at historically white universities from 1945 to 1955. From the mid-to-late 1950s, a few African Americans like Hansberry's Howard colleague E. Franklin Frazier were brought into the new African Studies community that culminated in the founding of the African Studies Association in 1957. This membership made provisions and links to an alliance between state and federal government, private foundations and philanthropic organizations, and academics based mostly at white universities.

Although the pre World War II African American historians and Africanists like Hansberry received no recognition or membership in the new African Studies movement, their influence on the African politicians and intellectuals and African American (and diaspora) activists and intellectuals bore fruit in the 1960s. Hansberry attended the independence celebrations of Ghana (1957) and Nigeria (1960) at the personal requests of African Nationalists and Pan-Africanists Kwame Nkrumah and Nnamdi Azikiwe, respectively. In 1964 Emperor Haile Selassie I awarded Hansberry the first African Research Prize Trust for his earlier efforts in behalf of Ethiopia during the Ethiopian-Italian War and for his subsequent research. Finally, after his death in 1965, which coincided with the re-emergence of the 1920s African/Black Studies movement, Hansberry's former students continued his pan-Africanist tradition of studying Africa. They founded the African Heritage Studies Association (AHSA), which was initially formed as a Black Caucus (1969) within the African Studies Association, the leading Africanist professional body.

The founding of the AHSA links William Leo Hansberry's paradigm for African/Black History/Studies and the Black Studies movement of the 1960s and solidifies a direct relationship between the African American intelligentsia and activists in this movement and Hansberry's teachings. While these former students never implemented Hansberry's paradigm in its entirety, fragments of it materialized through their efforts at major universities, community groups, and other organizations that promoted Black pride throughout the African diaspora. One of his more accomplished and prolific students, historian John Henrik Clarke, seized the mantle of opportunity and spread this model to several venues. Ultimately, the gap between Hansberry's death in 1965 and the modern Black Studies movement initiated in 1969 left the discipline dubious and controversial in the minds of mainstream academic circles. Accordingly, Clarke and others like William M. King, Ronald W. Walters, Arvrah E. Strickland, and James Turner have kept the discipline alive and well.

In summation, Hansberry's initiation, establishment, and development of African Studies as an academic discipline and his attempt to secure support for a movement in the United States resulted from his interdisciplinary research experience at Harvard, his first appointment as professor and director of the Department of Negro History within the Social Sciences division at Straight University and independent advanced research at Oxford Univeristy. With these credentials, Hansberry employed his academic and professional accomplishments as a springboard for movement activity. He launched an unprecedented self-promotional campaign as an Africanist. More specifically, he projected himself as "an expert on Africa." In this regard, his outreach program sought moral and financial support from mainstream and Black organizations. He sent letters to groups he considered "leading organizations engaged in the uplift work among peoples of African descent." To be sure, after he secured a position at Straight University and established African Studies in the Social Sciences division, Hansberry launched a more public career and a promotional campaign for a mass movement. Although several opportunities arose during his early academic and public career, his research commitments, teaching schedule, and lecture tour shielded him from distractions, at least through the 1920-1921 academic school year. The more exposure he received, the more confidence he secured.

Finally, the importance of this essay lies in its analysis of how Hansberry's African/Black Studies paradigm/model and curriculum made an impact on the political and social thought of people of African descent. He made it palatable to the world community in general. Hansberry's resurrection and significance shows his influence on African/Black Studies in the United States, Africa, and the Caribbean. He provided the perfect conduit for the practical applications of pan-Africanism. Consequently, from a pan-African perspective, this discussion reveals Hansberry's influence on early African heads of state and therefore the African independence movement, particularly the years between 1954 and 1964. The major contribution of this essay serves as revision to the historiography and literature regarding the origins of the African/Black Studies movement in the United States that matured in the 1960s.

Notes

1. For further analysis of Hansberry's early intellectual growth and development, see Kwame Alford, "The Early Intellectual Growth and Development of William Leo Hansberry and the Birth of the Discipline of African Studies," *Journal of Black Studies* (March, 2000). For further information on Hansberry's development of the African/Black Studies paradigm and movement, consult the following: Booker T. Coleman interview with Joseph E. Harris, 19 April 1984, Washington, D.C.; Carter G. Woodson, director, ASNLH, Washington, D.C. to the Committee on Fellowships (Alfred M. Tozzer), Harvard University, Cambridge, Massachusetts (Woodson's admiration and recommendation in Hansberry's behalf), 7 March 1921, Hansberry Personal and Private Papers (HPP).

2. August Meier and Elliott Rudwick, *Black History and the Historical Profession, 1915-1980*, 2-3, 52-53, 55-60; Hansberry, *Announcing*, 1921; Michael R. Winston, *The History of Howard University Department of History, 1913-1973*, 45-46.

3. Meier and Rudwick, 2-3; Alfred Moss, "Alexander Crummell: Black Nationalist and Apostle of Western Civilization, 246-247.

4. See John Hope Franklin and Alfred Moss, *From Slavery to Freedom: A History of African Americans, Black Leaders of the Twentieth Century*, 318-320; Franklin and Meier, 88-102.

5. W. Augustus Low and Virgil A. Clift, eds., *Encyclopedia of Black America*, (New York, N.Y.: McGraw-Hill, 1981), 402, 823; Claude Andrew Clegg III, *An Original Man: The Life and Times of Elijah Muhammad*, 70-71; John Henrik Clarke, *Notes for an African World Revolution: Africans at the Crossroads*, 127-138.

6. Hansberry, *Circular* 1921; William Leo Hansberry to James Weldon Johnson, Executive Secretary, NAACP, 29 April 1921; William Leo Hansberry to W.E.B. Du Bois, Editor, *Crisis Magazine*, and Director of Publicity and Research, NAACP, 29 April 1921; W.E.B. Du Bois, Editor, *Crisis Magazine*, and Director of Publicity and Research, NAACP, to William Leo Hansberry, 20 June 1921; all in HPP.

7. William Leo Hansberry, "Material Culture of Ancient Nigeria," *Journal of Negro History* 6 (July 1921): 261-295, HPP; James G. Spady, "Dr. Cheikh Anta Diop and the Background of Scholarship on Black Interest in Egyptology and Nile Valley Civilizations," *Presence Africaine*, 50 (1992): 300.

8. See Booker T. Coleman, "The Life and Works of William Leo Hansberry," 14; William Leo Hansberry to W.E.B. Du Bois, Editor, *Crisis Magazine*, and Director of Publicity and Research, NAACP, 29 April 1921; Carter G. Woodson, Director, ASNLH, Washington, D.C. to the Committee on Fellowships (Alfred M. Tozzer), Harvard University, Cambridge, Massachusetts (Woodson's admiration and recommendation in Hansberry's behalf), 7 March 1921; William Leo Hansberry to Alfred M. Tozzer, Peabody Museum, Cambridge, Massachusetts, 24 March, 1921; all in HPP.

9. Myron W. Adams, Treasurer and Acting President, Old Atlanta University, Atlanta, Georgia, to William Leo Hansberry, 3, 11 August 1922, HPP; Winston, The History of Howard University Department of History, "Hansberry," 14; Low and Clift, 192. Spady, "Diop," 300-301.

10. William H. Ferris, "The Harvard Expedition into Ethiopia," *Negro World*, (11, February 1922), 4; Spady, "Diop," 300-301.

11. Myron W. Adams, Treasurer and Acting President, Old Atlanta University, Atlanta, Georgia, to William Leo Hansberry, 3, 11 August 1922; Winston, History, 49; Coleman, "Hansberry," 14; Low and Clift, 192.

12. See Hansberry, *Announcing;* Hansberry, *Circular*; William Leo Hansberry to James Weldon Johnson, Executive Secretary, National Association for the Advancement of Colored People (NAACP), 29 April 1921, in HPP.

References

Clarke, John Henrik. *Marcus Garvey and the Vision of Africa*. New York, N.Y.: Vintage Books, 1974.

_____. *Notes for an African World Revolution: Africans at the Crossroads*. Trenton, N.J.: Africa World Press, 1991.

Clegg, Claude A. III. "An Original Man: The Life and Times of Elijah Muhammad, 1897-1960." Ph.D. dissertation, University of Michigan, Ann Arbor, Michigan, 1995.

_____. *An Original Man: The Life and Times of Elijah Muhammad*. New York, N.Y.: St. Martin's Press, 1997.

Cliff, Virgil A. and Augustus W. Low. eds. *Encyclopedia of Black America*. New York, N.Y.: McGraw-Hill, 1981.

Coleman, Booker T. "The Life and Works of William Leo Hansberry." Master's thesis, Hunter College, New York, 1989.

Cowan, Tom, and J. Maguire, eds. *Timelines of African-American History: Five Hundred Years of Black Achievement.* New York, N.Y.: Roundtable, and Perigee Books, 1994.

Du Bois, W. E. B. "The Higher Training of Negroes." *Crisis* 22 (July 1921): 105-112.

_____. *The Negro.* 1915, Reprint, Millwood, N. Y.: Kraus-Thomson, 1975.

Ferris, William H. "The Harvard Expedition into Ethiopia." *Negro World*, 11 February 1922, 4.

Franklin, John H., and August Meier, eds. *Black Leaders of the Twentieth Century.* Urbana and Chicago: Illinois Press, 1986.

Franklin, John H., and Alfred Moss. *From Slavery to Freedom: A History of African Americans*, 7th edition. New York, N.Y.: McGraw-Hill, 1994. Goggin, Jacqueline. *Carter G. Woodson: A Life in Black History.* Baton Rouge and London: Louisiana State University Press, 1993.

Hansberry, Gail. William Leo Hansberry's daughter, Washington, D.C. Telephone interview by author. 9 August and 9 September 1997.

Harris, Joseph E. Interview by Booker T. Coleman, April 1984. Washington, D.C.

_____. *Pillars in Ethiopian History: The William Leo Hansberry African History Notebook, Vol 1.* Washington, D.C.: Howard University Press, 1974.

Meier, August, Rayford W. Logan, and Elliott Rudwick. *Black History and the Historical Profession, 1915-1980.* Urbana and Chicago: University of Illinois Press, 1986.

Moss, Alfred. "Alexander Crummell: Black Nationalist and Apostle of Western Civilization." In Black Leaders of Nineteenth Century, ed. by Leon Litwack and August Meier. Urbana and Chicago: University of Illinois Press, 1988.

Posey, Josephine McCann, to Kwame Wes Alford, letters dated 30 October 1996, Historical data on Elden Hayes Hansberry, Lorman, Mississippi.

– – -. "Dr. Cheikh Anta Diop and the Background of Scholarship on Black Interest in Egyptology and Nile Civilization." *Presence Africaine* 50 (1992): 292-312.

_____. "Legacy of an African Hunter." *A Current Bibliography on African Affairs* 3, 10 (November-December 1970): 25-40.

Spady, James G. "Pioneer Black Historian Passes On: The Distinguished Career of Benjamin Quarles." *Philadelphia New Observer*, Black History Month Supplement, 19 February, 1997, 13, 17.

Winston, Michael R. *The Howard University Department of History, 1913-1973.* Washington, D.C.: Department of History, Howard University, 1973.

7

AFRICOLOGY: CONSIDERATIONS CONCERNING A DISCIPLINE

Winston A. Van Horne

INTRODUCTION

If, at the outset of the twenty-first century, one were to ask what was particularly distinctive of the twentieth century and set it apart from bygone ones, I should dare say: It was a century of untold technoscientific achievements that overspread socioideological extremes and endless sociocultural confrontations. It is in this context that africology – the normative and empirical inquiry into the life histories and life prospects of peoples of primary African origin and their descent transgenerationally, transmillennially, and universally – began to acquire formal, structural recognition as an academic discipline in the American academy through the naming of academic departments. In 1994, the Department of Africology at the University of Wisconsin-Milwaukee was the first department to be so named. Though its subject matter covers millennia, africology in a departmentalized form is of late twentieth century vintage.

Given its subject matter, africology is truly enormous in scope. The enormousness of its scope, conjoined with an array of adverse transepochal historical forces, muddled and confounded africology to the point where only the barest few could conceive of it. And the few who did conceive of its disciplinary nature by subject matter were, almost uniformly, without institutional frameworks to enliven the discipline of which they conceived. They understood well the distinction between *subject-matter discipline* and *institutional discipline*, and pursued africology as subject matter discipline. Happily, late in the twentieth century institutional structures began to appear that made possible the emergence of africology as a subject-matter discipline and an institutional discipline conflated into one complex whole.

The subject matter of africology now comes alive through institutional structures, which have six basic purposes: 1) educate and train scholars who will discover, recover, construct, deconstruct, and reconstruct knowledge pertaining to the subject matter of the discipline; 2) reposition Africa and its significance in the evolution and development of human life, society, and civilization; 3) open new paths in the advancement of society and civilization; 4) provide rigorous and substantively rich education, at both the undergraduate and graduate levels, for those who desire to pursue careers outside of the discipline; 5) win the respect of competing disciplines through the conceptual rigor and empirical soundness of its scholarship; and 6) bring distinction to the institution(s) of which it is a part through the research, instruction, and service of its scholars, the broad-gauged value of its scholarship, as well as the work of the students that it produces. Given the purposes just mentioned, a three-fold question, most compelling in its significance, confronts everyone who either engages or would engage the contemporary discipline of africology: Is africology really an academic discipline, given the interests and purposes in culture, political economy, and society that it serves? What measures of intellectual stringency ought to ground inquiry and discourse in the discipline? Is its scholarship an open or closed domain of inquiry and discourse?

AFRICOLOGY: INTERESTS AND PURPOSES THEREOF

At first blush, it seems odd, unscholarly, and downright unacademic for one to speak of the social, cultural, economic, and political interests and purposes of africology as an academic discipline. Are not academic disciplines frameworks for free, open, rigorous, unencumbered, and value-neutral inquiry and discourse pertaining to distinctive ranges of phenomena and subject matters of universal scope? The rhetorical import of this question is most obvious; it presumes its own affirmation – the soundness of which is open to much doubt.

In an unpublished paper, read at the First Symposium on Africology at the University of Wisconsin-Milwaukee in April of 1987, Professor Lawrence J.R. Herson calls attention to the *Oxford English Dictionary*, which notes that the term discipline is rooted etymologically in the Latin words *disciplina* and *discipulus*, from which come the English terms discipline and disciple. He observes that "[t]hese terms, in their several meanings, entered our language from the 14th to the 17th centuries, and indicate: instruction imparted to disciples (1360); a branch of instruction; a department of learning (1386); a particular course of instruction imparted to disciples (1680); instruction having for its *aim to form pupils to proper conduct and action* by exercising them in the same; the order maintained or observed among pupils (1680); and more recently, a system or method for maintaining order."[1] Herson goes on to point out that "[a]cademic disciplines are branches of learning, usually sited within an organization or collective dedicated to such learning. Disciplines are mostly self-governing in two senses of the term: they give disciples a sense of order, proper conduct, and the *intellectual content* of the discipline; and are self-governing in that they emerge and develop mostly in accord with the *intent and purposes* of those who provide the instruction in their discipline."[2]

Academic disciplines arise neither in a natural, cultural, nor social vacuum. They emerge in order to serve ranges of interests and purposes, and accordingly, are not, and cannot be, value-neutral. All interests and purposes are value-grounded. I learned this in undergraduate school, and discussed it ad nauseam in classes in graduate school, a long time ago. Moreover, being much closer to the end rather than the beginning of my academic career, I find it both tiring and tiresome to make this point. Yet, the need to do so persists. It is as if fire has to be continually rediscovered and the wheel reinvented. What one need worry about constantly is not whether there are value-neutral (read value-free) interests and purposes but, instead, what values are in play in a given situation, and whose interests and purposes do they serve. Since there is no value-neutral interest or purpose, as the interests and purposes of those who may nonpejoratively be termed disciplinary disciples diverge, intersect, or conflate, so too will the intellectual contents of their disciplines.

Intellectual content impresses design and form upon the amorphous, incoherent, and malleable elements of the subject matter of a discipline. But design and form, discrete conceptual categories, are inseparable from the interests and purposes of the ones who construct them. Inasmuch as interests and purposes arise contextually, that is, in specified or specifiable interactions in culture, society, and political economy, the intellectual contents of academic disciplines are but formal and informal expressions and extensions of varieties of preference. Of what significance is this observation?

I should like to begin by noting that it is sheer folly, even dangerously disingenuous, to claim that disciplines such as astronomy, mathematics, physics, chemistry, biology, anthropology, sociology, history, philosophy, or political science are not contingent upon the social and cultural interests and purposes of those who construct and transmit their intellectual contents. Did Pythagoras' mathematics not arise in the service of his religious convictions? – of course, Pythagoras' theorems served the purposes of his religious dogmas. And one need only reflect upon the intellectual contents of, say, Cheikh Anta Diop's *The African Origin of Civilization: Myth or Reality* and *Civilization or Barbarism: An Authentic Anthropology,* as well as Daniel J. Boorstin's *The Creators: A History of Heroes of the Imagination* and *The Discoverers: A History of Man's Search to Know His World and Himself* to discern a clear and distinct line of demarcation in the social and cultural interests and purposes that animate their historical anthropologies.[3]

Diop scrutinizes the globe in order to deconstruct the putative marginality of Africa and Africans in the origin and rise of society and civilization, and reconstruct the centrality of the continent and its peoples to the many branches of human learning and development. Boorstin, on the other hand, surveys the world in order to establish what may be termed civilizational polymorphisms, absent the hub which Diop ascribes to Africa.

In his *re*construction of Africa in the growth and development of *Homo sapiens sapiens*, Diop posits the recovery of ancient Egypt to be an intellectual imperative, given the necessity of creating sound conceptual maps for the purpose of guiding the revitalization of the cultures of Africans and their descent, and the reconstitution of their societies globally in a postcolonial world. To Boorstin, ancient Egypt is but one of many rich sources, albeit a particularly striking one, in the evolution of human societies and civilizations. Thus, whereas in Diop one feels the force of Africa in the transmillennial civilizing of *Homo sapiens sapiens*, in Boorstin one senses the power and primacy of the Indo-European world in this process. Put differently, divergent interests and purposes in culture, society, and political economy enliven their historical anthropologies.

The range of conceptual and empirical questions, problems, and issues pertaining to Africa, *Homo sapiens sapiens,* and civilization that engaged Diop, finds grounding in the discipline of africology, which he advanced notably, becoming the greatest africologist of the twentieth century. Putting the subject matter of africology in the service of Africans and their descent globally, Diop sought to "restore the historical consciousness of... African peoples."[4] Africology reconnects unborn progeny with dead ancestors through the living, making known "the laws governing the evolution of African [grounded] sociopolitical structures, in order to explain the direction that historical evolution has taken [worldwide]."[5] A crucial purpose here is the eliciting and guiding of behaviors and activities designed to foster mastery over congeries of historical processes, for the sake of promoting and advancing the interests and good of Africans and their descent universally.

This disciplinary purpose is such that africologists neither can abide putative Weberian value-free inquiry and discourse nor countenance purported Mannheimian scholarly detachment. As a discipline, africology has as one of its primary aims the reconstruction and revitalization of the societies, cultures, and political economies of Africans and their descent globally. Accordingly, its scholars cannot be "ignorant, cowardly, and neurotic"[6] knaves, as Diop pejoratively characterizes "[t]he African historian who evades the problem of Egypt."[7] Africology thus necessitates a measure of fearlessness, self-confidence, and composure in every africologist who would advance the intellectual contents of his/her discipline.

In its departmentalized form, africology instructs students concerning the life histories and prospects of peoples of primary African origin and their descent. Through such instruction, students are exposed to, and have the opportunity to become steeped in, the defining attributes of culture – *species being, species life, language, religion, literature-art-music-science-technology, institutions, and transgenerational memory* – and political economy (*the normative and empirical relations between political phenomena and economic phenomena in given sociocultural formations*) in relation to the contours of the lives of Africans and their worldwide descendants. By scrutinizing paradigms of recovery, paradigms of discovery, and paradigms of engagement, students discern short-term trends as well as long-term patterns that occasioned and/or sustain either desirable or undesirable outcomes in the cultures, political economies, and societies of Africans and their descent.

Africology thus makes known ranges of behaviors, practices, actions, and events whose generational and transgenerational signal value is reliable and lively in relation to cultural and social enfeeblement, decline and decay, as well as sociocultural survival, growth, and development. Within the domain of its intellectual contents, the matter of cultural survival is of the utmost importance.

As a young assistant professor, I took strong issue with B.F. Skinner when he wrote: "Survival is the only value according to which a culture is eventually to be judged, and any practice that furthers survival has survival value by definition."[8] As a middle-aged full professor, I take much less issue with Skinner, in point of fact agreeing with him insofar as the elasticity of the term "the only value" conflates both empirical and normative elements.

Empirical behaviors, practices, actions, and events that foster the survival of a culture are of value within the limits of that culture. Yet, those very behaviors, practices, actions, and events may elicit stern normative judgments from without that culture, and even from within it, where they abridge transcultural norms of human decency. Cultures that survive, especially over innumerable cross-sections of historical time, are ones which unite empirical and normative attributes in adaptive ways that expand their domains of human decency. Those that adapt empirically to changes in their environments without sound normative moorings usually become overspread with human indecency and rot. How very well is this point instantiated in Christopher Dawson's observation that

> Hellenic civilization collapsed not by a failure of nerve but by the failure of life. When Hellenic science was in full flower, the lifeof the Hellenic world withered from below, and underneath thesurface brilliance of philosophy and literature the sources of the life of the people were drying up.... Yet throughout the period of...decline, the intellectual achievements of Hellenic civilization remained,and Greek culture, in an abstract and standardized form, was spreadingEast and West far more than it had done in the days of its living strength.

> If intellectual progress – or at least a high degree of scientific-achievement – can co-exist with vital decline, if a civilization can fall topieces from within – then the optimistic assumptions of the last twocenturies concerning the future of our modern civilization lose theirvalidity. The fate of the Hellenic world is a warning to us that thehigher and more intellectually advanced civilizations of the West maybe inferior in point of *survival value* to the more rudimentary Orientalcultures.[9]

Hellenic culture and civilization rotted from within even as they glittered from without. Is there a warning most poignant and ominous for American culture and civilization here? I shall not engage this question in this chapter, but it is nonetheless one that is most germane to africology as what has been termed "the American century" ends.

The survival of a culture is contingent on the sorts of empirical and normative elements that ground it. Through its intellectual contents, as well as its instructional and research practices, africology calls out present and past conduct that occasion/have occasioned the survival, as well as the demise, of the cultures and societies of Africans and their worldwide descendants.

As an academic discipline, africology entails a broad framework within which intellectual content is impressed upon a specified subject matter of universal scope. Though it is not an ideology of African cultures, political economies, and societies, in the conceptualization and organiza-tion of the discipline's intellectual contents, purposive considerations that are social, cultural, economic, and political do, however, come into play both intuitively and rationally.

Intuitively, the subject matter of africology signals as an imperative the revitalization of the cultures and the reconstitution of the societies of peoples of primary African origin and their descent. Rationally, such revitalization and reconstitution are an objective necessity. The subjective reality of intuition and the objective reality of rationality conflate in the social and cultural utility of the intellectual contents of africology. Social and cultural utility thus makes africology a highly purposive discipline. Thus, through its conceptual organization, africology calls out behaviors and practices of varying social and cultural usefulness in relation to the promotion and advancement of the interests of Africans and their global descendants.

The social and cultural utility of africology makes the discipline highly adaptive. The twentieth century opened in the Industrial Age and closed in the Information Age. The twenty-first century opens in the Information Age and will, perhaps, close at the dawn of the Postbiological Age. The radical changes in political economy that have occurred in the shift from an industrial society to an information society, and are likely to be even more dramatic in the transformation of an information society into a postbiological one, will affect profoundly the character of societies and cultures worldwide.

If William Bridges is correct, a crucial defining attribute of an information society is the de-jobbing of its work force, as jobs are supplanted by fields of work. Speaking of the United States, he writes:

> We used to read predictions that by 2000 everyone would work 30 hour weeks, and the rest would be leisure. But as we approach 2000 it seems more likely that half of us will be working 60-hour weeks and the rest of us will be unemployed....

> The reality we face is [particularly] troubling, for what is disappearing is not just a certain number of jobs – or jobs in certain industries or jobs in some part of the country or even jobs in America as a whole. *What is disappearing is the very thing itself: the job. That much sought after, much maligned social entity, a job, is vanishing like a species that has outlived its evolutionary time....*

> The modern world is on the verge of another huge leap in creativity and productivity, but the job is not going to be part of tomorrow's economic reality.... In fact, many organizations are today well along the path toward being "de-jobbed."... Today's organization is rapidly being *trans-formed from a structure built out of jobs into a field of work needed to be done.*[10]

As information societies are more and more de-jobbed, the capacity of individuals to adapt to a variety of fields of work and perform well in each field will increasingly determine their life chances. Here the development of intellectual capital is of the utmost importance. The larger the reserves of this capital that individuals possess, the greater will be their chances of participating successfully in the legal and legitimate political economies of their societies. And so, most poignant is Thomas A. Stewart's observation that "[a]ccounting for intellectual capital is more than an exercise for the cloistered or the fad-struck. What's at stake is nothing less than learning how to operate and evaluate a business when knowledge is its chief resource and result."[11]

In political economies where knowledge is ever the more resource and result, a fundamental purpose of the intellectual contents of africology is to prepare the ones who engage the discipline to be effective participants in the societies of those political economies. Given the cultural foundations on which all political economies rest; given the interplay between culture and political economy; and given the range of societies, from simple agrarian to highly complex technologic ones, in which Africans and their global descendants live, the intellectual contents of africology necessarily preclude a one-dimensional approach either to culture, or society, or political economy.

Just as africology's intellectual contents facilitate the creation of intellectual capital that is of value to the culture and political economy of an information society, they also foster the development of a range of attributes that could be of much value in, say, a simple agrarian society. The crucial point that emerges here is that regardless of the form which the culture and political economy of a given society take, a sound knowledge of the subject matter of africology positions one to advance interests and purposes that are relevant to the scope of the discipline.

Africology thus affords pathways of engagement with a variety of cultures, political economies, and societies universally. Given the fact that all cultures share the defining attributes of culture qua culture, africology admits of comparative analyses that facilitate accurate diagnoses, proffer well-grounded prescriptions, and stimulate concerted actions concerning constellations of societal concerns, issues, and problems. Sound africological descriptions, explanations, evaluations, and prescriptions pertaining to ranges of social phenomena are neither culture-bound catharses nor masked African particularisms. They are, strictly speaking, articulations of the way societies are organized and expressions of how they should be.

In the twenty-first century, africology cannot fail to build large reserves of intellectual capital in the ones who study its subject matter. This is especially important to those of African descent whose societies will literally have to leap-frog the Industrial Age if, at the outset of the twenty-second century, they are not to be hopelessly left behind in technoscientific transformations of the planet and, by extension, human life. Great social and cultural responsibility thus falls on those who impress design and form upon the subject matter of africology through the intellectual contents of the discipline.

Future and past must be made to come alive in the africological present, in ways that enable individuals to demonstrate rational self-mastery in the advancement of their interests in an ever the more de-jobbed universe. It is thus socially and culturally imperative that the curricular offerings of Departments of Africology evince great sensitivity not only to the value of paradigms of recovery, but also to ones of discovery, and engagement. This should assure a leading role for africology in the efficaciousness of intellectual capital in the twenty-first century and beyond.

MEASURES OF INTELLECTUAL STRINGENCY IN AFRICOLOGY

More than two generations ago, Thomas Kuhn occasioned great excitement in the academic world with his concept of *paradigm*. Since that time, the term has been the subject of intense critical scrutiny. This has resulted in its integration into the ordinary language of scholarly inquiry and discourse. As is true of many of the terms of ordinary language, however, there is no universal agreement about the substance of the concept. But given its entrenchment in the vocabulary of inquiry and discourse pertaining to natural as well as social phenomena, it is well that the ones who participate in architectonic roles in the institutionalization of a discipline should articulate paradigms designed to organize the subject matter of the discipline.

The intellectual contents of paradigms afford descriptions, explanations, evaluations, and predictions pertaining to the phenomena that constitute the subject matter of a discipline, as well as provide justifications for paradigmatic behaviors. The sounder the descriptions, explanations, evaluations, and predictions the more stringent are justifications grounded in them. Accordingly, descriptive, explanatory, evaluative, predictive, and justificatory rigor enables the paradigms of a discipline to better withstand free, open, unencumbered, and searching critical scrutiny. In this regard, a critical scrutiny of its disciplinary paradigms is an, perhaps the, ultimate measure of intellectual stringency in africology. This is a point of compelling importance.

No one-to-one correspondence now obtains, or ever will obtain, between africology, as an academic discipline, and any of the many paradigms that organize its subject matter. The very concepts of academic discipline and paradigm preclude this, since paradigm entails some measure of general acceptance of a particular organization of given phenomena, while academic discipline presumes a subject matter that is amenable to more than one design in the construction of its intellectual contents. Competition among paradigms for dominance marks academic disciplines, and over time one or two usually emerge as dominant in a particular discipline, sooner or later to be challenged by others that seek to displace it/them. Such competition fosters disciplinary strength over the long haul, as weak paradigms are discarded and strong ones are supplanted by even stronger ones. In africology, then, a crucial measure of intellectual stringency is the encouragement and facilitation of paradigmatic competition. For it is through such competition that the ideas, concepts, hypotheses, theoretic sketches, theories, empirical generalizations, law-like statements, and perhaps even laws, of the discipline are developed, honed and refined.

The flourishing of paradigmatic competition in africology presumes tough-minded, critical inquiry and discourse, which aim at disclosing truths that are amenable to intersubjective testing and corroboration. Regardless of whether such truths are rational, empirical, or intuitive, they must be open to searching scrutiny by disinterested observers. Paradigmatic competition is thus antithetical to paradigmatic cloistering, which discloses "truths" only to initiates and their disciples. If truths are disclosed through true statements and propositions rather than declarative sentences; if true statements and propositions are open to intersubjective testing and corroboration; and if such testing is not the private province of any one or any group, paradigmatic competition constitutes a stringent means whereby the truths of africology are disclosed to the world.

At the outset of the twentieth-first century, fierce paradigmatic competition continues to encompass africology. Paradigms employing descriptors such as afrocentricity, *Kawaida* theory, cultural nationalism, Pan-Africanism, Africana womanism, among others, all strive for dominance within the discipline. This is, of course, not unusual, for it is quite consistent with patterns that Kuhn has observed in the rise and decline of paradigms in science across the centuries. He points out:

> At the start a new candidate for paradigm may have few supporters, and on occasions the supporters' motives may be suspect. Nevertheless, if they are competent, they will improve it, explore its possibilities, and show what it would be like to belong to the community guided by it. And as that goes on, if the paradigm is one destined to win its fight, the number and strength of the persuasive arguments in its favor will increase.... [Eventually,] only a few elderly hold-outs [will] remain [as the]

hardheaded arguments.... produced and multiplied [by adherents of the new paradigm occasion an ever] increasing shift in the distribution of professional allegiances."[12]

Adherents of the now dominant paradigm are won over in part because of its problem-solving/puzzle-solving capability, and also in part because of its aesthetic appeal. "Probably the single most prevalent claim advanced by the proponents of a new paradigm," writes Kuhn, "is that they can solve the problems that have led the old one to a crisis. When it can legitimately be made, this claim is often the most effective one possible."[13] In addition to this, though, "more subjective and aesthetic considerations... [come into play. For] the man who embraces a new paradigm at a very early stage must often do so in defiance of the evidence provided by problem-solving. He must... have faith that the new paradigm will succeed with the many large problems that confront it, knowing only that the older paradigm has failed with a few. A decision of that kind can only be made on faith."[14]

Rational inferences from empirical observations conjoin with intuitive hunches from aesthetic stimuli to incline one in the direction of a new paradigm, which may, or may not ultimately attain dominance in a given community. Inclinations will vary with the initial attractiveness of a new paradigm, especially where a dominant paradigm is under constant and severe attack or there is no dominant paradigm in play. As one reflects on the sorts of attacks that have been leveled at afrocentricity – perhaps the dominant paradigm in africology – at the end of the twentieth century, for example, one is reminded of the disaffections that astronomers came to have concerning the Ptolemaic paradigm in the sixteenth century. Again, Kuhn is most helpful here. He writes:

> When... the Ptolemaic system was first developed during the last twocenturies before Christ and the first two after, it was admirablysuccessful in predicting the changing positions of both stars and planets.No other ancient system had performed so well.... [However, w]ithrespect both to planetary position and to precession of the equinoxes,predictions made with Ptolemy's system never quite conformed withthe best available observations....[15]

By the early sixteenth century an increasing number of Europe's best astronomers were recognizing that the astronomical paradigm wasfailing in application to its own traditional problems. That recognition was prerequisite to Copernicus' rejection of the Ptolemaic paradigm andhis search for a new one.

Kuhn also notes that "Copernicus' co-worker, Domenico da Novara held that no system so cumbersome and inaccurate as the Ptolemaic had become could possibly be true of nature. And Copernicus himself wrote... that the astronomical tradition he inherited had finally created only a monster."[16]

I know of no harsh critic of afrocentricity who has accused it of creating a "monster." Nonetheless, one can readily discern in broadsides on afrocentricity the sort of acrimony that invariably accompanies attacks on a dominant paradigm.[17] In a state of paradigmatic flux, the ability of a dominant or near-dominant paradigm to stand up to hardheaded arguments – the obverse of the dogmas of a discipleship of true believers – and tough-minded, close critical scrutiny is more serious for its continued ascendancy than in times of paradigmatic calm, when its acceptance is nigh taken for granted.

Should afrocentricity be superseded by a competing paradigm, it will not simply dissolve into ether, as it were, in africological inquiry and discourse. It will continue to enliven scholarship in africology, though its status will be different, just as the Ptolemaic paradigm persists in astronomy. Kuhn observes that "for the stars, Ptolemaic astronomy is still widely used today as an engineering approximation; for the planets, Ptolemy's predictions were as good as Copernicus.'"[18] Afrocentricity *re*centers Africa in the rise, growth, and development of society and civilization globally; it *re*positions Africans and their descent as subjects rather than as mere objects in the evolution and revolution in ideas and societal structures from the Agrarian Age through the Information Age; and it *re*directs the consciousness of those who have, for whatever reason(s), marginalized Africa. In africology, afrocentricity is thus of much corrective, restorative, and prescriptive value, paradigmatically pointing one in new directions *vis-a-vis* Africans and their descent over innumerable cross-sections of historical time. It is not, though, coextensive with the range or scope of the discipline. Africology and afrocentricity are not coterminous.

As the phenomena of subjective reality and objective reality that form the subject matter of africology are scrutinized and organized by reason and intuition, the intellectual contents of the discipline evince both rational and intuitive attributes. Intuitive insights and rational judgments make lively inquiry and discourse in africology, as on occasion the dictates of reason collide with the directives of intuition. Where reason and intuition guide differently in the construction and articulation of the intellectual contents of africology, a choice invariably has to be made. By what criteria? The openness and amenability of the choice to inspection and corroboration by disinterested others. This is especially important where insights of intuition overrule judgments of reason.

Where intuition overrides reason in relation to choices concerning the intellectual contents of africology, relevant means for the disinterested corroboration of those choices may not be immediately available. If such means do not obtain, the choices that have been made should be allowed, unless compelling and incontrovertible evidence that they would occasion harm dictates otherwise. Where sound intuition impels towards risk-taking, creative outcomes often obtain. But neither risk-taking nor creative outcomes are inherently inconsistent with intellectual stringency. Hence, tolerable risks that have a potential for advancing the intellectual contents of africology are consistent with stringency within the discipline.

Tolerable risk-taking ought to be encouraged by the structures that institutionalize africology. Still, it is well to ask: What moral and ethical questions and/or costs attend such risks? Here the stringency of the ethical and moral categories of the discipline come into play. The limits of this chapter do not allow an expansive discussion of these categories, anyhow the following points need to be made.

Africology does not countenance ethical and moral flaccidity. It does not fudge that which is indubitably wrong for the sake of a desired outcome. Firm and clear statements and propositions concerning right, proper, fair, honorable, permissible and praiseworthy conduct, as well as wrong, improper, unfair, dishonorable, impermissible, and unpraiseworthy behavior mark the intellectual contents of the discipline.

Moreover, the moral and ethical categories of africology afford no justification for behavior that wrongfully diminishes the self-respect, self-esteem, dignity, integrity, and freedom of the individual qua individual. Conduct that unnecessarily puts oneself or others at risk of injury or harm – whether physical and/or psychological – finds no ethical or moral justification in africology.

Finally, though within the discipline itself no moral or ethical cost may attend any given risk that is deemed to be tolerable for the sake of advancing the intellectual contents of africology, institutional costs may nonetheless obtain. Yet, if one is confident of one's position in relation to the moral and ethical categories of africology, one cannot but stand one's ground where an acceptable disciplinary risk collides with an institutional (department, college, university) stance against it. But this is not easy; it is downright tough, since severe career and financial costs could really test one's mettle. Thus, intellectual stringency in africology does not necessarily free one from institutional risk.

Intellectual stringency is not an abstract concept. It is, rather, an empirical construct designed to guide the behaviors of individuals and groups. Concerning academic disciplines, it applies to research, instruction, and service whereby the intellectual contents of particular subject matters are continuously expanded, sharpened, refined, and transmitted. Intellectual stringency inclines – it cannot really compel – succeeding generations of scholars and students never to be fully satisfied with their accomplishments, and to strive continually to improve upon the work of their predecessors. The intrinsic striving purpose of intellectual stringency precludes one from ever resting on one's laurels, knowing that decline and decay are parasitic upon achievement.

A continuous expansion of, and improvement in, the intellectual contents of africology are a sure and certain measure of intellectual stringency within the discipline. This necessitates high expectations by africologists of themselves, as well as of their students. Whether it is the design and execution of a particular research project, the preparation and delivery of a given lecture, the setting and grading of an in-class examination, or the guiding of a master's thesis or a doctoral dissertation, africologists advance and improve their discipline insofar as they give of the very best of their idea-power and creativity, and elicit the same from their students.

Measures of intellectual stringency are, as it were, guideposts of becoming. They signal what might be, encouraging one to strive to become all that one can be. In africology, at the dawn of the twenty-first century, they serve to position the newly departmentalized discipline to meet the challenges that lay in front of it. By undergirding the discipline with rigor and tough-mindedness, intellectual stringency enables africologists to stand toe-to-toe with their peers in other disciplines in the arena of intellectual combat.

AFRICOLOGICAL SCHOLARSHIP: AN OPEN OR CLOSED DOMAIN OF INQUIRY AND DISCOURSE?

It is well to begin with an anecdote. Each October the University of Wisconsin-Milwaukee hosts an Open House entitled *Showcase for Learning*. Thousands attend this two-day event at which programs, departments, schools, and colleges throughout the institution showcase their wares to the public at large. The Department of Africology consistently has an impressive booth. Standing by this booth at the Open House of 1998, I became engaged in conversation with a white student in my course entitled *Introduction to African-American History to 1865*. I congratulated the individual for having received 99 out of 100 marks on the first midterm, which consisted of a major essay plus a set of identifications. (In then thirty-three years of grading blue books, numbering thousands, I do not recall ever having given those marks to any student before.) The student expressed great delight in having done so very well on the examination, and proceeded to inform me of the discouragement that had occurred prior to signing up for the course, noting: "I was told not to take africology, for they [instructors in the Department of Africology] either fail white students or give them bad grades." Given this advice, I asked: "What prompted you to take the course?" The individual replied: "I just had to come and find out for myself."

The preceding anecdote is of interest and important on at least four counts. First, what the student said was no news to me. All too many have been the times that I have heard it. Still, it is not of passing consequence, for it signals clearly and distinctly that there is a belief among white students – and I dare add those of other racial/ethnic groupings – that africology is for blacks; that it is intolerant of nonblacks. This belief is in no little measure a product of transgenerational sentiments pertaining to the mass movements, especially the civil rights movement and the black power movement, of the 1960s out of which africology as an institutional discipline arose. And it has fostered what may be termed dispositional isolation, that is, a prevailing tendency or inclination among nonblacks to perceive and to believe that africology is the private domain of blacks. There is abroad a sense that africology represents a cloister, to which outsiders (read racial/ethnic) are admitted only with the permission of afrocentrically baptized disciples. This is, of course, a corruption both of africology and afrocentricity. Nevertheless, it remains a hard reality that must be confronted head on by africologists who have a reverence for critical inquiry and discourse that is free, open, and unencumbered.

By law, africology cannot be a closed institutional discipline in the American academy, and as a subject matter discipline it is wide open to all. Dispositional isolation thus distorts and disfigures africology, an open-textured academic discipline with considerable conceptual elasticity and extraordinarily rich empirical substance, by closing it to putative outsiders. This is not good. Timidity, arrogance, and indifference are drawn together in dispositional isolation to exclude many from africology – some are simply afraid to engage those whom they perceive, usually wrongly, to be unwelcoming, if not downright hostile; others set themselves apart because of a vulgar superiority complex; and still others just go along with what they discern to be the prevailing sentiment and exclude themselves from participation in the discipline, with little or no thought given to the reasons for their self-exclusion. There is a strong undertow of intolerance here, and it issues less from a presumed cloister of africological insiders than the apartness fostered by the dispositional isolation of supposed outsiders.

Second, rumors of africological intolerance go hand in hand with a presumptive incompetence of africologists. White students receive bad grades in africology where all too many of the instructors are incompetent – so the gossip goes. Now, the notion of presumptive incompetence is most troublesome. In one of his infamous tapes, President Richard Milhous Nixon declares: "With blacks... you can usually settle for an incompetent, because there are just not enough competent ones, and so you put incompetents in and get along with them, because the symbolism is vitally important."[19] Given the preponderance of black instructors (tenured, tenure-track, and nontenure-track) in africology; given the objective reality that Nixon's blunt talk was expressive not only of a personal sentiment but also of a wider cultural belief in the Euroworld; and given also the objective reality of dispositional isolation among nonblacks *vis-a-vis* africology, one can readily grasp the propensity of many to label africology as a closed universe overspread with incompetents. This is a brutal weight upon the discipline, as its practitioners are buffeted endlessly for demonstrations – both substantive and symbolic – that they are not incompetents. But how shall one demonstrate that one is not incompetent? By what criteria shall one be judged? And by whom shall one be judged? These are not rhetorical questions; they were broached in the preceding section.

Presumptive incompetence draws a tight and hard circle around africology, and forces africologists everywhere to take the risks necessary to break out of the closed universe (of putative incompetents feeding off incompetents) that it imposes upon them. Without the luxury of presumptive competence and its corollary advantages, africologists, at least the ones who are black, must necessarily open up their work to protagonists and antagonists alike, as they continue the process of institutionalizing africology. Hence, as an institutional discipline, it is empirically impossible for africology to be closed in the face of the frontal assault on the intellectual integrity of africologists, which the presumptive incompetence of black people represents. In this regard, does the *Bell Curve* not proclaim: "One of the great losses of preferential affirmative action has been to dilute the effects of the university credential for some minorities [read blacks]. Today the same degree from the same university is perceived differently if you have a black face or a white one."[20] Presumptive competence accompanies a white face, presumptive incompetence a black one. Africology abides neither of these. For its enduring aim is none other than to make ever wider the frontiers of intersubjectively corroborated knowledge in relation to Africans and their descent worldwide.

Third, as the fountainhead subject matter discipline from which all other subject matter disciplines have flowed – Africa gave birth to the mind, spirit, soul, intelligence, and body of *Homo sapiens sapiens* – africology necessarily embraces humankind in its entirety. All of the life histories and life prospects of Africans and their descent through innumerable cross-sections of historical time conflate in africology.

Accordingly, the subject matter of africology touches every one on the planet in some way or form – from the bodies that carry *Homo sapiens sapiens,* to the cultures without which s/he could not, and would not survive, to the sorts of value that are ascribed to persons, things, objects, and events – regardless of the consciousness of individuals and groups of this objective reality. The subject matter of africology is thus of a strikingly open and inclusive texture. None is excluded from it by subject matter – just as political science encompasses *all* political phenomena in their totality, and history enfolds *all* historical phenomena in their entirety – even though the imperative of being an institutional discipline necessitates the drawing of boundaries that are sufficiently clear to give academic integrity to the discipline.

Just as philosophy as an institutional discipline in the American academy at the outset of the twenty-first century is drawn much more narrowly than it was in say, Plato's Academy of fourth century (B.C.E.) Athens, africology in the academy is limited largely to its domains in culture and political economy. Through these domains of inquiry and discourse, the subject matter of africology is opened wide to whomever would study it, despite the particular approaches, techniques, methods, conceptual frameworks, hypotheses, theories, and paradigms that are brought to bear upon it. Africological studies are open to all since none has possessory title to them, and these studies are germane to the lives, freedom, and well-being of *Homo sapiens sapiens* in toto, the ignorance, as well as dismissive personal and cultural arrogance, of particular individuals and groups notwithstanding.

Finally, it is a commonplace to hear students ask: "What can I do with a degree in africology?" "Is africology about Africa?" "Isn't africology for blacks?" One need not linger on the second and third questions, since they have been disposed of through observations made earlier in this section. I would, however, like to tarry on the first question, which is a constant refrain of students (black, white, and other racial/ethnic groupings) contemplating a major in africology.

Another anecdote is in order here. In the early 1970s, William E. Nelson, Jr., then chair of the Department of Black Studies at The Ohio

State University, launched a major initiative to increase the department's quarterly enrollments. One element of this initiative involved faculty and staff from the department going to the dormitories to talk with students. As a young assistant professor in the Departments of Black Studies and Political Science, I was engaged heavily in the effort. One student with whom I spoke, a black individual, enrolled in *Introduction to Black Studies*. The student also enrolled in courses in English, mathematics, philosophy, and another subject matter discipline that I cannot recall. Once the student's mother learned that the individual had elected to take a course in Black Studies she came to the department in tears. She wondered aloud whether Black Studies involved serious university work, and called attention to the cost of the student attending the institution. Happily, she was persuaded by the reasons that were presented to her, and the student did take the course – later declaring a major in Black Studies as I recall.

To this mother, before her rational faculties were engaged through conversation, taking Black Studies was a waste of time and money, for it was simply about black people in the United States, and her youngster did not have to go to the university to learn of black people. Black people already knew about black people. Here one observes a closed perceptual universe, which is all too common among blacks, who knew little or nothing then about the range or scope of Black Studies, or have more than a rudimentary knowledge of africology today.

As an institutional discipline, africology evolved out of Black Studies, which it now subsumes as one approach to the discipline. In the process of its continued institutionalization, it is vital that black students be made cognizant of its open-textured subject matter. In this way, they can begin to discern that like philosophy, or mathematics, or political science, or history, or chemistry, or biology, africology affords them disciplinary preparation for both specialized and nonspecialized "fields of work." Once this discernment is clear and distinct, the mundane question of what can one do with a degree in africology dissolves away for black students.

For white students and other racial/ethnic groupings, the problem is more formidable. Africology is perceived, for the most part, to be remote from their lives. The task at hand, then, is to diminish the perceptual, intellectual, emotional, cultural, and social distancing of nonblacks from the discipline. This is done by exposing them to the open-textured subject matter of africology through a variety of forms that the classroom takes. Such exposure not only diminishes distancing – even though for some it may actually increase distancing by challenging long-held, and cherished beliefs of which they are unwilling to let go – but also clarifies and redirects values as they become conscious of the relevance of the discipline's subject matter for their own lives. Consequently, the hard, the really hard job is to break through the initial barriers of resistance to the discipline. Mandatory requirements are sometimes the most efficacious, though not the sole, means of doing this. The breaching of the barriers of resistance often paves the way for nonblack students to transcend the fears, anxieties, insecurities, uncertainties, and limitations inherent in the question: "What can *I* do with a major in africology?"

Given my abiding belief concerning the universality and openness of africology, it is well to end with a paradigmatic sketch pertaining to the discipline. I shall call it *transgenerationalism*. By transgenerationalism I mean processes of creation, adaptation, decline, decay, and *re*creation in culture and political economy whereby common and uncommon traits are observable across generations in the behavior of individuals and groups. Common traits are ones that mark the spontaneous and unconscious behaviors of individuals and groups, as well as the conscious, intentional, and deliberate conduct of most members of a particular community or society. Uncommon traits are ones that single out individuals and groups by the distinctiveness and/or uniqueness of the behavior that they occasion. Rational and irrational, intuitive and observational, corroborative and uncorroborative elements cluster in both common and uncommon traits. And it is the relative weighting of these elements that makes a given trait either common or uncommon. The relation between common and uncommon traits on the one hand, and survival, growth, development, stagnation, destruction, and reconstruction in culture and political economy across generations of Africans and their descent globally on the other, form the conceptual and empirical core of transgenerationalism in africology.

There is conceptual beauty and empirical rigor here. Conceptually, transgenerationalism allows one to construct a range of conceptual frameworks by drawing upon a variety of traits that make conceptual sense regarding, for example, the survival of a particular culture over a specified period of historical time. Empirically, it calls upon one to test out these frameworks against the available evidence, or to seek out new evidence that either corroborates or confutes them. Rigorous comparisons of different conceptual frameworks across generations bounded by the same period of historical time, or the testing of the soundness of a given conceptual framework through many generations in different periods of historical time is a paradigmatic imperative of transgenerationalism.

Rigor and testing aside, transgenerationalism has an inherent attractiveness about it in that it not only bridges generations, thereby preserving their distinctiveness while allowing for crisscrossing influences, but also delineates patterns that cover two or more of them at varying points in time. From these patterns one can derive clues, hunches, insights, and draw inferences concerning the sorts of behaviors that were of greater or lesser value in fostering the freedom and well-being of one or more generations at specified periods of historical time. Given that generations are not homogeneous entities, one can discern in these patterns the sorts of forces that were at work that enabled some to get ahead, others to make little or no headway, and still others to stagnate and wither away. Transgenerationalism thus affords a powerful tool for societal archaeology, construction, and reconstruction.

At this stage, I have termed transgenerationalism a paradigmatic sketch, because the work that needs to be done to transform it into a paradigm has not yet been done. Nonetheless, I do believe that transgenerationalism has the potential of becoming a major paradigm in africology, given: i) its intrinsic dynamism; ii) its conceptual bridging of generations over both narrow as well as broad cross-sections of historical time; iii) the necessity of comparison and testing in establishing the conceptual rigor and empirical soundness of a given hypothesis or framework that emanates from it; iv) the descriptive, explanatory, evaluative, and predictive richness that inhere in it; v) the normative judgments that may be grounded in it; and vi) its simple utility as a conceptual toolbox for solving problems/puzzles[21] in the cultures and political economies of Africans and their descent.

A final point concerning transgenerationalism may be in order. As a paradigmatic sketch, it is not unique to africology. It can readily be applied to other disciplines. What makes it especially valuable in africology is its universality and timelessness. Bridging past and future through the present, transgenerationalism brings into focus images of generations of the dead, the unborn, and the living that call out clear and distinct pathways of societal progress and regress to Africans and their descendants. In doing this, it should be embraced not as an ideology but as a source of tough-minded arguments that hold out the possibility of making better the lives of individuals and groups.

CONCLUSION

As one reflects upon this chapter, an overriding point of singular significance emerges. There is no incongruity between measures of intellectual stringency and openness of inquiry and discourse on the one hand, and an array of interests and purposes in culture and political economy that africology serves on the other. This true statement calls out the animating imperatives of the discipline: passionate articulation and advancement of a range of social, cultural, economic, and political interests and purposes, conjoined with an unswerving commitment to the disclosure of truth through rigorous, critical inquiry and discourse. Both of these are of great moment as one extrapolates from the present state of Africans and their worldwide descendants to that which is likely to obtain in the twenty-first century, absent fundamental, radical changes designed to improve their lots.

Given the continual displacement of human labor-power by machine labor-power as idea-power increasingly dominates the Information Age, and given the relation between the intellectual capital of idea-power and the de-jobbing of the work force, a transcenturial responsibility falls upon africology. It is obligatory that the discipline prepares well the ones who become steeped in its intellectual contents, as well as acquaints those who are only exposed to it, to discern the sorts of structures, as well as participate in constellations of activities, which are likely not only to maximize their life chances as individuals in the new century, but also to strengthen and regenerate their societies. And so, africology calls out and opens paths of particular as well as universal value in the global regeneration of Africans and their descent.

Notes

I should like to thank Teresa W. Shannon, former program assistant in the Department of Africology, for her keen philosophic eye and very close reading of an early version of this chapter. I also should like to thank my faculty colleagues for their rigorous scrutiny of a later draft of the text at one of the department's Faculty Seminars. Finally, a very special word of thanks to my son, Maxwell A. Van Horne, who majored in africology, read this essay a number of times, and pushed me to broach themes on which I otherwise might have passed.

1. Lawrence J.R. Herson, "The Emergence of Disciplines in the American Academy: Notes on the Sociology of Knowledge" (Columbus, OH.: The Ohio State University, 1989), pp. 9-10. Author's emphasis.
2. Ibid., p. 10. Author's italics.
3. Cheikh Anta Diop, *The African Origin of Civilization: Myth or Reality*, trans. Mercer Cook (Westport, CT.: Lawrence Hill & Company, 1974), and *Civilization or Barbarism: An Authentic Anthropology*, trans. Yaa-Lengi Meema Ngemi; ed. Harold J. Salemson and Marjolijn de Jager (Brooklyn, N.Y.: Lawrence Hill Books, 1991). Daniel J. Boorstin, *The Discoverers: A History of Man's Search to Know His World and Himself* (New York: Random House, 1983), and *The Creators: A History of Heroes of the Imagination* (New York: Random House, 1992).
4. Diop, op. cit., *The African Origin of Civilization*, p. xv.
5. Ibid.
6. Ibid., p. xiv.

7. Ibid.
8. B.F. Skinner, *Beyond Freedom and Dignity* (New York: Alfred A. Knopf, 1971), p. 136.
9. Christopher Dawson, *Progress and Religion: An Historical Inquiry,* (Westport, CT.: Greenwood Press, 1970), pp. 65-66. This volume was originally published in 1929 by Sheed and Ward, 35 London. Author's italics.
10. William Bridges, "The End of the Job," *Fortune* 130: 6 (September 19, 1994): 62, 64. Author's italics.
11. Thomas A. Stewart, "Your Company's Most Valuable Asset: Intellectual Capital," *Fortune* 130: 7 (October 3, 1994): 68.
12. Thomas S. Kuhn, *The Structure of Scientific Revolutions* (Chicago and London: The University of Chicago Press, 1964) , pp. 158, 157.
13. Ibid., p. 152.
14. Ibid., pp. 152, 155,157.
15. Ibid., pp. 68-69.
16. Ibid.
17. Afrocentricity has been attacked for making its boundary coterminous with the discipline of africology; for the limits of its problem-solving/puzzle-solving capability; for the narrowness of its scope; and for the severe limits of its "hardheaded arguments."
18. Kuhn, op. cit., p. 68.
19. "Tapes show side of Nixon he would've hidden, lawyers say," *Milwaukee Journal Sentinel,* December 27, 1998, p. 15A.
20. Richard J. Herrnstein and Charles Murray, *The Bell Curve: Intelligence and Class Structure in American Life* (New York: The Free Press, 1994), p., 474.
21. See Margaret Masterman, "The Nature of a Paradigm," in *Criticism and the Growth of Knowledge,* ed. Imre Lakatos and Alan Musgrave (Cambridge: Cambridge University Press, 1970), pp. 59-89.

Bibliography

Boorstin, Daniel J. *The Discoverers: A History of Man's Search to Know His World and Himself.* New York: Random House, 1983.

_____. *The Creators: A History of Heroes of the Imagination.* New York: Random House, 1992.

Bridges, William. "The End of the Job," *Fortune 130: 6* (September 19, 1994): 62-74.

Dawson, Christopher. *Progress and Religion: An Historical Inquiry.* Westport, CT.: Greenwood Press, 1970. This volume was originally published by Sheed and Ward: London, 1929.

Diop, Cheikh Anta. *The African Origins of Civilization: Myth or Reality.* Translated into English by Mercer Cook. Westport, CT.: Lawrence Hill & Company, 1974.

_____. *Civilization or Barbarism: An Authentic Anthropology.* Translated into English by Yaa-Lengi Meema Ngemi. Edited by Harold J. Salemson and Marjolijn de Jager. Brooklyn, N.Y.: Lawrence Hill Books, 1991.

Herson, Lawrence J. R. "The Emergence of Disciplines in the American Academy: Notes on the Sociology of Knowledge." Unpublished essay. The Ohio State University, 1989.

Herrnstein, Richard J. and Murray, Charles. *The Bell Curve: Intelligence and Class Structure in American Life.* New York: The Free Press, 1994.

Kuhn, Thomas. *The Structure of Scientific Revolutions.* Chicago and London: The University of Chicago Press, 1964.

Masterman, Margaret. "The Nature of a Paradigm." In *Criticism and the Growth of Knowledge*, edited by Imre Lakatos and Alan Musgrave, 59-89. Cambridge: Cambridge University Press, 1970.

Skinner, B.F. *Beyond Freedom and Dignity.* New York: Alfred A. Knopf, 1971.

Stewart, Thomas A. "Your Company's Most Valuable Asset: Intellectual Capital." *Fortune* 130: 7 (October 3, 1994): 68-74.

8

AFRICOLOGY: FROM SOCIAL MOVE-MENT TO ACADEMIC DISCIPLINE

William E. Nelson, Jr

THE STRUCTURE AND MEANING OF AMERICAN SOCIAL MOVEMENTS

Since the middle 1960s, American higher education has undergone significant transformation. The most visible signal of significant change is the existence of a wide variety of multiethnic academic programs at major colleges and universities. This paper focuses on one of' the earliest forms of multiethnic programming in higher education, Black Studies. The emphasis will be on the emergence of Black Studies as an institutional option, and the transformation of Black Studies from a social movement to an academic discipline, which we will label, for analytical purposes, Africology.

Black Studies is a social movement with organic roots planted firmly in the soil of patterns of social development endemic to the American social and political system. Any meaningful analysis of Black Studies as a political force in higher education must place this phenomenon in the context of social, economic, cultural, and political forces shaping the character of social movements in America in general. The best analytic interpretation of the life history of American social movements is Roberta Ash, *Social Movements in America*. Ash defines a social movement as "a set of attitudes and self-conscious action on the part of a group of people directed toward change in the social structure and/or ideology of a society and carried on outside of ideologically legitimated channels or which uses these channels in innovative ways" (Ash, 1).

Ash develops from this definition an analytic paradigm that postulates the division of society into three distinct levels: the level of production, including techniques, material culture and technology, work, organization and relations to the environment; a social-structural level, including the relations of production (class relations) and political structure; and the superstructural level, the ideology and value system level (Ash, 4). It is the structure of society, particularly the system of production, that determines the basic organizational and ideological character of society, for example, the nature and number of class systems, the distribution of political power, the character of the economic order. In the unusual case when compatibility between the substructure and the superstructure is lacking, a society will manifest severe stress and conflict. Thus, stable societies are always in search of ways to harmonize their political arrangements and belief systems with their systems of production.

Over time, the large-scale industrial economy of the United States has produced a superstructure characterized by "extremely concentrated political power and control over wealth, an important, subservient, highly rewarded intelligentsia, and widespread welfare measures and redistribution of income" (Ash, 5). American institutional development in its early stages was characterized by isolation from Europe and the creation of a liberal bourgeois ideology. These factors produced class relations in America that were in sharp contrast to those prevailing in Europe. The liberal ideology of the American state helped to mute class conflict, giving to diverse groups a broad sense of common societal interests. The strong conflict between the intelligentsia and the ruling classes that has long plagued European politics has been virtually absent in the United States, because in America the political interests of the intelligentsia and those of the ruling class have been fused. This convergence of interests has held violent conflict in America in check and helped to forge a broad consensus in America among politically active groups about the appropriate limits of state authority. In this regard, it is significant to note that no matter how desperate or violent the struggle of classes and special interests in America, no one has "seriously suggested an alternative organization of society" (Ash, 30).

The liberal ideology of the state, the absence of sharp class conflict, and the concomitant absence of a rebellious intelligentsia have all helped to shape in important ways the organizational behavior of social movements in America. These movements have almost invariably been reform movements. They have not sought revolutionary ends such as changing the relations of production or replacing an incumbent ruling class; rather, they have used constitutionally sanctioned or legitimate means designed to win concessions from or manipulate elites. The American emphasis on limited government and open elections has undercut the adoption of revolutionary programs that call into question the legitimacy of central values or central institutions by social movements. The American two-party system has sharply limited the options available to social movements, removing from public attention a range of issues not directly at stake in elections. "In a multiparty system, voters are offered markedly different choice; that they have not been confronted with such choices is heralded as a victory for American consensus and a means of preventing serious conflict" (Ash, 34).

One of the crucial by-products of the American Revolution was the shared conviction by Americans that they were a chosen people with a unique destiny. Basic values arising during the colonial experience – civic responsibilities, individual opportunity, and achievement, became permanently etched in the American social system. These values reinforced a broad commitment to constitutional democracy and held in check the propensity for socially mobilized groups to seek radical solutions to societal problems. The frontier, slavery, and immigration have in their own way helped to constrain the radical impulse of American social movements by obscuring the level of misery suffered by the white working class under state capitalism and by transmuting class into ethnic conflict (Ash, 35-44).

In the final analysis, social movements in America have served the interest of elites rather than the masses. The revolutionary propensities of dissatisfied groups have been muted by the absence of sharp class conflict and the prevalence of a liberal ideology that stresses the resolution of public issues through reform and compromise. Social movements in the educational arena have tended to follow religiously the pattern of behavior manifested by social movements operating in other spheres of interest. Nevertheless, a number of interesting distinctions can be made regarding the operational norms of Black and white oriented movements. Within the American social order, racial factors serve to modify the orientation of politically mobilized groups in their quest for power and upward mobility.

THE EMERGENCE OF WHITE SOCIAL SCIENCE

In contrast to the American emphasis on the propagation of democratic values and the expansion of social development opportunities to broad segments of society, American institutions of higher education, from their very inception, have been elitist enterprises. The nine original colonial colleges – Harvard, Yale, Princeton, Dartmouth, Rutgers, Brown, Columbia, Pennsylvania, and William and Mary – were all established to train the male children of wealthy merchants and landowners for the ministry or positions of power and influence in the mercantile economy. Control of the colleges was placed in the hands of trustees drawn from the ranks of ministers and businessmen. The pivotal obligation of the trustees was to ensure that the colleges served the social, economic, and intellectual needs of the upper-crust (Meranto, Meranto, and Lippman, 14). During this period higher education was expected to be the chief vehicle through which special privileges to a small educated elite could be funneled and maintained. The college curriculum was designed to serve the basic needs of this special group; faculty members were expected to adhere to the basic orthodoxy in classroom instruction and personal character and deportment.

While the enrollment and the curriculum of American colleges expanded during the 19th century, little alteration took place in the basic elitist foundation of higher education. This remained true despite the passage of the Morrill Act in 1862, which established the basis for the creation of state-supported land grant institutions. Publicly owned, newly emergent state universities sought to emulate the social values and educational philosophies of prestigious older private institutions. Thus, it was out of an environment heavily weighted toward the promotion of elitist values and interests that American social science disciplines emerged (Higham, 9-10).

The molding of American social science disciplines in their early years was highly influenced by elite educational patterns employed in German higher educational institutions. Most of the early leaders of these professions were trained in German universities. In many instances, these American students were so impressed with German social science research and teaching methods that they attempted to replicate the German experience in American schools when they returned to the United States. John W. Burgess is regarded as the founding father of American political science. Burgess traveled to Germany for graduate study and was highly impressed with the German emphasis on unfettered research; he also delighted in the fact that German universities placed no administrative restrictions on the freedom of students to learn. Burgess returned to the United States and established the first graduate programs in political science at Columbia University. The founding of the Columbia school marked the beginning of the emergence of political science as a discipline. This emergence took the form of the vigorous spread of graduate education in the field, spirited debates regarding methods of' inquiry, the founding of the American Political Science Association in 1902, and the development of independent departments of political science in the period 1903-1921 (Somit and Tanenhaus, 15-85).

The emergence of history as a professional discipline followed a similar pattern. Consolidation of the field of history into a professional discipline began with the founding of the American Historical Association (AHA). The central figure behind the creation of the association was Herbert Baxter Adams, a graduate of the University of Heidelberg and director of historical studies at Johns Hopkins University in the 1880s and 1890s (Higham, 11-15). From the outset, professional historians controlled the AHA. Considerable expansion of the organization's public influence derived from its control over the *American Historical Review*, and its influence on the teaching of history in colleges as well as secondary schools. The expansion of doctoral programs in history at the turn of the century also significantly increased the stature of history as an emerging academic discipline. Much of the credit for the growth of history as a profession after 1900 can be attributed to John Franklin Jameson, one of the early presidents of the association. Jameson promoted scholarly research in history by accepting the editorship of the *American Historical Review*, and by spearheading the establishment of a center for historical research in Washington under the sponsorship for the Carnegie Institution. Out of the association emerged an invaluable annual bibliography entitled *Writing American History* (Higham, 16-23).

An analysis of the life histories of political science and history as academic disciplines suggests that their quest for status and recognition was greatly enhanced by a number of factors that do not apply with equal force and relevance to newly emergent disciplines. The fact that these disciplines began at the graduate level lent to them a considerable amount of instant prestige. Questions regarding their academic credibility dissipated in the wake of the emergence of strong Ph.D programs at Harvard, Johns Hopkins, Columbia and Yale. Graduates of these programs became the natural constituents and cheerleaders of the disciplines. Accepting positions as professors of political science and history at colleges and universities, these graduates had a self-interest in lobbying for the creation of independent institutional networks, such as autonomous departments and research libraries, to support the rapid institutional development of their disciplines.

These disciplines also had the advantage of emerging at a time when the formal organizational structure of American colleges and universities had not fully crystallized. The organizational core of the American university was still in flux. No particular field of study – especially in the social sciences – had unchallenged control over subject matter. Problems centering on questions of academic turf were usually resolved by splitting off one field of academic interest from another. Thus, as history and political science gained separate identities from economics and sociology, each of these fields could legitimately claim the right to function autonomously.

The professional and political interests of social science disciplines was advanced immensely by their adherence to a worldview, a sociology of knowledge, that was in keeping with the interests of the patrons of the university and the dominant white population at large. In their search for truth and objectivity, these disciplines relied on research methods and epistemological assumptions that served to justify and promote the subordination of minority interests to the power and preferences of white elites. Robert Staples has described the racial impact of traditional or "white" sociology in the following terms: "White Sociology refers to those aspects of sociology designed more for the justification of racist institutions and practices than objective analysis of human institutions and behavior. It is this body of theory and research that has been employed by the powers that be to sustain white racism and the instruments of its implementation. White sociology has provided not only the scientific covering for the exploitation of the Black masses, but the ideological rationale for the arrangement of power and the ascendancy of the powerful in human society" (Staples).

Traditional social science has been extremely functional for the dominant classes and interests in America. It has not only opened the door to the pursuit of higher learning for the dominant elite, it has also instilled patriotism and an instinct for system support into the hearts and minds of the masses. Although often claiming to be value free, traditional social science has embraced a racist ideology that has given a veneer of legitimacy to the perpetual subordination of Black power and authority in the social system. Given their historic role, it is not surprising that the leaders of corporate capitalism have been among the strongest supporters of traditional social science disciplines. By the middle years of the 20th century, these disciplines had seemingly gained an intractable foothold in the political structure of the American academy. Few people were prepared for the challenge to the academic hegemony of these disciplines that would emanate from the movement for Black Studies in the 1960s and 1970s.

THE BLACK STUDIES MOVEMENT

As an intellectual enterprise, Black Studies has long and honorable roots. Scholarly studies on Black people in the New World date back to the antebellum period. The writings of former slaves, abolitionists, and 19th-century intellectuals laid a solid foundation of scholarship upon which 20th-century students of the Black experience could build. Scholarship on the Black experience began to take on systematic qualities as a result of the pioneering of early 20th-century scholars such as W. E. B. Du Bois, Carter G. Woodson, Charles J. Johnson, and Lorenzo Turner. Movement in this direction was reflected in the establishment in 1915 of the Association for the Study of Negro Life and Thought and in the publication of *the Journal of Negro Life and History*. More recent studies by intellectual giants such as John Hope Franklin, Charles H. Wesley, E. Franklin Frazier, and Benjamin Quarles have taken the study of the Black experience out of the shadows of intellectual activity and into the bright light of serious, penetrating, and enduring scholarly analysis and development.

As a social movement, the movement for Black Studies found its immediate roots in the student protest movement of the 1960s (Edwards, 17-60). In this regard, the movement for Black Studies differed sharply from earlier movements designed to create new disciplines in higher education. Unlike the campaign to build the disciplines of history and political science, the campaign for Black Studies was not led by a well-entrenched social elite. Rather, the campaign to establish Black Studies was promoted by Black students and intellectuals instilled with a high sense of racial consciousness by their involvement in militant Black protest campaigns (Brisbane, 223-228). In the 1960s Black protests spilled from the streets onto the campuses. These protests were fueled by the growing realization by Blacks that American universities were important citadels of power and potential influence. Noting the absence of significant Black involvement in the life of major American universities, students began to demand the recruitment of more Black students and faculty. They also began to demand the establishment of Black Studies courses so that Black students could understand the total dimensions of the problems of Black people across the world. Eventually the demand for courses would be translated into a demand for comprehensive programs to institutionalize the systematic examination of the Black experience into the organic framework of the university (Brisbane, 226-236).

The political demand for Black Studies by Black students resulted in the establishment of over five hundred Black Studies programs at American colleges and universities over a five-year period. Efforts to inaugurate, stabilize, and institutionalize Black Studies programs on major college campuses unleashed a storm of controversy and conflict. The demand for Black Studies was more than just a call for the construction of new courses. At bottom, Black Studies represented a powerful critique of traditional American values, institutions, and political arrangements. Black Studies questioned both the methods and the epistemological assumptions of traditional social sciences. It called into question not only the content of specific courses but the ideological network that undergirded the fundamental approaches to human questions of entire disciplines (Turner, V-XXV). Furthermore, on a practical level, Black Studies threatened to siphon away both students and financial resources from traditional departments during a period of emerging fiscal crisis in higher education. Thus from the very beginning, the demand for Black Studies was met with strong resistance by individuals deeply committed to preserving the historic character of higher education. On many campuses, the resistance was designed to keep Black Studies from coming into existence at all (Chrisman, 222-232). On others, the strategy was to establish a program to placate student demands, but to limit the reach and impact of the program. This was usually accomplished by keeping the staff and the resources of the programs small and by maintaining the programs as coordinating units rather than autonomous departments. Even in those places where comprehensive departments were established, strong efforts were made to keep the movement for Black Studies from translating itself into university-wide curriculum reform. Black Studies departments would be confined to developing and teaching their own courses. Collaboration across disciplinary lines between Black Studies and other departments would be discouraged. Few Black Studies courses could be entered into the university's basic education curriculum. The notion that Black Studies courses should be required of all students was considered subversive. Students who took Black Studies courses who were not Black Studies majors would not be allowed to use those courses for graduation by their home departments.

The battle for Black Studies was destined to be severe because the movement for Black Studies was a movement propelled from the bottom up rather than from the top down. This movement was not sanctioned by the dominant elite and did not work in its interest. It was, in many ways, a radical movement with revolutionary potential. Racial and class distinctions that had been suppressed from public attention were illuminated by the debate over the "relevance" of traditional American education. Given the gravity of the threat, the reactions from elite sectors to the threat were predictable. Second, the coalition that brought Black Studies into existence was tenuous and transitory. Militant Black student boycotts and demonstrations could not be maintained over a significant period of time. When the marching stopped, the forces of reaction began to turn back the clock. Third, Black Studies was faced with the challenge of attempting to achieve in a matter of months feats of organizational development that had been accomplished by traditional disciplines over a period of years. The challenge to move from a social movement to an academic discipline remains one of the most critical items on the agenda of the Black Studies movement.

AFRICOLOGY: BUILDING AN ACADEMIC DISCIPLINE

The term *Black Studies* has served a number of useful purposes for the Black academic community. Adoption of this term illuminated in the 1960s the determination by Blacks to become the subjects not merely the objects of serious intellectual endeavors. As the movement for human understanding popularly known as Black Studies proceeds toward the goal of becoming a discipline, it should be assigned a name that captures the essence of the enlarged perspective implied by the term discipline.

One possible choice of a new term is Africology, a concept that evokes images of the rigorous scientific pursuit of knowledge about individuals of African descent.

Transition from social movement to academic discipline requires, of course, more than just the assignment of a new Rome. According to Professor Maulana Karenga, a discipline is, by definition, "a self-conscious, organized system of research and communication in a defined area of inquiry and knowledge" (Karenga, 5). The building of a discipline of Africology is uniquely challenging because of the absence of a widely accepted paradigm. The search for an appropriate paradigm is an essential precondition for the development of the discipline of Africology. An appropriate paradigm in Africology must be interdisciplinary in nature, that is, it must be a conceptual framework that can cut across routine disciplinary lines to produce order, coherence, and understanding out of a vast array of social scientific materials. Professor James Stewart has referred to such a paradigm as an "expansive model of Black Studies" (Stewart). His expansive model transcends the ordinary boundaries of traditional disciplines and creates a new inter-discipline.

An appropriate paradigm for Africology must also be an alternative and corrective to traditional scholarship. Such a paradigm must, of necessity, be Afrocentric in its basic orientation. This requirement entails more than just the substitution of Black concepts for white concepts, it means the construction of a new epistemic based upon the unique position of African people in the world social order. In the words of James Turner, the challenge for the new Black intellectual is not "simply to pick and choose among the conceptual and methodological toys of traditional disciplines but to reconceptualize social action and rename the world in a way that obliterates the voids that halve inevitably occurred as a result of artificial disciplinary demarcations" (Turner, x-xi). The discipline of Africology must give us a prism through which we can correctly interpret the world around us. It must give us the capacity not simply to ask different questions, but to ask the right questions, and to test the truth of the answers we receive on the basis of realities emanating uniquely from the African experience. If Professor Russell Adams is right that epistemology is a social code for mapping a group definition of various levels of reality, an epistemology for Africology must be one that allows us to determine our reality and speak to the world about our plans for transforming the world as we know it (Adams, 208). An appropriate paradigm for Africology must be a liberating paradigm, that is, it must allow us to shed the straight jacket of Western culture and to begin the quest for self-knowledge and self-realization called for by Karenga.

An appropriate paradigm for Africology must also combine self-knowledge and self-realization with social action. In contrast to the parochial, self-limiting practices of traditional disciplines, Africology must move its boundaries beyond the borders of academia and register a concerted impact on the broader community. Africology must symbolize the search not only for a new discipline but also for a new community of political activists. Traditional boxes and squares that have separated the research enterprise from the moral obligation to create social change contradicts the philosophical essence of Africology. As a reincarnation of the militant impulses of the 1960s revolts, Africology must not seek knowledge for the sake of knowledge alone but must vigorously pursue positive social change.

From a practical standpoint, Africology must command the allegiance of Afrocentric scholars and promote effective communication within the discipline. As a discipline, Africology must also develop multiple avenues for communicating its accomplishments to the outside world. Issues centering on the imperative of standardization must be resolved in the context of the Afrocentric paradigm. Critical decisions will have to be made regarding disciplinary priorities with respect to undergraduate and graduate programming. The discipline must also establish minimum standards of professional conduct. It must insist that those who wish to wear the disciplinary name must be committed unswervingly to promoting the social and cultural objective of an Afrocentric community of scholars. Finally, Africology must come to grips with the new methodologies and new technologies of the social sciences and humanities. The miracle of communication has made possible the creation of a global village of African people. Technological breakthroughs in this field have produced exciting new research possibilities; they have also given to us enormous challenges and responsibilities.

The task of building the discipline of Africology as an alternative and corrective to traditional scholarship is an extremely challenging one. In its quest for coherence and permanence, Africology faces obstacles not present during the formative years of history and political science. The distinctions that can be made here are quite marked. First, Africology does not trace its origins to forces within the academic establishment but emanates from an external grassroots movement designed to open doors for Blacks in higher education that have been closed for centuries. Professional educators with influence and power were not the key actors in the early campaign for Black Studies. Programs in Black Studies could not draw upon linkages with prestigious departments in foreign universities to undercut the cloud of suspicion surrounding their claims to academic legitimacy. In the eyes of university administrators, these programs represented political prizes to the Black community; questions concerning institutionalization, substantive content, and longevity would be intimately tied to the mobilization of political support for the programs in arenas both within and external to the university.

Second, Black Studies was introduced at a time when the lines of power, authority, and jurisdiction within the academic community had already been tightly drawn. Black Studies threatened to disrupt formal and informal organizational agreements that had been settled for decades. The artificial lines of demarcation that separated political science, history, sociology, and economics have been crafted through protracted experimentation and negotiation. As an interdisciplinary enterprise, Black Studies not only blurred traditional distinctions but sought to carve out for itself a separate and unique position by drawing into its purview courses and related activities impinging on the academic terrain of traditional disciplines. Established disciplines were not prepared, without a fight, to concede to Black Studies the right to teach Black related courses that fell within their alleged jurisdiction. Thus when the Black Studies Department at Ohio State University introduced 10 African courses in 1972, the courses were seized by the History Department and added to History's course list. The rationale given by History for this action was that all courses with history in the title properly fell within the jurisdiction of the History Department and could only be legitimately taught by members of that department's faculty. A serious political struggle had to be waged by Black Studies for two years before its "right" to teach courses in African history was firmly established.

Third, Black Studies represented an innately radical critique of the ideology, methods, and objectives of traditional social science disciplines. It rejected the elitist assumptions of tradition social science, seeking instead to use education to promote the broadscale distribution of social economic and cultural benefits across all sectors of the population. Black Studies questioned the validity of the Eurocentric assumption endemic to traditional social science that the whole of society could be effectively examined and explained on the basis of the values, needs, and interests of the dominant culture. It sought to transform the concomitant hostility toward African values, needs, and interests, and to provide an intellectual forum where Black activist-scholars could begin to examine Black life from an African-centered perspective.

The dual emphasis on social change through social action and academic creativity and on educational reform through a transformation of the values and practices of social science serves as the pivotal touchstone for the construction and evolution of the discipline of Africology. Given the present structure and ideological framework of American higher education, how can these objectives be realized? This question illuminates the most pivotal dilemma facing Black Studies today. If it remains firmly rooted within the structural nexus of American academic life, Africology will be required to assume some of the behavioral characteristics of other disciplines. Members of the discipline will be required to teach, do research, provide guidance for student projects, read papers at conferences, answer requests for support by community constituents, and conform to the bureaucratic requirements and expectations of the universities where they work. The discipline of Africology must support the work of its members and forge the kind of broad linkages throughout the academic community required to achieve respectability and influence. Can Africology achieve the practical objectives outlined above while fulfilling its challenge to radically transform traditional approaches to education? There is a great danger that, as Africology seeks to become institutionalized, it will abandon its commitment to radical social change and community uplift. This danger is reflected in the tendency for second-generation Black Studies scholars to change the focus of the discipline by acceding to university demands for joint appointments, and to cut their ties to student groups and community organizations. The new orthodoxy is that Black Studies can best do its work by cementing formal relations with parallel academic units across the university, while simultaneously relinquishing its claims to institutional autonomy and academic independence. Structural decentralization, under this formulation, becomes the functional twin of ideological disintegration. The emphasis on Afrocentric analysis is muted by a concern for "objective" scholarship, which places issues germane to the Black experience within the broader context of Western developments and the contributions of dominant white interests.

Clearly, the task of building the discipline of Africology is fraught with pressure, complexity, and contradictions. The American academy has not been a receptive host to those attempting to adhere religiously to the original goals of the Black Studies movement. Still, the challenge faced by the advocates of Africology are not insuperable. A strong, dynamic, functional discipline of Africology can be built without unduly sacrificing its commitment to educational reform and social change. In contrast to history and political science, Africology must be built from the bottom up and not from the top down. The building process must begin in the broader Black community with the establishment of a firm political network dedicated to good quality, radical academic programming. American universities are deeply immersed in the political process. Pressure by organized interests both within and outside the university can have an appreciable effect on the ability of Africology programs to achieve their objectives without making major concessions. The community base of the Africology building process cannot be emphasized enough. The quest for Africology must be viewed as an extension of the civil rights campaign that first brought Black Studies into existence. Africology represents a continuing phase in the struggle for Black liberation through education. Its substantive interests are coterminous with those of the community and exist in symbiotic relationship with a range of other objectives propelled by the immense actual and potential power, of community mobilization.

Africology must also establish a base of strong political support on the campus. The central target here must be undergraduate students, who will be motivated not only to take courses in the program but also to rally to its support on a continuous basis. Because of its history as an overtly political movement, Africology cannot afford to follow in the footsteps of history and political science by concentrating its initial efforts on graduate education. While graduate education is a critical component of the overall developmental process, a heavy concentration in this area must await the construction of a solid academic and political base at the undergraduate level.

Africology must seek to cultivate an image of disciplinary integrity through the creation of standardized curricula and the establishment of procedures and criteria for evaluation and accreditation. A clear sign that the field has begun to move toward disciplinary consolidation will be the disappearance of a multitude of approaches to Black Studies courses and the institutionalization of a uniform curriculum across the country. Such a curriculum will be important not only in clearly defining the central ideology and core subject matter of the discipline but also in erecting disciplinary boundaries so that the essence of' its contributions will not be diluted through external penetration from rival disciplines.

Africology must create a nationwide institutional network to support the fundamental objectives of the discipline. Efforts should be made to establish autonomous departments of Africology. Academic departments are the lifeblood of successful disciplinary movements. They serve as important recruitment vehicles for students into the field. They are also the essential instruments of power in the effort to promote the creative institutionalization of disciplines within the central structure of the university.

An accent on professional growth must be an essential component of plans for the long-term evolutionary development of the discipline of Africology. The professionalization process begins with the imitation of sound graduate programs. It continues with the creation of a national organization, the holding of annual conferences, and the publication of a national journal. The national organization must be both a political instrument and a service organization. As a political instrument, it must coordinate the establishment of functional networks to mobilize organizational support behind the discipline's premier objectives. In its service capacity, it must keep members of the discipline informed of important developments, promote their career interests, and coordinate the raising of support funds from public and private sources. The unorthodox ideological perspective of the discipline may make it impossible to obtain government grants and major corporate support, which may make it more difficult for disciplinary leaders to find ways to make the contributions of the discipline visible and relevant to grassroots citizens.

At this moment in our history we have reached that magical cross-section in time where human aspirations can be transformed into academic programs that can liberate the world from hundreds of years of human suffering. African people bring to the human condition special insight and a unique gift for progressive social development. If carefully constructed, Africology can be the instrument of enlightenment and political triumph that will transform the human condition around the world into a model of social responsibility and magnificent achievement.

References

Adams, Russell L. "Intellectual Questions and Imperatives in the Development of Afro-American Studies" *An Assessment of Black Studies Programs in American Higher Education*, ed. Carlene Young. *Journal of Negro Education* 53.3 (Summer, 1984).

Ash, Roberta *Social Movements in America* Chicago: Markham Publishing Company, 1972.

Brisbane, Robert H. *Black Activism: Racial Revolution in the United States, 1954-1970*. Valley Forge, Pa: Judson Press, 1974.

Chrisman, Robert. "Observations on Race and Class at San Francisco State," *Black Power and Student Rebellion* ed. James McEvoy and Abraham Miller. Belmont California: Wadsworth Publishing, 1969.

Edwards, Harry. *Black Students* New York: The Free Press, 1970.

Higham, John. *History: The Development of Historical Studies in United States*. Englewood Cliffs, N.J: Prentice-Hall, 1965.

Karenga, Maulana. "Black Studies and the Problematic of Paradigm: The Philosophical Dimension," unpublished paper prepared for publication in *Phylon: The Atlanta University Review of Race and Culture*, June 1986.

Meranto, Philip J., Oneida J. Meranto, Matthew R. Lippman, *Guarding the Ivory Tower: Repression and Rebellion in Higher Education*, Denver: Lucha Publications, 1985.

Somit, Albert, and Joseph Tanenhaus. *The Development of Political Science: From Burgess to Behavioralism*, Boston: Allyn and Bacon, 1967.

Staples, Robert. "What is Black Sociology? Toward a Sociology of Black Liberation," in *The Death of White Sociology* ed. Joyce A. Ladner. New York: Vintage Books, 1973.

Stewart, James B. "Toward Operationalization of an "Expansive" Model of Black Studies," Atlanta, Ga.: Institute of the Black World, 1983.

Turner, James E. *The Next Decade: Theoretical and Research Issues in Africana Studies.* Ithaca, New York: Africana Studies and Research Center, Cornell University, New York, 1984.

9

FOUNDATIONS OF A "JAZZ" THEORY OF AFRICANA STUDIES

James B. Stewart

INTRODUCTION

This analysis uses "jazz" as a metaphor to describe the field and function of Africana Studies. The metaphor encompasses characteristics of jazz music, performance techniques of musicians, demographics and socialization of performers, audience involvement, consumption patterns, and musicological analyses. This approach is designed to clarify aspects of Africana Studies obscured by typical interpretations based on either scientific or literary/artistic models. The "jazz" model of Africana Studies outlined here is designed to bridge these two interpretative modalities.

A cursory review of the Africana Studies literature reveals how major Africana Studies theorists have used Western models of science to either describe Africana Studies or differentiate the field from Western intellectual traditions (see for example Ani, 1994; Asante, 1990; Karenga; 1982; Stewart, 1992). On one hand, useful aspects of Western scientific praxis have been endorsed and adapted successfully into the disciplinary matrix of Africana Studies. On the other hand, overemphasis on "scientific" explanation has created unnecessarily restrictive notions of what constitutes knowledge and how it is generated and disseminated.

There is an equally well-established tradition of emphasizing the artistic/humanistic dimensions of Africana Studies. For example, Ford's early effort to define the enterprise included the assertion that "Black Studies are concerned primarily with the history, literature, art, music, religion, cultural patterns and lifestyles developed in America by a race of people cut off completely from all contact with the land of their origin" (Ford 225). Over time the increasing visibility of artists/literati has created confusion about the boundaries between Africana Studies and other disciplines. Given these competing images of Africana Studies it is first necessary to clarify the relationship between different approaches to knowledge production.

CULTURAL TRANSFORMATION AND AFRICANA STUDIES

It is well established that distinctions among ways of knowing were largely absent in traditional African societies. The point of contention is whether specialized approaches to knowledge production (illustrated, for example, by scientific reasoning) are more functional than traditional approaches. It should not be surprising that Eurocentric commentators have generally concluded that Western science is the most highly developed strategy for knowledge generation, in some cases basing this claim on comparisons of the relative efficacy of scientific and traditional African knowledge-production strategies. To illustrate, although Horton's classic comparison of traditional African and Western approaches to knowledge creation identified many similarities, in the end Western scientific approaches were deemed to be more powerful in terms of explaining events (Horton, 1967a; 1967b). Similarly, Hanson and Martin (1973) argued that Western anthropologists can replicate traditional thought processes and can manipulate traditional cultural constructions in ways inconceivable to indigenous members of a culture because of access to a broader frame of reference.

I argue here for the complementarity of different ways of knowing using the critique of Pitrim Sorokin's theory of cultural dynamics advanced by W. E. B. Du Bois and Rushton Coulburn in 1942. Sorokin (1937-1941) argued, in effect, that in all societies humans employ three epistemological approaches or "attitudes of mind" to understand reality – the ideational, corresponding with intuition; the idealistic, corresponding with reason; and the sensate, corresponding with sense perception. At any given time, Sorokin claimed, one epistemological approach is dominant in a particular society and is embedded in its main cultural systems. This dominant epistemological approach, Sorokin asserted, is defined by the most powerful forces in a society. Coulburn and Du Bois summarized the argument as follows:

> [Sorokin] sees the functioning of society and the making of history as man's struggle to know himself and to know the cosmos, passing eternally through a threefold rhythm of epistemological phases. The process may be described briefly as 'intuition over sensation, reason, and matter; reason over intuition, sensation, and matter; sensation over reason, intuition, and matter' (Coulburn and Du Bois, 500).

Note that in this formulation, reason (presumably the hallmark of science) is not the most advanced way of knowing if, as claimed by Sorokin, a society goes through only one developmental cycle, that is, reaches a developmental apex, followed by a subsequent decline in power and influence.

Coulburn and Du Bois revised Sorokin's model to incorporate the potential agency of groups like African Americans to participate in shaping the ethos of a culture. First, they rejected the idea that one attitude of mind is dominant at any given period of time, arguing that "surely no human mind can think in terms of ideation, which is to say, intuition or belief, alone; to attain, develop, and defend the belief there must be some sense-perception and some reasoning." Instead, they asserted, "the mind must employ – in systematic relation with one another – all three methods of cognition" (Coulburn and DuBois, 519). Second, unlike Sorokin, Du Bois and Coulburn insisted that change is not unidirectional and sometimes requires retrogression in order for transition to a new stage to proceed (Coulburn and DuBois, 513). Thus, it may be necessary for an "idealistic" culture to resurrect some "intuitive" elements in order to progress to the "sensate" stage.

Coulburn and Du Bois rejected those aspects of Sorokin's framework that relegated members of non-dominant groups to the status of recipients of constructs imposed by the dominant culture. Instead, they modified the framework such that different cultural groups could have overlapping but still distinct mixes of ways of knowing during a particular era, roughly comparable in degrees of sophistication. This formulation avoids absolut-ist claims that impenetrable barriers exist between cultures, thus allowing cultural borrowing.

Using the Sorokin-Coulburn-Du Bois framework as a point of depar-ture, Africana Studies can be interpreted as an attempt to synthesize all three ways of knowing in a manner that retains the synergies present in traditional African societies. Depending on the subject matter and circum-stances, one mode of knowledge production may be emphasized over the others. Du Bois provided an illustration of this dynamic in his challenge to historically Black colleges and universities:

> Starting with present conditions and using the facts and the knowledge of the present situation of American Negroes, the Negro university expands toward the possession and the conquest of all knowledge. It seeks from a beginning of the history of the Negro in America and in Africa to interpret all history; from a beginning of social development among slaves and freedmen in America and Negro tribes and kingdoms in Africa, to interpret and understand the social development of all mankind in all ages. It seeks to reach modern science of matter and life from the surroundings and habits and attitudes

of American Negroes and thus lead up to understanding of life
and matter in the universe. (Du Bois, 1973: 95-96)

Note the priorities assigned by Du Bois. History and hermeneutic
cultural interpretations are the foundations upon which generation of "scientific" knowledge proceeds. This strategy reflects the fact that Western
scientific modalities have had relatively less influence on the experiences
of peoples of African descent than ideation and sense perception.

The type of synthesis of ways of knowing pursued through Africana
Studies is actually at the cutting edge of a broader de-emphasis of science
(as distinct from technology) as the principal source of socially useful
knowledge. This erosion of scientific influence is signaled by several
developments. Within the scientific establishment itself there is increasing soul-searching among practitioners in various social and behavioral
disciplines regarding the value of the current "incrementalist" approach
to knowledge. The growing prevalence of "meta-analyses" and review
essays is a manifestation of a desire to generate broader interpretations
from potpourris of small-scale scientific studies. Popular culture, with its
decided sensate emphasis, has supplanted science as the major purveyor of
cultural imagery, values, and (most important), sensory stimulation. This
shift in attitude of mind finds its intellectual expression in deconstruction
and cultural studies paradigms that challenges both the claims of universalism and the linguistic assumptions associated with scientific explanation.
The growing significance of popular culture media is, of course, linked
directly to the increasing commodification of culture and the associated
scramble for profits in the global cultural marketplace. Du Bois foresaw
this trend some fifty years ago when he warned about a "leveling of culture
patterns" that would emerge from the unbridled expansion of monopoly
capitalism. He forecasted direly that, "If this [leveling of culture patterns]
is going to continue to be the attitude of the modern world, then we face
a serious difficulty in so-called race problems. They will become less and
less matters of race, so far as we regard race as biological difference. But
what is even more important, they will even become less and less matters
of conflicting cultures" (Du Bois, 247).

From this vantage point, one of the challenges of Africana Studies is
to preserve culturally specific sources of innovation and to resist market
tendencies to commodify cultural forms in ways that lead to cultural leveling. In addition to the increasing role of sensate approaches to understand
reality, there are also ideational challenges to scientific discourse, including
various "new age" philosophies and resurgent traditional religious movements. Not surprisingly, many of the new age philosophies borrow heavily

from non-Western cultures. This resurgence of idealistic ways of knowing constitutes an expanded search for spiritual guidance in a rapidly changing world. Technology plays a critical role in propagating shifts in attitude of mind. In particular, new technologies of information acquisition and dissemination, especially the Internet, are accelerating shifts in patterns of knowledge production and information acquisition as well as changes in patterns of human-to-human and human-to-machine interactiosn.

Within African and African American communities the preoccupation with popular culture is especially pronounced. In an interesting way, "hip-hop" culture serves as a counter-force to the escapist tendencies of emergent attitudes of mind that ignore persistent and growing patterns of inequalities and unspoken cross-cultural contestations. On the other hand, the growing commodification of rap music, the principal artistic expression of hip-hop culture, limits this genre's liberatory potential. However, the synthesis of jazz and rap has extensive transformative possibilities, and the beginning of such a synthesis is underway. Rap music serves as the action -inducing counterpart to the theoretical direction provided by jazz. At the same time it must be recalled that jazz emerged "in the streets," as did rap. Buddy Bolden is credited with organizing community parades in New Orleans in which jazz was first played. These origins are captured in the following lines from David Henderson's (1993) poem, "A Coltrane Memorial":

my first day in new orleans
Home-hous of jass
coltrane dead
In my dreams
among marching creoles
among marching blacks
bojangling jass parade (Lange and Mackey, 1993: 263-4)

The contemporary renewal of interest in jazz as a musical genre is only partially relatedto its artistic merits and entertainment function. Although the attitude of mind embodied in jazz is most closely aligned with the African and African American cultural ethos, many admirers from a variety of cultural backgrounds are drawn to its deeper meanings.

The unique ability of jazz to express the complexities of the experiences of peoples of African descent has long been recognized. Langston Hughes (1926) once declared: "Jazz to me is one of the inherent expressions of Negro life in America: the eternal tom-tom of revolt against weariness in a white world, a world of subway trains, and work, work, work; the tom-tom of joy and laughter, and pain swallowed in a smile." In *Invisible Man*, Ralph Ellison observed:

I'd like to hear five recordings of Louis Armstrong playing and singing "What Did I Do to Be so Black and Blue" – all at the same time.... Perhaps I like Louis because he's made poetry out of being invisible. I think it must be because he's unaware that he *is* invisible. And my own grasp of invisibility aids me to understand his music.... Invisibility, let me explain, gives one a slightly different sense of time, you're never quite on the beat. Sometimes you're ahead and sometimes behind. Instead of the swift imperceptible flowing of time, you are aware of its notes, those pointswhere time stands still or from which it leaps ahead. (Ellison, 8)

The linkage between cultural invisibility and jazz suggested by Ellison is an illustration of how an oppressed group can create an alternative mode of defining reality and seeking meaning. Khephera Burns's (1987) description makes the point more directly: "jazz is the father of hipness, the mother of invention, and a Black philosophy of life without words. Jazz is about the business of the isness of being."

The epistemological and ontological characteristics of jazz are some-times obscured by the manner in which it has been and is being appropri-ated by external forces. One form of appropriation involves revision of the history of jazz to de-emphasize its African and African American roots and to highlight contributions of European Americans, paralleling efforts to rewrite the history of the Harlem Renaissance. A second type of appropria-tion involves what can be described as "musicalogical reductionism." This entails an emphasis, especially in jazz studies programs, on translation of compositions into standard musical notation, thereby allowing replication of the music while detaching it from its cultural roots. This reductionism even attempts to model improvisation, thereby negating the spontaneity and intuitiveness of the music. A third form of appropriation involves censored representations of jazz on FM radio stations that have adopted a "Smooth Jazz" format. The play lists are dominated by European Ameri-can musicians playing "pop jazz" compositions. African Americans are disproportionately represented by female vocalists, many of whose songs do not fit standard definitions of jazz.

Africana Studies faces similar challenges. Europeans and European Americans are increasingly attempting to appropriate the study of the expe-riences of peoples of African descent. The principal approach in these analy-ses involves efforts to force-fit the experiences of peoples of African descent into models developed to explain the experiences of European Americans.

The interpretive process is controlled externally through privileged access to the most powerful information dissemination technologies.

A JAZZ MODEL OF AFRICANA STUDIES

In the jazz model of Africana Studies presented here, a musical composition performed by a jazz ensemble is the analog of an interdisciplinary investigation by a team of Africana Studies specialists. The live performance of the jazz composition is the equivalent to the presentation of scholarship at a professional conference or similar venue. Recording a composition is the equivalent of the publication of a study. The rehearsals that precede performances or recording sessions mirror the research conducted as part of a research project. Individual rehearsals are the equivalent of self-study to hone research techniques or to acquire background information as part of the research process. Jam sessions are the equivalent of informal discussions of research and can involve nonprofessionals in a type of teaching environment or outreach activity.

Extending the analogy, individual instruments are the counterparts to individual academic disciplines with the unique sound produced by each corresponding to the specific emphasis of each academic discipline. Each performer develops an individual style in the same way that each scholar develops an individual approach to the tools of an academic discipline. One of the highest compliments that can be paid to a jazz musician is that he or she makes the instrument "talk." The combined voice of the instruments tells a story like a narrative account produced by a researcher.

Langston Hughes emphasized the importance of the drum as the keeper of time, the equivalent of the discipline of history. The saxophone was originally developed specifically to mimic the human voice. Charles Christian was the first modern jazz guitar soloist to treat the guitar as a peer to the saxophone. As Albert Murray (1987) has emphasized: "Jazz is the ancestral down home voice at its highest level of refinement. Jazz tells us what we African Americans have done with our experience on these shores."

Although one instrument (discipline) may be showcased through solos, the basic model of the ensemble is democratic. To illustrate, legendary drummer Max Roach (1987) has observed: "Jazz is a very democratic musical form. It comes out of a communal experience. We take our respective instruments and collectively create a thing of beauty. Everybody's allowed to be out front and supportive during a composition. Everybody's free." Thus this collective model still allows for a high level of individuality. Solos are the equivalent of a more in-depth examination of a particular facet of the subject matter. To illustrate, consider the following lines from Jayne Cortez's (1993) poem, "Solo Finger Solo":

Count Basie
you reach through the bottom of the music
way down beneath cross rhythm vamps
below air stream of the lowest octave
into depths of a sacred drum
and Count Basie Count BasieCount Basie
how powerful a dignified and exquisite and direct and sharp
(Lange and Mackey, 1993: 196-197)

Cortez's reference to the drum again underscores its centrality and its special role in African cultures. However, the obvious question is how does the model accommodate the fact that most other instruments are of European origin? The answer is that through the development of innovative techniques jazz performers have found ways to "Africanize" the sounds produced by the instruments. This is, in fact, the same challenge that faces Africana Studies scholars in applying and adapting research and dissemination techniques that originate in Western scientific or humanistic disciplines..

Various examples of the processes whereby jazz musicians have Africanized instruments can be offered. Compositions written for the piano by African Americans generally make more extensive use of the black keys than compositions by musicians from other backgrounds, and also greater use of the left hand. These innovations were necessary because the piano's pitch could not be bent as is the case for other instruments. One technique that was developed to overcome the technical limitation on the range of string instruments to two octaves was playing double notes. John Coltrane's technique sometimes involved playing "off the register sounds." Sonny Rollins and Miles Davis are noted for "phrasings across the bar" that introduce structural asymmetry into compositions..

The often discussed "blue note" (flatting the third, the fifth, and the seventh) is not abnormal in African musical forms, but it is difficult to represent in European musical notation. Jazz musicians often "bend notes," which entails a type of symbolic inversion that alters the "meaning." Finally, the syncopation patterns found in many African American musical genres reflect the African musical tendency to emphasize the downbeat.

The prevalence of polyrhythms in African music and its derivative genres is well established . In the context of the model, these can be interpreted as creating more complex explanations of events that incorporate several historical forces. History is also preserved through the technique of "quoting," that is, playing portions of other pieces in a jazz composition. This practice obviously correlates to the standard practice of citing previous research in scientific studies.

Finally, the process of improvisation is an integral characteristic of jazz performance. Improvisation can be interpreted as the exploration of new ideas, building on an established body of knowledge. The best improvisation occurs when the musicians have a large repertoire of possible techniques and compositions to build on. As noted by William Cook (1988); "We are here, charged with the task of completing... ourselves. The process is jazz. It requires improvisation, the daring to strike out on your own coupled with a sure grounding in and respect for the tune on which you are working changes."

The combination of the various characteristics discussed above enables jazz ensembles to create the equivalent of an interdisciplinary Africana Studies analysis that is more than simply the sum of the individual performances. The composition is transformed into a collective statement that is irreducible. This is equivalent to how Maulana Karenga (1982) describes interdisciplinarity in Africana Studies:

> Black Studies...as an interdisciplinary discipline has seven basic subject areas. These intradisciplinary foci which at first seem to be disciplines themselves are, in fact, separate disciplines when they are outside the discipline of Black Studies, but inside, they become and are essentially subject areas which contribute to a wholistic picture and approach to the Black experience. Moreover, the qualifier Black, attached to each area in an explicit or implicit way, suggests a more specialized and delimited focus which, of necessity, transforms a broad discipline into a particular subject area. (35-36)

Jazz has processes of training practitioners and evaluating performance that parallel those associated with academic disciplines. However, at least traditionally, there has been less emphasis on formal training than in the case of academe. Historically, the typical process involved self-taught practitioners honing their craft through individual practice building on their "feel" or "ear" for the music and mentorship by established performers. In the context of the model described here it is significant that the early developers of jazz were called "professors." In a similar vein, the progenitors of Africana Studies were largely self-trained. In the cases of both jazz and Africana Studies the outcomes of a greater emphasis on technical training have been mixed.

Irrespective of the type of training received, jazz performers face a tripartite level of scrutiny from peers, audiences, and formal critics. The analogs for Africana Studies specialists are academic peers, students, constituencies served through Africana Studies outreach, and academic administrators. Individual jazz performers and ensembles are formally and informally evaluated using various criteria including technical precision, phrasing, and clarity of sound. At the other end of the evaluative spectrum, one of the ultimate tests is whether people purchase recordings. The obvious equivalent for Africana Studies scholars is sales of monographs.

The different types of jazz, such as be-bop, hard bop, and free jazz are the equivalent of the different schools of thought or paradigms within Africana Studies. From time to time paradigm shifts have occurred as is the case in academic disciplines. And, as in scientific revolutions (see Kuhn, 1970), paradigm shifts in jazz have involved radical changes in the style, content, and technique. When radical new styles emerge, traditional evaluative criteria become irrelevant, just as in the case of scientific revolutions.

Jazz has had a major impact on other forms of expressions in a manner similar to Africana Studies. Perhaps the penultimate example is Toni Morrison's explicit use of jazz characteristics in the novel "Jazz." As noted by Randle (1998) "this novel does not... merely evoke muscial forms, it *defines* itself, by title as jazz." One manner in which Morrison accomplishes this is through the absence of chapter designations such that, "one chapter flows directly into the next, taking up precisely – yet unexpectedly – where the previous one has ended, usually in sentence fragments, not sentences, the result of which is both a seamless transition and a jarring rift." Randle (1998) Al Young has, developed a new literary genre, the musical memoir," grounded in a jazz motif (see Carroll, 1998). This pattern represents the perpetuation of historical praxis. During and following the Harlem Renaissance there was extensive interaction between jazz musicians and artists, and some jazz musicians were also accomplished artists.

One of the critical characteristics that differentiates Africana Studies from traditional disciplines is its emphasis on direct engagement in processes that foster social change in order to improve the conditions of peoples of African descent. Africana Studies has eschewed the generation of knowledge for knowledge's sake and has encouraged its practitioners to foreground perspectives that identify, critique, and offer defenses against forces that perpetuate the oppression of peoples of African descent. Similar perspectives can be found in jazz. Examples include Charlie Mingus's albums "Fables for Faubus" and "Scenes of the City," Max Roach's "We Insist: Freedom Now" and "Garvey's Ghost," and Sonny Rollins's "Freedom Suite." It is interesting that, despite the resurgence of popularity of jazz and the re-release of many standards, none of these titles is currently available (Porter, 1998).

The discussion to this point has emphasized how analogies to jazz help clarify the positive dimensions of Africana Studies. However, the analogy can also be used to describe less progressive features as well. Jazz has a comparatively small audience relative to many other musical genres, similar to the circumstances facing Africana Studies. This means that opportunities to convey messages are limited. One strategy employed by jazz musicians to confront this problem involves capitalizing on the greater popularity of jazz in Europe. Africana Studies scholars have had some success with a similar strategy in the cultivation of contacts in various African countries. In the case of jazz overseas, exposure has increased European musicians' appropriation of the genre. Similarly, the European colonial legacy has engendered efforts to appropriate the study of experiences of peoples of African descent.

On the other hand, some jazz musicians have attempted to broaden their reach by altering styles to expand commercial opportunities. Similarly, some Africana Studies specialists have refocused their writing to appeal to nonprofessional audiences. In both cases this strategy runs the risk of diminishing the value of information conveyed through the two media.

The description of the ideal function of a jazz ensemble is not meant to minimize the possibility of intragroup conflict. Disputes within ensembles have erupted for various reasons including conflicts in styles, professional jealousies, personality conflicts, lifestyle conflicts, and so on. Personnel changes can occur frequently. As a consequence of the preceding caveats, long-standing associations are the most likely to yield exemplars of the type of ensemble dynamics envisioned in the model.

The expression of women's experiences and their roles in production have been circumscribed in both jazz and Africana Studies. In jazz, women have performed disproportionately as vocalists, rather than as musicians. In Africana Studies, systematic efforts to address the gender bias via prioritizing the triple plight (race, class, and gender) of Africana women under the auspices of Africana Womanism is a relatively recent development (see Hudson-Weems, 1993). An analysis of gender conventions in jazz from an Africana Womanist perspective could be extremely valuable in generating new insights.

The lifestyles of many jazz artists have exhibited self-destructive behaviors. A growing number of biographies and autobiographies are emerging that provide useful insights into the "sociology of jazz" and the relationship between creativity and various coping behaviors. In contrast, although the broad parameters of the emergence and evolution of the field of Africana Studies are well known, no comparable body of case studies exists that examines individual programs and departments or presents biographical or autobiographical profiles of Africana Studies specialists.

Finally, jazz, like Africana Studies, suffers from ambiguity of definition. In both cases the lack of a clear definition serves as a catalyst for misinterpretations and misrepresentations. The model presented in this section attempts to avoid this problem by specifying which dimensions of each respective enterprise are amenable to inclusion.

IMPLICATIONS OF A JAZZ MODEL OF AFRICANA STUDIES

The jazz model of Africana Studies here outlined in the previous section synthesizes the more useful features of scientific and humanistic models while overcoming some of their most debilitating weaknesses. The jazz model exhibits all of the characteristics of a scientific disciplinary matrix as described by Kuhn (1970). Kuhn argued that disciplinary matrices have four components: (1) a metaphysics that provides a context for the search for knowledge; (2) values shared by practitioners; (3) symbolic generalizations, observational language, and research methods; and (4) exemplars or concrete examples of the application of the theoretical and empirical framework.

The jazz model relaxes the requirements associated with the generation and verification of knowledge. In particular, the criterion that exact replication of results be possible is discarded in favor of an approach that assigns a crucial role to improvisation in generating new insights. Improvisation in this sense consists of intuitive departures from previous methods and interpretations. However, critical core elements must not be altered to the point that the original problem and solution are not readily identifiable. This type of verification procedure generates a representative, as opposed to a differentiated problem solution. The characteristics of such knowledge are clarified in a passage from C. Eric Lincoln's novel, *The Avenue, Clayton City*:

> These stories may well have been factual, but the genius of such stories, factual or not, is that they assemble the informal data of larger truths transcending the particular individuals to whom they claim to refer. The... stories were undoubtedly *culturally* true, and as such they were adequate explanations for whatever gaps there were in the factual histories of the individuals to whom they were applied. Whether or not the details were true, they were well within the conventional cultural format, and having some of the required characteristics. (Lincoln, 45)

The jazz model shifts attention from the individual scholar or researcher to a collective or team, working cooperatively to generate new knowledge by moving beyond traditional disciplinary limitations. Unfortunately this model is currently rare in Africana Studies despite the verbal commitment of its advocates to interdisciplinary scholarship. Perhaps the closest approximation to this model entails edited volumes comprised of contributions by individual scholars trained in different disciplines but writing about a common theme. However, the production of the individual chapters rarely involves any dialogue among contributors prior to the publication of the monograph.

The jazz model suggests that participant observation and other qualitative research protocols have the greatest potential to generate information appropriate for Africana Studies analyses. Laboratory research protocols or other designs requiring sharp demarcations between the roles of observer and subject are seen as unduly limiting. The jazz model imposes structure on the standard model of the unfettered individual artists or humanistic scholar and focuses attention on collective roles, rather than on individual outputs. The type of artistic collaboration highlighted in the jazz model is consistent with the perspective advanced by Du Bois:

> For the development of Negro genius, of Negro literature and art, of Negro spirit, only Negroes bound and welded together, Negroes inspired by one vast ideal, can work out in its fullness the great message we have for humanity....For the accomplishment of these ends we need race organizations, a Negro school of literature and art, and an intellectual clearing house, for all these products of the Negro mind, which we may call a Negro Academy. Not only is all this necessary for positive advance, it is absolutely imperative for negative defense.(1897, 79)

The assertion of a Black Aesthetic by literary critics during the 1960s is a more modern example of the articulation of a set of artistic values consistent with the jazz model (Gayle, 1971).

The jazz model's synthesis of the scientific and artistic models has the potential to introduce a balanced approach to knowledge generation instead of exacerbating tensions among the different ways of knowledge described by Sorokin, Coulburn and Du Bois. To operationalize such a balanced knowledge-production process, however, will require some modifications to the current praxis of Africana Studies. There is a need to incorporate the study of jazz, and Black music in general, systematically into Africana Studies research and instruction. The most useful approaches would de-emphasize formal musicological analyses in favor of analyses that decode the messages embedded in jazz. This will require structured dialogue between Africana Studies scholars and jazz composers and performers. Such dialogues will hopefully produce a common observational language and eventually lead to the development of interdisciplinary multimedia instructional approaches and associated products using CD-ROM and Web technologies. A jazz-focused Africana Studies initiative could broaden the field's impact in the global arena and serve as a counter force to the global cultural-leveling process described by Du Bois. The rationale for such an initiative was described cogently by Du Bois himself in *The Souls of Black Folk*: "Art is not simply works of art; it is the spirit that knows Beauty, that has music in its soul and the color of sunsets in its handkerchief, that can dance on a flaming world and make the world dance too" (Du Bois, 1903).

References

Ani, M.. *Yurugu: An African-Centered Critique of European Thought and Behavior*. Trenton, N.J.: Africa World Press, 1994.

Asante, Molefi. *Kemet, Afrocentricity and Knowledge*. Trenton, N.J.: Africa World Press, 1990

Burns, K. Cited in "Jazz Men: A Love Supreme," *Ebony Man* (April 1987).

Carroll, M.. "Al Young: Jazz Griot," *Mimeo*. 1998.

Cook, W. In "The Meaning of Life," *Life* (December 1998).

Cortez, J. "Solo Finger Solo," In Lange and Mackey, *Moment's Notice*, 196-197. (1993)

Coulburn, R., and Du Bois, W. E. B. (1942). "Mr. Sorokin's Systems," *Journal of Modern History*, 14, (1942): 500-521.

Du Bois, W. E. B. "The Conservation of Races," American Negro Academy Occasional Papers, No. 2. Reprinted in P. Foner (ed.) W. E. B. Dubois Speaks, Speeches and Addresses 1890-1919. New York: Pathfinder Press, 1970, 73-85.

_____ "The Field and Function of the Negro College." Alumni Reunion Address, Fisk University, 1933. Reprinted in *W. E. B. Du Bois: The Education of Black People, Ten Critiques 1900-1960*. H. Aptheker, Amherst: University of Massachusetts Press, 1973. 83-102.

_____ "Race Relations: 1917-1947," *Phylon* 9. 3 (1948): 234-247.

_____ . *The Souls of Black Folk*. New York: Verso. 1903.

Ellison, Ralph. *Invisible Man*. New York: Random House, 1980.

Ford, Nick Aaron. "Black Studies Programs," *Current History* (November 1974).

Gayle, Addison ed. Garden City, N.J.: Doubleday, 1971.

Hanson A. and R. Martin, "The Problem of Other Cultures," *Philosophy of the Social Sciences* 3, (1973): 191-208.

Henderson, D. "A Coltrane Memorial," In Lange and Mackey, *Moment's Notice*, 263.

Horton, R. "African Traditional Thought and Western Science," part I, *Africa* 37. (1967a): 50-71.

_____ "African Traditional Thought and Western Science," part II, *Africa* 37 (1967b): 155-187.

Hudson-Weems, Clenora. *Africana Womanism: Reclaiming Ourselves*. Troy, Mich: Bedford Publishers, 1993.

Hughes, Langston. "The Negro Artist and the Racial Mountain," *Nation* 23 (June 1926).

Karenga, Maulana. *Introduction to Black Studies*, Los Angeles: University of Sankore Press, 1982.

Kuhn, T. *The Structure of Scientific Revolutions*, 2nd edition. Chicago: University of Chicago Press, 1970.

Lincoln, C. Eric, *The Avenue, Clayton City*. New York: William Morrow and Co., 1988.

Murray, A. In "The Soul of Jazz," *Ebony Man* (April), 1987.

Porter, T. "The Social Roots of Afro-American Music." Mimeo, 1998.

Randle, G. "Lady Sings the Blues: Toni Morrison and the Jazz/Blues Aesthetic." Mimeo, 1998.

Roach, Max. "Jazz Men: A Love Supreme," *Ebony Man* (April 1987).

Sorokin, P. *Social and Cultural Dynamics*, 4 Vols. New York: Bedminster Press, 1937-1941.

Stewart, James (1992). "Reaching for Higher Ground: Toward an Understanding of Black/African Studies," *Afrocentric Scholar* 1.1 (1992): 1-63.

PART III
THE BLACK AESTHETIC

Black Aesthetic is a black criterion for judging the validity and/ or beauty of a work of art... "art for people's sake,"...judged according to its presentation of the tradition and styles stemming from African and African American cultures...[with] a separate symbolism mythology, critique, and iconology. (Hill, *Call and Response*)

10

THE GARVEY AESTHETIC

NOTE: THIS CHAPTER IS REPRINTED WITH PERMISSION FROM TONY MARTIN, *LITERARY GARVEYISM: GARVEY, BLACK ARTS AND THE HARLEM RENAISSANCE* (DOVER, MA: THE MAJORITY PRESS, 1983). MARCUS GARVEY'S UNIVERSAL NEGRO IMPROVEMENT ASSOCIATION (UNIA), WHICH FLOURISHED IN THE POST-WORLD WAR I YEARS, REMAINS AFRICAN AMERICA'S LARGEST MASS MOVEMENT EVER. ITS *NEGRO WORLD* WAS THE WORLD'S MOST WIDELY CIRCULATED AFRICAN NEWSPAPER.

Tony Martin

However great his interest in art, Garvey was still a political figure. And art, for him had to serve the cause of freedom, justice and equality. His view of the place of art in his people's struggle was a succinct statement of what, in the 1960s came to be known as the "Black aesthetic." "We must encourage our own Black authors who have character," Garvey postulated, "who are loyal to their race, who feel proud to be Black, and in every way let them feel that we appreciate their efforts to advance our race through healthy and decent literature."[1]

This did not mean that the Black author must necessarily confine himself solely to racial themes. Garvey himself did not do so. His own poetry included items on racially neutral topics. Yet, the briefest of glances through any collection of Garvey's poetry would clearly indicate what his primary concern was.

There was considerable debate within the columns of the *Negro World* over this question of the Black aesthetic. Most contributors tended to follow Garvey's view of art as a weapon in the struggle for African advancement. But the occasional dissenting voice was not unheard of. In this regard the *Negro World* simply mirrored the vexing controversy that raged throughout the 1920s and beyond, among Black artists in general.

Marion S. Lakey, one of the better *Negro World* poets, reflected Garvey view in a 1922 poem entitled "Mission" –

> I'm struggling far afield today.
> Son of a lowly race;
> Fortune her gifts must yield to me
> In spite of my black face.
> I'm fighting my people's cause today
> To down an ancient wrong.

And to lift this yearning race of mine
In lofty take and song.[2]

Garvey's concern with encouraging "our own Black authors who have character" implied, of course, that the race should itself decide who its worthy artists were. "We must inspire a literature and promulgate a doctrine of our own," he wrote, "without any apologies to the powers that be. The right is ours and God's. Let contrary sentiment and cross opinions go to the winds." This was in his powerfully eloquent essay on "African Fundamentalism."[3]

John Edward Bruce echoed Garvey's concern. He argued that Afro-American too often refused to accept its literary figures until they had received a stamp of approval from the dominant race. Writing on "The Negro in Poetry" in the *Negro World* in 1923, he stated that those Black poets who "have achieved any distinction, owe it to the fact that some white author, more liberal than is usual, has put the seal of his approval upon their work and thus given them prestige and standing, which they could not otherwise have got. Thus [Paul Laurence] Dunbar jumped into fame at almost a single bound. He came to his own, but his own received him not. William Dean Howells recognized his ability and with a stroke of his pen gave him international fame." Bruce lamented this abdication of responsibility on the part of the Black public. "The white man, he said, "designates our poets, political leaders and moral advisers. We accept the designees...."[4]

The problem that Bruce described was well illustrated in the case of Claude McKay, arguably the best poet of the Harlem Renaissance. Mckay's first breakthroughs into print in North America came via the white publications, *Seven Arts* (1917) and *Pearson's Magazine* (1918). The poem, "The White Fiends," which Pearson's printed had earlier been rejected by W. E. B. DuBois' *Crisis*, organ of the National Association for the Advancement of Colored People. A selection of his poems had also previously been rejected by William Stanley Braithwaite, Black literary critic for the white Boston *Evening Transcript*.[5] McKay's career, from his early days in Jamaica, was characterized by a succession of white mentors, godfathers and bankrollers. Perhaps DuBois and Braithwaite, in rejecting his work, lost an opportunity for Afro-America to corral one who should have been its own. For McKay, as will be seen, never could fully reconcile himself to the role of race man, his excellent racial poetry notwithstanding. His novel, *Home to Harlem*, caused Garvey in 1928 to place him among those guilty of "prostituting their intelligence, under the direction of the white man, to bring out and show up the worst traits of our people...." The book was, in Garvey's view, "a damnable libel against the Negro."[6]

During the late 1930s, Garvey, now living in England, kept up a similar barrage of criticism against Paul Robeson, by then one of the world's best known actors on stage and screen. He considered Robeson a good actor but a poor representative of his race. Robeson, like McKay, he accused of being manipulated by whites, this time in the playing of racially demeaning roles.[7]

One of Robeson's films, *Emperor Jones*, had been the subject of *Negro World* upset since its first appearance on Broadway in 1920. Written by white playwright, Eugene O'Neill, it originally starred Charles Gilpin in the title role of an ex-convict turned buffoonish emperor of a Caribbean island. William Bridges, editor of the *Challenge* and a regular contributor of the *Negro World*, called the *Emperor Jones* a travesty of the African race.[8] Hubert H. Harrison surprisingly wrote a very favorable review of the play. He was taken by task by a *Negro World* reader, Mrs William A. Corbi of Cambridge, Massachusetts.

Mrs. Corbi's letter illustrates the willingness of the *Negro World* to engage in real debate, even when the paper's own editors came out on the losing end. On this occasion it was Mrs. Corbi, the reader, who found herself articulating the correct Garveyite aesthetic as against one of the *Negro World*'s own editors. She wrote,

Mr. Eugene O'Neill's co-called wonderful play, described as a study of the psychology of fear and of race superstition, which Mr. Harrison so readily commends to Negroes as a work of genius, cannot and will not be accepted by race-loving Negroes as a work of genius. Surely "Something is rotten in Denmark" when Hubert Harrison lauds "Emperor Jones." That is the trouble with our educated and intelligent men. They are using their brains to keep down their own race.

Harrison had expressed surprise that such a serious play could succeed so well on Broadway. To Mrs. Corbi, this fact was not surprising at all. The reason was the same as that which had made the film *Birth of a Nation* a success. For, she informed Harrison,

> Anything that causes the white man to believe that the Negroes are superstitious, immoral and illiterate...can make a hit on Broadway....

One does not need "an understanding of drama and its laws," to quote Mr. Harrison, to realize that "Emperor Jones" is of no racial value to the Negroes of the World. The play does not elevate the Negro, and such plays never will.

Mrs. Corbi ended with parting shots against Harrison, Gilpin and white writers:

> Such men as Mr. Harrison who encourage white playwrights by lauding them to the skies, are of no racial value to the Negroes. Remember always the man who allows a man to make a fool of him will always be a fool. Charles Gilpin has won fame in "Emperor Jones." Now let them bring him back in one of the higher plays, and see how long he will remain on the great white way.

> The time has come when Negroes will not accept such plays as great. Let the white man write them of himself and the Negroes will say "Atta Boy."[9]

Ten years after the Harrison-Corbi exchange another *Negro World* editor became involved in a similar difference of opinion. This time editor H.G. Mudgal praised the *Pittsburgh Courier* for its campaign against the "insulting" radio comedy show, "Amos 'n' Andy," where white actors portrayed two dim-witted Black characters. Arthur S. Gray, a regular *Negro World* contributor, disagreed with Mudgal. He thought that the show was to be laughed off, rather than to be upset over.[10]

For most commentators within and without the *Negro World*, the question of a Black aesthetic was usually raised in the form of debate on the place of "propaganda" in art. Art consciously enlisted in the cause of struggle was considered by some to be mere propaganda and not worthy of true art. Those of Garvey's persuasion saw "propaganda" as a desirable element in art, if art was to have any purpose.

The *Negro World* in 1920 praised the advent of the *Promoter* magazine, edited by a regular contributor, Hodge Kirnon. The magazine was "radical and racial at the same time," and therefore good.[11] At times the Black artist might suffer in terms of recognition and wider short term critical acclaim because of a propagandist stance. But this was not an unreasonable price to ask of the racially committed. Marion S. Lakey made this point in a 1923 critique of the work of fellow *Negro World* poet, Ethel Trew Dunlap. He wrote, "One comes to realize more and more as one reads Miss Dunlap's poems that it will be the women of the race who will lead the race to a higher and more genuinely cultured spiritual plane....Miss Dunlap is – yes – a poetess laureate and a heroine to her race, in that she has dared to write for a cause that means everything to the future well-being of her race at a time when that cause is the object of the supercilious ridicule and contempt of many of her own people, thus, to a certain extent, sacrificing for the time her chance to win a larger but what could not be other than a less altruistic fame."[12]

Even among those who favored propaganda, however, there were different shades of emphasis. *Negro World* literary editor, William H. Ferris, consistently advocated a subtle and understated propaganda. Propaganda that was too strident and preachy might, in his view, detract from the niceties of plot, characterization and style that went to make, say, a good novel. By some strange dialectical process, the masterfully written, subtly propagandistic novel would be a much more powerful weapon than a strident, poorly constructed work. "The Novel," he argued, "has been a potent method of arousing the public conscience. Harriet Beecher Stowe's *Uncle Tom's Cabin* won more converts to the slave's cause than did the brilliant addresses of Sumner, Phillips and Douglass and the forceful editorials of Garrison." It followed from this argument that the task facing the Black novelist of the 1920s was to create great fiction – "Novels which can powerfully picture the civilization of Africa during the Middle Ages, novels which can powerfully envisage the struggles of an aspiring Negro in a hostile Anglo-Saxon civilization, will undoubtedly add to the prestige and standing of the Negro Race."[13]

If the fiction of the second Mrs. Garvey (Amy Jacques Garvey), is any indication, then Marcus Garvey was less troubled by overt propaganda than was Ferris. Mrs. Garvey was as perfect a companion for her husband as any political leader could hope for – powerful orator, efficient private secretary, excellent editor (she edited his two books of poems and his seminal two volume *Philosophy and Opinions*), sometime associate editor of *The Negro World*, later her husband's biographer and a devoted wife and mother. Garvey certainly could not have asked for more.

In 1923 Amy Jacques Garvey published a short story in the *Negro World* entitled "Whither Goest Thou?" The main character was a Black Mississippian. The man's friend had been lynched and he himself beaten up and thrown unconscious into a train's jim crow coach. A note pinned to his coat advised him to get out of town. He did. He went to Arkansas. But before he could settle down there his host Black community was given twenty-four hours to remove itself. Our protagonist thus found himself involuntarily on the road again, this time to New York. But New York was no place to be cold, penniless, unemployed and destitute. Driven by unfathomable desperation, he decided to commit larceny and turn himself in. In jail at least there would be a warm place to sleep and food to eat. But the judge refused to jail him under these circumstances. He had no choice but to face a hostile world once more, vowing this time to make it to jail by committing "one of the most fiendish robberies" imaginable. Mrs. Garvey ended her story like this –

"The door closed behind him and the blizzard raged before him.

"Negro; whither goest thou?"[14]

This was powerful stuff, though Ferris may have considered it unsubtle. One aspect of the story of which he would definitely have approved, however, was Mrs. Garvey's starkly realistic treatment of an inelegant theme. For herein lay an element which frequently entered into the debate over propaganda and art. Should the Black writer reveal the joys and sorrows, even the misery and degradation that were to be found among the mass of people, or should he or she emphasize only the genteel and refined?

Ferris opted for the former. His criticism of Black artists here is reminiscent of E. Franklin Frazier's later classic, *Black Bourgeoisie*, which so cruelly exposed the world of make-believe wherein much of the Black middle class has traditionally sought respite from its frustrations. "One of the stumbling blocks in the pathway to Negro progress," Ferris wrote, "is the Negro's false conception of art. Art to him, be it music, poetry, drama, sculpture, painting [or] literature, is a thing that appeals exclusively to the cultural-minded, to the bourgeoisie, to the lords and ladies who try, and fail miserably, to develop a genuine Bohemianism...." Black artists have before them the examples of Shakespeare, Robert Burns, and Paul Laurence Dunbar, all of whom had shown that great art does not have to lose touch with the masses. But they had largely rejected these models. "Instead, by virtue of social pressure, Negro artists are forced to produce works that bring out 'the higher aspirations of the Negro,' works that with a brutally sterile puritanism steer clear of the beauty and simplicity of true art."[15]

Here, however, as with other aspects of the propaganda question, the nuances were finely drawn. For it was one thing to write about ordinary folk, but quite another to hold their foibles up to ridicule in the name of realism. This would explain Garvey's language, previously noted, in reference to Claude McKay's *Home to Harlem*, to the effect that some writers were "prostituting their intelligence, under the direction of the white man, to bring out and show up the worst traits of our people...."[16] The same debate reappeared in the 1970s, over the depiction (some would say glorification) of prostitution, drugs and violence in "Black exploitation" films.

The generality of *Negro World* writers were much more pro-propaganda than most of the better known figures of the Harlem Renaissance. Novelist and poet Jessie Fauset spoke for many of the latter when she urged the Black actor to become "an artist first and only secondarily...

a Negro."[17] Inherent in her argument was the supposition that one had to purge oneself of one's identity in order to achieve artistic perfection, a sacrifice which Fauset and her ilk seemed not to require of white artists.

The anti-propaganda school found its only consistent *Negro World* voice in Eric Walrond, an associate editor from 1921 to 1923. For Walrond, propaganda tended to detract from good art. And according to his way of thinking, the propaganda trap was one that the Black writer in the United States was more or less forced into by the prevailing climate of racism. "One reason why the Negro has not made any sort of headway in fiction," he wrote in the *Dearborn Independent*, "is due to the effects of color prejudice. It is difficult for a Negro to write stories without bringing in the race question. As soon as a writer demonstrates skill along imaginative lines he is bound to succumb to the temptation of reform and propaganda."[18] Walrond did not adequately explain why the Black writer should not deal with racism, given, as he himself admitted, that the experience of racism represented the Black writer's most pervasive reality. His position was anomalous within the context of the *Negro World*, and will be discussed later. He come close to the classically a-social stance of art for its own sake. This position received extreme endorsement from the painter Salvador Dali in 1980 when he said that "nobody knows whether the Venus de Milo was a fascist or a Communist."[19]

The debate over propaganda was a debate over the use of art for positive social ends. Where art was harnessed to the cause of oppression there was little if any disagreement. Even those unwilling to countenance pro-Black propaganda unwittingly acknowledged the power, even of unsubtle propaganda, in their frenzied reactions to the racist noels of, say, a Thomas Dixon. *Negro World* columnist (later editor) H. G. Mudgal in 1922 provided some expressive commentary on the arch propagandist, Rudyard Kipling, the "poet laureate of British imperialism." For him, Kipling was "the only great artist in the history of humanity who has proved capable of misusing his art for dark purposes and destructive ends...." On reflection he even contested Kipling designation as a "great artist." For Kipling seemed "a stinking carcass with gaudy clothing and fragrant flowers on."[20] It was doubtless with the Rudyard Kiplings of this world in mind that UNIA conventions in New York in 1924 and Jamaica in 1934 suggested a literary censor to safeguard the race from unfavorable literature.[21]

While the pro and anti-propaganda lines may have seemed clear to some on theory, they were often muddled in practice. The fine distinctions drawn in the arguments of the main protagonists made this inevitable. The non-UNIA artists especially, usually exhibited considerable lack of clarity on this question. Sometimes they vacillated between one position and the other. Often they tried to eat their cake and have it too, arguing in theory against propaganda while being unable in practice to escape the all encompassing reality of North American racial prejudice.

For the leading figures of the Harlem Renaissance this confusion was fed in large part by a political fact. Most of them depended on white mentors and/or worked for predominantly white or at least white financed organizations. Thus Claude McKay drifted from one white patron to the next, whether in Jamaica or the United States or Europe. Jessie Fauset worked for W.E.B. Du Bois' *Crisis* magazine, the organ of the then white dominated NAACP. William Stanley Braithwaite worked for the white Boston *Evening Transcript*. In the case of Jean Toomer, he could pass for white anytime he felt like and he eventually ended his days as a white Quaker in Pennsylvania. Zora Neale Hurston was significantly helped along by white patrons.

Langston Hughes had his fair share of white mentors, too, but he somehow managed to maintain a more widespread credibility within his community than most of the others. In fact, Amy Jacques Garvey was quite excited by his famous essay on "The Negro Artist and the Racial Mountain." She probably would not have agreed with every single word in it, but there was enough in it to transport her into rapturous joy. Hughes had begun his essay by telling a little story that could easily have been written by a Harrison or a Garvey—

> One of the most promising of the young Negro poets said to me once, "I want to be a poet – not a Negro poet," meaning, I believe, "I want to write like a white poet;" meaning subconsciously "I would like to be a white poet;" meaning behind that, "I would like to be white." And I was sorry the young man said that, for no great poet has ever been afraid of being himself. And I doubted then that, with his desire to run away spiritually from his race, this boy would ever be a great poet. But this is the mountain standing in the way of any true Negro art in America – this urge within the race toward whiteness, the desire to pour racial individuality into the mold of American standardization, and to be as little Negro and as much American as possible.[22]

Mrs. Garvey was "delighted with the frank statement of Mr. Hughes in a white magazine." She did not know whether he was "a registered member of the Universal Negro Improvement Association," but "in any event his closing paragraph" showed him to be "a keen student of Garveyism, and with stamina enough to express its ideals...." For Hughes had declared therein, "Why should I want to be white? I am a Negro – and beautiful." "Bravo, Mr. Hughes!" Mrs. Garvey rejoiced, "...let the canvas come to life with dark faces; let poetry charm the muses with the hopes and aspirations of our race; let the musicians drown our sorrows with the merry jazz; while a race is in the making, and steadily moving on to nationhood and to power."[23]

Hughes was somewhat of an exception. His follow luminaries of the Renaissance mainstream more typically tended to follow the dictates, expressed or implied, of their white patrons. Nor were these patrons always reluctant to foist their anti-propaganda ideas onto their Black protégés. Carl Van Vechten, White Patron No. 1, addressed this controversy in his novel, *Nigger Heaven*. In his cold, sometimes incisive, arrogant and presumptuous way, he said of this character Byron, an aspiring young Black writer – "Try as he might, he could not get away from propaganda. The Negro problem seemed to hover over him and occasionally like the great, black bird it was, claw at his heart. In his stories this influence invariably made itself felt, and it was, he was sometimes convinced, the very thing that kept him from doing better work."[24]

White support for major Renaissance figures inevitably brought with it some commitment to an integrationist political perspective. And the anti-propaganda position was, more often than not, an integrationist position. For why use one's artistic gifts on behalf of racial struggle when one's larger purpose was to escape race altogether into a colorless world? Unlike the Garveyite intellectual, Ferris, who argued that great art, B la Shakespeare, Burns and Dunbar, could have universal appeal despite a parochial base, the anti-propagandists of the 1920s were more apt to believe that great art must be "universal" to begin with, in the sense of shedding itself of its primary sectional appeal.

William Stanley Braithwaite expressed this position very well in comments on Jessie Fauset's novel, *There Is Confusion*, which was set among the Black middle class. The strength of the work lay for him in the fact that it avoided "the limitations of propaganda on the one hand and genre fiction on the other [and therefore] emerges from the color line and is incorporated into the body of general and universal art." Braithwaite liked Jean Toomer's *Cane* even more, since "So objective is it, that we feel that it is a mere accident that birth or association has thrown him into contact with the life he has written about." Toomer, he thought, would write equally well about Irish or Russian peasants if a chance opportunity should bring him into contact with them.[25]

Braithwaite tied his anti-propaganda position very explicitly to his political integrationism, in what sounded like an upside down propagandist position of his own. The task of the Black artist, he said, was to "lift the Negro into the only full and complete nationalism he knows – that of the American democracy."[26]

Yet even so committed an anti-propagandist and integrationist as Braithwaite could exhibit some confusion on this question. Despite his love for the de-racialized Jean Toomer, who could write equally well of Black, Irish or Russian peasants, he could contradictorily assert in the same article that only a Black person could write a really accurate Black novel.[27]

W.E.B. DuBois, always confused and vacillating on things ideological, exhibited this confusion in an acute way. In 1921 he inveighed against the growing tendency among Black artists to "insist that our Art and Propaganda be one." By 1926 he was equally vehement that "All Art is propaganda.... I do not care a damn, for any art that is not used for propaganda."[28] This about face represented the first stirrings of what was eventually to blossom forth into a short lived flirtation with Garvey style separatism.[29]

The contradiction besetting Braithwaite and so many others was that they were drawn into an integrationist position at a time when the Black masses (and some sections of the middle class, too) were giving organizational expressions to Black nationalism on an unprecedented scale. For the Garvey Movement, with its 35,000 members in the New York local alone, represented a force from which none could escape. Some fallout from Garvey's insistent message of race pride, self-reliance and African redemption could not help but settle, even on conservative elements within the mainstream of the Harlem Renaissance. This, and the all-embracing nature of North American racism, which refused to release from its grasp even those who would ignore it.

The Garveyite propagandists of course rejected the integrationism espoused by many of the Renaissance leading lights. An unsigned *Negro World* editorial of 1922 (probably written by Ferris), looked forward "to a period when DuBois, James Weldon Johnson and the other high-brow black Americans who think white, will have abandoned the shadow of a spurious American citizenship for the more solid advantages of African co-operation and repatriation."[30]

These conflicting attitudes to propaganda can be observed in the works of other contemporary figures. Claude McKay, for example, could at times be the most powerful of propagandists. Recalling Braithwaite's rejection of his early offerings because they betrayed his race too much, he commented – "Need I say that I did not entertain, not in the least, Mr. Braithwaite's most excellent advice?.... My poetic expression was too subjective, personal and tell-tale... a discerning person would become immediately aware that I came from a tropical country and that I was not, either by the grace of God or the desire of man, born white." Like Ferris, McKay was aware that many of the world's white literary figures – "Byron, Shelley, Keats, Blake, Burns, Whitman, Heine, Baudelaire, Verlaine and Rimbaud and the rest" – had made no effort to submerge their identities. "In their poetry," he wrote, "I could feel their class, their roots in the soil...."[31]

McKay's propagandism was fueled not only by considerations of race, but by his few years of flirtation with left wing radicalism. While in the Soviet Union in 1922-23 he was commissioned to write a book on *The Negroes in America*. Here, in an effort to please his communist hosts, appeared perhaps his strongest endorsement of propaganda. "The only [Black] literature which merits any attention," he argued, "is that which has the character of national propaganda. Almost any Negro writer, however much he might appear to be minding his own business, is really drawn into active work in the area of propaganda. Such a great, urgent need can be felt here that not a single thinking person can stand aloof."[32]

Yet McKay was not entirely without confusion on this question. Recalling later his break with his white colleagues on the radical New York based *Liberator* magazine, he commented, "I cannot be convinced of a proletarian, or a bourgeois, or any special literature or art."[33]

McKay of course wrote excellent propaganda as well as non-propaganda verse. His contemporaries were divided, for the most part along predictable lines, over which they liked better. Robert Lincoln Poston, *Negro World* editorial writer and secretary general of the UNIA, thought that McKay's propaganda poems "for the present....serve a splendid purpose." He harbored the fear, though, that some of McKay's verse might suffer the fate of John Greenleaf Whittier's anti-slavery poetry – future generations with new preoccupations might pass them by.[34] Poet Countee Cullen thought that "Claude McKay is most exercised, rebellious, and vituperative to a degree that clouds his lyricism in many instances, but silhouettes most forcibly his high dudgeon...."[35] Braithwaite seemed to see McKay's propaganda poetry as definitely second best to his "poetry of expression," a temporary, perhaps pardonable aberration into which younger Black poets were invariably drawn. He also saw the fact that McKay wrote both propaganda and neutral poetry to be reflective of a wavering "between the racial and the universal notes."[36] This was not necessarily the case, for an espousal of propaganda did not necessarily carry with it any obligation to refrain from writing about springtime in New Hampshire or Harlem dancers.

Though the anti-propaganda position was mostly confined to integrationists the converse was obviously not true. Black nationalists, though normally pro-propaganda, obviously did not have any monopoly on this tendency. W.E.B. DuBois, coming out (in the 1920s) of the radical integrationist protest school, arrived in due and roundabout course at a propagandist position, as already seen. His colleague at the NAACP, James Weldon Johnson, though more ambiguous, at least summed up the complexities of the propaganda debate very well. He noted that the Renaissance poets had largely failed to live up to the anti-propaga/nda rhetoric which many of them preached. Countee Cullen, for instance, might "with justification chafe under any limitation of art to race, for he is a true lyric poet," but yet "the best of his poetry rises out of the idea of race and is permeated with it." He felt the same way about the race poetry of Langston Hughes.[37]

He felt the same way, indeed, about the whole Renaissance generation, whose race poetry seemed to him to be its best. Addressing himself to the whole corpus of Afro-American poetry he observed that "not in all of it do I find a single poem possessing the power and artistic finality found in the best of the poems rising out of racial conflict and contact."[38] History has not diminished the correctness of Johnson's view. Certainly the most famous, most loved and most often quoted poem of the Harlem Renaissance has to be McKay's fighting sonnet, "If We Must Die" – "...If we must die, Oh let us nobly die...."[39]

References

1. *Negro World*, September 29, 1928, quoted in Martin, *Race First*, p. 26.
2. *Negro World*, December 2, 1922.
3. Amy Jacques Garvey, ed., *Philosophy and Opinions of Marcus Garvey, II* (New York: Atheneum, 1969, first pub. 1923 and 1925), n.p.
4. *Negro World*, June 9, 1923.
5. Claude McKay, *A Long Way From Home* (New York: Harcourt, Brace and World, 1970, first pub. 1937), pp. 26, 27.
6. *Negro World*, September 29, 1928, quoted in Martin, *Race First*, p. 26.
7. See Chapter 6.
8. *Negro World*, March 26, 1921.
9. Ibid, July 30, 1921.
10. Ibid, June 20, July 11, 1931.
11. Ibid, August 21, 1920.
12. Ibid, July 7, 1923.
13. Ibid, July 31, 1920.
14. Ibid, March 31, 1923.
15. Ibid, April 15, 1922.
16. Ibid, September 29, 1928, quoted in Martin, *Race First*, p. 26.

17. Locke, ed., *The New Negro*, p. 167.
18. *The Dearborn Independent*, May 13, 1922.
19. *Time*, November 10, 1980, p.77.
20. *Negro World*, October 7, 1922.
21. Martin, *Race First*, p. 26.
22. Reprinted in Addison Gayle, Jr., ed, *The Black Aesthetic* (Garden City, N.Y.: Anchor Books, 1972), p. 167.
23. *Negro World*. July 10, 1926
24. Carl Van Vechten, *Nigger Heaven* (New York: Octagon Books, 1980, first pub. 126), pp. 175, 176.
25. Alain Locke, ed., *The New Negro*, pp. 43, 44.
26. Ibid, pp. 40, 41.
27. Ibid, pp. 43, 44.
28. Arnold Rampersad, *The Art and Imagination of W.E.B. DuBois* (Cambridge: Harvard University Press, 1976), p. 184.
29. Martin, *Race First*, pp. 309, 310.
30. *Negro World*, June 17, 1922.
31. Claude McKay, *A Long Way From Home* (New York: Harcourt, Brace and World, 1970, first pub. 1937), p. 28.
32. Claude McKay, *The Negroes in America*, ed. by Alan L. McLeod (Port Washington, N.Y.: Kennikat Press, 1979, first pub. ca. 1923), p. 73.
33. McKay, *A Long Way Home*, p. 139.
34. *Negro World*, July 8, 1922.
35. Countee Cullen, *Caroling Dusk* (New York: Harper and Brothers, 1927), p. xiii.
36. In Locke, ed., *The New Negro*, p. 40.
37. James Weldon Johnson, *Black Manhattan* (New York: Atheneum, 1968, first pub. 1930) p. 267.
38. James Weldon Johnson, *The Book of American Negro Poetry* (New York: Harcourt, Brace and World, 1959, reprint of 1931 edition), pp. 5,6.
39. McKay, *A Long Way From Home*, p. 227.

11

LEGACY REVISITED: VISUAL ART AND THE BLACK LIBERATION STRUGGLE IN THE TWENTIETH CENTURY

H. Ike Okafor-Newsum

The retention of African cultural expressions in the Black diaspora is a profound acknowledgment of the ancestral legacy of Africa. The regenerative force of the African heritage in Black life is a prominent characteristic of Black culture, even in the mundane existence of Black people. This can be seen in both the unconscious and the intentional performance of cultural expressions. One cannot deny an African sensibility in Black American language, dance, music, dress, and worship. Those things often taken for granted, such as grave and yard adornment, are also pregnant with African meanings. As is true of the mundane aspects of Black life and culture, African American art celebrates and reifies the expressive traditions and tendencies of the African ancestors. Artist and art historian David Driskell observes that African American artists "have reconstructed in various media the spiritual impetuosity of the multimedia-oriented forms of a bygone African past" (Driskell, 15). African American artists employ a variety of materials in the production of artwork, and objects of everyday use that may not appear as art to the outsider (a junked bicycle in a Thonton Dial sculpture, for example) function as artistic media.

The present discussion explores the stylistic and spiritual continuity of African aesthetic expression in African American art with particular interest in the functional role that art, artistic expression, and art producers play in the psychological, spiritual, and political uplift of Black people. We hope to further elaborate on the role of self-conscious visual art in the creation of a counter-narrative in the late twentieth century. The stylistic, spiritual, and political continuity of Black art and art producers derives from the historic experience of Black people from the pre-colonial period to the present. The continuity of style, spirit, and politics that can be identified with Black art and the psychological and ideological elements and currents of the Black experience that accompany it occur in direct response to Black people's encounter with the white or European world, and as a result of their collective memory of an African past. The culture war of the Reagan-Bush era questioned the cultural movement of the sixties that celebrated the expressions of racial minorities, women, and other marginalized groups, especially Black Americans. The buzzword of the eighties and nineties, multiculturalism, became the rallying point for the various hegemonic centers, each vying for space upon an American cultural landscape. But for some, multiculturalism threatened what was thought to be the cultural center of society and the signifiers of its value. The opponents of the "great canon" – such as so-called liberals like Henry Louis Gates and Werner Sollors, feminists like Alice Walker, Gloria Anzaldúa, and Cherrié Moraga, and the post-colonialists and Marxists like Gayatri Spivak, Edward Said, and Frederick Jameson – defend multiculturalism but with great reservation about the commercial and corporate academic kind of multiculturalism typical of "the university's" rhetoric of "academic excellence" (Lee, 201). Multiculturalism "is seen as having become part of a boutique or consumerist market culture, a 'symbolic ethnicity' in flight from both politics and history " (Lee, 202). In the nineties multiculturalism represented a strategy that sought to appease marginalized cultural groups with symbolic gestures of legitimacy and inclusion, while at the same the expectation (myth) of cultural assimilation remained an important element of success and status in the society.

AN ANCESTRAL LEGACY

The rhetoric of cultural assimilation was authorized by conservative ideologues of industry, church, and state during the Reagan-Bush years and appears to be a feature, albeit an illusory one, of the social contract America offers the Black middle class in the nineties. Many intellectuals have criticized the utility and appropriateness of an assimilationist strategy but have also suggested that African Americans share with other American ethnic groups certain characteristics that speak to the adaptability of cultural groups to their environment. "The major myth of America – that of assimilation – does not apply to African-American civilization. But many others do: the adaptation of 'Old World' culture to a new set of circumstances, the retention of culture and memory through literature, art, music, and pop culture, and the appropriation of "Old World cultural elements as crucial components of a 'New World' identity" (Brettell, 7). The collective survival of African American communities required a confluence and transformation of cultures into a symbolic system that expressed their humanity under the specific conditions of their social reality in the "New World." The forced exportation of Black people from Africa and the physical separation of Black communities by law and custom in the United States in the pre-civil rights era laid the conditions for the fragmented replication of an African/Afrocentric culture in Black America. Black communities have existed as labor and consumer colonies, and as vessels of culture and ancestral memory; hence a neo-African sensibility has flourished in all aspects of Black life in the colony as well as in the dominant society of the colonizer.

It is the interaction between the colonized and the colonizer that accounts for the African American flavor in American culture. Some forms of African-derived expression have been more readily integrated in the American cultural matrix than others. In his essay "Heritage Reclaimed" Edmund Barry Gaither notes that "music has always been the preeminent cultural form in Africa. While Black churches in the American South served to preserve aspects of traditional music, they failed to become institutional patrons of Black visual artists. An integral part of funerals and other African ceremonies, the ritual use of visual arts was discouraged by Protestantism. And other social institutions which might have sponsored development of the visual arts, such as universities or museums, were virtually absent in the rural South until the mid-nineteenth century" (Gaither, 18). The disassociation of visual art from the African aesthetic canon was lamented by Alain Locke in the 1920s. He observed in his essay "The Legacy of the Ancestral Arts" that Black visual art was for the most part imitative, and far too dependent on European art. As a result of their enslavement and the systematic destruction of their former self-conception, African Americans were psychologically devastated, their cultural and racial identity mocked by the cultural system of white society. Such devastation could only be overcome by pulling away the veil of racism and ignorance that perverted the American worldview. But Black visual artists first of all sought legitimacy in the white world, so they thought to prove themselves by imitating their white counterparts. African American artists of the nineteenth century such as portrait painter Joshua Johnston (1765-1830) and landscape artists Robert S. Duncanson (1821-1872) and Edward Mitchell Bannister (1826-1901), are recognized as master painters and novel professional artists, but only in terms dictated by the Euro-American academy and private art enthusiasts. They were "to establish [for African Americans] a place in that class of Western society that was considered able to appreciate and participate in 'high culture'" (Holland, 26). Locke believed that Black art lacked direction and recommended African art as a source of creative invention (Locke, 256).

The penetration of Black southern culture in urban centers due to migration, along with a new militancy expressed by Black soldiers returning from World War I and by intellectuals like Ida B. Wells-Barnett, WEB. DuBois, A. Philip Randolph, Marcus Garvey, and Alain Locke, combined with the growing influences of twentieth-century Modernism on the arts, gave birth to the dynamic commonly referred to as the Black Renaissance (or Harlem Renaissance). DuBois, Garvey, and Locke each espoused a rhetoric of African identification. Evidence of Africa as a source of creative expression is present in the work of some of the early twentieth-century artists. For example, the sculpture *Ethiopia Awakening* by Meta Warrick Fuller (1914) "symbolized the complex meaning of Africa for Black Americans" (Gaither, 19), predicting the importance of race in the twentieth century and the centrality of the African continent in African American identity.

In a Jungian sense (the collective unconscious), DuBois and Locke believed that African aesthetic sensibility was naturally inherent in the Black body, but the Black American visual artist had become detached from his ancestral roots by slavery and therefore needed to be redirected back to the original source of his racial and cultural identity. Initially, African expressions and themes in African African visual art were heavily influenced by the Modernist tendency toward the exoticization of all things African or otherwise foreign to Euro-American taste, rendering Africanity to a state of superficiality. As Fanon would describe it, the Africa embraced at this stage was "in fact the castoffs of thought, its shells and corpses, a knowledge which has been stabilized once and for all" (Fanon, 225).

As their exposure to Africa and Africans increased as a result of visits to the continent and interaction with Africans studying at historically Black colleges in the United States. Black American artists reestablished continuity with their African heritage, and in the period between the two wars, produced more genuinely earnest representations of Africa and African inspired themes. Lois Mailou Jones' *Les Fetiches* (oil painting, 1937), a stylistic precursor to Africobra, is testimony to the energy of African-identified expression in Black American art between the two world wars. Also important to this period was the presence of Black southern folk themes and iconography in African American artistic production.

The Black-belt South was the greatest retainer of African-derived cultural elements in North America, and it offered some of the best examples of the African New World synthesis in American culture. Author and folklorist Zora Neale Hurston was one of the leading voices advocating the cultural relevance of Black southern folk experience in the matrix of African American creative expression. Southern folk sensibility is seen in Ellis Wilson's paintings *Field Worker* (n.d.) and *Funeral Procession* (1940) and Clementine Hunter's *Church Gathering* (n.d.) and *Among the*

Lilies (1943). Hunter's depictions are often reminiscent of the days she spent on the Melrose plantation in Louisiana. "Hunter used art to lend dignity to her community of people: field hands, churchgoers, fishermen, and others" (Lewis, 111).

Black "folk" aesthetics sometimes conflicted with the sophistication of the New Negro urbanites who sought to distance themselves from the perceived unsophisticated rural personality. This chasm, however, also represents the class dynamic of culture, that is, the gulf between an "assimilated" Black elite who believes itself culturally superior, and the masses of Black people believed to be without culture (Cabral, 143-46). This "high"/"low" culture dichotomy is one of the organizing character-istics of a racist class system in capitalist democracy. Since the turn of the century, the urban/rural (cultured/uncultured) dichotomy has figured significantly in Black identity discourses. Richard Wright and Zora Neale Hurston, for example, disagreed vehemently over the issue. Among the northern Black working class, however, there was little confusion.

The Black urban working class continued to embrace and practice elements of southern culture. Cities like Chicago, Kansas City, and St. Louis became known for the Mississippi Delta Blues, because their clubs and lodges catered to the music's listening audience, which continued to grow as a result of Black migration to urban centers along the Mississippi. After the forced exportation of Africans to the "New World," Black south-ern cultural migration to the North represents the second transformation of African culture in North America. In various modifications, the Black southern culture flourished in the daily lives of Black northerners, in their kitchens, restaurants, barbershops, bars, and in formal and "informal" reli-gious practices. Stylistically, the work of creative writer Langston Hughes is one of the great examples of the rural-urban synthesis in the African American creative arts. Visual artist Jacob Lawrence's Migration Series,... *And the Migrants Kept Coming* (1940-1941), captures the feelings of would-be migrants in the south and their northern counterparts, "Johnny-Come-Latelies," impoverished and destitute in a strange land that would become home to their generations.

In the twenties and thirties, the Garvey Movement and Ethiopia's prominence in the Black American social consciousness accounted for the popular awareness of Africa, but after World War II, Black America's identification with Africa decreased as the ideology of racial integration became a popular discourse. However, Black nationalist opponents of integrationism, some Garveyites, continued to emphasize the importance of Africa to Black America.

The urban north experience provided for the intersection of a variety of "old" and "new world" Black cultures. The culture of North American Blacks encountered that of Blacks from all parts of Africa and from the francophone, anglophone, and Afro-Latin Caribbean, causing a creative explosion in music, dance, and the visual arts, accompanied by a spirituality (Voodoo, Santeria, Yoruba) that drew Black America deeper into its African past. During the next renaissance of Black culture, a generation of African American spiritual patrons would become devotees and students of Classical Yoruba religion and Egyptian civilization. The double axe of Shango and the Egyptian ankh are frequently occurring icons in the visual lexicon of the sixties as can be witnessed in Ademola Olugebefola's *Shango* (n.d.), David Driskell's *Shango Gone* (1972), and Mikelle Fletcher's *Guardian* (1971) (See Lewis 145, 151, 156). During this period, creative artists like New York-based drum master Olatunji and the South African musical artists Hugh Masakela and Miriam Makeba would become cultural icons of American entertainment culture.

In the fifties and sixties, the anglophone discourse of "The African Personality" and the francophone Negritude movement captured the Black American imagination and fueled the cultural components of the Civil Rights and Black Power movements. Africa's importance in Black American social consciousness was growing as a result of the celebratory mood throughout the Black world in response to Ghana's independence in 1957. The country's charismatic leader Kwame Nkrumah invited Black people all over the world to participate in the building of a strong independent Africa. African American intellectuals were drawn to Ghana and the African continent as a whole. The spirit of Africa was rekindled for a new generation of artists. The Black Arts Movement, as it has become known, is considered the second Black Renaissance in the same way that Manning Marable identifies the social movements of the sixties as the second Reconstruction.

THE FIGHTING PHASE

The Negritude Movement of the fifties and the Black cultural nationalism of the nineteen sixties provided a discourse of identity politics and decolonization that further energized Black intellectuals and cultural workers in the diaspora. Leopold Senghor was the architect of the Negritude movement and a popular figure of the times, but the francophone Black world introduced to the sixties generation another major intellectual who was sometimes critical of Negritude, Frantz Fanon.

As the sixties generation echoed Marcus Garvey's early twentieth-century claim of "Africa for the Africans," Fanon's *The Wretched of the*

Earth (1963*)* provided a psycho analysis of the colonized Black subject under European domination and suggested that the return to the African past is a good and necessary stage in the psychological development of Black intellectuals and Black people generally, but that it is not sufficient for their total liberation. In the course of their development, Black artists of the sixties, like Fanon's "native intellectual" (poets, writers, musicians, and painters) questioned the customs and culture of the dominant power. Such questioning is still indicative of a psychological journey that Fanon refers to as the second phase, which sends the colonized subject in search of "truth," and a cultural identity that is antithetical to the white culture and inevitably rooted in the ancestral past. This second phase follows a period of assimilation, represented in the nineteenth-century United States by artists like Duncanson, Bannister, and Johnston.

Fanon's three phases – which can be summed up as "Assimilation," "Immersion," and "Revolution" (or Fighting Phase) – each represent stages in the stylistic, psychological and political development of Black artists who dare scale the racial mountain. These phases represent also the journey undertaken by the Negritude and Harlem Renaissance artists who sought to break with Western conventions and to identify with Africa and African-derived elements. In his essay "On National Culture," Fanon expresses concern for the romanticism and lack of political clarity that accompanies this second phase of cultural identification.

Fanon's writings were instructive to the sixties' generation, in as much as they provided an explanation of the psychological and intellectual impact of European domination of the Black subject, including the artist. The ideas expressed in *Wretched of the Earth* facilitated a clearer understanding of the development of Black art and artistic identities. These ideas were not strange to the North American Black, for they echoed similar ideas expressed by DuBois (father of the American social sciences) and Locke (dean of the Harlem Renaissance). The "immersion" phase, which Locke called for in the twenties when he encouraged Black American artists to study African art, was necessary in the reconstruction of a Black self that is confident in its racial heritage and self-reflective in its material culture. Complementary to this calling, Fanon suggested that the past should be used "with the intention of opening up the future, as an invitation to action and a basis for hope" (Fanon, 232). He believed that the substance and future of Black culture is realized in the struggle of Black people to liberate themselves from all forms of oppression. The advancement of Black culture (any of its aspects), according to Fanon, required practical participation in the liberation struggle, "that material keystone which makes the building of a culture possible" (Fanon, 233).

The historical and political context of Fanon's ideas, the turbulent sixties, encompassed the African Independence Movement on the continent and the Black Pride Movement in North America, but this generation was able to draw examples from their antecedents of the Black Renaissance. As a thematic property, the third phase, which Fanon called the "fighting phase" can also be recognized as an African American art tradition. DuBois once asserted that he had little patience for any art that was not committed to the service of the Black struggle, so artists like Jacob Lawrence and Hale Woodruff used art to call attention to the injustices done to Black people. Lawrence and Woodruff did not want others to believe that Black people were passive victims of white domination.

Jacob Lawrence's depiction of John Brown's efforts against slavery (1941) is not only a record of the people's struggle but also an appeal to white America to stand up against racial discrimination (Bearden and Henderson, 304). His *Migration of the Negro*, Panel 50, "Race riots were very numerous all over the North.... "(1940-1941) speaks to Lawrence's artistic temperament and to his commitment as a creative artist and recorder of the Black experience. He placed his command of pictorial organization and use of primary colors in the service of social awareness about racial injustice (Lewis, 130-131). In Lawrence's opinion, "it is most important for an artist to develop an approach and philosophy about life-if he has developed this philosophy, he does not put paint on canvas, he puts himself on canvas.... the most important part of painting is the feeling towards the subject and what the artist wishes to say about it" (qtd. in Bearden and Henderson, 305). His stylistic development paralleled his studies in history. Lawrence turned to Haiti's revolutionary example in the heroic figure of Toussaint L'Ouverture, "Statesman and military Genius, esteemed by the Spaniards, feared by the English, dreaded by the French, hated by the planters and reverenced by the Blacks" (Bearden and Henderson, 298). The *Toussaint L'Ouverture Series* (1937-38) consists of forty-one paintings (gouache on paper), including scenes of the French brutality unleashed upon the Haitian people and Black freedom fighters in hand-to-hand combat with the enemy. Also included in the series is a majestically fashioned portrait of Toussaint L'Ouverture (Powell et al. 144-51).

Further evidence of the thematic interpretation of the fighting phase in African American art can be seen also in Hale Woodruff's mural painting, the *Amistad Mutiny* (1939), located in Savery Library at Talladega College and unveiled for the centennial anniversary of the 1839 revolt at sea. This depiction of Black men wielding machetes in a bloody battle against their Spanish captors stylistically resembles the Mexican murals of Diego Rivera, David Alfaro Siqueiros, and José Orozco, and possesses the same revolutionary spirit (Patton, 144-45; Taylor and Warkel, 132-36). Woodruff's smaller work is equally powerful. For example, in Panel 4 of the Art of the Negro Series (1946), a twenty-three-by-twenty-one-inch oil painting, a slave mother and her would-be fugitive son are surrounded by Blacks bearing swords, rifles, and spears; the same panel includes a scene of Douglass's meeting with Lincoln. The painting depicts Black people on the move for freedom (LeFalle-Collins and Goldman, 176). Black history offered many examples of the people's efforts to free themselves from the tyranny of whites, and progressive Black art attempted to represent "the whole body of efforts made by a people in the sphere of thought to describe, justify, and praise the action through which that people has created itself and keeps itself in existence" (Fanon, 233).

The African sensibility that had been lost in the nineteenth-century Black artists in the New World could always be found in the customs of the people, and it could be observed in their everyday creative expression. The fighting spirit of the people is also demonstrated in their ability to resist cultural genocide (erasure) and to reproduce an African culture in spite of attempts by the dominant society to destroy and distort their ancestral identity. The regenerative powers of Black culture caught the attention of Black artists who were also attracted to the African motherland, who saw themselves psychologically and spiritually connected to an Afrocentric cultural continuum. The generation of the sixties and seventies Black artists identified with the people's culture and with African culture as a matter of political commitment. They demonstrated in their individual work and in their group efforts a certain understanding of the relationships among art, cultural legacy, and political struggle. Literary figure and cultural leader Amiri Baraka contributed to the politicization of art when he proclaimed that Black art is to be art by Blacks, for Blacks, and to Blacks. In doing so he fueled the Black Aesthetic debate. Baraka and cultural critic Larry Neal were among the key spokespersons of the Black Arts Movement of the sixties and seventies. Progressive art groups and institutions were formed, and the Black Arts Movement was born out of the political struggle for racial justice taking place on the larger social stage.

MOVEMENT ART

The Black Arts Movement of the sixties and early seventies was the cultural arts expression of the political struggle of the times. By the late sixties a new breed of Black radicals was emerging, and the Black Panther Party was an organized political expression of this new breed. One characteristic of the movement that was clarified by the Panthers was the Left orientation of young radicals, as could be seen for example in the leadership of the Student Non-Violent Coordinating Committee (SNCC). Prominent Black intellectuals like DuBois, George Padmore, C.L.R. James, Lorraine Hansberry, and Paul Robeson called attention to socialist revolutions taking place throughout Asia and Africa, and in some places in the Western Hemisphere. The international scene, with its challenges to capitalist and racist domination, was brought into consideration with the black struggle in the United States. Both Malcolm X and Martin King, Jr. advocated this international perspective before their tragic deaths. And the contradictions of the Vietnam War were beginning to irritate the American public. A critical understanding of these international struggles among movement activists arguably represented an advanced stage of the fighting phase in political and artistic expression and led to new radical formations including artist collectives.

During this period the young radicals also caught the attention of the Federal Bureau of Investigation (FBI) and other local state agencies that were dedicated to destroying revolutionary groups and/or any group deemed to be involved in activities against the government. The Counter-Intelligence Program of the U.S.government (Cointelpro) infiltrated the Black movement, and by the late sixties, it had destroyed Black organizations through scandal, assassination, and overt brute force. The raid on Panther Party headquarters in Chicago in 1968 ended in the death of several party members including Fred Hampton and Mark Clark and suggested how volatile race relations were in the Windy City. One response to the situation in the city came from artists who had earlier made up the visual arts workshop of the Organization of Black American Culture (OBAC), and who had painted a huge mural in the Black community. This magnificent mural painting known as *The Wall of Respect* (1967) is a monumental example of how art functions socially and politically. "On this wall, larger than life figures of African-American heroes were venerated, celebrated, and most importantly exposed to the common people" (Kai, 6). The inspirational power of this mural painting surpassed the imagination of its creators. The whole project conveyed a new sense of responsibility to artists of the period. "The project was a seminal, collective effort among OBAC artists who volunteered and used their own funds to finance the work. The mural became the visual symbol of Black pride in Chicago and was soon to have an infectious impact on visual artists throughout the country. 'Walls of Respect' sprung up in Detroit, Cleveland, New York, Oakland, Memphis, Philadelphia, Los Angeles, and Atlanta. But its influence did not stop here. The movement became international, crossing over the borders into Third World countries and in Europe" (Kai, 6).

After the break up of the OBAC visual art workshop, Jeff Donaldson and Wadsworth Jarrell and others of their art cohort founded the African Commune of Bad Relevant Artists (AfriCobra) in 1968. Their philosophy as artists was based upon three principles: an atavistic aesthetic, technical excellence, and social responsibility. AfriCobra artists believed that Black aesthetic sensibility is derived from an ancestral link to African culture and traditions, and is a product of collective memory. "An atavistic art transcends any limitations of time and space, though it defines, directs and fashions historical evolution. It is art carried in the blood, passed on through generations, and tends to re-emerge full force as a sort of protective guardian spirit during periods of social crisis" (Kai, 6,7).

AfriCobra artists believed that technical excellence was a prerequisite in traditional African society for artistic recognition and acceptance. Their regard for technical excellence in the Black art heritage echoed Locke's observation that the spirit of the ancestral arts, by and large, is disciplined and sophisticated (Locke, 254). Emphasis on technical excellence has long been particularly evident among jazz artists notorious for their critical preoccupation with technique. Technical excellence is seen by AfriCobra as "the artist's responsibility to the people to communicate at the highest possible level." Further, social responsibility, according to AfriCobra, "is the natural role of the artist." An art that is not socially responsible is not art at all, "since it fails to fulfill the purpose for which art is cosmically designed," within an African understanding of art (Kai, 7). AfriCobra's philosophy appealed to artists around the world who believed similarly in the social functioning of art.

Their stylistic contribution represents an understanding of color, symmetry, and luminosity that marks the work of Black artists everywhere and reifies the Afrocentric atavism at the core of Black aesthetic sensibility. AfriCobra artists merge a modern African American aesthetic sensibility with formal elements of African art and in so doing illuminate Africanisms in the mind of their viewers. Jeff Donaldson's *Message from Tehuti (Toth)* employs vibrant color, traditional African line patterns, symbols, and shapes to evoke Africa's cultural heritage in textiles, music, and science. The best example of AfriCobra's neo-African aesthetic can be seen in the group's symbol, a Yoruba gelede mask with sunglasses.

While Africa is prominent in the work of AfriCobra artists, it is not classical or traditional African art that serves as their immediate inspiration. Similar to the ideas of Fanon and Cabral concerning the class characteristics of culture and the role of the oppressed class in the liberation struggle, the cultural life of common people in the Black ghetto has been central to the aesthetic and stylistic development of AfriCobra. Frantz

Fanon and Amilcar Cabral argued that those at the very bottom of the socioeconomic system possessed the greatest potential for social change. It is from the vantage point of this social category that the liberation movement must proceed and it is within the culture that one finds "the germ of challenge which leads to structuring and development of the liberation movement" (Cabral, 143). The forces of domination always seek to replicate the culture of prestige that they see as their own, and to deny the culture of the dominated group. The culture of prestige (that is, the culture of the oppressor) is symbolic of social, political and economic domination. "We see therefore that, if imperialist domination has the vital need to practice cultural oppression, national liberation [the salvation of the oppressed] is necessarily an *act of culture*" (Cabral, 143). The challenge to cultural oppression requires then a valuing of the grassroots culture created by the oppressed group, the polar opposite of the oppressor's culture. The Afri-Cobra artists "were inspired by the popular artifacts of African-American street culture: the polished shine of Cadillacs and patent leather shoes, the greasy shine of pomade hair-dos, the gaudy shine of cheap jewelry and clothes" (Kai, 8). Progressive activists of the period argued that the interest of the common people in Black communities had to be at the center of the liberation struggle, and therefore at the center of Black Arts Movement.

Based in Harlem and founded in 1965, the Weusi art group saw as their mission the preservation and promotion of African and African American culture through the visual arts. The act of institution-building was strongly encouraged during the Black Liberation Movement of the sixties. One important way to combat the cultural oppression suffered by Black people was to build structures that affirmed the aesthetic value of Black cultural expressions. The Weusi group attempted to fulfill this mission by founding a gallery and an academy for the advancement and study of African and African American fine art. The group's members (Otto Neals, Abdullah Aziz, Kay Brown, Gaylord Hassan, Ademola Olugebefola, James Phillips, and others) wanted to expose ordinary people to African and African American art and to make artworks available at affordable prices.

In "Heritage Reclaimed," Gaither suggests the prominent role of Afri-Cobra and Weusi in establishing a synthesis of cultural heritage and political responsibility. This synthesis is probably the most important aspect of the Black Arts Movement. The Conference on the Functional Aspects of Black Art (CONFABA), held at Northwestern University in May 1970, gives testimony to this fact. "The heart of the Black Artist's ideology is the dedication of his art to the cultural liberation of his people. It is in this sense that Black art is decidedly functional, politically and spiritually, and it is not to be confused by the alienation concept of 'art for art's sake' rather than art for people's sake" (qtd. in Gaither, 25). Gaither believes, and we concur, that "[b]oth AfriCobra and Weusi helped to establish an iconography expressive of Black art and Neo-African themes" (Gaither, 29).

THE PRESENT

The influence of the Black Arts Movement generally, on contemporary artists and art groups is clearly seen in the continuing embrace of the African heritage and the creative vernacular expressions of Black people. The difference between the art groups of the sixties and those today, however, can be seen in the absence of an overt political rhetoric and social program on the part of the latter, and this development has everything to do with the fact that there is no organized political movement of national proportions like the one witnessed in the sixties. What appears to be the end of nationalism and the national liberation movement is actually the absence of moral imperative and collective will on a mass level. However, small efforts continue to demonstrate the role of socially committed art and artists in African American communities.

In Houston's Third Ward, artist Rick Lowe has organized Row Houses Project, a public art project that not only facilitates the production of art but also salvages housing stock slated for demolition, provides cultural education, revitalizes the neighborhood, and provides a home for community services such as a women's center, daycare center, and housing for teen mothers. The Kwanzaa Playground in Columbus, Ohio, represents the collective efforts of artists in that city – Shirley Bowen (project administrator), Lavern Brown, Larry Winston Collins, Queen W. Brooks, Bill Agnew, Barbara Chavous, Pheoris West, Andrew Scott, and the William H. Thomas Gallery – who were concerned about providing recreational space for local youth that reinforces their African/Black heritage. Each artist involved in the project contributed interactive artwork suitable for outdoor entertainment. Community service such as this is not rare among contemporary artists but in the absence of a national social movement as in the sixties, such efforts are seen as isolated examples of charitable work.

Even without the political reenforcement of a national social movement, the African heritage in African American art is so powerful today that virtually all of the Black artists in North America have at one time or another produced African-inspired artworks. The exception would be rare. "[T]hese works have differed considerably in the ways in which Africa's impact has been rendered.... Some artists have been content to pursue African themes as subject matter; some have sought to integrate its formal elements with their own personal style, and still others have assigned themselves the extraordinary task of creating a new-perhaps even hybrid-

189

art that will result from merging formal and psychological elements of black American and African cultural traditions." (Gaither, 30)

Present-day African American artists are the inheritors and guardians of ancient ancestral traditions, and the heirs of the Black Renaissance of the twenties and thirties, and the Black Arts Movement of the sixties and seventies. They represent also something else: the cultural vanguard of a new social movement in waiting.

References

Bearden, Romare, and Harry Henderson. *A History of African-American Artists.* New York: Pantheon Books, 1993.

Brettell, Richard R. Preface. *Black Art, Ancestral Legacy: The African Impulse in African-American Art.* Dallas Museum of Art. New York: Harry N. Abrams, Inc., 1989. 7-9.

Cabral, Amilcar. *Unity and Struggle.* London: Heinemann, 1980.

Denino, Kae. "The City vs. the Nigerian Sign: Art Gallery Fuels Tension on the Near East Side." *The Other Paper,* 19-25 August 1999, 8-9.

Driskell, David. Introduction. In *Black Art, Ancestral Legacy.* 15-16.

DuBois, W. E. B. *The Souls of Black Folk.* 1903. Greenwich, Conn.: Fawcett Publications, 1961.

Fanon, Frantz. *The Wretched of the Earth.* New York: Grove Press, 1963.

Gaines, Sallie. "It's True Artistry." *Chicago Tribune,* 31 March 1996, sec. 16, 1, 5A.

Gaither, Edmund Barry. "Heritage Reclaimed: An Historical Perspective and Chronology." In *Black Art, Ancestral Legacy.*

Goldberg, Vicki. "In Houston, Rebuilding by Creating." *New York Times,* 16 July 1995: sec. 2, 26, 27.

Higgins, Connie A. "Festival to Open Playground: Three-Day Celebration Scheduled for Afrocentric Play Area." *Columbus Dispatch,* 5 May 1995, 04B.

_____. "Decaying Play Area Is Revived: Boy's Wish Leads to Playground with Afrocentric Theme." *The Columbus Dispatch,* 12 July 1994, 02B.

Holland, Juanita M. "The Color of Art: African-American Artistic Identities in the Twentieth Century." In *Narratives of African-American Art and Identity: The David C. Driskell Collection.* The Art Gallery and the Department of Art History and Archeology, University of Maryland at College Park. San Francisco: Pomegranate, 1998. 23-44.

Kai, Nubia. "AfriCobra Universal Aesthetics." *AfriCobra: The First Twenty Years.* Atlanta: Nexus Contemporary Art Center, 1990.

"Kwanzaa Playground to Open in October." *Call and Post,* 18 August 1994, 8A.

Lee, A. Robert. *Designs of Blackness: Mappings in the Literature and Culture of Afro-America.* London: Pluto Press, 1998.

LeFalle-Collins, Lizzetta, and Shifra M. Goldman. *In the Spirit of Resistance: African-American Modernists and the Mexican Muralist School.* New York: American Federation of Arts, 1996.

Lewis, Samella. *African-American Art and Artists.* Berkeley and Los Angeles: University of California Press, 1990.

Locke, Alain. "The Legacy of the Ancestral Arts." In *The New Negro*, ed. Alain Locke, 1925. New York: Atheneum, 1968, 254-267.

Patton, Sharon F. *African-American Art.* Oxford History of Art. Oxford: Oxford University Press, 1998.

Pellicer, Carlos, and Rafael Carrillo Azpeitia. *Mural Painting of the Mexican Revolution.* Mexico: Editorial Fund for Mexican Plastic Arts, 1985.

Powell, Richard J., et al. *Rhapsodies in Black: Art of the Harlem Renaissance.* Berkeley and Los Angeles: University of California Press, 1997.

Taylor, William E., and Harriet G. Warkel. *A Shared Heritage: Art by Four African Americans.* Bloomington: Indianapolis Museum of Art and Indiana University Press, 1996.

Tucker, Sheryl G. "Reinnovating the African-American Shotgun House." *Places* 10.1 (summer 1995): 64-71.

12

CRITICAL THEORY
AND PROBLEMS OF CANONICITY
IN AFRICAN AMERICAN LITERATURE

Richard K. Barksdale

Note: This chapter is reprinted with permission from University
of Illinois Press, which published Richard Barksdale's book,
Praisesong for Survival (1992).

When I first began the study of literature as an undergraduate English major at a small New England liberal arts college some fifty-five years ago, I had absolutely no misgivings about what we were told to study as English literature. It was "Beowulf to Thomas Hardy," with as much crammed in between these two formidable gateposts as possible. In fact, for the convenience of those dedicated few who ventured to travel on the strange, silent seas of literary study, someone had provided a two-volume text entitled *Beowulf to Thomas Hardy*. Not one of us asked a single question about the canon. For instance, no one asked why there was no American literature included. Nor why there was no twentieth-century or contemporary literature. And, in my case, why there was no literature on or about Black Americans, or, as we said then, colored people.

Apparently, no one anywhere else asked any such questions, for when we applied to graduate schools, our transcripts were readily accepted and we were all admitted for further and more exacting study of the literature from "Beowulf to Thomas Hardy." In fact, in graduate school the terms "general" and "special" were used to describe what one as a graduate student should know about English literature. We were told that, generally, one should know everything, literarily speaking, from "Beowulf to Thomas Hardy," and there was something called a "general" oral examination whereby properly designated authorities determined the extent of one's "general" knowledge of literary events and history over the some thirteen centuries spanning English life and history from Beowulf to Thomas Hardy. In addition, one was required to focus on or develop a "special" area of interest; from this area one mined a thesis or dissertation. One poor chap, I recall, chose the year 1859 as his "special" area; some years later when I asked him at an MLA meeting about his special interest in 1859, he stated that he still had a special interest in 1859 but only in the life of Melville, an author in whom he had now developed a special interest. Incidentally, my own "specialty" in that faraway time was the Arnolds – Dr. Thomas Arnold of Rugby and his famous poet-critic-school-supervising son.

Not only did we meekly accept the canon presented to us as fixed and immutable, but we became career generalists and specialists within the fixed parameters of that canon. We also accepted very restricted notions about the meaning and function of literature. Literature, we were informed, had moral, emotional, and spiritual meaning; it was stimulating, inspiring, ennobling; and it was thought that those who loved and studied literature moved on a higher plateau of humanistic concern than lesser folk who merely invented or engineered or, even worse, politicked. Thus, literature had no political meaning or political content; if there were political content, then that was not literature; that was propaganda. So Milton in his magnificent sonnet on the slaughter of the Piedmontese Protestants during the Reformation was not making a political statement; he was making a moral statement. Nor was his cutting censure of Eve as but "second" in *Paradise Lost* a political statement but an observation based on Old Testament law, and hence a moral judgment. Similarly, the satirical literature flowing forth from the partisan political imbroglios of the Restoration was, when taught, divested of its political content and presented as good, solid examples of satire, a genre with deep roots, particularly in Roman history and culture. So the satires of Dryden and Pope were good neoclassical imitations of the classical satires of Juvenal and Horace, shorn, of course, of political content.

Fortunately, for most of us who were nurtured on the standard pre-World War 11 literary canon, change began to come with the war and with the events that followed the war. By the 1950s, there was no longer any safe and reclusive literary ivory tower to hide either pendant or pedagogue from intense scrutiny. A madly erratic Senator McCarthy from Wisconsin found that he could make political capital by charging most professors and college personnel with various kinds of Marxist-related forms of treason and political heresy. Not only did the senator's attack on the academy fuel distrust of the professoriate everywhere, but it had a particularly devastating effect on Black professors who were trying to survive under intense segregation pressures at Black public institutions in the South. Under these pressures, all literature became political, and all writers of literature and all teachers of literature became politicized. If one became exhilarated by reading or studying or reciting a poem, it was first a political exhilaration, and only later an emotional exhilaration. Indeed, the argument advanced then by man in the white literary establishment that a Black literature protesting white America's discrimination against its Black minority was not acceptable as literature was, in the 1940s and 1950s, challenged on every front. As you can recall, the successful civil rights protest of the 1960s blew the last vestige of that erroneous idea out of the water. Some folk still read Baldwin's "Everybody's Protest Novel," but everyone, white and Black, now agrees with Richard Wright's assessment that all literature is a protest against something and that. without a protesting and politicized literature, needed changes will never be recognized, discussed, or successfully implemented.

Thus it was that when Keneth Kinnamon and I, following some of the other anthologists of Back literature who emerged in the 1960s, began to assemble what became *Black Writers of America*, we were more on fire with political energy than inspired by literary insight. I had been in Atlanta for one of the most exciting decades of my life; I had seen the South change almost before my eyes; and I, my wife, and my youngest son had been in the long line that snaked its way across the Spelman campus to Sisters Chapel to view a martyred leader's remains on a warm April sabbath day.

So, driven by the political furies of the times, Kinnamon and I forged a Black literary canon full of political content. I remember setting aside the poetry of Anne Plato, Claudia Ray, Georgia Douglas Johnson, and Lucy Terry's "Bar's Fight" because I thought it lacked sufficient political content. And I recall fighting to include a unit on the "literature" of the Black man in the Civil War because it was an event filled with political protest. And I remember losing the fight to include a unit on the literature of the Black man in the struggle to win the West, simply because we had, in the view of our Macmillan editor, run out of word space.

The Barksdale and Kinnamon anthology is now seventeen years old. He and 1, and I assume the profit-mongers at Macmillan, are glad that our politicized and protest-filled anthology has served several college and university generations. Obviously, given the history that I have presented, *BWA* represents a far cry from my somewhat humble beginnings as a student of literature. Now for me a literary act is a political act, and I now view even the so-called sacrosanct standard English literature canon as a political arrangement designed to glorify English history and the British Empire. For, as I have pursued my research in British antislavery literature, I have found that not one iota of the volumes of writing produced in that genre has ever been included in the official canon of English literature. Newman's *Apologia* and the dull trivia of the Oxford Movement made the canon but James Montgomery's magnificent 1809 epic on the slave trade did not, nor did any of the poetry included in three volumes of antislavery verse. Apparently, the reason behind the exclusion of antislavery literature is that that literature was, in the final analysis, harmful to empire interests. Newman and his Oxford associates left the empire undisturbed and thus met the major criterion for canonicity.

So as we prepare the way for effective formation or reformation of our African American literary canon, we will have to assess, with astute care, the cultural, sociopolitical, and demographic factors which will affect anything occurring in America as we approach the twenty-first century. For instance, demographers pretty generally assert that, by the year 2025, ethnic minorities will in all probability outnumber the current Caucasian majority, especially in urban America. The question can now be asked, To what extent should our canon be enlarged to reflect broader minority interests? Should there be more literature reflecting the urban Hispanic experience, the literature of the Puerto Rican emigré, the literature of the Native American? And then there is the Black literary ferment of the Caribbean (some say that there is a pulsating Caribbean aesthetic that leaps racial and cultural boundaries). Should the poetry and folk songs and stories of Jamaica, Trinidad, Barbados, Cuba, and Haiti be included in our canon? Historically, the jazz drumbeat that came out of New Orleans had its birth in the drums of Haiti. To what extent should we renew old cultural linkages? Even as we consider these problems of forming a more encompassing canon, let us be ever mindful that something is developing in the vestiges of the British Empire called Commonwealth literature. Black literary scholars who are graduating from Canadian universities, for instance, are seeking employment in American universities as specialists in Commonwealth literature. How should African Americans cope with this development? Remember what the Beatles did to or with black music!

A major problem in African American literary canon formation, however, is the burgeoning influence of the very fanciful critical theories which have come from France and are currently spreading throughout our major graduate schools. Ours is a profession certainly not immune to faddish change, but the adherents and practitioners of the new critical approaches are increasing in large numbers. Indeed, teachers who have developed skills in these new areas of critical interpretation quickly attract advisees, and their growing power and influence in any given English or comparative literature or modern foreign language department have interesting and provocative political consequences. They not only have become the major dissertation directors, but they have a very strong voice in search and hiring decisions. Inevitably, an alert doctoral candidate quickly sees future publishing and employment leverage in associating with the critical-theory power clique in any given graduate department. As a consequence, a large number of graduate students have written and are writing dissertations in the new critical theory mode, and a large number of "theory-grounded" articles are appearing in the professional journals. Indeed, one wonders whether *PMLA* has not become completely enamored of the dense and jargon-ridden style and format practiced by the critical theorist.

In other words, there is a certain amount of professional success associated with the practitioners of the new critical theory. For instance, members of one major Big Eight English department, after a long and frustrating search for a chair, announced with great pride that they had secured a chair who not only had superb administrative skills but was a Lacanian specialist as well.

So critical theorists have built power bases of influence in many departments of literature, not only in the literary bastions of the East and the West coasts, but throughout the departments of the Big Eight and Big Ten universities. Where the universities have publishing presses, critical theorists also usually exercise some influence on publishing decisions, either as press readers or members of press boards. Inevitably, wherever there are minority students or students specializing in minority literature, these students have been affected by the intradepartmental political maneuvering over the status of critical theorists in the departments. Usually, these students become mini-critical theorists.

What is the basis of the appeal of the French-based theories of textual criticism to the American literary academy? As we all know, over the centuries, nations the world over have found French products alluring and attractive. French perfumes are irresistible; French couturiers dominate the clothing styles of the West; and the world's best wines come from French vineyards. The French themselves have even declared that, at some point during their hundred-year conflict with England, the English stopped eating their food with their hands and learned to use French-made knives, forks, and spoons. Also the Western world well knows that out of France's revolutionary turmoil of the late eighteenth century came the democratic ideas that are still basic in Western democracies. But nothing imported from France has caused as much concern as Derrida's critical notions of poststructural textual analysis and Paul de Man's ideas about textual deconstruction.

What has always been puzzling is the enthusiasm with which our somewhat conservative literary academics imported these new approaches to textual exegesis. One writer, Frank Lentricchia, in a work entitled *After the New Criticism*, argued in the early seventies that the erosion of the authority of the New Criticism left "a theoretical vacuum" which was quickly filled with European critical theory. Even then, critics like Frank Lauter who were unhappy with the New Criticism's emphasis on ignoring history and personal experience were just as unhappy with the new critical theory's emphasis on an ivory towerish sense of intellectual mystification. Indeed, the continental critical theories seemed to deemphasize totally literature's needed concern for man's social and political welfare. At this point, some of the critical theorists began to discuss with each other the merits and deficiencies of the imported critical theories. One, Frederic Jameson, a neo-Marxist at Duke University, published in 1981 a work entitled *The Political Unconscious,* in which he contended that the theories of Derrida, Lacan, and Ricoeur could be used for textual interpretations that would unmask capitalistic contradictions in our postindustrial society. Jameson's work, like most of the works intended to illuminate a neo-Marxist approach to the effective use of the new theories, is not easy reading. Nor is Lentricchia's1983 response, *Criticism and Social Change*, in which he argues against the social isolation engendered by textual deconstruction and encourages the use of theories advanced by Gramsci and Foucault for promoting individual empowerment.

Arguments between neo-Marxists and non-Marxists about the proper interpretation and employment of critical theory techniques and practices continue to this day. These arguments are long and jargonistic and written in the dense and opaque style that only the truly dedicated critical theorist can understand. In the meantime, notwithstanding conflicts about approaches and interpretations, the use of continental critical theory finds even more defenders, practitioners, and fundraisers than many other humanistic enterprises on the campuses of large research institutions. For instance, in the early 1980s when I was an associate graduate dean at the University of Illinois at Urbana- Champaign, an associate vice chancellor for research told me that the only humanistic organization on campus worth funding was the Unit on Criticism and Interpretive Theory.

So, as we contemplate expanding and broadening our African American literary canon in preparation for an exciting new century, what recognition will we, or must we, give to continental critical theory? My recommendation is that, as we broaden our canon, we ignore deconstruction, poststructural textual exegesis, and continental hermeneutics. African American literature cannot effectively survive critical approaches that stress authorial depersonalization and the essential unimportance of racial history, racial community, and racial traditions. For instance, when I offer a course next spring in "Hurston, Hughes, and the Folk Vernacular," at the outset I shall explain to my students that I will welcome astutely formulated textual criticism of the works of the two authors, but don't travel all the way to Paris's Left Bank for an elucidating theory; just take an imaginative trip to Eatonville, Florida, or New York's Harlem, using either Hemenway's book on Zora or Rampersad's book on Langston. Or use me, the teacher, to elucidate and expatiate and clarify, for I believe not in avoiding history but in elucidating history. Admittedly, I am that old-fashioned kind of historical critic who still stresses the three M's – the man, the moment, the milieu – in approaching a literary work; and, when we get to the text, I stress more M's – matter, manner, mode, meaning. As a graduate student once told me after we finished with an author, "Professor Barksdale, we emmed all over that man!"

But it is easy to state here that we can cavalierly ignore the critical theorists as we build our literary canon for the years that await our scholars in the next century. Actually, it is possible that the pressure on the canon builders will be too great to muster total resistance to the critical theorists. In departments in which they wield power, they will shut Black literature programs off and cancel your course or courses. For instance, I am being somewhat naively hopeful that my next semester's seminar will materialize; there is always a chance that the requisite number of students will be advised away and guided into another course or seminar. In fact, I strongly suspect that that is how the University of Illinois's very vibrant program in African American literature withered away to nothing in less than three years. After a record production of eighteen Black doctorates in African-hhhh American literature between 1973 and 1986, there are now no Black graduate courses in the timetable and no Black candidates in the pipeline.

So, I recommend that as we build our literary canon for the tomorrows that lie ahead in the next century, we remain ever mindful of the need to utilize the politics of survival. This is something to be found in the text of our racial history that ahistorical theorists like a Derrida, a Gramsci, or a Lacan would not begin to understand. And let us not be casual about the struggle that we might have to face as we attempt to compromise an accommodation with a brother or sister who had to accept training as a critical theorist in order to win his or her degree but who still wants to teach African American literature. As a young black man a few days ago commented on TV on the still-ruinous aftereffects of Hurricane Hugo in rural Black coastal South Carolina: "Dis heah ral seius. Dis shit *ral* seius!"

199

Translated into academic language, he means, for Blacks, "Life ain't no crystal stair," but I prefer his version. It has a realistic ring to it.

Note
This lecture was delivered to the Langston Hughes Society in 1989.

PART IV
HEGEMONIC DISCOURSE

We must use Diop's concept of harmonious dualism to endorse the best of revolutionary nationalism and socialism ideologies, as well as the best of cultural and struggle-oriented studies. (Mary Hoover)

13

GLOBAL AFRICA AND COMPARATIVE LEADERSHIP: WALTER RODNEY, JULIUS K. NYERERE, AND MARTIN LUTHER KING, JR.

Ali A. Mazrui

This was the inaugural lecture to launch the Walter Rodney Chair in History and Governance at the University of Guyana, Georgetown, Guyana, March 16, 1998. In attendance were Prime Minister Samuel Hinds, former President Desmond Hoyte, Minister of Education Dale Bisnauth, Prochancellor of the University Martin Bhoodhoo, and other dignitaries. The Deputy Vice-Chancellor of the University presided.

Let me begin by saying how pleased I am to be back in Guyana and to experience once again the warmth, friendliness, and genuine smiles of its people.

On my last visit in 1988, I was the guest of President Desmond Hoyte to mark the 150th anniversary of emancipation from slavery. It was a great honor then, and I was well looked after by the president and his people. This time I am the guest of both the University of Guyana and President Janet Jagan's government. Again it is indeed a great honor.

I have occupied a number of academic chairs in my professional life. None has given me greater pleasure or a greater sense of privilege than this Walter Rodney Chair. But with this chair I see myself mainly as a launching pad to get the chair started. A resident incumbent would later have to occupy it. What is very important is that the name of a great son of Guyana – Dr. Walter Rodney – should now be honored in an appropriate academic manner in the country of his birth.

Totally independently of me, and without even knowing that I had been appointed the Walter Rodney Professor of the University of Guyana, students at the State University of New York at Binghamton (where I teach) are organizing an international conference in November 1998, dedicated to the memory of Walter Rodney, and marking the 200th anniversary of the Haitian revolution and the hundredth anniversary of the Spanish-American-Cuban war. In the words of the brochure of the students calling for papers, "Rodney's life and work evoke the Caribbean, Africa and the Americas, the Black Atlantic and the African Diaspora. Rodney's highly imaginative work questioned boundaries between peoples as well as ideas, and provides rich ground from which to think nationalist movements, multicultural organizing, and historiography itself."

These particular students are recommending that the Binghamton Student's Union as a whole be renamed "The Walter Rodney Memorial Student Union." The recommendation is ambitious, considering that Binghamton University is primarily white, and half the white students are Jews. But the recommendation is a measure of student enthusiasm for Walter Rodney.

The deadline for abstracts and panel proposals for the Rodney conference is August 25, 1998.

Because this is an inaugural lecture to launch a chair in honor of Dr. Walter Rodney, I chose a theme that would be as much about Walter Rodney as about some of the wider issues he was concerned about. But given that I intended to use the canvas of "Global Africa"(meaning Africa and its diaspora), there was a case for analyzing the *comparative Black experience*. Should I compare a Caribbean country with an African country through Walter Rodney's eyes? Should I compare a Black community in North America with a Caribbean society through Walter Rodney's eyes? Should I simply compare and contrast regional experiences through Walter Rodney's eyes?

I have chosen to compare three historical figures from different parts of global Africa in the context of wider political and ideological issues. I have chosen to compare Walter Rodney first with Julius Kambarage Nyerere of Tanzania for whom Walter indirectly worked for a while and then Martin Luther King, Jr., as two victims of violent premature death. I could have entitled this lecture: "Global Africa and a Tale of Three Leaders Walter Rodney, Julius Nyerere and Martin Luther King, Jr."

For the purposes of this lecture it will not be necessary to compare Julius K. Nyerere with Martin King, Jr., although that is a most worthy comparison in its own right for a future lecture. But it is worth noting that 1998 marks the thirtieth anniversary of Martin Luther King's assassination. It also marks the thirtieth anniversary of Walter Rodney's pilgrimage to the University of Dar es Salaam to teach revolutionary historiography.

RODNEY AND THE MWALIMU

Walter Rodney and Julius K. Nyerere had a number of things in common and of course a lot of differences. By an accident of history they were both born in the month of March, but almost exactly twenty years apart. Rodney was born in 1942; Nyerere in 1922.

They were both partly British educated – but Rodney in England, Nyerere in Scotland. They both became Socialists – but Rodney became a Marxist while Nyerere consciously distinguished his brand of socialism from Marxism.

They were both Pan-Africanists – but Rodney was a *global* Pan-Africanist (thinking of the unity of the African peoples worldwide) whereas Nyerere was a *continental* Pan-Africanist (thinking of uniting the people of Africa, and initially the people of eastern and southern Africa.)

Nyerere and Rodney were both defenders of the Indian populations in their own respective countries against racial prejudice – but the Indian population of Tanzania was urban and often conspicuously rich; the Indian population in Guyana was originally primarily rural and was historically relatively underprivileged.

Rodney and Nyerere both had profoundly ambivalent feelings about the Western world as the oppressing hegemon – but Nyerere was not above constantly looking for Western aid for Tanzania, provided the conditions respected Tanzania's dignity. Rodney and Nyerere also had ambivalent feelings about Great Britain as the former colonial power of their countries – but while Rodney was almost bitter about the School of Oriental and African Studies, London, where he obtained his doctoral degree, Julius Nyerere translated two Shakespearean plays into the Swahili language – *Julius Caesar* and *The Merchant of Venice*, translations which are now widely used in East African literature classes, both in Tanzania and in Kenya.

Rodney and Nyerere both believed in the reality of class struggle and of race conflict – but Nyerere believed that race was more salient for Africa than class, while Rodney believed that race was a *derivative* of class worldwide. In the 1960s Nyerere was defending the One-Party State partly on the grounds that Tanzania did not really have sustainable class differences. Rodney was totally unconvinced.

Rodney and Nyerere combined the skills of teaching with the skills of political activism: they were both teachers before they became active politicians. Rodney was a global teacher (teaching in four continents) but a regional activist in the Caribbean; Nyerere is still a global activist (involved in North-South relations) but a regional teacher [the *Mwalimu* (the great teacher) of East Africa].

Rodney and Nyerere lived in multi-religious societies. Observers say that in Guyana 50% of the population is of Indian origin. Observers also say that 50% of the Guyanese population is Christian. But clearly the 50% *racial* category does not coincide with the 50% *religious* category. The majority of the *Christian* category are not *Indians*. Guyana seems to have 30% Hindus and 15% Muslim from the Indian population mainly.

Tanzania's triple religious heritage is primarily *Christian, Muslim*, and *African traditional religion*. Are there more Muslims than Christians in Tanzania? Almost certainly there are more Muslims in Tanzania. The political process has, however, decided to alternate the presidency – *Christian* Julius Nyerere followed by *Muslim* Ali Hassan Mwinyi, followed by *Christian* Benjamin Mkapa – a presidential system of alternating incumbency?

Rodney and Nyerere believed in regional integration as a bulwark against underdevelopment – Nyerere believed in East African integration but his socialism got in the way of his Pan-East Africanism. Rodney believed in the integration of the Caribbean but his socialism would similarly have clashed with his Pan-Caribbeanism.

Socialism in a multi-ideological region finds it hard to accommodate other ideologies. But nationalism is also often isolationist. In East Africa Pan-Africanism fell victim to socialism in Tanzania. In the Caribbean Pan-Caribbeanism fell victim to nationalism in Jamaica and elsewhere.

In East Africa a socialist revolution in Zanzibar gave birth at least to the union between Zanzibar and Tanganyika, creating the United Republic of Tanzania – a case of *unite and rule*. U.S. President Lyndon Johnson and Prime Minister Alec Douglas Home of the U.K. *pressured* Nyerere to unite with Zanzibar in order to stop Zanzibar becoming another Marxist-Cuba. Socialist anti-colonialism in Guyana, and later socialist self-assertion in Grenada, resulted in regional opposition to socialism. This was a case of *divide and rule*. The United States pressured the rest of the Caribbean to distance themselves from Guyana and, later, from Maurice Bishop's Grenada.

If Rodney had become President of Guyana, would there have been a U.S.-led invasion of Guyana comparable to the U.S.-led invasion of Grenada in 1983? The scenario is by no means out of the question. An English-speaking Marxist government in the hemisphere was always more feared by Washington than a Spanish speaking one.

Rodney and Nyerere both served Tanzania at a crucial moment in the country's history when Tanzania was beginning to move to the left under the Arusha Declaration. But while Nyerere was the architect of the new Tanzania, Rodney was a sympathetic critic from the left. According to Rodney, the Arusha Declaration was not scientific socialism.

Like Julius Nyerere, Walter Rodney aspired to lead his country one day into an era of progressive change. Nyerere got the opportunity by becoming President of his country; Rodney was denied the opportunity when he was killed prematurely.

BETWEEN THE DUAL AND THE PLURAL SOCIETY

Now a word about the ethnic configuration of their respective countries. Tanzania is a plural society – whose Black population consists of multiple linguistic groups. But Tanzania is also a multiracial society – with significant minorities of Asians, Arabs and Europeans.

The overwhelming majority of the population is Black. It is one of the blessings of Tanzania that none of the Black ethno-linguistic groups are large enough to be regarded as a threat to others – unlike the situation in neighbouring Kenya or neighbouring Uganda where ethnic fears of larger groups have sometimes resulted in deadly rivalries. The dispersal of Tanzania's groups over a large territory, giving breathing political space, is another feature which has helped to stabilize Tanzania.

Walter Rodney's country, Guyana, is closer to being a *dual society* than a plural society. A dual society is one in which two ethnic groups add up to nearly ninety percent of the population. While the total population of Indo-Guyanese and Afro-Guyanese is in the *mid-eighty percent* rather than ninety, the figures are close enough to dualism to make us pause and take stock.

Dual societies present problems which are sometimes different from those of plural societies. In dual societies there is a higher risk of stalemate unless special care is taken – a higher risk of polarization. That is one reason why Walter Rodney was so bitter that the original People's Progressive Party of Guyana split up into two different parties each of which became ethnic-specific to large extent.

Nevertheless, our hopes as outside observers are still pinned on Guyana and Trinidad as countries which would help prove that dual societies are indeed viable. Elsewhere in the world dual societies which were not guided in wise directions have ended up in either stalemate, violence or a breakup.

Cyprus is a dual society of Greek and Turkish Cypriots. It has been in a bitter political stalemate on a divided island since 1974. Czechoslovakia used to be a dual society – until the leadership decided in 1990 that it was time to part and form two separate republics, the Czech and Slovak republics.

Northern Ireland has been a dual society of Protestants and Catholics. They have yet to find a satisfactory formula of living together – though the British Government thinks there is at last light at the end of the Irish tunnel. Sri Lanka (formerly Ceylon) is a dual society of majority Sinhalese and minority Tamils. The country has been landed with a violent struggle waged by a Tamil movement for separate independence.

The worst African cases of dual societies are Rwanda and Burundi, each of which has majority Hutu and minority Tutsi. At the moment the minority Tutsi are in power in both Rwanda and Burundi. The scale of violence has cost hundreds of thousands of lives in the 1990s alone. There were earlier eruptions of comparable deadliness.

What solutions are available to dual societies? There are three approaches – two of them desperate and the third more hopeful. One approach is to move from *dual* to *single* society. This is a cry of despair because it means breaking up the country – as in the case of the split of Czechoslovakia or the special case of East Pakistan. (The old Pakistan was a dual society in a different territorial sense.)

The second approach towards a solution is to move from *dual* to *plural*. This would involve regional integration. My own recommended solution for Rwanda and Burundi has been to unite them with Tanzania. The armies of Rwanda and Burundi would be pensioned off, the Hutu and Tutsi would discover how much they really have in common with each other in the peaceful political process of an enlarged Tanzania. I have discussed this issue with President Julius Nyerere – who agreed with aspects of my plan and disagreed with others.

The third redemptive approach for a dual society is neither to break it up into two single societies nor to unite it with a plural society but to find satisfactory solutions *within* the country. This must be the way for Guyana. It has been the way for Belgium – a dual society which was long divided between French speakers and Dutch-speakers, but which, beginning with the Egmont Pact of 1977, has inaugurated a system of federal reconciliation between Dutch-speaking Flanders, French-speaking Wallonia and Brussels.

Guyana is too small for a federal solution internal to itself. But there are other ways which can be explored to find satisfactory answers not only for Indians and Africans, but also for the Amerindians and other minorities in Guyana. Walter Rodney would have preferred a socialist revolution to achieve those goals. But finding a working formula for national integration can itself be revolutionary.

THE REVOLUTIONARY AND THE REVEREND

Let us now shift our focus. We have compared dual societies with each other and with plural societies. We have also compared Walter Rodney with a historical figure in Africa, Julius Kambarage Nyerere. Let us now compare Rodney with a historical figure in North America, Martin Luther King, Jr.

Nyerere was a foil to Rodney within the fraternity of Black socialism. Reverend Martin Luther King was outside the fraternity of Black socialism. Dr. King was a Black liberal and a Black racial integrationist. But if so, why was the Civil Rights movement in the United States part of Walter Rodney's dream of a world revolution?

There is indeed a concept called "Global Africa". Walter Rodney symbolized it. It means the people of Africa and those of African descent who are scattered all over the world. C.L.R. James talked about "who should know of cricket who only cricket know". But, in fact, much more relevant is to paraphrase the sentiment in the following way:

> Winds of the world give answer
> They are whimpering to and fro
> Who should know of Africa
> Who only Africa know.

When he was in Africa, Walter Rodney knew when to forget that he was Guyanese. When Rodney was in Guyana he knew when to forget that he was an African. Identity is a many-splendored thing. Walter Rodney called upon Africa to re-Africanize itself – but called upon Guyanese to fall short of being either too African or too Indian.

There was a *deficit* of Africanity in postcolonial Africa. But in the Guyana of Walter Rodney's day, was there a *surplus* of Africanity in the political process?

In the postcolonial situation, were Africans in East Africa not African enough? In the postcolonial situation in Guyana, were Diaspora Africans too African? Walter Rodney never fully resolved these dilemmas, but at least he was looking for answers.

The dilemma of Martin Luther King, Jr. in the United States was of a different kind. He was torn between his identity as a Black man and his identity as an American. In his capacity as a Black man he confronted a nightmare which resulted in his own assassination. In his capacity as an American he was brought up with a "Dream", the *American* Dream, which he revised and refashioned in the language of racial integration.

Walter Rodney's dream of racial integration was between Indians and Africans in Guyana. Martin Luther King, Jr.'s dream of racial integration was between Whites and Blacks in the United States.

Somewhere between them stood Malcolm X (El-Hajj Malik El-Shabazz) – closer to Walter Rodney in radicalism and militancy, closer to Martin Luther King, Jr. in the experience of white racism.

Three Diaspora Africans touched my life very briefly – and each symbolized something important to Global Africa. Each of those Diaspora Africans was assassinated, although Rodney's precise fate is still in dispute.

One of those remarkable Diaspora Africans was Martin Luther King, Jr. I met him in New York when I was a graduate student at Columbia University. I was of course just an enthusiastic young African – but King was already an international figure. I was impressed that King knew so much about Kenya – and knew Tom Mboya personally, who was then a rising political star of Kenya.

Partly because he was a Reverend, and partly because of his Biblical oratory, I might have regarded Martin Luther King, Jr. as a link between Global Africa and Christendom, though I could not have articulated it in quite that fashion at that age.

The second Diaspora martyr who touched my life briefly was Malcolm X. I also met him in New York in either 1960 or 1961 – I am not absolutely sure of the month. Since I had myself been brought up a Muslim, I was fascinated by Malcolm's creed. I disagreed with his racial approach to Islam at that stage of his life, but I was thrilled by his political militancy. He also had a magnetic personal presence. In terms of Global Africa, was he one of its important links with the world of Islam?

The third Diaspora martyr who touched my life was Walter Rodney. At a personal level I interacted with him more extensively than I ever did with either Martin Luther King, Jr. or Malcolm X. Walter Rodney and I were, after all, colleagues at the University of East Africa – he in Dar es Salaam and I at Makerere. We had a number of highly publicized academic and ideological clashes – I from the liberal center, he from the Socialist left.

Once in the Main Hall at Makerere University in Uganda our debate was televised live. Although he was debating me on my home turf, many of my own students were converted to his side. Walter was a brilliant debater.

Walter Rodney was born in Guyana in the middle of the second World War – in March 1942. I suppose a prophet might have known how tumultuous his life was going to be. When he was banned from returning to

Jamaica after attending a Black Writer's Conference, there were riots in the streets of Kingston in protest with many casualties. And after he returned to Guyana in 1974 there was one political emergency after another. A man of charisma was caught up in a country in crisis.

There were confrontations – beginning with Walter's deprivation of his professorship at the University of Guyana, threats of legal action, and Walter being encouraged (reportedly at the highest political level) that he should write his will!

Tensions became particularly difficult after he became more directly part of a political movement, and then a political party. The stage was being set for much more than a confrontation. We now know that the stage was being set for a tragedy.

Some people write history but never make history. Other people make history but never write it. Walter Rodney, like Winston Churchill, was one of those who tried to do both. Winston Churchill first made history and then wrote it. Walter Rodney first wrote history and then made history. The sequence was different. But though vastly different in ideology, Churchill and Rodney belong to that fertile category of activist historians.

If Martin Luther King, Jr. was a link between Global Africa and Christendom, and Malcolm X was a link between Global Africa and Islam, Walter Rodney was in part a link between Global Africa and the world of Socialism.

Curiously enough, Walter spent many years in countries which were to the left of their own regions – but were nevertheless to Walter Rodney's right. Tanzania under Nyerere was to the left of East Africa if not eastern Africa – but Nyerere was nevertheless to the *right* of Walter Rodney.

Guyana profoundly disappointed Walter Rodney – but the regime was to the left of most of the Caribbean and definitely most of South America. Guyana was to the left of its region – but to Walter Rodney's right.

Since Martin Luther King, Jr. was a link between Global Africa and Christendom, his memory found it easier to acquire legitimacy in the Western world. Martin King, Jr.'s birthday has even acquired greater official status than Abraham Lincoln's birthday. Although harassed by the Federal Bureau of Investigation (FBI) when he was alive, and constantly under the shadow of right wing extremism in the United States, Reverend King was, in the ultimate analysis, a preferred antagonist to the Establishment.

But, as we shall indicate, this Black man's legitimacy to the Euro-Christian establishment in America was ultimately due to the influence of a major figure in *India*. This Black agitator touched the conscience of white America partly because he was a disciple of an *Indian*. But more about that later.

However, partly because Malcolm X was a link between *Blackness* and *Islam*, he has yet to be restored to national legitimacy in the United States. No scholarships named after him, no major schools.

Rodney was a link to *Socialism* – not to Islam. In spite of his *socialism,* Walter Rodney used to be honoured more in the United States than in Guyana – fellowships, publications, panel discussions. This Walter Rodney Chair at the University of Guyana is a major step towards correcting that anomaly.

In my lecture at the 150th anniversary of emancipation from slavery in Georgetown, I appealed to President Desmond Hoyte that Walter be restored to national legitimacy. President Hoyte was in attendance when I made that appeal, and he was most gracious to a presumptuous guest.

In reality, Walter was not just a link between Global Africa and Socialism. Walter Rodney was *a living connection even in death* between Global Africa abroad and Global Africa at home.

He traversed the Black world like Mr. Global Africa – taught in Africa, Jamaica, and elsewhere, lectured in North America, conferred in Europe, crusaded in Guyana – and died for greater social justice.

According to Walter's paradigm, that social justice at the global level demanded that Global Africa should one day be in a position to underdevelop Europe – just as Europe had once underdeveloped Africa. But Global Africa would be more magnanimous to Europe. More realistically, Walter Rodney called upon Africa just to reverse the underdevelopment perpetrated by Europe – and redevelop itself. Walter Rodney in Tanzania was part of the clarion call for Africa's awakening and Africa's own rededication to self-empowerment.

BETWEEN DREAMS AND DEEDS

Let us now return to that other victim of assassination. As I indicated, I was privileged to meet Dr. Martin Luther King, Jr. when I was a graduate student at Columbia University in New York. King was already sensitive to issues beyond the American shores. The period was 1960-1. This was several years before I met Walter Rodney.

Let me repeat that Dr. King and I talked about that dear man called Tom Mboya, at that time the second best known East African politician after Jomo Kenyatta. Mboya and King were about the same age. Of course, we had no idea that the lives of both King and Mboya would be cut short by an assassin's bullet before the decade of the 1960s was out.

But although Martin Luther King, Jr. was so sensitized quite early to issues beyond these shores, was his dream too parochial? Was his dream too U.S. based? Of course King never became as Pan-African as Walter Rodney did.

Nevertheless, King did respond quite early to intellectual influences from beyond the American shores. He particularly emphasized his moral debt to Mahatma Mohandas Gandhi, the Indian leader of resistance against British rule in India. King once observed: "It is ironic that the greatest Christian of the modern age was a man who never embraced Christianity" – that is, Mahatma Gandhi.

As the author Keith D. Miller has reminded us, Gandhi's protests against British repression were done in such a way that it was "a collective expression of Christ-like love." While Walter Rodney's life was a continuing interaction with people of Indian origin, Martin Luther King's life was transformed by one single and particular Indian.

Did King first get interested in Gandhi when he heard Mordecai Johnson of Howard University preach about Gandhi's achievements? The presentation was to King "so profound and electrifying" that King "bought a half-dozen books on Gandhi's life works."

But was King inadequately attentive to the larger questions of the world? DID KING have the wrong dream? Should he have gone global – and dreamt about the end of the cold war – East and West, Socialist and Capitalist, reconciled at last?

"Free at last! Free at last! Thank God, Almighty, we are free at last!" *Was King more parochial than Rodney?* After all, the great reconciliation of the last decade of the 20th century has not been racial, not religious – but *ideological*. Martin King did start agitating against the war in Vietnam before he died – was he getting internationalized?

Let us take a closer look at Martin Luther King's dream articulated from Martin Luther King, Jr.'s "I HAVE A DREAM".

"I have a dream that one day on the red hills of Georgia, sons of former slaves and the sons of former slave owners will be able to sit down together at the table of brotherhood.

"I have a dream that one day even the state of Mississippi, a state sweltering with the heat of injustice, sweltering with the heat of oppression, will be transformed into an oasis of freedom and justice.

"I have a dream that my four little children will one day live in a nation where they will not be judged by the color of their skin, but by the content of their character.

"I have a dream today! I have a dream that... one day right there in Alabama, little black boys and black girls will be able to join hands with little white boys and white girls as sister and brothers....

"And when this happens, and when we allow freedom to ring, when we let it ring from every village and every hamlet, from every state and every city, we will be able to speed up that day when all God's children, black men and white men, Jews and Gentiles, Protestants and Catholics, will be able to join hands and sing in the words of the old Negro spiritual: 'Free at last. Free at last. Thank God Almighty, we are free at last.'"

Is that dream too parochial, too U.S.-based? And even within the USA what is the balance sheet?

How much of that dream has been realized? There have in fact been gains and losses since the 1960s.

King said *"We can never be satisfied as long as the Negro is the victim of the unspeakable horrors of police brutality."* In the 1990s it took the video tape involving a man combining the name of Rodney and the name of King – Rodney King – to shock the world into the full realization that police brutality against Blacks is alive and well, at least in some parts of the country. That part of King's dream still poses problems.

Reverend Martin King said *"We can never be satisfied as long as our bodies, heavy with the fatigue of travel, cannot gain lodging in the motels of the highways and the hotels of the cities."*

Here there is some gain. Overt discrimination in hotels, restaurants, and other public places has almost disappeared though *de facto* discrimination in some Christian *churches* persists, as President Carter once reminded us.

Discrimination in private clubs is still rampant, but less so than in the 1960s. Walter Rodney's visits to the United States in the 1970s displayed a great awareness of these contradictory trends. He and I compared notes on these issues when he visited the University of Michigan, Ann Arbor, where I was Director of Afro-American and African Studies.

Dr. King said *"We cannot be satisfied as long as the Negro's basic mobility is from a smaller ghetto to a larger one."* For many U.S. Blacks, this condition still persists – the Black underclass is larger than ever. Poverty, crime, infant mortality, drugs and now AIDS have been decimating large sections of ghetto populations. This particular concern of both King and Rodney has, in some respects, become worse.

Dr. King said: *"We can never be satisfied as long as our children are stripped of their self-hood and robbed of their dignity by signs stating "For Whites Only."* The actual visible signs have all but disappeared – but there are still obstinate psychological signs which say to many African-Americans "For Whites Only." The colour-bar has gone *invisible* in large areas of life. Is that *invisibility* a gain or a loss? There are controversial arguments which say that better open prejudice than subversive undercurrents of racism. This would apply to relations between Whites and Blacks in the USA as well as between Indians and Africans in Guyana and Trinidad. But other people would strongly disagree and say that open prejudice is worse.

Reverend King said: *"We cannot be satisfied as long as the Negro in Mississippi cannot vote and a Negro in New York believes there is nothing for which to vote."* There has been a change in Mississippi – the so-called "NEGRO" now can vote. But there has been no change in New York – the so-called "NEGRO" still believes there is nothing for which to vote.

The question for Guyana is whether there is indeed something for which to vote – even if the disagreements are sometimes passionate.

Reverend King proclaimed loudly *"No! No, we are not satisfied, and we will not be until justice rolls down like waters and righteousness like a mighty stream."* Justice in the legal sense is certainly not rolling down like waters – the U.S. Supreme Court has moved further to the right than ever. And many Civil Rights gains in the United States are in jeopardy.

Hotels in the United States are no longer restrictive racially but police brutality continues – e.g., the beating of Rodney King. Segregation by law has ended; but segregation in fact persists. De facto segregation in housing, in clubs, in churches has not disappeared.

The Congress has become more Republican and the Supreme Court has become more conservative. The judicial and penal system continues to be hard on Blacks – *40%* of those on death row are Blacks – more Blacks in *jail* than in *colleges*.

Who walked with Martin Luther King, Jr.? An Indian assassinated in the 1940s walked with King in the 1950s and 60s. King said: "It is ironic, yet inescapably true that the greatest Christian of the modern world was a man who never embraced Christianity" – Mahatma Gandhi. To King Gandhi's protests amounted to a collective expression of *Christ-like love*.

The Black predicament in the USA is full of contradictions. Martin Luther King, Jr. preached non-violence but saw Blacks disproportionately represented in the U.S. Army. Was *Muhammad Ali* a better Gandhian when he refused to fight in Viet Nam? *Is violence in uniform less violent than violence in the streets*? With the end of the ideological war, is there an intensification of the racial war world-wide?

215

There is the possible birth of GLOBAL APARTHEID. The white world is closing ranks – there is now greater Pan-Europeanism than anything since the Holy Roman Empire. The European Union is admitting new members. The cold war has ended a deep ideological split which once existed within the white world. Is the shadow of global apartheid looming over us – a new racial hierarchy on a global scale? Perhaps Walter Rodney would have recognized such a danger more readily than Martin Luther King, Jr. Who knows?

MARXISM-LENINISM AND THE JESUS-GANDHI NEXUS

Both Walter Rodney and Martin Luther King Jr. were politically moulded by two personal ties external to the Black experience. In the case of Rodney the external personalities were Marx and V.I. Lenin. In the case of King the two external personalities were Jesus Christ and Mahatma Gandhi.

Rodney believed that Lenin operationalized Marx from the world of ideas to the world of policy. King believed that Gandhi operationalized the love-ethic of Jesus from the world of ethics to the world of action.

Both of Martin Luther King's ultimate mentors were, in a sense, assassinated. The Jesus of Christianity was assassinated through the crucifixion. Mahatma Gandhi was assassinated by a bullet from a fellow Hindu.

Neither of Walter Rodney's ultimate mentors were assassinated, though each was constantly in the shadow of violence. Karl Marx died of natural causes in 1883 – just a year before the 1884-5 Berlin Conference which helped to seal the colonial fate of Africa. Lenin died almost exactly forty years later after launching a revolution which changed the course of the twentieth century.

King used the legacy of soul-force from Jesus and Gandhi as a means to an end. The end was the liberation and dignification of Black people. Rodney accepted the legacy of Marxism-Leninism as a means to an end. But Rodney never fully made up his mind whether *revolution* was a means *or* an end in itself. Nor did he resolve the issue of whether revolution was for oppressed *races* or for oppressed *classes*.

For Martin Luther King, Jr., the union between Jesus Christ and Mohandas Gandhi was indissoluble. If Christianity had been – like Hinduism – a religion based on *reincarnation*, Reverend King would have wondered whether Mohandas Gandhi was a reincarnation of Jesus Christ.

Although Rodney was intrigued by the *Trotsykite* thought of C.L.R. James, Rodney did believe that Lenin and Marx too had an indissoluble union. But Rodney did not live to see the union between Marx and Lenin put to the test in the final years of the twentieth century. The collapse of communism in the Soviet Union and Eastern Europe has been a collapse of Leninism but not necessarily a failure of Marxism,

Historically, Marxism had served three functions – as an *ethic of distribution, as an ideology of development and as a methodology of analysis*. As an *ethic of distribution*, Marxism distrusted private property on any significant scale. It also sought to contain class inequalities.

As an *ideology of development* Marxism-Leninism moved towards central planning, the vanguard party as the core in the political process, and the state as the core in the economic process. Marxism as a *methodology of analysis* has tended to lean on class analysis, on economic determinism and more recently on studying imperialism as a stage in capitalist development and exploitation.

What has failed in Eastern Europe and the former Soviet Union is *only Marxism as an ideology of development*. In this role, Marxism did not really deliver *development*. And when you look closely, it was the *Leninist* additions which let Marxism down – such as excessive statism, the tendency towards a vanguard party, and the whole doctrine of "democratic centralism."

On the other hand, Marxism as an ethic of distribution may still be valid. We should still be on the alert against gross class inequalities. We should still be aware of the dangers of unregulated private property on a certain scale.

Walter Rodney was at his best in the field of Marxism as a methodology of analysis. This methodology has not necessarily been invalidated by the collapse of communism in eastern and central Europe. There is still a need for class-analysis in understanding society. There are occasions when economic determinism is the only sensible explanation for a particular social phenomenon or a particular historical change.

If Leninism has been substantially discredited while Marxism may still be valid, is there a case for the *de-Leninization of Marxism*? We need not throw out the Marxist baby with the Leninist bath water.

CONCLUSION

Walter Rodney did not live long enough to face the crisis of Leninism at the end of the century. How would Walter Rodney have responded to the challenge of having to de-Leninize Marxism?

Martin Luther King, Jr. would not have had to de-Gandhi-ise Jesus. At least so far the union between Jesus and Gandhi has turned out to be more truly indissoluble than the union between Marx and Lenin.

Martin Luther King, Jr.'s dream remains relevant – but it needs to be globalized. Walter Rodney's dream was already global, but did it need more focus in goals and strategies?

So let freedom ring from the high plateaus of Ethiopia, let freedom ring from the deep valley of the Brahmaputra and the Euphrates, let freedom ring from the isles of the Caribbean and the deep recesses of the Amazon, let freedom ring from Hungary to Harlem, from the snows of Kilimanjaro to the winds of Chicago. As we continue to paraphrase Reverend King, let freedom ring from Georgetown to Capetown.

And when this happens and when we have allowed freedom to ring in every village and every city, in every country and every continent, we will speed up the day when all of God's children – Indo-Guyanese and Afro-Guyanese, indigenous and immigrant, men and women, white and Black, Jew and Gentile, Palestinian and Israeli, Muslim and Christian, Hindu and Buddhist, Saint and Sinner, will be able to join hands and globalize both Martin Luther King and Walter Rodney – "Free at last, Free at last, Thank God Almighty! We are free at last!"

Walter Rodney put it differently: "They call us a mob. We say, come together to draw strength from the traditions of resistance which have come down from the tradition of slavery and indentureship and anticolonialism to the present day... All power to the people."

And what would Julius K. Nyerere say? He would say, quite simply in Kiswahili, "*Ujamaa na kujitegemea, kwa hisani yako*" – "Socialism and self-reliance, by your leave, please." Walter Rodney would have nodded his approval. Even in your silences we still hear you, Walter!

14

THE MODERN CIVIL RIGHTS MOVEMENT

PERMISSION TO REPRINT THIS CHAPTER WAS GRANTED BY BEDFORD (ORIGINAL PUBLISHER FOR *EMMETT TILL: THE SACRIFICIAL LAMB OF THE CIVIL RIGHTS MOVEMENT*, 1994) AND AUTHORHOUSE (2006 REPRINT OF BOOK).

Clenora Hudson-Weems

> *Historians will talk about the good and the bad, but they don't want to deal with the ugly. . .The ugliness of racism is not a white man's telling a black woman to give him her bus seat—bad as that is—but the—confident home-invasion, kidnapping and murder of a fourteen-year-old black youth and the exoneration by jury of the youth's apparent killers.*
>
> Rayfield Mooty[1]

The subject here is the history of the Civil Rights Movement with regard to the Till murder case and how this case has been treated or ignored by traditional historians. Since the involuntary migration of black people from Africa (the motherland for all blacks), throughout the bloody transatlantic slave-trade, to the seasoning islands of the Caribbean, to the incomprehensible atrocities of American slavery, blacks have been struggling for human rights. During the earliest stages of American slavery (near the beginning of the seventeenth century) to its final legal period in the mid-nineteenth century (marked by the Civil War and the signing of the Emancipation Proclamation in September 1862, which went into effect January 1, 1863), emphasis on physical freedom from human bondage characterizes the black American struggle. Subsequent white retaliation and bitterness, resulting from the whites' displaced ownership of black people and their stubborn sense of white superiority, ultimately evolved into the establishment of the Jim Crow laws in the early 1880s. These laws, which according to Woodward were "the public symbols and constant reminders of his [black's] inferior position,"[2] legalized what W. E. B. DuBois metaphorically designates in *Souls of Black Folk* as the "veil," the wall or curtain of segregation. Just as blacks rose up against forms of oppression then, they continue to do so today. Extreme white opposition to the black resistance to oppression, in the form of heinous, brutal crimes such as rape and lynchings, clearly validates the need for black people to continue and even to intensify their struggle as a proud and historically determined people. This act of self-determination in turn would protect blacks against a designed vulnerability to which they are assigned in this dehumanization and blatant denial of their "inalienable rights" as fellow human begins.

The fifties mark the beginning of the era of the widely publicized struggle for the civil rights of African-Americans. No longer a question of emancipation, the key issue for the early part of that decade was the notion of being "separate but equal" as a way of life. This aspiration proved to be both hypocritical and unrealistic within the American system. The Supreme Court's landmark decision in the 1954 controversial *Brown versus Topeka Board of Education*, established the unconstitutionality of the "separate but equal" public school systems. Thus, desegregation in the public schools was officially ordered. Blacks, like any other people, desired to share in all the benefits American society had to offer—educational, political, economic, as well as social rights. However, the resolution to demand boldly their civil rights did not come without a high price. As in the past, blacks were severely dehumanized; but they were to be now alarmed into consciousness of the urgent need to remedy the powerlessness and insignificance of their lives as perceived by the dominant white culture. Such was the case in the infamous murder and mock trials of Emmett Till.

FROM 1877 TO 1965

The Till murder case has been vastly underappreciated as a main stimulus for the modern Civil Rights Movement, despite the fact that it was one of the most important events that occurred in African-American, and even American, culture in the fifties. It embodies the ugliness of American racism, effecting the most vicious form of violence to be bestowed upon a human being. Lynching is an atrocity that finds its victims both powerless and, more important, too often guiltless. After reflecting upon the nuances of the scores of atrocities heaped upon African-Americans between the years 1877 to 1965, marking the beginning to the end of the Till scenario, it appears that symbolically the stage for the Till slaying was set by Rutherford Birchard Hayes's infamous 1877 Compromise. The nineteenth president of the United States, Hayes won by only one electoral vote. As a strategy to win the presidential election, he agreed to a "laissez faire" policy on the matter of the laws and practices of the southern conservative states. One of the ramifications of the Hayes Compromise was that the

North ignored the plight of the African-American in the South, and the Till case, seventy-eight years later, forced America to take another look.

The ramifications of the Hayes Compromise would not be legally concluded until Lindon Baines Johnson, the thirty-sixth president of the United States, signed the 1965 Voting Rights Bill, that removed the legal shackles from African-Americans. Mooty has this to say:

> I have to go back to the presidential election of 1877... when all of the rights that we had (President Abraham Lincoln did give us a little relief of freedom) were taken from us by the stroke of one pen and only by one vote! One electoral vote ... In 1877 Rutherford B. Hayes made a compromise with the South that "if you give me your vote and make me president, I will pull the troops out of there." And the troops were what they called a toothache to the southerners, and he said, "I will pull that tooth out, and then you can do whatever you want to."[3]

Just prior to the Hayes election, whites were retaliating against the legal progress of the African-Americans, directly related to Lincoln's signing of the Emancipation Proclamation. They particularly resisted the newly acquired freedom of African-Americans in Reconstruction to exercise voting rights, so they used terrorist tactics at the polls.

During the mid-twentieth century, Till became part of that historical continuum, although voting was not the issue with him. The climate was much the same just before his lynching, when voting registration drives in Mississippi were posing a threat to the white power system. As in the 1870s, whites used lynching as a means of intimidation and of discouraging African-American participation in the voting processes. The Thirteenth, Fourteenth, and Fifteenth Amendments provided constitutional rights and protections for African-Americans; however, the established institution of black servitude and white supremacy was a way of life, and one that whites were not willing to surrender peacefully.

THE JIM CROW LAWS

Another critical event in the history of the modern Civil Rights Movement was the emergence of the Jim Crow laws of the 1880s. These were various laws that sprang up in different states, culminated by the *Plessy versus Ferguson* case in 1896, which was decided by the Supreme Court and which gave federal and constitutional sanction to "separate but equal facilities," thus making racial segregation both legal and constitutional. This legally established second-class citizenship for African-Americans during the nadir of the post-Reconstruction period. These limitations on African-Americans culminated in countless lynchings as terrorist political tools for social and economic control. And the lynchings continued, legally uncontested in the courts, until the Till lynching in 1955: the first of its kind to hold a trial of whites for the lynching of an African-American.

The Till lynching was a culminating experience in African-Americans' feelings of powerlessness. Demonstrations erupted and continued. Ten years later, in 1965, President Lyndon B. Johnson, with the stroke of a pen, granted African-Americans the voting rights that were needed to change this abject victimization. He cautioned that every African-American must register and vote, for one is not truly free until then, until one can ensure oneself proper protection through proper political representation. Johnson knew that the dominant culture would stop at nothing to secure the votes of African-Americans, once the latter had that privilege. And since over half of the African-American population lived in northern and western states where they had voting rights already, southern whites knew that once southern blacks had that right too, the whites would have trouble. Realizing that much of the democratic society lies in the voting power, Johnson moved all the more on the potential of the ballot for African-Americans. This represents the true meaning of the signing of the Voting Rights Bill, reflecting its significance to the plight of all African-Americans, and reversing Hayes's earlier regressive act.

As for Till, his death carried that race and sex inference. His murderers had the security that the law would not be implemented against them. The point of the trial following Till's lynching is that African-Americans did not and could not become jurors in Mississippi, and whites would not convict any other white for murdering any African-American. According to John Popham of *The New York Times*, race was a key issue with John C. Whitten, one of the defense attorneys, who established his confidence in the all-white jury: "Every last Anglo-Saxon one of you has the courage to free these men in the point that several people who handled the dead body testifies they thought it had been too decomposed to be identified."[4] That was just what happened: the jury unanimously found the defendants not guilty.

THE FEAR BENEATH

There is something beneath the surface in the meaning of Till's murder. It has always been said that opposites attract—men are attracted to women, women are attracted to men, and in some cases white men are attracted to black women, and black men are attracted to white women. According to Calvin Hernton, "Out of his [white mans'] guilt [because of his relationships with black women] grew fear—if he found it difficult to stay away from the 'animal' attraction of black women, was it not possible that his wife felt that same attraction to the black 'bucks'? Something had to be done."[5] Given the time period, the location, and the state of race relations during the pre-Civil Rights era in the South, the attraction between the different races (particularly of African-American men to white women) was not only illegal and unacceptable, but abhorred and dangerous. This was true because the fear that Hernton analyzes on the part of white men is that, given the freedom to choice, their women may demonstrate a mutual attraction to the African-American men. Wells explored this concept earlier with the following conclusions:

> I also found that what the white man of the South practiced as all rights for himself, he assumed to be unthinkable in white women. They could and did fall in love with the pretty mulatto and quadroon girls as well as black ones, but they professed an inability to imagine white women doing the same thing with Negro and mulatto men. Whenever they did so and were found out, the cry of rape was raised, and the lowest element of white South was turned loose to wreak its fiendish cruelty on those too weak to help themselves.[6]

Winthrop Jordan takes the fear to another level in *White Over Black*, in which he examines the white man's attitudes toward the African-American man. He contends that the white man fears the African-American man's sexual aggression:

> The concept of the Negro's aggressive sexuality was reinforced by what was thought to be an anatomical peculiarity of the Negro male. He was said to possess an especially large penis … If a perceptible anatomical difference did in fact exist, it fortuitously coincided with the already firmly established idea of the Negro's special sexuality; it could only have served as striking confirmation of that idea, as salt in the wounds of the white man's envy.[7]

The white, therefore, finds the need to prove to himself that he is the master.

According to William Bradford Huie, a white investigator of racial atrocities who wrote the celebrated story of Till's murderers for *Look* magazine after the trial, "They didn't take him out to kill him. The killed him because he had a white girl's picture in his pocket, and he told 'em that she was his girl. It was at that time that they thought that this sorta thing had to be stopped in order to defend the 'Southern way of life.'"[8] The thought that such an attraction might get out of hand and cause widespread miscegenation was regarded by the dominant culture as a critical problem, and hence was treated with utmost urgency and drastic measures. The scenario surrounding the Till incident was indeed explosive.

Arnold Rose asserts in his condensed version of Gunnar Myrdal's *The American Dilemma* that "a lynching is not merely a punishment against an individual but a disciplinary device against the Negro group."[9] Although the reaction and response of Till's murderers to such an issue was both extreme and unwarranted, it was, nonetheless, the trend. It was easy to repeat such an act, since it had happened over and over again. The difference with Till was that he was a teenager who could not have had the same ultimate intentions as a grown man. His lynching was called to the public's attention, and the ugliness of American racism became known to the world.

These insights into the socioeconomic and psychological ramifications of lynchings confirm that the motivations behind them are multifaceted, complicated, and intricate. The lynching of Till symbolizes the ultimate deterioration of race relations. His death reflects a three-fold victimization: of a human being denied his life, of an African-American man deprived of dignity, and of a child robbed of his future.

THE TILL CASE AND THE MODERN RIGHTS MOVEMENT

It appears that, for a number of reasons, there has been a conscious effort to neglect the fact that this incident is a key historical event in the record of the movement. To begin with, the victim of this incident was not a member of the upper-middle-class bourgeoisie, and his experience was more prone to happen among the lower and working classes than among the upper class. On the whole, established historians, as is the case of academicians in general, were members of the upper-middle class, the bourgeoisie, and generally tended not to focus on the particular plight of the lower or working-class African-Americans, except as their plight affected the whole race. In other words, the neglect of the Till case stems from a class issue.

Then the nature of Till's "crime"—wolf-whistling at a white woman—was ambiguous. At that time, it was considered taboo behavior, particularly in the Deep South. Finally, because Till was an outsider (a northern African-American youth visiting in the South who did not conduct himself according to white people's expectations, according to southern etiquette), the whole Till case posed an embarrassment to the movement, both for African-American leaders and whites. The respected black leaders and historians possibly feared that the incident would alienate them from white culture. For example, there has always been that segment of the African-American population who seeks approval of and direction from the dominant culture. During slavery they were generally among the "house niggers" and later they were generally among the "black bourgeoisie." Having been accepted by the dominant culture, this group directs its energies toward protecting that relationship to maintain the alliance, which necessitates protecting whites through avoidance of the embarrassment of having their shortcomings exposed. Therefore, in avoiding the Till incident as a significant part of the fabric of American culture, they protect both their established relationships with whites and the reputations of the whites as well.

Another possible explanation for the lack of attention to the Till case is that those historians, leaders, and reporters of the Civil Rights Movement had more to gain from a "peaceful" movement. This is true because they could that way appease both blacks and whites: the former by articulating and spearheading their demands to end segregation in the social and educational spheres, and the latter by addressing the eradication of their acceptable chosen issues of concern. The historians in particular acted to downplay Till's lynching, to downplay the embodiment of racial violence and the ugliness of racial victimization. They chose, instead, to celebrate the refusal of Rose Parks to relinquish her bus seat to a white man, a morally acceptable act of proclaiming one's common humanity through integration, a major issue with the NAACP. Unlike Till, Parks was not the object of brutal racism. Her symbolic act was a peaceful one and a more appealing media image than the slaughtered Till. Had the Till case continued to receive maximum attention, under the leadership of organized labor (with its legacy of marshalling the demands for economic parity as well as civil rights for blacks since the early forties), the direction of the then-evolving Civil Rights Movement would have probably taken on another dimension or even direction.

RANKING TILL WITH ESTABLISHED LEADERS

Although Till, technically, cannot be included among the martyrs who gave their lives in the pursuit of African-American freedom (for instance, two black Mississippians murdered shortly before Emmett, Rev. George W. Lee, who had just delivered a sermon giving a review of the history of black Americans' struggle for freedom on the Sunday before he was murdered by members of the white Citizen's Council for registering to vote, and Lamar Smith, also involved in voter registration efforts), Till's untimely death, and the public's reaction to it, helped set the stage for the Civil Rights Movement. Richard Aubrey McLemore in the second volume of *A History of Mississippi* concludes that "the effect of the crime and its aftermath was to intensify an already emotional atmosphere, and the state's preoccupation with a politics of race increased."[10]

Indeed, even Rosa Parks herself acknowledges the uniqueness and importance of this case. She asserts that "it [the Till murder case] was a very tragic incident. . . Many such incidents had gone unnoticed in the past."[11] Dr. King, too, referred to the Till case twice in *Stride Toward Freedom*. Discussing the impermanence of publicity and popularity, he asserted, "Today it is Emmett Till, tomorrow, it is Martin Luther King. Then in another tomorrow it will be somebody else."[12] Later he alluded to the fact that Till's murder is ever present in the minds of the oppressed who fear that there is no recourse for their victimization: "With the Emmett Till case in Mississippi still fresh in our memories, the Negroes held little hope of conviction."[13] Undoubtedly, this case bore heavy on their minds, as it did on the minds of many others.

Although Juan Williams does not postulate that the Till incident was the catalyst for the movement, in his work *Eyes on the Prize*, he does acknowledge that "the *Montgomery Advertiser* in Montgomery, Alabama, picked up the Till story and gave it prominent display. Three months later, the black population of Montgomery began an historic boycott of their municipal bus system."[14] He investigates the motivations behind the prime movers of the boycott, such as Rosa Parks' continuous refusal to relinquish her bus seat at times dating back as early as 1944; Jo Ann Robinson's traumatic and dehumanizing experience of being forced to relinquish her bus seat during the Christmas rush in 1959; and Edgar Daniel Nixon's leadership in waiting for the "right person" and soliciting the black ministers (one of whom was Martin Luther King, Jr., then a new minister in the town).

It should be noted there that, for a number of reasons, Till was not the "right person." The leaders of the Civil Rights Movement have always made choices. For example, according to Taylor Branch in *Parting the Waters*, approximately seven months before Rosa Parks' demonstration, there was the case of

> a feisty high school student named Claudette Colvin, who defended her right to the seat in language that brought words of disapproval from passengers of both races . . . Colvin was crying and madder than ever by the time the policemen told her she was under arrest. She struggled when they dragged her off the bus and screamed when they put on the handcuffs . . . Prosecutors had thrown the book at Colvin, charging her with violating the segregation law, assault, and disorderly conduct.

Unlike Parks, Claudette did not surrender peacefully. On May 6, Judge Eugene Carter:

> sentenced Colvin to pay a small fine—a sentence so much lighter than anticipated that it ruined her martyr status. Many Negroes who supported her case nevertheless came to believe she was lucky.[15]

The black leadership did investigate the situation. However, after the discovery that the teenager was also pregnant and unmarried, they decided that she would not be the proper model to rally behind. In other words, because her character and sense of morality were questionable, she was not selected as the perfect model for a movement against institutionalized racism.

Parks, on the other hand, was another story. Nixon, a black leader in Montgomery, went to Clifford Durr, and attorney and one of the few white liberals in the town, for consultation.

> He asked for Durr's legal opinion: was this the case they had been waiting for? Could they use it to win a victory over segregation on appeal? . . . The only flaw with the case as he saw it was that the charges would first be heard in state court rather than federal court. But there were ways to move cases. Otherwise, the circumstances were highly favorable. There were no extraneous charges to cloud the segregation issue, and Rosa Parks would make a good impression on white judges. This was enough for Nixon, who already knew instinctively that Rosa Parks was without peer as a potential symbol for Montgomery's Negroes—humble enough to be claimed by the common folk, and yet dignified enough in manner, speech, and dress to command the respect of the leading classes.[16]

A respectable, light-skinned gentlewoman, Parks was a perfect model, both impressive and appealing.

As for Till, particularly with his bloated brutalized face, and the whole white woman/black man sex scenario, he was not the proper model to choose. There were still those who said that Till should have known better, and who were angry with him for being mannish, and for stepping out of line. Williams' investigation in *Eyes on the Prize* (which is the most detailed account of Till in the traditional historical canon) is a demonstration of individual or personal history, reflections on the lives of the heroes or "great" people (or, as in the case of Parks and Robinson, established, respected citizens), rather than the history of the masses. His study would have been strengthened had he attempted to include an assessment of the mood of the black masses who in fact carried out the Montgomery Bus Boycott.

It seems that since blacks had been subjected to the segregated bus system there for sixty-five years, something more dramatic or traumatic than their "tired feet" was needed to carry them through this unyielding year-long bus boycott. And it seems plausible and natural to suggest that a people would react in the manner they did only after a supreme insult to their race—the radically motivated murder of a black youth, for example. Indeed, after Till's death, blacks in large numbers bravely demonstrated and publicly confronted the racial immoralities in the American system. Even though all were moved by the Till murder case, the movement itself physically needed a Rose Parks, the symbolic impetus for the movement.

TILL AND TRADITIONAL HISTORY

Prior to the Till case and the Montgomery Bus Boycott, the *Brown versus Topeka Board of Education* case had in a sense established a mood of optimism. The Till case exploded approximately a year after this legal landmark and jarred people back too the realization that black freedom would be achieved only through independent black efforts, since the Till case made it once again obvious that the courts would not take up the fight for equal justice. Moreover, the Till case occurred about a year before the Montgomery Bus Boycott, which points to the fact that there was the need for another vehicle—mass demonstrations—by which to achieve justice and exposure for black victims.

Until *Eyes on the Prize*, black and white historians alike have failed to recognize the significance of the Till case and even this work does not do it justice. Even though William's work introduced Till, still there has been no official full-length scholarly discussion of the implications of the Till case on the future development on the Modern Civil Rights Movement, particularly from an endemic perspective. Williams implicitly corroborates the thesis of this work: that Till's contribution to the growing militancy of the black community was significant, and worthy of a full-length scholarly examination.

Consider the historical account of the black American struggle in the fifties and the sixties as documented by the foremost black historian, John Hope Franklin. In his most recently revised edition, the 1994 seventh edition of *From Slavery to Freedom*, there is only one reference to the Till case, and it is not even indexed. Franklin wrote, in a brief catalogue of black victims during that period: "Near Greenwood a fourteen-year-old Negro boy from Chicago was murdered for allegedly whistling at a white store-keeper's wife."[17] He failed to even identify the victim. So much for the Till murder case in this standard textbook.

Consider Kenneth G. Goode's *From Africa to the United States and Then: A Concise Afro-American History.* Nowhere is Till mentioned in the text, not even in the chronological table of events, which appears in the back of the book.

Consider Peter M. Bergman's *The Chronological History of the Negro in America.* Here Till receives minimum coverage, as he appears in the list of three victims of lynchings occurring in Mississippi in 1955: "Lynching returned to the South. Mississippi accounted for three: Rev. George W. Lee at Belzoni, Lamar Smith at Brookhaven, and Emmett Till near Money."[18] While there is some elaboration on the other two, Rev. George Lee and Lamar Smith relative to their involvement with the Mississippi voter registration drive, no additional comment on the Till case is made.

Consider co-authors Albert P. Blaustein and Robert L. Zangrando who wrote *Civil Rights and the American Negro: A Documentary History.* In the entire 671-page book on the African-Americans' civil rights from 1619 until 1968, only one reference is made to Emmett Till: "Moreover, segregationist and states' rights opposition had encouraged the formation of such organized groups as the White Citizens' Councils and the initiation of such unorganized violence as the kidnap-lynching of fourteen-year-old Emmett Till at Money, Mississippi, in the summer of 1955."[19] Even then, the reference does not reflect the impact Till's murder and trial had on the American people, particularly African-Americans. On the contrary, it merely emphasizes intimidation of the black community by the dominant culture.

Consider one of the greatest black historians of the twentieth century, Benjamin Quarles and *The Negro in the Making of America.* Nowhere in his entire book is the Till murder case mentioned. In recapitulating the activities of the fifties, he asserts that "This movement [Civil Rights Movement] started on December 1, 1955, when seamstress Rosa Parks boarded a bus in downtown Montgomery, took a seat in the section reserved for whites, and refused to surrender it to a white man who subsequently entered the bus."[20]

Consider the recently published co-authored historical account of the black American by two highly credible black historians, Mary Frances Berry and John Blassingame, *Long Memory: The Black Experience in America.* Again the reference to the Till murder case is limited to one sentence, and like other historians they fail to put this case in the historical perspective of the Civil Rights Movement. Hence, "Emmett Till, a fourteen-year-old boy, was kidnapped and killed in Money, Mississippi, in 1955 because he allegedly whistled at a white woman."[21] Their reference to the Till case only exemplifies the taboo of the black man and the white woman in the long debated issue of sex and racism.

According to Gunnar Myrdal, who devised what he called "The Rank Order of Discrimination" in *An American Dilemma*, he found that whites contended that blacks wanted sexual relations and intermarriage with white women more than other forms of equality. When he questioned blacks, he found that they contended that they valued the sexual attraction least.[22] Calvin Hernton discusses this issue in *Sex and Racism in America*, in which he concluded "that the race problem is inextricably connected with sex . . . The sexualization of the race problem is a reality, and we are going to have to deal with it even though most of us are, if not unwilling, definitely unprepared."[23]

Finally, consider the interpretive historian Vincent Harding in *The Other American Revolution*. Till is not mentioned at all.

Others, too, have been guilty of side-tracking or by-passing the Till case, as reflected in the records of both *The World Almanac* and the *Reader's Digest*. In recording the significant events of the month and year, the World Almanacs cite the Rosa Parks incident, but fail to mention Till. The *Reader's Digest*, too, mentions Parks, but not Till. Clearly, the Till murder case is a lost chapter in the history books on the Civil Rights Movement.

There is a discrepancy between the underplayed account of the Till case in history and the detailed media coverage it received. Only through reviewing the Till case as interpreted by journalists, as well as everyday people, photographers, creative writers, singers, and autobiographers, can the oversights of historians be corrected. One important publication (important because of its accuracy on the Till murder case), which documented testimonies by persons with insights on it, was one of several small pamphlets covering this atrocity. Published in 1956, *Time Bomb* was written by Olive Arnold Adams, editor of *Global News Syndicate*, with a foreword by Dr. T.R.M. Howard, the civil rights activist in whose home Till's mother, grandfather, and cousin Mooty resided during the murder trial. This book relates detailed information surrounding the murder. Mooty attests to the insights in this book, as he was an intricate part of the case from its inception. In all these testimonies, one crucial thing comes out: that at the outset of the Civil Rights Movement, a fourteen-year-old northern black youth fell prey to the treachery of American racism, both in his death and in the subsequent mock trials. The unrelenting restlessness, fervor, and anger of the African-American established on that day that obsequiousness, helplessness, and complacency had passed, at least for the moment.

In spite of it all, Till has yet to receive his deserved place in the historical chronicles of the African-American struggle. As Simeon Booker observes, "Today, only one stature of Emmett Till exists in the entire nation. That being in a city park in Denver. The black mother who changed the course of history is almost forgotten—except for a three-par series on the lynching, broadcast by Chicago's WMAQ-TV station's Rich Samuels."[24] Although Till has not been properly remembered or immortalized by Americans, Congressman Gus Savage of Chicago wrote in a moving letter addressed to the fallen victim that, "A monument to serve as a shrine has been suggested in your memory; but we know the only monument not decayed by time is freedom. So we shall fight for freedom in your memory."[25]

SACRIFICIAL LAMB

Emmett Till has been called the sacrificial lamb of the Civil Rights Movement. As Jordan asserts: "There was no way for progress to be made without someone dying ... There had to be sacrificial lambs and that is what Emmett Till was." The editor of *Freedom*, Louis E. Burnham, said shortly after Till's death: "The fights to avenge the murder of Emmett Louis Till has become a symbol of the Negro people's bitter struggle for first-class citizenship. [26]

Although many regard the Parks incident as the beginning of the Civil Rights Movement, it is a mistake to ignore the earlier impact of the Till murder, which occurred just three months and three days before the Parks incident. Inundating the world press, the Till murder case was thoroughly covered by the news media, but it has not been adequately chronicled in history books. In a 1956 *Ebony* article, Clotye Murdock wrote:

> The state (Mississippi) has been referred to in the foreign press at the "land of the Till Murder." Racial clashes between Negroes and whites there have made headlines in a Babel of languages. In lands far distant from America, where Mississippi is only a word, a name, for a state or a city or a province—many know not which—people frown in bewilderment as they hear it, and say: "Is that not the place where the Negro boy was killed?" [27]

LABOR UNIONS TAKE UP THE CASE

Since Till was neither the first nor the last black to be lynched, one may question why this case became a big issue. First of all, the Till incident happened at the right time, just as the age of modernity with mass media technology reached an all-time high in the area of communication. Radio, newspapers, and television ushered the news of the Till lynching into the homes of countless American citizens, making a traditionally isolated incident public information. With this new technology, events that would not have reached the national public were now known to all.

Another reason is that a major national labor-union organization, the AFL-CIO, had just merged in August, bridging the gap between the two most prominent black labor leaders—A. Philip Randolph, president of the Brotherhood of Sleeping Car Porters, and William S. Townsend, president of the Former Red Caps, president of the Transportation Services Employees—who embraced this case from the outset and obtruded it upon the American society for public censure. The following memorandum, dated September 27, 1955, from labor-union official Boyd L. Wilson to David J. McDonald, the president of the United Steel Workers, and I. W. Abel regarding the labor meeting on the Till case states that:

Monsignor Cornelius J. Drew, pastor, St. Charles Roman Catholic Church, before an impressive crowd of ten thousand people in New York City last Sunday, made an impassioned plea that the decent, right-thinking people of the United States rise up and make a repetition of the Till case impossible in America.

He was joined by A. Philip Randolph, president, Brotherhood of Sleeping Car Porters; Roy Wilkins, executive director, NAACP, and City Councilman Earl Brown, before a rally sponsored by trade unions and instigated by the Brotherhood of Sleeping Car Porters, AFL...

Resolutions were adopted calling upon Governor Hugh White of Mississippi, and the United States Department of Justice to investigate and establish the whereabouts of two missing witnesses. Likewise, to establish, beyond the shadow of a doubt, as to the identity of the body discovered in the river, if indeed it was not that of Till.

The Till case has been a rallying point for liberal movements and peoples within the United States in recent weeks, and it has been my considered judgment that it is to the best interests of the Steel Workers' Union to carry its share of the responsibility and to do what it can to further the case of justice of all people.

Mooty had much to say about the labor-union involvement: "The whole labor union was involved in it [the Till case] before it [public exposure] happened."[28] A relative of Till through his uncle Henry Spearman, Rayfield Mooty, a member of the Community Services Committee and the president of a steel labor-union local in Chicago, had spent years in the labor movement and was in the position to make the necessary contact with the right people who had the influence to expose this case nationally. As Mamie Bradley-Mobley recalls, "Mr. Mooty was the one who was sort of like steering me which way to go because he was quite active in the labor movement and he knew the politicians. I didn't know a politician."[29]

He first contacted one of the most influential blacks in the United Automobile Workers, vice-president of the Cook County Industrial Union, vice-president of the newly merged AFL-CIO, and vice-president of the NAACP (Chicago branch), Bill Townsend. Townsend, in turn, was able to bring the entire United Automobile Workers and the Cook County Industrial Council into the case. Some other influential persons who were drawn into the case included Boyd Wilson (personal representative of the United Steel Workers of America), Bill Abner (vice-president of the Cook County Industrial Union Council and vice-president of the NAACP Chicago branch), David McDonald (president of the United Steel Workers Union), Doug Anderson (former chairman of the Community Services Committee and manager of Senator Paul Douglas's office in Chicago), Senator Paul Douglass, Congressman William Dawson (of the First Congressional District in Illinois), and three executive board members of the union, Lucius Love (staff member of the United Steel Workers and executive board member of the Cook County Industrial Union Council), Charlie Hayes (Cook County Industrial Union Council), and Hugh Lewis (public school teacher with the school union). And finally the president of the International Brotherhood of Sleeping Car Porters himself A. Philip Randolph was brought into the case. These people had worked together for years and thus, as Mooty asserts, "It was easy to swing them into place."[30] Clearly they could together influence the entire labor movement to act.

Demonstrating the commitment of the Steel Workers' Union, it was revealed in *Steel Labor: The Voice of the United Steelworkers of America— C.I.O.* that "the brutal slaying of a 14 year-old Chicago Negro boy ... was vigorously condemned in a resolution on Civil Rights adopted by delegates at the annual conference of District 31, United Steelworkers."[31]

The following telegram to Rayfield Mooty from Theodore Brown, director of research and publicity for the Brotherhood of Sleeping Car Porters in New York, dated September 23, 1955, documents the national involvement of the labor union:

> Would appreciate deeply your acceptance of invitation of New York division of the Brotherhood of Sleeping Car Porters to attend and speak at mass meeting occasion to protest and organize New York public opinion against the brutal lynching of your nephew in Mississippi. This meeting first organized effort in New York on this unfortunate incident to take place this Sunday, September 25, at Williams Institutional C.M.E. Church located 2225 Seventh Avenue, New York City. Time is 2:30 pm. The organization's international president, Mr. A. Philip Randolph, will be chairman and speakers will include some

of New York's distinguished citizens, white and colored. We would also deeply be very happy to have Mrs. Mamie Bradley. I have talked to our mutual friend Boyd Wilson, of your union. The Brotherhood of Sleeping Car Porters will be happy to pay all expenses for you and Mrs. Bradley if it is possible for you to accept this invitation. Kindly wire or telephone me collect at Monument 2-5079.

> Theodore Brown, Director of Research and Publicity,
> Brotherhood of Sleeping Car Porters
> 217 West 125th Street, Suite 301
> New York 27, New York.

The involvement of the National Labor Union and particularly the Brotherhood of Sleeping Car Porters offered an interesting diffusion of sentiments and information. In the case of the porters, they talked to the passengers on the trains, which was assumed to be a part of their job. People had heard about the Till case and naturally wanted to talk about it, and so, oftentimes for hours at a time, the porters, who had become themselves involved in the national movement against this murder, would share their information with the passengers.[32] This sort of activity, passing the information by word of mouth, served as an information channel from the North to the South, from the East to the West.

Communist organizations, too, expressed demands for action against the Till lynching; however, efforts to conceal their interest were undertaken, as revealed in the following memorandum from Boyd Wilson dated September 28, 1955, to Mr. Mooty:

> Reliable information from New York supports the suspicion that the meeting now being arranged for that city, October 2nd, involves some questionable possibilities.

> You probably noticed a number of telegrams received at last Sunday's meetings. You will recall none of them were read. The reason was some of these wires were from known communists. We could not properly read some of these telegrams and not read others without having demands made for reading all of them, hence rather read communists demands for action, none of the wires were made public.

> I am reliably informed that next Sunday's meetings will provide an opportunity for these communists telegrams to be read, thereby furnishing an opportunity for communists to be identified with our movement. I fear this will tend to kill the support and give hundreds of liberal people an excuse to refuse

to support our demand for redress in the brutal murder of an innocent boy in the State of Mississippi.

To be sure, the labor-union officials knew that involvement from the communists could alienate other legitimate organizations, which considered communists as illegitimate organizations, which considered communists as illegitimate and un-American, from continuing their involvement in the case.

THE NAACP AND THE TILL CASE

It should be noted that (in keeping with the tradition of intervening in racial incidents) the NAACP did embrace the Till case, although not until late October.

Photograph 1 documents the key participants in the first demonstration meeting, September 1955, after the trial for the Chicago Chapter of the NAACP. Seated at the table is Vivian Moore, the Chicago secretary of the Chicago Chapter, with Mamie Bradley and Rayfield Mooty seated to the left behind. In all of their faces, the message of the Till story is the same—that this senseless act should not have taken place. They (the family and the officials of the NAACP) came together to devise a strategy for ending such racial atrocities. It was noted that the membership drive for the NAACP escalated following their involvement with the Till murder case, thereby empowering them more in their war against racism.

In a letter dated September 23, 1955, the president of the West Side Unit of the Chicago Branch of the NAACP wrote to Rayfield Mooty: "We would be honored to have you as a guest on the platform at our Mass Rally on Sunday, Oct 2, 1955, 3:00 P.M. at Stone Temple Baptist Church, 3622 W. Douglas Blvd., to protest the lynching to (sic) Emmett Till." This was after Roy Wilkins, the executive director of the NAACP, and Theodore Brown, public relations director for the Brotherhood of Sleeping Car Porters, who set up the meeting, with Wilkins, Mamie Bradley, and Rayfield Mooty in New York. Bradley recalls in a recent personal interview that Wilkins' primary reluctance about taking the case on stemmed from the fact that too often the organization had taken on people and their cases who later demanded too much money. As it turned out, a financial dispute between Mamie Bradley and Roy Wilkins did ensue. She agreed to a $3,500 honorarium, an amount with which one of the NAACP leaders, Mr. Odum of the West Coast, had also agreed. However, when she discussed the financial matter further with Roy Wilkins, "He became very distraught . . . Roy Wilkins just put his foot down, and he said he would not do it, and he accused me of capitalizing on my son's death, and he broke the relationship, and that was the end."[33] Wilkins withdrew his support and subsequently canceled all her scheduled engagements under the auspices of the organization. This act discredited her with the organization, and thus the NAACP's supporters likewise pulled away.

Alphonse Lewis, Jr., president of the Grand Rapids branch of the NAACP, said the following in a letter dated October 31, 1955, to Mr. Mooty:

> Please acknowledge our thanks for the fine down-to-earth message that you brought to our mass meeting on Friday, October 21, 1955. I truly hope that Mrs. Bradley's bravery through her long suffering will not be forgotten by this or any other community in this nation. I trust the message that Mrs. Bradley and you bring will be long remembered..

Everywhere, the Till murder case was discussed, according to the *Chicago Defender*, it had become an international "cause célèbre."[34] Not only were there written denunciations of the Till lynching, but there were financial communities as well, most of which were channeled through the NAACP, early on before it pulled away from the case, to combat injustices against blacks in the South and elsewhere. For example, the display of Till's body, according to Juan Williams in the book *Eyes on the Prize*, "without question, it moved black America in a way the Supreme Court ruling on school desegregation could not match. Contributions to the NAACP's "fight find," the war chest to help victims of racial attacks, reached record level. Only weeks before, the NAACP had been begging for support to pay its debts in the aftermath of its Supreme Court triumph."[35] After the mock trials, there were numerous speaking engagements under the auspices of the NAACP.

Simeon Booker, the Washington bureau chief for *Jet* magazine, asserted thirty years later, that "a black Chicago mother, Mrs. Mamie Till Mobley [Mrs. Mamie Bradley} unknowingly, but decisively jolted 'the sleeping giant of black people'"[36] The young thirty-three-year-old grief-stricken mother, Mamie Bradley Mobley, emerged heroic, publicly vowing to honor her son's memory with a lifetime commitment to the black struggle. The Rev. Smallgood Williams of Washington, D.C., arranged the speaking engagement in which she "spoke before a crowd of 6,000 who filled the Uline Arena in Washington. Four thousand more who waited outside were given a chance to hear her at a second special service that evening . . . The Uline rally launched a spiritual nation-wide mobilization drive against intolerance and racial bigotry in Mississippi and elsewhere."[37] Clearly the strength of this mother to define her loss as public and political was unusual. The numbers were there to witness this;

the crowd was evidence that the Till murder case had a profound impact upon the black masses. While in D.C. Mamie visited the Capitol, and Photograph 2 of Mamie Bradley, Rayfield Mooty, Elizabeth Wright (wife of Mose Wright), and Bishop Isaiah Roberts in October 1955 at the Capitol Building in Washington, D.C., makes a powerful statement. The Capitol Building is at the center for obvious reasons. Moreover, Mamie Bradley collaborates with the photographer, in this posed photograph, by pointing to the Capitol as the others, at an angle, face both her and the Capitol with the American flag of justice and freedom waving in the background. Given the fact that she had just experienced one of the greatest injustices to befall a mother, whose child's brutal death was ruled non-consequential, it is ironic, as well she knows, that she should be standing on the steps of this building which supposedly houses the executors of American justice, smiling as she muses to the others that "Maybe I can get justice there." Justice was never rendered in the murder case of Till and, thus, it remains an unresolved issue in the minds of many Americans.

Emmett Louis Till lived and died. His murder and trial were a mockery of the value of African-American life. This incident exemplified racial atrocities in modern history. As the people were keenly cognizant of this case then, through mass media, so should they be today through recorded history. Indeed, it so pressed upon the minds of Americans then that is ultimately exploded into the Civil Rights Movement. It is crucial for the civil rights struggles of today, yesterday, and tomorrow that the importance of Emmett Till to the Modern Civil Rights Movement be written, understood for its merit, and become a focal point for positive, consciousness-raising thought and action for all American citizens who love the ideas of trust, truth, integrity, and justice.

Photograph 1. Mamie Till Bradley, Ethel Payne (reporter for *The Chicago Defender*), Rayfield Mooty, Vivian Moore (Secretary for the Chicago Chapter of the NAACP) at first meeting of the Chicago Chapter of the NAACP after the trial. [Rayfield Mooty]

Photograph 2. Mamie Bradley, Rayfield Mooty, Elizabeth Wright and Bishop Isaiah Roberts at the Capitol in D. C. (*The Chicago Defender*)

Notes

1. Video-tape-recorded interview with Rayfield Mooty, Chicago, Illinois, April 1986.
2. C. Vann Woodward, *The Strange Career of Jim Crow* (New York: Oxford Univ. Press, 1957), p. 7.

3. Video-tape recorded interview with Rayfield Mooty, Chicago, Illinois, April 1986.

4. John N. Popham, "Mississippi Jury Frees 2 in Killing," *The New York Times*, 24 Sept. 1955.

5. Calvin C. Hernton, *Sex and Racism in America* (New York: Doubleday & Company, Inc., 1965), p. 16.

6. Alfreda M. Duster, ed. *Crusade for Justice: The Autobiography of Ida B. Wells* (Chicago: The University of Chicago Press, 1970), p. 70.

7. Winthrop D. Jordan, *White Over Black* (Baltimore, MD: Penguin Book Inc., 1968), pp. 158-159.

9. Quoted in Howell Raines, *My Soul Is Rested* (New York: Viking Penguin Books, 1983), p. 393.

10. Arnold Rose, *The Negro in America* (Boston: The Beacon Press, 1948), p. 185. Richard Aubrey McLemore, *A History of Mississippi, Volume II* (Hattiesburg: Univ. & College Press of Mississippi, 1973), p. 153.

11. Rose Parks quoted in Joe Atkins, "Slain Chicago Youth Was a 'Sacrificial Lamb,'" *The Clarion-Ledger Daily News*, Jackson, MS, 24, Aug. 1985:1.

12. Martin Luther King, Jr. *Stride Toward Freedom* (New York: Ballantine Books, 1958), p. 127.

13. King, p. 145.

14. Juan Williams, *Eyes on the Prize: America's Civil Rights Years, 1954-1965* (New York: Viking Penguin Inc. 1987), 57.

15. Taylor Branch, *Parting the Waters: America in the King Years 1954-1963* (New York: Simon and Schuster, 1988), 120, 123.

16. Branch, p. 130.

17. John Hope Franklin, *From Slavery to Freedom: A History of Negro Americans* (New York: Alfred A. Knopf, 1980), p. 459.

18. A Peter M. Bergman, *The Chronological History of the Negro in America* (New York: The New American Library,1969), p. 542.

19. Albert P. Blaustein and Robert L. Zangrando, *Civil Rights and the American Negro: A documentary History* (New York: Washington Square Press, Inc., 1968), p. 471.

20. M Benjamin Quarles, *The Negro in the Making of America* (London: Collier-MacMilland Ltd., 1969), p. 250.

21. Mary Frances Berry and John W. Blassingame, *Long Memory: The Black Experience in America* (New York: Oxford University Press, 1982), p. 124.

22. Gunnar Myrdal, *An American Dilemma* (New York: Harper & Brothers, 1944).

23. Calvin C. Hernton, *Sex and Racism in America* (New York: Doubleday & Company, Inc., 1965), pp. 4-5.

24. Simeon Booker, "30 Years Ago: How Emmett Till's Lynching Launched Civil Rights Drive" in *Jet* (17 June 1985), Booker, p. 14.

25. Gus Savage quoted in "30 Years Ago" by Booker, p. 18.

26. C Louis Burnham, *Behind the Lynching of Emmett Louis Till* (New York: Freedom Associates, Inc., Dec. 1955), p. 5.

27. Clotye Murdock, "Land of the Till Murder," *Ebony* (April 1956), p. 91.

28. Mooty, Interview, 1986.

29. Mamie Bradley-Mobley in my tape-recorded interview with her, Chicago, IL, 6 January 1988.

30. "Mooty, Interview, 1986.

31. "Steelworkers Condemn Racial Slaying of Boy," *Steel Labor: The Voice of the United Steelworkers of America—C.I.O.* (Indianapolis, IN, Oct. 1955), p. 11.

32. Mooty, interview, 1986..

33. Tape-recorded interview with Mamie Bradley, Chicago, IL, 24 March 1988.

34. Ethel L. Payne, "Army Gave Till Facts to Eastland," *Chicago Defender* (Chicago, IL, 22 Oct. 1955), p. 1.

35. Juan Williams, *Eyes on the Prize: America's Civil Rights Years*, 1954-1965 (New York: Viking Penguin Inc., 1987), p. 44.

36. Simeon Booker, "30 Years Ago, pp. 12-13.

37. Ethel L. Payne, "Army Gave Till Facts to Eastland," *The Chicago Defender* (Chicago, IL, 22 Oct. 1055), p. 2.

15

EBONICS: RECLAIMING
AND REDEFINING OUR LANGUAGE

Robert L. Williams

In January 1973 I called a national conference of Black and white scholars to discuss the cognitive and language development of African American children. It was at this conference that I experienced an epiphany, a defining moment, a sudden creative and intuitive insight. I coined the term *Ebonics* by combining two words: Ebony (Black) and phonics (speech sounds). The coining of the term *Ebonics* was accomplished during a creative discussion group with Black scholars and in the spirit of the second Nguzo Saba principle Kugichagulia (self-determination) as defined by Dr. Maulana Karenga (1965). The following is a re-creation of part of the discussion that occurred:

> Dr. Robert Williams: Ladies and gentlemen, we need to define what we speak. We need to give a clear definition of our language.
>
> Dr. Ernie Smith: Let me tell you something. If you notice, every language in the world represents a nation or a nationality. What we are speaking has continuity not only in the Unites States, but also outside of the United States and all the way back to the mother country. We need to get the term completely off the English scale and start calling it what it really represents.
>
> Dr. Williams: Let me make a point here. Language is a process of communication. But we need to deal with the root of our language. What about Ebo? Ebo-linguistics? Ebo-lingual? Ebo-phonics? *Ebonics*? Let's define our language as *Ebonics*.
>
> The Group: That sounds real good.

Dr. Williams: I am talking about an Ebony language. We know that ebony means Black and phonics refers to speech sounds or the science of speech sounds. Thus, we are really talking about the science of Black speech sounds or language.

Dr. Ann Covington: That's beautiful.

Dr. Williams: With *Ebonics*, we mean black pronunciation, vocabulary, syntax, structure, and the whole ball of wax.

Dr. Grace Holt: That's beautiful. Now we can go to a new term and really define it and say what our language really is.

Dr. Smith: *Ebonics* may be defined as the linguistic and para-linguistic features, which on a concentric continuum represent the communicative competence of the West African, Caribbean, and U. S. slave descendants of African origin. It includes the grammar, various idioms, patois, argots, idiolect, and social dialects of Black people. *Ebonics*, also, includes nonverbal sounds, cues and gestures that are systematically and predictably utilized in the process of communication by African-Americans.

Previous to the above conference, White linguists (Stewart, 1969; Dillard, 1972; Fasold, 1972) defined and described the language of African Americans. Their definitions of our language were pejorative descriptions: "Black English," "substandard speech," "deviant speech." "deficient speech," " non-standard English," and other negative terms. Thus, *Ebonics* clearly represented a response to the need for the proper naming (*Nommo*) and self-defining of our language. Toni Morrison (1987) aptly puts it in her celebrated novel *Beloved*: "Definitions belonged to the definers – not the defined" (190).

We needed to define our language, not let others define it for us. Creation of new terminology and definitions, as in the case of *Ebonics*, however, was not a precedent. Other Black scholars had previously coined relevant terms and continue to do so. Karenga (1965, 1976, 1980) introduced the terms *Kwanzaa* and *Nguzo Saba* principles, both of which have gained significant acceptance among African Americans. Dr. Bobby Wright (1976) coined the term *Mentacide*, which means "the deliberate and systematic destruction of an individual or group's mind" by distorting and omitting its history. Dr. Winston Van Horne coined the term *Africology*, which was proposed as a new name for the discipline of Black Studies at a University of Wisconsin Symposium on African American Studies. Dr. Clenora Hudson-Weems (1987), coined the term *Africana Womanism*, earlier called Black Womanism, in the mid 1980s, which she defined as "an ideology created and designed for all women of African descent. It is grounded in African culture, and therefore, it necessarily focuses on the unique experiences, struggles, needs, and desires of Africana women" (20-22).

Prior to December 18, 1996, not too many people had heard of the term *Ebonics*. On that date, the Oakland California School Board passed a resolution legitimizing *Ebonics* as a language to be used as a bridge to teach Standard English. The school board's decision created a firestorm of controversy. Following the resolution, there was, however, a disturbing rush to judgment on the merits of *Ebonics*. The media's negative spin on *Ebonics* created many misconceptions about the term.

The issue in the school board's decision was not whether *Ebonics* qualified as a legitimate language but whether Black children were getting the education they deserved. Because evidence suggested they were not, the school system faced a crisis; 53 percent of the students in the Oakland school district were Black. Their mean grade point average was 1.8 (D plus) and a disproportionate number of students in special education classes was Black (71 percent); 64 percent of the students retained were African American. 80 percent of all suspended students were African American. In addition, almost 20 percent of the Black students who reached the twelfth grade did not graduate. Combining these statistics with the fact that sixty-one percent of the teachers in the Oakland school district were white, one can easily see that the district faced a crisis, which the board attempted to resolve.

If *Ebonics* is not a language, then tell me what is it? Is it a dialect? Is it slang? Is it deficient speech? Is it the speech of the uneducated? There are two schools of thought on the origin of *Ebonics*: (1) the Pidgin/Creole theory and (2) the African retention theory.

First the Pidgin/Creole theory states that on the plantation, a common language by necessity emerged among the captives or the prisoners. A simplified version of the English language emerged that was defined or called the pidgin language. This language served as the lingua franca, or the language used for communication between persons of different mother tongues. Pidgin is not the native language for any of the speakers. Pidgin has no native speakers. Pidgin language is reduced in vocabulary. One theory is that pidgin language developed from the Portuguese language. Others have been unwilling to accept this version of Black language and say that these pidgins are not merely distortions of European language, but bear some resemblance to West African languages. Creole has pidgin as its source. It is the language that the children of the captives learned as their first language.

Another point is that when you superimpose a second language on the native tongue, an interesting combination occurs, and this depends on the basic structure of the native language. For example the Chinese have no "R" in their language. So they pronounce "fried rice" as "flied lice."

The second school of thought is that of the Africanist or African Retention School. Africans, in spite of whites attempting to strip away their culture, retained much of their cultural identity. Because they were isolated and segregated on the plantation, they retained their religion, philosophy, culture, folkways, beliefs, tales, and storytelling, naming practices, art, kinship, and music. How can we not be aware of the transmission of such a rich African oral tradition that kindles our communicative behavior?

From the outset the art of storytelling, song, praise-singing, myth-making, poetry was retained. The Brer Rabbit folk-tales, lullabies of Black mothers, work and blues songs of enslaved women and men laborers, street cries of vendors, spirituals, call and response sermons of Black preachers, fables, rhymes, proverbs, and healing chants – all are clear examples of an African retention.

Africanisms represent the deep structure of *Ebonics*. Many West African languages such as Ibo, Twi, Fon, Yoruba, Wolof, Fante, Mandinka, and others are relatives of *Ebonics* or Black Language. In a videotape, Smith in 1977 asserts that "Ebonics is the African American's linguistic memory of Africa applied to English words. It is the linguistic continuation of Africa in Black America." To dismiss or negate Ebonics as a legitimate language of African-descended people is to negate our universal memory of Africa.

Many whites would have us believe that the Africans arrived on this continent empty-handed: no culture, dumb, and ignorant. That is not the case. Holloway (1996) reported on the Bantus as an example of African Retention:

> Once the Bantu reached America they were able to retain much of their cultural identity. Enforced isolation of these Africans by plantation owners allowed them to retain their religion, philosophy, culture, folklore, folkways, folk beliefs, folk tales, storytelling, naming practices, home economics, arts, kinship and music. The Africanisms were shared and adopted by the various African ethnic groups of the field slave community, and they gradually developed into African American cooking (soul food), music (jazz, blues, spirituals, gospels), language, religion, philosophy, customs and arts. (17)

Several studies have suggested that the use of *Ebonics* raised standardized test and reading scores of African American children. The first study by Williams and Rivers (1975) translated (code switched) test items contained in a standardized test of basic concepts from Standard English to *Ebonics* or into a language that was familiar to the children. The results were striking. The children who scored low on the Standard English version performed exceptionally well on the *Ebonics* version. The following are two examples of how we changed the test items:

(1) Standard English: Mark the toy that is *behind* the sofa.

Ebonics: Mark the toy that is *in back of* the couch.

(2) Standard English: Point to the squirrel that is *beginning* to climb the tree.

Ebonics: Point to the squirrel that is *fixing to* climb the tree.

In another study involving the Peabody Picture Vocabulary Test, Dr. Wendell Rivers (1977) translated (code switched) items from the standard version to an *Ebonics* version. Instead of asking the child to identify a "crib" as the test item required, the child was asked to identify a "baby bed." The word crib to many African children meant a house or an apartment. With the code switching the children's IQ scores increased significantly.

What we discovered was that the standard versions contained blocking agents or noise. In many ways the Standard English version did not activate the Black children's linguistic conceptual systems. Rather, the blocking agents or noise interfered with the children's understanding of the question. This does not mean that Black children lack the capacity to process standard language. Instead, the children's linguistic intake gates were not activated by the stimulus properties of Standard English. Many African American children must be taught to code switch – to move from *Ebonics* to Standard English, just as Asian or Hispanic children must be taught to move from their native tongues to Standard English.

Dr. Savannah Young (1997) provides an excellent guide for teaching Standard English to *Ebonics*-speaking children. She provides exercises for parents and teachers and demonstrates how to help children learn Standard English.

Simpkins, Holt and Simpkins (1974) conducted an important study using *Ebonics*. They developed The Bridge Reading Program that places emphasis on initially using language skills already in the child's repertoire. Bridge is a transitional process whereby students proceed from the familiar *Ebonics* to the less familiar (Standard English). It embraces the axiom "Start where the child is." The Bridge program uses three readers to present the same story. The first story is written 100 percent in *Ebonics*, the second 50 percent in *Ebonics* and 50 percent in Standard English and the third 100% in Standard English.

Two groups (a Bridge-exposed group and a non-Bridge group) were each given different reading programs over a four-month period. At the end of the training period, they were given the Iowa Test of Basic Skills. The Bridge group showed a 6.2-month increase in their reading scores whereas the non-Bridge group reading scores increased only 1.6 months. These findings were significant. Clearly these studies demonstrate the effectiveness of recognizing and using the home language (in this case Ebonics) as a bridge to teach Standard English.

There is considerable confusion surrounding the education of African American children. We have been led to believe certain fallacies concerning the education of Black and other minority children. Further, the rising number of high school dropouts is one of the most dramatic indicators suggesting that school systems may have dual purposes for educating or mis-educating Black children. Does the American educational system have a dual purpose for Black children?

What is the purpose of American education? Is it to educate children or is it to prepare them to take their place in American society? On the one hand, the educational system is failing to educate our African American children who are disproportionately represented in special education classes. One in every four Black students enrolled in the ninth grade drops out before high school graduation. Drop-out rates for Black students are just under twice as great as for white children.

On the other hand, the educational system has not failed Black children, especially if the purpose is to prepare them to take their place in society. Schools are doing what they are supposed to do. They are organizing Black children for the purpose of taking their place in society. And they are succeeding at what they are designed to do. Thus the school systems really have not failed. They are doing a good job at preparing Black children to take their place in society – at the bottom of the rung of the economic ladder. Perhaps, it is not explicitly stated as a policy, but this is what is happening; it is de facto, existing in fact but without a policy.

A recent study suggests that Black and Hispanic elementary school children enjoy school more and have greater confidence in their own academic abilities than their white classmates. This study was written by three researchers at the University of Michigan's Center for Human Growth and Development. It challenges the popular belief that minority children's poor academic achievement is a function of low self-esteem, a lack of educational motivation, and low academic ability.

More significant are the questions the study raises about what goes wrong for these children later on, in junior high and high school. At that point, their academic performance and attitudes toward school often deteriorate markedly. Blacks and Hispanics show the largest percentages of dropouts and failure to complete high school.

Kunjufu (1986) argues that despair sets in much earlier than junior high school. He posits a "fourth grade syndrome" in which Black males, in particular, become disillusioned with school. This is a period when they begin psychologically to drop out or fall out of school. Previously bright eager young boys begin to hate school.

If our Black men and women, our Black boys and girls can become super athletes, Olympic gold medalists, they also can become super businessmen and women, doctors, professors, lawyers, accountants, rocket scientists at all the high level positions. We must demand that the educational systems develop Black scholars and Black scholar athletes. We must require more scholastic trophies in addition to the numerous athletic trophies in the halls of elementary schools and high schools.

The question concerning the education or mis-education of Blacks is explicated in a metaphor used by Professor Lani Guinier of Harvard University Law School. She points out that years ago coal miners used a canary to detect dangerous levels of methane gas present in the mines. The bird, having a more delicate respiratory system than the miners, would succumb to the gas long before the miners detected it, thereby warning the miners of the dangers of toxic substances in the mines. In a similar fashion, Blacks are more sensitive to and aware of the deficiencies in the educational system than are whites because as victims we have a keener awareness of its lethal effects.

The overrepresentation of Blacks in special education programs is a grim warning to the general population that the educational system is toxic to many Black children. Just as the canary warned the miners of toxicity in the mines, these warnings from the African American children must be heeded. Instead, the problem is being located in the vittims – the canary or the African American children rather than in the environment or in the educational system. Professor Guinier warns how we pathologize the canary and act as though the solution is to fix the canary, to fit it with a tiny gas mask, so that it can withstand the toxic atmosphere. She maintains that we must cease arguing about what is wrong with the canary and seek to remedy the conditions under which it exists and make changes in those circumstances. We must use the overrepresentation in special education classes to fix the educational system in order to eliminate the toxic effects on the Black children. Professor Guinier says that perhaps Black kids are America's canaries; their failure, their social dysfunction warns us of the toxins in the classrooms. The question is what do we do about what these Black canaries are telling us? Instead of trying to find out what is wrong with the canary or compiling statistics on the canary, we need to pay more attention to the atmospheric toxicity. The canaries have told us enough.

Now that we have entered the twenty-first century, this nation cannot afford to leave undeveloped the talents of millions of children who happen to be born different by virtue of race, language, sex, income status or mental ability. Nor can this nation ignore, under the pretense of educational excellence, the unfinished national task of offering every child – Black, Hispanic, Native American, Asian, and white – an equal chance to learn and to become a self-sufficient, and productive citizen. President Bush's policy of "No child left behind" is a clear mandate to educators.

It is my firm belief that education is a fundamental right deserving protection under the Fourteenth Amendment, which guarantees all Americans equal protection of the law. Democracy does not guarantee success but it is supposed to guarantee equal opportunity. I further believe that progress for African Americans will accelerate when we are able to build on the knowledge provided by our ancestors and pass it on to the succeeding generations. When we forget this knowledge, or when we omit this information in our educational process, or when this knowledge is distorted by either accident or design, a terrible condition is created.

Thus, as we survey the historical and current state of affair of African Americans, we notice a familiar litany of rather negative and pathological descriptions or euphemisms of African Americans. For example, for Blacks we associate words and phrases like *slavery, underprivileged, gangs, drugs, crime, unemployment, teenage pregnancy, school failure, school dropout, welfare* and, seemingly, an endless litany of euphemisms suggesting deficits and weaknesses of African Americans. I believe that when we write and infuse our educational system afrocentrically with an African-centered perspective, as advanced by Molefi Asante (1987), we will have a different group of African American children who will be eager and willing to learn.

I am suggesting a bold, new educational paradigm for our African American students. Afrocentric education is a systematic and comprehensive method of equipping our children with the proper education to effectively deal with life's problems and to meet the challenges that confront them. Afrocentric education represents a paradigm shift. And this is what we need in public schools, because too many educational systems have developed what Barker (1986) called a "paradigm paralysis" – getting stuck on a particular method, playing it safe, and refusing to look at alternative methods of teaching.

Barker (1986) provides a classic example of paradigm paralysis involving Swiss watchmakers, who in 1960, commanded approximately 65 percent of the world market in watch-making. When one of their watchmakers invented the Quartz watch, the Swiss corporate executives rejected the new paradigm because, to them, a watch without a mainspring was not a watch. Because it did not have any movable parts, it did not fit their "watch paradigm." Since the Swiss executives rejected the new paradigm and did not protect the Quartz patent, Seiko and Texas Instruments pre-empted their discovery and became world leaders in watch-making. The Swiss lost their preeminence in watch-making because they refused to change their paradigm. They were guilty of paradigm paralysis.

I firmly believe that progress will evolve from the *Ebonics* controversy and debate. I also believe that the debate gave our nation an opportunity to engage in serious discussion and dialogue that could lead to new policies and practices in teacher-education programs. The real issue remains: the academic underachievement of our African American children. It is clearly in the nation's best interest to produce African American children who can speak, read, write, and comprehend Standard English and at the same time preserve the rich cultural heritage of our people. *Ebonics* offers a means by which the end goal can be realized.

Notes

The 1990 version of the Encarta World English dictionary defines *Ebonics* as "Black Americans English considered as a language in its own right....most scholars prefer the term AAVE (African American Vernacular English)." In a recent study by Williams (2002) 92 percent of the participants were familiar with the term *Ebonics* whereas only 26 percent were familiar with AAVE.

References

Asante, M. K. *The Afrocentric Idea.* Philadelphia: Temple University Press, 1987.

Barker, J. "Discovering the Future: Business of Paradigms." Videotape, 1986.

Dillard, J. L. *Black English: Its History and Usage in the United States.* New York: Random House, 1972.

Encarta World English Dictionary. *Ebonics.* New York: St. Martin's Press, 1999.

Fasold, R. W. *Tense Marking in Black English.* Washington, D.C.: Center for Applied Linguistics, 1972.

Guinier, Lani. Quoted in William Raspberry. "Death and Incivility." *St. Louis Post-Dispatch*. Wednesday, May 27, 1998. B7.

Hill, P. L., ed. *Call and Response: The Riverside Anthology of the African American Literary Tradition*. Boston: Houghton-Mifflin, 1997.

Holloway, J.E. "The Origins of African American Culture." In *Africanisms in American Culture*, J. E. Holloway, ed. Bloomington: Indiana University Press, 1996.

Hudson-Weems, C. *Africana Womanism: Reclaiming Ourselves*. Troy, Mich.: Bedford, 1993.

Karenga, M. *Kawaida Theory: An Introductory Outline*. Inglewood, Calif.: Kawaida Publications, 1980.

_____. *Kwanzaa: Origin, Concepts, Practice*. Los Angeles: Kawaida Publications, 1976.

_____. Nguzo Saba. San Diego: Kawaida Publications, 1965.

Kunjufu, J. *Countering the Conspiracy to Destroy Black Boys*. Vol. 2. Chicago: African American Images, 1986.

Morrison, T. *Beloved*. New York: Alfred A. Knopf, 1987.

Rivers, L. W. "Black Language: A Moderator Variable in Intelligence." National Institute of Mental Health Grant 5R 01 MH 24454-03, 1977.

Simpkins, G., G. Holt and C. Simpkins. *Bridge: A Cross-Culture Reading Program*. Experimental edition. Boston: Houghton-Mifflin, 1974.

Smith, E. "Ebonics: A Threat to White Supremacy: A Presentation at the United African Movement (U.A.M.) Forum," New York.Videotape. January 22, 1997.

Stewart, W., J. C. Baratz and R. Shuy, eds. *On the Use of Negro Dialect in Teaching of Reading*. Washington, D.C.: Center for Applied Linguistics, 1969.

Van Horne, Winston. "Africology: Normative Theory." Symposium on Africology, Department of African American Studies, University of Wisconsin, Milwaukee. April 24, 1987.

Williams, R. L. "A Language Survey of African American Vernacular English, Black English and Ebonics." Unpublished manuscript, 2002.

Williams, R. L. and L. W. Rivers. "The Effects of Language on the Test Performance of Black Children." In *Ebonics: The True Language of Black Folks*, R. L. Williams, ed. St. Louis: The Institute of Black Studies, 1975.

Wright, B. "Mentacide: The Ultimate Threat to the Black Race." Unpublished manuscript, 1976.

Young, S. *A Guide to American English*. St. Louis: Miller-Young, 1997.

16

POLITICO-PSYCHOLOGICAL CONTROL AND OPPRESSION OF BLACKS THROUGH THE MEDIA

Talmadge Anderson

THE INSTITUTION OF THE AMERICAN MEDIA: NATURE, STRUCTURE AND POWER OF THE MEDIA

Media is defined here as the spoken, printed, and audiovisual means of intermediately presenting and disseminating information and images of events, occurrences, or issues to targeted groups or to mass audiences. These means in contemporary society involve newspapers, magazines, radio, movies, television, and various other technological and electronic methods. Each method constitutes a medium that produces and circulates social or political messages, which, if internalized, may affect the perception, attitude, or psyche of an individual or an entire community.

Beginning in the mid or late 1950s, the media – collectively – have emerged as the most powerful intervener and influence between government, industry, academe, and the people. While there are constitutional guarantees of freedom of speech for persons and the press, the news media and the film industry have become "artificially personified" to the extent that they may possess powers going beyond the original intent of the Constitution. The medium of television is the most powerful persuasive and pervasive information and imagery force in contemporary society. Television and its concomitant news, film, or movie programming have provoked concern and protest from various societal groups relative to a myriad of ethical and moral issues. Consequently, the news media and the popular imagery of the film or movie industry have significant political and psychological effects on societal groups, and on especially African Americans.

The mass media, primarily, is a composite of business enterprises motivated by profit and receiving their revenues from commercial sales of space and time. Each major industry segment (print media, radio, television, film) has an oligopolistic market structure effected through subsidiary, franchise, or associative arrangements. This means that each industry area of the media is composed of a few firms that control 70-80 percent of a market with smaller firms sharing the remainder. The owners and management are predominantly white American or European. Staff personnel of media organizations such as writers, correspondents, producers, and editors are predominantly well- educated and well-paid white males in their thirties and forties. The American mass media is managed and operated by a small group of people of European descent with similar socioeconomic status who control national political news and sociocultural events or agenda. They are aptly described as the "media elite."[1]

Perceptibly, those who own, manage, execute, and perform mass media functions and objectives are socially, economically, and often ethnically different from the various mass audiences they are purposed to serve as information intermediaries. The result is that media productions are politically serving the socially powerful and business interests. The majority media is too often indifferent or counterproductive to the interest and welfare of Blacks and other racial-ethnic minority populations. The American media institution is not a cultural democracy. It has not proven capable of upholding the ethics of value neutrality; of balancing information, interpretation, and analysis; or of adhering to the egalitarian principles of democracy.

All media industry areas (periodicals, radio, movies, and, especially, television) are purveyors and manipulators of news and cultural imagery to the extent that corporate profits are increased and the cultural dominance of the ruling class is sustained. The news and programming of major print media the radio and television commercial networks, and the cultural messages and imagery in movies produced by major movie studios, all have the effect of managing the minds of readers, viewers, or audiences.[2] The receivers of news, information, and cultural messages may be lulled into passivity, aroused emotionally, or recommitted to the status quo. The objective is to appease those closer to the top of the social pyramid and to have Blacks, other racial-ethnic minorities, or the lower classes conform to the will of the gatekeepers of the dominant culture, and to the interests of the political and corporate establishments.

AFRICAN AMERICANS AND THE MEDIA

Historically, Blacks have lacked significant access to employment and have not been allowed fair and equitable representation, voice, or viewpoint within the American print, electronic, and movie media. Thus, the media is not socially, culturally, or politically democratic in terms of equitable representation and fair portrayal of Black Americans. There are well over 30 million African Americans in the United States. While some studies indicate that Blacks are represented in the media to the equivalent of about three-fourths of their proportion in the population, the nature or circumstance of their appearance is predominately related to sports, entertainment, or negative social events and issues. In television, Blacks seldom appear with whites and actually interact with whites only about 2 percent of their total appearance time.[3]

Beyond crime, delinquency, and other so-called social pathologies, the vitality, creativity, relevant concerns, and activities of the Black community are not usually covered, portrayed, or reported in the media. The media have traditionally been unwilling to present the views of African Americans, which might be inconsistent with white concepts and perceptions. There is no element of the media complex that Blacks are more under-represented and misrepresented in than in the film or movie industry. Blacks are customarily cast in the roles of auxiliaries to white people. Low status, stereotypical, comic, and negative character roles for Blacks continue to prevail even through the 1990s. The crux of the matter is that there are virtually no African Americans in media decision-making positions, and only a minute number of Black media executives, managers, and producers. The result is that the media reflect white concepts and perspectives of Black life and experiences.[4]

There exists a considerable amount of literature substantiating and explicating the various characterizations of the media mentioned. However, there is a paucity of writings or research focusing on the political and psychological power of the media to socialize many Blacks into accepting or acting out the racist oppressive messages and imagery propagated and transmitted. What I am proposing here is that a person or group may be induced voluntarily to submit to the control of an "alien" society and to accept a social stigma or condition through the influence or stimulus of the media.

The theory that the media have the potential to control or manage the minds of people is not new. For example, Herbert I. Schiller introduces his book *The Mind Managers* by stating that "America's media managers create, process, refine, and preside over the circulation of images and information which determine our beliefs and attitudes and, ultimately, our behavior. When they deliberately produce messages that do not correspond to the realities of social existence, the media managers become mind managers."[5] The process constitutes a form of politico-psychological manipulation, which as served to preserve, metaphysically, the master/slave relationship between Blacks and whites since before and after the antebellum period in the United States. Generally, the media assign negative imagery and models to Black life and experience. Media production

253

and transmission of messages, imagery, or models of white omniscience and supremacy induce some Blacks voluntarily – subconsciously or consciously – to submit to social and political control, economic dependency, and oppression. Only if the unreal messages, imagery, and models are rejected and not internalized will true political and psychological liberation be achieved by Black Americans.

MEDIA SOCIALIZATION OF BLACKS: ANALYSIS, PURPOSE, AND EFFECT

Social psychology offers the most valid framework for the study of media influence and socialization power. It is concerned with the study of individual behavior in a social setting or with the influence of other people on individuals. The American media primarily represent and promote the culture and values of white Americans. It is predominantly Eurocentric in ethos, philosophy, and worldview. Racism, oppression, and the dehumanization of African/Black people are germane to the Eurocentric ethos. Consequently, the messages, imagery, and models transmitted through the media reflect, explicitly or implicitly, the attitudes, beliefs, and interests of the dominant white society. A social psychology approach would determine the degree to which African American individual or group behavior is affected by the American media.

While parents, siblings, peers, teachers, and adults are the primary socialization factors in the life of children, the media are agents of socialization for children and adults alike. The social process of the media is one of stimulus and response. The politico-psychological racial messages, imagery, and models communicated by the media may provide the stimuli that can result in negative psychological response and social consequence for Black Americans. Every society provides for and requires some form of socialization of its population. However, in a racist society certain elements of socialization function as a system of control over diverse racial-ethnic groups.[6]

The media also functions as an auxiliary to the education institution. It defines and enforces the social norms of the dominant society (whites) upon the individual and/or other racial-ethnic groups (Blacks and other oppressed minorities). Furthermore, through its racial messages, imagery, and models the media define and construct the social role, position, and pattern of behavior expected of the minority racial-ethnic individual or group. With few exceptions, the media reflect the social norms, values, and culture of white Western Euro-American culture. Through media programming, Blacks are inundated with the arts and literature, and the social and scientific achievements of white Americans and European peoples. The paucity or absence of positive Black messages, imagery, and models of achievement is intended to affirm the supremacy of white culture and values. The predominance of white aesthetic expressions induces respect for the established order, and creates within the psyche of many Blacks an attitude of political and psychological submission to the ideological myth of white cultural supremacy.

IDEOLOGICAL IMPLICATIONS AND FUNCTIONS OF THE MEDIA

Ideology embodies a set of cultural, social, economic, and political ideas for survival and for the future mental and material development of a person or group. Culture strongly influences the nature and course of an ideology. If an individual, group, or race is culturally confused and diffused, the result is a weak and disoriented ideology. The media is the most efficient and forceful reproducer and reinforcer of social, cultural, and political ideology.

Historically, Blacks have demonstrated a proclivity toward ideological weakness and divisiveness because of the formidable power of the American media to reproduce and reinforce white supremacy ideology. Without an effective counter-media measure, African Americans are inevitably afflicted with a cultural syndrome W.E.B. DuBois described as "double-consciousness... two-ness... and warring ideals..."[7] Consequently, the politico-psychological and racist nature of Euro-American ideology and media has made Blacks subject to white control and oppression.

Political and psychological control of Blacks is effected through manipulated and distorted media messages, images, and models of Black life and social reality. For example, Herman Gray points out that "In television representations of blacks, the historical realities of slavery, discrimination, and racism or the persistent struggles against domination are displaced and translated into celebrations of black middle class visibility and achievement."[8] Thus, television and the other media attempt to ideologically conceal America's racial inequality, injustice, and repression on the one hand, while publicizing or featuring Black social deviance and political marginality on the other. The media's messages support racial integration in theory, while in practice the most wretched form of separation (segregation) exists. The effect on Blacks is ideological confusion and disorientation.

The media act as a tool and accessory in the practice of ideological management, disseminating unrepresentative and distorted messages, images, and models of Blacks to the public to foster and preserve the notion of white supremacy and the status quo. However, sometimes ideological management can have contradictory effects.[9] The dominance of Eurocentric culture and images on television and in the movies has not caused all Blacks to want to emulate whites, but to counter with Afrocentric symbols and values of their own. Thus, the affirmation and fortification of Black culture are the first steps toward formulating a strong and viable ideology of Black liberation.

POLITICAL PSYCHOLOGY OF NEGATIVE MEDIA PORTRAYALS OF BLACKS

Negative media messages, imagery, and models of Blacks are purposed politically to influence public opinion, and psychologically to form group attitudes that in turn will affect behavior. The media have the capability of creating and conveying negative opinions with the effect of justifying or legitimizing prejudice and discrimination against Blacks. In the news media (television and newspapers) and in popular movies, Blacks are portrayed as drug dealers, violent offenders, thieves, failing or drop-out students, welfare recipients, disease carriers, and disease prone.

In reality, it is obvious and well documented that the greatest percentage (85 percent) of drug users are white Americans, and whites are the chief entrepreneurs in the billion-dollar illegal drug industry.[10] On a national aggregate scale, whites commit the most violent murders including psychopathic sex and child murders, and mass and serial killings. The million and billion-dollar thefts are committed by whites (white-collar crimes). On a relative basis, there are no more functional illiterates and school failures among Blacks than whites; and numerically, whites are the major recipients of government welfare payments and subsidies. Blacks are no more disease laden or prone than whites except that whites have better access to and greater means to secure health care.

Yet, invariably, in television news and documentaries, and in various print and visual media, Blacks are depicted as the principal representative models associated with all these negative or deviant acts and conditions. The American – media, intermediary, reproducer, and promulgator of much racist ideology – distort social reality for political purposes. In doing so, the media compound and reinforce racial stereotypes about Blacks causing the formation of public attitudes insupportable of equal opportunity and civil rights."[11] Blacks viewing and internalizing negative imagery of and about themselves may suffer a loss of self-esteem or they may subconsciously accept and act-out the distorted and false messages and models of the media. The media have the potential of reproducing messages, imagery, and models for hope and liberation or, conversely, for despair and oppression.

BLACK LEADERSHIP AND THE MEDIA

It is undeniable that the media play a strategic and dominant role in the selection and election of American social and political leaders. However, Black leaders and leadership roles have always been different from those of whites. Therefore, the media have been utilized by and have affected the two races in different ways during different times. During the era of slavery, the print media of the Northern abolitionists were the primary instruments for fighting for the freedom of Africans. Much of these periodicals and underground newspapers were owned and initiated by Black leaders and spokespersons of the time. However, with few exceptions, the white-dominated media have historically engaged in the defamation of true Black leaders and in the destruction of Black true leadership initiatives. Indeed, this poses the question as to what and who is a true Black leader? For history reveals and some scholars may affirm that the white media have not condemned all African Americans who have paraded as Black leaders.

Various definitions and types of leaders and leadership have been set forth in the literature. While the general definition of a leader might be one who influences the life, actions, and welfare of his or her constituents, group, or community, American racialism and racism requires a modified and more unique description of a Black leader. Black leaders have evolved out of social and protest movements for Black liberation. Therefore, the task of true Black leadership necessarily must include the disruption of order and the initiation of change. Milton D. Morris posits that "black 'leaders' traditionally have been prominent blacks who came to be recognized by blacks and whites in any of a variety of ways as spokesmen for, and on behalf of, the race."[12] This definition implies mutual Black/white criteria in Black leader or leadership determination. In fact, white perception and recognition of Black leaders are often inconsistent with those of Blacks. In contemporary society, whites commonly select and promote as African American leaders those media-popularized Black athletes and entertainers who are generally apolitical or ideologically neutral.

Furthermore, the problem with Morris' definition is that it is not in the interest of the white power establishment to recognize a true Black leader if that person is committed to disrupting the status quo, liberating the Black race, and initiating change. Consequently, whites have always sought to bestow their recognition of Black leaders on those who do not seek to significantly change the system and who can be controlled by the white establishment. Maintaining "good" race relations within the established order is the forte of white-recognized Black leaders. Daniel C. Thompson describes this typology of Black leadership as "racial diplomats."[13]

The Black masses do not or hold in high regard the racial-diplomat type of Black leader. Nevertheless, it is necessary for the white power structure to have Blacks to function as "leaders" or liaisons with the African American community. Traditionally, the media have been used to endow certain

Blacks with the image of leadership. Those with the appropriate background and compatible race-relations philosophy are given frequent space, time, and forums in the media. Because of frequent media exposure and approval of whites, these Blacks are assigned Black leadership roles and parade in the polity as Black leaders. Thus, the media have the power to create Black "leaders" without input or sanction of the Black community.

Black spokespersons are not necessarily suspect because they are courted by the media. The media can be valuable in the struggle for human equality and social justice. True Black leadership is evident in "[t] hose persons who have historically or who presently stand ready to risk their personal well-being in order to press for the liberty and uplift of Black people."[14] If this guideline for appraising African American leadership is not followed, the politico-psychological control and oppression of Blacks through the media will continue.

MEDIA EFFECT ON BLACK IDENTITY AND PERSONALITY: OBFUSCATION AND BIFURCATION OF BLACK IDENTITY

The media, especially television, have a powerful influence in the shaping of Black identity and beliefs relative to social reality. In terms of race relevance, Blacks watch television at a higher rate than whites. Since over 95 percent of the characters, actors (virtually no Black heroes or heroines), images, and culture portrayed on television and other media are white, the effect may cause serious psychological identity and self-concept problems for Blacks. The deluge of culture, social experiences, speech patterns, and physical traits peculiar to the white race presented in television or in various other media can have obfuscating or bifurcating effects on Black self and group identity, self-esteem and social reality.[15] An obfuscated identity is evident when one is confused or unclear as to one's individual or racial identity. Identity bifurcation is related to W.E.B DuBois's "dual-consciousness" theory mentioned previously.

On a cognitive individual basis, racial and group identification is essential to normal psychological functioning. Identification is a psychological phenomenon that serves to increase feelings of worth and importance by identifying with, or taking on the characteristics, values, or cultural attributes of some person or group perceived as ideal or superior. Inequitable race biases and representations incorporated in media content reinforce the myth of white supremacy. The dangers of the oppressed assuming the identification of the oppressor are clear. White political and psychological control and oppression are assured to the extent that Black individuals consciously or subconsciously renounce their African/Black identity in favor of an "alien" European/white identification.

MEDIA EFFECT ON BLACK AFRICAN PERSONALITY

The essence of this discussion is how negative or stereotypical race messages, imagery, and models of the white-dominated media can be counterproductive to the political and psychological liberation of Blacks. Specifically, this topic is an attempt to examine and question how the habits, attitudes, values, and motives of whites, which dominate the media, are implanted in the individual personalities of the African American – child and adult. The socializing tendency of the media can result in learned behaviors pertinent to and prevalent in white culture that are extrinsic and contradictory to Black social reality. For example, what influence does the media's invariable secondary, tertiary, and "minority-status" depictions of Blacks have on Black self-esteem and personality? Blacks may learn early from the superior roles of whites in the media that their employment or career advancement may be in direct relationship to their successful emulation of white personality traits. Thus, white personality or behavior is perceived to be more attractive and beneficial.[16] This often means that collective African/Black cultural and freedom objectives become subordinate to individual economic achievement. Those Blacks who, consciously or subconsciously, adopt white behavioral characteristics including speech (tonal and vernacular) and mannerisms risk becoming alienated from those in the Black community who value and maintain own-race personality traits. If and when this happens, the media may be partially blamed for contributing to the sociopolitical stratification and psychological disunity of the Black community. Without positive Black messages, imagery, and models in the media, the psychological oppression of the Black race will be perpetuated.

Extreme conscious or preconscious adoption of white cultural and behavioral traits by Blacks may be indicative of psychological misorientation, mentacide, alien-self disorder, or anti-self disorder.[17] While there is insufficient empirical research to affirm qualitatively the politico-psychological influence of the media on Blacks, the logic and probability of such a contention is irrefutable. More study and research are needed pertaining to the politics and psychology of oppression, relating not only, to the media, but also to various other dominant influences of white culture and society.

Notes

1. S. Robert Lichter, Stanley Rothman, and Linda S. Lichter, *The Media Elite* (Bethesda, M.: Adler and Adler, 1986, 21-22).

2. Herbert I. Schiller, *The Mind Managers* (Boston: Beacon Press, 1973) 8-31.

3. The literature is replete with studies substantiating these claims. See Doris A. Graber, ed., *Media Power in Politics* (Washington, D.C.: CQ Press, 1984, 119.

4. For an in-depth view of Blacks and the media, see Carolyn Martindale, *The White Press and Black America* (Westport, Conn.: Greenwood Press, 1986), and Bernard Rubin, ed., *Small Voices and Great Trumt)ets: Minorities and the Media* (New York: Praeger Publishers, 1980).

5. Schiller, *The Mind Managers*, p. 1.

6. Some of the social psychology theory presented here has been adapted from Fillmore H. Sanford, *Psycholociv* (Belmont, Calif. Wadsworth Publishing, 1965), and from Richard R. Bootzin et al, *Psychology Today* (New York: Random House, 1983).

7. W.E.B. DuBois, *The Souls of Black Folk* (New York: Signet Classic, the New American Library, 1969), 45.

8. Herman Gray, "Television, Black Americans, and the American Dream," *Critical Studies in Mass Communication* 6 (1989): 378.

9. For a discussion of the limitations of ideological management, see Joel Spring, *Images of American Life* (New York: State University of New York Press, 1992), 263-64.

10. Numerous reports verify the higher percentage of white drug users and major drug entrepreneurs. See Sam Meddis, "Drug Arrest Rate Higher for Blacks," *USA Today,* 20, December 1989, A-1.

11. Any student of media criticism should read Teun A. Van Dijk, *Racism and the Press* (London: Routledge, 1991).

12. Milton D. Morris, *The Politics of Black America* (New York: Harper and Row, 1975), 285.

13. Daniel C. Thompson, *The Negro Leadership) Class* (Englewood Cliffs, N.J.: Prentice-Hall, 1963), 68-70.

14. Talmadge Anderson, *Introduction to African American Studies* (Dubuque, Iowa: Kendall/Hunt Publishing, 1993), 209.

15. See Richard L. Allen and Shirley Hatchett, "The Media and Social Reality Effects: Self and System Orientation of Blacks," *Communications Research*, 13, 1 (January 1986): 97-123.

16. For a look at a Black personality evaluative instrument, see Joseph A. Baldwin and Yvonne R. Bell, "The African Self-Consciousness Scale: An Af ricentric Personality Questionnaire," *The Western Journal of Black Studies* 9.2 (summer 1985):61-68. Further related to the theory of personality adoption and oppression is the book by Franz Fanon, *Black Skin, White Masks* (New York: Grove Press, 1967).

17. Daudi Ajani ya Azibo, "African-Centered Theses on Mental Health and a Nosology of Black/African Personality Disorder," *The Journal of Black Psychology 15.2* (spring 1989): 173-214.

17

FROM AFRICA TO AFROCENTRIC INNOVATIONS SOME CALL "JAZZ"

Karlton Edward Hester

AFROCENTRIC ORIGINS OF "JAZZ"

Music, dance, and visual arts remain reliable means through which Africans communicate with God, perpetuate their sociocultural history, and harmonize with nature. In America, music inherited a dominant role in nurturing spiritual, intellectual, and philosophical aspects of African culture for displaced people in a hostile environment. Throughout the history of America, the impact of African American music has gradually affected all who managed to shed their cultural biases long enough to witness the evolution of its innovative beauty, grandeur, and cultural significance. It is small wonder, therefore, that so many people in the world now want to claim African American music as their own.

It is important to examine the African past carefully if we are to recognize the elements of African tradition that lie at the foundation of African American music and culture. Avoiding Afrocentric perspectives in discussions of the development of American culture only postpones the inevitable serious study of the music some call "jazz." Just as we examine European music from European antiquity to the present, we must study the complete history of African American music. Since African culture is much older, and more obscure to Western readers, the task of surveying the history of the vast African continent is formidable. In this study we can only manage to scratch the surface.

The Afrocentric innovations that some call "jazz" are now recognized as classic American music and as an American treasure. This music, the invention of Africans in America under the pressures and limitations of an oppressive society, is America's premier indigenous art form. Tracing the history of African American music carefully from African roots to the present leads to the discovery of the point at which "jazz" evolved from the categories of "Nigger music" and "race records" to the more lofty status of an American art form. It also forces the question, Can "jazz" be referred to as "American" music when the people who created it were not recognized unconditionally as American (as opposed to African American)?

The diversity of languages, sociocultural customs, religious practices, political structures, and metaphysical systems among the numerous African nations served to undermine possibilities of unification among those who later became captive "New World" slaves, especially within the regions that eventually became the United States of America. An extremely eclectic culture was apparent even within the small radius of the Gulf of Guinea, the region from which most slaves were obtained by means of bargaining or larceny. Some areas of Africa remained untouched by slave traders. Other northern countries (particularly desert areas such as Egypt) contributed only a few slaves. The difficulties in communicating between fellow Africans, as well as the weak communication between Africans and Europeans, made it difficult for Africans to appreciate and anticipate the severe consequences of the malfeasance that fell upon their continent. To the foreign European slave traders, the social and cultural diversity within African society was interpreted as uncivilized, disorganized, and backward.

In 1990, CBS Records released an album by the controversial, and highly popular, rap artists Public Enemy entitled *Fear of a Black Planet*. The media reprimanded the group for its "explicit lyrics," perhaps because the clarity, precision, and unreserved nature of the artists' Afrocentric perspective is exactly the thing that America labored arduously to suppress for centuries. Clearly the Public Enemy artists, like many other African American citizens, wonder to which "good old days" in the incessant history of slavery and oppression European Americans often refer when attempting to thwart social progress in America.

The development of the notion of European supremacy and the perpetuation of a slave culture required the destruction of the history of African people. Oppression required an attempt at the total repression of the minds, bodies, and spirits of not only those captives imported from Africa as hard laborers, but also those forced to live under the countless lies, delusions, and psychological baggage that also enslaved European American society. Slave-era mentality remained a dominant force in American culture while "jazz" and other African American music evolved. African American music becomes distorted or obscured if divorced of its African heritage. The melodies, harmonies, timbres, textures, and formal construction of traditional African music are all elements that African American music has retained in various form of the music labeled "jazz," blues and spirituals.

African Americans, Native Americans, and other victims of colonial conquest were forced to abandon their indigenous religions and adopt Christianity. Paradoxically, African Americans used this same religion – intended to pacify and subdue them – as one of their primary tools for liberation. Similarly, when the drums were taken away from Africans in America (and African music forbidden) to further annihilate tribal, familial, and sociocultural structure, African polyrhythms were transformed into a new brand of stylistic syncopation unlike any rhythms the world had ever known. Africans forced to sing European hymns did not merely fuse African and European music. European hymns were subjected to an extraordinary fissional process that combined a multiplicity of musical elements and social convergence, experienced by Africans in America, into a socio-nuclear reactor producing billions of musical "electron volts." "Jazz" was the most electrifying result of this experimentation. Not only were the musical elements and concepts novel, but the composers of twentieth-century "jazz" were more fluent in the performance practice of their musical language than most other twentieth-century composers. European twelve-tone and serial composers created exciting new musical concepts and languages, but few could improvise with their new vocabularies the way most baroque, classical, and romantic composers did during their respective eras.

This investigation involves the historical legacy of musical development that evolved from traditional African music and emerged into the African American innovations labeled "jazz." It is not intended to deny or diminish the participation and contributions of people of European, Hispanic, Asian, Native American, or other descent in the history of African American music. All modern art forms are influenced by numerous ancient determinants from the global community. Consequently, as Henry Wadsworth Longfellow said, "Music is the international language of all mankind." Nonetheless, particular art forms evolve from cultural traditions, patterns, and dialects that determine the shapes, colors, and styles of a given artistic manifestation. We cannot confine "jazz," one of the world's most ecumenical and influential musical genres, to a color like black, brown, red, white, or any other hue or ethnicity. It most certainly does have a specific cultural origin, however, and the African American innovators responsible for its evolutionary development are the focus of this study.

People say that defining "jazz" is a difficult task. Without a doubt, the music some call "jazz" is an African American invention evolved in the musical world essentially during the twentieth century. Its evolution from traditional African music into an array of related forms involves African American field hollers, spirituals, blues, ragtime, classic "jazz," swing, rhythm and blues, bebop, cool, hard bop, free "jazz," funk, soul, fusion, neo-classic "jazz," and rap music. Each new African American musical invention retains elements of traditional African music. It will certainly continue to evolve and retain Afrocentric musical vocabulary in the next millennium.

A clear relationship exists between the African American use of "blue notes" and similar traditional African stylistic elements in music such as the traditional Fulani song "Nayo" (as sung by Juldeh Camara). Within the context of some African songs we hear emphasis on a pentatonic scale embellished with a flexibility of pitch. These qualities were conspicuous characteristics of early rural blues. Certain Baoulé traditional songs demonstrate a pitch set that has much in common with rural blues tonality. Qualities identifiable with African American swing "feel" and "riff" technique, as well as the use of ostinato patterns as grounding structures for polyrhythms and heterophony, have parallels in Malinké and other African music from south of the Sahara. A comparison between "All Blues" by Miles Davis with the bass pattern heard in the Malinké "Dance of the Hunters" displays striking resemblance. The blue notes, call-and-response patterns, and other musical elements and devices found in blues and "jazz" are also apparent in various traditional musical forms throughout the African continent. African music is often directly associated with dance and the multidimensional effect in most performance presentations.

The inclinations toward blue notes in African music were difficult for Europeans and European Americans to understand before they were exposed to African American blues. The ability of tonal systems to support both the major and the minor third within a single chord of a given key baffled Europeans when they first heard it in Africa. The frequent employment of the unresolved tritone (interval composed of three whole steps) in African music (also a prominent characteristic of African American "jazz") made African music sound dissonant to the European ear. Likewise, the structuring of musical intonation along flexible lines of tuning aligned with the natural harmonics of vibrating objects (tube, string, wooden or metal bar, and so on) stood in opposition to the even temperament of the European piano. A European American missionary arrogantly reports:

But it is surprising that – since our scales are new to them – they at first need a little careful training, or at least the lead of a clear-toned organ reasonably played? Otherwise they are not unlikely to substitute the tones of their own scales. The result is indescribable. Imagine a large congregation singing the doxology with all their might, and about half of them singing G minor instead of G major! But the comparison is inadequate. The singing in some mission congregations is enough to cause a panic (Milligan, 78).

The blues introduced a harmonic orientation based on an Afrocentric attitude regarding tonal resolution (unstable dominant seventh chords became stable harmonically) and the verticalization associated melodic anomalies. Later, bebop masters heard more involved implications inherent in older blues forms and explored the upper regions of the harmonic series to justify harmonic expansion. Rural blues was not originally the 12-bar standardized type that was popularized later. The rural blues players invented their own personal forms, refusing to be restricted to standard 4/4 (or any other) meter, choosing instead to treat meter in a flexible manner as well. Lightnin' Hopkins singing Willie Dixon's song "My Babe" (either live or on studio recordings) is a case in point:

> My Baby don't stand no cheating, my Babe. [circa 4 bars]
> My Baby don't stand no cheating, my Babe. [circa 4 bars]
> My Baby don't stand no cheating, no back-talking or midnight creepin', [circa 4 bars]
> My Babe... two little children by My Babe... don't let me catch you with
> My Babe.... etc. [circa 5-6 bars]

A connection with sacrosanct or the more ethereal essences of music can be traced through Bantu rain songs, African American work songs, sea shanties, ring shouts, spirituals, blues, and other Afrocentric musical forms. Relationships between sacred and secular music and art are evident whether you are observing presentations of the *pokot* witch doctor of Kenya (who draws evil spirits out of patients in the *liakat* ritual) or listening to Lightnin' Hopkins (who reminds us that the "Blues Is a Feeling" on *Mojo Hand: The Lightnin Hopkins Anthology*) and other African American blues singers. The close harmonic, melodic, and rhythmic kinship between blues and spirituals is an indication of the bond that joins these forms.

Recordings of voodoo ceremonies in Haiti are good examples of interdisciplinary Afrocentric celebration and African retention in the "New World" regions where Africans were not completely denied their African heritage. Music for such spiritual occasions resembles traditional African ceremonial sources more closely than any African American musical style. Nonetheless, the music of "jazz" artists such as Sun Ra, the Art Ensemble of Chicago, and other modern innovators embrace African tradition and are strongly influenced by African music and culture.

A student once asked, "Isn't most of society naturally inclined toward tonal music because it is a natural musical phenomenon to which we grow up listening; and avant-garde music apparently opposes this (sonic) orientation?" This question has some merit, but it reveals what is often a Western indoctrination, that presupposing that Eurocentric orientation is pandemic and "natural" for all of world society. An early twentieth-century book (a part of the Schomburg collection) containing discussions on musical practices in Central Africa shows elements of the European American bigotry, fascination, and ambivalence that many people carried with them throughout Africa.

The native songs are elementary but fascinating. Few white men, however, can sing them; for the scales, or tone-systems, upon which most of them are based, are entirely different from our major and minor modes. Their scales have not a distinct tonic, that is, a basal tone from which the others in the system are derived, as, for instance, the first tone, do, of our major scale. It follows that the cadences of their music are not clearly defined; or, as a friend of mine would say, "They don't taper off to an end like ours" (Milligan, 78).

Every analysis Robert Milligan made regarding African music tends to assume an Eurocentric aesthetic musical model as the supreme standard. Typically, he makes little effort to discover whether African musicians organized their music around an array of fundamental tones that might have evaded his ear. Yet, he admits, "although their music is so difficult for the white man, the natives learn our music with astonishing ease, even their oldest men and women, and sing it well – if they have half a chance" (Milligan, 78).

Technically speaking, placing the musical focal point on the lower portion of the harmonic series (musical intervals including the tonic, octave, fifth, fourth, and major and minor third) is no more natural than the modern emphasis on the upper intervals of the same series (namely, major and minor seconds, quarter tones, and so on). African music, and later many African American counterparts, have preferred to include a wide range of intervalic, timbral, and rhythmic possibilities. This too is a very natural inclination, though many Westerners initially considered such musical choices as chaotic or dissonant. Understanding the relationship between those stylistic inclinations shared between African and African American culture is key to developing a knowledgeable appreciation for the Afrocentric innovations labeled "jazz." A thorough and systematic sociocultural journey, from the dawn of African culture through early African American music, is necessary to expose the Afrocentric roots of "jazz."

Despite Milligan's difficulties, he spent enough time in Africa to gain an awareness of the close relationship between African and African American music:

So great a musician as Dvorak, when he came to America, was pro-foundly moved by the original melodies of the American Negro, and became their enthusiastic champion. Indeed, they inspired the most beautiful of all his symphonies, the one entitled, "Aus der Neuen Welt." I do not refer, of course, to the so-called Negro melodies composed by white men. Some of these are beautiful; but they are not Negro melodies. They do not express the Negro's emotional life and he does not care much for them. Those wonderful songs of the Fisk Jubilee Singers are the real thing. Some of the very melodies may have originated in Africa. Others are more developed than any that I heard in Africa; but they are very similar, and they use the same strange scales, which makes them unfamiliar to our ears and difficult to acquire. Among them, I really believe, are occasional motifs as capable of development as those of Hungary.

For a long time the music of Africa defied every attempt on my part to reduce it to musical notation. Very few persons have made the attempt; for it is easier to reduce their language to writing than their music. At first it seemed as inarticulate and spontaneous as the sound of the distant surf with which it blended, or the music of the night-wind in the bamboo (Milligan, 79).

What are other distinguishing features of this music with African roots? In addressing an audience at the African Heritage Studies Association's 30th Annual Conference (March 1998), Dr. Clenora Hudson-Weems of the University of Missouri-Columbia suggested that the most conspicuous difference between most Eurocentric and Afrocentric literary approaches is that the former emphasizes form while the latter prefers to focus on content. Regarding Afrocentric literature, Hudson-Weems implies that structure is better determined if extracted from content, and that form itself is not fascinating as an empty package alone.

Transferring this theory to the analysis of music, I find a similar tendency among Eurocentric theorists and musicologists to emphasize the analysis of musical forms and formulas. Central to their investigations, for example, we find the examination of music based on the sonata form, the application of Schenkerian and other forms of musical analysis, the tracing of the Golden Section (also known as Golden Mean, Golden Ratio), the cataloguing of materials, or the search for tonal coherence. Afrocentric discussions more often attend to personal styles, musical anomalies, virtuosity, and elusive elements such as spiritual or aesthetic concerns. The two approaches are certainly not mutually exclusive, but the different emphases may reflect aspects of cultural orientation.

Analysis can often help our understanding of a musical subject, but usually only if the system of analysis is derived from the music under investigation. Western analysis generally involves tearing the subject apart without regard for a particular creative goal. At the conclusion of the analysis of music, for instance, often little is produced other than catalogues of rhythms, scales, chords, and cadential formulas. Once isolated, these elements are like the brushes, paints, canvasses, and colors used to produce a beautiful painting: isolated ingredients used in the production of art that tell little of the power and beauty produced from the wellsprings of artistic imagination. Music involves the direct transference of human emotions and thought through sonic images. Musical meaning remains beyond the reach of words. Therefore, we often look to the environment upon which artists reflect to find greater appreciation and understanding of their music.

Many African American "jazz" artists insist that a spiritual orientation is the foundation of their music. As their titles and comments often suggest, some African American innovators and practitioners insist that their musical expression is inseparable from African American spirituals, gospel, and other religious music.

Dean C. J. Bartlett and the Reverend John S. Yaryan invited Ellington to present a concert of sacred music in Grace Cathedral San Francisco. A review of the September 16, 1965, concert in the *Saturday Review* entitled "The Ecumenical Ellington" stated: "These were musicians offering what they did best – better than any others in the world – to the glory of God." Hundreds of newspapers across America carried a UPI report of the concert under the headline "Duke Ellington Talked to the Lord in Grace Cathedral Last Night." Ellington discussed his attempts to "see God" in his autobiography:

If you can see by seven caroms to the seventh power, then you can see God. If you could see total carom, to total power, you would be thought of as God. And since you can't do either, you are not God, and you cannot stand to see God, but if you happen to be the greatest mathematician, you will discover after completing carom that God is here with you. So be wise and satisfied with the joy that comes to you through the reflection and miracle of God, such as all the wonders and beauty we live with and are exposed to on earth.

There have been times when I thought I had a glimpse of God. Sometimes, even when my eyes were closed, I saw. Then when I tried to set my eyes – closed or opened – back to the same focus, I had no success, of course. The unprovable fact is that I believe I have had a glimpse of God many times. I believe because believing is believable, and no one can prove it unbelievable (Ellington, 260).

In addition to the bond between sacred and secular dimensions, African American art forms tend to remain inseparable. Albert Murray considers the sounds contained in music of composers like Ellington onomatopoetic renderings that reflect the dialect, motion, and styles of African American culture. Ellington was a modernist who developed a rich vernacular African American compositional language (in collaboration with the creative members of his orchestra) capable of orchestral variety and excitement that remains inimitable. With Ellington and other masters of African American music in mind, Albert Murray's literature uses "jazz" and blues as a model. The works of visual artist Romare Bearden (1912-1988) were also heavily influenced by "jazz" and blues (*Jazz Village, At the Savoy, Fancy Sticks, In E Sharp*, and so on). Bearden leads the viewer through a prism of his ideas and perspectives with vivid color and textures. His subjects involve collages that create rhythm and form that reflect his childhood in Harlem during the Harlem Renaissance. Fats Waller, Ellington, and other well-known artists visited Bearden's home frequently during their childhood.

Denying Africans in America direct access to past traditions forced them to become the most culturally free people in the world. While American composers continued to express their creative ideas through Eurocentric musical language, they could not expect to achieve a high degree of affinity with an indigenous American musical language. Ellington's musical dedications to Harlem, on the other hand, contain the power, subtlety, elegance, pain, complexity, intensity, and emotion found within that community during the first half of the century. No composer could produce such vivid American imagery without engaging both African American and European American culture directly the way Ellington managed. Albert Murray suggests that most Americans preferred attempts at building European edifices, social constructs, and cultural emulation on the American landscape. It is easy to distinguish between music that reflects original cultural patterns created by people of a given cultural milieu music that is created through imitation of stylistic innovations from the fringe of a culture and other such derivative products.

Those musicians and music scholars who refuse to seriously consider the importance of African American music enter into debates over where to find a definitive American Music. At a lecture at Cornell University, when composer Lucas Foss mentioned that he abandoned improvisation because he could not master it, a student in the audience asked the appropriate question: Why didn't [Foss] study with any of the countless number of African American "jazz" masters in New York City? Albert Murray discusses the significance of African American blues and "jazz":

And anybody who introduces even the sleeping bag sequence in *For Whom the Bell Tolls* as evidence that Hemingway was out to reduce the world to the gratification of the sex urge would be as intellectually irrespon-sible as those who describe so-called black Africans as childlike, simple creatures of sensual abandon. An outsider – say, a blonde from the jet set – who comes into a down-home-style hall and pulls off her shoes, lets her hair down, and begins stomping and shaking and jerking and grinding in the spirit of personal release, liberation, and abandon, does not represent freedom; she represents chaos, and only an outsider would do it. Only an outsider could be so irresponsible to the music. Insiders know that the music and dance, like all other artistic expression, require a commitment to form. As is the case with all other artistic expression, they achieve freedom not by giving in to the emotions but through self-control and refinement of technique. Swinging the blues and swinging to the blues, however free they may seem to the uninitiated listener and onlooker, are never acts of wild abandon; they are triumphs of technical refinement and are among the most sophisticated things a human being can do (Murray, 206).

Many contemporary "Young Lions" and other artists reconstruct musical images from the past, while neglecting the relevance of their own rich contemporary environmental contexts. The best of these Young Lions, performing music that shadows bygone eras, enjoy popularity. African American innovators, however, remain ostracized from the mainstream music industry. Younger players do not have a thriving music community like Ellington's Harlem from which to absorb and paint as music composi-tions. "Jazz" programs at most universities in America generally employ European American faculty, ignoring the potentially rich educational resources that the former members of bands led by Ellington, Count Basie, and other seminal African American ensembles could provide. Although many African Americans died fighting for their country during two world wars, music innovators such as Charlie Parker, Dizzy Gillespie, Miles Davis, Ornette Coleman, and John Coltrane, were never among those musicians employed by American universities and symphony orchestras. American society lost a great deal, as a consequence, when African Ameri-can artists could not share their skills and musical knowledge and could not be honored as eminent American composers. Thus young students are denied direct exposure to the process of musical experimentation, inno-vation, and mentoring enjoyed by earlier developing musicians. Most African American musicians today learn a significant amount of their music through recordings alone, or within Eurocentric studies at conserva-tories and university music departments.

EUROCENTRIC DOCUMENTATION AND CONTROL OF AFRICAN AMERICAN MUSIC

People on the fringe of the progenitors' culture generally define African American creative expression. This condition stems from the hegemony of Eurocentric discrimination. The contemporary African American community is less a victim of slave mentality and oppression than in the past, yet problems related to the exploitation of African American music continue to intensify. The recent reduction of African American "jazz" to "neoclassic" imitation by talented African American musicians is telling. Clearly a movement driven more by business capital than revolutionary artistic motivation, the music of recent decades stands in striking opposition to the legacy of evolutionary experimentation and innovations of earlier years.

During the era of slave exploitation, language and culture were manipulated to erase African heritage from the minds of Africans in the Americas and to promote negative images of things associated with Africa. Terms such as "jazz," "serious music," "race records," and other politically charged labels perpetuate social notions that foster racial division and economic control. According to many labeling practices in American society, African Americans produce "popular" music regardless of the actual level of popularity enjoyed by a given style, or despite degrees of musical sophistication and complexity involved. This "popularity," consequently, erodes the music's credibility and deems it unworthy of institutional support or serious study. Only European or certain European American music is "serious" music. Labels change as needed, however. The increased popularity and prestige of "jazz" finally brings forth the modern phrases "vernacular American music" and "America's classical music." Some innovators in America prefer to find their own labels, such as the Art Ensemble of Chicago's "Great Black Music" or, as Makanda Ken McIntyre puts it, simply "African American music":

> The indigenous music of America is not "jazz," but rather it is music in the African and American tradition since the elements that make up the music come from the African slave and the European. The African Slave brought rhythm, timbre and melody; and integrated them with the European instruments and the twelve tones that make up Western European music. Hence, we have African American music.

Not that the African slave in America did not have instruments, but rather, they were taken away-unlike slavery in the Caribbean, where the slaves were allowed to keep their instruments. Consequently, the connection with Africa is more direct, since the vast majority of musical instruments utilized in the Caribbean are built similar to West African instruments.

Duke Ellington never liked the term "jazz" but acquiesced at times for the sake of clarity. Ellington felt that "jazz is based on the sound of our native heritage. It is an American idiom with African roots – a trunk of soul with limbs reaching in every direction, to the frigid North, the exotic East, the miserable, swampy South, and the Swinging West" (Ellington, 436). When elements of African American music are freely employed, they are often paradoxically described as too complex, too simplistic, chaotic, or excessive. On the other hand, baroque polyphony is considered ingenious because it conforms to a complex, systematic, Eurocentric musical logic. With each new generation, nonetheless, the understanding of ecumenical musical principles evolves, and a gradual softening of social bigotry takes place. Ellington realized many years ago that this brings an ever-increasing number of serious music students and new listeners to study "jazz."

> Yet I have reason to be optimistic, for with all those good musicians graduating from the conservatories, the future has got to be bright. Of course, the same people who say they don't like electrically amplified guitar and basses will often add that they "just love a string section." The basic concern should not be the instrumentation, but the taste and skill of the person who plays it.... The American listening audience is actually growing more mature every day. I believe the brainwashing will soon subside, because all the brainwashers have become wealthy. Their problem now is that their children, too, have been brainwashed. (Ellington, 410)

Much of the labeling and documentation of "jazz" is done by people with little musical training or understanding of "Black" culture. If those who make decisions regarding the documentation, dissemination, and artistic status of "jazz" were required to pass through Afrocentric musical training, a new governing hierarchy would be established. The progenitors of innovative African American music might then be regarded as those best qualified to define and control their art form. Miles Davis's remark regarding the comment of a woman in the audience at one of his performances is clear and appropriate. The listener complained she couldn't understand Davis's music; Davis's sagacious reply – "It took me twenty years study and practice to work up to what I wanted to play in this performance. How can she expect to listen five minutes and understand it?" (Ellington, 244). Ethnomusicologists stopped referring to African polyrhythms as chaotic cacophony and simplistic only after beginning to transcribe African music: their transcriptions revealed levels of rhythmic complexity and metrical organization transcending the rhythmic concepts of Eurocentric composers. Andrew White was the first theorist/musician to transcribe all of Coltrane's solos, exposing their richness and complexity (to the embarrassment of those who claimed Coltrane was playing strains of "meaningless notes"). Most of those who transcribe "jazz" extract a single instrument and write out portions of that part in standard Eurocentric notation. More challenging and adventurous performances of African American masters are rarely subjected to total transcription. Total transcription, of all instrumental or vocal parts involved in a composition, would be the starting point for serious theoretical study of "jazz." Rarely do theorists transcribe entire compositions such as Ornette Coleman's "Free Jazz," John Coltrane's "Ascension," Cecil Taylor's "Unit Structures," or Sun Ra's "Of the Other Tomorrow."

The problems that surround the documentation of African American music are complex. Anthony Braxton discusses some aspects of the problems rooted in the African American community in Graham Lock's *Forces in Motion*:

> Here we are, you and I, sitting in this room because you're interested enough in my music to do the book. So OK, that's great. For those African American intellectuals who look at this book and say, "Well Graham Lock is white."... Ted Joans, for instance, put down Ross Russell for *Bird Lives* – that was ten years ago, we're still waiting for Mr. Joans's book! I can name – I won't do it, but I could – fifteen African American intellectuals, so-called, who would protest to heights if they see an article or a book on Benny Carter, say, written by a white American intellectual. They would cry out – and rightfully – that a black guy could have written this too. OK, but where are these people? I see only a handful of African Americans at my concerts – well, Braxton's the so-called White Negro, I'm not a good example – but I don't see many at Art Ensemble's concerts, I don't see many at Dexter Gordon's concerts. Are we gonna blame this on white people too? (Lock, 276-77)

Braxton later acknowledges, "Dr. Yosef ben-Jochannan: this is an African American intellectual who is like a shining tower in an ocean of despair, an ocean of negligence." Curiously, Braxton fails to mention that African American authors are less likely to find publishers eager to publish their controversial manuscripts. He also ignores the literary and theoretical contributions of Alain Locke, Amiri Baraka, Bill Cole, Eddie Harris, Wendell Logan, Albert Murray, Andrew White, George Russell, David Baker, and other African American musicians and scholars. Many musicians would prefer to write about their music themselves. Unfortunately,

Louis Armstrong, Duke Ellington, Charles Mingus, and Miles Davis are among the few African American master musicians who were able to get their autobiographies published. Nevertheless, Braxton is accurate in pointing out the scarcity of African American listeners found at "Black jazz" concerts.

European theorists and musicologists write most European music history and theoretical analysis. Social context is often an important element of such studies. Histories of Jewish music during World War II benefit from ample descriptions of the horrible social and political circumstances surrounding the artistic production in Germany under the Nazi regime. Historical research that avoided mentioning the intense brutality and genocide of the time would be poor and insensitive indeed. People may well feel that such histories are better told by qualified Jews than by Aryan Germans. A related set of considerations must be applied to African American music scholarship and theory.

Jehoash Hirshberg's *Music in the Jewish Community of Palestine 1880-1948* presents a social history that begins with the Jewish immigration to Palestine and ends with the declaration of the state of Israel. Hirshberg discusses the lives of Jewish musicians in the context of two world wars, local skirmishes, and a full-scale national war, then considers the effect that waves of immigrants and refugees had on the development of Jewish music in Palestine. Few would criticize such comprehensive and candid research as polemic. Yet writers often consider frank Afrocentric viewpoints "disturbed and disturbing," as Gene Lees describes *Miles: The Autobiography*. There are those who seem to view any frank Afrocentric position as polemic. The difference in perception is difficult to reconcile.

Although many of the progenitors of the African American music some call "jazz" have always considered that label for their music derogatory, it becomes increasingly clear that artists have little control over the labeling, presentation, documentation, and dissemination of their work. Christopher Harlos feels this is why African American musicians have wanted to write autobiographies, in order to define their music themselves.

One motivation behind the jazz player's move to autobiography, for example, is signaled in the opening of *Treat it Gentle* where Sidney Bechet states flatly, "You know there's people, they got the wrong idea of Jazz," and then a few pages later he asserts it was only "a name white people have given to the music." Likewise, in *Music Is My Mistress*, Duke Ellington makes a point of the fact that he was disinclined to use the term "jazz" as a way of classifying his own musical endeavors (Harlos, 134).

People did not apply the label "America's Classical Music" to African American music during the eras in which the music of Scott Joplin, Buddy Bolden, Louis Armstrong, Fats Waller, Jelly Roll Morton, Art Tatum, Fletcher Henderson, Duke Ellington, or Count Basie evolved. Those referred to as "Black," "white," "Asian," "Indians," "Hispanic," "Africans," "Europeans," and so on, have composed and performed twentieth-century African American music. Unfortunately, there are no people referred to as simply Americans in the United States. Is "jazz" becoming a catalyst for the long overdue transformation of this unfortunate social tradition? How has American society come to produce vernacular American music?

If the system used to label citizens is a strong indicator, then there is little chance of creating legitimate vernacular American music in the twentieth century. French composers may compose French music; Japanese composers compose Japanese music; Russian composers compose Russian music. Alexander Pushkin did not produce Afro-Russian literature. But who are the creators of native American music? There are only Native Americans ("Red"), African Americans ("Black"), European Americans ("white"), Hispanic Americans ("brown"), Asian Americans ("yellow"), biracial Americans (here we run into serious problems with colorful labels!), and other such people. There is no category on employment or college applications for anyone who is just "American". Since African Americans are the creators of blues, spirituals, "jazz," and other "race" music, why is the music produced by African American innovators referred to as American music? This does not occur with Latin "jazz" (even when performed by Pamela Wise, an African American), European American country music (when performed by Charlie Pride, an African American), or Jewish klezmer music (in the hands of Don Byron, an African American) in America.

In a country that has often asserted that African Americans have contributed little to American culture, should labeling "jazz" American Classical Music arouse skepticism, suspicion, and trepidation? Will African American innovators and music scholars finally enjoy appropriate equity and economic benefits commensurate to their European American musical colleagues? If so, this change should be reflected in a new attitude toward the performance and preservation of African American music. The conventional terms used by European American industries to identify African American music thus remain severely flawed, as McIntyre suggests in the liner notes to his recording *Home*:

> There have been volumes written about "jazz" and the word/term has become synonymous with the music created in America. I have problems with accepting the term "jazz" as the title of the

music since the creators of the music did not title the music,
but rather it was the writer F. Scott Fitzgerald who coined the
phrase which has become the box for the music created by the
African slave in America. Moreover, the term "jazz" was part
of the African American vernacular, however, the meaning had
nothing to do with music, but it did relate to sex. In fact the
definition of the word during the first and second decades of the
twentieth century was to copulate.

The term is rather nebulous regarding its heritage. Moreover, it raises
questions. For example, What is "jazz"? Are there "jazz" people? Where
do they come from? Where did it originate? Who were the creators? What
caused it to happen? Is it racial or is it national? Unquestionably, the questions can never be answered by someone who has the ability to manipulate the language. But when one is seeking logical answers, the questions
become unanswerable.[8]

The music once sold on "race records" is now a slightly more cherished commodity locally and abroad and is recognized as America's only
indigenous art form. One of the consequences of the small measure of
success "jazz" and other African American musics now enjoy is the fight
over whether the "jazz" art form is community property.

The function and purpose of many general labels used to identify cultural components, social artifacts, and other aspects of our environment,
remain fairly unchanged. Such terms are often geared toward justifying
actions, maintaining control, and perpetuating prevailing political agenda.
It could be argued, for example, that under the cloak of the terms war, religion, and slavery, "New World" men have killed and raped more people,
stolen more property ("from sea to shining sea"), and altered or suppressed
more information than any other people since antiquity. Propaganda disseminated by black-faced minstrels of the nineteenth century, who promoted racial stereotypes and hatred, seem now converted into media portrayals of criminal African American men or Hispanic American men, and
unwed African American or Hispanic American women. Although African
American citizens represent around 15 percent of the population in the
United States, this statistic is not reflected in any positive way in American
society. For example, well over half of the prison population is composed
of African Americans and other "minorities."[9]

Many Americans still refer to Native Americans as "Indians" although
none of the numerous tribes labeled as such ever had anything to do
with India. Just as African American musicians resigned themselves to
accept the term "jazz," some Native Americans eventually began to refer
to themselves as "Indians." Other labels invented by Europeans, such as

"Negro", "Nigger", "Colored", "Mulatto", and so on, share similar histories, political purposes, and social patterns. Labels (for music or anything
else) can serve political agendas, therefore, and are not always simply for
the purpose of organization and clarity.

THE IMPACT OF RACISM AND SEXISM

It is often difficult to approach modern issues involving residual
racism, sexism, and other social malfeasance stemming from European
colonization. The theory that "might makes right" has enabled conquering
armies to dictate the gods that people worship, the history they believe,
the marriages that are socially appropriate, and the art that is aesthetically
significant. While a dominant culture may shape fragile and temporary
historical records, it in no way changes the course of historical actuality.
Nonetheless, those who suffered the limitations and hardships of slave
– era brutality and oppression could expect punishment if they complain
about social conditions or attempt to assert perspectives that contradict
prevailing notions.

Racism is one of the primary factors that thwarts an understanding
and appreciation of African American music. Racism has been a topic of
numerous debates and articles in "jazz" publications over the years. It is a
complex topic that cannot be investigated meaningfully when Europeans
or European Americans are the sole authors and participants in such discussions.

Given the history and nature of American society, one cannot assume
that non-African Americans have documented and evaluated African
American music in an objective, knowledgeable, and equitable fashion.
Systematically institutionalized racism and sexism remain a prominent
feature of contemporary American society and a constant reminder of even
more offensive conditions in the not-so-remote past. Just three decades
ago in many regions of America it was highly unusual to find European
American males prosecuted for raping African American women or for
lynching African American men. Although less overt today, such conditions have not been eradicated. Bigotry is evident statistically among the
students and faculties of American colleges, among gainfully employed
professionals, and among citizens enjoying economic prosperity. A few
years of limited affirmative action policies have hardly eliminated the attitudes that perpetuate racism and sexism in America.

Some people feel that "serious" art is a mirror of the conditions within
which it resides. A glance at the history of "jazz" in America reveals few
integrated bands that remained together for a number of years. Even when
musicians were willing to integrate, socioeconomic factors often prevented

anything more than tokenism of various kinds. Consequently, musicologists can write two separate histories of American "jazz," each revealing tangible differences reflective of our general American society. There will be distinct African American and European American "jazz" forms as long as American socioculture is strongly segregated along racial and ethnic lines.

Today there are many debates over the ownership of the music some call "jazz." While there is agreement that the roots of African American music are in Africa, some have always claimed that "jazz" evolved from a mixture of almost equal proportions of African and European influences. Regardless of the inaccuracy of the claim, this is a step up from earlier times when Nick LaRocca claimed that "jass" was a European American invention African Americans had nothing to do with. LaRocca claimed that his Original Dixieland Jass Band invented "jass" and insisted that he and his musical colleagues were completely unaware of (and therefore escaped the possible influence of) the music of African Americans in his native New Orleans.

It is not entirely surprising that LaRocca could gain support for his assertion from at least one individual, the German researcher Horst Lange.[10] It is not clear how much time (if any) Lange spent in America listening to African American music. Nevertheless, the effects of LaRocca's exposure to African American stylistic influences (ranging from "front-line" funeral band music, ragtime, and jig bands to other forms extant within the musical community of the day) are obvious in the derivative style of the ODJB's music. It is also obvious that LaRocca and his colleagues were not enclosed within a cultural void as they suggested. If nothing else, the ODJB members received distorted or diluted exposure to African American music through the media.

If we are to believe the historical documentation of European American writers, then Paul Whiteman was the "King of Jazz" and Benny Goodman the "King of Swing," and George Gershwin made "jazz a lady."[11] Each musician brings something special to "jazz." Nonetheless, when the various stylistic forms of African American music are carefully and thoroughly examined from a more objective position, none of the above claims to royalty can be justified in musical terms. European American musicians have the economic and social advantage over their African American counterparts (as well as a greater percentage of musicians), yet the evolution of "jazz" innovations has remained entrenched among African American musicians. If we extract the major innovators from the various sectors of "jazz" history, then it is undeniable that "jazz" is a musical style invented and evolved primarily by African American progenitors.

Because Eurocentric and Afrocentric musical worlds are most often segregated in America, Eurocentric American "jazz" understandably exhibits different characteristics than the Afrocentric music of Scott Joplin, Jelly Roll Morton, Louis Armstrong, Mary Lou Williams, Basie, Ellington, Bird, Monk, Coltrane, Miles Davis, Sun Ra, Ornette Coleman, and Cecil Taylor. This is a question not of musicianship or creativity but, rather, of style and authenticity. Origins and originality itself cannot be fabricated or duplicated.

The economic and political factors that impinge upon the development of African American music make the question of racism significant. William Julius Wilson is a noted author and professor of sociological and public policy at Harvard University. On November 13, 1995, Wilson spoke on the topic "Power, Racism and Privilege" before a packed hall at Goldwin Smith Hall on the Cornell University campus. He acknowledged that the problems of the poor and underserved sectors of the American population (especially in inner cities) are exacerbated by racism, but he felt that the roots of the issue lie within the unequal and discriminatory economic class structures: "It's not just simply a matter of race or racism. I assume the race factor. Besides the fact that these places are segregated based on a history of racial discrimination, something else is happening here. We need to go beyond race to explain the impact of these economic and political factors."[12]

Once "Black" music migrated away from the economic infrastructure of segregated African American neighborhoods, the European American music industry influenced the definition, the success, and the audience acceptance of "jazz" and other African American music to a much greater degree. Additionally, as a result of American socioeconomic constructs, European American "cover" bands that performed music based upon African American prototypes received much wider acceptance and economic returns than the African American innovators.

Books written by Eurocentric authors have claimed that women were inferior, that Native Americans were savages, that Columbus "discovered" America, and that Africans were only three-fifths human. Sun Ra said, "History is 'his'-story... You have not heard my story.... My story is a mystery [my-story].... Because my story is not his-story. "Self-proclaimed Eurocentric "jazz" authorities frequently display arrogance and lack humility, regardless of their level of knowledge or experience, because these men (traditionally, they rarely are women) are seldom challenged. Writer Gene Lees, for example, insists that Bill Evans is the most significant force in "jazz" and in the history of music. He never feels the need to support his claim with any evidence beyond his personal opinion, which he apparently feels is sufficient:

> Given the musical character of the two lands of origin, the question "What would an American jazz pianist of mixed Welsh and Russian background sound like?" deserves the answer: Bill Evans. Yet Bill had explored every aspect of jazz. One night late at the Village Vanguard, when the audience was almost gone, he began to play blues. His gorgeous golden tone was abandoned. He was playing hard and funky, dark Southern blues. After that final set, he said to me with a grin, "I can really play that stuff when I want to." And so he could.

But why should he? It wasn't him. He had assimilated many influences, but the result was what we think of as Bill Evans, one of the most distinctive, original, and finally influential forces in the history of jazz, and one of the most original in the history of music (Lees, 238).

While such a statement would never be taken seriously among African American innovators, this is irrelevant to Lees. There is no need to ask a blues musician whether he or she feels Evans can "really play that stuff." Lees implies that Evans is more important to the evolution of "jazz" tradition than Armstrong, Tatum, Ellington, Parker, Coltrane, Coleman, Davis, and other African American innovators. He somehow concluded from hearing Evans play the blues that he could also play ragtime, stride, bebop, free "jazz", and all other "jazz" styles. His bigoted comments also imply that Evans was required to abandon "his gorgeous golden tone" to play blues.

Likewise, the systematic exclusion of women, children, and people of color from historical records renders subjectively grounded reporting negligible. Sexism minimized the roles women musicians have enjoyed in music throughout the Western world. Although women managed to play a significant role in the development of African American music, sexism exists to varying degrees in "jazz" as well. The cycles of exploitation and development that women have witnessed tell us something significant about the attitudes and conditions surrounding their musical creations and the music of their male counterparts.

In the minds of marginalized musicians, social insularity, inequality, and institutional malfeasance consequently relegate Eurocentric critics, club owners, or record company executives to positions of "plantation store" parasites. The music industry, therefore, appears bent on destroying "Black" artists who fail to conform to Eurocentric authority. This condition continues virtually unchallenged in America. Labels, catch words, and cryptic signals are assigned by tacit (if subliminal) agreement by an entertainment industry controlled by a social "majority" that benefits economically and egotistically from the exploitation of "minority" artists. The manipulation of seemingly innocuous terms like "jazz" obfuscates the origins of African American music while facilitating the commercial goals and interests of a music industry born out of a slavery-era mentality. Thus the acknowledgment that "jazz" is America's only indigenous art form has rarely been coupled with the recognition that it is an African American manifestation.

If reasonably objective music scholarship is a desirable goal, then the elimination of racism should be of mutual concern. Irrational and bigoted propaganda leads to confusion. Many champions of the music of Elvis Presley, for instance, attempt to defend his recordings against attacks from listeners who assert that Elvis stole music from African American musicians. Ironically, a few broadcasters have presented programs where they played original versions of numerous African American blues songs followed by Elvis's versions of those songs. While seeking to prove Elvis's ownership of the music by claiming that Elvis "refined" the original African American songs to the point of creating a brand new music, these broadcasters inadvertently substantiated the accusations and claims of those they sought to disarm.

Rhythm and blues artists such as Louis Jordan, Fats Domino, Little Richard, and others derived their singing and instrumental style from the Afrocentric speech patterns, dance movements, and other sociocultural nurturing on which they were reared. Rock and roll merely became a "distilled" derivative of rhythm and blues. Since Elvis and other European American artists had limited direct contact with African American culture, it is understandable that they could only create parodies of African American styles. Elvis even adopted the style, clothing, and fake "processed" hairdo of rhythm and blues artists of the 1950s. Despite individual aesthetic preferences, the original creators of the songs Elvis "covered" were indeed African American.

During the 1960s some European performers who used African American music or stylistic elements in creating their own music (such as the Beatles) acknowledged their debt to original artists. Why do many Americans find it hard to admit they love, learn from, and borrow African American music?

SUMMARY

Most American children know more about Bach, Mozart, Beethoven, Picasso, Michelangelo, and Rembrandt than about Ellington, Bird, Davis, Coltrane, Bearden, Sargent Johnson, and Augusta Savage. Perhaps this is because an embarrassingly disproportionate number of the people who teach, compose, perform, document, theorize, criticize, sell, and distribute innovative African American music are non African American. Braxton again discusses some possible reasons for the unfortunate and often absurd notions and attitudes that many Americans hold regarding music.

The fact that we have not had a real understanding of the great African Masters, the great Asian masters, or that many of the great European white masters too have not been understood... is to do with the way everything is defined in this time period. The notion that the Europeans are the superior races and that every philosophical and scientific idea which has helped the cause of human evolution is related only to the European male is a profound misuse of thinking. Yet this is what young children have to grow up under – the weight of misdefinition, the weight of gradualism, of racism, of sexism (Lees, 238).

Gradualism, according to Braxton, refers to the redefining of information in the interest of those engaged in the redefinition. He uses as an example "the way Egypt has been written out of classical Greek history, and the white 'takeovers' of both big band swing and rock 'n roll" (Lees, 313). Traditionally, the question of ownership takes on a more prominent role in European cultures than it did in many traditional African societies. European culture traditionally proposes that whoever is in possession of an official European document granting the bearer ownership to a property is the "legal" owner. It makes little difference whether the property owned is in Africa, South America, the moon, or just happens to be a particular style of music.

I propose, therefore, that "jazz" be divided into several subdivisions. There are distinct approaches involving African American, Latin, European American, Asian American, Asian, African, and European styles, for instance. Each variation shares basic roots based on evolving American music transplanted from African tradition. Of course, African music has been influenced by local environmental elements everywhere it landed. Nevertheless, each subdivision of music is largely a factor of the specific sociocultural values, attitudes, history, and styles of the various segregated units in which music practitioners find themselves. As we grow closer socially, so too will we begin to produce music that is clearly, and unqualified, American.

People say that music is potentially a universal healing force capable of bringing peace, understanding, and harmony to the inhabitants of our world. As we rapidly begin a new century, how much of the bigotry, selfishness, and ignorance that has retarded the progress of humanity will we take as baggage into the next millennium? Can we find a few answers to relevant questions concerning solutions to our contemporary social problems and strife within a careful study of Afrocentric innovation some call "jazz"? "Jazz" has managed to bring people together from all backgrounds, occupations, and places on earth. Even those who despise and discriminate against African American people have not escaped their alluring music. In time, given the opportunity, perhaps Afrocentric music might demonstrate even greater positive potential. Reflected in the patterns retained in African American music, sermons, quilting, painting, dance, and nutritional arts are the oral histories, motivic patterns, and cultural nuances inherent within the songs of the African griots. The psychological, educational, economic, and spiritual benefit of this rich heritage enabled the Africans in America to endure severely debilitating slavery-era conditions.

The mentalities that slavery produced are extremely difficult to overcome. If the African American music some call "jazz" suffers today under adverse economic and social conditions worldwide, this is more a consequence of its progenitors' African American identity than of any reasonable aesthetic criteria. The introduction of dodecaphonic music,[13] aleatory music,[14] musique concrPte,[15] and minimalism into European and certain American academic musical circles has received far less resistance than the influential art forms created by African Americans.

Racism and sexism, like other ridiculous notions, manifest in ludicrous ways that make it clear that only quest for power, sociopolitical privilege, and economic advantage could motivate people to accept weak justifications for their insensitivity and greed. The absurdity of such delusions is clear when society presumes that a woman of African heritage cannot have a "white" child, yet a woman of European ancestry can have a "Black" baby. How did a "white race" evolve so rapidly during the slave era? It took time for Italians and Jews to become "white" in America and parts of Europe. The socioeconomic and psychopolitical frameworks that support such conditioning weigh heavily upon the development of African American music.

Bishop Desmond Tutu heads the Truth Council in South Africa. This transitional organization grants amnesty to those who confess to atrocities committed under apartheid. Tutu feels that, as painful and inadequate as this process may be, it is necessary to expose facts of history and to arrive at some measure of truth that can aid in the promotion of healing throughout his country. Perhaps by looking squarely and sincerely into the American mirror some call "jazz" we can achieve similar ends. "Prejudice, intolerance, and discrimination are vain and hollow luxuries in which none but the ignorant, the idle, and the indolent can indulge. Courage,

competence, and comradeship come in many colors, and these characteristics have meaning to men who stand together in the face of adversity"
(Drotning, ix).

Notes

1. *Mandinka and Fulani Music of the Gambia: Ancient Heart.* Axiom 314-510
148-42. 1990. CD. Mandinka group: Sukakata Suso, Karnnka Suso, Bolong
Suso, Manjako Suso, Jewuru Kanuteh (kora); Mahamadou Suso, Mawudo
Suso, Salun Kuyateh (balafon); Saiko Suso, Lamin Suso (batakonkon);
Dembo Kanuteh, Mahamadou Suso (dundungo); Bobo Suso, Mahame Camara
(voice), Fulani group: Juldeh Camara, Korreh Jallow (nyanyer, voice); Alieu
Touray (flute); Amajou Bah, Karimu Bah (calabash); Amadou Jallow (lala);
Ousman Jallow (jimbeh), "Hamaba," "Nayo," "Dangoma," "Sanjon Bilama,"
"Kumbusora," "Nyanyer Song," "Julajekereh," "Galoyabeh," "Lanbango,"
"Borasabana," and "China Product."

2. *African Tribal Music and Dances.* Legacy International CD 328. No year
listed. No personnel listed. Music of the Malinké: "Festival Music," "Solo
for the Seron," "Hymn of Praise," "Percussion Instruments," "Festival of the
Circumcision," "Dance of the Hunters," and "Dance of the Women." Music
of the Baoulé and others: "Invocation, Entrance, and Dance of the Glaou,"
"Duet for Flutes," "Solo for Musical Bow," "Xylophone Solo," "Male
Chorus and Harp," "Dance of the Witch Doctor," "Sicco," "Toffi," "Ibonga,"
"Gnounba Gnibi," "Dianka Bi," "Sibi Saba," "Sindhio," "Didrenquo," and
"Bonomiollo."

3. See *Mojo Hand: The Lightnin Hopkins Anthology.* 1993 Rhino Records (R2
71226). 4. Listen to *Voodoo Ceremony in Haiti: Recorded Live on Location.*
Olympic Records 6113. 1974. LP. No personnel listed. "Voodoo Drums,"
"Nibo Rhythms," "Prayer to Shango," "Petro Rhythms," "Nago Rhythms,"
"Invocation to Papa Legba," "Dahomey Rhythms: 'The Paul'," "Maize
Rhythm,"and "Diouba Rhythm: 'Cousin Zaca'."

5. A way of dividing a fixed length in two sections, expressed in mathematical
terms as $b/a = a/a+b$ (also known as Golden Mean, Golden Ratio).

6. Liner notes from McIntyre's album *Home.* Steeple Chase SCS-1039, 1975.
McIntyre plays alto sax, flute, oboe, bassoon, and bass clarinet on this recording.

7. Ibid.

8. The number of people referred to as minorities in America collectively
compose over 50 percent of the population.

9. James Lincoln Collier, *Jazz: The American Theme Song* (New York: Oxford
University Press, 1993), 200.

10. The latter idea was Leonard Bernstein's.

11. See *Cornell Chronicle*, 30 November, 1995, 6.

12. The term dodecaphonic music pertains twelve-tone musical technique or compositions.

13. Aleatory music is music involving the introduction of chance or unpredictability into the process of performance or composition.

14. A conceptual term first coined by Pierre Schaeffer in Paris around 1948, *musique concréte* involves the recording of any number of sounds (voice, street noises, musical instruments, sounds of nature, and so on) that undergo electronic manipulation, modulation, and enhancement in the recording studio.

References

Collier, James Lincoln. *Jazz: The American Theme Song*. New York: Oxford University Press, 1993.

Drotning, Phillip T. *Black Heroes in Our Nation's History*. New York: Washington Square Press, 1970.

Ellington, Duke. *Music Is My Mistress*. Garden City, N.Y.: Doubleday, 1973.

Harlos, Christopher. "Jazz Autobiography." In *Representing Jazz*, ed. Krin Gabbard. Durham: Duke University Press, 1995.

Lees, Gene. *Cats of Any Color: Jazz Black and White*. New York: Oxford University Press, 1994.

Lock, Graham. *Forces in Motion: The Music and Thoughts of Anthony Braxton*. New York: Da Capo, 1988.

Milligan, Robert. *Fetish Folk of West Africa*. New York: Fleming H. Revel, 1912.

Murray, Albert. *The Blue Devils of Nada: A Contemporary Approach to Aesthetic Statement*. New York: Pantheon, 1996.

PART V
TOWARD AFRICANA WOMANISM

The fact of the matter is that Africana womanism is a response to the need for collective definition and the re-creation of the authentic agenda that is the birthright of every living person. In order to make this shift to authenticity, Hudson-Weems has called us back to the earliest days of African cultural history. In this antiquity she has discovered the sources of so much commonality in the African world that there is no question that Africana womanism has a distinct and different approach to relationships than, say, feminism. It is the African woman=s own voice emerging from the debris of a vast cultural waste-land in the Western world. Having been the victims of so much brutality in the West, the African woman, in all of her guises, comes now to the forefront of the struggle for centeredness. (Asante, Afterword for *Africana Womanist Literary Theory*)

18
NOMMO/SELF-NAMING, SELF-DEFINITION, AND THE HISTORY OF AFRICANA WOMANISM

Clenora Hudson-Weems

Definitions belonged to the definers – not the defined.

– Morrison, *Beloved*

Africana Womanism, emerged from the acknowledgment of a long-standing authentic agenda for that group of women of African descent who needed only to be properly named and officially defined according to their own unique historical and cultural matrix, one that would reflect the co-existence of a man and a woman in a concerted struggle for the survival of their entire family/community. The process by which this phenomenon, a concept I named and defined in the mid-eighties (then called "Black womanism"), took shape, and the open acknowledgment of its pre-existence was articulated in a 1998 publication, several years after my 1992 presentation at the First International Conference on Women of Africa and the African Diaspora at the University of Nigeria-Nsukka :

> For nearly a decade, I have been actively working on naming and defining, via identifying and refining an African-centered paradigm for women of African descent. In observing the traditional role, character, and activity of this collective group, identified by their common African ancestry, I concluded during the early stages of my research that the phenomenon I named and defined as Africana womanism had long been in existence, dating back to the rich legacy of African womanhood. Therefore, I did not create the phenomenon in and of itself, but rather observed Africana women, documented our reality, and refined a paradigm relative to who we are, what we do, and what we believe in as a people. [Hudson-Weems, "Self-Naming" 449]

The activity surrounding Africana/black womanism itself commenced in the fall of 1985, when, during my first semester as a Ph.D. student at the University of Iowa, I challenged Black feminism. At that time I used the terminology "Black womanism," which later evolved to the present terminology--Africana womanism. From the research paper I wrote that semester, entitled "The Tripartite Plight of the Black Woman–Racism, Classism and Sexism–in *Our Nig, Their Eyes Were Watching God* and *The Color Purple*," I was motivated to set up a panel for the 13-16, March 1986 National Council for Black Studies (NCBS) Annual Conference in Boston. I presented a paper there entitled "Black Womanism versus Black Feminism--Racism First, Sexism Last: The Survival of the Black Race," wherein an obvious paradigm is outlined in the title itself. While many black women at the conference, including two established sociologists, Delores Aldridge, then president of the NCBS, and Vivian Gordon, author of the 1987bpublication *Black Women, Feminism and Black Liberation: Which Way?*, concurred with my thesis of prioritization; others insisted on the simultaneity of these obstacles–race, class, and gender respectively–in the lives of black women.

For the three years standing, from 1985 to 1988, and even to my first publication in 1989 on the subject, I relentlessly spoke out on this crucial subject at national conferences, most notably at a panel entitled "The Tripartite Plight of Black Women" for the 24-28, June 1987 National Women's Studies Association Convention in Atlanta, Georgia. That fall, the challenge presented to my work on black women continued and was taken up on an Iowa City local television program, "The Silver Tongue," where I debated a senior doctoral student, who would complete her studies there in 1989, approximately a year after I did. Later that semester, I continued to challenge Black feminism in a paper presented at a 1987 University of Iowa Black Survival Conference: "Black Womanism versus Black Feminism: A Critical Issue for Human Survival." The seed for two subsequent presentations came from this work, with some revisions–work that was well received at the 7-9, April 1988 National Council for Black Studies and later at the 28-30, April 1988 African Heritage Studies Association Annual Conferences. In fact, some of my colleagues acknowledged that feminism/black feminism, for some reason or another, did not quite work for them, and they expressed their gratitude for this new distinction.

The following year, the fruition of this long continuous work culminated in two publications: One was "Cultural and Agenda Conflicts in Academia: Critical Issues for Africana Women's Studies" which was released in the 1989 Winter Issue of *The Western Journal of Black Studies.* The other was "The Tripartite Plight of African-American Women as Reflected in the Novels of Hurston and Walker" which was released in the December 1989 issue of *The Journal of Black Studies.* A call for new terminology for articulating the historical and cultural reality of women of African descent was issued forth in the first article:

> Africana women might begin by naming and defining their unique movement "Africana Womanism." The concept of Womanism can be traced back to Sojourner's [1852] speech that began to develop and highlight Africana women's unique experience into a paradigm for Africana women. [Hudson-Weems, "Cultural and Agenda Conflicts" 187]

This new terminology, coupled with a new paradigm, expressed discontent with other female-based constructs (e.g.: feminism, black feminism, and womanism) that had not clearly expressed an agenda for Africana women relative to the prioritizing of their triple plight. To be sure, this sense of prioritizing is clearly delineated in Sojourner Truth's self actualization oration "And Ain't I a Woman," where she was obligated to address the race factor first, then the class factor, before she could even begin to entertain the absurd notion of female subjugation, the gender factor.

Four years later, in 1993, the publication of the book on this topic, *Africana Womanism: Reclaiming Ourselves,* was released, despite the fact that several publishers initially expressed hesitancy in publishing the manuscript. Their reluctance was in no small part due to the controversial issues surrounding black women's rejection of "mainstream" feminist ideology, that is, its caustic beginnings and its inapplicability for women of African descent. Significantly, *Africana Womanism* was at the center of existing debates and at the forefront of a new, even bolder controversy in its radical pronouncement of the abandonment of feminist terminology in labeling black women. Describing my work in the biographical headnotes preceding my contributed article to their text, the editors of *Call and Response: The Riverside Anthology of the African American Literary Tradition* asserted the following:

> Taking a strong position that black women should not pattern their liberation after Eurocentric feminism but after the historic and triumphant women of African descent, Hudson Weems has launched a new critical discourse in the Black Women's Literary Movement. [Hill 1811]

At the same time, those black women (black feminists) who continued to use the term feminism as a theoretical construct for their analysis received unnumbered support for their research. Aligning themselves with the acceptable framework of feminism was unquestionably one of the most reliably strategic means of becoming initiated into that established community, which rendered many perks, such as visibility, prodigious employment possibilities, and publications. Clearly, such a *reward system* has been influential in black feminists and black feminist critics' allegiance to and identification with dominant feminist ideologies. Moreover, it is my conjecture that many may very well have viewed their acceptance of Africana womanism not only as risking their professional security, but as invalidating their years of research from the Black feminist perspective. This, indeed, is unfortunate, for instead they should have viewed "it as a natural evolutionary process of ideological growth and development" for the black women's movement from black feminism to Africana womanism (Hudson-Weems, ". . . Entering the New Millennium" 17). In the final analysis, then, in an attempt to reshape the feminist/black feminist agenda to suit their needs by ignoring an existing practical, theoretical, and more compatible construct, these prominent black feminists, having been "appropriated and reshaped into a revised form of black feminism," often duplicate much of the work that has already been done in Africana womanism, distinguishable only, for the most part, by misnaming (Hudson-Weems, "Africana Womanism: An Overview" 206).

Exemplifying this practice is black feminist Evelyn Brooks Higginbotham in "African-American Women's History and the Metalanguage of Race," published in 1992, approximately six years after the inception of many powerful debates and publications delineating the importance of self-naming and self-defining for black women, which encompasses formulating one's own name, agenda, and priorities as highlighted in black womanism/Africana womanism. To be sure, Higgenbotham was well aware of the fact that race had not been properly factored into the burgeoning field of Women's Studies, and thus, she called for "Feminist scholars, especially those of African-American women's history, [to] accept the challenge to bring race more prominently into their analyses of power" (Higginbotham 252), a call issued several years earlier in the announcement of Africana womanism. Black feminist bell hooks, who unrealistically urged black women to move from the peripheral to the center of the feminist movement, which was founded by white women and justifiably tailored to their particular needs, later incorporated many of the descriptors outlines in *Africana Womanism* in one of her mid-nineties publications. Moreover, Patricia Hill Collins, in a 1995 article, "What's in a Name? Womanism, Black Feminism, and Beyond," inaccurately asserts that "No term currently exists that adequately represents the substance of what diverse groups of black women alternately call womanism and black feminism" (Collins 15). The truth of the matter is that the so-called non-existent term to which Collins refers had already been articulated years before in *Africana Womanism*, which was, at the time of her article, in its third revised edition. As the term Africana womanism had been in existence since the mid-eighties, it is clear that, along with the terminology, a well-defined paradigm was also established. Even Alice Walker's "womanism" pronouncements–literally a page and one-half–does little more than present a brief commentary on the shade differentiation between what Collins notes as "alternately call[ed] womanism and black feminism"– purple vs. lavender. (See Walker's introduction to her collection of essays entitled *In Search of Our Mother's Gardens.*) Restating in her own words in *Black Feminist Thought* what Africana womanism had pronounced a decade earlier, but without any reference to *Africana Womanism* itself, Collins contends:

> Several difficulties accompany[ing] the use of the term "black feminism" . . . involves the problem of balancing the genuine concerns of black women against continual pressures to absorb and recast such interests within white feminist frameworks. . . the emphasis on [of white feminist] themes such as personal identity, understanding "difference" . . . and the simplistic model of the political . . . "personal is political," that currently permeate North American white women's feminism in the academy can work to sap black feminism of its critical edge. [15]

More important than the way the Academy, in collusion with feminism, has effectively diluted the "critical [black feminist] edge" is the tacit consent that black feminism has given both to the Academy and white feminism through its short-sighted forfeiture of the highly political edge that Africana womanism offers. Even as black feminism attempts to correct its myopic vision through its incorporation of the substance of Africana womanism, it fails to admit (while it omits) Africana womanism's essential and underlying foundation– *nommo, its name.*

Collins' own shift to what she incorrectly claims to be a more culturally/globally centered approach to theorizing black women's resistance to all oppression is even more pronounced in her tenth and most recent edition of *Black Feminist Thought* (2000). Here she vividly points to the confusion and dysfunctionality that the term Black feminism engenders: "whereas this edition remains centered on U.S. black women, it raises questions concerning African American women's positionality within a global black feminism" (xii). Obviously, this type of confusion and these types of questions with regard to Africana women within any type of feminism is directly and clearly addressed within the authentic agenda put forth by Africana womanism. Conversely, scholarship like that expressed in Collins' black feminism finds itself in a socio linguistic and cultural maze. Sadly, Collins demonstrates, through her own language, confusion about what aspects of black feminism she sees as part of a global address/append-age—Africana womanism's prioritizing race, class, and gender-based paradigm or white feminism's gender-based system. Collins' misnaming of black women's resistance and thought through supposed "renaming" or appropriation of a "black" additive to an already baggage-laden feminist center does much to belie her claims to "global black feminism" and most certainly supports Africana womanism's long-standing argument concerning the inherent and fundamental contradiction in the concept of black feminism itself. Collins unwittingly turns a light of truth on her own flawed system of naming as she addresses the problem of terminology with regard to paradigms like Africentricity She glaringly and perhaps unconsciously supports Africana womanism's thesis about the importance of naming and the incongruent relationship between the theory and practice of black feminism and the Africana women it claims to represent. Thus, Collins' contends that "When the same language continues to be used, whereas the meaning attached to it changes . . . the term becomes too value laden to be useful" (Collins xi). Her assertion here, which she later contradicts, clearly echoes and appropriates the underlying premise for Africana womanism without so much as citing the source—as scholars must ethically do. For example, in "Cultural and Agenda Conflicts in Academia: Critical Issues for Africana Women's Studies," I insisted that "When the Black feminist buys the White terminology, she also buys its agenda" (Hudson'Weems, "Cultural" 188). Collins contradicts her notion of a non-existing alternative terminology for black women in her earlier publication, "What's in a Name?," yet later acknowledges its existence in *Black Feminist Thought*, tenth edition, does, in fact, list alternative terminologies:

> Rather than developing definitions and arguing over naming practices–for example, whether this thought should be called Black feminism, womanism, Afrocentric feminism, Africana womanism, and the like–a more useful approach lies in revisiting the reasons why black feminist thought exists at all. [Collins 22]

Clearly, from this quotation, we see that she has missed the point. Obviously she does not comprehend the concept of *nommo*, or she would not have ended by proposing such a question in the first place. More relevant is the question of why Collins retains the term, "feminist" and refuses a more authentic one? This is the dilemma within which black feminism, through its dysfunctional association with gender and illogical disassociation from race, finds itself. Pointing to the relationship between terminology, Africana womanism, and its potential for effecting political change, Afrocentric scholar Ama Mazama highlights Hudson-Weems' Africana womanism in rendering particularly useful contributions to the Afrocentric discourse on African women and men. Hudson-Weems coined the term *Africana Womanism* in 1987 out of the realization of the total inadequacy of feminism and like theories (e.g., Black feminism, African womanism, or womanism) to grasp the reality of African women, let alone give us the means to change that reality. [Mazama 400]

Notwithstanding the failure of black feminists to utilize Africana womanism as a tool for analyzing Africana women's lives, and the way this original paradigm has affected our perception and fostered a deeper understanding of our agenda in the past twelve to fifteen years is evident. But the voice of Africana womanism will not and cannot be silenced, and like the true Africana womanist, who has never really needed to "break silence" or to "find voice," the expressed sentiments of many feminists, I have continued–through my ever-evolving critical paradigm–to uphold the Africana womanist agenda and priorities within Africana historical and cultural contexts. Such contexts are reflected in our on going struggle for the human rights of our entire family–men, women, and children.

Using Africana womanism as a spring board, Valethia Watkins, in "Womanism and Black Feminism: Issues in the Manipulation of African Historiography," interrogates Nancie Caraway's critique of the failure of white feminists to document black women's role in the feminist movement. While Caraway's critique appears a sincere gesture to "correct" the past regarding its omission of black women from the feminist arena, the Black Feminist Revisionist Project, a response to Caraway's work, was flawed at its inception for various reasons. To begin with, the very intent and design of the project to reclaim *all* black women as feminists, particularly activists in our on-going liberation struggle – e.g.: Sojourner Truth, Harriet Tubman, Anna Julia Cooper, Ida B. Wells, Rosa Parka - presupposes the primacy of a white history of resistance. Thus, the Black Revisionist Project problematically locates black activism, dating back in antiquity, outside of its historical reality. In other words, naming black women activists after white women, black feminists, is in essence "duplicating a duplicate," since in reality, feminists often modeled their strategies after black activists models, such as antislavery abolitionism, the civil rights movements, and other political frameworks for survival that are found in black history and black communities (Hudson-Weems, *Africana Womanism* 22). In fact, they go so far as to claim any and all activities and perspectives related to (black) women as black feminist. One blatant example of this is in placing Toni Morrison's 1971 *New York Time Magazine* article "What the Black Woman Thinks about Women's Lib" in a 2000 feminist publication entitled *Radical Feminism*, edited by Barbara A. Crow, which, by its very inclusion in the text of such a title, presumes or more significantly suggests that the article belongs to a feminist arena. Nobel Laureate, Morrison is clearly not espousing a feminist agenda for female empowerment; rather she asserts that "the early image of Women's Lib was of an elitist organization made up of upper-middle class women with the concerns of that class and not paying much attention to the problems of most black women" (Morrison, quoted. in *Radical Feminism*, 455). Moreover, in Wendy Harding and Jacky Martin's *A World of Difference: An Intercultural Study of Toni Morrison's Novels*, which was published in 1994, quoted Morrison as saying that she "feels too much emphasis is placed on gender politics," and hence her emphasis on the cruelties and horrific after effects of slavery are justified (Harding, 61). If anything, her focus here is on race– i.e., on the exclusion of black women's concerns. And this is only two examples of unconscionable acts of in the academy.

Tragically, dating back to the inception of the Black Feminist Revisionist Project, black women scholars, according to this project's documentation, stood "silent" on mislabeling black women activists, thinkers, etc. as black feminists. Critiquing this practice, Watkins contends:

> Despite the sheer magnitude and scope of the Black Feminist Revisionist Project, it has gone virtually unchallenged, and it has been met with silence, by and large, by the community of African-centered scholars. One notable exception to our complicity with this project, through our silence, has been a critical commentary written by Clenora Hudson-Weems . . . [who] contends that this revisionist process of inappropriately labeling African women is both arbitrary and capricious. Similarly, she argues that a feminist procrustean agenda de-emphasizes and recasts the primary concern of African women of the nineteenth and early twentieth century. According to Hudson-Weems, the primary concern of the women and men of this era was the life-threatening plight of African people, male and female. Black feminist revisionism changes this focus into a narrow feminist concern which prioritizes the plight of women as delinked and somehow different from the condition of the men in their community. [258]

Of course, refusal to surrender the authentic agenda for Africana women, notwithstanding the many personal and professional sacrifices, has paved the way for contemporary black women to follow, even though many, some them are cited above, have failed to acknowledge Africana womanism as a legitimate paradigm and model. They have too often camouflaged their so called "new black feminism," as proposed by Hortense Spillers, wherein they can more equally deal with gender and race issues, suggesting that an adequate model of resistance against female oppression for black women in a racist society does not already exist within Africana cultures and society. With their revised theory, they position themselves straddling the fence and thus, remain ideologically acceptable by the dominant culture.

It should be here noted here that in the wake of more recognition of the cultural diversity that exists within the general population and by extension its concomitant global perspectives on gender, the dominance of mainstream gender perspectives is waning and Africana womanism, at the center of the debate for well over a decade, is at the forefront of this Tran cultural revisitation of a woman's place in society. In addition to an interview that Kay Bonetti conducted in 1995 for *The American Audio Prose Library, Inc.* on *Africana Womanism*, many scholars have asked me for chapters, articles, or reprints of my work that deal with Africana womanism for their publications. Thus, my work has been included in such publications as *Call and Response: The Riverside Anthology of the African American Literary Tradition* (1997); *A Historiographical and Bibliographical Guide to the African American Experience* (2000); *Out of the Revolution: The Development of Africana Studies* (2000); *Sisterhood, Feminisms and Power* (1998); and *State of the Race, Creating Our 21st Century* (2003). Other book chapters will appear in *Black Studies: From the Pyramids and Pan Africanism and Beyond* (2002), and *Keepers of the Flame* (2003). In my edited book entitled *Contemporary Africana Theory and Thought* (2003), there is an entire section devoted to scholarship on the application of Africana womanism. Additionally, I received and accepted an offer to be contributing editor for a special issue on *Africana womanism* for the 2002 Spring Issue of *The Western Journal of Black Studies*, which includes several articles by Africana womanist scholars. Thus, Africana womanism is indisputably creating a new wave for black women and the black women's movement in particular on all fronts.

Be that as it may, many were impressed with this new paradigm from the very beginning, and I received numerous invitations to speak at institutions across the nation, including an invitation from Winston-Salem State University's 1988 Black History Month Program, where I had the occasion to meet and converse with renowned scholar, the late Dr. C. Eric Lincoln, Professor Emeritus of Duke University, who endorsed *Africana Womanism: Reclaiming Ourselves.*

> Hudson-Weems's *Africana Womanism* sent unaccustomed shock waves through the domain of popular thinking about feminism, and established her as a careful, independent thinker, unafraid to unsettle settled opinion. [Lincoln quoted in *Africana Womanism*]

Demands for colloquy on this controversial topic grew, complimented by invited speaking engagements – sometimes as many as fifteen a year on this subject alone – at such national/international colleges and universities as the University of Nigeria-Nsukka, University of Utah, Bryn Mawr College, Mary Washington University, Cornell University, Texas Southern University, Illinois Wesleyan University, University of Rhode Island, Central State University, University of Michigan-Flint, University of Illinois-Springfield, LeMoyne-Owen College, Northern Illinois University, Kean University, Drew University, California State University-Long Beach, Virginia Commonwealth University, Wayne State University, Stillman College, Southern Utah State University, Kentucky State University, University of Wisconsin-Milwaukee, Temple University, University of the West Indies-Barbados, and the University of Guelph (Canada). In addition to numerous invitations as guest speaker at institutions of higher learning, I have also been the keynote, plenary, round-table, banquet and luncheon speaker at national/international conventions, among them the National Council for Black Studies Annual Conference, the African Heritage Studies Association Annual Conference, the Annual Meeting of The Association for the Study of African American Life and History, College Language Association Annual Conference, the International Conference on Women of Africa and the African Diaspora, Chicago State University's Black Writers' Annual Conference, the Annual Third World Conference, the National Conference on Civil/Human Rights of Africananas, the Annual Diop International Conference, and the U.S. Army Ft. Leonard Wood Black History Month Luncheon (keynote address). Finally, faculty in several institutions of higher learning in far away places like England, South Africa, Germany, Nigeria Brazil, Japan, and the Caribbean Islands, utilize *Africana Womanism*. National universities also utilize it, among them California State University-Long Beach, University of North Texas, Florida A & M University, Western Michigan University, Indiana State University, Northern Illinois University, San Francisco State University, Temple University, the University of Arizona, the University of Michigan-Flint, the University of Missouri-Columbia, and the University of Utah to name a few.

Having presented the history of the emergence, evolution, and subsequent dominance of Africana womanism, I will now turn to a brief history of the critical acceptance of Africana womanism within cultural and literary studies, focusing on the relationship of these endorsements to the specific agenda. The Editors of *Call and Response: The Riverside Anthology of the African American Literary Tradition* credited me as the "first African American woman intellectual to formulate a position on Africana womanism [in her] groundbreaking study *Africana Womanism: Reclaiming Ourselves*" (Hill 1811).

In the foreword to *Africana Womanism*, the late 'Zula Sofola, the internationally renown scholar revered as Nigeria's first female playwright, describes the work as not simply a scholarly work, one of those in the mainstream, but our own. It is a new trail blazed with incontrovertible revelations on the African heritage and gender question. Hudson-Weems bravely takes the bull by the horns, confronts the Eurocentric avalanche of works on questions of gender, and puts forward the Afrocentric point of view [Quoted in *Africana Womanism* xvii].

Daphne Ntiri-Queman, the Sierra Leonean scholar recognized as an expert on women's issues, spent years as a delegate to the United Nations and consultant to Senegal, Kismayo, and Somalia under the auspices of UNESCO, and in her Introduction to *Africana Womanism* she insists:

> This landmark pioneering treatise of Africana woman's realities cannot be ignored. . . . It will unlock closed doors and usher in a spirit of renewed plentitude. *Africana Womanism* is reminiscent of a comparable avant garde movement of the 1930s by diasporan [sic] Black scholars Leopold Sedar Senghor, Leon Damas, and Aime Cesaire, who struggled to seek reassurance of their blackness. [Quoted in *Africana Womanism* 10-11]

In "The WAAD Conference and Beyond: A Look at Africana Womanism," in *Sisterhood, Feminisms and Power: From Africa to the Diaspora*, Ntiri Queman contends that "Its [Africana womanism's] purpose is multifunctional as it serves as the conceptual tool which harnesses the transformative energies and strategies embedded in Africana women's rise from oppression" (Ntiri 462). Later in "Africana Womanism: Coming of Age" in [*Contemporary Africana Theory and Thought*], she concludes:

> Just as there are compelling reasons to reclaim the power to ascribe names to African people (e.g., colored, Negro, African, African-American) in the United States (to reaffirm their race and establish stronger African affinity), so are there reasons to advocate an Africana womanist theory that is properly labeled, more attuned, and appropriate to the needs of the Africana woman.

Delores Aldridge, holder of an Endowed Chair in Sociology and Africana American Studies at Emory University, endorsed the book in 1993 as "unquestionably a pioneering effort whose time has come." Her edited book, *Out of the Revolution: The Development of Africana Studies*, in which I have contributed a chapter, "Towards Integrating Africana Women into Africana Studies," presents her juxtaposition of Black women's activities and Africana Studies with Women's Studies. Here she discusses the history of the caustic beginnings of feminism as presented in *Africana Womanism*, , which cites Carrie Capman Catt's contention that white men must recognize "the usefulness of woman suffrage as a counterbalance to the foreign vote, and as a means of legally preserving white supremacy in the South" (quoted in Hudson-Weems, *Africana Womanism*, 21). Aldridge concludes that "it is from this perspective of Africana womanism that this discourse [on integrating Africana women in Africana Studies] is developed" (Aldridge 193). She also refers to my thesis on Africana womanism as a "revolutionary work [that] has no parallel as a new way of understanding Africana women" (196). Finally, in her forthcoming article "Black Male-Female Relationships: An African Centered Lens Model" in the book *Contemporary Africana Theory and Thought*, she adds me to her "chorus of voices [that] have criticize[d] feminism (LaRue, 1970, Duberman, 1975, Gordon, 1987, [and] Hudson-Weems, 1989 and 1993)."

Talmadge Anderson Professor Emeritus at Washington State University, and Founding Editor for *The Western Journal of Black Studies*, concludes in his book endorsement that the "work captures the essence of the true meaning of Black womanhood and resolves the classical debate relative to the prioritizing of race, class and sex in American society." Similarly, Robert Harris, vice provost and former director of the Africana Studies and Research Center at Cornell University, asserts the following:

> In the triple marginality of Black women, race rises above class and gender in this remarkable book. With it, a reunion, a much needed healing, a human philosophy emerge for men and women of African ancestry and ultimately for all caring men and women. [Quoted. in *Africana Womanism*]

The late Maria Mootry, Respected literary critic, original Black Bio-ethicist, and author of the seminal work in this area, "Confronting Racialized Bioethics: New Contract on Black America" (*Western Journal of Black Studies* 2000), taken from her unpublished manuscript *Brain Games: Race, Bioethics and the Seduction of the American Mind*, stated the following in her review of *Africana Womanism*:

> Now comes a voice, cool and clear, rising above the chorus, offering not only lucid insights into the status of Africana women and their literature, but a blueprint to help us find a way out of confusion and despair. In *Africana Womanism: Reclaiming Ourselves*, in its second revised edition after only seven months, Clenora Hudson-Weems examines the perceptions women in the African diaspora have of their historical and contemporary roles. She treads fearlessly through the maze

of tension between mainstream feminism, Black feminism, African feminism, and Africana Womanism. The result, in the words of Professor Charles Hamilton, is "an intellectual triumph." [*WJBS* 244]

Daisy Lafond, former editor of *Voice: The Caribbean International Magazine*, writes the following in *Class Magazine*:

Molefe Kete Asante gave us Afrocentricity, to help us relocate ourselves from the margins of European experiences to the centrality of our own. Now, Clenora Hudson-Weems, in her second book *Africana Womanism: Reclaiming Ourselves*, is helping black women relocate themselves from the margins of white feminism to the centrality of their own experiences. [Lafond 57]

Finally, April Langley proclaims, in "Lucy Terry Prince: The Cultural and Literary Legacy of Africana Womanism," in *The Western Journal of Black Studies*, that

It is Africana Womanism as originated, developed, and outlined by Hudson-Weems that enables a reading which restores and revises the African origins of the earlier African American writing. . . . the import of this critical paradigm for the earliest Africana writers is essential for recuperating what is "African" in early African American literature. [Langley 158]

Other scholars who view Africana womanism as a viable concept include P. Jane Splawn ("Recent Developments in Black Feminist Literary Scholarship: A Selective Annotated Bibliography?" in *Modern Fiction Studies,* 1993;, Philip L. Kilbride ("Africana Womanism" in *Plural Marriages for Our Times: A Reinvented Option?*, 1994); Mary Ebun Modupe Kolawole (*Womanism and African Consciousness*, 1997); Tolagbe Ogunleye, aka: Dr. Martin Ainsi ("African Women and the Grassroots: The Silent Partners of the Women's Movement" in *Sisterhood, Feminisms, and Power: From Africa to the Diaspora*, 1998); Robson Delany, (Ninteenth-Century Africana Womanist: Reflections on His Avant-Garde Politics Concerning Gender, Colorism, and Nation Building" in *The Journal of Black Studies*, 1998); Olabisi Regina Jennings ["Why I Joined the Black Panther Party: An Africana Womanist Reflection" in *The Black Panther Party Reconsidered*, 1998, "Africana Womanism in the Black Panther Party: A Person Story" in *The Western Journal of Black Studies*, 2002 and "Africana Womanist Interpretation of Gwendolyn Brooks' in *Maud Martha*, 2002]; (First International Conference on Women in Africa and the African Diaspora: A View from the USA" in *Sisterhood,* 1998); Janette Y. Taylor ("Womanism: A Methodologic Framework for African American Women" in *Advances in Nursing Science,* 1998); P. S. Brush ("The

Influence of Social-Movements on Articulations of Race and Gender in Black Women's Autobiography" in *Gender and Society*, 1999); Yolanda Hood ("Africana Womanism and Black Feminism: Re-reading African Women's Quilting Traditions," AFS Annual Meeting, 1999); Laverne Gyant ("The Missing Link: Women in Black/Africana Studies" in *Out of the Revolution: The Development of Africana Studies*, 2000); Carolyn Kumah ("African Women and Literature" in *West Africa Review*, 2000); Deborah Plant ("African Gender Trouble and Africana Womanism: An Interview with Chikwenye Ogunyemi and Wanjira Muthoni" in *Signs*, 2000); JoAnne Banks Wallace ("Womanist Ways of Knowing: Theoretical Considerations for Research with African American Woman" in *Advances in Nursing Science*, 2000); Madhu Kishwar ("Feminism, Rebellious Women and Cultural Boundaries: Re-reading Flora Nwapa and Her Compatriots," 2001); Ama Mazama ("The Afrocentric Paradigm: Contours and Definitions" in *The Journal of Black Studies*, 2001); Adele Newson-Horst ("Gloria Naylor's *Mama Day*: An Africana Womanist Reading" in *Contemporary Africana Theory and Thought*, 2007); ("Maud Martha Brown: A Study in Emergence" in *Maud Martha: A Critical Collection*, 2002); Pamela Yaa Assantewaa Reed (*"Africana Womanism* and *African Feminism*: A Dialectic" in *The Western Journal of Black Studies*, 2001); Anne Steiner ("Frances Watkins Harper: Eminent Pre-Africana Womanist" in *Contemporary Africana Theory and Thought*, 2003); Betty Taylor Thompson [("Common Bonds from the U.S. to Africa and Beyond: Africana Womanist Literary Analysis" in *The Western Journal of Black Studies*, 2001) and (*Contemporary Africana Theory and Thought*, 2003)]; Antonio Tillis (*Hispanic Review,* "Cuba's Nancy Morejon: Caribbean Poetic Voice of Africana Womanism" in 2002), Barbara Wheeler ("Africana Womanism: An African Legacy—It Ain't Easy Being a Queen" in *Contemporary Africana Theory and Thought*, 2002). Theoretical constructs that have been influenced by Africana womanism include Kawaida womanism, emerging from Maulana Karenga's Kawieda, and Afrocentric womanism, coming out of the school of Afrocentricity as popularized by Molefe Asante.

Even those who have either consciously or unconsciously appropriated Africana womanism demonstrate the overarching presence and validity of this concept. Notably, we have among many Tuzyline Jita Allan (*Womanist and Feminist Aesthetics*); Doris M. Boutain ("Critical Nursing Scholarship: Exploring Critical Social Theory with African American Studies" in *Advances in Nursing Science*, 1999); Michelle Collison ("Race Women Stepping Forward" in *Black Issues in Higher Education* 1999); Nah Dove ("African Womanism: An Afrocentric Theory" in *Sage*, 1998); Lynnett Harvey (*Why Black Women Reject Feminism: Racism in the Femi-*

nist Movement, 1997); Anthonia Kalu ("Women in African Literature" *African Transitions* 2000); and Gail M. Presby ("Culture, Multicultural- ism, and Intercultural Philosophy" in *Forum for Intellectual Philosophiz- ing*, 2000).

Considering the history, the acceptance, and the pronounced demand for its dynamic critical framework, I have been challenged to re-articulate and to further develop the critical principles of Africana womanism. Since Africana people have long been denied not only the authority of naming self, but, moreover, of defining self (as inferred by the narrator of Mor- rison's *Beloved*, Pulitzer Prize-winning novel –"Definitions belonged to the definers--not the defined") it is now of utmost importance that we take control over both these determining interconnected factors in our lives if we hope to avoid degradation, isolation, and annihilation in a world of greed, violence and pandemonium (190). Self-namer and self-definer, two of the eighteen characteristics of the Africana woman, are seminal descrip- tors that delineate the first step in establishing an authentic paradigm rela- tive to the true level of struggle for women of African descent, as this gets to the very crux of the matter and the history of Africana womanism. From the authentic act of self-naming and self-defining, this critical paradigm emerged. At its very core/center lies *nommo, an* African term that cultural theorist, Molefi Kete Asante, calls "the generative and productive power of the spoken word" (Asante 17). It is a powerful and useful concept holding that the proper naming of a thing will in turn give it essence. Par- ticularizing and advancing the concept, Harrison contends that "Nommo, in the power of the word . . . activates all forces from their frozen state in a manner that establishes concreteness of experience . . . be they glad or sad, work or play, pleasure or pain, in a way that preserves [one's] humanity" (Harrison xx). In African cosmology, the word *nommo*, then, evokes material manifestation. Thus, as Barbara Christian summarizes, "It is through nommo, the correct naming of a thing, that it comes into existence" (157-158), a profound statement to which she herself fails to adhere in calling herself a black feminist. While initiating a call for proper naming, I also insisted on our own agenda and our particular priorities of race, class, and gender respectively, contrary to the feminists' female-cen- tered agenda with female empowerment as their number one priority. The other descriptors outlined in *Africana Womanism* are family-centered (in concert with the men in the liberation struggle), strong, genuine in sister- hood, whole, authentic, respected, recognized, male compatible, flexible role player, adaptable, respectful of elders, spiritual, ambitious, mothering, and nurturing.

The long-standing focus on the woman and her role in the greater society continues to be at the center of controversy today. For over a century and a half, dating back to pre-Civil War/Emancipation Proclamation, women have been engaged in shaping their role within the context of a particular social reality, one in which white males predominate within a racist patriarchal system. Although racism is clearly a seminal component of the overall system of oppression, white women in general, and the feminist movement in particular, have been driven almost exclusively by issues related solely to gender oppression. However, the vast majority of black women have necessarily focused their energies on combating racism first before addressing the gender question. As a consequence, it is clear that the two groups ultimately have disparate goals for meeting their specific needs. In short, for black women, who are family-centered, it is race empowerment; for white women, who are female-centered, it is female empowerment. Because of this difference in agendas, distinct naming, then, is critical.

Noted black psychologist Julia Hare makes a profound comment on the reality of the difference in the politics of black life and that of white life, particularly in terms of the difference in certain meanings and ideals relative to the two parallel groups.

> Women who are calling themselves black feminists need another word that describes what their concerns are. Black feminism in not a word that describes the plight of black women. In fact, ... black feminists have not even come together and come to a true core definition of what black feminism is. The white race has a woman problem because the women were oppressed. Black people have a man and woman problem because Black men are as oppressed as their women. [Quoted in Phillip, 15]

Hare's 1993 call for another name for the black woman's movement, because of the problematic dynamics of the terminology black feminism, offers insights into the significance of self-naming, and by extension self-definition, for the integrity and survival of Africana people. While her call indicates that she was unaware of the existence of the term Africana womanism as a paradigm for all women of African descent, dating back to the eighties, her seminal statement, nonetheless, echoes the underlying concept of Africana womanism in the on-going undercurrent debate both within and beyond the Academy surrounding the politics of black and white life. What is particularly disturbing here is the dominant culture's failure to acknowledge proper names, identifications, and systems even when they do exist, as is the case of Africana womanism. Rather, the dominant culture too often promotes distortions of black life and models, the one constancy in an ever-changing climate of dissension and confusion revolving around the lives and destinies of black women and their families. Commanding different terminologies to reflect different meanings, this proper self-naming and self-defining, as a means of establishing clarity, will at the same time offer the first steps towards correcting confusion and misconception regarding one's true identity and the true level of one's struggle in terms of agenda. Hare's statement, then, reflects the nuances of the relativity of a particular terminology and concept—feminism—as issued forth by whites, and its inapplicability to black women as well as their male counterparts who are trapped first and foremost by the race factor rather than by the gender factor so prevalently addressed today. Hence, it is the crucial need for self-naming and self-defining, an interconnecting phenomenon, that becomes penultimate as we come to understand truly that *giving name to* a particular thing simultaneously gives it meaning.

Because of the critical race factor for blacks, another scholar, Audrey Thomas McCluskey, insists that "Black women must adopt a culturally specific term to describe their racialized experience, " as she is astutely cognizant of that reality for black women, whether or not black women on the whole pursue this issue to the point of independently naming themselves. McCluskey contends that "the debate over names reflects deeper issues of the right to self-validation and to claim intellectual traditions of their own" (McCluskey 2). Another scholar, Linda Anderson Smith, also writes about the importance of naming. In her article, "Unique Names and Naming Practices among African American Families," she asserts:

> Names are universally recognized as having power–as evoking images or signifying membership in a particular collective. Names are of great significance to African Americans, who, because of the history of slavery, have had to fight for the right to choose their names." [Smith 290]

Ben L. Martin, too, notes the importance of naming in "From Negro to Black to African American: The Power of Names and Naming," where he states that "names can be more than tags; they can convey powerful imagery. So naming–proposing, imposing, and accepting names—can be a political exercise" (Martin 83).

While this process seems to be a natural course of action, society, on the contrary, has not taken this route. Rather, it has ignored the true operational existence of this long-standing phenomenon and has elected to name and define Africana women outside of their cultural and historical context via the superimposition of an alien construct—Eurocentrism/feminism. In essence, the dominant culture has held the position of identifying who we are and how we fit into the scheme of things with little regard for what we ourselves perceive as our authentic reality and identity. Instead of respecting our lives as representative of self-authentication, the dominant culture obtrudes itself upon Africana people. Pointing to Africana womanism as a successful strategy and corrective for this obtrusion, Mazama asserts that "the term Africana womanism itself is the first step toward defining ourselves and setting goals that are consistent with our culture and history. In other words, it is the first step toward existing on our own terms" (Mazama 400-401). It must be noted here that "it is true that if you do not name and define yourself, some else surely will" (Hudson-Weems, "Africana Womanism and the Critical Need" 83). And they usually do so miserably. Thus, in the midst of this legacy of continued European domination through improper identification, Africana people must actively reclaim their identity, beginning with self-naming and self-defining. To be sure, without reinventing pre-existing wheels, we could then move more expediently towards resolving the problems of human survival through family cohesiveness, which Africana womanism most certainly offers.

References

Aldridge, Delores. "Black Male-Female Relationships: An African Centered Lens Model" in *Contemporary Africana Theory and Thought*. Clenora Hudson-Weems, editor. Trenton: Africa World Press, 2007.

------. "The Structural Components of Violence in Black Male-Female Relationships" in *Journal of Human Behavior in the Social Environment*. Vol. 4, No. 2 & 3, (2001): 13-24.

------. "Towards Integrating Africana Women into Africana Studies" in *Out of the Revolution: The Development of Africana Studies*. Delores Aldridge and Charlene Young, editors. Lanham/New York: Lexington Books, 2000, 191-203.

Asante, Molefi Kete. *The Afrocentric Idea*. Philadelphia: Temple University Press, 1987.

Christian, Barbara. *Black Feminist Criticism: Perspectives on Black Women Writers*. New York: Pergamon, 1985. Collins, Patricia Hill. "What's in a Name? Womanism, Black Feminism, and Beyond." *The Black Scholar*. Vol. 26, No. 1 (Winter/Spring 1996): 9-17.

------. *Black Feminist Thought: Knowledge, Consciousness and the Politics of Empowerment*. 10th Anniversary, 2nd revised edition. New York: Routledge, 2000.

Harding, Wendy and Jacky Martin. *A World of Differences: An Intercultural Study of Toni Morrison's Novels*. London: Greenwood Press, 1994.

Hare, Julia. "Feminism in Black and White." Quoted in *Black Issues in Higher Education*, by Mary-Christine Phillip. 11 March 1993: 12-17.

Harrison, Paul Carter. *The Drama of Nommo*. New York: Grove Press, 1972.

Higginbotham, Everly Brooks. "African-American Women's History and the Metalanguage of Race." *Signs: Journal of Women in Culture and Society*. 17,2 (Winter 1992): 251-275.

Hill, Patricia Liggins, et al., eds. *Call and Response: The Riverside Anthology of the African American Literary Tradition*. Boston/New York: Houghton Mifflin, 1998.

Hudson-Weems, Clenora. "Africana Womanism: An Overview." *Out of the Revolution: The Development of Africana Studies*. Delores Aldridge and Charlene Young, eds. Lanham/New York: Lexington Books, 2000, 205-217.

------. "Africana Womanism and the Critical Need for Africana Theory and Thought." *The Western Journal of Black Studies*. Vol. 21, No. 2 (1997): 79-84.

------. "Africana Womanism: Entering the New Millennium." *State of the Race—Creating Our 21ˢᵗ Century: Where Do We Go from Here?* Kamara, Jermadari, and Van Der Meer, T. Menelick, eds. Boston, MA: Diaspora Press, 2004, 7-26.

------. *Africana Womanism: Reclaiming Ourselves*. Troy, Michigan: Bedford, 1993.

------. "Cultural and Agenda Conflicts in Academia: Critical Issues for Africana Women's Studies." *The Western Journal of Black Studies*. Vol. 13, No. 4 (Winter 1989): 185-189.

-----. "Self Naming and Self Definition: An Agenda for Survival." *Sisterhood, Feminisms and Power: From Africa to the Diaspora*. Obioma Nnaemeka, ed. Trenton: Africa World Press, 1998, 449-452.

LaFond, Daisy. "Book Review of *Africana Womanism: Reclaiming Ourselves*." *Class Magazine*, 57.

Langley, April. "Lucy Terry Prince: The Cultural and Literary Legacy of Africana Womanism." *The Western Journal of Black Studies*. Vol. 25, No. 3 (Fall 2001): 153-162.

Martin, Ben L. "From Negro to Black to African American: The Power of Names and Naming." *Political Science Quarterly* 106, 1 (Spring 1991): 83-107.

Mazama, Ama. "The Afrocentric Paradigm: Contours and Definitions." *Journal of Black Studies*, Vol. 31, No. 4 (2001): 387-405.

McCluskey, Audry Thomas. "Am I Not a Woman and a Sister?: Reflections on the Role of Black Women's Studies in the Academy." *Feminist Teacher*. Vol. 8, No. 3 (1994): 105-111.

Mootry, Maria K. "Book Review of *Africana Womanism: Reclaiming Ourselves*." *The Western Journal of Black Studies*. Vol. 18, No. 4 (1994): 244-5.

Morrison, Toni. *Beloved*. New York: Alfred A. Knopf, 1987.

------. "What the Black Woman Thinks about Women's Lib." *Radical Feminism: A Documentary Reader.* Barbara A. Crow, ed. New York: New York University Press, 2000, 453-459.

Ntiri, Daphne. "The WAAD Conference and Beyond: A Look at Africana Womanism," in *Sisterhood, Feminisms and Power: From Africa to the Diaspora.* Obioma Nnaemeka, editor. New Jersey: Africa World Press, 1998, 461-463.

------. Introduction to *Africana Womanism: Reclaiming Ourselves.* Troy, Michigan: Bedford, 1993, 1-13.

------. "Africana Womanism: The Coming of Age" in *Contemporary Africana Theory and Thought.* Clenora Hudson-Weems, ed. Trenton: Africa World Press, 2007.

Smith, Linda Anderson. "Unique Names and Naming Practices among African American Families." *Families in Society.* Vol. 77, No. 5 (May 1996): 290-298.

Sofola 'Zulu. "Foreword." *Africana Womanism: Reclaiming Ourselves.* Troy, Michigan: Bedford, 1993, xvii-xviii.

Walker, Alice. "Introduction." *In Search of Our Mothers' Gardens.* San Diego: Harcourt, 1983, xi-xii.

Watkins, Valethia. "Womanism and Black Feminism: Issues in the Manipulation of African Historiography." *The Preliminary Challenge.* Los Angeles, CA: Association for the Study of Classical African Civilization, 1997.

19
AFRICANA WOMANISM: THE COMING OF AGE

Daphne W. Ntiri

The Primary goal of Africana women, then, is to create their
own criteria for assessing their realities, both in thought and in
action. (*Africana Womanism*, 50)

In 1993, Clenora Hudson-Weems broke new ground with the publication of her seminal work, *Africana Womanism: Reclaiming Ourselves*.
Continuous dialogue and *discourse* on the place and agenda of Africana
women in the Black women's movement dating back to her controversial
stance on Africana womanism in the mid-eighties reflect the impact of this
paradigm both inside and outside the academy. Within six years, this work
reached the second printing of its third revised edition. Adopted as a text
at several major universities, it has also been adopted by faculty in several
higher education institutions in as faraway places as United Kingdom,
Japan, several African countries and the Caribbean Islands. Lauded for
having added a crucial perspective on understanding the complex landscape of recent literature on the construction of race in the evolution of the
women's movement, Hudson-Weems challenges some of the ideological
inaccuracies of the movement and intensifies her message of cultural identity and collective consciousness among Africana women as central to the
ultimate goal of family survival.

Hudson-Weems coined the concept Africana Womanism in the
mid-eighties. This coinage resulted in the 1989 publication of "Cultural
and Agenda Issues in Academia: Critical Issues for Africana Women's
Studies," in the *Western Journal of Black Studies*. The term *Africana* ties
black women to their ancestral homeland in Africa and the term *womanism*
evokes Sojourner Truth's open challenge to an all-white-women's rights
convention in 1852, where she was snubbed on the basis of her race. Her

rebuttal, "And ain't I a woman," sparked a lasting attachment to the truth and worth of her words.

The paradigm of Africana Womanism has its foundation in the dissimilarities between women of African descent and those of European origins. The establishment of the feminist movement hardly conceals the chasm between these two groups. One of its nineteenth- century leaders, Carrie Chapman Catt, pushed for women's voting rights, while being sure to stress the preservation of white supremacy and racial purity (Hudson-Weems, 1993, 21). Thus, while the feminist movement evolved from its initial thrust to addressing women's civil rights and social injustice following slavery to sexual parity in the United States, and then to worldwide concerns about sex discrimination against women in a world of male power and privilege, its exclusion of other important issues (such as, race and class) resulted in the alienation of women of color (Collins, 1996; Ntiri, 1993; Splawn, 1993; Ntiri, 2001; Hudson-Weems, 2004).

This peripheralization of non-Western women hastened this group's rejection of the central tenets of mainstream feminist ideology and necessitated the formulation of a perspective on the role and place of black women in the women's movement. Feminism came to be seen as problematic and incapable of addressing all the needs of all women all the time. Predicated on patriarchy-based, Western-oriented ideas, the basic premise of feminist ideology is rooted in historical hegemony and a separatist and non-inclusive agenda for Africana women.

This is the basis for Hudson-Weems's theory. She operationalizes her theory on the assumption that race is of paramount importance in any deliberation of or about Africana women. Since any discourse involving Africana people cannot escape the historical realities of Eurocentrism, oppression, and domination, it makes sense to articulate a clear and firm position that is inclusive of those realities. In this regard, Hudson-Weems states:

> feminism was conceptualized and adopted by white women, reflecting an agenda which was designed to meet their particular needs. Therefore, Black or African feminism that originates from mainstream feminist theory is in a sense a postscript or afterthought and therefore, extremely problematic as labels for the true Africana woman (1993, 18).

Hudson-Weems continues the spirit of this argument in her analysis of what the feminists represent. She states

> While white feminists today are not necessarily hostile to the most dominant issues that impact more upon the lives of Afri-

cana women, the majority are not sensitive to the magnitude of these concerns (1993, 49).

Support for this argument is captured in the Introduction to *Africana Womanism,* which I authored and in which I identified four key issues related to the dubious relationship between white and Africana women. These pronouncements spoke first to the temporary and short-lived embrace of the feminist movement as a consequence of the absence of any structured or organized Black women's socio-intellectual groups. Second, I stated that reclamation of the Africana women was a prerequisite for the new Africana women's voices. Third, the loose alliances between the racial sectors were on a weak foundation. Finally, an identity crisis was inevitable as the struggles and expectations of the races remained on a different footing (Ntiri, 2001; Ntiri, 1993).

These sentiments are not new. African Americans in most areas of life have found themselves in similar predicaments, that is, where they are not considered "full-status anything." In particular, African American literary expression took centuries to enter the mainstream genres and even then, the moves have been guarded. Patricia Hill Collins (1996) echoes similar doubts concerning feminism as a viable methodology for Black women in her article, "What's in a Name? Womanism, Black Feminism and Beyond," even though she fails to cite Hudson-Weems's earlier works with the same perspective. Like Hudson-Weems, she challenges the acceptance of the concept of feminism *ipso facto* by Black women because of some of the same reasons given above. Also Collins, argues that some of the characteristics of white feminism are in conflict with the moral ethos of an oppressed people whose past is marred by the collective actions of the oppressor group. She takes liberties to highlight what she considers major drawbacks to buying into a feminist ideology that is outside of one's culture. First, she points out, gender works with racism to maintain oppression. Second, an acceptance of feminism by Africana women translates into the rejection of Africana men, given the theoretical underpinnings of the movement. Third, the practice of feminist ideology is based on individualism rather than communalism, a lifestyle and value more akin to African Americans and their ancestry.

Thus, the question arises: Whose feminism is it? For those Africana women in the academy who aligned themselves with feminism, such an embrace should not be misconstrued as insensitivity to these factors identified above. According to Hudson-Weems, it can be explained as an effort to become a legitimate part of a woman-focused discourse that was

311

timely and needed and had theoretical and methodological legitimacy in the academy (1993, 18).

Henry Louis Gates, Jr., in his book *Reading Black, Reading Feminist* (1990), reaffirms the intellectual integrity and historical continuity of Black women writers. However, he labels almost all the giant Black women writers and activists, including some whose texts and activity do not represent a feminist agenda, as feminists. By using this characterization, Gates does an injustice to the Black women writers he esteems. For him, it seems, if you are a woman, a writer, and successful, you are automatically a feminist even when the content and theme of your writing remains within the locus of race without any treatment of gender issues.

A few examples crystallize Gates's act of misnaming. Gloria Naylor's (1982, 1985) preoccupation with the forced displacement of the African American community in her choice of Brewster Place and Linden Hills as settings is no mistake. Race and class – not race and gender – form the basic premise of her protagonists' plot whose "dead-end" lives in the Black community are the result of victimization by the majority culture which is white and racist. Her theme is familiar to the African American community. New insights into Naylor's study of race and class are presented by Montgomery (2004) in her *Conversations with Gloria Naylor.* Equally symbolic is the portrayal of the characters caught in a Eurocentric dilemma. Instructive also is Paule Marshall's depiction of Jay Johnson in *Praisesong for the Widow* (1984) which is less concerned with gender as is, for that matter, Toni Morrison's portrayal of Macon Dead in *Song of Solomon* (1977) or Zora Neale Hurston's portrayal of Jody Starks in *Their Eyes Were Watching God* (1978). In each, the conflicts are located in race and class distinctions, illuminating basic issues that have more to do with who has more to eat than who and how to deal with a white world that continues to impose its values on Black people.

> demonstrates the value of Africana Womanism as a critical paradigm for analyzing early African American literature. Based on an analysis of Terry's personal and poetic narrative, my reading resituates her life and poem within the context of key characteristics as outlined in the structure of Africana Womanism (153-4)

As evidenced in these women's writings, social and economic mobility is a central conflict within the Black world. Black women as key players, just like Black men, are victimized directly and indirectly by the system. How then can our first-rate African American writers accept the label feminists? One answer to this question is provided by April Langley (2001) in her article "Lucy Terry Prince: The Cultural and Literary Legacy of Africana Womanism" in which she

With a close perusal of the various Black women's movements, editors of *Call and Response: The Riverside Anthology of the African American Literary Tradition* conclude the following: "Of all the theoretical models, Black feminism, African feminism, Womanism, and Africana Womanism, Hudson Weems's [Africana Womanism] best describes the racially based perspective of many Black women's rights advocates, beginning with Maria W. Stewart and Frances W. Harper" (Hill, 1997).

Feminism for them is clearly a misnomer. The term Africana Womanism conveys a spirit that is more in tune to the realities of a racially unjust society.

The controversy about the naming process dates back to the 1970s when Black women academics reformulated new definitions and paradigms for self-empowerment. The search for the right labels to convey Black thought and practice became an engaging exercise for those dissatisfied with feminism. John Henrik Clarke (1992), a contemporary writer on lost identity and Black consciousness, referred to naming as a critical variable to a race of people. How people have been classified and named in the social order in the past has serious implications for the performance, expectations, and subsequent portrayal of such people. Naming cannot be delegated to the oppressor whose abuse of power has put Blacks in various predicaments in Western circles. Clarke says, "We have been named; we should now become namers" (21). Africana people's need for self-naming, self-defining, and self-identity has led to the emergence of labels such as Black feminism, African feminism, womanism, and Africana womanism. This cannot be taken for granted; the process of naming is vital to the survival of the group. "Nommo: Self-Naming and Self-Defining" finds a place in Hudson-Weems's new theoretical work, *Africana Womanist Literary Theory* where she goes beyond just laying claim to a concept. (Hudson-Weems, p. 1, 2004) Hudson-Weems addresses this troubling issue by drawing a distinction between labels: "Africana womanism and its agenda are unique and separate from both white feminism and Black feminism; moreover, to the extent of naming in particular, Africana womanism differs from African feminism. Clearly, there is a need for a separate and distinct identity for the African woman and her movement" (1993, 155; 2001, 1). She continues her discourse in "Self- Naming and Self-Definition: An Agenda for Survival" in 1996 and 1997 publications (Nnaemeka, 1998).

At another level, Alice Walker exposes the oppression of Black literary women in her historic collection of essays, *In Search of Our Mothers' Gardens* (1983). In it, she coins the word *womanism*, which she defines as the "Black feminist or feminist of color who loves other women, sexually and/or nonsexually, appreciates and prefers women's culture (and) sometimes loves individual men, sexually and/or nonsexually. Committed to the survival and wholeness of an entire people, male and female. Womanist is to feminist as purple to lavender" (xii). This definition of womanism is indistinguishable from Black feminism except for the mention of color, and it provokes feelings of alienation from men and evokes lesbian possibilities. The survival and wholeness of the Black family appear not to be central to Walker's womanism.

None of these symbols (Black feminism, African feminism, and Walker's womanism) is sufficient in its coverage of the full range of the black woman's experience because each gives primacy to gender, rather than race and class. Hudson-Weems charges:

> It becomes apparent, then, that neither the term Black feminism nor African feminism is sufficient to label women of such complex realities as Africana women, particularly as both terms, through their very names, align themselves with feminism (1993, 20).

In addition, these descriptors automatically link the Africana woman to a racist, white feminist ideology. Collins (1996), in much the same way as Hudson-Weems has been arguing for years, concludes that:

> ...in this situation, those black women who identify with feminism must be recorded as being either non-black or less authentically black" (13).

If a black woman chooses to identify herself as a feminist, whether she is African or African American, then gender automatically takes center stage, not race. Yet, gender works in tandem with race to maintain oppression. To claim feminism, then, is to suggest that gender oppression is the primary issue in the black community. This can violate certain African American community rules and undermine the collectivism necessary to struggle against the group's oppression. Africana sociologist Joyce Ladner (1972) noted that "black women do not perceive their enemy to be black men, but rather the enemy is considered to be oppressive forces in the larger society which subjugate black men, women and children" (277- 78). Within the Africana womanist circle, men are not excluded from women's issues. On the contrary, they are invited as partners in problem-solving and social change. Challenges to power and oppression within the black community necessitate a dialogue between black men and women as a way to acknowledge the heterogeneity within the community.

Within the global configuration, the African feminist perspective is subjected to a set of different factors. The victim of neocolonialism and cultural domination, the African feminist is often cast by Westerners within a misrepresented interpretation of what Western values purport her to be. Her brand of feminism is based "on the tradition of autonomy in the performance of sex roles" (Steady, 28). The African woman's primary role in traditional society is that of mother, and this role is central to society as a whole. The African woman joins the common struggle to end discrimination against women; the importance of motherhood and the value of the child-bearing capacity is primary to meet community needs. Nnaemeka (1998) argues that feminism on the continent is so "complex and diffused that it is intractable" (5). This complexity heightens within the context of various cultural imperatives, historical forces, and localized realities that shape the face of women's activism in Africa. With the rapid pace of global change, African feminism, as it is supported by African women, cannot in all sincerity be defined within a monolithic framework. Only a pluralistic framework can capture the various transitional stages of the continent.

Taking into account all the issues raised here, the onus of responsibility for the destiny of the Africana woman lies with the Africana woman herself. The growing need to be self-named and self-defined, the desire for reclamation of her historical past, the search for a stronger sense of belonging, and a greater call for cultural roots provide the rationale and justify the urgency and necessity for a new direction for the Africana woman. Should the acceptance of black feminism imply an admission of alienation and marginalization of the Africana woman within mainstream feminism, "what we have then is not a simple issue of sex or class differences but a situation which because of the racial factor, is caste-like in character on both a national and global scale" (Steady, 18-19). And if black feminism recognizes its peripheral status and clearly espouses a move "from margin to center" of the feminist movement (hooks 1984), then Africana Womanism as proposed by Hudson-Weems is timely, theoretically fitting, and intrinsically advantageous to the Africana woman. It has charted a new direction for self-naming and self-control. *Africana Womanism* fills a void created by the disassociation of Africana women from movements that foster inequality and keep them languishing on the fringes of the white world – exploited, unfulfilled, and alienated.

This novel advocacy solidifies the commonality of political and socio-economic goals, gives legitimacy to their claim for equality, demonstrates clarity of mission in our Africanness, and adds originality to the collective voice of Africana women (Ntiri 1993, 5). This is why Hudson-Weems states that Africana womanism is "an ideology created and designed for all women of African descent. It is grounded in their culture, and therefore, it necessarily focuses on the unique experiences, struggles, needs, and desires of Africana women" (1993, 24).

Just as there are compelling reasons to reclaim the power to ascribe names to African people (such as, colored, Negro, African, African American) in the United States (to reaffirm their race and establish stronger African affinity), so are there reasons to advocate an Africana womanist theory that is properly labeled, more attuned and appropriate to the needs of the Africana woman. The proper label must take into consideration the unique experience and realities of the Africana woman. The status, struggles, and experiences of the Africana woman in forced exile in Europe, Latin America, the United States, or at home in Africa remain typically separate from those of other women of color, and of course from those of white women.

The prevailing primacy of race (over gender) is clear in Weems's sharing of the words of an observer about the Africana woman in any given situation. She writes: "From so many feet away, her race was noticed; as she got into closer proximity, her class was detected; but it was not until she got in the door that her sex was known" (1993, 41). Not only is it apparent that race precedes sexism in a racist world, but is it not also true that society has conditioned its observers to see race before sex, and that racism and classism go hand in hand? In South Africa, just as in the United States, race wars were primary galvanizing instruments to fight oppression and defend human dignity. In many African countries, organized movements, such as the Mau Mau in Kenya, toppled European colonial administrations whose exploitative policies are still felt today. The question that arises repeatedly then is, Why should an Africana woman, disabled by a global system of oppression and racism, support the feminist movement with its distinct orientation to Eurocentric ideals?

As is now evident, "the implications of the feminist movement for the black woman are complex" (Steady, 23). Hudson-Weems, therefore petitions Africana women to construct "their own set of criteria for assessing their realities in thought and action" (1993, 50). The true and loyal Africana womanist is a self-namer and a self-definer. She is family-centered and a partner with males in the struggle for social change. She is strong, spiritual, and nurturing. According to Steady, "several factors set the black woman apart as having a different order of priorities. She is oppressed not simply because of her sex, but ostensibly because of her race and, for the majority, essentially because of their class" (Steady, 23, 24).

316

In conclusion, one must remember that women in general belong to different socioeconomic groups as they do not represent a universal category. Suffice it to say, because the majority of black women are poor and illiterate, the process of reflection in language use and naming their struggles is reserved for the privileged in the academy and may have little direct or immediate consequence for the woman trapped in the segregated ghettos of America or the resourceless villages in southern Africa. However, that there is an inextricable relationship between Africana women and their communities. Clearly, the survival and the growth of the black community rest largely on the acceptance, understanding, and appreciation of the Africana woman, which includes her participation in the livelihood of her family. That said, it is no surprise that Hudson-Weems' theory of Africana Womanism has gained popularity and respect in the Academy. Her first book is now in its fourth revised edition since its release date in 1993 and now there is the sequel to it, released 2004, eleven years later.

References

Alridge, D. *Focusing: Black Male-Female Relationships*. Chicago: Third World Press, 1991.

Amdahl, J. *My Voice, My Choice: Identity Issues in Black Feminist/Womanist Discourse*, English 8720, University of Minnesota, on line, 1998. (Received from m1.boston.juno.com in March 1999.)

Anderson, M. L. and Collins, P. H. Race, Class, and Gender: An Anthology. Thomson Learning, 2006.

Calloway, Licia M. (2003). *Black Family (Dys)function*. New York: Peter Lang.

Clarke, J. H. "To Name Ourselves." *The Voice Holiday*, 3.4 (1992): 20-21, 41.

Collins, P. Hill. "What's in a Name? Womanism, Black Feminism and Beyond." *The Black Scholar* 26 (1996): 9-17.

_____. Black Feminist Thought: Knowledge, consciousness, and the Politics of Empowerment (Perspectives on Gender) New York: Routledge, 2000.

Gates, H. L., Jr., editor. (1990) *Reading Black: Reading Feminist*. New York: Meridian Books, 1990.

Hill, P. Liggins. *Call and Response: The Riverside Anthology of the African American Literary Tradition*. Boston: Houghton Mifflin,1997.

hooks, b. *Feminist Theory: From Margin to Center*. Boston: Southend, 1984.

Hudson-Weems, Clenora (2004). *Africana Womanist Literary Theory*. Trenton, NJ: Africa World Press.

_____. "Africana Womanism: A Historical Global Perspective for Women of African Descent." In Hill, *Call and Response:* 1812-1814.

_____. *Africana Womanism: Reclaiming Ourselves*. Troy: Bedford Publishers, 1993.

_____. "Cultural and Agenda Conflicts in Academia: Critical Issues for Africana Women's Studies." *Western Journal for Black Studies* 13.4 (1989):185-189.

_____. "Self-Naming and Self-Definition: An Agenda for Survival." In Nnaemeka, O. *Sisterhood, Feminisms and Power*, 449-452, 1998.

Hurston, Z. N. *Their Eyes Were Watching God.* Urbana: University of Illinois Press, 1978.

Kolawale, Mary E. Modupe. *Womanism and African Consciousness.* Washington DC: Africa World Press, 1998.

Ladner, J. *Tomorrow's Tomorrow: The Black Woman.* Garden City, N.Y.: Anchor, 1972.

Langley, April. "Lucy Terry Prince: The Cultural and Literary Legacy of Africana Womanism" in *The Western Journal of Black Studies* 25:3 (2001): 153-162.

Levin, Amy K. (2003). *Africanism and Authenticity in African American Women's Novels*, University Press of Florida.

Marshall, P. *Praisesong for the Widow.* New York: A Dutton Belisk, 1984.

Montgomery, Maxine L. (2004). *Conversations with Gloria Naylor.* University Press of Mississippi Morrison, T. *Song of Solomon.* New York: Knopf, 1977.

Naylor, G. *Linden Hills.* New York: Tucknor and Fields, 1985.

_____. *The Women of Brewster Place.* New York: Penguin Contemporary American Fiction Series 60, 1982.

Nnaemeka, O., *Sisterhood, Feminisms and Power: From Africa to theDiaspora.* Washington, D.C: Africa World Press, 1998.

Ntiri, D. W. "An Introduction." In Hudson-Weems, *Africana Womanism.* Troy: Bedford Publishers, 1993.

Radford-Hill, S. *Further to Fly: Black Women and the Politics of Empowerment.* Minneapolis: University of Minnesota Press, 2000.

Splawn, P. J. *Recent Developments in Black Feminist Literary Scholarship: A Selective Annotated Bibliography? Modern Fiction Studies* 39. 3& 4, (Fall/Winter 1993): 819-21.

Steady, P., ed. *The Black Woman Cross-Culturally.* Rochester: Schenkman Books, 1985.

Walker, A. *In Search of Our Mothers' Gardens.* San Diego: Harcourt, 1983.

20

AFRICANA WOMANISM – AN AFRICAN
LEGACY: IT AIN'T EASY BEING A QUEEN

Barbara A. Wheeler

> Descending from a lineage of strong, proud African women
> activists and culture bearers, dating back to the advent of the
> colonization of Africa by Europe, notwithstanding African
> warrior queens in antiquity... [African queens] demonstrate
> unquestionable persistence.... (Hudson-Weems, *Africana Wom-
> anist*, 51).

I am indebted to Clenora Hudson-Weems whose presentation at the 1988
National Council for Black Studies annual conference in Philadelphia helped my understanding of the necessity for making a distinction
between (Black) Africana Womanism on the one hand and Euro-American
feminism on the other. Subsequently, Hudson-Weems' definition of Africana Womanism in her book. *Africana Womanism: Reclaiming Ourselves*
proved salient. According to the author, "there are eighteen distinct and
diverse characteristics of Africana Womanism; the true Africana womanist possesses all of these qualities to a varying degree, encompassing all
aspects of her life" (55).

In Chapter IV of the text, entitled "The Agenda of the Africana Womanist," Hudson-Weems defines these descriptors, contending that she is first
self-naming, and self defining. She is also family-centered and in concert
with males in the broader struggle for humanity and the liberation of all
Africana people. Other characteristics include flexible role player, genuine
in sisterhood, psychologically as well as physically strong and male compatible. She is respected and recognized while seeking both wholeness
and authenticity in her life. The Africana womanist demonstrates belief
in a higher power, spirituality, and is respectful of her elders. Finally, she
is adaptable, ambitious and committed to mothering and nurturing, all

of which are seminal features of the true Africana Womanist (Hudson-Weems, 55-73).

This paper will begin with a little of what is known, in legend and in fact, about the achievements and characteristics of African queens in antiquity. It goes on to make some observations about the influence of African women on the origins and evolution of the world-wide institutions of marriage and family. The conclusion contains thoughts regarding of the visible legacy of ancient African queens, queen warriors, and ordinary African women, and their impact upon contemporary women of African heritage.

I am indebted to my father, who first told me about ancient African queens during my early years in Boston's South End, a mixed neighborhood of Irish, Jews, Italians, Poles, Syrians, Lithuanians, and other ethnic Caucasians. When I think back on that time and place, I recall a joke Richard Pryor told about a kid whose mother was Black, whose father was Puerto Rican, who lived in a Jewish-owned tenement building in a predominately Italian neighborhood where he attended a Catholic school during the week and a Baptist church on Sundays. When he went out to play, the rest of the kids would shout, "Get him! He's all of them!"

Ethnic consciousness has always been a dominant part of America's cultural heritage and the streets of Boston's neighborhoods were laboratories for learning and reinforcing one's ethnicity. The games we played usually had an ethnic lesson; whether jump rope, dodge ball, or street ball, the lyrics always dealt with ethnicity. The kids were obsessed with ethnic identification, proudly proclaiming: I'm Irish, I'm German, I'm French, I'm Italian, and so on. I recall I was about eight years old when I was questioned about my ethnic heritage. Frankly I was not really sure what I was, but not to be outdone, I replied that I was Mexican. In retrospect I realize I may have been reluctant to say "Negro," the accepted terminology of that era, for fear of ridicule or exclusion. I had read that Mexicans had a lot of names, so I told them mine was Barbara Ann Marie Louise Jones. However, when I went home I told my father about the episode and asked him to tell me who I was. His reply was profound and has stuck with me throughout my life: "You are the descendant of a long line of African kings and queens; that makes you an African princess." He went on to assure me that I would be an African queen when I grew up. In 1972 my father died, just as I was finishing my doctoral dissertation and I recall whispering into his casket, "It ain't easy being a queen, Daddy."

As the Black revolution of the sixties gathered strength, Black scholars were stimulated to research African history for an understanding of a past, which for so long had been distorted to make us despise ourselves. They brought to light documentation of ancient Africa with attesting to a high level of civilization and culture, which forms the basis of a proud legacy.

> Black people have survived on this earth at least two million years – for at least as long as man has been known to exist. We are an old people with wisdom to share.... Black people have built complex, humanistic social systems which served our ancestors well in their time and from which much good can be learned today,... while rearing children in an increasingly dehumanizing and mechanized society.... Black people have continually fought for freedom from tyranny and oppression, sometimes winning and sometimes losing, all the while learning the art of survival.... In interpreting the acts of birthing, loving, living and dying, in the form of dance, music, art, and literature, black people have immortalized expressions of life that transcend racial distinctions and speak eloquently of the universality of the human condition. This is SOUL. And it's hard to identify with our history and not have it (Bennett, 194-98).

This understanding is vital for Africana women. In the Quest for historical truth, we are raising questions about ourselves as Blacks and as females. "What can we learn," we ask, "from the Black and female experience? What themes evolve from African history that might provide insight into our struggle against both racism and sexism? And what African models can be used as we raise the timeless question: "Who and what and why am I?"

It has now been acknowledged that humankind originated in Africa; that is, that the continent of Africa is the cradle of humanity. We also know that the hand that rocks the cradle historically has been the hand of a woman, the culture bearer. It is for this reason that we must laud Lewis, Mary, and Richard Leakey for resurrecting the oldest known African queen. In 1962, from the diggings of Olduvai Gorge, in Tanzania, the Leakeys unearthed the fossil that helped establish that humans, as we know them today, did originate in Africa. The Leakeys' discovery was of paramount interest because it established this fossil as a concrete record of a female who had lived approximately 800,000 years ago. The Leakeys nicknamed their fossil Cinderella, a very "ofay" name for an African woman of any era. She also had a scientific name, Homo Habilis Woman, meaning "woman with ability," and that is a distinction of note. We are able to learn a great deal about the conditions of life in prehistoric times from Cinderella – including her ability to speak, walk, and eat meat. It is also believed that she worked with tools, perhaps even made them. It is appropriate that

Cinderella entered the human record with the designation "woman with ability," because ability has consistently characterized African women – the ability to work with tools in antiquity, and other implements in later times; the ability to toil relentlessly so that her family might survive and her people advance; the ability to laugh, sing, and create, in good times and bad – all abilities that mark the history of the African woman. *Homo Habilis Woman*: a worthy ancestor!

We do not learn about ourselves from archaeology or written records alone. Legends (many of them handed down through oral tradition, a communication technique widely used in Africa) enter the human consciousness and form impressions, attitudes, and feelings. Legends and facts, the latter subject to the biased interpretations of historians, combine to give a people a sense of their worth. Important in the legends of Africa are the stories of women, most of which give us a sense of the esteem, even the fear, felt toward other women. These legends describe the characteristics so highly valued in Africana women.

First there is the legend of Queen Moo who demonstrated the ultimate in strength, male compatibility, and spirituality, all key descriptors for the true Africana womanist as defined by Hudson-Weems. There are many gaps in the story of human evolution and the Americas represent a fertile land for future exploration. Perhaps in years to come, the story of Queen Moo, an Africana woman who, according to legend, engineered the building of the Sphinx along the banks of the Nile in Egypt, will be lifted from legendary speculation to truth. Legend tells us that when the Egyptians were just beginning a civilization, there already existed on the Western continent a nation called Maya. The exact boundaries of Maya are unknown, but it included the Yucatan, where important archaeological discoveries have now been made. Its people were exceptional navigators and explorers whose seagoing feats are illustrated in the epic ARamayana." Queen Moo was forced to flee from Maya to the banks of the Nile where she commanded the building of the Sphinx to honor her brother-husband, Prince Coh. How Moo got to the Nile is a mystery. However, the fact that she actually existed and built a temple and mausoleum in Maya to house her husband's remains is fairly well established. It should be noted that in many ancient European, African, and Asian kingdoms, brothers and sisters married each other in order to preserve royal lineage. Thus, Moo and Coh, brother and sister, were a happy couple and benign rulers of Maya. Coh's brother, Prince Aac, who was jealous of both their reign and their marriage, assassinated him and attempted to force Moo to marry him. Heartbroken by the death of her husband, Moo rejected Aac and devoted herself to her husband's memory. In a grand gesture of love and respect for Coh, she ordered the building of a memorial hall and mausoleum in Maya. The cruel Aac resented Moo's rejection and her efforts to keep her husband's memory alive. He finally plunged the country into civil war and threatened her life. Moo fled Maya and sought refuge among her fellow countrymen in the land now called Egypt. Here she was worshipped as a goddess, and she designed and ordered the building of the mysterious Sphinx, whose features were exactly like those of Coh. Centuries later, LePlon claims that, in his excavations in the Yucatan, he found the charred heart of Coh. He makes comparative notes on the similarity of the inscriptions found both in the Maya temple and at the base of the Egyptian Sphinx. Particularly convincing is his comparison of the two languages and the portrait in the monument of the leopard with a human head, so alike in both countries. It is thought that Moo associated this leopard with the strength of her husband. The solution of the Sphinx mystery may very well be found in the ancient Maya archives, where it is waiting to be mined by future scholars and archaeologists. Additionally, among the hypotheses to be tested is the idea that a woman – an Africana woman in many respects, including her respect for male-female compatibility and her strength in enduring the hardships of her personal lost – may have, indeed, designed the Sphinx (Noble, 7-9). Thus, "the Africana womanist comes from a long tradition of psychological as well as physical strength... out of both awesome courage and true love for her family" (Hudson-Weems, 66). To be sure, Queen Moo's fidelity and persistence – which is reminiscent of the resilience of another pre-Africana womanist, Isis, who faithfully searched for the body parts of her loved one, Osiris, scattered by Seth in the Abydos drama, is a testimony of the rich legacy of the Africana womanhood.

Herodutus the Greek, acknowledged by Western civilization as the father of history, tells us about the Ethiopian queen Nitocris, who was placed on the Egyptian throne after the Egyptians killed her brother. Demonstrating remarkable engineering insight during her reign, she routed the Euphrates via a large basin so that the river could form a reservoir. Displaying an unusual interest in conservation, she lined the embankment with stones and constructed a stone bridge across the largest span of the river to unite the two halves of her city. She constructed it in such a way that the bridge planks could be taken up at night, thereby discouraging nocturnal crimes. It appears that Nitocris was also revengeful, In retaliation her brother's death, she invited his enemies to a banquet held in a chamber she had designed with a secret duct, which allowed the water from the river to flow in and drown them (Noble, 7-9).

Africa has, in fact, produced an unusual number of queens, remembered not because they were consorts of kings but because they were rulers in their own right. It should be noted here that, because Ethiopia was the mother of Egypt, it produced the mother and grandmother queens of the now popular Cleopatra and Nefertiti. Makeda, the queen of Ethiopia whom we know as Sheba, was described in the *Song of Solomon* as black and comely. She makes her mark in history as an eager student, anxious to learn everything possible from Solomon. Law and order and social justice were her preoccupations, and she besieged Solomon with questions and debates. Happy to oblige such an inquisitive student, Solomon became an agreeable teacher but, inevitably, sought a more romantic relationship. She repeatedly refused his advances, but Solomon finally tricked her into bed by daring her to agree that if she ever took anything from him, she would have to accede to his wishes. Sheba, wealthy and independent, accepted this as a wager she could easily win. Solomon then staged a banquet with a menu of highly spicy foods, forbidding the serving of water and wine during the meal and later in her bedroom. That night, half-crazed with thirst, Sheba crept into Solomon's bedroom looking for water. As she drank from the pitcher beside Solomon's bed, he said, "Aha, you have taken something of mine!" "But it is only water," replied Sheba. "Yes, but what more important to take than water from a friend?" She lost the bet and so a love relationship began. Menylek, a son, was born and when Sheba returned home to Ethiopia, her people accepted the boy as their future king. Solomon's parting gift to Sheba was a royal ring and his promise that if Menylek presented the ring in the future, Solomon would acknowledge him as his son. Menylek grew strong and brilliant under his mother's tutelage and was brought up to observe Solomon's religion and philosophy. With Sheba's blessing, he later took the royal ring to his father and studied with him.

Between 748 and 644 BC, a period of more than eighty years, Ethiopia again ruled Egypt. During that time a series of eight Ethiopian queens called Mistresses of Kush reigned. One of them, Queen Amenertas, bore the full insignia of authority. Both her mother and father were of royal lineage. Her Ethiopian father, Kashta, is often depicted with his daughter on his right hand. A princess-sovereign devoted to the service of Amon, Amenertas was noted for her beautification of Thebes and the restoration of the works of her predecessors that had been destroyed in war. She built chapels in her own name and left many examples of her beautification program in other cities, including Aswan and Memphis. Queen Amenertas, "a vigorous ruler, administered her kingdom in peace and prosperity, both as its political and spiritual leader." A black granite statue of Amenertas, found in mutilated condition, still remains. Her daughter, Shepen-apt, was the last of the Ethiopian queens to rule Egypt (Noble, 12-13). A long line of near-goddesses and great Africana women have also played a significant role in Ethiopian life. The Ethiopian women of antiquity may have established the model for modern Africana ideas of male-female complementarity and equality. Indeed, a close study of Ethiopian women in antiquity would help Africana women today understand something of the resoluteness and independence that has come to characterize us as a group. Regardless of Ethiopian attitudes toward women today, it is certain that the concept of "regality" came from the women of ancient Ethiopia long before European colonialism introduced male chauvinism.

Egypt has produced great and illustrious queens, excitingly glamorous queens. The world has long romanticized and idolized them, particularly Cleopatra and Nefertiti. But this fascination is not new; for many of the Egyptian pharaohs took their wives from Ethiopia. Indeed it was said that an Egyptian ruler who married an Ethiopian wife would one day produce a crown prince who would restore the lost paradise and bring about univer-sal brotherhood. For all this continuous interest, surprisingly little atten-tion has been paid to two of the greatest Egyptian queens of earlier times, Nefertari and her great-granddaughter Hatshepsut. Dynasty XVIII, in which both of these earlier queens lived, is generally considered to be the greatest age of Egyptian history. Arts, crafts, and literature flourished. The quality of life, especially the people's dedication to justice and compas-sion, marked this age as one of the most humane in history. The treatment of women as equals and the respect for their minds and talents created an atmosphere in which their competence was allowed to flourish. The concept of matriarchy seems to have started here. These Egyptian women were first-class citizens, who could own, inherit, build, buy, and sell prop-erty. Enjoying great independence, they participated in government of the family, religious ceremonies, and business affairs conducted outside the home. It is not surprising then that these two ambitious Africana woman-ists, Nefertari and Hatshepsut, grew in stature to astonishing heights of power and eminence scarcely matched in the Western world (Noble, 14).

Nefertari's husband, King Amose I, was the founder of the 18th dynasty. He would certainly be considered a liberated man today. He wrote of his deep love for the women of his family, and he accorded them authoritative powers that equaled his own. His deepest love and respect, however, was reserved for his wife, Nefertari, who, in an Africana womanist fashion, shared the throne of Egypt with her husband for twenty years, establish-ing a peaceful and humane reign, and even after his death she refused to resign her authority. She was the first queen who scorned the inactivity of the harem and actively fulfilled the duties of a sovereign. Even when her son, Amenhotep I, came to power she continued to wield influence and continued guiding and building projects, including the shrines and temples in Upper Egypt. Nefertari was one of the most venerated queens in history. An Africana womanist, grounded in spirituality, there was a kind of religious mystique surrounding her. Her husband had bestowed on her the title "God's Wife" as well as "Great Royal Wife" (Noble, 14).

Hatshepsut was groomed to reign like no other queen in Egypt. She was her father's favorite, and despite the existence of other royal children, there appeared to be no question that her intelligence and manner made her the ideal choice to assume the throne. Wearing a boy's kilt, Hatshepsut learned to hunt and participate in sports. Priests and scholars tutored her in all the lessons needed to rule Egypt. Her father gave her the title ACrown Prince." However advanced this society, it would seem there was still a greater premium put upon a Aprince" than on a Aprincess"! Departing from custom, her father decided to make Hatshepsut co-regent of Egypt before his death. When she was barely twenty, in an elaborate coronation that took the royal party to two cities, Thebes and Heliopolis, she was crowned AKing of Upper and Lower Egypt, Living Forever". By the time Hatshepsut came to full power, Egypt had been used to the strong male presence of her father, and even for Hatshepsut, her sex became a liability. She was the only remaining fully royal Thotmesid, a line of royal descent, and the first sole woman regent. For a time, this strong Africana womanist ruled alone, but in accordance with royal obligations and social pressure, she finally chose a half-brother to rule with her as her husband. He took the name of Thothmes II, though his mother was not of royal birth. He was not aggressive (perhaps Hatshepsut liked it that way) but he gave her two daughters to assume the continuation and fulfillment of royal expectations. Thothmes II died young and once again Hatshepsut ruled alone; but this time, to put down a palace coup, she had herself crowned King. Using all of her dead father's royal titles, she assumed a stronger reign and was able to go on to build some of Egypt's greatest monuments, including her Deir elBahari temple. Everywhere, splendid new temples and buildings were rising. Egypt was prosperous, art flourished; there was good government and lively commerce. An astute politician, Hatshepsut recognized the claim to the throne of Thothmes III, her husband's son by Isis, his concubine. Thus, Thothmes III was married to Hatshepsut's daughter, making him co-regent; but he waited impatiently in the wings, for Hatshepsut continued to rule in total power. Thotmes III then started a propaganda campaign to get rid of this peace-loving woman. The Egyptians, goaded by Thothmes's friends and apparently tired of prosperity and peace, overthrew the queen. Her violent, ruthless son-in-law then plunged Egypt into an era of war and aggression. Not content just with replacing Hatshepsut, Thothmes erased her name and face from most of her lovely monuments. Until fairly recent times, even historians scarcely realized that Hatshepsut was, indeed, a woman.

This story of Egyptian queens would be incomplete if we neglected that outstanding Africana womanist Nubian regent, Queen Tiye, wife of Amenhotep III. Queen Tiye was the mother of Amenhotep IV who is better known to us as Akhenaten. Queen Tiye and Nefertiti, Akhenaten's wife, served as co-regents of Egypt while Akhenaten pursued his monotheistic religious beliefs. Known for her beauty, Queen Tiye demonstrated monumental influence over both Egypt and her son. Other African countries also produced outstanding queens of great intelligence and varied talents. Many of them were forced to prove their abilities on the battlefield and thereby became known as Africa's Queen Warriors. Judith, the Fire of Ethiopia; Zinga, queen of Angola; and Chaka, the Zula queen; they all deserve more attention than history accords them today. Additionally, there are those African women who illuminated the earliest beginning of African national or tribal history. For example, the history of the Sala people of northwestern Rhodesia started in 1820 when a queen named Namumbe appeared from a district to the northwest of Lusaka and "founded a village." When Namumbe died in 1835, her sister Maninga inherited the chieftaincy. The names of the African women who fought to stave off enslavement by the Europeans are also numerous and worthy of further study. The stories of these queens and female warriors of Africa will document the fact that strong brave African women have always helped to shape African history.

AFRICAN WOMEN IN MARRIAGE AND FAMILY LIFE

A mere cataloging of ancient African queens and queen warriors tells us too little about the everyday themes of human struggle and the role of Africana women in that struggle. An Afrocentric perspective of history moves us away from an emphasis on the "great women" theory to that of ordinary Africana women as a collective force in molding world civilization, particularly the institutional life of marriage and family. Heuristically, the prominent position of African women in the family led generally to a prominent position of women in government. No people, ancient or modern, has accorded women so high a legal status as did Egypt and the other ancient African states. Throughout Africa, ordinary women occupied equal social positions with men. Thus, when outside explorers and colonizers sought to impose their male chauvinistic views on African social systems, they met polite resistance. For example, when Mohhamed Askia the Great attempted to reform Timbuktu, he ordered the women draped from head to toe. But when he died, the country returned to the accustomed freedom and equality between men and women. Paternalism did not easily fit into the traditions of Africa.

The matrilineal system of kinship – in which inheritance, succession, and political allegiance are determined by the female line of descent – was widespread in Africa, a situation often associated with a matriarchy. Lay people all too often conclude that in such a system the women exercise domination over men similar to that exercised by men over women in modern patriarchal society. In African societies, both men and women were producers and both had power positions in the accumulation and disposition of property and wealth. Furthermore, the African social system was more family-oriented than marriage- minded. Decisions were made for the good of the entire family, and marriage between a man and a woman represented a Acoming together" of two families. Since only a woman can truthfully certify the paternity of children, authority over kinship lines rested with her in a matrilineal system. John Jackson assists our understanding of the origins of matrilineal descent as follows:

> In the Old Testament of the Bible the first human group, we are told, was a married couple, Adam and Eve. This pair and their children were the first family. The idea of the primacy of the patriarchy, with its male head and a subordinate position for women, was held to be the very foundation of human society. This theory is no longer tenable, for we now know that the patriarchal family was *not* the first human group. The first type of family was matriarchal, since the role of the father in procreation was unknown. The evidence at hand points to the conclusion that the primordial human group consisted not of a father, mother, and their descendants, but instead of a mother and her descendants in the female line, since no other line of descent was then known. This system of female descent is known among anthropologists as Mother-right. (Jackson, 51)

African people appear therefore to be the first to understand the still-popular saying "mother's baby, father's maybe." This knowledge helps us understand the role of African women as originator of nation or tribe, as presented in the legends of most African people.

Jomo Kenyatta, an anthropologist, who later became president of Kenya, tells us in *Facing Mount Kenya* that women were the original rulers of the Kikuyu people. He goes on to explain how men plotted to overthrow their female rulers, and carried out the plan: "After several centuries, man slowly began to realize that he played a role in procreation; that nine months after conception, a baby was born. Using that information the men schemed to get all the women drunk on the same night, to impregnate them on that night and then they waited the nine months. While all the women were in labor, the men took over and we've had inequality ever since" (Kenyatta, 8-9).

John Jackson tells us that this plan to overthrow the women coincided with the origins of private property or capitalism. The system of collectivism or communalism was superseded by the institution of private property. This was a momentous change, and in many parts of the world it led to the decline of female egalitarianism, which was succeeded by a state of male dominance.

> Men who had acquired private property in cattle, slaves and weapons inevitably sought to transmit such possessions to their children. This was incompatible with the existence of the matrilineal clan. Mother-right meant that the children belonged to their mother's clan, not to their father's, and that when a man died, his property, in order to remain in the clan, passed to his nearest clan relations, to his brothers and sisters or his sisters' children – but not to his children. Thus, MotherBright had to go. Man's ownership of cattle, slaves, and weapons gave him the upper hand. So in due course... inheritance was shifted to the male line.... At the same time, in order to secure the legitimacy of children, the bond of marriage was tightened and chastity imposed as a duty on women, but not men. Thus along with private property and slaves, arose the patriarchal family – the man with *his* house, *his* wife, *his* maidservant, *his* ox, *his* ass, and everything that was his. (Jackson, 55)

CONCLUSION

Our saga would be incomplete without mention of the impact of enslavement in the Americas upon our queens. Nobody knows how many descendants of these African queens were brought to the shores of the New World during the long centuries of the transatlantic slave trade from the 1400s to the mid 1800s. Nor do we know how many skeletal remains of those queens who preferred death and drowning to slavery now line the bottom of the Atlantic ocean. Historical attempts to guestimate numbers range from 30 million to 100 million Africans taken from the continent and, of course, not all survived the Middle Passage. For our purposes today, let's just say that countless numbers of African women have ennobled the fabric of American life. The social system from which our African ancestors were captured and enslaved produced a woman whose self-concept, values, loyalties, and lifestyles foretold an impossibly difficult adjustment to America. The individualistic, competitive social system of the Americas was strikingly different the sharing, collective group life these women had lived. Though some had been accustomed to African slavery, it was certainly never as inhumane, never as life-binding as American slavery. Our African foremothers were thrown into the most brutalizing and humiliating institution in the history of mankind – American slavery – and their survival and that of their children is the greatest monument to humanity ever yet recorded.

The overriding summation of the Africana woman's past is simply the fact that she has always demonstrated strength and self-reliance – necessary qualities for survival. As the women of Africa were captured, bound, and dragged to the shores of the Caribbean, and North and South America, the historical characteristics handed down to the true Africana woman, which made them strong, flexible, adaptable, and ambitious were those same traits that enabled them to survive. Frail "clinging vines," overly dependent shrinking violets become extinct, like *Homo Erectus*. The strong, family-centered, self-defined Africana woman survived – as did Cinderella – Africa's first queen – *Homo Habilis Woman* – Woman with ability! And survive we have! We've multiplied, endured, built, resisted, and persisted.

> It Ain't Easy Being A Queen
> We black women have been called many things
> Foxes, matriarchs, Sapphires, and recently... Queens
> I would say that Black women have been a combination
> of all them words...'cause if we examine our past history, at one
>   time or another, we've had to be like them words be saying.
> But today, there are some words we can discard,
> There be some we must discard,
> For our survival, for our own sanity,
> For the contribution we must make to our emerging Black
>   nation.
> And we must move as the only Queens of this universe
> To sustain, keep our sanity, in this insane3messed up...
> Diet conscious, pill taking, masochistic,
> Miss Ann oriented society
> Got to be dealt with cause that's us.
> Y'all hear me? US! Black Women!
> The only Queens of this universe
> Even though we be stepping unqueenly sometimes
> Like... It ain't easy being a Queen in this unrighteous world
>   Full of...

Miss Anns and Mister Anns
But we be steady trying! (cited in Noble 291)

References

Bennett, Lerone. *The Challenge of Blackness*. Chicago: Johnson Publishing, 1972.

Hudson-Weems, Clenora. *Africana Womanism: Reclaiming Ourselves*. Troy, Michigan: Bedford Publishers, 1993.

_____. *Africana Womanist Literary Theory*. Trenton, NJ: Africa World Press, 2004.

Jackson, John. *Introduction to African Civilizations*. Secaucus, N.J.: Citadel Press, 1974

Kenyatta, Jomo. *Facing Mount Kenya*. New York: Vintage Books, Random House, 1962.

Noble, Jeanne. *Beautiful, Also, Are the Souls of My Black Sisters*. Englewood Cliffs, N. J.: Prentice-Hall, 1978.

21

FRANCES WATKINS HARPER:
EMINENT PRE-AFRICANA WOMANIST

Anne Steiner

Of all the theoretical models, Hudson-Weems' best describes the racially based perspective of many black women's rights advocates, beginning with Maria W. Stewart and Frances Watkins Harper in the early nineteenth century. (Hill, 1997)

Frances Watkins Harper was poet, orator, and abolitionist. Her "astute readings of the subtle nuances of race, gender and class" helped in shaping America away from its inhumane practices of the enslavement of African Americans throughout this country (Hill, 349). Her literary works reveal her purpose in life, which was to uplift African Americans by working to improve all aspects of their lives. Her life and her works, therefore, are inexorably connected. As she asserts in *Iola Leroy,* her mission was to awaken in the hearts of our countrymen a stronger sense of justice and a more Christlike humanity in behalf of those whom the fortunes of war threw homeless, ignorant and poor, upon the threshold of a new era (282).

Harper's efforts aimed at achieving justice and equality for the entire race of African Americans newly released from slavery and lacking immediate means of gaining parity in a new world order. Voicing her concern for the entire race, not just its female portion, Harper insists that her efforts are not to improve any separate subgroup of African Americans. In fact, her entire canon reveals her commitment to the betterment of African Americans through abolishing slavery and lynching, achieving civil rights and human rights, obtaining education for blacks, instilling racial pride, and fostering a Christian ideal. In this quest for all African Americans, Harper emerges as an eminent pre-Africana womanist, fully aware that because American society oppresses and represses all African Americans, she must direct her efforts toward the whole. Indeed, "until her entire people are free, she is not free" (Hudson-Weems, 59). In dedicating her entire life to this cause, Harper exemplifies some of the major tenets of Africana womanism – self-namer, self-definer, family-centered, strong, in concert with male in struggle, whole, authentic, male compatible, adaptable, ambitious, mothering and nurturing (Hudson-Weems, 55-74).

Harper reveals her Africana womanist inclinations in how she used her natural talent and education to become a writer and teacher, and in how, she worked incessantly to improve the race. Her quest for freedom for herself and others led her to become an outspoken lecturer and abolitionist. She voiced her allegiance to her people to William Still, one of the main figures associated with the underground, vowing that she would utilize her "time, talent, and energy in the cause of freedom" (Hill, 346). To be sure, her commitment to the abolition movement was so strong that she risked her own freedom and, indeed her life, to end slavery. Thus, Harper worked to create for herself and all Africanans a new definition – that of a free people. She was respected and recognized for her attempts to create an authentic, realistic existence for all Africanans. She struggled for an authentic existence that recognized and acknowledged the need for family, connectedness, and a sense of community. Harper's own life had taught her to value these concepts.

Born in Baltimore, Maryland, to free parents, Harper was left orphaned at the tender age of three, her mother's premature death. She was nurtured and educated in the loving family of her uncle, William Watkins, who provided the foundation on which she built her life of service to African Americans. When she became a wife and mother, she established for her family the same type of nurturing environment that had nurtured her. She resumed her career as lecturer after the premature death of her husband, Fenton Harper, in 1864, thereby exemplifying several characteristics of Africana womanism – male compatibility, mothering and nurturing, and adaptability. Working with other abolitionists, including Frederick Douglass, Sojourner Truth, and Robert and Harriet Purvis, Harper further presents herself as a model Africana womanist, by working collectively with her male counterparts as well as with other females toward the betterment of the race.

Though certain aspects of Harper's philosophy converge with that of mainstream feminists, the points of difference are too significant to label Harper a feminist. Carby describes Harper as a feminist who "had to confront the contradictions between advancing the cause of equal rights for her race and the predominantly white movement for women's suffrage" (Carby, 67). Carby also states that Harper did not advocate the feminization of society but, rather, a "transformation of the social order achieved through a unity gained in the grand and holy purpose of uplifting the human race" (70). She goes on to say that Harper could not separate the issue of suffrage from the issue of race because voters tortured and lynched blacks (Carby, 70). That Carby accurately states Harper's perspective in these statements and yet labels her a feminist underscores the difficulties some critics face in truly establishing Harper's worldview, and that of Black women in generalBand particularly to where properly naming or defining her is concerned. This practice of misnaming and ill- defining the writings and activism of Black women has been called out by Hudson-Weems ever since the mid-eighties. Moreover, another scholar, Valethia Watkins, has not only called this practice out in her 1998 definitive article entitled "Issues in the Manipulation of African Historiography: The Black Feminist Revisionist History Project," she also analyzes this practice by such critics as bell hooks, Patricia Hill Collins, and Beverly Guy Sheftall, to name a few.

Thus, Carby's statements actually contradict the notion of Harper as a feminist. Indeed, Harper's vision of African Americans' progress as a race precluded any focus on gender-based issues as primary. Harper believed and acted upon her idea that "there are no people that need all the benefits resulting from a well-directed education more than we do. The condition of our people, the wants of our children, and the welfare of our race demand the aid of every helping hand" (in Sterling, 159). As indicated in this letter to William Still, Harper viewed her involvement in the abolitionist movement as equally crucial to its victory. Hence, "a woman's work, and a woman's heart" (in Sterling, 406) would play a significant role in this racial uplift. She also held that becoming involved in such a noble goal required "a deep earnestness and a lofty selfishness" that would around out our lives" (106). Again, Harper, the pre-Africana womanist, emphasized racial progress. Because she believed that women could play a major role in uplifting the entire race, Harper called for true women to work in unison with true men to achieve this goal, an agenda that fits the paradigm of Africana womanism.

This is exactly what Harper did in working with Frederick Douglass to secure the franchise for black men as opposed to white women. Harper's position was unequivocal:

> Understanding that obtaining the ballot for part of the race was far better than none, she pleaded for the greater urgency of black men's attainment of the vote. Without her help, Douglass would not have been able to turn back the tide of the white feminist-Sojourner Truth power bloc, which had mounted enormous support for the women's vote (Hill, 346).

Harper's activism in this situation clearly evinces her Africana womanist inclinations. Not only did she work with the Africana man, she also
worked to achieve a goal that most directly benefitted men. A feminist
agenda would have precluded her supporting an agenda in which men's
(voting) rights superseded those of women. Her work with Douglass in
support of this issue is, in fact, testament to her belief that racial uplift took
precedence over any narrow, gender-based concern. Harper believed that
this benefit to men would in fact benefit the entire race. Hence, she worked
with Douglass for passage of the Fourteenth and Fifteenth Amendments:
"with the support of Frances Watkins Harper and other black abolitionists, Douglass led the fight for the passage of the Fourteenth and Fifteenth
Amendments to the Constitution. Hence, he played a vital role inlaying a
foundation for subsequent challenges by law against what would become
institutionalized segregation of the races"(Hill, 274). As Lerone Bennett
states, these "amendments [are] permanent and indispensable contributions to American democracy" (Bennett, 252). Further testament to
Harper's activism for the race, she advocated for these amendments as a
means of achieving for African Americans all the rights and privileges of
citizenship, including the right to vote. Despite the fact that these rights
were later challenged and largely negated, passage of these amendments
"had immediate impact on the lives of black Americans" especially in economic, political, and social gains (Bennett, 252).

Harper's life of service also reflects the idea of "true" African American men and women as expressed in her essay "Our Greatest Want":

> It does not seem to me that money is our greatest want. We want
> more soul, a higher cultivation of all our spiritual faculties. We
> need more unselfishness, earnestness and integrity. Our greatest
> need is not gold or silver, but true men and true women. We
> need men and women whose hearts are the homes of a high and
> lofty enthusiasm, and a noble devotion to the cause of emanci-
> pation. (in Sterling, 163)

This call for true men and women is tantamount to a call for Africanans to commit themselves to uplifting the race, for indeed, "until her
entire people are free, she is not free" (Hudson-Weems, 59). She is the true
woman working with her male counterpart for the good of the Africana
community. While Harper's entire canon reiterates this philosophy, her
most famous work, *Iola Leroy,* clearly provides a more comprehensive
illustration of this paradigm. As Carby indicates, *Iola Leroy* was written to
intervene in and to influence political, social, and cultural debate concerning the status of "the Negro" as Jim Crow practices threatened to extin-
guish the last hopes for a black political presence in the South (Carby, 64).

This novel provides sufficient revelation of Harper's Africana womanism in the characterization of true women, including Iola, Mrs. Stillman, and Lucille Delany, who devote their time and talents to uplifting the race through education as well as moral instruction and spiritual uplift. These women realize, as did Harper herself, that alleviating the deplorable state of the entire race took precedence over any notion of gender exclusivity. Similarly, the Africana men in the novel are true men, working in conjunction with these women to achieve the same goal of racial uplift.

First, the novel depicts the Africana womanist secure in her position within the context of her family's struggle for liberation. Iola, the main character, best exemplifies the Africana womanist firmly positioned within the family, even when physically separated. This is most evident when Iola learns her racial heritage, and that by law she is a Negro. Like any normal individual whose life undergoes a major upheaval, Iola first responds by bursting into a "paroxysm of tears" (*Iola Leroy*, 106). However, she is not "the stereotypical fragile, passive, and refined tragic mulatto beauty of late nineteenth-century fiction"(Hill, 347). She immediately reassesses her thoughts on slavery, grows calmer, and discovers who is responsible for her family's reversal of fortune. This true Africana womanist does not attempt to save herself by escaping to the North as her mother suggests. Instead, she vows to stay with her mother, increasing her resolve as her dying sister tells her to "stand by mother" (*Iola Leroy*, 108). But Iola extends this commitment to her entire family. It is this mantra that gives her the strength and courage to unite her family and to work toward racial uplift.　　Hence Iola exemplifies the Africana womanist's refusal to view herself as a victim. Birnbaum states that "Iola survives what is for others a fatal verdict of race, yet she inherits not only the >condition of the mother' – the historical euphemism for slavery, but also her mother's... racial anxiety about enslavement" (Birnbaum, 9).

Actually, Iola is more specifically concerned about her family's fate as slaves. Despite having lived a privileged life before her father's death, Iola never laments her new situation. She accepts her new status, realizing that her fate is inseparable from that of the entire Africana community. This only strengthens her resolve to liberate her people through education, moral instruction, and spirituality. Harper clearly delineates Iola's relationships to family and community by depicting the various segments of the Africana community that are involved in reuniting Iola with other members of her immediate family, her mother, brother, and sister, as well as with Aunt Linda. Though Aunt Linda had been a slave before Iola's change in status, she, also the Africana womanist, reconnects with Iola as an Africanan. Their interactions reveal a bond based on their heritage as Africanans and reiterate the fact that the Africana womanist is family-centered. Even though Iola and Aunt Linda are not related by blood, their emotional bond makes them family.

The characterization of Iola also exemplifies another concept crucial to the quest for liberation,the belief in the concept of self-naming. In fact, for the Africana woman, naming and defining are prerequisite to liberation, for only through self-naming and self-definition can Africanans negate the limitations of others' definitions. This is exactly what Iola does. When Mr. Lorraine attempts to define Iola as slave and usurp her inheritance, Iola refuses to be so defined. She becomes "committed to a definition of self in relation to community" (Carby, 75). She defines herself as educator and liberator of Africanans and thereby further establishes herself as an Africana womanist. Soon after discovering that she is a Negro, she recognizes and identifies with the condition of her people. She ultimately refers to herself as one of the "colored children" on her father's plantation (145).

Believing that her experiences as an African American make her stronger and secure her reason (273-74), Iola ultimately appreciates her life more after her father's death and her resultant lowered status. In fact, she believes that her new life is more significant because it awakens her to reality. This awakening manifests itself in her work to improve herself, her family, and her community. Thus identifying her true self brings forth her real identity as an Africana womanist. As such, her "cultural identity supersedes self-definition" (Hudson-Weems ,58). Her work for her family and her race becomes the hallmark of Iola's life. Beyond her strivings for racial progress, Iola seeks nothing for herself because as an Africana womanist, she has no other desire.

Iola also exemplifies Harper's Africana womanist perspective in her focus on educating women, for Harper believed that educating women would translate into better lives for African American families. Iola's first lecture, "On the Education and Elevation of the Colored Race," is not simply a call for women's education for women's sake, but rather for the entire family. Hence, for her, the objective was to educate women in order to provide the structure upon which to build strong, effective families capable of nurturing and supporting their children. She met with women to discuss how to raise their daughters and foster racial progress within their own homes. She appealed to women to accept their role in the struggle by focusing sufficient attention on managing their homes and raising their children properly so that they could become useful, self-reliant, and self-respecting.

Harper held in high esteem those Africana women who worked in or outside the home to support their families or to educate their children.

In her novel, Iola clearly expresses Harper's Africana inclinations in the statement that every woman should earn a living, thus preventing much sin and misery which result from "the weakness and inefficiency of women" (*Wonan's Political Future*, 205). This was not a condemnation; as slaves African American women had not been granted the opportunity to maintain and nurture families or to manage their own households. In short, Iola expresses Harper's view that work makes women stronger and more efficient at home, thus making marriages happier. Harper believed that "women were potentially capable of transforming society, but although this vision was not limited to what women could achieve from the hearthstone Harper did regard the home as a crucial sphere of women's influence" (Carby, 69).

Iola and Lucille Delany definitely illustrate this aspect of Africana womanism in their willingness to work. Iola is happy to work, even in establishments that prefer not to hire African Americans. She ultimately works in schools and in the church to support her community. Harper also depicts this characteristic of the Africana womanist in her portrayal of Lucille Delany as working outside her home teaching women to become effective mothers. In establishing a school to teach young women to be wives and mothers and thus helping women provide for their families, Miss Delany also fosters racial progress.

Harper's view that women should honor labor "undermines the doctrine of separate spheres for the sexes" (Birnbaum, 10). The Africana womanist usually works with men to achieve the goal of racial uplift, for, as Hudson-Weems asserts, "Africana men and women share a similar space as oppressed people, and thus, they cannot afford this division between the sexes" (Hudson-Weems, 63). That Iola works with males to achieve liberation for Africanans is, therefore, very significant. The Africana womanist realizes that in America, race limits Africanans more directly and more significantly than gender. She also knows that Africana men and women must work together in order to survive. Understanding that race, not gender, is the major obstacle to achieving parity in American society, Iola works with her uncle Robert, her brother Harry, and ultimately with Dr. Latimer to "uplift the race." When she first meets Robert, she is unaware that they are related. As far as she knows he is merely an African American man who distinguished himself in the Civil War. She works with him and the community to reunite their family.

Iola also works very closely with Dr. Gresham, a white doctor who seems to be unprejudiced, but who wants to marry her only if she agrees to pass for white. When she meets Dr. Latimer, an African American doctor, they form a bond based on racial uplift and work together to help the race.

In fact, this is the basis of their relationship. They are united "[i]n their desire to help the race.... One grand and noble purpose was giving tone and color to their lives and strengthening the bonds of affection between them" (*Iola Leroy*, 266).

Here again, Iola and Dr. Latimer are not only concerned with the uplift of the race, but with its capacity to survive the harsh American reality. Iola works with the minister, children, and their families; Dr. Latimer becomes an effective, caring doctor and a community leader. Together they become a model of Africana male- Africana female relationship in the context of the Africana community.

Their relationship also illustrates the Africana womanist's desire for positive male companionship. Such compatibility is essential for racial survival, and the Africana womanist seeks to fulfill this aspect of her life. Iola seeks such a relationship but refuses to establish a relationship with Dr. Gresham, the white doctor, because he requires that she sacrifice her race for the privilege of being white – passing. For her, this would not be a positive male- female relationship because it would force her to negate a crucial aspect of herself, her true identity. Iola's refusal to accept such an existence indicates the strength of her bond with the race, as well as her insistence upon a realistic life for herself and her people. It is her true Africana womanist identity that disallows such a relationshipwith Dr. Gresham. Connected with the Africana community, she is indebted to her race: "It was through their unrequited toil that I was educated, while they were compelled to live in ignorance. I am indebted to them for the power I have to serve them" (*Iola Leroy*, 235). Since to reject the race is to reject her essential self and replace it with a false identity, she rejects Dr. Gresham's offer, which would preclude her ability "to do something of lasting service for the race" (*Iola Leroy*, 262).

Frances Watkins Harper devoted her entire life to the social, political, and spiritual progress of Africanan people. For her, this was not a situation in which she sacrificed her personal desires for the greater good of the race. The truth is, Harper's only real desire was to leave a legacy of service to improve the condition of her people. Though she often focused on women's issues, as do all other gender- based theorists, she always did so within the context of their impact on racial progress. Hence, African and gender-based theorists "may share strategies for ending sexual discrimination, but they are divided on how to change the entire political system to end racial discrimination and sexual exploitation" (Hudson-Weems, 37). Harper personified the view that she expresses in "Women's Political Future": "The world cannot move without a woman's sharing in the movement, and to help give a right impetus to that movement is woman's highest privilege" (363). To be sure, Harper's contribution to that movement cannot be overstated, and the Africana community continues to benefit from her contribution. Her life and works so well fit the paradigm of Africana womanism that she emerges, indeed, as an eminent pre- Africana womanist.

References

Bennett, Lerone Jr. *Before the Mayflower: A History of Black America.* Chicago: Johnson, 1987.

Birnbaum, Michele. "Racial Hysteria: Female Pathology and Race Politics in Frances Harper's *Iola Leroy* and W. D. Howells's *An Imperative Duty.* *African American Review* 33.1 (1999): 7- 23.

Carby, Hazel V. *Reconstructing Womanhood: The Emergence of the Afro-American Woman Novelist.* New York: Oxford UP, 1987.

Harper, Frances W. *Iola Leroy, or Shadows Uplifted.* 2nd ed. Maryland: McGrath, 1969.

_____. "Woman's Political Future." In Hill, *Call and Response,* 363-365.

Hill, Patricia Liggins, ed. *Call and Response: The Riverside Anthology of the African American Literary Tradition.* Boston: Houghton Mifflin, 1998.

Hudson-Weems, Clenora. *Africana Womanism: Reclaiming Ourselves.* Troy, Mich.: Bedford, 1993.

Sterling, Dorothy, ed. *We Are Your Sisters: Black Women in the Nineteenth Century.* New York: Norton, 1984.

22

COMMON BONDS FROM AFRICA TO THE U.S: AFRICANA WOMANIST LITERARY ANALYSIS

Betty Taylor Thompson

> The true Africana womanist novel is the manifestation of the Africana woman in literature. Most of the earlier cited features of the Africana womanist can be found in the main characters in these works. (Hudson-Weems, 78)

There is a distinct link between the concerns of African and African-American women writers in the characters, themes, and women's issues and concerns that appear in their fiction, dramas, and essays. The specific response of Africana Women writers on the continent to the common concerns of Africana women will be explored through the texts of Flora Nwapa of Nigeria, Mariama Ba of Sengal, and Tsitsi Dangarembga of Zimbabwe. Representing the African American women writings are *Toni* Morrison's *Song of Solomon* and *Beloved* and Gloria Naylor's *Bailey's Cafe*, all of which demonstrate strong Africana womanist concerns. To be sure, women literary artists of the continent and the diaspora demonstrate a unity of concerns, backgrounds, images, visions, and methodology which culturally bind their creative productions.

Adeola James in *Their Own Voices* asserts that the

> Common themes in African Literature have been the devastating effect of Africa's contact with Europe, and the rehabilitation of Africa's cultural heritage to mitigate, heal or correct some of the injuries inflicted by colonialism. Some writers have addressed the conflict of the traditional world with the modern world Africa is aspiring to build; specifically, the problems of polygamy, infidelity, corruption, and abuse of power, and the anomaly of human sacrifice" (James, 1).

Kofi Anyidoho (a director of the National Endowment for the Humanities Institute, Literature and the Modern Experience in summer, 1996 and

Professor at the University of Ghana) in *The Pan African Ideal in the Literatures of the Black World* remarks that

> All over the Black World, literature has frequently functioned as a weapon for revolutionary change. Literature of combat is a natural product of any situation of enslavement or oppression.... In all of these cases, we find also that the literary dimension of the struggle sometimes assumes even greater significance not so much in written literature as it does in oral literature. (Anyidoho, 25-27)

In *Africana Womanism: Reclaiming Ourselves* (1993) Clenora Hudson-Weems affirms a unique method of looking at the culture of Africana women and establishes a paradigm for the goals of Africana women on the continent and throughout the diaspora. Moreover, Hudson-Weems acknowledges that many of these means of thinking and ways of acting have existed for centuries and that, in fact, Africana women have surrounded themselves particularly with sisterly support and family support as they attempted to negotiate their way through the triple problem of race, class, and gender prejudices. In her philosophical and practical treatise on Africana women, the author explains why the tenets of *feminism* and even *black feminism* are inadequate to overcome and understand the triple threat of prejudice that affects Africana women. Africana women, therefore, in order to survive, need a different paradigm because their problems are unique and more disparate than those of any other group of women throughout the world. Furthermore, in *Africana Womanism*, Hudson-Weems cites certain Africana womanist novels that support her thesis; thus linking the Africana Womanism paradigm with the artistic and literary production of Africana women's activies (Taped "Interview").

In responding to their triple threat in their literary texts, Africana women writers highlight the beneficial theme of sisterly kinship necessary to support themselves against the horrific assaults of society. In *Africana Womanism*, Hudson-Weems asserts that her theory of Africana Womanism is a plausible and workable concept which provides a theoretical framework useful for expressing that context of the Africana community (Hudson-Weems, *Africana Womanism*, 75). With a theoretical context providing a basis for analyzing the literature of Africana women, we find that the literature of many Africana writers continues to espouse Africana Womanist concerns. In Part Two of her work, the author analyzes five Africana Womanist novels – Hurston's *Their Eyes Were Watching God*; Ba's *So Long A Letter*, Marshall's *Praisesong for the Widow*; Morrison's *Beloved*; and Macmillan's *Disappearing Acts*.

When Black women began to write creative works, they looked back to their foremothers in Africa and throughout the diaspora for creative inspiration. Although the line of communication between African and African-American women was forcibly broken by slavery, African-American women have had to take another step and "envision" their African foremothers who used the oral traditions of story telling to impart cultural values which have been passed down from generation to generation. Toni Morrison in her essay, "Rootedness: The Ancestor as Foundation," espouses a basic tenet of Africana Womanism when she affirms that the ancestors found in African-American writing "are not just parents, they are sort of timeless people whose relationships to the characters are benevolent, instructive, and protective, and they provide a certain kind of wisdom" (Morrison, 343). Morrison further notes that if we don't keep in touch with the ancestor, we become lost and when you kill the ancestor you kill yourself (Morrison, 344). Marjorie Pryse in *Conjuring* also notes that "Black women have long possessed magical' powers and told their daughters stories" (Pryse, 3). Writing out of the urgency to record her mother's life, Alice Walker discovers her ability to write her "mothers'" lives. These mothers need not be biological mothers alone, but literary mothers as well (Pryse, 3). The respect and veneration of the ancestors is a principle of Africana Womanism. Thus, literary foremothers like Harriet Jacobs, Frances Harper, Zora Nealse Hurston, Nella Larsen, and Jessie Fauset serve as models for creativity.

In *Afrocentricity*, Molefi Kete Asante concludes that Afrocentricity takes a simulsense form once it is a fact in one's life (or one's critical stance); it is not linear, cannot be analyzed in a single line, is inherently circular, and has a transforming nature because it transforms attitudes, beliefs, values and behaviors, leading to the conclusion that we have one African cultural system manifested in diversities (Asante, 1-2) When one looks at African and African-American women's writers with the Afrocentric perspective, one cannot deny the circular lineage of tradition reflected in their writings.

Audre Lourde, an African American writer and a self acclaimed feminist, lesbian, and socialist mother of two, states that

> In a society where the good is defined in terms of profit rather than in terms of human need, there must always be some group of people who, through systematized oppression, can be made to feel surplus, to occupy the place of the dehumanized inferior. Within this society, that group is made up of Black and Third World people, working-class people, older people, and women (Lourde, 352).

Lourde further states that for Black women, violence weaves through the daily tissues of life – in the supermarket, classroom, elevator, clinic, school yard and in the homes (355). Therefore, Lourde writes:

> Black women's literature is full of the pain of frequent assault, not only by a racist patriarchy, but also by Black men. Yet the necessity for and history of sharedbattle have made us, Black women, particularly vulnerable to the false accusation that anti-sexist is anti-Black. Meanwhile, woman hating as a recourse of the powerless is sapping strength from Black communities and our very lives (Lourde, 356).

To be sure, for Hudson-Weems and the entire Africana community, sexism is a very important component of the triple plight of the Africana woman. Just as we cannot omit the importance of racial and cultural integrity, neither can we omit the importance of gender equality for the woman, resulting in a profound respect for her overall personhood. According to Hudson-Weems, "The Africana man, too, must do his part, beginning with total respect for his female counterpart. If he disrespects his women, he disrespects self in a real sense (68-9). The answer to the problems that especially beset African American women, then, is rooted in mutual bonding and support.

There is a movement by those involved with scholarly research on Africana women writers to develop a broad-based critical approach which explores dimensions on generational and cultural continuity for people of African descent which does not rely on Eurocentric critical traditions nor male oriented scholarship. This challenge has received its reply in Hudson-Weems' *Africana Womanism* and especially in its subtitle, *Reclaiming Ourselves*.

Hudson-Weems, as originator/recorder of the Africana Womanism theory, asserts that

> Africana men and women do not accept the idea of Africana women as feminists. There is a general consensus in the African community that the feminist movement, by and large, is the White women's movement for two reasons. First the Africana woman does not see the man as her primary enemy as does the White Feminist, who is carrying out an age-old battle with her White male counterpart for subjugating her as his property. Africana men have never had the same institutionalized power to oppress Africana women as White men have had to suppress White women (Hudson-Weems, *Africana Womanism,* 23).

Her theory of African Womanism thus forms the basis for looking at the literature created by Africana women in an original way. Moreover, literature by Africana women is rooted in their own specific problems in dealing with racial oppression in a society which considers race as a classification strategy before looking at gender. Thus, the Africana woman must focus on her particular and peculiar circumstances, and her literature takes on that perspective.

African and African-American writings transcend national boundaries, reflecting a cultural lineage beyond even that of familial ancestry. Until recently there has been little focus on women's roles as creative writers in this diasporic tradition and on the commonalities that exist in female modes of literary production throughout the African diaspora. Specifically the role of women and the collective nature of women's work – especially the rearing of children and the responsibility for children's socialization – have impacted and informed the communities in which they lived. The agenda of the Africana Womanists includes eighteen distinct and diverse characteristic: Self namer; Self definer; Family centered; In concert with males in struggle; Flexible roles; Genuine sisterhood; Strong; Male compatible; Respected and Recognized; Whole and Authentic; Spirituality; Respectful of elders; Adaptable; Ambitious; and Mothering and Nurturing (Hudson-Weems, *Africana Womanism*, 53-71). The heroines of Africana women's literature demonstrate a multiplicity of these characteristics.

Mariama Bâ's *So Long a Letter* has the distinction of being one in which there is important social criticism by a woman, regarding the problems of polygamy and the status of women in Senegalese society. Bâ ably penetrates the feminine universe of an African woman as wife, mother, dutiful daughter, intellectual, professional, politically aware female and devout Muslim. The heroine cooperatively juggles this multiplicity of roles, never complaining until her husband breaks the collective struggle with his desertion of her. As devastating as this blow to her family structure is, she adapts and copes, hence demonstrating two more characteristics of the Africana woman as defined in Africana Womanism, flexible role player and Adaptable. Through letters to her friend, Aissatou, Ramatoulaye in this epistolary novel exposes her inner conflict after her husband's second marriage and the subsequent desertion of her and their ten children. Aissatou has also experienced a similar circumstance; however, unlike Ramatoulaye, Aissatou has chosen to leave Africa and make a new life for herself in the United States where she has prospered. She is able and willing to support her friend through her trials since Ramatoulaye is unwilling to leave her husband whom she still loves. In the novel, the reader encounters the remarkable durability of two African women caught in the throes of their rapidly developing nation of Senegal and their developing selves. While in conflict and stress, their relationship bends and stretches to accommodate their inner growth and expanding personalities. (Wallace, 85) Nevertheless, Bâ's character accepts the new challenges brought on by her role as sole supporter both financially and psychologically of her family, but unlike the women in many African as well as African-American women's novels, she is not happy with her new role and would not have chosen it for herself (Wallace, 20). The protagonists continues to long for a family centered existence and for a loving companion. In fact, she misses her husband even though he has rudely cast her aside. Notably, according to the postulates defined as characteristic of Africana women, there is the desire to have fulfilling relationships with Africana men, contrasting with the feminists desire to free themselves entirely from male influence.

The reader's sympathy is engaged when Ramatoulaye's husband dies, and she must adhere to the customs of Senegalese Muslim society and watch as her belongings are taken away by her in-laws. She also has previously endured the pain and humiliation of seeing her husband take as a second wife the friend of one of her daughters who has laughingly called him a "sugar daddy." She has watched as her husband squanders his wealth to please a young wife. Also she has watched an avaricious mother-in-law plot to deprive her of her standing as first wife and her husband's financial support. Although polygamy is a traditional part of Muslim society, Rama-toulaye is still devastated by the occurrence and the disrespectful way in which she is informed of her husband's second marriage. Although both she, the second wife, and the mother-in-law are left destitute by the death of the husband, Ramatoulaye finds no comfort in this ironic turn of events. Fortu-nately, the protagonist is an educated woman with a job and is able to fend for herself with the psychological and financial support of her friend, Ais-satou. Through a continuous letter, the novel focuses on the decisions each woman makes in order to achieve a sense of inner well-being after being disenfranchised socially and personally (Fetzer, 9). In Bâ's novel the friends find sisterly support and comfort in a long term friendship, which overcomes the distraction of distance in a traditional historical cultural milieu.

Nigeria's first woman novelist and the first African woman write publish a novel in English, Flora Nwapa and her pioneering work, *Efuru* (1966), cannot be overlooked in any consideration of West African women writers. In this work, like in *So Long A Letter*, the women form support systems to encourage, console, and inspire the heroine in troubled times. In this novel, Nwapa brings a fresh perspective to West African culture and modern Nigeria in literary works by exploring a woman's point of view in pre-colonial African society. The novelist uses folk idiom and oral traditions to underscore the concepts of generational continuity, and the commitment of women to pass the traditions of their fore-mothers. Nwapa demonstrates a keen ear for village voices with an oral literary form based on the tales she heard as a child. Although she has been criticized by Eurocentric African critics for writing a novel that embodies the culture and spirit of her tribe, she continued in her pursuits to capture the traditional and changing role of women in a communal village society, while emphasizing the importance of the woman in passing on cultural values to future generations encoded in women's voices.

Efuru is the story of a beautiful independent "remarkable" woman who marries two worthless men of her own choosing in spite of the traditions of the community. After losing her first and only daughter, she is childless and finally becomes a worshiper of the lake deity, Uhamiri. In fact, one of the first descriptions of Efuru by a farmer pertaining to her great beauty is that "You would think that the woman of the lake is her mother" (Nwapa, 8). Efuru is also known to be a very kind, fair and resourceful woman, qualities believed to come from the benevolent water spirit, Uhamiri. Thus, Efuru's relationship with the water goddess develops gradually, reflecting her spiritual destiny.

The women in the community, while providing a support system for Efuru when both her husbands desert and wrong her, are also the demanders of adherence to strict social codes for women, including "the bath" (female circumcision). The practitioner who gives Efuru her "bath" warns her of the disasters of those who do not follow the tradition. Of Nwakaego who refused the tradition, and whose child died, the practitioner says to Efuru's mother-in-law. "Foolish girl. She had a foolish mother, the folly costs them a son, a good son" (Nwapa, 10). The practitioner also offers Efuru a proverb for consolation, "The pain disappears like hunger." As for marriages, in Igbo communities, as in most African cultures, the choosing of a wife or husband is a lengthy process which involves the extended family. Because Efuru eloped with her first husband, she is in total opposition to her family and to tradition. After her elopement, Efuru works hard at trading, in spite of a lazy husband, to get the dowry necessary to give to her father so that he can formally bless her marriage, formally acknowledging the importance and respect for elders indemite in African culture; however, Efuru is more interested in performing this traditional act than her husband. She also chooses to submit to the circumcision in spite of her seeming independence of tradition. The novelists, therefore, suggests that there is a penalty for not consulting the voice of the elders and flaunting the tradition of one's ancestors. In addition the failure of Efuru at childbearing makes her unable to conform to the society's role for women and reiterates that not having children is a curse. The maternal nurturing of children has always been of great importance in Africana communities.

Thus, the enforced separation of mothers and children, fathers and children, and husbands and wives during slavery caused psychological havoc in Africana family life.

The reclamation of Africana women of this role as mothers and family protectors has often caused them to be misnamed as "Sapphires", "Matriarchs", and "super women"; however, if one looks at the dislocation of families that slavery enforced, the Africana woman's proclivity for protecting her children is understandable and has been quite necessary for child survival. Again, a racist society has decided to make this strength seem a weakness, rather than celebrating the power and fortitude of the Africana woman. Toni Morrison's, *Beloved*, examines how far (even as far as infanticide) an Africana woman will go to save her children from the horrors of slave life and exploitation, in the defining action of Sethe, who kills her child, Beloved, to spare her "from the unspeakable fate to which most female slaves were heiresses" (Samuels and Hudson-Weems, 94).

The textual background of the novel revolves around the community of women advising, instructing, commenting, sympathizing, and gossiping. When the community of women speak, they do so as a collective. When Efuru returns to her father's house after her first husband deserts her, the women of the village comfort her. Ajanupu, Efuru's aunt-in- law, and her mother-in-law, provide a solid support system for Efuru. Her mother-in-law never deserts Efuru and acknowledges the neglect of her son and is saddened. Ajanupu is always there to comfort and help Efuru and to illustrate the benefits of the communal system. Nwapa reflects the traditional role of women in African culture through the novel while depicting an Afrocentic and Africana womanist family-centered literary universe which reflects the significance of the Africana values of community bonding and support.

In *Nervous Conditions* by Tsitsi Dangarembga, the communal spirit is still preeminent, especially in the realm of family connections, and the patriarchal condition. In this novel Dangarembga vividly illustrates the havoc that modern world values create in a traditional society, the unenviable position of women in a patriarchy, as well the mental or, if you will, "nervous conditions" that women and young females experience because the inevitable movement into a new society threatens the men while allowing the women a place to grow and learn. The novel also depicts the strength and determination of women as they demand acceptance and freedom in a new contemporary society. In this work, the women suffer from race, class, and gender prejudices, while having to cope with the negative aftermath of European colonialism.

On the cover jacket of the novel, Alice Walker stated that *Nervous Conditions* was a rare novel whose characters were unforgettable and that the author had created memorable and fascinating female characters. The narrator begins the novel with a jolting opening declaration, which exposes her character and portends to the reader that this will not be simply an African novel that generalizes on the destruction and upheaval of colonialism, post colonialism, and political unrest. The narrator asserts

> "I was not sorry when my brother died.. Nor am I apologizing for my callousness as you may define it, my lack of feeling.... For though the event of my brother's passing and the events of my story cannot be separated, my story is not after all about death, but about my escape and Lucia's; about my mother's and Maiguru's entrapment; and about Nyasha's rebellion." (Dangarembga, 1)

Significantly, the death of the narrator's brother allows the young female narrator to attend school, and the reader learns that her brother was selfish, arrogant, and generally unlikable; however, his attitudes about women and society were reflective of the standard tradition.

The novel centers around Tambu, the narrator, and her cousin Nyasha, who are on the threshold of understanding almost "too much" about the bitter reality of women's lives in modern Africa. Nevertheless, they persist in their determination to be both free Africans and free women in a patriarchal society (Walker, back cover). The title *Nervous Condition* refers to the anorexia that Nyasha gets when she is frustrated by her father's (Tambu's uncle) attempts to control her life and emotions. The anorexia (refusal of eating and throwing up when she is made to eat) occurs as a rebellion to the control that the patriarchal society exerts. Babamukuru, the head of the family, returns to the village with a British education and asserts his place and takes seriously his duties as head of the family. He considers it his duty to support and arrange for someone in his brother's family to be educated so that they may uplift the family. When Tambu's brother dies, she becomes that person, and she is overjoyed. Tambu's mother, however, is devastated by the loss of her son, who had already forgotten how to speak Shona, and now she is dashed by the idea of losing her daughter also. When Babamukuru and his wife, Maiguru bring the message of Nhamo's death to his parents (he has suddenly died from meningitis type illness, though it is never spelled out or confirmed), his mother senses that something is wrong and begins to scream: "First you took his tongue so that he could not speak to me and now you have taken everything for good" (Dangarembga, 54).

His mother is voicing the confusion and despair that come about when young Africans are exposed to modern education and leave home, only to return with a distaste for their traditional culture or never to return at all. More modern conflicts occur as Babambakuru takes social and economic control over the extended family. He orders Tambu's parents to formally marry in a Christian wedding ceremony. Her parents have been together for fifteen years and have had several living children and some who have died and/or miscarried. The idea of a marriage ceremony between Jeremiah and Mainini is ridiculous to Tambu and Nyasha, and the thought of it makes Tambu physically sick. Her conflict arises when she considers all that her uncle has done for her so that she feels guilty about her anger with him over this matter. This psychological conflict causes Tambu to get an "hysterical illness" which leads to her inability to attend the wedding. To complicate the matter further, Tambu's mother has a rebellious and strong willed sister, Lucia, who insists on arguing and disobeying the patriarchal hierarchy of the family and going her own way. In addition, the sister voices her opinions loudly. All this conflict between the old and the new causes great confusion in the extended family, and when Tambu expresses her concern about the effects of modernity to her free thinking cousin, Nyasha, Tambu tells us:

> Because the more I saw of worlds beyond the homestead the more I was convinced that the further we left the old ways behind the closer we came to progress. I was surprised that Nyasha took so much interest in the things our grand parents and great great grandfather had done. We had quite a debate about it, but I was sure that I was right. Because Babamukuru himself had opted for a wedding rather than the cleansing ceremonies. When I confronted Nyasha with this evidence of the nature of progress, she became quite annoyed and delivered a lecture on the dangers of assuming Christian ways were progressive ways. AIt's bad enough she said severely when a country gets colonized, but when the people do as well that's the end, really that's the end." (Dangarembga, 147)

Thus, Nyasha, a product of the new generation of educated Africans, with her exposure to British schooling and culture, nevertheless, comes to appreciate tradition and questions the value of taking on the entire culture of colonialism and modernity. Nyasha demonstrates the inability of Eurocentric culture to embrace the needs of Africana women in adolescence or at any level of maturity Nwapa portrays the traditional role of women in African culture through the novel and depicts an authentic Africana womanist, family centered literature reflective of the significance of African values of communal support among women, a from of sisterhood, which can also be seen in the works of African-American women writers such as Toni Morrison.

Song of Solomon, like Morrison's other novels, has several communities of women which are eclectic. For example, there is Ruth and her daughters, and First Corinthians and Magdalene called Lena who live hollow virginal lives abandoned by men. There is also Pilate, her daughter Reba and her granddaughter, Hagar who share a loving supportive relationship among themselves; however, Pilate's daughter and granddaughter do not seem to benefit from Pilate's example of self actualization (Samuels and Hudson-Weems, 73). African values and African culture are exemplified in Pilate, for Pilate has all the qualities Morrison associates with an ideal African woman: she has stature, strength, and presence. Pilate is as tall as her brother, Macon, and constantly has a "chewing stick" between her lips, much like a West African market woman. Like Efuru, Pilate also has mystical powers, for she is born without a navel which allows her the special privilege of a conjure woman. Moreover, like Efuru 's childlessness and dedication to the water spirit, Pilate's spirituality separates her, as with any religious figure, from the community of women. Pilate's house resembles one in an African village compound, since it has no electricity or gas, but rather candles, kerosene, and a three stone fireplace. Also reflecting her African heritage, Pilate offers food and hospitality to all who enter.

There is in addition, great familial bonding in Pilate's house reflecting the grandmother who has a profound influence on the socialization of children in African and African-American society. As a culture bearer in touch with her ancestors, Pilate holds conversations with her dead father.

She forms the basis of the women's as well as the men's support system in the novel. She enables the protagonists, Milkman, to be born even though his father has previously sexually abandoned his mother. Mimicking Efuru's visit to the diaba (Medicine Man) in order to conceive, Ruth goes to Pilate to conceive Milkman. Through the reincarnation of his great grandfather and the instruction of his ancestor aunt, Milkman symbolically flies home to Africa.

Hudson-Weems specifically discusses Morrison's *Beloved* in *Africana Womanism, wherein* she highlights the co-existence of the spiritual and physical worlds, an African cosmological reality, and the importance of positive male/female relationships as demonstrated by that special relationship between Sethe and Paul D, an African womanist mandate for human survival. But there is also a strong emphasis on the community of women in this text as well, led by Ella, who had helped Sethe when she first came to Ohio. This community of women is incensed upon learning of the intrusion of the ghost child, Beloved, into the lives of Sethe and Denver with its debilitating effect on their family. Thus, the women converge upon 124 singing songs and bringing all the magic and charms they knew in order to rid the house of the vengeful spirit. When the white man, Mr. Bowdin, approaches the house to pick up Denver for work, Sethe relives the visit of her former slave master, schoolteacher, and picks up an ice pick with murderous intentions of oncre again "saving" her child. Beloved, thus, vanishes. A complex novel full of African traditions, the novel provides the avenue for a resurrected female slave narrator's voice. "And it is not only Sethe who speaks: it is her mother, Patsy, "the Thirty - mile Woman," and Sethe's two girl women, Denver and Beloved, and Baby Suggs whose broken hip is the physical legacy of sixty years of bondage. Barbara Christian correctly notes that "Afro-American women writers rewrite the established history by embodying their ancestors' memory in fiction"(Christian, 9). It is within the realm of the Black women's novelists' effort to reclaim their history by writing from "the inside out" according to Christian (Samuels and Hudson-Weems, 98).

In the novels of Gloria Naylor, she devotes attention to the special bond that can exist between women characters, including women of different generations. For example, in *Mama Day* this support system is portrayed through the passing of folk wisdom from the ancestors to the contemporary women. In *Bailey's Cafe* a mythical eatery provides a place where women can heal and regenerate after psychological and physical suffering has completely disabled them, and they can no longer live in the world of reality. Naylor has used art, realism and mysticism to transform the details of the lives of outcasts into a world of spirituality and myth. It is a tale of prejudice, oppression, and inhumanity healed in a realm of the supernatural. Naylor uses a centralized location where diverse characters meet and are compelled to communicate. Her novels rely on a unified physical setting as a spirit of place which causes close contact, thus making the women's confrontation with others inescapable and their mutual support compelling (Andrews, 4).

"Geographically Bailey's Cafe is everywhere. It can be entered from the real world at any point; its address is despair" (Fowler, 26). It is only a way station, Eve tells us, with no guarantees. Bailey's Cafe is presided over by Bailey and his wife, Nadine, and it is a magnet that draws a variety of society's outcasts, each with their own story. The characters include Sadie who has an addiction to alcohol and a mania for cleanliness, and Eve who runs a bordello which accepts only fresh flowers as payment. In the bordello reside Esther, who takes only white roses for payment, and

Peaches, who has a mutilated face and a magnificent body. The novel is further populated by Jesse Bell, who cannot overcome her lust for heroin even for the love of a woman, Miss Maple, a transvestite who makes a living by entering soap flake contests, and Miriam, an Ethiopian child, who is pregnant but denies ever having sex. The ancestor figure in the novel is Eve, who understands the pain and needs of the women who fill her bordello and the support system for the women of this novel is further enhanced by the unique caring, humanity, and non judgmental understanding of Bailey and his wife. The proprietor, musing on the reason for the continuing customers at the cafe in spite of its obvious failures as a eatery, states:

> And it can't be for the company like others think. Our customer-sare all so different I've yet to see anybody get along in here.... They don't come for the food and they don't come for the atmosphere. One or two of the smart ones finally figure that out, like I figured out that I didn't start in this business to make a living – personal charm is not my strong point – or stay in it to make a living – kind of hard to do that when your wife is ringing up the register and it's iffy when and how much she'll charge. No I'm at the grill for the same reason they keep coming.... There's a whole set to be played here if you want to stick around and listen to the music. (Naylor, 4)

Bailey is loquacious, but his wife is supernaturally taciturn. Her silence has such a powerful effect that when she begins to talk there is a great impact. Nadine gives us the story of Mariam, a story she warns us that is so horrifically female that Bailey has sneaked off rather than repeat it. (Bailey later says that this is a lie). The story tells the reader why Mariam (a pregnant fourteen year old Ethiopian Jewess) has had to make the mystical journey from Ethiopia to Bailey's Cafe. She has become pregnant without marriage, which makes her an outcast in her society, but she continually asserts (and all, including the reader, begin to believe her) that she has never had a sexual experience. Her assertion is made more poignant by Eve's magical telling of Mariam's story. How does Eve know step by step what happened? How can Eve know and understand the feelings of Mariam's Ethiopian mother when she agrees for Mariam for the rights of female clitorectomy, which in this case involves the sewing up tightly of the vulva so that urination is almost impossible and sex without extreme pain and screams that can be heard all over the village is impossible. Mariam is still sewn tightly; therefore, she is the true violated innocent, a Christian Mary without a Joseph She can go nowhere except Bailey's Cafe. Even though a child had never been born on the street, and, in fact, a child isn't supposed to be born on this street, at the end of the novel, Mariam's son is born on that street. Bailey notes: "the Baby's arrival didn't make this street disappear"(Naylor, 227).

Africana womanist family centered literature highlights the significance of women in the Africana community as reflected in the literature of African and African-American women writers. Africana women writers speak their heritage to their children, the community and the reader through female characters passing on their legacies, cultural traditions, and histories through the world of books. Through their creative efforts, women writers of the African diaspora, such as Ba, Nwapa, Dangarembga, Morrison, and Naylor, provide support to one another as audience, fellow artists and critics. These authors demonstrate not only the tenets of African Womanism, but more significant these texts speak the soul of Africana women through their stories. These texts give voice to Nwapa's Efuru, Dangarembga's Nyasha and Naylor's Miriam. Ba's sister friends and Morrison's Africana women of mystery live in the voices of their unforgettable, tantalizing characters. Africana women writers of the continent and the diaspora continue to speak to their sisters, binding them together through tales of their ancestor foremothers and the strength, flexibility and adaptability of their resilient characters.

References

Andrews, Larry R. "Black Sisterhood in Naylor's Novels." in Gates, Henry L. and K. A. Appiah, eds. *Gloria Naylor: Critical Perspectives Past and Present.* New York: Amistad, 1993.

Anyidoho, Kofi. *The Pan African Ideal in Literatures of the Black World.* Accra: Ghana Universities Press, 1989.

Asante, Molefi Kete. *Afrocentricity.* New rev. ed. New Jersey: Africa World Press, 1988.

Bâ, Mariama. *So Long A Letter.* London: Heinemann, 1989.

Christian, Barabara. *Black Feminist Christicism.* New York: Pergamon, 1985.

Dangarembha, Tsitsi. *Nervous Conditions.* Seattle, Washington: Seal Press, 1988.

Fetzer, Glen. "Women's Search for Voice and the Problem of Knowing in the novels of Mariama Ba. *CLA Journal.* (September, 1991): 31-41.

Fowler, in Gates, Henry Louis (editor). *Gloria Naylor: Critical Perspectives Past and Present.* New York: Amistad, 1993.

Frye, Marilyn. "Oppression." in Paula S. Rothenberg , ed. *Racism and Sexism: An Integrated Study.* New York: St. Martin's, 1988.

Hudson-Weems, Clenora. *Africana Womanism: Reclaiming Ourselves.* Troy, MI: Bedford Publishers, 1993.

_____. *Africana Womanist Literary Theory*. Trenton, NJ: Africa World Press, 2004.

"An Interview with Clenora Hudson-Weems." Columbia Mo.: American Audio Prose Library, 1407-9, 1995.

James, Adeola. *In Their Own Voices*. London: Heinemann, 1990.

Lourde, Audre, "Age, Race, Class, and Sex: Women Redefining Difference." In Paula S. Rothenberg, ed. *Racism and Sexism : An Integrated Study*. New York: St. Martin's, 1988.

Mazrui, Ali A. "The Black Woman and the Problem of Gender: An African Perspective." *Research in African Literatures*. 24, 1 (April, 1993): 87-104.

Morrison, Toni. "Rootedness: The Ancestor As Foundation." In Mari Evans, ed. *Black Women Writers (1950-1980)*. New York: Anchor/Doubleday, 1984.

_____. *Beloved*. New York: Alfred A. Knopf, 1987.

_____. *Song of Soloman*. New York: Alfred A. Knopf, 1977.

Naylor, Gloria. *Bailey's Café*. New York: Harcourt, 1992.

_____. *Mama Day*. New York: Vintage Contemporaries, 1989.

Nwapa, Flora. *Efuru*. London: Heinemann, 1966.

Samuels, Wilfred and Clenora Hudson-Weems. *Toni Morrison*. New York: G.K. Hall, 1990.

Wallace, Karen. "Women and Identity: A Black Francophone Female Perspective." *Sage*. Vol. II, No. 1 (Spring, 1985): 19-23.

23

GLORIA NAYLOR'S *MAMA DAY*: AN AFRICANA WOMANIST READING

Adele S. Newson-Horst

... For Black women, who are family centered, it is race empowerment; for white women, who are female-centered, it is female
empowerment. Because of this difference in agenda, distinct
naming, then, is critical. (Hudson-Weems, *Africana Womanist*,
19)

In the last few decades feminism and Black feminism have gained such a
stronghold in the academy that the activities of most all of the important
women writers have been stamped as feminist enterprises. While feminism
provides a refreshing alternative to patriarchal hegemonic discourse, it is
nevertheless, inadequate to account for the numerous and varied works
produced by Africana women. This is especially true when one considers
that the masses of Africana women do not identify themselves as feminists.
Hence, the appropriation of Africana women writers, that is the naming
of them as feminists, emergent womanists, prototypical feminists, or pre-
feminist, is, indeed, a disturbing trend, sanctioned by some of our most
visible critics and theorists. This inherent contradiction, an ahistorical
impulse, in defining a Black tradition and a theoretical preoccupation as
feminist, commands that a distinction be made between feminist impulses
and feminism. Phyllis Marynick Palmer best sums up the way in which
appropriation serves feminists when she explains:

> White feminists who may know almost nothing else of Black
> women's history are moved by [Sojourner] Truth's famous
> query, "Ain't I a woman?" They take her portrait of herself
> as one who ploughed, and planted, and gathered into barns as
> compelling proof of the falsity of the notion that women are
> frail, dependent, and parasitic (Palmer, 167).

Palmer goes on to suggest that, while the image of Truth is embraced, the interests of black women in the feminist movement are ignored:

> White academics, in particular, have formulated theories grounded in notions of universal female powerlessness in relation to men, and of women's deprivation relative to men's satisfaction. Often treating race and class as secondary factors in social organization, feminist theorists write from experiences in which race and class are not felt as oppressive elements in their lives. Having theorized from a position in which race and class are unimportant because they are unexperienced elements in their oppression, white feminists then engage in practical political work on issues that do not seem so compelling to black women. Similarly, the emphasis on sexism enables white women to deny their own history of racism and the benefits that white women have gained at the expense of Black women (168).

While Euro-Americans appropriate our cultural and historical products, we seem ever intent on validating ourselves with products of the majority culture. Indeed, the current use of the label "Black Feminist" establishes an unwitting connection with and validation of the white feminist agenda. It is akin to a literary colonialism that is suggestive of second-class citizenship.

In the mid-eighties, Clenora Hudson-Weems advanced the theory of Africana Womanism. She began the process by "naming and defining, via identifying and refining an African-centered paradigm for women of African descent" (1998, 439). As she points out,

> Terminology is critical to definition, since words are loaded with meaning. Therefore, when you name a particular thing, you are simultaneously giving it meaning. The African term for proper naming is *nommo*, a powerful and empowering concept. In African cosmology, *nommo* evokes existence, which carries with it the total package. Since Africana people have long been denied the authority of defining self, as inferred in the words of Toni Morrison's narrator in *Beloved* – to the effect that definitions belonged to the definers, not the defined – it is important to seize control over these determining factors now, lest we risk eternal degradation, isolation, and annihilation (1998, 449).

Notwithstanding Hudson-Weems's long-standing insistence upon self-naming and self-defining, many Black women scholars, who have built their careers on aligning themselves with feminist theory, insist upon making feminist theory fit Black women's activities. The ultimate misrepresentation of this practice is the Black Feminist Revisionist Project, which

Hudson-Weems questions in "Cultural and Agenda Conflicts in Academia: Critical Issues for Africana Women's Studies" (*WJBS* 1989):

> But procrusteans have mis-labeled Africana women activists, like Sojourner Truth and other prominent African women freedom fighters such as Harriett Tubman (who spent her lifetime aiding Africanana slaves, both males and females, in their escape through the Underground Railroad in the North for freedom), and Ida B. Wells (an anti-lynching rebel during the early twentieth century), simply because they were women (186).

The naming of women as *feminist* (except where they are obviously so) is tantamount to appropriating the historical and literary traditions of these figures. The practice is wide and all-consuming in the academy today. In his introduction to the critical anthology *Reading Black, Reading Feminist*, Henry Louis Gates, Jr., opens his observations with a reference to Anna Julia Cooper as a "prototypical black feminist whose 1892 book of essays, *A Voice from the South*, is considered to be one of the founding texts of the black feminist movement"(1). Yet, Gates *references* the contradictions inherent in the anthology when he offers:

> black feminist criticism has been empowering for a whole community of critics; almost all worthwhile criticism of black literature written in the past decade has been profoundly informed by its insights and perspectives. And for all its current diversity, it has taken Davis's warnings about the perils of narrowly interest-based politics to heart. Again, rather than attempt to construct a monolith of the" black woman's experience, black feminists have sought to chart the multiplicity of experiences and perspectives .Perhaps, then, the contradictions that *Reading Black, Reading Feminist* contains (and is contained by) will themselves prove instructive (Gates, 8).

At the heart of the contradiction is the name itself – feminist. Black feminism is inadequate to contain the multiplicity of writings by historical black women.

Particia Liggins Hill best summarizes the current state of scholarship in her anthology *Call and Response*. In surveying today's critical landscape Hill notes that since the 1970s, black women theorists and critics from the academy

> have attempted to formulate new definitions and conceptual models for African American women who seek empowerment. In a large camp are black feminist critics. Although these women differ on various issues, a *black feminist*, is in general, a woman who insists on the simultaneity of gender, race, and

class even though her obvious alignment with feminism is dictated by the fact that most of her energies go into the gender
question. Closely akin to the black feminist is the *womanist*, as
defined by Alice Walker. However, with the exception of Walker's inclusion of women of color, there is little differentiation
between the womanist and black feminist. An *Africana womanist*, as defined by theorist Clenora Hudson-Weems in her book
Africana Womanism (1993) is a black woman activist who is
family-centered rather than female- centered and who focuses
on race and class empowerment before gender empowerment.
Of all the theoretical models, Hudson-Weems's best describes
the racially based perspective of many black women's rights
advocates, beginning with Maria W. Stewart and Frances W.
Harper in the early nineteenth century (Hill, 1378-79).

Africana Womanism as theory is characterized by affirmation and
engagement. Distinct from feminism, black feminism, and womanism in
its insistence on family- centeredness and prioritizing the triple plight of
Africana women in order of race, class, and gender, it ultimately seeks to
unite the Africana woman and man in the struggle for human survival.
Moreover, by taking the most useful/best of the traditions of Africana
peoples, it enables them to advance their positions in their communities,
their countries and the world. At its center is the concept of place, and
it is the concept of geographical locale that enables identity, more specifically "an African" identity with its attendant heritage. The essence of
the concept is featured in Gloria Naylor's *Mama Day* (1988), which a
close reading will reveal one of the author's most successful novels, as it
departs from her earlier works and moves toward being an authentic Africana womanist novel. In the prologue to this work, the narrator reflects on
a resident of the island (Reema's boy) who goes to the mainland for an
education and returns "to put Willow Springs on the map"(Naylor,7). The
result of his efforts is a book in which he comes to the naive conclusion
that the community's use of the phrase A18 & 23" is not really A18 & 23"
at all. Rather the residents actually mean A81 & 32" – the logical lines of
longitude and latitude marking off where the island sits on the map.

The use of the phrase is, in fact, an act of self-definition, which leads to
an authentic existence. The community has defined certain features of its
life through the linguistic rendering of experience with the phrase A18 &
23." The phrase reflects back to the community's origin: in 1823 Sapphira
Wade accomplished feats that are no less than mythical and that ultimately
ensure a place (with a strong heritage) in the world for the residents of
Willow Springs.

The fact that Western education renders people of color in general, and Africana peoples specifically, objects in a perpetual state of invented nativism is not lost on the narrator.[1] Indeed, the narrator comments on the author's assertion, Awe were just so dumb that we turned the whole thing around" (Naylor, 8). By way of explanation the narrator offers:

> Not that he called it being dumb, mind you, called it "asserting our cultural identity,"
>
> "inverting hostile social and political perimeters." Cause, see, being we was brought here as slaves, we had no choice but to look at everything upside-down. And then being that we was isolated here on this island, everybody else in the country
>
> went on learning good English and calling things what they really was – in the dictionary and all that – while we kept on calling things ass-backwards. The people who ran the type of schools that could turn our children into raving lunatics – and then put his picture on the back of the book so we couldn't even deny it was him – didn't mean us a speck of good (Naylor, 8).

By turns, both the plans of the would-be developers and the notion of education are discredited in this prologue. Moreover, the prologue establishes both an African-centered community and a community that is proudly self-defined as well as autonomous. This act of self-definition speaks to the precept that the Africana woman alone defines her reality. Hudson-Weems asserts that "Africana Women's activities have always been by and large collective, [Africana women] defined themselves and their community in terms of their Africana cultural experiences, retaining the African ways in African-American culture" (1993, 57). As theory for literature, not unlike the cautionary tale offered by Naylor's narrator, African womanism emerges organically from the text, representing fidelity to the text. The field of inquiry saw its genesis over a decade ago with Hudson-Weems's "naming and defining, via identifying and refining an African-centered paradigm for women of African descent" (1998, 439). The process involved "observing Africana women, documenting their reality, and refining a paradigm relative to who they are, what they do, and what they believe in as a people" ( ).

Distinct from feminism and black feminism in its insistence on family-centeredness and prioritizing the triple plight of Africana women in order of race, class, and gender, Africana Womanism ultimately seeks to unite the Africana woman and man in the struggle for economic empowerment and survival. Moreover, the new paradigm accounts for certain features of Naylor's text that are essential to the body politic of the author. It neither imposes nor extrapolates as it explicates and clarifies; rather it advances a theoretical framework for assessing African-centered works. Additionally it gives the Africana woman an ancestral land base that identifies her with a geographical and historical reality. Finally, it accounts for what some critiques have identified as texts speaking to other texts or revising ideas raised in texts. In this instance, Naylor's efforts in *Mama Day* may be seen as a revision of Morrison's efforts in *Beloved*. Morrison's community of women who come together to expel the evil plaguing sister Sethe is called to mind here.

Gloria Naylor's *Mama Day* is an Africana Womanist novel. It features, in large part, the eighteen descriptors identified by Hudson-Weems:

> Critical to understanding and appreciating the Africana woman is recognizing her common 18 features: (1) a self-namer and (2) a self-definer, (3) family-centered, (4) genuine in sisterhood, (5) strong, (6) in concert with male in struggle, (7) whole, (8) authentic, (9) a flexible role player, (10) respected, (11) recognized, (12) spiritual, (13) male compatible, (14) respectful of elders, (15) adaptable, (16) ambitious, (17) mothering and (18) nurturing (1993, 143).

Among the eighteen features, three figure most prominently in *Mama Day*: the desire for positive male companionship, family-centeredness, and spiritual awareness. Just as important is the prioritizing of the triple threat (racism, classism, and sexism) in the way of being in the world for the people of Willow Springs. Central to the novel is the agenda for survival of not simply the central characters but of the entire community of Willow Springs. The features that suggest the work as an Africana Womanist novel are not distinct from each other, rather they work in concert to produce the overall effect that would situate Willow Springs as a model community for Africana peoples surrounded as it is by an unfriendly world.

FAMILY-CENTEREDNESS

Central to the Africana Womanist Project is family – a critique of family, a celebration of family, and innumerable gradations between. Within African cosmology the concept of family is large and spacious, inclusive of aunts and uncles, often biologically unrelated persons, as well as elders. At the center of *Mama Day* is motherhood or a maternal figure who is both conjurer and nurturer of her community. Similar to Maryse Condé's character Tituba, Mama Day has powers directed exclusively to the good of her community. Consider the definition of witch provided in *I, Tituba:*

> Isn't the ability to communicate with the invisible world, to keep constant links with the dead, to care for others and heal,

a superior gift of nature that inspires respect, admiration, and gratitude?" (Condé 17)

Earlier she advises: AI was born to heal, not to frighten" (12). Similarly, Mama Day possesses the power to communicate with the invisible world as she offers up to her community this superior gift.

In her foreword to *I, Tituba*, Angela Davis dubs Condé's effort as one of retrieving fragments of an intentionally ignored history to reshape them into a coherent, meaningful story. According to Davis: "It is the same consciousness that has motivated contemporary women of African descent – both scholars and artists – to explore the infinite possibilities of our lost history" (in Conde, xi-xii). What Davis describes here might be identified as the Africana Womanist Project and this includes key works of Zora Neale Hurston, Toni Morrison, Paule Marshall, and Naylor, among others. Central to the project is the reclamation of an "African way of knowing," of religion as a technology for living (to paraphrase Toni Cade Bambara), and of giving voice to the seemingly mute.

Abigail and Amanda, in *Mama Day*, are central to both Cocoa's family and the community of Willow Springs. Sisters, immersed in true sisterhood, they share the parenting of Cocoa who is actually Abigail's granddaughter. Abigail is the mother of Grace, who is the mother of Cocoa. Amanda never married – opting instead, in the tradition of true conjure women, to devote herself exclusively to her community. Yet, it is the attainment of true sisterhood, elevating "sisterhood" to the level of art, that is noteworthy here:

> "You there, Sister?" Miranda says.
>
> "Uh, huh."
>
> There ain't no other way for Miranda to greet her, or for Abigail to respond – not after eighty years. It don't matter when and it don't matter where: Abigail bringing a fresh bunch of collards from across the main road, Miranda sliding into the pew beside her at church, them running into each other at the post office.
>
> "You there, Sister?"
>
> "Uh, huh" (Naylor, 35-36).

MALE COMPANIONSHIP

Naylor's Mama *Day* is set both in New York City and on the mythical island of Willow Springs. The story begins with Ophelia (Cocoa) Day's quest for companionship against the backdrop of the modern problems of dating and finding "suitable" Black male companionship. Location is important, as it speaks to the transient nature of the people of New York and the absence of tradition and heritage that would support viable relationships. There are no guardians here or keepers of traditional courtship patterns. Yet, in Willow Springs, Cocoa's two surrogate mothers extend through the distance their goodwill (with various aids, which some might call charms) to aid her in her quest.

Cocoa meets George, a Black professional, who epitomizes the plight of the transplanted city-dweller, and later marries him. It is five years before she takes him home to Willow Springs to meet her family: her great-aunt Miranda (Mama Day) and her grandmother Abigail. At the start of the novel, George is the product of the rational world exclusively. Raised in an orphanage and literally a self-made man, he recognizes none but a Western cosmology:

> Until you walked into my office that afternoon, I would have never called myself a superstitious man. Far from it. To believe in fate or predestination means you have to believe there's a future, and I grew up without one. So until you walked into my office everything I was – all the odds that I beat – was owed to my living fully in the now (Naylor, 22, 27).

Deprived of affection in his youth, George finds in Cocoa "a woman who has the power to turn [his] existence upside-down" (33). Cocoa, who is bi-cosmological, finds in George the companion for life.

Willow Springs is forty-nine square miles situated toward Georgia on the south end and South Carolina on the north. The bridge to the island sits as the dividing line between the two states. The people of the island take pride in the fact that it belongs to neither state – rather "It belongs to us – clean and simple. And belonged to our daddies, and our daddies before them" (5). It has at its center the memory of Sapphira WadeBan African, a true conjure woman, a slave woman who secures the land for her descendants.   Sapphira Wade represents the long history for a place that is in full contrast to George's living "fully in the now."

In the second part of the novel, George and Cocoa make the excursion across the bridge to the island of Willow Springs. Rich in tradition and color, the island is a place outside of time and outside the influence of the disruptive nature of American progress. George immediately develops an affinity for the two old ladies whom he finds a bit eccentric. The women, in turn, admire his work ethic and love of Cocoa. Here George completes his education in "authenticity." He learns about magic, human nature, his own nature, and loss. In the end, George remains and Cocoa leaves (Newson, 56). Returning to part I, Cocoa and George, alternately speak to each other and reminisce. Together, they tell the complete story of his education with both sides – George's the product of the rational world, and Cocoa's the product of both the rational and nonrational worlds – accounted for. That the dialogue continues is testament to the powers of their connectedness. Even though in the present, Cocoa has remarried and lives in Charleston, she returns "to meet up with her first husband [George] so they could talk about that summer fourteen years ago" (10). That summer includes a great tempest, which destroys the bridge (George's connection to the other side).

Cocoa, as defined by Hudson-Weems, is budding Africana womanist as the story begins. She shares a special relationship with Mama Day – a relationship born of mutual respect and similar temperaments. Mama Day's influence over Cocoa is widely evident in the novel; yet, Cocoa, for all her familiarity with the folkways of Willow Springs, cannot detect the spell of a jealous woman, Ruby, that ultimately leads to the death of her husband, George. Many critics have identified Naylor's ambivalent characterization of Cocoa as the only weak spot in the novel. In New York, Cocoa is strong-willed, witty, tough – a casualty of the mobile society in which she lives. In Willow Springs, however, she is shallow and unperceptive, amazingly ignorant of the activities of the island (Newson, 57). What these critics fail to realize is that there is no true contradiction in Cocoa's character here. Comparing her physical and rational intelligence, as reflected in her ability to successfully negotiate the New York city life, reveals her lack of spiritual savvy reflected in her naivete regarding folk knowledge. She does, however, evolve to this level of spiritual sophistication later in the novel, as she maintains a spiritual connection with George after his death. This is quite reminiscence of the coexistence of the spiritual and physical worlds in the emotional lives of Hurston's Janie Mae Crawford in *Their Eyes Were Watching God* and of Morrison's Sethe in *Beloved* after their great losses.

Reflecting on the phenomenon of male-female relationships, Mama Day observes that Cocoa had mellowed since marrying George—"soft around the edges without getting too soft at the center" (Naylor, 203). Ever extending from self to the reaches of her community and its well-being Mama Day muses:

> You fear that sometimes for women, that they would just fold up and melt away. She'd seen that happen so much in her time, too much for her to head on into it without thinking. Yes, that one time when she was way, way young. But after that, looking at all the beating, the badgering, the shriveling away from lack of true touching was enough to give her pause. Not that she mighta hooked up with one of those. And not that any man – even if he

367

tried – could ever soaked up the best in her. But who needed to wake up each morning cussing the day just to be sure you still had your voice? A woman shouldn't have to fight her man to be what she was; he should be fighting that battle for her. (203)

The key to Africana Womanism in her relation to her man is found in the above passage. It predisposes characters to being in concert in a common struggle.

The novel also suggests that in the struggle for dominion over the self and for understanding the complexity of existence, magic, God, science, and nature are constants. To embrace one alone is to be doomed to an unsatisfying existence or death. Cocoa is undone because Ruby, consumed by jealousy, is after her—"ain't no hoodoo anywhere as powerful as hate" (157). George dies trying to save his wife because he would not acknowledge the power of magic. But George and Cocoa's relationship ultimately endures because, at the end, he embraces magic. Thus, he lives on in death.

SPIRITUAL AWARENESS

An account of the beliefs of the people of Willow Springs, from the Candle Walk celebration to the observance of the hallowed grounds of the burial place of Sapphira Wade, speaks to an African way of knowing the world. Featured in the novel are at least two levels of spiritual awareness: the ability to affect godhead and the power to heal. In addition to these elements (which remain the province of Mama Day, the conjure woman who springs from the seventh son of a seventh son), the residents themselves are immersed in a religious existence. Consider, for example, the event termed "Candle Walk":

Candle Walk night. Looking over here from beyond the bridge, you might believe some of the more far-fetched stories about Willow Springs: The island got spit out from the mouth of God, and when it fell to earth it brought an army of stars....Over here nobody knows why every December twenty-second folks take to the road – strolling, laughing, and talking – holding some kind of light in their hands. (110)

The traditional practices of Candle Walk evolved over the generations, but at its center is A a slave woman who *took* her freedom in 1823. Left behind sons and a dead master as she walked down the main road, candle held high to light her way to the east bluff over the ocean" (111). It is the continuous reckoning of this event in the community that is important here. According to John S. Mbiti:

> Africans are notoriously religious, and each people has its own
> religious system with a set of beliefs and practices. Religion
> permeates into all the departments of life so fully that it is not
> easy or possible always to isolate it (Mbiti, 1).

The belief system of the people of Willow Springs is both complicated and expansive. In the prologue to the novel, the narrator, who is
reminiscent of the informed narrator of Hurston's novel *Their Eyes Were
Watching God*, attempts to interpret the framework – the long history that
prevails – of the society/community. Naylor's narrator speaks directly to
the reader in the eight-page prologue that explains the community in terms
that are only accessible with careful listening. The work begins:

> Willow Springs. Everybody knows but nobody talks about the
> legend of Sapphira Wade. A true conjure woman: satin black,
> biscuit cream, red as Georgia clay: depending upon which of us
> takes a mind to her (3).

In the consciousness of the island's inhabitants, Sapphira Wade is
a phenomenon of a traditional African way of knowing. Mbiti asserts that
an African concept of time is key to understanding of the basic religious
and philosophical concepts of peoples. For traditional African peoples:

> [T]ime is simply a composition of events which have occurred,
> those which are taking place now and those which are immedi-
> ately to occur. The most significant consequence of this is that,
> according to traditional concepts, time is a two-dimensional
> phenomenon, with a long *past*, a *present* and virtually *no future*.
> This time orientation, governed as it is by the two main dimen-
> sions of the present and the past, dominates African understand-
> ing of the individual, the community and the universe (Mbiti,
> 21-23).

Not only does the time frame for which she accomplishes the feats
suggest an African way of knowing, but Sapphira Wade exists in the
memory of the people and she does not Alive in the part of our memory
we can use to form words" (Naylor, 4). Rather, her name is associated with
A18 & 23" – a way of describing grown-up doings, disasters, scams, and
all manner of foolishness. She stands as a symbol – a constant watch over
the community. So the notion of a religious way of knowing the world, the
perimeters of the world, and conjuring are tied together and packaged in
the legendary symbol of Sapphira Wade. And the threat to the community
is the threat of developers held at bay by the keeper of the community,
Mama Day. According to the narrator:

> Sure, we coulda used the money and weren't using the land.
> But like Mama Day told em (We knew to send em straight over

there to her and Miss Abigail), they didn't come huffing and sweating all this way in them dark gaberdine suits if they didn't think our land could make them a bundle of money. Weren't gonna happen in Willow Springs. >Cause if Mama Day say no, everybody say no. There's 18 & 23, and there's 18 & 23 – and nobody was gonna trifle with Mama Day's, >cause she know how to use it – her being a direct descendant of Sapphira Wade, piled on the fact of springing from the seventh son of a seventh son – uh, uh. Mama Day so no, everybody say no. No point in making a pile of money to be guaranteed the new moon will see you scratching at fleas you don't have, or rolling in the marsh like a mud turtle (Naylor, 6).

Then too the expansive nature of the community and its beliefs are revealed in the character of Dr. Buzzard, who is not a true conjure man but who is tolerated by Mama Day as she deems him harmless. Occasionally she chides him for his contrivances – warning him, for example, against aiding the misguided Bernice Duvall, a woman desperate for a child. Consider their exchange:

I am just what I say I am. You do things your way and I do em mine. And it hurts my feelings no end that you won't call me *Doctor* Buzzard:I gives you respect.

here ain't but one Dr. Buzzard, and he ain't you. That man is up in Beaufort County, South Carolina, and he's *real*. You may fool these folks in Willow Springs, but ain't nobody here older than me, and I remember when your names was Rainbow Simpson. But what you do ain't none of my business...

If Bernice comes to me for help, I'm helping her....And in all due respects, like you said, it ain't none of your business.

It ain't, Buzzard, it really ain't. And that's why it would cause me no end of sorrow to make it so. >Cause the way I see it, you been walking round on this earth a long time and got just as much right as the next fella to keep walking around, health and all – living out your natural life (51).

The implicit threat is not wasted on Dr. Buzzard. He understands the source of the power in the community and is suitably cowed by Mama Day's admonitions. Additionally, the rational and nonrational exist side by side in this community, which has a healthy sense of its heritage and survival. The society is matrilineal, and at the center is the legend of a woman who in 1823 killed her master and inherited the land. Because of her way of knowing the world, the narrator suggests that the situation that gave rise to the community is not a question of Aright or wrong, truth or lies, it's about a salve woman who brought a new meaning to both them words" (51). Hence if Sapphira Wade stands as the symbol of the religious awareness (again, religion here is meant as a technology for living), Mama Day represents the character of the island in its authentic self. She is the community agent who affects godhead to protect her own and she is the healer and keeper of a healthy society.

The survival of African America's cultural products are dependent upon the need for paradigms that would adequately address, in this instance, the text. For too long and much too often what passes for criticism of Africana works are theoretical discourses external to the body politic of the author. In an interview with Phyllis Robinson, Naylor speaks to the "female experience that is coming through now in our literature from females of all cultures" (Robinson, 4). Situating herself geographically as well as philosophically, Naylor adds:

> I am from the Western hemisphere. I think and write in the English language. I also come from a culture that is indigenously mine, the African-American culture. Without having and embracing all of that, I would not have been able to find a vision I could call my own (Robinson, 4).

Scholar Maria Mootry suggests that "Africana Womanism critiques and corrects the ideological inadequacies of Black women intellectuals often cited as spokespersons" (Mootry, 244). Scholar Patricia Liggins Hill explains:

> African American women writers, the novelists in particular, have set the tone for the American literary scene of the 1980s and 1990s. Morrison, Alice Walker, Gloria Naylor, and Terry McMillan have given new life to the novel form with their distinctive use of the African American folk idiom and mythology and their continued emphasis on black female lives (Hill, 1380).

Black Feminism, Womanism, and Africana Womanism have at their center the exploration of black female lives. But, as Hill adds, "Of all the theoretical models, Hudson-Weems' best describes the racially based perspective of many black women's rights advocates, beginning with Maria W. Stewart and Frances W. Harper in the early nineteenth century" (Hill, 1379). Additionally as Hill points out, the critics and writers of the three schools "have exposed the oppression of black literary women" (Hill, 1379). Africana Womanism goes beyond, to embrace family and community, characters in concert with their men, as well as the authenticity of self of an African self. *Mama Day* renders this aim of the Africana Womanist Project in narrative form.

Notes

1. Hudson-Weems has suggested that developing paradigms and critical theories, "make possible for better monitoring interpretations of our works in an effort to keep them both authentic and accurate in order to maintain their originality in meaning and value" (Critical Need, 79).
2. Interview with Clenora Hudson-Weems, May 17, 1999

References

Agoawike, Angela. "Beyond 'bra-burning' Womanism as Alternative for the 'Africana' Women." *Nigeria Daily Times*, 27, July 1992, 1.

Condé, Maryse. *I, Tituba: Black Witch of Salem*. Charlottesville: University Press of Virginia, 1992.

Gates, Henry Louis, Jr., ed.. *Reading Black, Reading Feminist*. New York: Penguin Book, 1990.

Hill, Patricia Liggins, et al. *Call and Response: The Riverside Anthology of the African American Literary Tradition*. New York: Houghton Mifflin, 1998.

Hudson-Weems, Clenora. "Africana Womanism and the Critical Need for Africana Theory and Thought." *The Western Journal of Black Studies* 21:2 (1997): 79-84.

_____. *Africana Womanism: Reclaiming Ourselves*. Troy, Mich.: Bedford Publishers, 1993.

_____. "Self-Naming and Self-Definition: An Agenda for Survival." *Sisterhood, Feminism and Power: from Africa to the Diaspora*, ed. O. Nnezmeke, 449-52 Trenton, N.J.: Africa World Press, 1998,

Mbiti, John S. *African Religions and Philosophy*. New York: Anchor Books, 1970.

Mootry, Maria. "Review of *Africana Womanism: Reclaiming Ourselves*." *The Western Journal of Black Studies* 18:4 (1994): 244-45.

Naylor, Gloria. *Mama Day*. New York: Ticknor and Fields, 1988.

Newson, Adele S. "A Review of *Mama Day*." *Sage* 6:2 (fall 1989): 56-57.

Palmer, Phyllis Marynick. "White Women/Black Women: The Dualism of Female Identity and Experience in the United States." *Feminist Studies* 9:1 (1983): 151-70.

Robinson, Phyllis. "A Talk with Gloria Naylor." *Book of the Month Club* 4.

PART VI
CONSTRAINTS AND SOLUTIONS

A truly free people possess the power to produce, as well as to consume. (Weems, Jr. *Desegregating the Dollar* 131)

24

A TRAGIC AMBIVALENCE: AFRICAN AMERICAN CONFUSION REGARDING ECONOMIC SELF-INTEREST

Robert E. Weems, Jr.

It has been more than a generation since the passage of the Civil Rights Act of 1964 and the Voting Rights Act of 1965. This important legislation helped African Americans gain access to a variety of public facilities, including the voting booth. Yet, as Blacks enter the twenty-first century, a disturbing proportion of African Americans remain unemployed, under-educated, or incarcerated. Ongoing American institutional racism, undoubtedly, is chiefly responsible for this situation. Nevertheless, Black America's ongoing confusion regarding its economic self-interest must also be blamed.

Just as African Americans collectively cannot decide whether they want to blend into the American "mainstream" or strengthen existing Black communities, African Americans' views concerning business and economics are likewise muddled . Some believe that African Americans' only hope for substantive progress is through the aggressive development of more individually owned Black business enterprises. Others contend that African Americans' best hope lies in the destruction of the capitalist system and the establishment of an egalitarian socialist state. Most African Americans, probably, are somewhere between these two ends of the spectrum.

While African Americans have been caught up in an intellectual stalemate concerning the "correct" formula for Black economic empowerment, other groups, with more clearly defined goals, have made considerable business inroads in our community. At this important juncture in history, two questions literally scream out for an answer. First, how did African Americans become so confused about their own economic self-interest? Second, what can be done to alleviate this problem?

To begin to understand African Americans' confusion regarding their economic self-interest, we must first examine historic and contemporary attitudes about Black businesspeople. Significantly, no segment of the African

American community, with the exception of preachers, has received more ambivalent analysis. Perhaps, the most pointed criticism directed at both historic and contemporary Black businesspeople is the belief that they are (inherently) not as competent as their white counterparts. The roots of this ongoing discussion concerning the competence of Black business appear linked to the dynamics of the transatlantic slave trade.

The subsequent forced migration of millions of Africans began as a simple commercial transaction between European merchants and African chiefs. Europeans traded guns, rum, and various trinkets for Africans captured in inter-ethnic warfare. Europeans subsequently took these Africans to the Western Hemisphere and used their slave labor to build, among other things, what is now known as the United States. On the other hand, the guns African chiefs acquired from European traders accelerated African inter-tribal tensions and contributed to profound social and political destabilization (whose reverberations are still felt to this day). In simple economic terms, Europeans clearly profited the most from their early business dealings with Africans. Moreover, I would argue that the commercial consequences of the transatlantic slave trade subsequently conveyed a (not-so-subtle) subliminal message that blacks are not as competent in business as whites.

This assertion appears especially convincing when we examine black business activity during the Jim Crow era. Contrary to popular belief, African American businesses did not monopolize the black consumer market during American apartheid. Although blacks were residentially and socially segregated from whites, the stores of white merchants were not off limits to black consumers. Moreover, many African Americans chose to patronize white merchants rather than those of their own race. This reality has been, perhaps, best portrayed by the infamous "ice" anecdote. According to the story, a black merchant in a particular southern locale became increasingly concerned that his sales of ice were plummeting while those of his white competitor were skyrocketing. When he asked a local black consumer what was going on, he reportedly received for a reply, "the white merchant's ice is colder."

Despite the fact that many turn-of-the-century African American consumers apparently believed that white merchants provided them with "colder ice" and better goods, a significant black business infrastructure did emerge in the United States. Booker T. Washington's 1907 book *The Negro in Business* represents the best overview of early twentieth-century African American economic development. The enterprises and entrepreneurs discussed in this work, most of whom were affiliated with Washington's National Negro Business League (NNBL), founded in 1900, shared

Washington's belief that African Americans had to create a solid economic base to truly become a viable force in the United States.

Significantly, much of the ongoing confusion regarding black economic self-interest is related to ongoing confusion in the African American community regarding Booker T. Washington's historical role and legacy. Traditionally, Washington's critics have asserted that his emphasis upon black economic development, in lieu of seeking political empowerment, represented a capitulation to white racism.[1] Undoubtedly, some aspects of his public career can be described as an exercise in accommodation.[2] Still, Washington's promotion of internal African American business sentiment had militant, nationalistic connotations.

The Black nationalist orientation of Booker T. Washington's economic agenda, ironically, is put in clearer perspective by an examination of European immigrant (foreign language) newspapers in early twentieth-century Chicago. *The Chicago Foreign Language Press Survey (CFLPS)*, compiled and translated by the Works Progress Administration (WPA) in 1942, clearly indicates that immigrants from eastern and southern Europe, similar to Booker T. Washington and his adherents, viewed internal business development as a positive goal. Moreover, these same groups regarded ethnic business development as a prerequisite for full "acceptance" in America. For example, the December 14, 1910, issue of *Dziennik Zwinazkowy*, a daily Polish newspaper, featured an editorial entitled "Polish Trade" which asserted:[3]

> "If our people do not develop agriculture, trade, and commerce in this country as others have developed them, then our lot will always be hard labor in factories, coal mines, forests, and city streets. We must understand that only through mutual strength and support can we hope to raise Polish industry and commerce in America to a place where it will be at least equal to that of strangers."

If the Poles and other southern and eastern European immigrants viewed the establishment of a voluntary internal business structure as necessary, one can plausibly assume that African Americans would have sought to establish an internal business community even without the imposition of legalized racial segregation. Exploring this assumption opens up new areas of consideration.

During the late nineteenth and early twentieth centuries, even without being subjected to Jim Crow apartheid, recently freed blacks, similar to newly arrived immigrants from southern and eastern Europe, would have faced a competitive society grounded in the principles of Social Darwinism. In a "dog eat dog world" where "only the strong survive," group and individual survival were all-consuming preoccupations. Significantly, some African Americans (as personified by Booker T. Washington), along with some eastern and southern European immigrants, came to the conclusion that ethnic economic enterprise, based upon mutual cooperation, would greatly assist their respective quests for survival. More important, the attempt to establish racial/ethnic business, while based in part upon reacting to certain unpleasant realities, had clearly proactive dimensions of group pride and achievement.

Although historic black business development possessed positive, proactive characteristics, scholars have been slow to acknowledge them. This, in large part, has been due to the popularity of two distinct paradigms. First, what can be described as the black businessman as villain thesis has contributed to a long-standing dismissal of black business enterprise as a subject worthy of serious, objective, examination. Second, the "racial integration" and "civil rights" paradigms of the 1950s and 1960s, which focused upon black movement into the American mainstream, made community-based black business enterprises appear outdated and anachronistic.

For years, the anti-black-business scholarly tradition has impeded a serious assessment of historic black business enterprise. Significantly, this school of thought, despite the vehemence of its arguments and the prominence of its proponents, appears replete with faulty assumptions and outright sloppy scholarship. The first major anti-black-business treatise, Abram Harris's 1936 book *The Negro as Capitalist: A Study of Banking and Business*, exemplified how ideology can sometimes cloud analytical precision. Written during the midst of the Great Depression, this work reflected contemporary anti- black-business sentiment in America. Among other things, Harris found considerable fault with black businessmen's apparent self-serving promotion of racial solidarity. As James O. Young noted in *Black Writers of the Thirties*, Harris, along with his then-Howard University colleagues Ralph Bunche and Edward Franklin Frazier, firmly believed in the possibilities of interracial trade unionism. Consequently, this trio considered black business development as an irrelevancy that kept the black working class from linking with their white counterparts.[4]

Perhaps the most controversial (and debatable) aspect of Abram Harris's book was its direct association of black business with an exploitative black middle class. Harris, using this model of African American community development, concluded that the black middle class promoted racial pride and unity as a subterfuge to elicit black mass support for middle class-controlled businesses.[5] He also suggested that black businessmen were responsible for anti-Semitism among African Americans. Harris, in reference to black businessmen's complaints about Jewish competition, concluded:[6]

> In their confusion, the masses are led to direct their animus against the Jew and against whiteness. The real forces behind their discomfort are masked by race which prevents them from seeing that what the Negro businessman wants most of all is freedom to monopolize and exploit the market they provide. They cannot see that they have no greater exploiter than the black capitalist who lives upon low-waged if not sweated labor, although he and his family may and often do, live in conspicuous luxury.

Abram Harris's observations, despite their vivid imagery, represent a Marxist rhetorical flourish rather than careful scholarly analysis. An examination of U.S. Census data all but dispels the notion of a (numerically significant) "predatory" African American employer class. For instance, in 1929 the Census Bureau enumerated 25,701 black retail enterprises with net sales of $101,146,043. The average net sales of these 25,701 black retail establishments was $3,935. This compared to average annual net sales of over $32,000 for the 1,513,592 white-owned American retail establishments.[7] Also, the 25,701 black retail enterprises employed only 12,561 full-time employees (excluding proprietors).[8] Consequently, even if Harris's assertions contained a modicum of truth, it appears that the majority of African American enterprises during this period were either single proprietorships or tenuous partnerships and corporations.

Despite such inconsistencies, Abram Harris's book profoundly affected subsequent research relating to historic black business enterprises. Not surprisingly, later anti-black- business treatises, similar to their flawed progenitor, were filled with questionable assumptions and conclusions. Ralph Bunche's 1940 Research Memorandum for the Carnegie-Myrdal Study, entitled "The Programs, Ideologies, Tactics, and Achievements of Negro Betterment and Interracial Organizations," provided another example of the shortcomings associated with the black businessman as villain thesis.

A substantial section of Bunche's essay dealt with Booker T. Washington's NNBL. Bunche, after summarizing NNBL history and describing certain local chapters' community improvement projects, inexplicably concluded that, "despite his appeal to race pride and loyalty, the Negro businessman is not distinguished by his civic-mindedness, his efforts and sacrifices in behalf of his group."[9] Bunche's strange line of reasoning, considering the evidence that he presented, graphically illustrated his tunnel vision concerning black businesspeople. He and Abram Harris, both African American scholars, would have felt insulted by white racists seeking to characterize all blacks as lazy and shiftless. Yet, they eagerly perpetuated a stereotypical characterization of black business. Moreover, Edward Franklin Frazier, the third member of the influential Howard University anti-black-business triumvirate, ultimately presented the black businessperson as villain to an even wider audience. Few scholarly studies have attracted the widespread attention and discussion that accompanied the 1957 publication of his *Black Bourgeoisie: The Rise of a New Middle Class in America.* Still, despite the hoopla generated by this book, it appeared seriously flawed.

Professor Frazier, in his preface, noted that "it was not my intention to make a comparative study."[10] This decision resulted in gross distortion. For instance, he later described black business as "one of the main elements in the world of make-believe which the black bourgeoisie has created to compensate for its feeling of inferiority in a white world dominated by business enterprise."[11] Frazier's assertions did contain an element of truth. Nevertheless, the *Chicago Foreign Language Press Survey*, replete with examples of European immigrant economic nationalism, clearly refutes Frazier's notion that African American businessmen were afflicted with a unique, racially based, neurosis.

Perhaps the two most significant later works to perpetuate the black businessman as villain thesis were Earl Ofari's The *Myth of Black Capitalism* (1970), and Manning Marable's *How Capitalism Underdeveloped Black America (1983).* Both of these widely discussed books, written from a Marxist perspective, dismissed black business and black businesspeople as impediments to African American progress.

Besides being assailed by certain influential African American scholars, the mid- twentieth-century civil rights movement also diminished the stature of black-owned businesses. Between the years 1954 and 1965, African Americans achieved important gains in the areas of education, employment, voting rights, and accessibility to public accommodations and facilities. Consequently, as blacks increased their focus upon opportunities outside of traditional African American enclaves, and as black neighborhoods (or ghettoes) became areas that one "escaped" from, community-based black enterprise appeared increasingly anachronistic.

Although many African Americans, during the mid twentieth-century, were apparently afflicted with severe cases of "Desegregation fever," others offered a more cautious assessment of changes in U.S. society. For instance, as George S. Harris, the president of the black-owned Chicago Metropolitan Mutual Assurance Company noted in an important 1965 speech:[12]

I know that many advances have been made in the opening of new avenues and new levels of employment for Negroes. Well and Good. But this is only one side of economic democracy. While we have fought hard for advancement as Employees, we are not fulfilling our mission, our place in the sun, as Employers. Economic Democracy is no one-way street. What I am trying to say is that we are waging some pretty effective campaigns in the direction of over-all civil rights, while neglecting our potential as employers and entrepreneurs. Full equality to me includes the right to Hire, not just to be Hired: the power to own the company, not just work for the company. If we can make appreciable gains in this struggle, we will increase the self-respect and the self-dignity of the Negro people a hundred-fold.

Despite the inherent logic in George Harris's observations, many African Americans, since 1965, continue to (incorrectly) view increased employment with white-owned companies as black economic empowerment. Yet, increasing attacks upon Affirmative Action and a changing national and global economy (which has generated an increasing number of worker layoffs) clearly indicate the limits of linking black economic empowerment with employment in white companies.

The limits of linking employment in white companies with substantive black economic empowerment become even clearer when the issue of consumerism is examined. On the one hand, it is indisputable that enhanced black employment opportunities with white companies has contributed to a dramatic increase in collective African American spending power since the 1960s.[13] In fact, the typical African American family today, compared to a similar family a mere generation ago, generally eats a wider variety of food, wears better-quality clothing, drives a more prestigious model automobile, and listens to a more powerful stereo system. Yet, the evidence also suggests that African Americans are not the biggest beneficiaries of their increased consumer presence in this country. If one were to take a stroll through most urban black enclaves in contemporary America, one would be hard-pressed to see where increased African American spending has improved the infrastructure and ambiance of these neighborhoods. Black consumers, who spend the vast majority of their nearly $700 billion collective spending power in shiny downtown and suburban malls, enhance the economic bases of these outside areas to the detriment of their own enclaves.

Perhaps, the most ironic aspect of increased African American consumerism has been the simultaneous decline of black consumer support of black-owned businesses. During the World War I era, African American consumers spent approximately one-third of their collective disposable income with black businesses. As late as 1944, African American consumers made nearly 28 percent of their major purchases at stores owned by fellow blacks. Today, it is estimated that black consumers spend only 7 percent of their disposable income with black-owned enterprises.[14]

This lack of African American support for black businesspeople appears all the more paradoxical when one considers the nuances of the 1960s Black Power Movement. This sociocultural phenomenon, among other things, has been credited with enhancing the psyche and self-worth of African Americans. For instance, blacks' evolution from "Negroes" to "African Americans" clearly validates this assertion. Nevertheless, a closer look at the Black Power Movement offers important insights regarding the recent decline of black business in America. Although the Black Power Movement placed a special emphasis upon insular African American economic development, [15] persons like Stokely Carmichael (Kwame Ture), H. Rap Brown, and other visible Black Power advocates, had never started and maintained a business enterprise. The input and expertise of older black businesspeople could have benefited the Black Power Movement. Unfortunately, since much of the Black Power Movement focused upon such external considerations as wearing Afros and dashikis, many older black businessmen, who kept their hair short and continued to wear suits, were often labeled "Uncle Toms." In retrospect, this condemnation of established black businessmen appears to have been a serious error. Without the active input and expertise of persons who had spent their professional lives providing goods and services to the African American community, the militant Black Power Movement's call for community economic development never developed into anything more than mere rhetoric. At the same time, had Black Power advocates spoken enthusiastically of the need for blacks to actively support existing black enterprises, this might have slowed the growing defection of black consumers to white-owned businesses.

The legacy of this "missed opportunity" of the 1960s continues to affect African Americans to this day. In fact, since the late 1960s, blacks have been unable to either build new community-based economic structures or to sustain preexisting enterprises such as black insurance companies. Thus, in lieu of being employers and producers, African Americans have become one of U.S. corporations' most profitable consumer "markets."

Besides the corporations that sell "big ticket items" (cars, appliances, and so on) to the African American community, non-black small businessmen successfully compete against the dwindling number of black small business owners operating in African American enclaves. In fact, in most urban African American neighborhoods today, Arab and Asian entrepreneurs literally control grassroots commerce in these areas.

Significantly, when African Americans do question their economic situation in contemporary America, there is a tendency to criticize the activities of Arab and Asian small businessmen in black communities. Decrying the disproportionate presence of Arab and Asian entrepreneurs in African American enclaves is, indeed, appropriate. Yet, creating Arab and Asian "bogeymen" does not bring the African American community any closer to economic self-determination. It would, perhaps, be more useful for African Americans to discuss why there aren't more black entrepreneurs seeking opportunities in the black community.

In the early 1970s, the musical group Funkadelic recorded a song entitled "Free Your Mind and Your Ass Will Follow." Despite its crude language, this song title describes the path to true African American economic self-interest. While many of our collective problems are based upon external factors, others are based upon our distorted thinking, resulting from centuries of negative mental conditioning. Moreover, African Americans' apparent inability to demonstrate true economic self-interest is caused as much by our collective lack of self-determination as by white racism. This assertion is borne out by examining the experiences of other non-white groups in this country.

African Americans have not been the only non-white group to suffer economic discrimination. The same European American-controlled banks that historically refused to offer business loans to prospective and established African American entrepreneurs, likewise refused to assist Chinese, Korean, Arab, and Vietnamese businesspeople. These groups, however, spent their time developing means whereby they could independently fund their own ethnic economic development, rather than complain about what they could not get from European American financial institutions. Although other groups have experienced economic discrimination, we are the only ones to have experienced slavery. Moreover, this important distinction appears to be at the root of African Americans' collective economic plight. As former slaves we, at times, appear to be hoping against hope that at long last we will receive our "forty acres and a mule" or some other tangible compensation for our centuries of forced labor. While some types of reparations for African Americans are, indeed, appropriate, we should not postpone or disregard the process of community economic development in anticipation of some future windfall.

At this point, it is both appropriate and imperative to address the vital question, How can African Americans best pursue their collective economic self-interest? One long-standing proposed answer is that blacks should work with other groups to destroy the capitalist system. Unfortunately, while egalitarian socialism, on a theoretical level, appears difficult to criticize, the actual implementation of such a society appears problematic. Carter G. Woodson, in his 1933 classic *The Miseducation of the Negro,* capably described this situation as follows:[16]

> The impatient, "highly educated" Negroes say that since under the present system of capitalism the Negro has no choice to toil upward in the economic sphere, the only hope for bettering his condition in this respect is through socialism, the overthrow of the present economic regime, and the inauguration of popular control of resources and agencies which are now being operated for personal gain. There can be no objection to this radical change, if it brings with it some unselfish genius to do the task better than it is being done under the present regime of competition. Russia so far has failed to do well this particular thing under a proletarian dictatorship in an agricultural country. But whether this millennium comes or not, the capitalist system is so strongly entrenched at present that the radicals must struggle many years to overthrow it; *and if the Negro has to wait until that time to try to improve his condition, he will be starved out so soon that he will not be here to tell the story.* The Negro, therefore, like all other oppressed people, must learn to do the so-called "impossible." (emphasis added)

If socialism doesn't adequately answer the question, then is Black capitalism the "key to the kingdom"? Significantly, boosters of "bigger and better" individually-owned black businesses, similar to devout African American Marxists, appear to be divorced from present-day reality. For instance, between 1962 and 1997, the number of African American insurance companies shrank from fifty to thirteen.[17] This is especially significant because insurance companies, historically, have represented the cornerstone of African American economic development. Moreover, the evidence suggests that the creation of more individually owned black businesses, while it may result in more black millionaires, may not necessarily "trickle down" into real community wealth.

Considering the shortcomings associated with both capitalism and socialism, as they relate to African American economic self-interest, it may appear impossible for African Americans to truly achieve self-determination. However, there does exist a strategy, which incorporates the best elements of capitalism and socialism and, that *can* economically revitalize the African American community. Elements of this system, among other things, enabled African Americans to survive the holocaust of slavery and U.S. apartheid. This magic word, or concept, is "cooperation."

Presently, African Americans can draw inspiration and instruction from both a Western and a traditional African method of economic cooperation. Consumer cooperatives, along with the rotating credit concept (which the Yoruba call esusu), appear to offer African Americans real opportunities to substantively pursue our economic self-interest.

The consumer cooperative movement, which began in England in the early nineteenth century, represented a proactive response to the inequities associated with the capitalist system. The following excerpt from the movement's first publication, *The Co-operator*, is both illuminating and instructive:[18]

> Union is strength in all cases, and without exception. What one man cannot do, two may. What is impossible for a few is easy for many. But before many can work they must join hand in hand; they must know their objective and feel a common tie. At present, in working for others, we get for ourselves only a small part. If in any way we could work for ourselves, [we] could get the whole. As we have no capital, we are obliged to find a master to give us employment, and we must work for common wages. It is capital we want. Union and savings will accumulate it. We must form ourselves into a Society for this especial purpose. This capital may be employed in any way the Society may think advisable. Since its origins, the consumer cooperative spirit has manifested itself in a variety of enterprises including cooperative grocery stores, credit unions, and cooperative housing societies. In fact, there are few enterprises that cannot be run cooperatively.[19]

In African American history, one of the more significant black consumer cooperatives was the Consumers' Cooperative Trading Company organized in Gary, Indiana, in 1932. This organization sought to lessen the adverse effects of the Great Depression upon Gary's black community.

In 1932, nearly 50 percent of Gary's African American population was on public relief. In this setting of despair and frustration, a local high school teacher, after familiarizing himself with the principles of organized cooperation, started the Consumers' Cooperative Trading Company (CCTC) as a buying club for fifteen families. Significantly, the group's initial working capital was a minuscule $24. Within three years, after an extensive community education program about the power of consumer cooperatives, the CCTC had grown to 400 member families. By 1935 the organization coordinated several enterprises including a cooperative grocery store with annual sales of $35,000, a community credit union, and a cooperative ice cream and candy shop run entirely by children. Although it appears that a breakdown of the cooperative spirit led to the CCTC's untimely demise in 1940, its earlier success could serve as an inspiration to contemporary African Americans seeking to revitalize black neighborhoods.[19]

Rotating credit associations provides another means by which African Americans could pursue their real (collective) economic self-interest. This economic strategy, has been defined as:[20]

> an association formed by a core of participants who agree to make regular contributions to a fund which is given, in whole or in part, to each contributor in rotation. In many parts of the non-Western world, this type of association serves or has served many of the functions of Western banks.

In the United States, the Chinese and Japanese communities, historically, have experienced the most success in implementing rotating credit associations. Called "hui" by the Chinese and "ko" by the Japanese, prospective Asian entrepreneurs used hui or ko to circumvent the discriminatory lending practices of white American financial institutions.[21] Moreover, the Koreans' use of the rotating credit association has helped them establish a formidable business presence in black communities since the 1970s.

It appears that the rotating credit association concept provides African Americans with a workable system to break free from the crippling inertia that keeps us from pursuing our economic self-interest. As shall be demonstrated, it is flexible to the extent that blacks, who utilize this economic strategy, can focus upon either individual entrepreneurial or communal development projects. Moving from the abstract to the concrete, the following scenario illustrates how a rotating credit association would work in the real world. Suppose there is a group of fifty African Americans who want to establish an esusu whereby each individual agrees to pay $25 a week into the collective pool for fifty weeks. The total worth of this esusu is then $62,500. The members of the esusu could disburse this sum in a variety of ways. First, the members may decide to pay each member a lump sum of $1,250 on a rotating (weekly) basis during the life of the esusu ($1250 x 50 = $62,500). Second, members of the esusu may decide not to take their weekly individual shares. This would provide these individuals with $62,500 to collectively invest in a particular project. Lastly, the members of an esusu may decide to take a portion of their individual weekly shares and invest the rest in a group project.

It should be noted that the above scenario represents just one esusu cycle. Ideally, members of an esusu will continue their special relationship on an ongoing basis. Tables 1 and 3 illustrate how the esusu would work for African Americans from a variety of economic backgrounds.

Perhaps, the ideal vehicle to promote the esusu concept within the African American community is through the family. In recent years, large-scale family reunions have proliferated among blacks. If families used these gatherings to discuss establishing an esusu, this could represent a giant step in the right direction. Moreover, other groups that share a communal bond such as churches and fraternal organizations also appear to be ideal places to establish an esusu.

In sum, the esusu and consumer cooperatives represent two strategies that could graphically reacquaint African Americans with the practice and virtues of re-circulating our money within our own community. In fact, using African American dollars to revitalize African American communities represents true economic self-interest. Any other use of our resources, as current trends suggest, will ultimately lead to the physical and spiritual destruction of African American enclaves.

TABLE 1: The African American Esusu*

(50 members)

	Number of Weeks	Number of Weekly Shares Disbursed	Lump Sum Amount	Total Pool
$10	50	1	$ 500	$25,000
$25	50	1	1,250	62,500
$50	50	1	2,500	125,000
$100	50	1	5,000	250,000

* The number of weeks listed, along with the number of members, are arbitrary figures for the purpose of illustration. The life cycle of an esusu can be less than 50 weeks. Moreover, the number of esusu members can be less than 50. Flexibility is one of the strengths of the esusu.

TABLE 2: The African American Esusu

(100 members)

	Number of Weeks	Number of Weekly Shares Disbursed	Lump Sum Amount	Total Pool
$10	50	2	$500	$ 50,000
$25	50	2	1,250	125,000
$50	50	2	2,500	250,000
$100	50	2	5,000	500,000

TABLE 3: The African American Esusu

(500 members)

	Number of Weeks	Number of Weekly Shares Disbursed	Lump Sum Amount	Total Pool
$10	50	10	$500	$ 250,000
$25	50	10	1,250	625,000
$50	50	10	2,500	1,250,000
$100	50	10	5,000	2,500,000

Notes

1. William Edward Burghardt Du Bois, *The Souls of Black Folk* (Chicago: 1903), 41-59; Francis L. Broderick, *WEB Du Bois: Negro Leader in a Time of Crisis* (Stanford: 1959), 62-77.
2. Ann L. Lane, *The Brownsville Affair* (Port Washington, N.Y.), 90-109.
3. *Chicago Foreign Language Press Survey*, Microfilm roll # 49.
4. James O. Young, *Black Writers of the Thirties* (Baton Rouge: Louisiana State University Press, 1973), 35-63.
5. Abram Harris, *The Negro as Capitalist: A Study of Banking and Business* (Philadelphia: American Academy of Political and Social Science, 1936), 49-50.
6. Ibid., 184.
7. Charles E. Hall, *Negroes in the United States, 1920-1932* (Washington, D.C.: Bureau of the Census, 1935), 496-498.
8. Hall, *Negroes in the U.S.,* 497.

9. Ralph J. Bunche, "The Programs, Ideologies, Tactics, and Achievements of Negro Betterment and Interracial Organizations," Research Memorandum, Carnegie-Myrdal Study of the Negro in America, 1940, 317.

10. Edward Franklin Frazier, *Black Bourgeoisie: The Rise of a New Middle Class in America* (New York: Collier, 1957, 1962), 13.

11. Frazier, *Black Bourgeoisie*, 129.

12. Editorial, *Urban Life* (first quarter, 1965): 8. *Urban Life* was the in-house publication of the Chicago Metropolitan Mutual Assurance Company.

13. See Robert E. Weems, Jr., *Desegregating the Dollar: African American Consumerism in the Twentieth-Century* (New York: New York University Press, 1998).

14. Monroe N. Work, *ed., Negro Year Book and Annual Encyclopedia of the Negro 1916-17* (Tuskegee, AL: Negro Year Book Company, 1916), 318; *Negro Year Book 1918-1919*, 355; David J. Sullivan, "How Negroes Spent Their Incomes, 1920-1943," *Sales Management* 54 (June 15, 1945): 106; Joseph A. Pierce, *Negro Business and Business Education: Their Present and Prospective Development* (New York: Harper and Brothers, 1947), 52; "We Must Stop the MADNESS!!!" *Black Heritage Products Inc. Nationwide Co-op* 22 (October/November 1996): 1.

15. William L. Van Deburg, *New Day In Babylon: The Black Power Movement and American Culture, 1965-1975* (Chicago: University of Chicago Press, 1992), 116-20; Juliet E.K. Walker, *The History of Black Business in America: Capitalism, Race, Entrepreneurship* (New York: Macmillan, 1998), 271-72.

16. Carter G. Woodson, *The Miseducation of the Negro* (Washington, D.C.: Associated Publishers, 1933), 43-44.

17. Robert E. Weems, Jr., "A Crumbling Legacy: The Decline of African American Insurance Companies in Contemporary America," *The Review of Black Political Economy* 23 (fall 1996): 29-30, 31; Frank McCoy, "Life Sustaining Measures," *Black Enterprise* 28 (June 1998): 182.

18. V.S. Alanne, *Fundamentals of Consumer Cooperation* (Superior, WI: Cooperative Publishing Association, 1946), 6.

19. Weems, Jr. *Desegregating the Dollar*, 59.

20. Ivan H. Light, Ethnic *Enterprise in America: Business and Welfare Among Chinese, Japanese and Blacks* (Berkeley: University of California Press, 1972), 22-23.

21. Ibid., 20-21, 26-30.

References

Alanne, V.S. *Fundamentals of Consumer Cooperation*. Superior, Wisc.: Cooperative Publishing Association, 1946.

Broderick, Francis L. *WEB Du Bois: Negro Leader in a Time of Crisis*. Palo Alto, Calif.: Stanford University Press, 1959.

Bunche, Ralph J. "The Programs, Ideologies, Tactics and Achievements of Negro Betterment and Interracial Organizations." Unpublished research memorandum, Carnegie-Myrdal Study of the Negro in America, 1940.

"Chicago Foreign Language Press Survey." Chicago: Works Progress Administration, 1942.

Du Bois, William Edward Burghardt. *The Souls of Black Folk*. Chicago: McClurg, 1903.

Frazier, Edward Franklin. *Black Bourgeosie: The Rise of a New Middle Class in America*. New York: Collier, 1957.

Hall, Charles E. *Negroes in the United States, 1920-1932*. Washington, D.C.: Bureau of the Census, 1935.

Harris, Abram. *The Negro as Capitalist: A Study of Banking and Business*. Philadelphia: American Academy of Political and Social Science, 1935.

Light, Ivan. *Ethnic Enterprise in America: Business and Welfare among Chinese, Japanese, and Blacks*. Berkeley and Los Angeles: University of California Press, 1972.

Pierce, Joseph A. *Negro Business and Business Education: Their Present and Prospective Development*. New York: Harper and Brothers, 1947.

Sullivan, David J. "How Negroes Spent Their Incomes, 1920-1943." *Sales Management* 54 (June 15, 1945): 106.

Van DeBurg, William L. *New Day in Babylon: The Black Power Movement and American Culture, 1965-1975*. Chicago: University of Chicago Press, 1992.

Walker, Juliet E.K. *The History of Black Business in America: Capitalism, Race, Entrepreneurship*. New York: Macmillan, 1998.

Weems, Robert E., Jr. "A Crumbling Legacy: The Decline of African American Insurance Companies in Contemporary America." *The Review of Black Political Economy* 23 (1996): 25-37.

_____. *Desegregating the Dollar: African American Consumerism in the Twentieth Century*. New York: New York University Press, 1998.

Woodson, Carter G. *The Miseducation of the Negro*. Washington, D.C.: Associated Publishers, 1933.

Work, Monroe N., ed. *Negro Year Book and Annual Encyclopedia of the Negro 1916-17*. Tuskegee, Ala.: Negro Year Book Company, 1916.

_____, ed. *Negro Year Book and Annual Encyclopedia of the Negro 1918-1919*. Tuskegee, Ala.: Negro Year Book Company, 1918.

Young, James O. *Black Writers of the Thirties*. Baton Rouge: Lousiana State University Press, 1973.

25

EDUCATION FOR LIBERATION: PUBLIC BLACK COLLEGES UNDER SIEGE – DESEGREGATION VERSUS AFFIRMATIVE ACTION

Alvin O. Chambliss, Jr.

The historical record of education in this nation has never fully appreciated the Black struggle to achieve excellence at Public Black Colleges (PBCs). This nation's future is inextricably tied to its commitment to the Black Higher Education Agenda. Even at this late date, there are those who deny the existence of Black Higher Education.[1]

The 51 public black colleges and 49 private black colleges together with the two-year institutions totals 117 Historically Black Colleges and Universities (HBCUs) which are located in 14 southern states, six northern states, three midwestern states, California, the District of Columbia, and the Virgin Islands. These HBCUs are vital national resources, form the backbone of African American leadership, and make tremendous contributions to our nation and the world. Yet they are dying.[2]

HOPWOOD V. STATE OF TEXAS AND AYERS V. FORDICE: THE NEW ERA OF APARTHEID IN HIGHER EDUCATION

The question presented in Hopwood is a very narrow one, which focuses on affirmative action voluntarily imposed by the state because of its perceived notion of a need to have diversity and a more balanced student body. It is a difficult question in this context. The question for BPCs is whether Hopwood (which will be discussed later) and its limited scope will ultimately hurt the overall access movement. If this is so, how may BPCs would respond to this decision. We must start by saying that affirmative action Title VII is a voluntary program, but Title VI is the law and must be implemented. One is permissible and the other mandatory. It is very difficult for people to understand that in Adams v. Richardson – 356 F. Supp. 92 (D.D.C. 1973) 480 F.2d 1159 (D.C. Cir. 1973) – the court held that the 11 states of the confederacy and four broader states were not enforcing Title VI mandates applicable to higher education. The

Adams states were expanded to include Pennsylvania, Ohio, and several other northern and western states where BPCs were located. These states have been adjudicated law violators by both the court and the agency, which give them lots of money. There are 19 states that are considered subject to Title VI higher education mandates. Every state has submitted a plan, is working toward updating their plan of compliance, or is in litigation. The only state that never submitted a plan and is not in litigation is the state of Ohio. The federal government through the Office of Civil Rights has stated that all 15 states are subject to review pursuant to the Ayers v. Fordice standard, exception being the states of Tennessee, Mississippi, Louisiana, and Alabama where litigations on this issue are ongoing. The state of Texas is now on that list, "OCR" investigation notwithstanding. Title VI of the Civil Rights of 1964 (42 U.S.C. '2000d) declares:

> No person in the United States shall, on the ground of race, color, or national origin, be excluded from participation in, be denied the benefits of, or be subjected to discrimination under any program or activity receiving federal financial assistance.

Courts have generally held that Title VI incorporates the same standards for identifying unlawful racial discrimination as have been developed under the Fourteenth Amendment's Equal Protection Clause. The Supreme Court in United States v. Fordice held that

> Because the standard applied by the District Court did not make these inquiries, we hold that the Court of Appeals erred in affirming the district court ruling that the State had brought itself into compliance with the Equal Protection Clause in the operation of its Higher Education system (505 U.S. 732).

CAN A COURT OF APPEALS OVERRULE A SUPREME COURT DECISION?

In Hopwood v. State of Texas, circuit judges Jerry E. Smith and Harold Demoss struck down affirmative action in admissions at the University of Texas Law School. Stretching beyond the issues before them, the two judges denounced virtually all race-conscious affirmative action and made the extraordinary declaration that the Supreme Court's Bakke decision is no longer good law. The 1978 decision of the U.S. Supreme Court in Regents of the University of California v. Bakke has governed affirmative action by colleges and universities for almost two decades. A lower federal court is not empowered to overrule a decision of the Supreme Court, our country's highest court. The two Hopwood judges, sitting on an intermediate-level federal court in the Fifth Circuit Court of Appeals, rejected Justice Lewis Powell's conclusion in Bakke. Powell stated, "that a diverse student body enhances the learning environment for all students and therefore is a compelling interest supporting affirmative action." The third Hopwood panel member strongly disagreed with this part of the decision and filed an opinion concurring in part and specially concurring in part. The extreme position of two judges on the Fifth Circuit stands in the direct contrast with the moderate views of a majority of the Supreme Court. The Hopwood judges reasoned: "Justice Powell's view in Bakke is not binding precedent on this issue." In contrast, Justice Sandra Day O'Connor, widely viewed as the "swing" vote on the current Supreme Court has stated about the Bakke case: "I subscribe to Justice Powell's formulation" (Wygant v. Jackson Board of Education [285: 1986] concurring in part and concurring in the judgment). Justice O'Connor also has specially endorsed the diversity rationale set forth in Justice Powell's Bakke opinion, stating: "Although its precise contours are uncertain, a state interest in promotion of racial diversity has been found sufficiently 'compelling' at least in the context of Higher Education, to support the use of racial considerations in furthering that interest" (Wygant, 286).

The Hopwood judges predicted that the Supreme Court will turn back the clock and eliminate all nonremedial use of affirmative action: "subsequent Supreme Court decisions regarding education state that nonremedial state interests will never justify racial classifications." While the Hopwood judges refer to subsequent Supreme Court decisions regarding education, the only such decision is Wygant v. Jackson Board of Education, in which Justice O'Connor quite clearly stated the opposite, opening the door even for new compelling interests that have not yet been presented to the Supreme Court: "And certainly nothing... forecloses the possibility that the court will find other governmental interests which have been relied upon in the lower course but which have not been passed on here" (Wygant. Id.) The Hopwood judges conceded that affirmative action may be used to remedy past discrimination and its effects. Yet the judges defined past discrimination so narrowly, and required such a high burden of proof of causation, that few, if any, educational institutions will be able to use affirmative action if this decision stands. The Court ignored the Fordice decision (which will be discussed later).

The University of Texas Law School affirmative action program – created by order of the U.S. Department of Health, Education, and Welfare (HEW) in order to remedy a history of exclusion of African American students – was struck down by the U.S. Supreme Court Sweatt v. Painter case. Yet, according to the Hopwood court, even Texas Law Schools with this disgraceful past may not use affirmative action to level the playing field. Moreover, the Hopwood court held that the State of Texas Law Schools may not use affirmative action to remedy current or recent discrimination by the State of Texas – in its elementary, secondary, and college system. The Law Schools may, under this ruling, remedy only its own discrimination. Such a narrow view of the nature of the harm and the scope of the states remedial powers is unprecedented. But this is precisely what happens to southern states that push affirmative action plans over desegregation remedies. Desegregation is mandatory, but black colleges have to be at the table first, and this is where the conflict arises. Desegregation places obligations on both parties.

The Hopwood judges' constricted view of remedial affirmative action is contrary to Supreme Court doctrine. In 1995, the Court with Justice O'Connor writing for the majority stated that the constitutional standard is not applied to be "fatal in fact." The unhappy persistence of both the practice and the lingering effects of racial discrimination against minority groups in this country is an unfortunate reality, and government is not disqualified from acting in response to it. When race-based action is necessary to further a compelling interest, such action is within constitutional constraints if it satisfies the narrow tailoring test this court has set out in previous cases." (Adarand v. Pena, 1995). On July1, 1996, the U.S. Supreme Court denied review of the Hopwood decision. Justice Ginsburg, with whom Justice Souter joins, stated:

> The petition before us, however, does not challenge the lower court's judgments that the particular admissions procedure used by the University of Texas Law School in 1992 was unconstitutional. Accordingly, we must await a final judgment on a program genuinely in controversy before addressing the important questions raised in this petition. All concede this record is inadequate to assess definitively the constitutionality of the law school's current consideration of race in its admission process. (518 U.S. 1033, July 1, 1996)

On July 31, 1996, Judges Garwood, Jolly, and Duhe granted private plaintiffs Motion to Expedite the Appeal in Ayers v. Fordice No. 95-60431. Oral argument within sixty days. The question of whether or not affirmative action and race-based scholarship is lawful was finally before the Court. The question whether Hopwood v. Texas and its progeny Plessy v. Ferguson applied was at issue. The fifth Circuit precedent extends to the states of Texas, Louisiana, and Mississippi, but the Supreme Court decisions are the law in all 50 states. The State of Mississippi had many race-based scholarships, and race continues to be used along with other factors to determine valid educational goals as per the nearly 150 school-district desegregation decrees. The fifth Circuit ruling in Hopwood has been applied too broadly, and it was thought that states and cities would abandon affirmative action programs if the issue was not clarified. Mississippi, Louisiana, Texas, California, Georgia, and Virginia were just a few of the states that were in the process of changing their race-based scholarship. The Office of Civil Rights in the Department of Education contends that U.S. v. Fordice and Brown v. Board of Education apply to the 19 southern and border states, and, under Title VI of the Civil Rights Act of 1964, the states that have been found to be in violation of the fourteenth Amendment and/or Title VI have an affirmative obligation to remove the vestiges, remnants, and residual conditions caused by past discriminatory practices. The Office of Civil Rights (OCR) had reviewed the vestiges and/or remnants in Pennsylvania, Virginia, Florida, and Ohio. All four of those states now claimed they did not have an obligation to the PBCs even though the underfunding and other discriminatory practices persist. The states of Texas, Kentucky, Maryland, and Virginia were scheduled for review. Most observers did not believe that the judiciary would abandon the jurisprudence of Brown v. Board of Education. If Hopwood prevailed, all black people would be going back into the third reconstruction and back to the cotton patches they surmised. Without an education, black people would be enslaved within a decade, and this couldn't happen in America at this day and age, but it did. The Fifth Circuit did not even mention Hopwood. Moreover, it reaffirmed Cumming. It allowed for a remedy to decrease opportunities. It rejected open admission as a cure for years of a racially skewed policies. Many were disappointed and the One Dupont crowd said... We told you so. The word then and now is for PBCs to cool it and don't rock the boat.

The state of Ohio was first to take the Hopwood decision to the next level. Less than a week after the U.S. Supreme Court denied review in Hopwood, Governor George V. Volnovich, Dr. Elaine H. Hairston, Chancellor and the State Fire Marshall stormed Central State's campus and closed the school because of its poor living conditions (see Chronicle of Higher Education, August 2, 1996 A23). The State of Ohio had never cured the violations founded by then Clarence Thomas, now Supreme Court Justice. (see:, May 15, 1981, letter to James A. Rhodes from "OCR"). The State of Ohio refused to follow the Revised Criteria Specifying the Ingredients of Acceptable Plans to Desegregate State Systems of Public Higher Education. It is the author's belief that the effect (fallout from Hopwood) is being supported by the one Dupont Circle d/b/a Washington Educational Establishment, etc. Further, that the 68 or more organizations situated in and around one Dupont Circle are virtually all white elitist and anti-black colleges. One only has to ask longtime former NAFEO official Dr. Sam

Myers. There may not be a smoking gun. Nor is this an attempt to stroke all of these organizations with a broad brush. However, the educational establishment is not concerned with public black higher education and the proof is in their policy initiatives. ACE and NASULGC don't have a clue. There is no power-sharing, and they have remained mute in the face of genocidal tactics that they knew were destructive to black youth in Mississippi and the nation, yet they said nothing. The educational establishment followed Ray Cleere, former commissioner of higher education in Mississippi, and then Governor George V. Volnovich and their educational malpractices approaches.[3] See Journal of Negro Education 60. 4 (1991); Is Higher Education Desegregation a Remedy for Segregation but not Educational Inequality? by Dr. Elias Blake, Jr.; "Issues in Educational Policy and Practice: A Study of the Ayers v. Mabus Desegregation Case," in Phelps-Stokes Fund Newsletter, (September 1994); G. Kujovich, Equal Opportunity in Higher Education and the Black Public College," Minnesota Law Review 29 (1987); N. McMillen, Dark Journey: Black Mississipian in the Age of Jim Crow, 1990; James W. Loewen, Lies My Teacher Told Me, (1994) Kenneth S. Tollett, Sr. The Fate of Minority-Based Institutions after Fordice, The Review of Litigation, University of Texas School of Law Publication, (Summer 1994).

Again, the educational establishment at One Dupont Circle had a conflict between ethics and pragmatic politics. As Marva N. Collins of the Westside Preparatory says, "It's the maddening of America to build more prisons and close schools. Nobody is talking about where the real problems arise – namely in the places where we teach our children" (Essence Magazine, [Sept. 1994] 860). It is beyond doubt that all 19 Adams states and the District of Columbia have not equalized funding for their PBCs, but who cares in America? The constitutional mandates are not subject to legislative rationing if equal justice under the law is to be an overriding principle of our democracy. No one cares if black people don't care. Black people do not have an effective civil rights agenda, and they should adopt one soon with PBCs and civil rights enforcement being first priority. Resource allocation and a commitment to equal justice under the law should be the number one topic in America for us. Economic and consumer activism should be our business plan. For example, William Raspberry's piece on a "Powerful Strategy Affirmative Action", Houston Chronicle-November 12, 1999 46A is instructive. It starts, "Here's my nightmare; We'll wake up early in the new millennium to discover that Affirmative Action is dead and killed not just by prototypical angry white men but the opposition of the great American majority and the abandonment of the Courts." Homeboy is right on time about affirmative action in the 19

Adams states where black colleges exist, but what about enforcement of desegregation mandates that are being violated every day in the South? Why can't Jackson State University, the home of the late great Walter Payton, have a law school, a pharmacy school, an engineering school, and some type of medical mission? Why should white schools enjoy all of the fruits of taxpayers funds' in a state such as Mississippi, where the black population is at least percent? Why is Howard University the only research IHBCU on the planet? Why should rivil rights laws be ignored in these states? The children in the 19 Adams states deserve more, but homeboy and many others refused to look to the South for remedies and they must. See also: AA Time When 'White Only' Can Help Diversity" by Clarence Page, and "Civil Rights Fight Won and Time to Move On?" by William Raspberry, October 12, 1999 and October 19, 1999, Houston Chronicle respectively. (Raspberry is from Okolona, Mississippi.)

This situation can be explained only by race! In an effort to play David Duke by way of Kirk Fordice, the governors with the aid of the One Dupont Circle crowd threaten cajole, order, preach, commiserate with and even buy off our weak black leaders who go along to get along, in most instances. They will not touch higher education desegregation. It is safe to go to a UNCF event. It's tough to sue the southern states over college desegregation. No one will bother George W. Bush as his run for president but see Robinson v. Bush (A99-CA-303SS) and Benjamin v. Bush (A99-CA305SS), desegregation and tobacco litigation lawsuit for excluding Prairie View and Texas Southern from fund allocation. This is the choice that supporters of PBC's and Private Black Colleges face. The old trickle-down trick – the economic thing, apartheid 21st century style is at play here. President Reagan failed to deregulate a single industry or abolish any important government agency. He accomplished his purpose by "benign neglect" of government and beating down rather than legislative abolition of it. The states are doing nothing and PBCs are dying on the vine. The original intent of not educating black people is accomplished by non-enforcement. This is the Hopwood effect, and it cripples and causes a slow death. Why cause attention with closure when there are less painful avenues available? The issue is Title VI for blacks, or Title VII Affirmative Action for whites; and the blacks have chosen "the white dolls." This is the bottom line.

The uniform admission policy (one shoe fits all) in Mississippi was affirmative action for white people and racial exclusion for blacks. At the time of the adoption of the ACT in 1962 with James Meredith, whites averaged 18 on the test while blacks averaged 7.7. Raising the ACT from 15 to 16 excluded 2,500 blacks already in college and empowered 5,000 whites who were not in the system. Dr. Kenneth H. Ashworth with the, Higher Education Commission in Texas says it best: "We'll be casting a much broader net and taking in some deserving low-income Anglo students as well." (The Chronicle of Higher Education, July 19, 1996, A27). It is criminal that white people prey on the misfortunes of the weak brought on by state policy, which was designed to limit educational opportunities. Dr. F. Raymond Cleere, former commissioner in Mississippi said the exact same thing in 1995: "The new admission standards over time will bring a more broader range of students into the system." Decoded, this means push out blacks and bring in whites. Jackson State, Alcorn State, and Mississippi Valley State will lose up to 60 percent of their freshmen enrollment because of racism if the exclusionary state policies persist.

THE AYERS DECISION SUMMARY

The Fifth Circuit Court of Appeals reversed in part, affirmed in part, and sent the case back to Judge Neal B. Biggers' court in Mississippi. The Fifth Circuit Justices King, Jolly, and Dennis held that (1) portion of district court decree adopting uniform admissions standards and new remedial program proposed by state's governing board for higher education was proper, except for elimination of existing remedial courses; (2) use of college entrance examination scores as criterion for award of scholarships was traced to prior de jure system and had current segregative effects; (3) decree's provisions regarding addition of new academic programs to two historically black institutions (HBIs) were appropriate, but clarification was required as to issues affected by proposed merger of one HBI with historically white institutions (HWI); (4) district court's failure to alter state's current method of providing research and extension services to historically black and historically white land grant institutions was not clearly erroneous; (5) district court should, on remand, review findings on duplication of programs if proposed merger of HBI and HWI was rejected; (6) state's formula for funding institutions was not traceable to de jure system and did not require adjustment; (7) finding that no alteration to library allocations was required was not clearly erroneous, but district court was required to make further factual findings as to disparities in equipment at HBIs and HWIs; (8) state's hiring and salary practices for faculty and administrators were not traceable to prior de jure system; and (9) racial composition of governing board members and staff was not result of policy or practice traceable to prior de jure system. (Ayers v. Fordice, 1997).

The district court's decision in Ayers v. Fordice 1994 had made many finds on how the state of Mississippi had designed a system to limit educational opportunities for blacks. The lower court found that the Mississippi system of higher education was discriminatory and exclusionary from 1840/1848 (UM) until 1871 when ASU was established. Then it became racially segregated and discriminatory until 1962 and the James Meredith incident. The Supreme Court found that full compliance did not come until the mid 1970s when white students first attended HBCUs. Further, the Supreme Court found that Mississippi had never operated a lawful admission procedure. The Supreme Court in Fordice addressed the admissions standards for Mississippi's eight public universities. It noted the district court's finding that the system's adoption of the American College Test (ACT) was intentionally discriminatory.[4] The Supreme Court faulted the continuing use of the ACT for two reasons. First, were the uniformly higher cutoff scores for regular admission at the five historically white universities (HWUs) than at the three historically black universities (HBUs), and this was held to perpetuate segregation.

The Supreme Court also cited the failure to utilize high school grades along with the ACT in the admission process, contrary to the recommendations of the test's developer. The record suggested "that an admissions formula which included grades would increase the number of black students eligible for automatic admission to all of Mississippi's public universities." It is noteworthy that the second suspect feature of the admission criteria involved not simply segregation but also denial of access to the higher education system. As of the 1994 trial on remand, the five HWUs utilized a cutoff score for regular admission of 18 on the "enhanced ACT" and the three HBUs used a 15.[5] Moreover, students with ACT scores of 14-17 (for the HWUs) and 12-14 (for the HBUs) had considerable access via exceptions to the ACT minimum score requirements. Persons failing to satisfy one of these standards could gain admission only by satisfying the criteria applied in the new spring screening program, or the new summer remedial program (to run 10 or 11 weeks). The Fordice decision afforded the state the opportunity to justify the suspect features of its use of the ACT, which continued as of the remand hearing. The state chose not to do so. Rather, it preferred to revise admission standards.[6] The board's proposed standards, adopted below, are the same for all eight universities; they utilize ACT scores and high school grade point average and provide three paths for regular admission. Persons failing to satisfy one of these standards could gain admission only by satisfying the criteria applied in the new spring screening program, or the new summer remedial program (to run 10 or 11 weeks). If we compare of the standards in effect at the time of the remand hearing and the approved "remedy," this will allow us to identify high school graduates who formerly had access to one or more universities as regular or exceptional admittees but who can, under the new standards, be admitted only by succeeding in the new spring or summer phases. These high school graduates encompass:

> All students with ACT scores of 12-15;
>
> Students with ACT scores of 18 with high school grade point average below 2.0; and
>
> Students with ACT scores of 16 or 17 with high school grade point average below 2.5.

The evidence at trial revealed that approximately 51.3 percent of Mississippi's black high school graduates (2,999 persons) and 19.7 percent of white high school graduates (2,043 persons) were affected by the change.[7] The district court focused on diminished access by regular admission. It found, comparing the existing and the new standards, a reduction in the "overall percentage... of black students eligible for regular admission to the system" of 23.0 to 25.7 percent.[8] The district court also made this relevant finding: "Analysis of enrollment data spanning the years 1988 through 1992 indicates that over 60% of the students enrolled at the HBUs scored below 15 on the ACT compared with approximately 85% of the enrolled students at the HWUs scoring above 15 on the ACT. Of course, the 85% of students referred to includes both black and white students at HWUs." It is important to emphasize that the record contained data, based on studies of earlier admittees to the system, allowing conclusions regarding the prospects for success of students like the ones adversely affected by the board's remedial proposal. These students would be expected to earn at least a "C" average at the end of their freshman year at each of the HBUs, but not at the HWUs.[9] Should the lower courts consider that the new spring and summer options "could" have an ameliorative role regarding students affected by the changed discussed above? However, it is undisputed that these programs were incomplete in important respects, when approved by the district court. Review is also warranted by the split within the circuits. The Eleventh Circuit says open admission is an effective remedy while the Fifth Circuit says reduced opportunities and selective admission is constitutional.

Perusal of the district court's opinion allows identification of various incomplete features. A test known as the "Accuplacer" would be used in the new spring process. The district court found that "[i]t is not designed as a screening instrument or as a component of an admission process per se but rather as a placement device." The manner in which this test would be used in the spring process, and any norms to be used, had not been decided upon. Lastly, one does not find discussion of matters such as the ability of black youth, disproportionately from low-income families, to forgo working in the summer, or how the timing of the summer program would mesh with the end of high school for Mississippi high school graduates.[10] Indeed, the court of appeals seemingly sympathized with students capable of succeeding in college with remedial help "who self-select out of the spring or summer program because of the unique burdens, imposed by the program. The court of appeals discussed at length the planned reduction, as a component of the new admissions standards...of remedial courses that had been offered by all the universities at issue here." The appellate court found inadequate consideration of or justification for this feature of the proposal and required its reconsideration on remand.

THE FIFTH CIRCUIT DENIAL OF ACCESS IN AYERS V. FORDICE: MANDATED FURTHER REVIEW BY THE SUPREME COURT ON THE ACCESS QUESTION

At the outset of its analysis, the court of appeals wrote:

> We agree with the plaintiffs that it would be inappropriate to remedy the traceable, segregative effects of an admissions policy in a system originally designed to limit educational opportunity for black citizens by adopting a policy that itself caused a reduction in meaningful educational opportunity for black citizens. We do not, however, understand the District Court to have done so. The District Court considered and rejected alternative proposals as educationally unsound, and expressly contemplated that the remedial route to admission could alleviate any potential disproportionate impact on those black student who are capable with reasonable remediation, of doing college level work.

With several very important exceptions, black plaintiffs' quarrel with this approach is with the application of the standard set forth, rather than with the standard itself,"[11] even though we contend that both admission standards are legal and that they always choose whites over blacks. The Fifth Circuit, in part, faulted the admissions standards because the utilization of high school grades, as called for by the test developer, "would increase the number of black students eligible for automatic admission to all of Mississippi's public universities." This indicates that the remedial goal should have been increasing access to education not minimizing reduction, that is, attrition rates and saving the state money or, as the court emphasized, saving black students money. The court should not be so generous in this area given the history of the state of Mississippi during the days that exclusion of blacks from education saved their souls and allowed them to work the fields. One cannot handle these cases in isolation. The pivotal question in all educational settings when access for excluded victims is at issue is whether the proposed remedy will further the goals of full participation in the system. Stated another way, will the remedy kill the child or retard it in any way? Let us take a look at what the court did on remedy. Then, and only then, can we see the exclusionary pattern persisting.

THE SUPREME COURT SHOULD HAVE GRANTED REVIEW AND SHOULD GRANT REVIEW IN 99-6965

First, such a degree of incompleteness and concomitant uncertainty and speculation about the future should not be permitted in devising an admissions remedy "in a system originally designed to limit educational opportunities for black citizens." The state's proposal could not be deemed one "that promises realistically to work" (Green v. County School Board, 1968), when how it would work was so dependent upon future governing-board decisions. Yet, white educational experts testified that a summer program would better than a year-round remediation. This, Dr. Blake called educational fraud.

Second, the Supreme Court should decide whether the facts set forth above regarding the differences in access under the 1994 standards and the "remedial" proposal constitute "a reduction in meaningful educational opportunity for black citizens" or, indeed, "greater burden... being placed upon the black students... in Mississippi."[12] Of course, the court of appeals hedged its standard by referring to "meaningful opportunity for black citizens." This seemingly relates to the later references to predicted success only at HBIs and the permissibility of avoiding a proposal "under which students can do college level work at only three institutions in the system. " This apparent rationale is exceedingly troubling.

The district court made no relevant finding about the lack of good-quality education at the HBIs. There was no record basis for such a finding. The district court made express positive findings about Mississippi Valley State University. Where so much speculation was occurring, why wasn't the reasonable inference made that commitment of the type found at Mississippi Valley led to concrete efforts, yielding the success cited by the appellate court? The reference to students able to do college-level work at only three institutions also warrants discussion in light of the recognition that "the District Court credited expert testimony indicating that differential or tiered admissions standards are both sound and routinely used." Indeed, the evidence below was even stronger. Experts could not identify another state taking the same approach (that is, multiple universities all with the same admissions standards). This means that having students in different universities with, on average, differing levels of academic strength is common throughout the country. In summary, at the time when Mississippi was developing lawful admission standards, and for the first time in the history of the university system, the court tolerated some new notions of adequate college-level work. And these notions, based upon limited analysis, served to justify, at minimum, reduced access by regular admission. The Supreme Court needs to decide if this is acceptable.

The Supreme Court should decide whether the district court made adequate efforts to identify admission standards without the adverse effects discussed here. This court in Brown v. Board of Education, and indeed Fordice, provided for the development of remedies in the second stage of a bifurcated proceeding. If all of the admissions proposals before the court in the liability hearing were flawed, the court should have provided for the orderly preparation of other proposals. This was done in both the Louisiana and Alabama cases.[13] The findings and the evidence about the universality and the soundness of differential admission standards are also germane in this context. In the absence of a focused remedy hearing, the possibility for invoking this approach was not exhausted. The "desegregative" admissions standard and its summer remedial program have failed miserably – as black educators experienced and skilled in increasing educational opportunities for black citizens testified extensively that it would. The black educators put before the court a compelling and irrefutable case: educationally sound and practical alternatives must be and can be crafted so as not to reduce opportunities, but to meet Mississippi's unfulfilled legal obligation to dismantle and replace the policies of the design to limit higher education by race as a means of eliminating racial disparities in college enrollment and graduation. The court chose to believe the white educators who all agreed that the summer remediation program had never been tested anyplace.

The effect of the "desegregative" admissions standard has been to increase the disparities between whites and blacks by bringing a new population of white freshmen into the university system and increasing their numbers by potentially 25 percent while decreasing the number of first-time black freshmen by 45 percent. The three debilitating years of ricocheting up the destructive historic inferiority stigmatizing of the original "design to restrict the educational opportunities of black citizens" to "agricultural and mechanic training rather than the liberal education provided its white citizenry" must be stopped by all Americans. At the end of de jure desegregation in 1954, the court found "The Design" to have created the following disparities:

> Blacks earned 10 percent of the baccalaureates and were only 16 percent of the population, whereas they were the majority of the elementary and secondary population.

> Whites as a minority 48 percent were earning 90 percent of the degrees and 84 percent of the college enrollment.

In 1993-1994, the racial disparities were being perpetuated by racially discriminatory educational – policies in college preparation, in college admissions, in the limited mission, and in inequitable funding of the black colleges, and inequitable funding of higher education in general – that were still in force, traced to the original design and still limiting the higher educational opportunities of blacks to enroll in and graduate from the "liberal education" originally reserved for whites exclusively. Blacks earned 22 percent of the degrees while remaining 45 percent of the elementary and secondary school population, less than the 25.6 percent they earned in 1981. Blacks were still only 29 percent of the college enrollment, less than the 32 percent they represented in 1976. Whites increased from 74 percent to 78 percent of the degrees earned and from 68 percent to 71 percent of the enrollment while being only 55 percent of the elementary and secondary school population.

The Supreme Court must prohibit the defendants from instituting a new admissions program that will further disadvantage blacks and have them meet their prior obligation to "alleviate [the] disproportionate impact of the new admissions standards on those black students who are capable with reasonable remediation of doing college level work."

Nearly two years went by between the 1995 district court decision, the court of appeals decision, and a hearing on March 17, 1999. In the meantime, white students, taxpayers' and HWIs supporters decided to open a ninth university on the Gulf Coast of Mississippi. The University of Southern Mississippi Gulf Coast (USM-GC) would have been and still may become the largest public university in Mississippi. Jackson State is located in Jackson, Mississippi, in a metropolitan area of about 450,000. The Gulf Coast is second in population and first in growth in the state. The so-called urban mission of Jackson State has never been implemented... so why not start new programs in an underserved area of the state? which is what the state did.

Dr. Elias Blake, Jr., president of the Benjamin E. Mays National Educational Resource Center in Washington, D.C., lodged with the court an amicus memorandum in support of an order immediately restoring illegally reduced educational opportunities for black students at the March 17, 1999, hearing in Oxford, Mississippi, and opposing starting a ninth university. As originally indicated, the U.S. Supreme Court denied certiorari on January 22, 1998 (Ayers v. Fordice, No. 97-6811). The facts and circumstances have not changed materially except that the state now wants to start another university on the Gulf Coast. In the December 1997 submission in opposition to certiorari, the U.S. Department of Justice Seth P. Waxman, solicitor general agreed, with black students in every aspect but claimed review was premature and not ripe. Justice alleged before the Supreme Court that; the court of appeals erred in affirming the new admissions standards and approving the continued discriminatory funding formula. Justice also asserted that the court of appeals erred in allowing historically white universities to continue the practice of granting certain scholarship and out-of-state tuition waivers to children of alumni of those institutions. Finally, Waxman said he "agreed that Private Plaintiffs were right but the lower courts should be given more time." Nearly eighteen months passed and absolutely nothing of major significance happened. The Civil Rights Agenda started by DuVal Patrick and continued by Bill Lam Lee was to dispose of all higher education desegregation causes on the Justice Department docket. Nat Douglass was fired and Patrick never invited Fred Gray, Thomas Todd, Richard Dinkins, Dr. Fred Humphries, Dr. Elias Blake, and black counsel handling the Alabama, Tennessee, Louisiana, and Mississippi higher education cases to his civil rights meetings. DuVal refused to return calls or otherwise, and Dr. Benjamin Chavez refused to allow a sanction resolution to go forward at the annual Indianapolis national convention. Bill Lam Lee refused to meet or change Patrick's policy. With the exception of Elaine Jones, LDF personnel, and Raymond Pierce of "OCR" Department of Education, no blacks were at the table during the last eight years.

The U.S. Department of Justice, Civil Rights Division, Educational Opportunity continues to be puff. The creation of a ninth university in Mississippi took place with four U.S. Justice Department attorneys in attendance, but the Justice Department did not actively oppose the state of Mississippi. The Justice Department did not produce one witness nor did it participate in any of the proceedings. They were just there with nothing to offer. It is sad, criminal, and unforgivable. Dr. Blake, as well as Dr. Calvin Miller and Dr. Ivory Phillips, testified against the creation of yet another all-white university in Mississippi. The U.S. Supreme Court should now clear the record. Ayers v. Fordice, 99-6965, is back before the Court. The two issues are (a) whether the court of appeals had jurisdiction and (b) whether the mandate of Fordice is being followed by the lower courts.

WHAT YOU NEVER KNEW ABOUT BLACK HIGHER EDUCATION AND WHAT PEOPLE ARE AFRAID TO TELL YOU

"Higher Education, It's for all Americans." This is the theme song, this is the hope, the pray, the vision, the dream... (but will it ever include Blacks, African Americans, or if you prefer, people of African descent? It can – if we follow Robert E. Weems, Jr.'s prescription in "Desegregating the Dollar" (1998). The over 500 billion dollars, buying power of blacks must be exercised with restraint so that we support corporations, political candidates, and economic entities that financially support access to and support of black higher education.

The PBCs are not organized and HBCUs alumni, faculty, staff, and students are not exercising consumer activism. The 1965 Voting Rights Act is scheduled to run out soon...and very little voting is taking place at HBCUs. Even before one gets to the issue of organization, the question that no one mentions is whether black colleges should exist. Why are they here now? when qualified students can go to any institution they choose. Black colleges are racial enclaves that seek only black students, or HBCUs are vestiges. Jim Crow black colleges created by the state are impeding progress. These are issues we hear everyday. The issue is not entirely a black college issue but an elitist issue involving class distinctions, self-hatred, and the talented tenth concept of the few and the mighty. It is very difficult washing dirty linen publicly... but can we afford to ignore trains of thought that cause harm to PBCs? Intentional or unintentional, harm causes damage. Much of the debate on black colleges is a debate waged by old school thought and present-day realities of what is, not what ought to be. Much of the hidden discussion is a product of internecine conflicts and/or warfare between black college presidents, elitist corporate board members, Ad Council of America members, and the black middle class, as each seeks ideological dominance in African American life. Black history is left out of the discussion completely. Our collective amnesia has decontextualized and separated much of the current dialogue from any historical perspective so that we are not sensitive to the needs and aspirations of our brothers and sisters in the hood, in the Mississippi delta, or on the block. Perhaps a few examples will illustrate the deep feeling that emanates from the souls of people, and their Jim Crow schools which they will defend, regardless of the circumstances or risk. A recent work, Africana, the Encyclopedia of the African and African Experience, edited by Kwame Anthony Appiah and Henry Louis Gates, Jr., (1999), which was supposedly inspired by the dream of the late W.E.B. Du Bois. There were a couple of things that hurt and we will air a few. First, we turned to the Hall of Fame of the National Football League (NFL) and we found many deficiencies that true scholars would not have made if they cared. The history of the game is shallow, and, indeed, the racial strife of black players is not mentioned. The history and role of black coaches is not mentioned, nor is the economics of black ownership mentioned. In this section it does a disservice to HBCUs and tops it off by excluding one of the greatest players to ever play the game. Lem Barney, the Hall of Famer from Jackson State University who before Deion Sanders was the cornerback of all times. There is a reference to James Harris and Doug Williams as the first blacks to play quarterback on a high-profile level but the encyclopedia neglects to mention Grambling State University, the Public Black College they attended. Currently, there are 199 members of the NFL Hall of Fame. Roughly, 25 percent of the players are from HBCUs. The likes of Ken Houston, Texas Southern; Deacon Jones, Mississippi Valley; Leroy Kelley and Willie Lanier, Morgan State; Marion Motley, South Carolina State; Willie Brown, Willie Davis, Buck Buchanan, Charlie Joiner, Grambling; Art Shell, South Carolina State; and the list goes on. "In the South, football is a religion and on Saturday everyone goes to church," according to Mareno Casem, formerly of Alcorn State, Southern University, and Xavier University. There are some things you just have to get right. It is not the intentions of this writer to act like Howard Cosell's "I never Played the Game" (Monday Night Blues, 1985, 127-37). This is not about "Jockocracy" but about promoting the things that we do well. There are people who are knowledgeable – Collie Nicholson, Lloyd Wells, and coaches like Eddie Robinson and W.C. GordonB who would have helped, if asked.

The United Negro College Fund is referenced but there is no mention that I could find of the NAFEO nor the public/private distinction (p. 1920). The source was Encyclopedia of African-American Culture on HBCUs table 6.13, (Not only were Coahoma, Mary Holmes College left off in Mississippi but many other HBCUs. There were less than 95 colleges and, universities, and to add insult to injury, Berea College (1855) was listed as an HBCU. In Berea College v. Kentucky, in 1908 the Supreme Court affirmed the conviction of this private college, which had violated a Kentucky law that required the separation of the races in education. It is a good, nontraditional school, in the nature of Piney Woods Country Life School in Mississippi where everyone works. I strongly recommend it. It has never discriminated on account of race... but it is not an HBCU!

The encyclopedia references the black codes and lists 14 states (pp.248-49) and makes the distinction between slave codes and black codes. The Africana is an excellent source and the Africana a very good resource and should be supported by all of us. My constructive criticism

is with the substance per se but with the procedure as to how certain decisions were made. It is clear to me that white people in many instances,
when confronted with questions about our history, just don't care. Black
people might not know, but if we care, we would find someone who knows
and cares. Dr. Julius Chambers was the only person I recognized on the
encyclopedia board who was from a Public Black College. This is not to
suggest that HBCUs and Private Black Colleges cannot do or will not do.
It is to say that we must devote significant attention to matters of black
education, its delivery, its ideological posture, its history, the good, the
bad and the ugly and the prospects for its refinement and expansion. In all
things, Public and Private HBCUs must be at the table with an equal vice.
We must remember the Booker T. Washington and the Hampton-Tuskegee
accommodationist model of education. White northerners pushed on us
bad deals that were made because southern whites wanted no education
at all for us, so we stuck. We are beyond the "talented tenth" syndrome,
popularly attributed to Dubois but rightfully credited to Rev. Crummell
and the Academy leaders. (Anderson, 1988, p. 243). Lem Barney will be
ordained as a ministry into eternity on Watch Night, December 31, 1999,
by the Springhill Missionary Baptist Church, Detroit, Michigan. We go to
respect the cloth and the word.

Finally, I turn to where Notorious B.I.G. Biggie Smalls was listed as
an African American rapper murder in 1997 (p.1444). But I could not find
Dr. Aaron E. Henry, the father of the civil rights movement in Mississippi,
or Alfred "Skip" Robinson, founder of the United League of North Mississippi, and Morris Kinsey, educational director of the NAACP who filed
hundreds of education cases in Mississippi and the South.

Over the years, I have had arguments with Carl Rowan, Kenneth Clark,
Judge Robert Carter, and many other giants on the role and scope of Public
Black Colleges. Judge Constance Motley Baker's book, Equal Justice
under the Law (1998) brings the debate into sharp focus. In Fordice, it also
ruled that, in doing so, the states are required to root out any policy, practice, or procedure that would in any way affect a student's choice of which
institution to attend, such as continued maintenance of historically black
colleges, funding, types of curriculum, test scores, and college locations.
The court noted, specifically, that the continuation of all-black colleges
could affect choice.

After Fordice, in disestablishing their dual systems the southern states
may not act on the anomalous desire of some African American students
to have the states preserve black colleges that were set up under Jim Crow,
unless such continuation is "educationally justifiable" and an essential part
of an overall state plan to create a unified system of higher learning. The

burden is on the state to show such justification. In short, there is now a standard for determining when a state-run black college is to survive. The Supreme Court's decision in Fordice thus put to rest two arguments in favor of segregation at the college level that have emerged since 1954: that in order to comply with the Supreme Court's 1954 decision the southern states needed only to abandon their previously discriminatory admissions policies and practices; and that black colleges should be preserved as monuments to black culture, because they have history and traditions of their own, are a source of great pride to those who attend them, and are places where some black students feel more comfortable (p. 238).

Further, the book states: Justice Clarence Thomas's concurring opinion reveals the ambivalence in some parts of the African American community about the future of Public Black Colleges. Thomas pleaded for the preservation of black colleges on the ground that, "for many, historical black colleges have become a symbol of the highest attainments of black culture." I find the use of the term "black culture" in this context bewildering, since Western culture is the basis of the curriculum in traditional black colleges. I think Justice Thomas simply overlooks the distinction between black colleges established by the southern states under segregation and black colleges established by blacks themselves, abolitionists, missionaries, and churches to aid blacks after the failure of Reconstruction, and even before the Civil War. These latter are the repositories of black culture, if there is such a thing, but they are not the only repositories. Black churches, with their specially ornamented versions of Christianity, as revealed by Negro spirituals, may well be the only institutions that could be so designated. White folks claim to be the originators of jazz, but the blues is black, as I learned in Mississippi.

Obviously, some state-supported black colleges served blacks well during the segregation era, when blacks were totally excluded from white state colleges, but Jim Crow is dead. State-segregated black colleges bear the same stigma as the Jim Crow railroad car or the back of the bus; that era is gone with the wind. But a Private Black College may well be like the Negro spiritual, the blues, or a soul-food restaurant, a product of black culture carrying no stigma and attracting both black and white patrons. Justice Thomas acknowledged that, if the state continues to maintain a historically black college "pursuant to a sound educational justification," a vague court-designated test, then such a college must be open to all. But what about reality – as the Supreme Court's decision in the Green case, involving the failure of freedom-of-choice plans at the lower school levels, reveals? The reality is that, in a state like Mississippi with a large black population, black colleges will remain all black, or predominantly black, unless the state offers white students some highly desirable program that they cannot find anywhere else at state expense. It is, therefore, utterly confusing and too late in the day for the Supreme Court to emphasize that a black college could remain open for educationally sound reasons. With the burden of proof on the state, educationally justifiable reason sounds like an invitation to foot-dragging and disingenuousness on the part of state officials, such as occurred after the Court's 1955 Brown II decision. It would be clearer and more consistent with the Supreme Court's 1954 decision to say that these previously all-black colleges must be integrated by affirmative action to ensure white attendance, to erase the lingering stigma, and to eliminate something that plainly affects the choice of white and black students alike.

Private Black Colleges will survive as long as they are supported by alumni and private philanthropy, just like private predominantly white colleges. The United Negro College Fund raises money for PBCs. I attended such a school, Fisk University. Segregation was then fully entrenched. I rode a Jim Crow railroad car from Cincinnati to Nashville to get to Fisk. Back then, black people lived in a black world, and white people lived in a white world. During that Jim Crow era, I never thought I would see a desegregated America. As a northerner, I found the experience at Fisk broadening and invaluable and it lasted throughout my career; I learned some more black history firsthand and met some upper-middle-class black people whose lives were of a kind I did not know existed. But now, thanks to the Supreme Court, the world has changed; middle-class black people are everywhere.

We Americans entered a new phase in our history – the era of integration – in 1954. What will best serve those black youths of today who look to the state for a college education is an integrated education. Some formerly all-black state colleges are already integrated; now the remainder must be. People from narrow cultural backgrounds will simply not make it in twenty-first-century America, whether they are white or black. Now, there you have it, many of the old school leaders believe that only Private Black Colleges should exist. Judges, many of them, unlike Judge Biggers, state, "Why would one go to a broke down school when a better one is available?" Jack Greenberg, director and chief counsel of the NAACP Legal Defense Fund (LDF) who helped argue Brown said that, while carrying out the directive of the decision was unfinished in higher education, it had an "inspirational effect" because most colleges established affirmative-action programs that have led to larger enrollments of black and hispanic students and to better minority-group representation on faculties, staffs, and boards of trustees. "Without a doubt," Greenberg said, "the process had begun to dismantle segregated system." (In Darlene Clark Hine, Eyes on the Prize [1987, 74-75]). Not only is Mr. Greenberg wrong, and the evidence will not support his conclusion, but he and the NAACP-LDF made a policy choice not to pursue desegregation and enhancement of the black colleges so that they would be attractive to all but Title VII voluntary affirmative action, which consist of admission policies, scholarships and so on, all situated at the traditionally white institution. Why I still believe that white America is not yet prepared for fundamental changes toward justice especially changes involving redistribution of land, wealth and culture... a change must come ready or not. It is possible to decipher two interlocking mutually reinforcing strands in this southern reaction to Brown and Fordice; massive resistance and interposition by whites and quiet but defied rejection of Public Black Colleges and the nonsupport of them by certain elements in the black community. Perhaps, more disturbing than either is the general public's lack knowledge on the issues. If Public Black Colleges are declared illegal, surely Private Black Colleges will follow. The colleges needs each other, yet there is no real commitment to work together, or share power, that is, Ad Council "Higher Education... It's for all of Americans" projects or inform the public that when you give to the college fund... you are not giving to Texas Southern or Jackson State. From my limited nonscientific survey, 99 percent of white Americans, did not know the difference between Private and Public Black Colleges and 95 percent of blacks. The goal of HBCUs is to educate all who enter their gates. It is not integration, segregation, or desegregation – all of these are means – the end is education. If access was guaranteed all colleges – the closure proponents would have a better case, but access denied to Public Black Colleges is access denied in the system. I truly believe that everyone can and go to college. The experience is enriching and cannot hurt. However, most whites believe that only privileged persons should seek higher learning. There are blacks who believe that, unless you achieve a certain score on a standardized test, you are not college material. People have differences in opinion. However, using evidence of the Mississippi delta students at MVSU, 65 percent to 78 percent of remedial students passed their first year. The dropout was for financial and other reasons, not academic reasons. In Mississippi, as in other southern states, the means score on the ACT and SAT and below is where the critical mass of students are and I want to reach those students. If they are not educated, then this world has failed not just them but civilization. I do not accept the idea that blacks alone are responsible for their impoverished conditions... I think all of us share blame for the world.

CONCLUSION

The new millennium should bring a unified approach to desegregation litigation. Affirmative action as such is for the north, east, and west that did not segregate by law at the time of Brown in 1954. We can win the struggle only if we bring Public Black Colleges to the table and let them or their tenured faculty lead the charge in terms of access to higher education. The primary mission of PBC's is to educate black people, and all who enter their gates. The original intent of the states was not to educate black people, whom the state deemed unfit for higher learning. Nothing has radically changed these original understandings. Desegregation without regards to the primary mission of PBCs does damage to and is hostile toward access goals. The PBC's make full participation in the educational process a reality. If we must die for a cause, it must be a cause that empowers our communities. We're not necessarily talking about the physical but the mental. Desegregation must take into consideration the punitive measures the state has used throughout history to subrogate the theory of white supremacy. It is within this hostile environment that we must complete the unfinished work of Brown v. Board of Education and its original meaning of universal education for all black people. It is not affirmative action in the South but higher education desegregation. We need to get it right...then pass it on. Freedom ain't free, it costs money.

A couple of words on some of the cases should shed light on future directions. Wygant v. Jackson (1986), the role model theory in face of a reduction-in-force and reliance on societal discrimination, at best is weak and at worst seems to be a conscious effort by the white civil rights establishment to not think these things through. In Johnson v. Transportation Agency (1987). It appears odd that the women movement has never embraced effective, nation-building, civil rights strategies of grassroots people. This case was won for women but lost for blacks. Voluntary affirmative action plans should be grounded in statistical proof, plus historical discrimination, that is easy to find if the right people are looking. Richmond v. Croson (1986) is a rerun of the Regents of California v. Bakke case. Black people were never at the table from day one. It is amazing how little we look for historical discrimination that has lingering effects today. The prima facie case should always be the goal of plaintiffs, lawyers, and statistics plus must be pursued at all costs and in all situations. I will continue to believe that Croson was a set up, either consciously or unconsciously. The affirmative action cases do not help desegregation and we should not use them, and really, it is hard to explain them. Hopwood could never happen if Prairie View and Texas Southern were at the table. It is too late in the day to exclude the only viable entity that has a genuine claim of entitlement!

There are those who believe sincerely that the color-blind analysis within a historical context will improve black people's plight in the long run. Then, there are others who believe that education is important but that it is not sufficient to overcome racism. I disagree with both premises. While universal education may not be synonymous with black liberation, and approximation and disappearance are not the same, economic empowerment is the best shield for survival. We must not only desegregate the dollar, (Robert Weems [1998]), we must pay our debt down in 1999, save in 2000, and invest for our future in 2001. We are 500 billion strong in buying power, and we can do whatever we put our minds to doing. We must send the right signal to our children – which is, education for liberation. Access to Higher Education means more and better higher education desegregation for all, without the burdens and pains involved in being in places on the backs of black people exclusively. It means that the capacity of Public Black Colleges should increase by at least 100 percent within the next decade. It means that graduate and professional schools at all Public Black Colleges should be established, to dismantle the main tool of segregation, which was discriminatory exclusion and the banishment of all broad-based missions at Public Black Colleges (see Sweatt v. Painter). Texas Southern had the same mission as University of Texas and had a medical school. If the remedy for exclusion is inclusion, then the record should reflect that more, and better access can only be achieved by the establishment Public Black Colleges campuses, dis-establishment and dismantlement tools which are "highly unique" and have "high demand" and/or "special programs," which are the graduate and professional schools.

The *Adams v. Richardson* case (1973) held that Public Black Colleges should be enhanced: by placing "high-demand programs" and increasing the percentage of black academic employees in the system; by increasing the enrollment of blacks within the system and at historically black schools and increasing the flow of white students at Public Black Colleges; and by insuring that the state take the lead in substantially funding Public Black Colleges. As is often the case, desegregation has meant (1) closing black colleges, (2) applying Title IX sex discrimination remedies to black colleges as if they are financially as able as white colleges, (3) looking more closely at federal student loan default rates and placing sanctions on those colleges that are disproportionate in a comparison context, and (4) using all of the soft money to give white scholarships to white students who refused to even live on campus thus making it clear that desegregation remedies will not work. If courts were interested in attracting other race students, they would place highly selected programs on black campuses first, instead of paying white people to hold their noses. Desegregation is a two-way process. Not all black students attending TWIs place professional programs on PBCs campus. Fund them adequately and let's take a look after 10 years.

The hostile climate in the South should not deter us from using our 500 billion dollars, buying power to demand equal treatment as well as demand that the states reinvest in Black Public Colleges. We cannot mandate the state to do something we are unwilling to do. I am confident that members of our middle class will come around when they are sufficiently educated on the issue. The opening up of more opportunities in a broader range of programs is a first step. If we are to reach a watershed in the higher education desegregation area, it is imperative that black leadership manifests itself. Desegregation is an economic development issue and billions of dollars are at stake. Most Americans are inept and don't know the difference between a Public and a Private Black Colleges, but the debate has been to discourage this openness so it's understandable. If we are to solve the admissions, public contracts, and employment issues, we should start where the law is clear and on our side. Ayers v. Fordice is not dead and Brown is not dead... but if they are, we should at least give them a decent burial. Moreover, we must reclaim ourselves, as the noted author Clenora Hudson-Weems says, the black agenda dictates that we set new standards based on Africana views, values, and perspectives, and education is first on the list of priorities for the new millenium.

Notes

1. John D. Johnson, executive editor of the Clarion Ledger, A Gannett newspaper in Jackson, Mississippi, refused to allow the NAACP to meet the editorial board, had never heard of Black Higher Education, January 1991. The late Dr. Aaron E. Henry of Clarksdale, Mississippi, and the author had to reference the state NAACP Leadership Conference before the meeting was scheduled.

2. Fall 1995 enrollment data from HBCUs annual enrollment survey show sharp declines in enrollment in several states. PBS's in Texas, Louisiana, Mississippi, and Alabama are having accreditation problems. According to (Joffre T. Whisenton formally of SACS). *Ayers v. Fordice*, 879 F.Supp. (ND Miss. 1995) hereinafter *Ayers* tr. 186-89. Litigation in Louisiana, Mississippi, Tennessee, and Louisiana has resulted in gridlock and Central State University of Ohio was closed in July 1996 for repairs on all nine dormitories. *Chronicle of Higher Education*, August 2, 1996, A23." However, it is not just a matter of enrollment trends but rather a matter of structural incertitude; federal and state policy that have a disproportionate impact on HBCUs; and aggressively,

corporately funded, and professionally staffed year-round development/fundraising programs that the public colleges lack to compete.

It is at this junction where the road divides and one must be clear on whether the Institution is a private black college or a public black college. There are two primary organizations, United Negro College Fund (UNCF) with Dr. Bill Gray as its CEO and the National Association for Equal Opportunity in Higher Education (NAFEO) with Dr. Henry Ponder as its CEO. UNCF is run like a Fortune 500 Corporation with slick Madison Avenue ads supplemented by corporate and local fundraising in every major market in the country and a smart, aggressive and well-connected CEO. NAFEO is fraught with problems of leadership, finances, mission, and direction. Its two cofounders – Dr. Elias Blake, Jr., and Dr. Fred Humphries – and people like Dr. Joe Johnson i.e. the Old Guard seem to be on one side while the younger more laid back graduates of elite universities are less inclined to fight wars that must be fought for survival of Public Black Colleges. One can try to define Public and Private Black Colleges but to define them is to limit them, so we will just say that Private Black Colleges were the first black colleges in America and they are primarily controlled by black people and their institutions while Public Black Colleges are state-controlled and damned by their masters... the Southern states, by and large. They were created to miseducate, limit educational opportunities of blacks, and to keep black people in a subservient role in American society.

Private Black Colleges, which patterned their curriculum after the Harvard, Yale mode, opted for a liberal-arts type institution. The Booker T. Washington's Hampton-Tuskegee philosophy discouraged blacks from voting, running for political office, and pursuing civil equality. Education for Negroes was limited to vocational and teacher training in the South that stressed coercion by whites as the only safe means of keeping blacks in "their place." See James D. Anderson, *The Education of Blacks in the South*, 1860-1935, Chapter 3 (Education and the Race Problem in the New South) pp. 79-109. The point that must not be lost is that Private Black Colleges broke the mode and established for all times that black people could be educated. Had it not been for Private Black Colleges, there would not be Public Black Colleges today. The problem today, of course, is that the states have continued to limit Public Black Colleges' mission, funding, facilities, and academic programs in spite of *Brown v. Board of Education,* 347 U.S. 483 (1954), *Florida ex rel Hawkins v. Board of Control,* 350 U.S. 413 (1956) and *U.S. & Ayers v. Fordice,* 505 U.S. 717 (1992). Thus, it is not just a matter of development/fundraising but fighting to enforce congressional mandates and the supreme law of the land. It is here that the split between Public and Private Black Colleges is more profound. NAFEO and UNCF have failed to provide leadership in the area that the late Thurgood Marshall thought most important, the courts. Because corporate America feels safe if the National Association of State Universities and Land-Grant Colleges (NASULGC), American Council on Education (ACE), and the One Dupont Circle Good Ole Boy Network in Washington,

D.C. feel safe. Thus, not one of the One Dupont Circle, NASULGC, ACE, or any other white organization has pledged support for enforcement efforts in higher education desegregation. NAFEO and UNCF have followed the One Dupont Circle crowd and have paid lip service to the concept but little else.

This crab in the barrel approach to enforcement of *Brown* has led to disappointing failures in Congress, the executive, but not in the Courts, contrary to rhetoric proselytizing by clueless Washington establishment insiders. When one considers that neither NAFEO, UNC, nor the One Dupont Circle crowd and their foundations have not donated one dime to *Ayers v. Fordice* enforcement litigation and we are back before the Supreme Court *Ayers v. Fordice*, 99-6965 docket November 9, 1999, the miracle is that we are still alike. Winning becomes relative since the theory must be sought out first before the fruits manifest. Essentially, no black organization in America, major or minor, has dedicated itself to higher education desegregation, an issue that we can win and are winning despite the odds.

The Office for the Advancement of Public Black Colleges (OAPBC) and Dr. Joyce Payne are a part of NASULGC. She has been very helpful but there are constraints. She wanted to file an amici brief in 1990-1991 but was not allowed by her parent organization even though Alcorn State University life was on the line. UNCF has sent press releases but it takes money to fight legal battles and pretty much all of the white controlled foundations and organizations have said no to higher education desegregation. See: *Georgia Desegregation* case.

3. Dr. Elias Blake, Jr., desegregation expert, testified in Ayers that Dr. Hunter Boylan committed educational malpractice by testifying with peer review of the State's Summer Remediation Program. See also his Amicus on ninth university, March 17, 1999. Ayers hearing in federal court.

4. U.S. & Ayers v. Fordice, 505 U.S. 717, 734 (1992).

5. Ayers v. Fordice, 879 F. Supp. 1419, 1431 (N.D. Miss. 1995).

6. 879 F.Supp. at 1477.

7. Petitioners do not contend that all of these youth would have been admitted. Yet, all could have sought a place without participating in a spring or a summer program.

8. The calculations are as follows: 68.2 percent minus 52.5 percent is 15.7 percent; that figure divided by 68.2 percent is 23.0 percent; and 68.2 percent minus 50.7 percent is 17.5 percent; that figure divided by 68.2 percent yields 25.7 percent.

9. The District court made no finding faulting the quality of the education afforded at the HBUs (apart from resource-related problems traceable to the de jure system); nor would the record support such a finding. Indeed, that court praised the role of Mississippi Valley State University, located on the Mississippi Delta, "one of the poorest regions in the country " Ayers, 879 F.Supp. at 1491; see generally at 1491-92. The court found in part: "MVSU has developed a strong commitment to serving students from socioeconomic

backgrounds which, in the main, are vastly different from those of the clientele of the other public institutions of higher learning in the state, including its neighbor [Delta State University]." At 1491, citations to record omitted.

10. The absence of a plan for using the Accuplacer was of great concern because the district court found that two standardized tests had been misused. See Ayers, 879 F.Supp. at 1432, n. 18 (ACT); Id. at 1436 (Graduate Record examination). Regarding the absence of these standards, see the excerpts from the testimony which appear in the Appendix, at 151-93. The uncertainty of the situation is highlighted by the following portion of the district court's opinion: "While the new admission standards may reduce the number of black students eligible to be admitted into the system without remedial courses required, it is not evident that the new standards will actually reduce the number of black students ultimately admitted to the system as either regular or remediated admittees." Ayers, 879 F.Supp. at 1481.

11. The standard is supported by Fordice, 505 U.S. at 742, n.11; Milliken v. Bradley, 433 U.S. 267, 280-81, n.15 (1977); Knight v. Alabama, 14 F.3d 1534, 1546, 1551 (11th Cir. 1994). (Alabama Higher Education Case; and ARevised Criteria Specifying the Ingredients of Acceptable Plans to Desegregate State Systems of Public Higher Education," Federal Register, Vol. 43, No. 32, February 15, 1978, at 6658-64 and "Notice of Application of Supreme Court Decision, Federal Register, 59, 20, 4271, 4272 January 31, 1994 (discussing Fordice decision and reiterating reliance on the "Revised Criteria"). The "Revised Criteria" state: "However, as the Court had instructed, the transition to a unitary system must not be accomplished by placing a disproportionate burden upon black students, faculty, or institutions or by reducing the educational opportunities currently available to blacks" (6660).

12. Fordice, 505 U.S. 742, n.11.

13. Knight v. Alabama, 14 F.3d 1534 (11th Cir. 1994). United States v. Louisiana, 9 F.3d 459 (5th Cir. 1993).

26

CONFRONTING RACIALIZED BIOETHICS: NEW CONTRACT ON BLACK AMERICA

Maria K. Mootry

INTRODUCTION

Speaker of the House Newt Gingrich, in putting forward his ideas on reorganizing our social benefits and social burdens, has popularized the term, "Contract with America." This article will show how the 1990s brings not a contract with Black America, but a *new contract on Black America*. The contract on Black America pushes forward on three fronts: (1) at the grassroots level, terroristic, overt violence by skinheads, neo-Nazis, and other hate-groups; (2) on a middle-class (bourgeois) level, a middle-class compassion fatigue, featuring a withdrawal from inclusion-ary measures for people of color, including white-flight in the area of housing, and anti-affirmative action initiatives on university and college campuses; and (3) on an academic level, intellectual racism in the form of new theories, including sociobiology, and medical science's medicalization of social issues. At issue are the key questions of communication ethics and distributive justice. Will America tell the truth about its agendas? Is America willing to equitably share the goods?

HISTORICAL CONTEXTS FOR THE NEW CONTRACT

Nobel Prize-winning poet Derek Walcott, a West Indian from St. Lucia, said to Bill Moyers in an interview, "The immigrant's dream is inviolable, but the black man's dream is not – it is *made to be different*. The black man's dream is *not allowed to be the American dream*" (Moyers, 1989). Walcott talks about the language phenomenon, calling it the "language of empire," which is used as a mask to hide the will of the dominant culture to keep the goodies to itself. There is also the language of religion, which demonizes AIDS victims, asserting a deserving immorality for a genocidal epidemic that affects Black and Hispanic women of color disproportion-ately. However, the racist stereotype of bigoted lower-class uneducated whites is, to an extent lessening, as former liberals move to the right of center.

In the 1990s the cool, clear "objective" language of science, known officially as sociobiology, is heard. Nowhere is this clearer than in the intellectual history of American higher education. From our nation's founding, its scholars have participated in, initiated even, racist ideology based on and fostering the myth of white superiority. As Professor Luke Tripp has observed, "It is deeply imbedded in the culture of academe." (Tripp, 228).

In the eighteeenth century, physician Benjamin Rush, the "Father of American Psychiatry,"defined the black color of people of African ancestry as a *disease.*[1] Moreover, ignoring pleas from his enlightened French friends, Thomas Jefferson, noted American enlightenment philosopher and president, theorized that Blacks were inherently inferior in reason and imagination in *Notes on Virginia,* a classic text in American Studies courses. He considered Phillis Wheatley's heroic couplets parrotlike imitations of real poetry, refusing to grant that a black woman could possess a mind. That she was all body, he seemed too ready to believe, taking free sexual access to his wife's "half-black" sister, Sally Heming. And in the nineteenth century, William A. Dunning and John W. Burgess, Columbia University professors, argued that slavery was a benign institution and warned of the perils of newly freed Blacks who held political positions during Reconstruction as a threat from Black brutes.

Francis A. Walker, Yale professor of political economy and author of the most widely used work in the introductory course in college economics from 1883 to 1900, asserted that whites had a racially based "mechanical genius" imbedded in the "great inventive Teutonic race," which justified expansion of the trio science, economics, and technology over inferior peoples. Walker, later becoming president of the Massachusetts Institute of Technology, was also the commissioner of Indian Affairs. Little wonder that today's Native Americans struggle with pollution and nuclear waste dumped on the reservations they were forced to live on in resettlement policies of the Indian Bureau.

No mind, but all sex. This is what psychologist G. Stanley Hall maintained at the turn of the century. Racist novels depicting black men as leopard-like rapists leaping from open windows onto chaste white womanhood accompanied the greatest number of lynchings in American history. America's first great movie, *Birth of a Nation*, dramatized Thomas Dixon's novel *The Clansman*, debasing Black politicians as shiftless, lazy, or when active, crazed sex offenders. (The nation in the title was the Ku Klux Klan.)

Hall, the first Ph.D. in psychology in the United States and the founder of the psychology laboratory at Johns Hopkins (1883) and the *American Journal of Psychology* (1887), offered academic anti-Black propaganda that legitimized vigilante contracts on black male (and female) bodies, asserting that a peculiar emotional intensity of Black people was associated with unbridled sexuality. (Jordan, *White over Black*, 1968, and Fredrickson, *The Black Image in the White Mind,* 1974.) At the turn of the century, when white privilege was threatened by black assertion, as it is today, Robert Bennett Bean, a professor of anatomy at the University of Virginia Medical school, offered scientific support for the theory that Blacks were innately brutal, vicious, and stupid. The "Negro Brain," while normal in perception, memory, and motor responses, was deficient in logical critical thinking and in grasping abstract ideas, due to its arrested development. Even the distinguished Harvard historian Albert Bushel Hart – known for his "Germ Theory," which contends that each nation has a particular contribution to make, such as the political system of England – was quoted in Thomas Grossett's *Race*, theorizing that the "Negro mind" ceases to develop after adolescence.

The eve of Hitler's rise was a time when Hitler and his intellectual theorist, Alfred Rosenberg, found much of their racist ideology in American intellectual writings. In 1930, three years before Hitler took over and formed the Third Reich, Howard W. Odum, president of the American Sociological Society, published *Social and Mental Traits of the Negro: A Study in Race Traits, Tendencies, and Prospects,* in which he wrote of Blacks as outside the pale of morality and humanity. Odum theorizes that "The Negro has few ideals and perhaps no lasting adherence to an aspiration toward real worth. He has little conception of the meaning of virtue, truth, honor, manhood, integrity. His mind does not conceive of faith in humanity – he does not comprehend it" in (Tripp, 228).

It is interesting that was written in the post-abolitionist era, offering the bestial/demonic image of Blacks. Before this time, Blacks – as in Harriet Beecher Stowe's *Uncle Tom's Cabin*'s major characters Uncle Tom and the near-white Eliza and George – were theorized as repositories of an innate spirituality. Stowe claimed that they were "natural" Christians – kind, selfless, giving. She ends her novel with Uncle Tom being beaten to death as he refuses to fight back, and the near-white Eliza and George on their way to live in Liberia to Christianize the natives!

Ironically, in the late twentieth-century, both angelic and demonic images will be used to justify medical racism. Blacks will be enticed into being good Uncle Toms," representing disproportionate organ donors, by talk of gifts and sacrificial good. Go into any Black church and you will find copious copies of donation brochures, even though Blacks suffer from not getting transplants, either from lack of money, lack of access to efficient medical care, or lack of support in post-op settings at home (Spielman). Blacks are expected to be happy donees. Or, at the other end of the spectrum, when African Americans are demonic, seen as owing themselves to the body politic because of the terrible crimes they commit. Language of causality, of the prevalence of guns in our community, high unemployment, high density population, a younger, more active (violent) population is never entered into the equation, so solutions are not sought, except the happy solution of increased execution of prime bodies. All over, even Black legislators have joined whites in their desire to have juveniles tried as adults!

THE RISE OF RACIST SOCIOBIOLOGY

By the 1970s, when white academics and intellectuals launched an assault on affirmative action, their educational campaign was not so subtly buttressed by the theorizing of prominent psychologist Arthur Jensen, who ascribed intellectual inferiority among Blacks to a genetic basis. Jensen included in his assault the back-up measure of stockpiling white gametes, being among the first to participate in a sperm bank for "White genius."

Racist ideology masquerading as academic scholarship and fact continued with the rise of sociobiology in the 1980s. James Q. Wilson and Richard Herrnstein, Harvard professors, in *Crime and Human Nature* (1985) based crime on genetic predisposition and lower intelligence. Intelligence is determined not by environment but largely by genetics, and lower intelligence is positively correlated with crime; hence, the high crime rate among Blacks reflects their mental inferiority. Such theorizing justifies the belief and mental predisposition among whites to justify the high incarceration rate of Blacks; as of May 1995, 44 percent of all inmates were African American. Increased death penalties for punishment, for budgetary reasons, and for hidden schemes to attain organs for transplant, may be buttressed by such theorizing.

Herrnstein's publication of the controversial *Bell Curve* (1994) shortly before his death was a parting shot aimed at further demeaning Black status in American eyes by insisting on Black low I.Q. Black intellectuals organized to prevent a conference titled "Genetic Factors in Crime," to be held by David Waserman, a lawyer and research scholar at the Institute for Philosophy and Public Policy at Maryland, funded by the National Institutes of Health in the amount of $78,000.

Finally, the ideology of racial superiority, which may lead us to draconian, Hitlerian measures, continued in the 1980s in the works of scholars like J. Philippe Rushton, professor of psychology at the University of Western Ontario, who presented his views on racial differences at the American Association for the Advancement of Science, claiming that Orientals have "evolved" into the most intelligent race, Whites a close second, and Blacks a distant last (in Tripp, 229). His ideas complemented those of Harvard Medical School professor Emeritus Bernard Davis, occupier of an endowed chair. Adele Lehman, professor of bacterial physiology, who states that human races differ in their distribution of genetic potential, that trying to get equal performance from students from different groups is unrealistic because of genetic-based inequality.

THE RISE OF MEDICAL RACISM, MEDICAL ECONOMICS, AND MEDICAL NATIONALISM

When Americans look at the sites of the Human Genome Project initiatives, varied forms of genetic engineering projects, "assisted reproductions" of select gametes, and stockpiling of selected embryos, they include Yale, Harvard, and Johns Hopkins Universities.

Medical science is rushing toward a form of racist medical nationalism based on a biased belief in the primacy of genetics in racial inequality and propelled by anxieties of being overwhelmed by the "Other," which justifies incarceration, exploitation of the "Other's Body," and finally, by any means necessary, exclusion. In Tripp's words: "White intellectual giants of the academy... provided the theoretical and ideological underpinnings of racism and established it as a pillar in the traditonal canon of academe" (Tripp, 227). *Medical economics* stacks the deck against the have-nots versus those who are rich or have jobs with good insurance benefits. Few African Americans will be likely to be recipients of major transplant because they will have neither the money nor the job benefits. Deceptive language of "gift giving" – quasi-religious language about those who help others share the "miracle of life" – hide systematic, institutionalized racism inherent in the rationing process, driven by the inequality of economic status between blacks and whites.

The 1990s new contract for America is the alter side of the rewriting of a new contract *on* Black America. It is written in the "language of empire," dramatizing the *empire of language* and how language asserts itself in varied texts – legal contracts, media mush, academic textbooks, and colluding "discussions" of ethical issues in various interview formats.

AN END TO INNOCENCE: BRYANT GUMBLE'S DECONSTRUCTION OF MEDICAL EMPIRE TALK

On Friday, May 12, 1995, African American news anchor Bryant Gumble of the *NBC Today Show* announced that they would show a segment on a "miracle" baby, focusing on a couple and their physician from Loma Linda Hospital in California, who were discussing their "close call." Their baby, born with a defective heart, waited twenty days for a donor heart. (Here the camera shifted to the nursery's intensive care unit and you could see a fairly healthy looking baby with multiple tubes coming from its nose, head, etc.). Gumble questioned the three – the yuppie-looking couple, tired from their ordeal of staying up nights, and the happy, triumphant doctor.

It was a painful interview, which irritated and angered the couple, but this seemed to escape the doctor. He asked the doctor if the baby was out of danger, and he said, "No, not for two weeks." Then Gumble asked the couple if they participated in the new trend of getting to know the donor and the donor's family. They looked shocked, irritated, and angry. "No," the wife said curtly, "and we don't want to know." She rambled for a while, commenting that the donor gave life and speculating that perhaps several babies were living now because of the multiple donations possible from the sole donor. Gumble then lifted the veil from the language of "miracles" and "gift-giving." He asked the husband if he had considered donating his baby's organs, since the baby's heart had stopped beating before they could get the donor heart to it. (This was the "close call.") The husband was shocked and angry; he almost stammered. They had such a hard time; they wanted their baby so much, he said. In short, it never occurred to them to make a gift of their baby.

Lowering the boom, Gumble asked, "What if you were in the other parents' place? Would you have given consent?" The man was almost outraged. AI don't know," he said. Not once did the couple express regret at the death of the donor. The recipients' ruthless, selfish will to power, and the will for self-survival and for that of their progeny by money and by any means necessary emerged from this interview. And this was only possible because Gumble committed himself to a communication ethic that made visible those who are often erased from the picture.

In this interview, Gumble rejected a false dialogue that would speak only of medical "miracles" and "gifts." He turned the tables and revealed the true picture: the recipient baby, himself, could easily have been a donor; after all, his heart had stopped. In fact, some legislators wanted to enforce a rule that those who were not willing to donate would not be able to receive; but this case revealed the difficulty of that kind of legislation.

Finally, Gumble ostensibly softened and used the usual rhetoric of the sad shortage of organs, asking the doctor if there wasn't a "shortage" at his hospital. Happy with his success, the doctor walked right into the trap. "Yes," he said. "We never has enough organs. If only more babies would die so that others might live."

To even speak of a shortage of human organs is strange language that we would have found even stranger twenty-five years ago. The only people who spoke of needing human organs were cannibals or people engaged in sacrificial rites! In one interview, then, Gumble raised the troubling issue of ethics and the distributive justice of organ donation. The fact is that, with organ transplantation as our surgery of choice for major illnesses, there will never be enough; in fact, society will be driven to draconian measures to increase the supply.

It does not take a lot of brains to realize that any baby in a hospital from a poor family, who is on Medicaid, which pays for organ retrieval, would be at higher risk of becoming a donor as he nears death than another equally sick baby whose parents have the money or the insurance to pay for surgery and postoperative care that costs upwards of a quarter to a half million dollars. Health scientists and politicians must unmask the language of innocence, which is in reality the language of empire, raiding the body of the Other, raiding its precious jewels.

More public policies must be enacted, such as banning smoking in restaurants. The effect of firsthand and secondhand smoke is a major cause of heart disease and the potential need for hearts. Smoking not only is a leading cause of heart disease in adults, it affects the unborn and the baby who is brought home to an environment where sometimes both parents smoke. Some bioethicists have suggested a kind of "sin" tax, so that if a couple like the one Gumble interviewed had been smokers, their baby would not be eligible for a transplant if, in fact, its heart condition had seemed to be caused by exposure to smoking. Such management consti-tutes a version of *distributive justice.* It is like the Rev. Wayne B. Arnason's call in "Directed Donations" for affirmative action for organs for Blacks (Arnason, 13-19). Such measures will likely be what society will resort to, as the empire manages its body politic, but it is the kind of bureaucratic solution to an inherently evil practice. While the need for consoling habits is understandable, society must seek alternatives, not only in medical protocols but in a socially responsible public policy activism to save the commitment to equality, dignity, and the sense of community.

FATAL INNOCENCE

In this post-industrial, post-Soviet age, America must admit that it is an empire. But how can one have a "democratic empire," Walcott asked Moyers, dramatizing how the phrase is an oxymoron. Sometimes it takes an outsider to see your true self. Walcott wants America to accept responsibility, the responsibility of empire to protect and nourish its subjects. To deny empire status with slippery communication ethics is to promote inequitable distribution of goods.

American people in charge are not infants; they are not adolescents, but adults, responsible for their minds, their decisions, and their effects. This applies internationally and internally. When America can admit this, Walcott thinks, then it will admit that what it calls a series of crises is not that at all but, rather, a part of a pattern of cause and effect. America will see the interconnectedness of the privileged and the underclass, the sinner and the saint, as it were. Not to do this is hypocrisy.

What Walcott may underestimate is how America uses its very hypocrisy to mask its iron will. This will to power stunned English writer D. H. Lawrence into writing his brilliant essay on American character, *Studies in American Literature,* where he theorized that Americans, at heart, were "hard, stoic, killers." Perhaps it will be the Others in the body politic – women, the poor, the African Americans – who, in speaking out, will be corrective voices of conscience and prove him wrong.[1]

VIOLENCE, FAMILY, LANGUAGE ETHICS, AND THE SEDUCTION OF THE MIND AND BRAINS

Issues as bizarre as bioengineering, medical genetics intervention, and fetal brain transplants require deconstructing language, in part because deconstructing language often means uncovering violence. America is a violent country. Among the "advanced countries," the United States has the highest murder rate at 7.9 per hundred thousand.

From this perspective, the contract against the black body and the female body is merely an extrapolation of historicosocial trends. Slavery's inherent violence was described by Thomas Jefferson when he labeled it as a relation that fomented "boisterous passions." Historian Lerone Bennett felt that slavery was a state of "perpetual war," masking its violence with the metaphor of family. For pro-slavery arguers, a plantation was not an economic relation, any more than marriage is, but an affective set of relations with "Big Daddy," Aunties and Uncles, and children.

As late as the 1960s, southern whites argued an almost familial familiarity with "our" blacks, complaining that northerners were interfering in their family affairs. Similarly, the feminist movement of the antebellum period, the 1920s and the 1960s fought mythologies of family that masked dominance, patriarchy, and erasure of feminine identity.

Most people think of violence as overt murder, crime, gangs, etc. But we have a high degree of socially tolerated violence, including police violence, war, self-defense, riots. Wife-beating was legal, and until the 1980s a man could force his wife to engage in nonconsensual sex. By 1980, doctors targeted domestic violence as a medical problem, and emergency room personnel began obtaining training in identifying battered women.

One must wonder what the medical personnel in Orange County, California thought of surrogate mothers like Anna Johnson, when police were called to cut off phone service to her room, lock the door, and force her to sign papers giving up her rights to the baby she had just given birth to. In California, at that time, any woman who gave birth was the mother of the child she gave birth to. What kind of violence was this? One more form of socially tolerated violence.

The battering of Rodney King would have gone unnoticed as a social form of violence if it had not been caught on secret videotape. Even then, with a plain view of police battering a downed man, viewers could not make up their minds. The resulting exoneration of police violence led to the bloody, violent reaction, the burning uprising of April 29, 1991, in Los Angeles.

White American culture glorifies violence in its Westerns, its detective stories, its macho movie stars such as Sylvester Stallone and Arnold Schwartzennegger, and even in such TV re-creation of the "news" shows such as *Cops*. Similarly, many new medical protocols, from in vitro fertilization to genetic engineering and fetal transplants, are a form of medical science violence, appropriation of the body, often the black body and/or the female body, committed covertly but acting out the coded language of empire as appropriating the public body.

While the body politic is less and less allowed to have a mind (or brains) of its own, some "techno-rebels" are trying to speak out. The results are mixed. On Saturday, May 13, 1995, the *New York Times* reported that leaders from virtually every major religion in the United States would issue a joint statement the following week asking the government to ban the current patenting practices for genetic engineering. The newspaper reported that the statement had been signed by roughly one hundred Catholic

427

bishops, numerous Protestant and Jewish leaders, and groups of American Muslims, Hindus, and Buddhists. The religious leaders said they were not opposing genetic engineering or biotechnology on religious grounds, but rather because it *violates* the sanctity of human life. Ironically, researchers would love to have patents banned, since it slows down research. Absence of patenting practices for genetic engineering will simply leave the door wide open for all kinds of violent intervention into the pre-born body.

ATTACKING THE BRAIN: APPROPRIATING THE BODY POLITIC'S MIND?

Similarly, the issue of fetal brain transplantation is cloaked in the language of hope and "cautious optimism," that a "cure" has been found for Parkinson's disease, Alzheimer's, and Huntington's. What the public mind may not be aware of is the nature of intervention such 'hope" involves. Of course, the victims of the disease may not care. A director of the American Parkinson Association has been quoted as saying: "The majority of the people with the disease couldn't care less about ethical questions: They just want something that works" (Vas and de Souza, 81).[2]

In Bombay, India, a consultation workshop was triggered by a newspaper report of an alleged transplant of the head and brain of a young boy onto the body of his sister, both of whom were involved in an accident. The operation was said to have been performed in Erfurt, East Germany. A West German presenter at the workshop, Dr. B. L. Bauer, insisted that he had thoroughly investigated details of the reported case of whole brain transplant published in the newspapers, and concluded the report was a hoax (ibid., 70).

Nevertheless, many may be unaware that brain transplants fall under two rubrics: (1) whole or total brain transplant (TBT) and (2) the transplantation or implantation of fragments of tissue or cell cultures, that is, brain implantations or grafts (BI). The workshop concluded that TBT was unacceptably violent, gruesome, cruel. In its summary it reported that all the participants were unanimous in rejecting the performance of total brain transplants because the benefits were not commensurate with the cost and risk, but also for philosophical and theological reasons, which held that death was inevitable and had to be accepted with human dignity. The participants called for a moratorium on the performance of total brain transplants by scientific and medical conununities all over the world (ibid. 68-86, esp. 77).

The workshop also looked forward to a more acceptable form of agrifying human tissue, that is, growing human brain cells in the laboratory. Dr. Solomon Snyder, director of the neuroscience department at Johns Hopkins University at Baltimore, where the laboratory brain cells were grown, feels that culturing human brian cells is a breakthrough that will accelerate the range of basic research aimed at increasing our understanding of many serious disease problems (ibid. 85).

Ethical issues of violent appropriation of fetal tissue from captive women also were eased by an October 1989 report from Hungarian scientists at the World Congress of Neurosurgery, held in New Delhi, India, where they reported they had performed brain implantations for Parkinson's disease using stellate ganglia tissue instead of the substantial nigra required in more intrusive retrievals of brain tissue. If stellate ganglia tissue would work, the workshop participants suggested, ethics of getting fetal tissue from aborted human fetuses would not arise.

The World Congress called for an international moratorium on the performance of BI using fetal tissues until more satisfactory data was available. Use of live donors raised ethical issues and prospects of unacceptable violence that we now seem to be comfortable with. Yet Dr. Robert White, a neurosurgeon at Case Western Reserve, boasted that, "Transplanting an entire human head from one body to another is now possible" (Vas, 1). Dr. White had isolated the brains of monkeys and kept them alive for hours; he excised brains of dogs and transplanted them; in 1970, he transplanted the head of a monkey to another; in subsequent experiments he succeeded in keeping alive two transplanted monkey heads for a week.[3]

More gruesomely, P. Adam, N. Raiha, E. L. Rehilea, et. al. report in "Cerebral Oxidation of Glucose and D-BOH Butyrate by Isolate Perfused Human Head," that they used a protocol involving eight human heads obtained by abdominal hysterotomy at 12-17 weeks gestation, which were perfused through their internal carotid arteries. (in Vas, n. 63).

Violent research into the brain began as a result of the discovery that Parkinson's was due to dopamine deficiency in the brain's nigrostriatal complex. How to increase dopamine, to make up for the deficiency, became the challenge. Oral administration of L-Dopa was first thought to be the solution. However, revelation of the biochemical and clinical effect of a by-product of the procedures used for the manufacture of opiates (N.methyl 4 phenyl 1,2,3,6 tetarahydropipridine M.P.T.P.) led to the suspicion that neurotoxic and possibly environmental causes lead to the Parkinson's condition.

L-Dopa's failure led to the quest for brain implantation, a procedure that theoretically would lead to the natural production of dopamine by the infusion of living tissue from the fetal substantial nigra, which, if it attached itself and became integrated in its new site, would provide an ongoing supply. (Bergin, J. D., "Ethics of Brain Transplant," in Vas and de Souza, 7-21).

Dr. Bergin, a neurologist in Wellington, New Zealand, points out several problems regarding BI in Ms essay on the ethics. First, while most organ donation requires a pronouncement of brain death, brain implantation demands exactly the opposite – you have to use living brain tissue (Bergin, 14). Second, he cites other critics of BI, namely, P. McCullagh, in *Fetal Brain Transplantation: The Scope of the Ethical Issue* and P. J. Murphy, in "Moral Perspectives in the Use of Embryonic Cell Transplantation for Correction of Nervous System Disorders," (*Applied Neurophysiology* [1984]: 47: 65-68). McCullagh feels that use of fetal brain tissue for therapeutic purposes could increase induced abortions and lead to production-line abortion for that purpose (in Bergin, 15). Murphy feared a "crass commerce in aborted fetuses" and that transplantation of embryonic cell tissue for correction of nervous system disorders "coarsens humanity itself" and leads to the "grave loss of reverence for human life in its most helpless and dependent stage." This is a surrender of higher moral value that is too great a price to pay. Murphy refers in turn to philosopher Hans Jonas, author of *Experimenting with Human Subjects,* who warns against "progress" by any means necessary. Jonas warns that progress is an "optional goal," that the slower progress in conquering disease (as in "conquering" natives or the land!) may be more expeditious since the body politic's soul is threatened by loss of moral values caused by too ruthless a pursuit of scientific progress (Murphy, 67).

DeSouza raises questions of neuraonal continuity and maintenance of neuronal activity, that is, how well does brain implantation really work? She cites an experiment of quail embryonic tissue implanted into a chick embryo, leading to chicks that began to peep like quails; in short, brain transplants may be, in effect, mind transplants. Such violence into the body politic and its mind is what we face.

In the DeSouza case, there is the question of integrity of memory. Will the head remember what its body knew? Or what its new body knows? Nobody knows. The fact is that neural cells lose their histocompatability antigenicity and are less prone to rejection. The transportation of fetal substantia nigra and fetal medullary tissue to the caudate nucleus region of patients with severe Parkinson's disease seems to lead to an immediate improvement, but for how long and at what cost to the female "hosts" of fetal tissue and to the body politic's sense of decency and respect for human life? (Cf. Darab K. Dastur and S. A. Barodawala, "Neural Transplants," in Vas and DeSouza, 25-27)

Notes

1. For further reading see: Thomas Gossett, Race: The History of an Idea in America, 1963; Ron Takaki, Iron Cages, 1979; and B. Davis, Storm Over Biology: Essays on Science, Sentiment, and Public Policy, 1986.

2. For more discussion, see C.J. Vas and E.J. de Souza, eds., Brain Transplantation: Ethical Concerns, report on a consultation workshop organized by the FIAMC Bio-Medical Ethics Centre, held in Bombay in 1988. Report published in India by Mrs. P. Rodriquez for Rodrigo Enterprises: A-22, Seema Apts. Bandstand, Barndra, Bombay, India -400-050.

3. For further discussion, consult the following: R. J. White, Locke G.E., Albin M.S. "Isolated Profound Cerebral Cooling with a Bi-Carotid Head Exchange Shunt in Dogs," Resuscitation 1983: 10; 193-195; and White, R.J. "Experimental Transplantation of the Brain," in Human Transplantation, eds., Rapaport F.T. and Dausset J. Eds. 1968. Gane and Stratton, New York and London, 692-709.

References

Arnason, Wayne B. "Directed Donation: The Relevance of Race." Hastings Center Report. November/December, 1991: 13-19.

Dastur, Darab K. and S. A. Barodawala, "Neural Transplants." *Brain Transplantation: Ethical Concerns*. C. J. Vas and E. J. deSouza, eds. Bombay, India: Rodrigo Enterprises, 1988: 25-27.

Fredrickson, George. *The Black Image in the White Mind: The Debate on Afro-American Character and Destiny.* Connecticut: Wesleyan Press, 1987.

Gossett, Thomas. *Race: The History of an Idea in America.* Dallas: Southern Methodist University Press, 1963.

Jordan, Winthrop. *White Over Black: American Attitudes Toward the Negro.* Chapel Hill: University of North Carolina Press, 1968.

Lawrence, D. H. *Studies in American Literature.* 1924.

McCullaugh, P. *Fetal Brain Transplantation: The Scope of the Ethical Issue.* New York: Wiley, 1984.

_____. *Brain Dead, Brain Aabsent, Brain Donors: Human Subjects or Human Objects?* New York: Wiley, 1993.

Moyers, Bill. "A World of Ideas with Bill Moyers." An Interview with Derek Walcott, PBS Video, Public Broadcasting Service, 1989.

Murphy, P. J. "Moral Perspetives in the Use of Embryonic Cell Transplantation for Correction of Nervous System Disorders." *Applied Neurophysiology*, 1984, 47: 65-68.

Spielman, Bethany, "Directed Donation: Race Issues," Lecture at Sangamon State University (University of Illinois at Springfield), November 8, 1994.

Tripp, Luke. "The Intellectual Roots of the Controversy Around Cultural Diversity and Political Correctness." *The Western Journal of Black Studies*, Winter, 1994, 227-230.

Vas, C. J. and E. J. DeSouza, eds. Brain Transplantation: Ethical Concerns. Bombay, India: Rodrigo Enterprises, 1988.

Walker, Francis, A. *Political Economy*. New York: H. Holt & Co. 1883.

White, R. J. "Experimental Transplantation of the Brain." *Human Transplantation*. F. T. Rapaport and J. Dausset, eds. New York and London: Gane and Stratton, 1968, 692-707.

_____. Locke, G. E., Albin, M. S. "Isolated Profound Cerebral Cooling with a Bi-Carotid Head Exchange Shunt in Dogs," *Resuscitation*, 1983, 10: 193-195.

27

REPARATION PHASE III: REINSTITUTING THE PRIMARY COLLECTIVE VISION/WILL OF AFRICAN AMERICANS

Obedike Kamau

It can be argued that African American life and struggle in the United States of America, since coming here at an oppressor's impetus, can be divided into three broad, general eras or phases. The first phase is chronologically the longest and covers a time period that historians generally agree lasted from 1619 to 1865, during which time we were formally enslaved and legally classified as less than human. This period ended with the passage of the Thirteenth Amendment to the U. S. Constitution, which formally ended legal enslavement in the United States "except as punishment for crime whereof the party shall have been duly convicted" (The U.S. Thirteenth Amendment to the Constitution).

The primary collective will that the people now known as African Americans invoked during this era involved destroying chattel slavery and can be summed up in one word – freedom. Black people residing in the United States whether slave or "free" during the seventeenth-nineteenth centuries had very little, if any, collective material power. They had no aggregate political, social, economic, and certainly no institutional or systematic military capability. They were totally dedicated despite an overall disorganized collective effort, however, to obtaining their freedom and ending chattel slavery. The only source of power they could tap into during this era was the spirit; their collective spiritual and mental desire helped to create a situation that fundamentally changed their material and legal status. The only power they had access to was one which was and still is available to everyone, unseen, and immeasurable by the society that systematically oppressed them. Their will was finally able to create such a schism within this then infant nation-state, perhaps the only social phenomena powerful enough to topple the chattel slavery system, that evolved into a war.

Any analyses and conclusions concerning the root cause of the U.S. Civil War are sorely lacking unless they take into account the spiritual role Africans played. There has been a misplaced tendency on the part of both Black and white historians and other people in this country to give primary credit for the freeing of my Ancestors from enslavement to the U.S. government and the original Americans (people primarily of Anglo-European descent). The fact is that the U.S. Civil War is arguably the most seminal event in American history and is certainly the incident that is widely given credit as being primarily responsible for bringing an end to the chattel slave system, thereby creating the foundation for the quasi culturally diverse system in place today. This makes the dominant perspectives of its causes and effects particularly critical. The refusal on the part of most U.S. scholars to deal with the role that both African thought and action played in sparking the flame that legally ended slavery clearly places the descendants of enslaved Africans at a serious disadvantage. The continued tendency to see the Civil War as a primarily white enterprise (something that was done for us out of the goodness of America's hard heart) causes both Black and white Americans to have skewed perceptions of the role that Africans here have played in their own liberation.

Several authors have to some degree investigated the role that African spiritualism played in creating the war and destroying chattel slavery, but in a materialist and positivist culture (despite its declaration of postmodernism) the immeasurable is often overlooked, particularly if consideration of it refutes the dominant analysis. Civil War historians and others may want to overlook the role that Black desire played in the causation of this phenomena, but a quick review of the events that led to "the singular period/event in Europe's most important settler colony's history" (Cheatwood, 10) shows clearly in retrospect that there was no sound basis for the Confederate States of America to secede from the Union. Despite the rabble roused by the abolitionists, Abraham Lincoln was clearly not one of their number and actually went through a series of painful political postures in an effort to mollify the South, and to keep Africans and their social status from being perceived as the focus of this internecine family squabble.

The problems with the dominant analysis are at minimum two. First, there is little consideration given to the role that African desire – thought and action – played in the causation of the U.S. Civil War. This lack of consideration removes African responsibility for self-liberation, allowing a cultural tendency to develop, which gives credit to a general "White" America for liberating us. This tendency has prevented us from turning a collective, critical eye toward America and her inclination to oppress us to the extent to which we allow it, a social reality that unfortunately continues to exist. This tendency also forces us to look outside ourselves for our salvation, a social reality that unfortunately continues to exist. Recognition of this fact does not negate contributions non-Blacks have made to our evolution toward self-determination; rather it places responsibility where it accurately lies and reduces our impulse to relax after we have forced America to make concessions to us. America has developed an amazing ability to make what was forced appear to have been voluntary as time continues to pass, and history continues to be misrepresented. Second, this misrepresentation of history prevents us from critically assessing our efforts (since we are willing to assign them to others), and from logically building upon our former struggles. For example, our acknowledging that we, in fact, actively (if unconsciously) caused the Civil War, to some degree prevents us from understanding that physical freedom was ultimately a partial rather than a complete goal, and that we, because of our self-determination, rather than Chicago, should have been the promised land we sought from the beginning. One common attribute we share with our Ancestors in this land, regardless of the political landscape, is a state of dependence, particularly economic, upon white America (more on this later). Becoming collectively independent and thriving holistically should have always been the bull's-eye for which we were specifically aiming, on the target of gradational liberties at which we have been shooting.

To give due credit we must state that our Ancestors from the Civil War/Reconstruction eras were more nationalistic than we are. Things were much more black and white (forgive the pun) then. Our efforts at self-determination were ruthlessly thwarted by an implacable foe (white America), which was determined to prevent us from flourishing, at least as a community. Examples of this attitude abound; Rosewood, Florida, and Tulsa, Oklahoma, are two of the more infamous cases. An uncritical glance at U.S. history makes it clear that white America saw the flourishing of Africans, here, as a direct threat to their well-being, whether they were being "well" or not. We were, for all intents and purposes, abandoned by our white "friends" who assisted us in attaining our "freedom," and were told that we were blessed to be able to participate in the race, despite the fact that our legs had been cut off. I know that there are problems with the use of general statements such as white America, but history unfortunately teaches us that, even though this attitude may not have existed among all white Americans, those who were opposed to the dominant view were virtually powerless to reverse this tendency for very long periods of time.

White America's attempts in refusing to allow us to mobilize collective power proves, beyond a shadow of a doubt, that physical freedom was not enough in this context, which led us directly into the second phase.

The second period covers 1866 to 1968 and ended with the Civil Rights Bill passed that year, which together with the Civil Rights Acts of 1964 and 1965, as well as the 1954 *Brown vs. Board of Education* of Topeka, Kansas, and other federal court cases formally ended legal discrimination in this country. During this era we were able to legally attain both full human status as well as citizenship, win universal suffrage through the fifteenth and nineteenth Amendments (the fifteenth applied specifically to African American men), while also eliminating de jure segregation.

Perhaps the most significant occurrences during this hard day's night were the limitations built into Reconstruction as well as its eventual termination, and the civil rights movement. During this era Black nationalism made a determined stand but was eventually shunted to the side as integration was implemented, although perhaps not in the way that either Du Bois, Randolph, or King had in mind. The holistic terrorist methods either employed by or allowed by this country convinced us to push back just as directly and intensely, convinced us to insist on integration and inclusion and convinced us to insist on what we perceived was being denied us. Our insistence on primarily sharing white America's power rather than on developing our own, and consistently exercising it on our behalf, has once again left us shorthanded, and collectively dependent.

The primary will that we as a people employed during the second phase was invoked in the effort to attain equal opportunity – total equality. It became obvious to our elders and Ancestors that "freedom" in and of itself was not all that it was cracked up to be. They were systematically prevented from creating and nourishing independent Black power, as well as sharing white, or America's, power. It was clear that we were collectively living inferior material lives. We saw that the Fourteenth Amendment had made us "shitizens" rather than citizens. And my people moved mightily to correct this condition. We refused to accept the blatant oppression that America insisted on meting out to us under the legal guise of "separate but equal." We wanted less separate, more equal, and we fought to attain this. During the Booker T. Washington era, we saw that attempting to amass collective economic power without accompanying political power was ineffective. Perhaps because of this we shifted our efforts so completely from the economic to the political that our collective economic thrust has been all but completely abandoned.

Once again our thought and action, our desire to change our status, were powerful enough to force the federal government to move (to some degree) in our behalf. We feel more akin to our accomplishments in the civil rights/black power struggle than we do to the Civil War, however. First of all it is closer to us in time. We know people who saw and were involved in it; living testimony is available that can describe to us how things were during this time. Technology also helps; there are films and tapes available so that we can observe for ourselves the conditions under which we existed. We serve as witnesses to history. We enthusiastically give whites credit for assisting us in this battle, but we are also much more willing to claim ownership of the civil rights movement, because we were so out front in it. We, to a large degree, financed it; we put our bodies and those of our children on the line for it. We were clearly the leading spokes(wo)men for it, and to a large degree we determined the tone and nature of the conversation. We are able to concretely see our power, how it manifested, and the changes it has wrought.

The accomplishments we were able to actualize should not be taken lightly; they in many ways deserve the celebration that is accorded them. We were, in fact, able to continually break down America's insane obstinacy toward us. One of the more interesting facts concerning the ongoing relationship between Blacks and America is that every positive step we take for ourselves has ultimately been good for the country. We have literally dragged America kicking and screaming into new horizons, of moral decency and financial prosperity.

The steps we have made toward educational, economic, political, and social equality have certainly sweetened the physical freedom won by our Ancestors. The headway we made during the second phase has been very measurable; it has been something we can feel, as soul singer Aretha Franklin says. During this phase we were able to develop to a degree some of the concrete power that we did not have access to during the first phase. Some might argue that we have been victimized by our success during this stage of our development. After all, removing the legal barriers to equality falsely convinced us that the job was completed. Even though it was impossible to legislate morality, the legislation that we forced was significant, and many customs and traditions that were in place in this country, particularly in the South, were either eliminated or severely repressed. The physical atrocities we experience now are more often than not, despite an irregular James Byrd situation, administered through the criminal "justice" system. Despite the injustice in this situation we must admit that centralizing at least the physical violence we have had to face has significantly lessened it. We should also remember that we have forced every modification in America's thought and action toward us.

The third period has lasted from 1969 until the present, and it can be characterized by both its lack of significant collective African American social, economic, and political achievement, as well as its lack of a collective African American vision for continued cumulative empowerment.

Part of the problem in our seeming inability to logically continue our progress centers on how well we have done in eliminating the legal basis of our oppression. We must once again turn to the economic, Booker T's priority, in order to continue our journey to self-determination.

This paper suggests that the goal of the collective African American vision during this all-important third phase should be holistic, collective self-determination. It also focuses on the economic aspect of our collective lives and concerns itself with what is deemed a provocative and controversial way to strengthen our collective economic position. The primary method it suggests for this process is through attaining reparations for the group of people now currently called African Americans. It further posits that the demand for reparations is just as important and crucial as ending chattel slavery was during the first era, and ending Jim Crow and attaining 'civil rights' was in the second one. It goes on to assert that the realization of reparations is no more farfetched than eliminating either legal enslavement or destroying the imposition of an illegal and unconstitutional so-called second-class citizenship systematically fastened to African Americans by all American institutions during the second phase of our sojourn.

This paper maintains that the largest obstacle to our achieving reparations lies in convincing African Americans that our attaining it should be just as important to us presently as becoming "free and equal" was to our Ancestors and Elders. This paper also maintains that the illusion of equality makes it more difficult for our people to develop a collective vision and has negatively impacted our will to demand and work toward reparations. Furthermore, this paper maintains that during the first era ending our enslavement was the primary focus of our collective will, just as attaining citizenship and all of its obvious accouterments was the primary focus of our collective will during the second phase. In order for us to gain reparations and self-determination we must also make this goal the most current primary focus of our collective will, not a demand that is cyclical depending upon the treatment African American people receive from general American society.

Reparations, a term related to redress due one people by another, is sometimes referred to as damages or compensation. Its etymological root is the word *repair*, and at the international level reparation is required because of massive, national crimes committed by one people or nation against another. These massive crimes so disrupt the natural growth and development of the aggrieved people that monumental repair is needed to allow their national, self-determined contribution to human evolution. Reparations are well-established principles of international law, and the concept and practice extends back at least as far as the days of the Old

Testament Hebrew Israelites. It is also an international legal practice that the United States is very familiar with, having been involved in paying reparations, seeking and collecting reparations, as well as negotiating reparations on behalf of wounded states.

The term reparations as it applies specifically to African Americans is defined by Robert Brock, executive director of the Self-Determination Committee, and long- time reparations activist, as:

> the demand by U.S. slaves and their descendants, on the government of the United States of America and its individual white men, women and children and all others of the free structure and their heirs following in interest, inheritance, use and benefit through succession for payment and return and restoring and taking back, for damage, hurt, harm, injury, loss and wrong, in the form of
> 1. Money (Gold)
> 2. Goods
> 3. Service
> 4. Land, and
> 5. Treaty under international law not to recapture. (Brock, 7)

Reparations are due us for both the enslavement and the post-enslavement eras.

The concept of self-determination is inherently included in the concept of reparations, and it is clear that collective self-determination is a right that Africans have never had here, in either the colonial, dependent United Colonies of America or the independent, colonialist United States of America. Self-determination is collective or national free will and includes concepts such as self-defined culture, nationality, names and naming rituals, morals, religious worship, language, marriage and family, human status, and mental capacity (Brock, 14). All of these attributes were removed through the undeclared war by Europe on Africa through the misnomered "slave trade" and have never been restored. The right of self-determination has been taken and continues to be denied African Americans through physical slavery and mental captivity. Mental captivity is defined as "forceful and violent subjection to mental control or servitude through influences exerted over the intellect, affections, or will" (Brock, 18).

One of the more disturbing aspects of the whole Black Reparations issue is the seemingly noncommittal attitude African Americans seem to have toward it. Based on a nonscientific poll conducted by the author, most of us, once we minimally understand the concept, believe we should receive them but have absolutely no faith that it will ever happen and are, therefore, not willing to work toward it. This leads me to conclude that the primary job of those of us who advocate reparations is to first convince African Americans that they are, in fact, owed to us, and that we have not only the right but the responsibility to pursue them vigorously, using, as our Father/Brother El-Hajj Malik-el Shabazz said so many years ago, no self-imposed limits, but rather "by any means necessary!" Our unwillingness to attempt to systematically collect America's debt to us speaks directly to our understanding of our history, our collective self-respect, our understanding of the concept, wealth, and what we owe to our children. Our primary task is to make Black people here understand exactly what has happened to us, and to help us understand more directly exactly how our past here impacts our present and our future, in more than lip-service clichés. Anything less than the quest for self-determination through reparations and other means is simply repetition, leftovers, reruns, old wine in new bottles – a continued fight for rights that our Ancestors and Elders have already won and rewon. Self-determination through reparations is the fight for this generation of Africans in America! It is time for Blacks as Claud Anderson says,to "make acquiring reparations from the American government a major national issue" (Anderson, 182). If upon understanding why this is a requirement we do not manifest it, then we are moral and spiritual cowards who have no right to call upon our Ancestors! If all we are doing is continuing to fight for rights we have won, and that depending upon the political and economic conditions of this country, this country's leaders seem intent on wresting away from us once again then our Ancestors will no longer be interested in hearing from us anyway.

First we were captured – through acts of war – undeclared though they may have been. We were captured, not as prisoners of war, whose internment may be harsh, but nevertheless is temporary, but as slaves who purportedly were predestined to be born into this condition. The primary legal way to escape it was through death. The war did not stop in Africa, however, it was continually waged, even after we reached these shores. According to Obadele, the war here

> was of a more absolute kind. Its aim was to make slavery permanent, easy and peaceful. To accomplish this the American undertook to destroy all traces of African culture and dignity, while crushing mercilessly every revolt they could. The evolving Americans undertook to kill all the indomitable resisting Blacks and to terrorize the others. Such barbarous acts of the slave masters became fully sanctioned by colonial then United States law. The hope of the dominant whites was to remake these people of Africa into a new kind of people, a caste of

willing subservients who would fear to revolt and, ultimately
forget that they should. (Obadele, 3)

They were not able to accomplish this in either of the first two phases, but they have almost succeeded now.

Slavery, the kind of slavery that was practiced here, was not just physical; it was designed to destroy the cultural, modify the spiritual, and imprison the mental. Anderson elucidates some of the differences between Ancient enslavement and American enslavement:

Ancient Enslavement Slaves' basic rights were honored. The
Catholic church accepted slaves as humans and intervened on
their behalf.

BLACK SLAVES ASANTE SANA

"I Want My Money"
(The Reparations Rap)
Obidike N. Kamau
copyright 1989

Did somebody (what) mention reparations?
Well if so then check this information
they ripped us and they forced us into cash-free labor
The time when we were slaves and they were the slavers.
They stole us from our beautiful land
Reduced us to less than a man
Refused to let us take a stand and they made us wear animal brands.
They stole my children, stole my wife
They thoroughly fucked up my life
They stole my religion, stole my name
That's world history's biggest con game.
What do we get now – more of the same
and they want me to take all the blame.
They talk crazy, like they're on crack
Cause this country was built on my black back
But I'm tired of living as a slave
And now it's- time for me to get paid.

(Chorus)
I WANT MY MONEY!

(time to get paid in full)
I WANT MY MONEY!
(my forty acres and my mule)
I WANT MY MONEY!
(this devastation to my race)
I WANT MY MONEY!
(insures that I stay on your case)

They killed my father, and raped my mother
Molested my sisters one after the other,
and if that wasn't enough, what do I see?
They got my brother outside, hanging from a tree.
We've been frustrated, and castrated, systematically demotivated,
It's been bad, we been damn near eliminated
But we're Black and we're strong, as U see we can take it
Four hundred years, and still we have made it.
With dehumanization and mental slavery
Biological genocide's corrupting me.
All this because they raped my Black women,
These are some fact that I am just sending.
This is the message I have to relay
'Cause now is the time for me to get paid.

(Chorus)

See we are the victims of an undeclared war
We ain't fighting (Why?!) We don't know what for.
We've been manipulated by a diabolical mind
He's stolen our land, our life, and our time,
He's stolen our legacy, stolen our knowledge
and then all our rights as humans he abolished.
He's taken us people, completely degraded us
In seasoning labs, he then re-created us
Wanted to erase our cultural memory
Try and make us forget all of our history,
but I'm a time bomb
and I'm a loaded grenade

And I'll chase him and dog him – UNTIL I GET PAID!!
I WANT MY MONEY!!

References

Anderson, Claud. *Black Labor, White Wealth: The Search for Power and Economic Justice.* Edgewood, Md.: Duncan and Duncan, 1994.

Benton-Lewis, Dorothy. *Black Reparations Now! Solutions to the Crisis in Democracy and Black Survival in the USA.* Rockville, Md.: Black Reparations Press, 1978.

Brock, Robert. "The African American Case for Reparations." Unpublished monograph.

Clarke, John Henrik. *Notes for an African World Revolution: Africans at the Crossroads.* Trenton, N.J.: Africa World Press, 1991.

Lumumba, Chokwe, Imari Obadele, and Nkechi Taifa. *Reparations Yes! The Legal and Political Reasons Why New Afrikans – Black People in the United States – Should Be Paid Now for the Enslavement of Our Ancestors and for War against Us after Slavery.* Baton Rouge, La.: House of Songhay, 1993.

Munford, C. J. *Race and Reparations: A Black Perspective for the 21st Century.* Trenton, N.J.: Africa World Press, 1996.

Obadele, Imari. *America the Nation-State.* Baton Rouge, LA: House of Songhay. 1988.

Robinson, Lori. "Righting a Wrong," *Emerge Magazine* (February 1997): 43-49.

28

NGUZO SABA (THE SEVEN PRINCIPLES)

THIS CHAPTER, FROM *KAWAIDA: A COMMUNITARIAN AFRICAN PHILOSOPHY* (1997),
IS REPRINTED WITH PERMISSION FROM THE UNIVERSITY OF SANKORE PRESS.

Maulana Karenga

The *Nguzo Saba* are the core values of Kawaida philosophy. And they are the most widely known and used concepts of Kawaida. In addition to the millions of persons in the world African community who recite, discuss and organize their lives around them during the seven days of *Kwanzaa*, hundreds of organizations also use them as a fundamental value system for their members and the various projects they develop. Certainly, most independent African schools and rites of passage programs also use the Nguzo Saba as value-orientation and value-grounding. Likewise, the Nguzo Saba are used for value-grounding by various kinds of organizations including family maintenance and development programs, Black Student Unions, youth groups, school achievement and retention programs, ex-prisoner programs, prisoner and prisoner support groups, various dependency rehabilitation programs, cultural centers, Black caucuses, artist groups, priest and nun groups, cooperatives and various other organizations, programs and institutions.

The words Nguzo Saba are Swahili for The Seven (*Saba*) Principles (*Nguzo*). *Nguzo* also means pillar, buttress, palisade. As pillars, the principles are that which *support* and *sustain* the people, the construction and conduct of their lives, as in the phrase "pillar of the community." As a buttress, they are that which *uphold* and *reinforce* the people. And as a palisade, they are a wall of defense for the people. These Seven Principles are: Ujima (Unity); Kujichagulia (Self-determination); Ujima (Collective work and responsibility); Ujamaa (Cooperative economics); Nia (Purpose); Kuumba (Creativity); and Imani (Faith).

These seven principles are essential standards of personal and social excellence directed toward building and sustaining moral community, and strengthening and maintaining the community's capacity to define, defend and develop its interests in the most positive and productive sense. In addition to being standards of excellence, the Nguzo Saba are also categories of priorities and categories of human possibilities. As categories of priorities, they tell us some of the most important things in our lives, identifying a key set of views, values and practices which we should, even must, put first in our personal and social life. And as categories of possibilities, the Nguzo Saba offer us a set of principles which encourage thought and practice which help define, develop and enhance our humanity in the context of community and the world.

Furthermore, the Nguzo Saba, which serves as both the core values of Kawaida Philosophy and the central focus of the African American and pan-African holiday of Kwanzaa are a fundamental communitarian value system. They are posed as a moral minimum set of values African Americans need to rescue and reconstruct their lives in their own image and interest and build and sustain an Afrocentric family, community and culture. The Seven Principles were selected in terms of both tradition and reason, that is to say, they were selected from the African communitarian tradition, but were also chosen with an appreciation for where we are now as a people and what challenges we face and must deal with successfully as a people. The aim was to provide a common ground of values and resultant practice that would build, sustain and enhance family, community and culture.

Although there are many other communitarian values which could have been chosen, these seven core values, the Nguzo Saba, were specifically selected for four basic reasons. First, they were selected because of their prevalence and recurrence in communitarian African societies, therefore reflecting a Pan-African character. Secondly, these particular values were selected because of their perceived relevance to the liberational project of African Americans, i.e., their struggle for freedom, building family, community and culture and self-consciously contributing to a new history of humankind. Thirdly, these seven core principles were chosen because of the cultural and spiritual significance of seven in African culture. And finally, they were selected because of the manageability of the number seven in terms of teaching, learning and core emphasis.

Having accepted the centrality of culture and the values which undergird it, the task was to study communitarian African cultural values and choose and establish the ones which would best serve the interests and aspirations of the African American family, community and culture. In terms of the interest and aspirations of African American people, the Nguzo Saba were developed and offered as an Afrocentric value system which would serve the following basic functions: 1) organize and enrich our relations with each other on the personal and community level; 2) establish standards, commitments and priorities what would tend to enhance our human possibilities as persons and a people; 3) aid in the recovery and reconstruction of lost historical memory and cultural legacy in the development of an Afrocentric paradigm of life and achievement; 4) serve as a contribution to a core system of communitarian ethical values for the moral guidance and instruction of the community, especially for children; and 5) contribute to an ongoing and expanding use of Afrocentric communitarian values which would aid in bringing into being a new man, woman and child who self-consciously participate in the ethical project of starting a new history of African people and humankind. With these observations in mind, we can now turn to the rich meaning and message of the Nguzo Saba themselves, in the context of daily life.

UMOJA (UNITY)

> To strive for and maintain unity in the family, community, nation and race.

The first and foundational principle of the Nguzo Saba is Umoja, unity. For without it, all the principles suffer. Unity is both a principle and practice of togetherness in all things good and mutual benefit. It is a principled and harmonious togetherness not simply a being together. This is why value rootedness is so important, even indispensable. Unity as principled and harmonious togetherness is a cardinal virtue of both classical and general African societies. In ancient Egypt, harmony was a cardinal virtue of Maat, i.e., righteousness, rightness. In fact, one of the ways to translate Maat is to define it as harmony – harmony on the natural, cosmic and social level. Likewise, being among the Dinka means both morality and harmonious living together. Thus in both ancient Egyptian and Dinka society, one cannot live a moral life without living in harmony with other members of the community.

If unity is in essence a principle, it is not less a practice as are all the other principles. For practice is central to African ethics, and all claims to ethical living and commitment to moral principles are tested and proved or disproved in relations with others. Relations, then, are the hinge on which morality turns, the ground on which it rises or falls. In this regard, character development in African ethics in not simply to create a good person abstracted from community, but rather a person in positive interaction, a person whose quality of relations with others is defined first of all by a principled and harmonious togetherness, i.e., a real and practiced unity.

Unity as a value-orientation is also an active solidarity. This essentially means a firm dependable togetherness that is born, based and sustained in action. This applies to families, organizations, communities and people and expressed itself as building and acting together in mutual benefit. The key here is again practice. Finally, unity means a oneness, a similarity and sameness that gives us an identity as a people, an African people. And inherent in this identity as a people is the ethical and political imperative to self-consciously unite in order to define, defend and develop our interests, to speak the truth and beauty of our culture, and make our own unique contribution to the unfolding of history in the interest of humanity.

Unity as principle and practice begins in the family but presupposes value-orientation of each member. Adults and children must respect and approach unity as a moral principle to family and community not simply a political slogan. As principle and practice, this means principled and harmonious living with brothers and sisters, mothers and fathers – sharing and acting in unison. It means avoidance of conflict and quick, willing and principled resolution when it occurs. It means a yielding and gentleness of exchange as taught in Sacred Husia. The Husia teaches that each person and family must reject harshness and practice gentleness, stress coopera-tion and avoid conflict, and be very attentive to things that would divide or create differences negative to togetherness.

Especially important is the unity of the father and mother, for they are the models for the children and the foundation for the family in every sense of the word. Here the African concept of complementarily of male and female is instructive. In African complementarily, three principles internal to it are necessary and reinforcing of both the concept and practice: 1) equality; 2) reciprocity; and 3) friendship. We start from the principle of human equality and cultivate social equality as its logical and necessary complement. For respect for the dignity of the human person and the best of African ethical tradition demands it. Secondly, complementarily also requires reciprocity, a cardinal virtue in Kawaida ethics. This essentially means a mutually appreciative exchange which benefits all those involved. And it also means returning good given and giving good, to build the moral relation sand community we want to live in. Thirdly, complementa-rily requires friendship. Reciprocity among equals is morally and socially compelling. And friendship is the special loving relationship of equals, rooted in mutual investment in each other's happiness, well-being and development.

Finally the family must be, as in African culture, the focal point of unity not simply of siblings and of genders, but also of generations. One of the important expressions of family unity is the respect and collective concern and care for the elders. Respect for elders as Elechi Amadi points out is a "cardinal article of the code of behavior" of African society. One who does not respect his/her elders is seen as immoral and uncultured.

Elders are respected, like the ancestors they will become, for several reasons including: for their long life of service to the community; for their achievement; for providing an ethical model; and for the richness of their experience and the wisdom this had produced. Thus, elders are seen as judges and reconcilers. It is they who hear cases of conflict and problems and offer solutions. One of the most important aspect of African respect for elders is that it makes them useful and active in the community. Thus, it is clearly unAfrican to deprive them of meaningful roles and place them to the side, denying them their right and need to participate and relate fully.

In fact, the active participation and involvement of elders in the daily life of the family not only benefits them but the younger people. For it teaches them to understand and appreciate the process of growing old, gives them access to seasoned knowledge and experience and helps prevent the so-called generation gap so evident and advertised in the larger society. Key to this linking of young and old is the concept of lineage which links all the living, the departed and the yet unborn. This is translated in practice into the extended family and the practice and ritual of remembrance this involves. Early in life continental African children are taught to memorize and recite their family tree as far back as any ancestor is known. Moreover, at social occasions when we do libation, we participate in the communal practice of "raising the name" in which we call out and remember those who gave goodness and have now passed. This keeps historical memory alive and reaffirms respect for the living and departed who contributed to their coming into being and cultural molding.

Now, if one starts with the family when discussing unity, the community becomes of necessity the next level of the concern and practice of unity. The family, as it is written, is the smallest example of how the nation (or national community) works. For the relations, values and practice one has in the family are a reflection and evidence of what one will find in the community. Thus, although unity begins in the family, it must, of necessity, extend to the community. Malcolm X taught that community unity first depended on everyone's belonging to an organization, then all organizations uniting on the basis of common interests and aspirations. He posed community unity as morally compelling. It was for him irresponsible and self destructive not to unite around common interests and instead glory in differences. The principle of Umoja, then, stressed that which unites us and urges us to constantly seek and stand together on common ground.

Unity of the nations is unity of the national community as distinct from the local community. But the requirements for unity in the local community hold equally for the national community. In teams of "racial" unity, when one says race, one means the world African community. Thus, when Marcus Garvey says "Up you mighty race; you can accomplish what you will," he is talking to the world African community. The form of unity referred to here is Pan-Africanism, the struggle to unite all Africans everywhere around the common interests of freedom, development, cultural renewal and standing in strength and dignity among the people of the world.

KUJICHAGULIA (SELF-DETERMINATION)

> To define ourselves, name ourselves, create for ourselves and speak for ourselves.

The second principle of the Nguzo Saba is Kujichagulia, self-determination. This also expressed itself as both commitment and practice. It demands that we as an African people define, defend and develop ourselves instead of allowing or encouraging others to do this. It requires that we recover lost memory and once again shape our world in our own image and interest. And it is a call to recover and speak our own special truth to the world and raise images above the earth that reflect our capacity for human greatness and progress.

The principle of self-determination carries within it the assumption that we have both the right and responsibility to exist as a people, to speak our own special cultural truth, and make our own unique contribution to the forward flow of human history. This principle teaches us that as fathers and mothers of humanity and human civilization in the Nile Valley, we have no business playing the cultural children of the world. And it urges us as a people not to surrender our historical and cultural identity to fit into the culture of another. Openness to exchange is a given, but it presupposes that one has kept enough of one's culture to engage in exchange, rather than slavishly follow another's lead.

Self-determination requires that we understand and approach our culture as a rich resource and that we use it to seek answers to the fundamental questions of human life and society. Also, it means practicing freedom on the personal and collective level in the context of community and culture. As the ancient Egyptians taught, a strong respect for ourselves requires that we think with our won minds, see with our own eyes, hear with our own ears, speak with our own mouth and walk with the strength and dignity of our own person. Finally, the moral importance of the principle is beautifully stated in a verse from the Husia, "It is wrong to walk upside down and in darkness. Thus, I will come forth today and bring the truth which is in me."

UJIMA (COLLECTIVE WORK AND RESPONSIBILITY)

To build and maintain our community together and make our brother's and sister's problems our problems and to solve them together.

The third principle is Ujima, Collective Work and Responsibility, which is a commitment to active and informed togetherness on matters of common interest. It is also recognition and respect of the fact that without collective work and struggle, progress is impossible and liberation unthinkable. Moreover, the principle of Ujima supports the fundamental assumption that African is not just an identity, but also a destiny and duty, i.e., a responsibility. In other words, our collective identity in the long run is a collective future. Thus, there is a need and obligation for us as self-conscious and committed people to shape our future with our own minds and hands and share its hardships and benefits together.

Ujima, as principle and practice, also means that we accept the fact that we are collectively responsible for our failures and setbacks as well as our victories and achievements. And this holds true not only on the national level, but also on the level of family and organization or smaller units. Such a commitment implies and encourages a vigorous capacity for self-criticism and self-correction which is indispensable to our strength, defense and development as a people.

The principle of collective work and responsibility also points to the fact that African freedom is indivisible. It shelters the assumption that as long as any African anywhere is oppressed, exploited, enslaved or wounded in any way in her or his humanity, all African people are. It thus, rejects the possibility or desirability of individual freedom in any unfree context; instead it poses the need for struggle to create a context in which all can be free. Moreover, Ujima rejects escapist and abstract humanism and supports the humanism that begins with commitment to and concern for the humans among whom we live and to whom we owe our existence, i.e., our own people. In a word, real humanism begins with accepting one's own humanity in the particular from in which it expresses itself and then initiating and sustaining exchanges with others, in the context of our common humanity. It also posits that the liberation struggle to rescue and reconstruct African history and humanity is a significant contribution to overall struggle for human liberation.

In the context of a communitarian social order, cooperation is another key aspect of Ujima. It is based on the assumption that what one does to benefit others is at the same time a benefit to him/her. As Lady TaAset says, "Doing good is not difficult. In fact, just speaking good is a monument to those who do it. For those who do good for others are actually doing it for themselves" (Karenga, 1994: 229).

Here again, harmonious living is of paramount importance. Thus, being quarrelsome or contentious is one of the worst offenses of African ethics. And striving for uncoerced or free and willing agreement is the model of cooperative behavior. Moreover, reconciliation of conflict is patient and never coercive, and always done keeping the person in mind. And the fundamental objective in conflict is not to mechanically apply the rule but to reconcile the people. For as the Dinka teach, "if people do not agree, there can be no relationship." And, of course, if they have be coerced, there cannot be genuine agreement.

Finally, collective work and responsibility can be seen in terms of the challenge of culture and history. Work – both personal and collective – is truly at the center of history and culture. It is the fundamental activity by which we create ourselves, define and develop ourselves and confirm ourselves in the process as both persons and a people. And it is the way we create culture and make history. The challenge of our history and culture then is, through collective work and responsibility, to restore that which was damaged or destroyed and to raise up and reconstruct that which was in ruins as the ancient Egyptians taught. It is also to remember we are each cultural representatives of our people and have not right to misrepresent them or willfully do less than is demanded of us by our history and current situation as a community-in-struggle. We must accept and live the principle of shared or collective work and responsibility in all things good, right and beneficial to the community.

UJAMAA (COOPERATIVE ECONOMICS)

> To build and maintain our own stores, shops and other businesses and to profit from them together.

The fourth Principle is Ujamaa, Cooperative Economics, which is the principle and practice of shared work and shared wealth. Also, it means requires shared decision-making about the work and wealth. The concept Ujamaa which comes to also mean family-hood, suggests that we should approach economic activity in our relations as we would with family, i.e., in the spirit of kinship and willingness to cooperate to create goods and services and to share what we produce. This is what is meant by the call to build and maintain our own businesses and to profit from them together.

The principle of building and maintaining together speaks to the requirement of shared work. It is work to produce and work to keep and develop what is held in common. This suggests an appreciation for work and working together. Ujamaa stresses the essentiality of work to the well-being and development of persons, family and community. And it emphasizes working together to achieve what we need and what for both the personal and collective good. Working together means not only that we increase our productive capacity, bug also that we strengthen our claim to sharing what we produce. For a person who can help achieve a common goal and does not, cannot justify any claim to the benefits.

Thus, this principle speaks against laziness, slowness, triflingness and other negative and irresponsible approaches to work. In a situation which requires work, one must have a good reason not to. In ancient African societies even a guest was required to work after a few days of courtesy. In his essays on Ujamaa, Presisdent Julius Nyerere quotes an African proverb to illustrate this point. "A person is a guest for two days, on the third day give him a hoe." The giving of a hoe reflects an agricultural work situation and suggests the guests are expected to help cultivate the food the family hares with them. Therefore, the lesson here is that persons should only be guests for two days, on the third day, they should be invited to share in the work that benefits all.

Ujamaa, as a principle of shared wealth, speaks to the value of generosity. Thus, it is a principle which teaches us against selfishness and greed. Ujamaa encourages people to be other-directed, to be kind and considerate of others, and to be willing to share what we have that others need to could benefit from. This principle of sharing with others teaches us to be especially concerned for the most needy and the vulnerable. The Sacred Odu of Ifa (Yoruba) teaches that we can never simply restrict doing good to just those in our own house or family, but we must do good also for those outside. It says, "Those who restrict goodness to the inside of the house will never receive good from the outside. "Moreover, the Odu of Ifa that in our generosity of giving and sharing, we do it without fanfare or expectation of praise. The model of giving is the generous one, Ofun. The text says, "Ofun gives out goodness every-where. And he does not make any noise about it."

But in all our giving we must show a special concern for the vulnerable. The Husia teaches that we should show special care and concern for the most vulnerable. This teaching is summed up in the verse which says we should give good to the hungry, water to the thirsty, clothes to the naked and a boat to those without one. Ujamaa, then, is a principle with various lessons, but at the heart of its meaning is human sharing, cooperative work and collective decision-making about that which is shared and about the work directed toward producing, distributing and consuming the common good shared.

NIA (PURPOSE)

> To make our collective vocation the building and developing of
> our community in order to restore our people to their traditional
> greatness.

The fifth principle of the Nguzo Saba is Nia, Purpose, which is essentially a commitment to the collective vocation of building, developing and defending our national community, its culture and history in order to regain our historical initiative and greatness as a people, and stand in strength and dignity among the peoples of the world. The assumption here is that our role in human history has been and remains a key one, that we as an African people share in the great human legacy Africa has given the world. That legacy is one of having not only been the fathers and mothers of humanity, but also the fathers and mothers of humanity, but also the fathers and mothers of human civilization, i.e., having introduced in the Nile Valley civilizations the basic disciplines of human knowledge. It is this identity which gives us an overriding cultural purpose and suggests a direction. This is what we mean when we say we who are the fathers and mothers of human civilization have no business playing the cultural children of the world. The principle of Nia then makes us conscious of our purpose in light of our historical and cultural identity.

This again reminds us of Mary McLeod Bethune's point concerning our current status as heirs and custodians of a great civilization. She said, "We, as (African Americans) must recognize that we are the custodians as well as heirs of a great civilization. We have," she continues, "given something to the world as a race and for this we are proud and fully conscious of our place in the total picture of (humankind's) development" (Bethune, 1974). As noted above, Bethune is concerned that our purpose is derived from three basic facts. The first two are that we are both heirs and custodians of a great legacy. This means first that we must not simply receive the legacy as a formal historical and cultural transmission, but recognize and respect its importance. Secondly, it means that far from being simple heirs we are also custodians. And this implies an even greater obligation.

To inherit is to receive as legacy, place adequate value on and make a part of one's life. But to be a custodian of a great legacy is to guard, preserve, expand and promote it. It is to honor it by building on and expanding it and in turn, leaving it as an enriched legacy for future generations. Finally, Bethune asks us to recognize and respect our legacy in terms of where it places us in "the total picture of (humankind's) development." It is a call for us to see ourselves not as simple ghetto dwellers or newly arrived captives of the suburbs, but more definitively as a world historical people who have made and must continue to make a significant contribution to the forward flow of human history.

Inherent in this discussion of deriving purpose from cultural and historical identity is a necessary reference to and focus on generational responsibility. Fanon has posed this responsibility in compelling terms. He says, "each generation must, out of relative obscurity, discover its mission, (and then) fulfill it or betray it." The mission he suggests is always framed within the larger context of the needs, hopes and aspirations of the people. And each of us is morally and culturally obligated to participate in creating a context of maximum freedom and development of the people.

Finally, Nia suggests that personal and social purpose are not only non antagonistic but complementary in the true communitarian sense of the word. In fact, it suggests that the highest form of personal purpose is in the final analysis, social purpose, i.e., personal purpose that translates itself into a vocation and commitment which involves and benefits the community. As we have noted elsewhere, such level and quality of purpose not only benefits the collective whole, but also gives fullness and meaning to a person's life in a way individualistic and isolated pursuits cannot.

For true greatness and growth never occur in isolation and at others' expense. On the contrary, as African philosophy teaches, we are first and foremost social beings whose reality and relevance are rooted in the quality and kinds of relations we have with each other. And a cooperative communal vocation is an excellent context and encouragement for quality social relations. Thus, DuBois' stress on education for social contribution and rejection of vulgar careerism rooted in the lone and passionate pursuit of money is especially relevant. For again our purpose is not to simply create money makers, but to cultivate men and women capable of social and human exchange on a larger more meaningful scale, men and women of culture and social conscience, of vision and values which expand the human project of freedom and development rather than diminish and deform it.

KUUMBA (CREATIVITY)

To do always as much as we can, in the way we can, in order to leave our community more beautiful and beneficial than we inherited it.

The sixth principle is Kuumba, Creativity, and logically follows from and is required by the Principle of Nia. It is commitment to being creative within the context of the national community vocation of restoring our people to their traditional greatness and thus leaving our community more beneficial and beautiful then we, i.e., each generation, inherited it. The Principle has both a social and spiritual dimension and is deeply rooted both in social and sacred teachings of African societies.

Nowhere is this principle more clearly expressed than in the literature and culture of ancient Egypt. Creativity here is both an original act or imitation of the Creator and a restorative act also reflective of the Creator constantly pushing back the currents of chaos and decay and revitalizing and restoring the natural, spiritual and cosmic energy of the world. In ancient Egypt, there was a spiritual and ethical commitment and obligation to constantly renew and restore great works, the legacy of the ancestors, and the creative energy of the leader and nation. This was considered doing Maat, i.e., reaffirming and restoring truth, justice and righteousness, harmony, balance, order, rightness, etc. Each pharaoh saw his or her reign, then, as one of restoration of Maat, i.e., the reaffirmation, reestablishment and renewal of the Good, the Beautiful and the Right.

Therefore, Queen Hatshepsut says of her reign, "I have restored that which was in ruins; I have raised up that which was destroyed when the "amu were in the midst of Kemet, overthrowing that which had been made, as they ruled in ignorance of Ra (God)." And King Shabaka found a great work of the ancestors in ruins, the Memphite text on creation and be restored it "so that it was more beautiful that it was more beautiful than before" is also central to the concept of restoration and was a regular claim of the king, queen, priests and leaders. These concepts of restoration and progressive perfection are key concepts in the philosophy of Kawaida. Also, restoration as principle and practice is central to the fifth Principle of Nia whose essential thrust is "to restore our people to their traditional greatness." Thus, one has an interrelatedness and interlocking of principles and therefore a similar relationship in the practice of them.

Recovering and restoring African culture such as the creation of Kwanzaa falls within the restorative conception of creativity. For when I say I created Kwanzaa, the term "created" does not imply or mean "made out of nothing," for it is clearly not the case. What one has, then, is rather a creative restoration in the African spirit of cultural restoration and renewal in both the ancient Egyptian and African American sense of the practice as used in the 1960s.

It is, in fact, a restoring of that which was in ruins or disuse in many parts of Africa, and especially among Africans in America and attempting to make it more beautiful and beneficial than it was before as the Principle of Kuumba (Creativity) requires. This, as stated above, contains the interrelated principles of restoration and progressive perfection. To restore is what we called in the 60s "to rescue and reconstruct." Progressive perfection is a Kawaida concept that assumes an ability and obligation to strive always to leave what one inherits (legacy, community, etc.) more beautiful and beneficial than it was before. It is again, in this context and spirit of the cultural project of recovering and reconstructing African first fruit celebrations that Kwanzaa and other cultural production and reconstruction of Us was conceived and constructed.

The stress, then, is on leaving a legacy which builds on and enriches the legacy before you. It is again stress on generational responsibility. This reminds us of the ancient Egyptian teaching that if we wish to live for eternity we must build for eternity, i.e., do great works or serve the community in a real, sustained and meaningful way. And we are taught by the Husia to remember that "everyday is a donation to eternity and even one hour is a contribution to the future."

IMANI (FAITH)

> To believe with all our heart in our people, our parents, our teachers,
> our leaders and the righteousness and victory of our struggle.

The seventh Principle of the Nguzo Saba is Imani, Faith, which is essentially a profound belief in and commitment to all that is of value to us as a family, community, people and culture. In the context of African spirituality, it begins with a belief in the Creator and in the positiveness of the creation and logically leads to a belief in the essential goodness and possibility of the human personality. For in all African spiritual traditions, from Egypt on, it is taught that we are in the image of the Creator and thus capable of ultimate righteousness and creativity through self-mastery and development in the context of positive support. Therefore, faith in ourselves is key here, faith in our capacity as humans to live righteously, self-correct, support, care for and be responsible for each other and eventually create the just and good society, and better world.

Faith in ourselves is key, Bethun taught us, saying the greatest faith is faith in the Creator but great also is faith in ourselves. "Without faith," she states, "nothing is possible; with it nothing is impossible." Also, she taught that faith in the masses of our people is central to our progress as a people. "The measure of our progress as a race is in precise relation to the depth of faith in our people held by our leaders," she reminds us. As a community-in-struggle there is no substitute for belief in our people, in their capacity to take control of their destiny and daily lives and shape them in their own image and interests. This is fundamental to any future we dare design and pursue.

We must especially believe in the value and validity, the righteousness and significance of our struggle for liberation and a higher level of human life. This must be tied to our belief in our capacity to assume and carry out with dignity and decisiveness the role Fanon (1973) and history has assigned us. And that role is to set in motion a new history or humankind and in the company of other oppressed and progressive peoples pose a new paradigm of human society and human relations. Fanon says we can do anything as long as we don't do two basic things: 1) try to catch up with Europe (after all where is it going – swinging between spiritual and nuclear annihilation); and 2) imitate them so that we become "obscene caricatures" of them. We must, he says, invent, innovate, reach inside ourselves and dare "set afoot a new man and woman." The world and our people are waiting for something new, more beautiful and beneficial from us than what a past of oppression has offered us. We must not imitate them or be taught by our oppressors. We must dare struggle, free ourselves politically and culturally and raise images above the earth that reflect our capacity for human progress and greatness. This is the challenge and burden of our history which assumes and requires a solid faith. In constructing the order of the principles we place Umoja, unity, first to indicate that without unity we could not begin the liberational project. And we place Imani, faith, last to indicate that without faith we could not sustain it.

We must, then, have "faith in ourselves, in our Creator, in our fathers and mothers, our sisters and brothers, in our grandmothers and grandfathers, in our elders, our youth, our future, faith in all that makes us beautiful and strong, and faith in the righteousness and victory of our struggle, faith that through hard work, long struggle and a whole lot of love and understanding, we can again step back on the stage of human history as a free, proud and productive people" (Karenga, 1998:67).

EPILOGUE: THE "BELL CURVE," ANOTHER ENTITY IN THE LEGACY OF AMERICAN OPPRESSION

Irene Thompson

That the Black man in America still exists refutes the unfounded notion of inherent Black inferiority put forward by Richard Herrnstein, co-author of an earlier racial treatise (*Crime and Human Nature*, 1985), and Charles Murray in their book *The Bell Curve* (1994), which holds to the theory that Blacks, due to biological intellectual deficiency, are inferior to whites. Responding to such absurdity, in the vernacular of the brothers and sisters, Blacks say "I ain't stud-n it!" Nonetheless, we cannot under-estimate the rabble and babble of Herrnstein and Murray as it relates to the destiny of African-Americans. It is an extension of the paradox in the paradigm that seeks to destroy black people on every level, beginning with the public school educational system , which already serves as an insult to the idea of liberty, justice, and freedom for all. Therefore, Herrnstein and Murray's work must be refuted by intelligent human beings, Blacks in particular.

The advent of the "Bell Curve Theory," which has been presented as serious academic research, is a most heinous crime against the African-American people and must be denounced in the Halls of Justice by the world community. The premise of the "Bell Curve" is being used to reinforce the ideology of white supremacy, which is their academic panacea for a people who continually want to force racial oppression on its victims. Likewise, it represents a useful ploy of white racists who need to feel superior to other races in order to advance Caucasian hegemony.

The thinking engendered by the "Bell Curve" has had catastrophic consequences. It caused the "Enola Gay" to become a symbol of death to the Japanese people through the infamous dropping of the "A" bomb. These kinds of theories also created George Wallace, a born-again Christian, who stood in the door of the Halls of Education, axe in hand, to prevent African-American children access to minimal educational opportunities.

Historically speaking, Europeans' subjugation of non-Europeans, because of their alleged inequality or inferiority, evolved from a fifteenth-century papal proclamation, which stated that heathens and their lands could be divided among the Christian countries. Thus, using the cross as a sword, the Roman Catholic pope created a paradox that enabled "Christian" countries to satisfy their greed and the pillaging of other people. For oppressors to dominate and commit tyrannous acts, a plan or paradigm must be put in action that perpetuates and justifies their transgressions against humanity. This paradigm must have "just" laws that are paradoxical in nature in order for the oppressor to orchestrate the contradictions to fool himself as well as the oppressed. Like the Gorgon of Greek mythology, he cannot face himself on a moral plane without self-destruction. Can American face herself?

"The Great Paradigm," also known as the Declaration of Independence, declared that all men are created equal. Yet, the U.S. Constitution proclaimed that, for political purposes, enslaved Africans in America possessed three-fifths the worth of transplanted Europeans in America, indeed, a paradox in the "Great Paradigm, "which facilitates the assumptions in the theory of the "Bell Curve." In looking at a classical example of conquest, note the paradigm or plan of a certain king in the Bible's Book of Daniel as it relates to the education of the conquered:

> In the third year of the reign of Jehoiakim, king of Judah, came Nebuchadnezzar, king of the Babylon unto Jerusalem, and besieged it... And the king spoke unto Ashkenza the master of the eunuchs, that he should bring certain children of Israel and the king's seed and the princess; children in whom was not blemish, but well favored, and skillful in all wisdom, and cunning in knowledge, and understanding science, and such as had ability in them to stand in the king's place and whom they might teach the learning and the tongue of the Chileans....

> And the king appointed them a daily provision of the king's meat and of wine which he drank; so nourishing them three years, that at the end they might stand before the king.

Nebuchadnezzar, like the Americentric white man, understood very well the linkage between domination over a conquered people and the miseducation of the conquered people's future leaders.

Note the ongoing miseducation of the African American "talented tenth" (W.E.B. Dubois) by the universities and colleges of America and the unimaginable impact it has on the victims, as explicated in Dr. Carter G. Woodson's *The Mis-education of the Negro*. As students, the talented tenth is remade in the image of the oppressor, tied by psychological bonds that inhibit them from forging a separate ideology, which could throw off the shackles of oppression. Consequently, they then became oppressors unto themselves and their Black brothers and sisters. They cannot conceive of revolution or a time to kill.

Clarence Thomas, Supreme Court Justice serves and votes the convictions of the white majority, who are dedicated to the ideology espoused in the Bell Curve Theory. This theory has sounded the death knell for Affirmative Action in general, human rights legislation, and most of all, equal access to education.

Many of the Black intelligentsia apparently have forgotten, or were never taught, that the lambs who slept with the wolves were devoured. God: otiosis nuilus adsistit Deus – To Arms!!!

An Apologia
No Tears for a Brown Baby

There are no tears for you Brown Baby!
Your little head has been blown away by the police.
You never knew that you had worth.
I imagine the sun caressed your little face.
And the wind had blown so gently against your brown legs.

One day your laughter had been heard as you happily sucked
your little bottle. Perhaps your Black daddy thought you were
worth something. He held you as a shield against the wolves of
the world.
And he was blown away too.
He knew he was a zero,
but he never thought you were a zero, too!

So, little Brown Baby with soft wondrous eyes,
Little Brown Baby who lies soggy and bloody,
Little Brown Baby so cold and forever dead,
I am sorry not just for you
But for all the Brown Zeroes in America
Who have no value, no worth.

Like the ancestors whose blood cries out of the soil.
From the waters of the Atlantic ocean

To the mountains and prairies red with foam.
You see the Iranian Brothers knew this
And let the Brown Zeros go
during the hostage situation before your birth.

I can never say "I pledge allegiance to America"
I can never say "Under one God,
one nation with liberty and justice for all"
Therefore Little Brown Baby,
There are no tears left for you,
None for your Black Daddy
And most of all, none for me!

AFTERWORD

Mark Christian

A fricana Studies is at a crucial crossroads today in relation to both its development and future scope. The myriad themes and perspectives intelligently assembled and put forward in this massive volume by key scholars in the field are testimonies to the immense possibilities inherent in this multidimensional discipline. Indeed budding Africana scholars and seasoned scholars alike now have in one volume a theoretical foundation upon which to further develop and expand Africana studies, as we continue the on-going dialogue regarding Africana life, history and culture. We can confidently prepare for the inevitability of dynamic interdisciplinary and comparative approaches in comprehending the vitality and depth of global African descended peoples. The possibilities are endless, and this is both daunting and exciting for the neophyte and seasoned Africana scholar. Indeed Clenora Hudson-Weems has produced an edited volume that will provide the next generation of Africana scholars with a solid theoretical framework for examining Africana phenomena. In this sense, we are indebted to her as editor and to the other contributors as well for providing an intellectual orientation with data that offers clarity via multidimensional and interdisciplinary African centered paradigms. Crucially, this book represents a cerebral delight that weaves creatively through a labyrinth of Africana intellectual personalities, their thoughts and their practices.

Let us be certain and unequivocal. In a global context, peoples of African descent continue to grapple with the manifold social realities of white European cultural hegemony. Chapter after chapter confirm directly or indirectly both the existence of this domination and the resistance to it. More important, the authors offer pro-active analyses and methods in combating racialized discrimination via an African centered perspective. For liberation to become a reality, and not just a mere goal, the next generation of Africana scholars will require the varied intellectual tools offered in this book.

Engendering authentic and original Africana theories is arguably the most significant factor in this collection of essays. Africana scholars coming into this rich discipline need such a foundational text in order to make authentic contributions to the field themselves. Indeed without a clear understanding of the historical and contemporary struggles Africana scholars have endured up to this present age, the newcomers to the field could conceivably adopt intellectual paradigms that merely enhance or advance Eurocentric ideals. If junior scholars are to represent Africana phenomena in their works, it is of the utmost importance that they have at hand an Africana methodological frame of reference. Therefore, no longer should African agency be examined, explained, and enhanced via postmodernist analyses. To be sure, the approaches to Africana phenomena in this book provide us with cogent intellectual resources that go far beyond the current propensity toward essentially Eurocentric postmodernist perspectives. Moreover, if Africana scholars are to genuinely represent and empower African descended peoples, in terms of Aacademic excellence and social responsibility, we, therefore, require such a blueprint, as here presented, one that is both effective and resolute in its attempt to dislodge the continued domination of white European intellectual canons in the academy.

Another important role for the next generation of Africana scholars will be in establishing without compromise the crucial role of Africana women in particular. Within the same authentic Africana theoretical framework, an authentic African-centered paradigm designed for all women of African descent – Africana Womanism – has been put forth by the editor. As Africana studies focuses on the totality of Africana life and the interrelatedness of all African people – men women, and children globally – so must the Africana woman place the needs of her greater Africana family, who have for centuries suffered racial domination and exploitation, at the top of her list of priorities for ultimate human survival. Admittedly, the destiny of the collective Africana community lies within a concerted collective world-view wherein African centered thought and practice must co-exist on equal terms. The collective role of Africana women scholars, then, is to ensure that this part of the mission reaches fruition.

Finally, we are now in an age of unsurpassed technological revolution and the banks of knowledge will inevitably serve only those prepared to deposit resources. The next generation of Africana scholars have the potential to become key players in providing the necessary knowledge needed to combat what could be deemed "technological racism" and the exclusion of Africana paradigms in mainstream cyberspace. Our collective work ought to foster an acknowledgment that there is an "information war" taking place with regard to the creation of knowledge. Without being fully cognizant of this, Africana scholars may pay the ultimate price of continued marginalization and exclusion in the academy. Therefore, the next generation of scholars will not only need to build on the work of the past generations, it will also entail having an input into the production of knowledge via cyberspace. Hence, we suggest that this present volume be an impetus for the development of Africana cyberspace debates and discourse for the next step for interpreting, preserving and actualizing Africana theory and thought in this new millennium. Then on all fronts, we would be able to truly think, feel, and act within our own cultural zone.

ABOUT THE EDITOR AND CONTRIBUTORS

Delores P. Aldridge is the Grace T. Hamilton Professor of African American Studies and Sociology, Emory University where she also serves as Associate Director of the Program in Women's Health Service Research, School of Medicine, Center for Clinical Evaluation Sciences. She is the founding director of African American and African Studies at Emory and was two terms elected president of the National Council for Black Studies. Author of *Focusing: Black Male-Female Relationships*, her most recent publication is *Out of the Revolution: The Development of Africana Studies*, co-edited with Carlene Young.

Kwame Alford is an Assistant Professor of History, Texas Tech University. An editorial board member for *Africalogical Perspectives in Historical and Contemporary Analysis of Race and Africa Studies*, he is also the editor/curator of the *William Leo Hansberry Collection, Personal and Private Papers* and board and executive committee member of the Institute of African American Research at the University of North Carolina, Chapel Hill. His current work as a Ford Fellow is a complete biography of William Leo Hansberry, the father of African Studies.

Talmadge Anderson is Professor Emeritus in the Department of Comparative American Cultures and Marketing at Washington State University. He is the Founding Editor of *The* Western *Journal of Black Studies*, a leading professional periodical of African American and African studies. His publications include the book, *Black Studies: Theory, Methods and Cultural Perspectives*, and numerous articles relating to the Africana experience.

Molefi Kete Asante, considered the major proponent of Afrocentricity, is Professor of African American Studies at Temple University. He is the founding Chair of the first Ph.D. Department in Africana American Studies. The author of many books, book chapters, and articles on the Africana experience, his most referenced book is entitled *The Afrocentric Ideal*.

Richard K. Barksdale (deceased), Professor Emeritus of English, University of Illinois at Urbana-Champaign, is considered both a product and producer of the Africana literary tradition. Among his works are *Langston Hughes: The Poet and His Critics* and Black *Writers of America: A Comprehensive Anthology* (co-edited with Keneth Kinnamon), which was the first Black Aesthetic anthology, and *Praisesong for Survival*.

Jacob H. Carruthers (deceased) was Professor Emeritus at the Center for Inner City Studies, Northeastern Illinois University, Chicago and founding director of the Association for the Study of Classical African Civilization. He is also founding member of both the Kemetic Institute of Chicago and the Temple of the African Community of Chicago. Among his publications is *Intellectual Warfare*.

Alvin O. Chambliss, Jr. 2006 Charles Hamilton Houston Chair at North Carolina Central University School of Law, Durham, N.C. and Distinguished Visiting Professor of Indiana University in Bloomington, IN, he was the lead counsel for *Ayers vs. Fordice*, which the Supreme Court resolved on October 18, 2004. He is best known as "the last original Civil Rights attorney in America." He was taught, mentored and later practiced with the legendary Professor Herbert O. Reid. He worked on the preventive detention issue, involving excessive bond for Huey P. Newton and *Powell v. McCormick*, expulsion of Rep. Adam Clayton Powell from Congress. He has been actively involved in Higher Education litigation since 1972, beginning with Fairness Complaints filed against the television network on their racial exclusion of Black college sports activities.

Mark Christian is Associate Professor of Black World Studies and Sociology, Miami University-Ohio. The author of three books and a number of articles on the Black British and the African American experience, his latest book is an edited volume entitled *Black Identity in the 20th Century: Expressions of the U.S. and the U.K African Diaspora*. He is currently researching the Marcus Garvey Movement in Relations to Columbus, Ohio.

Karlton Edward Hester, formerly the Herbert Gussman Director of Jazz Studies, Cornell University, he is currently Director of Jazz Studies at the University of California at Santa Cruz. A composer, flutist and saxophonist, he has recorded ten albums for his own Hesteria Records label. His latest book is *Bigotry and the Afrocentric Jazz Evolution*. He has also worked with Dr. Donald Byrd in exploring connections between music composition and mathematical principles.

Clenora Hudson-Weems is editor of this volume and Professor of English at UMC. She co-authored, with Wilfred Samuels, the first Toni Morrison book, *Toni Morrison* (1990) and conceptualized theory of *Africana Womanism*. Her 1988 Ford doctoral dissertation, establishing Till's 1955 lynching as the catalyst of the civil rights movement, was published as *Emmett Till: The Sacrificial Lamb of the Civil Rights Movement* (1994). The book's sequel, *The Definitive Emmett Till: Passion and Battle of a Woman for Truth and Intellectual Justice*, was released in 2006. She also initiated and established the Nation's First graduate degree (MA and Ph.D.) in an English Department with and Africana Concentration, which other universities have since successfully implemented.

Obedike Kamau is Director of the library at Texas Southern University. His research is in the area of Africana studies and reparations. The co-host of a weekly radio talk show names Critical and progressive Review, he also has a spoken word CD entitled *A god talking to you*, which features "I Want My Money."

Maulana Karenga is professor of Black Studies at California State University, Long Beach. An activist-scholar of national and international-recognition, Dr. Karenga has played a significant role in Black intellectual and political culture since the 60's, especially in Black Studies and social movements. Also, he is the creator of the pan-African cultural holiday Kwanzaa and author of numerous scholarly articles and books, including: *Introduction to Black Studies*; *Kwanzaa: A Celebration of Family, Community and Culture*; *Kawaida: A Communitarian African Philosophy*; *Odu Ifa: The Ethical Teachings*; and *Maat, The Moral Ideal in Ancient Egypt: A Study in Classical African Ethics*. His fields of teaching and research within Black Studies are: Black Studies theory and history, Africana (continental and diasporan) philosophy; ancient Egyptian (Maatian) ethics; ancient Yoruba (Ifa) ethics; African American intellectual history; ethnic relations and the socio-ethical thought of Malcolm X. He is currently writing a book titled "Malcolm X and the Critique of Domination: An Ethics of Liberation."

Tony Martin is Professor of Africana Studies, Wellesley College. The foremost scholar on Marcus Garvey, his many publications include *The Jewish Onslaught*, which is his most controversial work explicating the role of the Jews in the slave trade.

Ali A. Mazrui is the Albert Schweitzer Professor in Humanities, Chair of Global Studies and Director of the Institute of Global Cultural Studies at SUNY-Binghamton. He is, the Albert Luthuli Professor-at-Large at the University of Jos, Jos, Nigeria, the Andrew D. White Professor-at-Large Emeritus and Senior Scholar in Africana Studies at Cornell University, Ibn Khaldun Professor-at-Large at the School of Islamic and Social Sciences, Leesburg, Virginia. He is also the Walter Rodney Professor of History and Governance at the University of Guyana, Georgetown, Guyana

Maria K. Mootry (deceased) was an Associate Professor of English and Director of African American Studie at the University of Illinois at Springfield. She is the author of numerous articles and co-editor of *Gwendolyn Brooks: A Life Distilled*. Her last publication is a collection of poetry entitled *Looking for Langston*.

William E. Nelson, Jr. is Professor of Political Science, Research Professor of African American and African Studies, Department of African American and African Studies and Director of the Center for Research and Public Policy at The Ohio State University. He is the founding Chair of the Department of Black Studies (OSU), and was former President of the National Conference of Black Political Scientists and the African Heritage Studies Association. He was also the Chair of the National Council for Black Studies and former Vice President of the American Political Science Association. Among his publications are *Electing Black Mayors: Political Action in the Black Community* (Co-author), and *Black Atlantic Politics: Dilemmas of Political Empowerment in Boston and Liverpool*.

Adele S. Newson-Horst is Dean, College of Arts and Letters, Missouri State University. Among her numerous publications is her book, *Zora Neale Hurston: A Reference Guide*. She also reviews works for both *Black Issues Book Review* and *World Literature Today*.

H. Ike Okafor-Newsum is Associate Professor of African and African Studies, Ohio State University. Among his publications are *Class, Language, and Education* and *United States Foreign Policy toward Southern Africa: Andrew Young and Beyond*. He is also an established visual artist; his most recent exhibit was an installation entitled *Levitation* 2005 at Project Row Houses in Houston, Texas. He is currently at work on a book-length study of Neo-Ancestralist artists of Ohio.

Daphne W. Ntiri is Associate Professor of Social Sciences in the Department of Interdisciplinary Studies, and Director of Detroit Area Lifelong Learning Coalition, College of Liberal Arts at Wayne State University, Detroit, Michigan. Her major areas of research interest focus adult literacy and gender studies both in the United States, and in Third World contexts. She has served as UNESCO consultant to Dakar, Senegal, and Kismayo, Somalia, where she worked to eliminate illiteracy and advance women's education. Some of her many publications appear in the *International Review of Education, Journal of Adult and Adolescent Literacy, The Western Journal of Black Studies*. Her forthcoming book is entitled *Literacy as a Social Divide: African Americans at the Crossroads*.

Anne Steiner is Professor of English and Associate Vice President for Academic Affairs at Central State University in Wilberforce, Ohio. She served as Chair of the Department of Humanities and has presented at numerous national/international conferences, including the Collegium for African American Research (Sardinia, Italy) and the International Conference on Mothering in Literature (Toronto, Canada), on her primary research on the literature of African American women writers.

James B. Stewart is Professor of Labor Studies and Industrial Relations and African and African American Studies at Penn State University. Author of numerous books and articles, he served as Vice Provost for Educational Equity, and also served as Director of Black Studies at Penn State. He was also president of The National Council of Black Studies and editor of *The Review of Black Political Economy*.

Betty Taylor Thompson is Professor in the of Department of English, Texas Southern University. She has numerous publication on the African American literary tradition; her current research is a full length book on Arna Bontemps.

Irene Thompson is a retired Memphis Public School Teacher and political activist. She is also a poet and a critic, who has written much on the intersection of Black life and literary creative activity.

Winston Van Horne is Professor and founding Chair of the Department of Africology at University of Wisconsin-Milwaukee. He is known for the coinage of the term Africology, which has been adopted as the discipline for Temple University's Department of African American Studies, the Nation's first Ph.D. program in the discipline.

Robert E. Weems, Jr. is Professor of History at the University of Missouri-Columbia. He is author of *Desegregating the Dollar: African American Consumerism in the Twentieth Century* and *Black Business in the Black Metropolis: The Chicago Metropolitan Assurance Company, 1925 to 1985*, as well as numerous book chapters and articles on African American history and Black economic history. This current work, co-authored with Lewis Randolph is untitled.

Barbara A. Wheeler, one of the founders of the Black Studies Movement, is Professor of Anthropology and founding Director of Africana Studies at Kean University. Author of *Human Uses of the University*, her film entitled *Mrs. DuBois: A Heritage Returned*, remains the only film documentary of Shirley Graham DuBois, wife of eminent scholar, Dr. W. E. B. DuBois.

Robert L. Williams is Professor Emeritus of Psychology and African American Studies, Washington University-St. Louis, and served as Visiting Distinguished Professor and Acting Director of Black Studies at the University of Missouri-Columbia. After developing the Black Intelligence Test of Cultural Homogeneity, he coined the term *Ebonics*. Author of *Ebonics: The True Language of Black* Folks and *The Collective Black Mind: Toward an Afrocentric Theory of Black Personality*, he has also published over 60 articles and scientific papers on cultural bias in testing and language development of Black children.

INDEX

Adams, Olive Arnold 83, 84, 118, 123, 128, 216, 378, 382, 383, 399
AFL-CIO 218, 219
Africana Womanism/Womanist 3, 8, 9, 13, 47, 58, 61, 63, 66-68, 70-72, 100, 141, 145, 228, 273, 275-290, 292-299, 301-307, 317, 320, 321, 327, 330-333, 342, 346, 348, 349, 354, 357, 450
Aldridge, Delores 4, 6, 9, 13, 45, 47, 49, 57, 276, 285, 286, 292, 293
Alford, Kwame 3, 75
American Audio Prose Library 297
Anderson, Talmadge 7, 219, 237, 286, 291, 294, 303, 394, 426, 427, 429
Asante, Molefi 5, 6, 19, 24, 25, 27, 48, 57, 66, 67, 131, 144, 273, 287-289, 292, 331, 342, 427
Authority/Authorities 32, 116, 120, 125, 179, 184, 265, 266, 289, 310, 311, 314, 346

Bergman, Peter M. 229
Berry, Mary Frances 229
Blassingame, John 215
Blaustein, Albert P. 215
Bloated Face 10
Bonetti, Kay 283

Booker, Simeon 79, 216, 222, 362, 363, 365, 394, 422, 424
Branch, Taylor 92, 212, 219, 221, 222
Brotherhood of Sleeping Car Porters 218-220
Brown v. Topeka, Kansas Board of Education 206, 214, 422
Brown, Theodore 220, 221
Burnham, Louis 217

Capitol 223
Catalyst 10, 212, 261
Cause Celebre 10
Chambliss, Alvin O. 7, 67, 377
Chicago Defender, The 222, 223
Child (ren) 8, 9, 11, 12, 38, 46, 58, 68, 70, 71, 117, 199, 200, 204, 227, 229-235, 240, 251, 258, 266-268, 281, 307, 312, 314-316, 321, 324, 326, 333, 335, 336, 339, 342, 349, 372, 383, 391, 399, 413, 423, 425-427, 433-436, 440, 446, 450
Christian, Mark 449
Civil Rights Movement 10, 105, 195, 205-207, 211, 212, 214-216, 223, 366, 394, 422, 423
Colvin, Claudette 212, 213
Continuum 10, 67, 171, 207, 228
Credit 119, 371, 372, 420, 421, 423

"Crime" 34, 200, 211, 234, 239, 408, 413, 419, 445

Definitive 52, 269, 335
Denver 128, 217, 340
Doctoral Dissertation 104
DuBois, W.E.B. 4, 5, 13, 16, 64, 133, 134, 144, 150, 158, 160, 161, 166, 169, 170, 172, 176, 205, 394, 446

Emancipation Proclamation 205, 207, 290
Emmett Till: The Sacrificial Lamb of the Civil Rights Movement 219
Entertainment Today (ET) 30, 31, 57, 170, 177, 293, 415
Eyes on the Prize 212-214, 222

Fact (s) Fact 17, 21, 31, 33, 35, 39, 40, 45, 46, 51, 62-64, 69, 77, 95, 97, 98, 118, 119, 133, 138, 139, 150, 151, 156, 157, 159, 166, 174, 175, 179, 185, 195, 200, 201, 206, 209, 210, 212-214, 221, 223, 229, 232, 243, 254, 260, 262, 265, 268, 269, 273, 276-278, 280, 281, 290, 306, 308, 310, 313, 316, 319, 322, 324, 326, 330, 331, 334, 341, 348, 349, 352, 356, 362, 367, 368, 371, 373, 380, 388, 391, 408, 411, 416, 420, 421, 423, 440, 426, 428, 433, 435, 437, 441, 442
Federal Bureau of Investigation (FBI) 172, 197
Forum 125, 289
Fox 330
Franklin, John Hope 33, 85, 119, 120, 154, 214, 364, 366, 423
Freedom 20, 39, 103, 107, 110, 118, 140, 149, 170, 171, 199, 200, 204, 205, 207, 209, 211, 212, 214, 217, 237, 245, 256, 307, 314, 320, 336,

347, 354, 365, 395, 398, 419, 421, 423, 432, 436, 437, 441, 445

Goode, Kenneth G. 229

Harding, Vincent 216, 282, 292
Hayes, Rutherford Birchard 206, 207, 219
Hernton, Calvin C. 208, 209, 216
Historians 30, 31, 78, 83, 85, 118, 197, 205, 210, 211, 214-216, 308, 313, 419, 420
Houston, Charles Hamilton 25, 176, 383, 393
Howard, T.R.M. 3, 26, 27, 83-85, 199, 216, 364, 383, 393, 407
Hudson-Weems, Clenora 3-5, 8, 9, 13, 19, 47, 54, 58, 61, 67, 71, 72, 141, 145, 205, 228, 253, 273, 275, 277, 278, 281, 282, 285-287, 292-297, 299-305, 309, 317, 320-322, 324, 325, 327, 329, 330, 332, 333, 336, 339, 340, 342, 343, 345-347, 349, 400, 449
Huie, William Bradford 209

Impetus 10, 214, 326, 419, 451

Johnson, President Lyndon B. 30, 40, 81, 82, 84, 120, 158, 160, 161, 181, 192, 199, 207, 208, 267, 298, 317, 327, 398, 413
Jordan, Winthrop 223, 231

King, Jr., Martin Luther 7, 56, 189, 190, 195-199, 201-204, 212

Labor Union 218-221
Ladner, Joyce 58, 129, 300, 304
Latimer, Lewis 325, 326
Lee, George 225, 229

Index

Legacy 8-10, 30, 57, 64, 141, 163-165, 171, 176, 177, 202, 211, 249, 257, 275, 287, 288, 292, 293, 299, 304-307, 309, 326, 340, 363, 368, 428, 433, 440, 442, 443, 445

Lewis, Marvin 58, 68, 167, 168, 170, 177, 219, 222, 307, 378, 429

Lincoln, C. Eric 142, 145, 159, 171, 207, 283, 420

Lynching (s) 10, 70, 81, 206-208, 210, 211, 215, 217, 219-222, 263, 319, 347, 406

Martin, Tony 6, 15, 39, 67, 149

Mississippi 10, 75, 167, 199, 201, 207, 208, 211, 212, 215, 217-219, 221, 222, 304, 378, 380-385, 387-395, 397

Mobley, Mamie Till 218, 222

Mock/Mockery 206, 216, 222, 223

Moore, Vivian 221

Mooty, Rayfield 219, 221, 230, 232-237

Morrow, Barry 145

Mother 35, 108, 136, 153, 171, 216, 217, 222, 223, 227, 229, 301, 306, 310, 312-315, 320, 323, 331, 333-341, 351, 413, 428, 434

Murdock, Clotye 217

Murphy, Eddie 416

Myrdal, Gunnar 216, 365

NAACP (National Association for the Advancement of Colored People) 30, 81, 82, 156, 160, 211, 218, 219, 221-223, 394, 396, 397

Nelson, Stanley 6, 59, 107, 115

Nixon, Edgar Daniel 106, 213

Parker, Charles Mack 256, 266

Parks, Rosa 9, 211-217

Passion 17

Payne, Ethel L. 223

Prior 15, 47, 78, 105, 143, 207, 214, 229, 384, 390

Quarles, Benjamin 120, 215

Racism 10, 21, 48-50, 54, 59, 72, 120, 155, 158, 165, 196, 201, 205, 206, 210, 211, 213, 215, 216, 221, 240, 241, 243, 263, 265, 267, 269, 276, 288, 290, 297, 302, 307, 342, 343, 346, 350, 361, 363, 369, 384, 405, 408, 409

Randolph, A. Phillip 180, 232, 233

Randolph, Lewis 68

Reed, Pamela Yaa Assantewa 288

Resurrect (ing) 133, 307

Rites of Passage 56-59, 431

Roberts, Bishop Isaiah 223

Sacrificial Lamb 205, 217

Samuels, Rich 67, 217, 336, 340, 343

Sankofa 85

Savage, Gus 217, 267

Shakespeare, William 154, 157

Silence (d)/ Silent 4, 8, 179, 282, 287, 341

Smith, Lamar 58, 84, 211, 215, 227, 228, 230, 265, 291, 294, 378

Steel Workers 218, 219

Stewart, James B. 20, 82, 137, 145

Stride Toward Freedom 226

Students 22, 30, 73, 76, 78, 80, 86, 92, 95, 104-109, 118, 120-122, 127, 128, 140, 168, 183, 185, 189, 190, 196, 229, 231, 232, 234, 242, 256, 258, 263, 379, 384-392, 394-397, 399, 400, 409, 447

Supreme Court 7, 71, 201, 207, 222, 378-381, 385, 387-391, 396, 447

Symbol 172, 173, 213, 217, 355, 357, 395, 445

Tennessee 70, 378, 391
Theft 256
Thompson, Irene 445
Till, Emmett 10, 205, 206, 212, 215-217, 221, 223
Till-Mobley, Mamie 222
Today Show, The 410
Turner, William 3, 15, 73, 86, 120, 121, 123, 129

Unearthing 321
University of Iowa 276

Victim 10, 192, 198, 210, 214, 217, 257, 301, 323

Weems, Robert E. 18, 81, 375, 406
Wells, Ida B. 16, 70, 166, 209, 281, 347, 393
Western Journal of Black Studies, The 7, 13, 57, 58, 61, 276, 283, 286-288, 293, 295, 304
Whitten, Jr., John 208
Wilkins, Roy 218, 221, 222
Williams, Juan 212, 222
Williams, Rev. Smallgood 222
Woods, Grandville T. 62, 393
Wright, Elizabeth 237
Wright, Mose 223

Zangrando, Robert L. 215